THE DISNEYLAND® ENCYCLOPEDIA

THE UNOFFICIAL, AUTHORIZED, AND PRECEDENTED HISTORY OF EVERY LAND, ATTRACTION, RESTAURANT, SHOP, AND EVENT IN THE ORIGINAL MAGIC KINGDOM®

CHRIS STRODDER

ILLUSTRATED MAPS BY TRISTAN TANG
PHOTOGRAPHS BY CHRIS STRODDER AND SHERYL PATTON

SANTA MONICA PRESS

Published by:

Santa Monica Press LLC
P.O. Box 1076
Santa Monica, CA 90406-1076
1-800-784-9553
www.santamonicapress.com
books@santamonicapress.com

Printed in the United States

Santa Monica Press books are available at special quantity discounts when purchased in bulk by corporations, organizations, or groups. Please call our Special Sales department at 1-800-784-9553.

ISBN-13 978-1-59580-033-6
ISBN-10 1-59580-033-6

Library of Congress Cataloging-in-Publication Data

Strodder, Chris
 The Disneyland encyclopedia : the unofficial, unauthorized, and unprecedented history of every land, attraction, restaurant, shop and event in the original Magic Kingdom / by Chris Strodder.
     p. cm.
 ISBN 978-1-59580-033-6
 1. Disneyland (Calif.)--Encyclopedias. I. Title.
 GV1853.3.C2S87 2008
 791.06'879496--dc22
                                    2008001801

Cover and interior design and production by Future Studio

Contents

Introduction

Writers are frequently asked how long it took them to write their works. Technically I wrote this one in about a year, from the summer of 2006 to the summer of 2007. But in truth, I've been working on it for over 40 years, dating back to the very first time I walked with my parents, brother and sister into Disneyland one hot summer's day in the 1960s.

Like most impressionable kids making their first pilgrimage to a park on the scale of the Magic Kingdom, I was overcome with sensations. There was simply too much to comprehend, too many sights and sounds to take in. Dazzled and dizzy, I came away with a swirl of overlapping memories, a T-shirt splattered like a Jackson Pollock painting, and my first Disneyland souvenir book. As soon as we got home I read everything I could find

about the park in our Northern California libraries, and I began to keep my eyes peeled for all the Disneyland-related TV specials I could tune into on our old rabbity-eared black-and-white TV. I was just a kid, but my encyclopedia research had begun, though I didn't know it at the time.

We didn't live near Anaheim, so repeat visits were rare. Every few years I'd get to go back, I'd acquire the latest souvenir book and a large wall map, and I'd mentally try to keep track of changes in the park. That last part was, I soon realized, a daunting, perhaps impossible task. Not only was the park huge, it was a moving target. Ambitiously evolving and growing, Disneyland seemed to be constantly turning its present into the past and its past into a prologue of the future. I'd notice restaurants coming and going; stores jumping from one side of Main Street to the other; new attractions replacing old ones; old at-

tractions getting subtle, unheralded name changes; entire lands appearing and disappearing. The souvenir books were helpful, but they weren't detailed enough to track all the changes, and their maps were too small and generic to show precise locations of everything in the park. The TV specials covered only the most obvious developments, such as the arrival of the Haunted Mansion, and the library books I found were usually Disney-produced promotions that certainly looked gorgeous but didn't offer historical details for every single entity in the park. I wanted more.

Well, they say you should write what you know; they also say you should write the book you yourself would want to read. On both counts "they" are right, I've learned. I sure knew Disneyland, at least as much as any casual visitor could. In the 1970s and '80s, my visits came more frequently while I was studying at UCLA and working in Los Angeles. Throughout those years I was observing Disneyland even more intently, content just to cruise the park and study the architecture with-

out needing to speed from one attraction to another. "Disneylanding" was my invented verb form to describe those fascinating rambles (as in, "I'm gonna go Disneylanding").

In the '90s and 2000s, I was actively buying up the old souvenir books and maps I'd missed and was swimming through the flood of text being written about Disneyland as it approached its 50th birthday. Some of the new books were lavish pictorial

retrospectives, but most were travel guides that told parents how to enjoy the park with their kids, rated the nearby motels, and pointed out other Southern California destinations. None of them was the exact book I wanted to read, which was a more scholarly history book that described in detail every restaurant, store, attraction, and event that had ever existed in Disneyland. In other words, the book you're now holding.

So here it is. As you read it, you'll see that my point isn't to glorify Walt Disney and his Disneyland—while much of the text praises the park, it also identifies lots of miscues and mishaps and mistakes. Nor is the point merely to list historical dates and facts; dates and facts may be knowledge, but they aren't wisdom. Instead, I've tried to explain how each thing in the park's history—each land, store, restaurant, attraction, and special event—is unique, how it's meaningful, and why it was created the way it was. These back stories, I think you'll see, are often just as fascinating as the attractions, stores, and restaurants themselves.

I've also included a couple dozen profiles of the park's prime movers. Some of the names are famous, some not so much, but all made mighty contributions to the overall Disneyland experience. Many were Imagineers, a hybridized term that merges imagination with engineering to describe those artists, architects, and designers who work creatively on the park and its attractions. Almost every one is a "Disney Legend," a title The Walt Disney Company has been using since 1987 to recognize key contributors to the Disney legacy. From the company's long list of movie stars, animators, songwriters, engineers, executives, and other honorees, I've selected those who did significant work at Disneyland, either behind or before the scenes. If you want to read more about them, long profiles of all the Disney Legends can be found at http://legends.disney.go.com/legends/index.

Also, I should mention that while I'm obviously a Disneyland fan, I've never been a Disneyland employee. As with every book I've ever written (this is number seven, the sixth one published since 2000), this encyclopedia was done while I held down a separate full-time job. In no way was that job, or any job I've ever had, related to the Disney Company. I always paid my own way into the park, and I did all my own research completely independent of, and

unauthorized by, the Disney Company. (I doubt if anybody at the park remembers me, but in recent years I was the guy pacing off long measurements throughout Disneyland while walking around for days with a huge notebook, a tape measure, a stopwatch, and a digital camera.) I did ask questions of a few park employees who happened to be on duty when I was visiting the park, and one extremely knowledgeable veteran cast member, Michael J. Phillips, was especially friendly and helpful as I tried to identify precise locations of extinct shops on Main Street. But again, I didn't consult or correspond with any Disney executives, officials, publicists, or archivists.

If I'm indebted to any one group, it's to the Mill Valley research librarians who scoured libraries across the country to find the obscure, often out-of-print books that I constantly requested. I'm also grateful to publisher Jeffrey Goldman and his team at Santa Monica Press for their faith in my ideas and their ability to execute them beautifully. And as per usual, I'm beholden to Sheryl Patton, who was tirelessly, brilliantly helpful every single day despite working her own more-than-full-time job. Sheryl's been an unwaveringly devoted and enthusiastic supporter of this book, which I lovingly dedicate to her.

As for the photos, they were taken during regular park hours with

no special access or photographic privileges. I snapped many of the pictures myself using a marvelous Canon digital camera loaned by Bryan Peariso, a cool carpool commando. Sheryl took the rest. Notice that our photos usually have no people in them, only buildings and scenery. That's intentional. Nearly every picture I've seen taken at Disneyland has got crowds in it, so I thought we'd

try to do ours differently. I quickly found out why most Disneyland photos are well-populated—taking a pretty picture of the photogenic castle or a picturesque Main Street corner is relatively easy if you simply show up on any nice afternoon, but it's relatively hard if you want to take it when there are absolutely no people walking through the shot. Still, after many photo safaris we pretty much managed to pull it off, so in many of our compositions it looks like the park was empty that day, even though it wasn't.

Tristan Tang made the amazing maps. Tristan's a gifted artist who's worked on numerous feature films and runs her own design company. She's also a long-time Disneyland visitor who remembers when. After I gave her a few simple suggestions and hundreds of my park photos to study, Tristan then painstakingly created and illustrated all the maps by hand, with marvelous results. That's also her 1959-style monorail that loops across the front and back covers. I'm still thanking my lucky stars that she so generously agreed to enhance this book with her remarkable talents. I can't imagine a better collaborator.

While researching and writing this book, I sometimes felt as dazzled and dizzy as I did when I first walked down Main Street lo those many years ago. There's still so much to see, so much to do, so much to know, that taking all of Disneyland in and capturing it all on paper sometimes seemed impossible. But as Walt Disney once said, "It's kind of fun to do the impossible." He was right.

Chris Strodder
Mill Valley, CA

Through the Turnstiles

Here at the beginning, just as you're about to pass through this book's metaphorical turnstiles, I thought I'd discuss Disneyland's popularity and try to explain why so many people have passed through the park's actual turnstiles. When I say popularity, I don't mean Disneyland is just a nice destination that many people have visited and enjoyed over the years. As the most-visited park of its kind in all of history, Disneyland's popularity is truly unparalleled. Over a half-*billion* people have stepped into the entrance tunnels since 1955, many of them repeatedly, despite famously high prices and potentially long lines. No other entertainment or sports venue

in the world has played to almost 30,000 paying customers virtually every day of the year for half a century (Walt Disney World has been drawing its crowds since the '70s, not the '50s, and it's got multiple parks, not just one). Think of it: except for a couple of sudden closures, that's over 18,000 consecutive days of Disneyland attendance approaching a full Fenway Park in Boston. Sure, sports stadiums and

concert halls can draw 30,000 people or more pretty regularly, but none have averaged that number daily, rain or shine, for five straight decades, with some days hitting 70,000, even 80,000 visitors.

Even people who aren't fans of Disneyland have to concede how important the park has been to American culture. Imagine if Walt Disney had never built his Magic Kingdom. The scenarios unfold like George Bailey's tangled connections in *It's a Wonderful Life*. The city of Anaheim, deprived of its biggest employer, probably would've grown up as an undistinguished bedroom community instead of as one of the state's 10 biggest cities, complete

Disneyland in July of 1955, the month the park opened. Note the original parking lot south of Disneyland's rounded triangle, the circular Plaza Hub in the center of the park, the white *Mark Twain* Riverboat docked in Frontierland's dark Rivers of America to the west, the large undeveloped area in Disneyland's northeast corner, and the orchards surrounding the park property on all sides. Photo courtesy of the Orange County Archives.

with major hotels, a busy convention center, a modern sports stadium, the Angels, and the Mighty Ducks. Orange County, minus its top tourist draw, might not have built its new commercial airport in the mid-'60s. Without Disneyland to learn from, Walt Disney wouldn't have considered launching an immense Walt Disney World in Florida, and today there wouldn't be Disney parks spread all over the planet. No *Pirates of the Caribbean* movies selling a billion dollars in tickets, since those movies were based on a Disneyland attraction. No Grad Nite memories for millions of high schoolers, no submarine experience of any kind for most people, and no maddeningly catchy It's a Small World theme song for the collective unconscious. Hmm, actually some would say that last one's a good thing (*de gustibus non est disputandum*).

So why is the park so popular?

Singularity is one enormous reason. Disneyland really is unique. It's the only Disney park completed in Walt Disney's lifetime, the only one he himself visited. Today the Disneyland name is unquestionably one of the most recognized in the world, and it's become common shorthand whenever someone is describing a place that's wonderful.

That uniqueness was even more conspicuous in Disneyland's first few decades, back before the global proliferation of Disney World, Universal Studios, and Six Flags parks. For a long time the things Disneyland offered really couldn't be found elsewhere. To name just one example, Disneyland routinely offered transportation systems unavailable to most people once they were outside the property. Roller coasters and little cars and carousels could be found all over the country, but not Disneyland's submarines and PeopleMovers and monorails. Even a simple amble down the park's Main Street, U.S.A. was special—thousands of towns still have Main Streets, but pedestrians have rarely been able to walk slowly down the middle of them (at least during the day), and they've never been able to count on a stupendous parade showing up every afternoon.

Propinquity accounts for much of the park's charm. Compared to some other theme parks that sprawl over mammoth geographies and soar to towering heights, Disneyland is relatively compact, making it more intimate, more manageable, more embraceable. The brilliant wagon wheel design of Disneyland's Plaza Hub puts paths to all the lands,

where vastly different experiences and moods await, just a few paces from each other. Guests are never more than a few minutes from a serendipitous stroll past an exotic jungle or a space rocket or a storybook village.

This shrewd hub-and-spoke layout has been copied and expanded in other parks and civic centers, but the Disneyland design is still definitive.

Every land in Disneyland adds a different dimension to the park's overall appeal. I'm not the first writer to identify Main Street, Frontierland, and Bear Country/Critter Country as expressions of Walt Disney's nostalgia—really everybody's nostalgia—for simpler times ("I love the nostalgic, myself," he once said. "I hope we never lose some of the things of the past"). Fantasyland celebrates childhood stories and dreams, high-tech Tomorrowland hums with exuberant optimism for the future, Adventureland finds its fun in the exotic, and Mickey's Toontown is a punster's paradise. Beloved Disney movies and TV shows come to life nearly everywhere you look, and the beauty of nature either saturates or punctuates every corner of the park. It's a cliché to say it, but there's truly something for everyone within the park's perimeter.

Once they've entered that perimeter, visitors often feel like they've stepped into some timeless, trouble-free realm. Surrounded by its protective berm, Disneyland sometimes seems like an enchanted island in an urban sea. This sense of separation from real life, its mundane problems and ineffable threats, probably contributes as much to Disneyland's ongoing popularity as any other factor. For many people, to be in Disneyland is to be free—free to play, to explore, to imagine, to remember, to forget. D.H. Lawrence wrote something similar about another isolated realm a century ago: "Australia is like an open door with the blue beyond. You just walk out of the world and into Australia." So too in busy Anaheim: visitors walk out of the world, pass through Disneyland's turnstiles, and enter a blue beyond of boundless imagination.

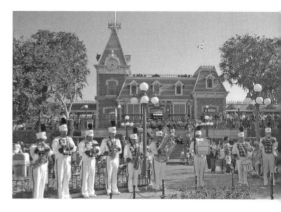

Every visitor can probably add his or her own additional explanation for Disneyland's popularity. Its cleanliness. Its friendly employees. Its joyful family spirit. The countless surprises of its endless evolution. The way it successfully "hides the wires" to sustain its enthralling illusions (at Disneyland, *not* seeing is believing). And more, always more, because there are as many reasons for the park's success as there are people giddily walking through it wearing mouse ears. Since 1955, over 500,000,000 have come, not just to a park, but to a kingdom. And they've found there, not mere amusements, but magic.

In ways personal and profound, Disneyland dreams can and do come

true. And why wouldn't they? "Anything," Walt Disney confidently and correctly declared on the 10th-anniversary episode of his TV show, "is possible in Disneyland."

C.S.

Notes on the Text

Some things to understand about this book before you begin. First off, know that it focuses exclusively on Disneyland in Anaheim. Occasional references are made to Disney's California Adventure (also in Anaheim), Walt Disney World in Florida, and Disney parks outside the U.S., but this book does not attempt to explicate anything in those other locations.

Next, for each one of this encyclopedia's 500 alphabetized entries, the descriptive text includes **bolded terms**. Bolding means there's a separate encyclopedia entry for that term.

To make the text more readable, the official names of some entities have been simplified. A brief alphabetical listing of some of these names includes Academy Award®, Disneyland® Park, Disney's Animal Kingdom®, Disney's California Adventure® Park, and Walt Disney World® Resort. Instead of these formal names I've used the abbreviated or colloquial forms commonly understood by the general public.

Each encyclopedia entry is marked on one of the maps (not the entries about people, obviously). These positions are indicated with a letter (for the map) and a number (for the spot on the map). A=Adventureland map, Fa=Fantasyland, Fr=Frontierland, TS=Town Square, and so on. In other books, including some of those published by Disney itself, "Main Street" often includes everything from the turnstiles up to the Sleeping Beauty Castle drawbridge; to help readers better envision where things are, I've trifurcated this large area into three separate parts—rectangular Town Square, slender Main Street, and circular Plaza Hub—each with its own map.

The dates used throughout the book are as accurate as I could make them without having access to the official Disney Archives. When I couldn't pinpoint an exact date, I occasionally resorted to less precise times like "Ca. 1992" or "summer 1967" (better to be general and right than specific and wrong).

Please forgive any mistakes, but do let me know about them by politely writing to me via the encycoolpedia.com Web site.

Park

(Map P)

14 BEAR COUNTRY/ CRITTER COUNTRY

15 FRONTIERL

13

12 NEW ORLEANS SQUARE

11 ADVENTURELAND

3

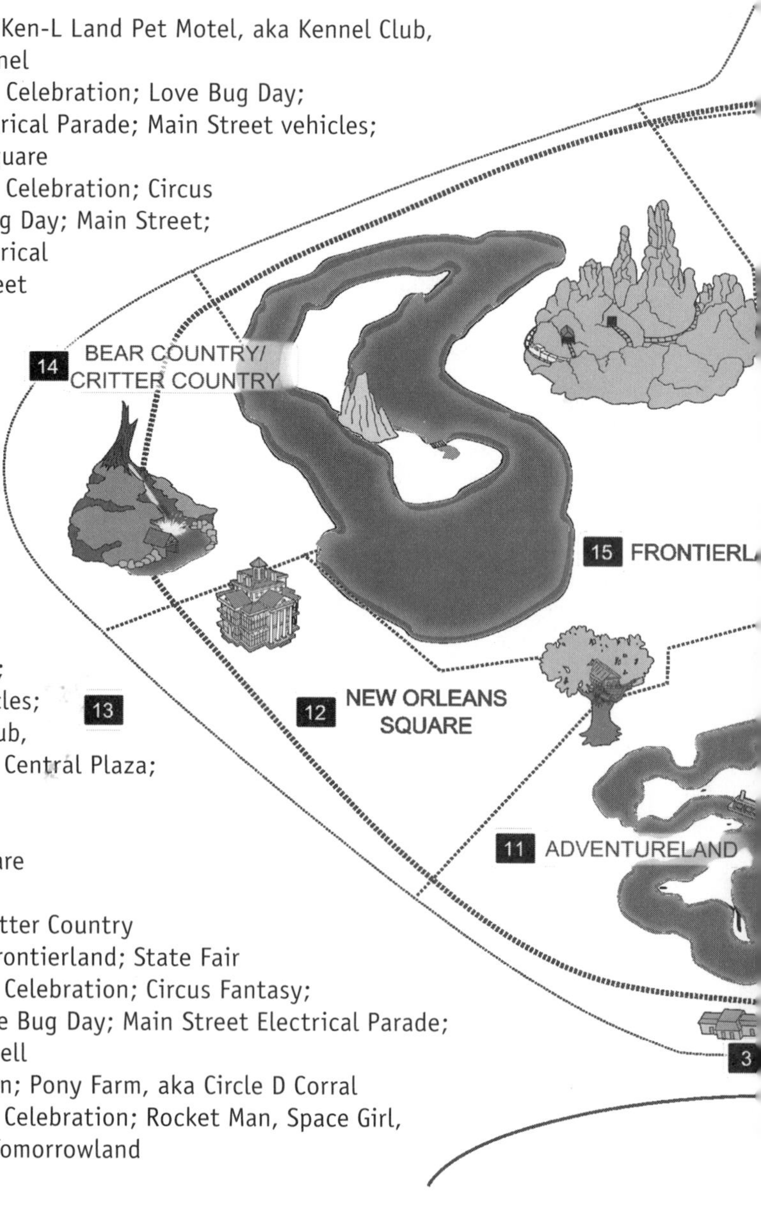

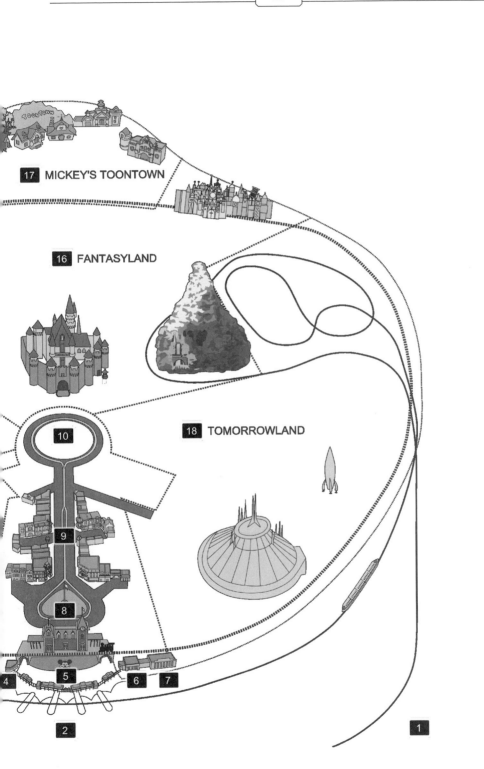

17 MICKEY'S TOONTOWN

16 FANTASYLAND

18 TOMORROWLAND

10

9

8

4

5

6

7

2

1

Town Square

(Map TS)

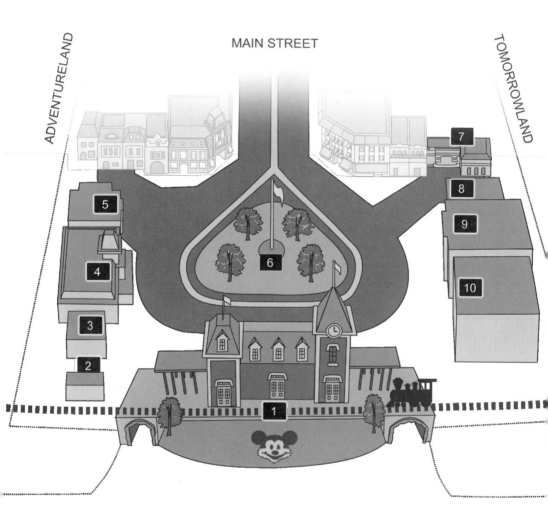

TS-1:   Santa Fe & Disneyland Railroad, aka Disneyland Railroad
TS-2:   Tour Guides
TS-3:   Police Station
TS-4:   City Hall; First Aid and Lost Children; Guest Relations; Tour Guides
TS-5:   Apartments; Fire Department, aka Fire Station
TS-6:   Flagpole
TS-7:   Dalmatian Celebration; American Egg House; Hills Bros. Coffee House and
        Coffee Garden; International Street; Liberty Street; Maxwell House Coffee
        Shop; Town Square Café
TS-8:   Jimmy Starr's Show Business Souvenirs; Mad Hatter of Main Street;
        Wonderland Music, aka Main Street Music
TS-9:   Babes in Toyland Exhibit; *Disneyland: The First 50 Magical Years*;
        Great Moments with Mr. Lincoln; Lost and Found; Mickey Mouse Club
        Headquarters, aka Mickey Mouse Club Shop; Opera House; Walt Disney
        Story, aka Walt Disney Story, Featuring Great Moments with Mr. Lincoln
TS-10: Bank of America, aka Bank of Main Street, aka Annual Pass Center;
        Town Square Realty

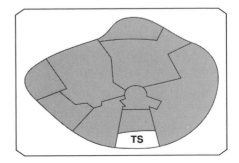

Main Street
(Map MS)

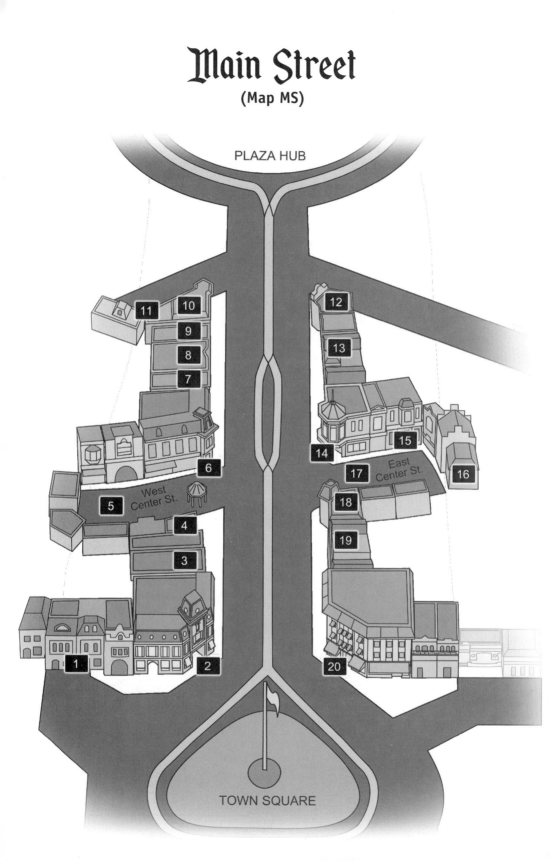

PLAZA HUB

West Center St.

East Center St.

TOWN SQUARE

MS-1: Carriage Place Clothing Co.; Locker Area, aka Main Street Lockers & Storage; Lost and Found

MS-2: Emporium, aka Disneyland Emporium

MS-3: Candle Shop; Crystal Arcade; Glass Blower; Story Book Shop, aka Western Printing Book Shop

MS-4: Disneyana; Hurricane Lamp Shop; New Century Watches & Clocks, aka New Century Timepieces and New Century Jewelry; Upjohn Pharmacy

MS-5: Carnation Café; Flower Mart, aka Flower Market

MS-6: Blue Ribbon Bakery; Carnation Ice Cream Parlor; Puffin Bakery, aka Puffin Bake Shop; Sunkist Citrus House

MS-7: Gibson Girl Ice Cream Parlor; Sunny-View Farms Jams & Jellies

MS-8: Main Street Shooting Gallery; Penny Arcade

MS-9: Candy Palace, aka Candy Palace and Candy Kitchen

MS-10: Refreshment Corner, aka Coke Corner, aka Coca-Cola Refreshment Corner

MS-11: Cole of California Swimsuits; Mad Hatter of Main Street

MS-12: Carefree Corner; Main Street Photo Supply Co.

MS-13: China Closet; Crystal Arts; Ellen's Gift Shop; Gallen-Kamp Stores Co.; Grandma's Baby Shop; Intimate Apparel, aka Corset Shop; Jemrock Shop; Kodak Camera Center, aka GAF Photo Salon, aka Polaroid Camera Center; Ruggles China and Glass Shop; Silhouette Studio; Watches & Clocks, aka Timex Shop; Wonderland Music, aka Main Street Music

MS-14: Card Corner; Disney Clothiers, Ltd.; Gibson Greeting Cards; Hallmark Card Shop

MS-15: Coin Shop, aka Stamp and Coin Shop; Pen Shop

MS-16: Locker Area, aka Main Street Lockers & Storage; Lost and Found; Main Street Cone Shop

MS-17: Chinatown; Flower Mart, aka Flower Market; Main Street Fruit Cart

MS-18: Market House

MS-19: Disneyana; Fine Tobacco; Jewelry Shop, aka Rings 'n' Things; Main Street Cinema; Main Street Magic Shop; Patented Pastimes, aka Great American Pastimes; 20th Century Music Company; Yale & Towne Lock Shop

MS-20: Disneyland Presents a Preview of Coming Attractions; Disney Showcase; Legacy of Walt Disney; Wurlitzer Music Hall

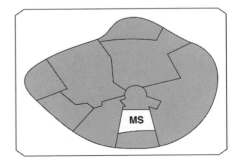

Plaza Hub

(Map PH)

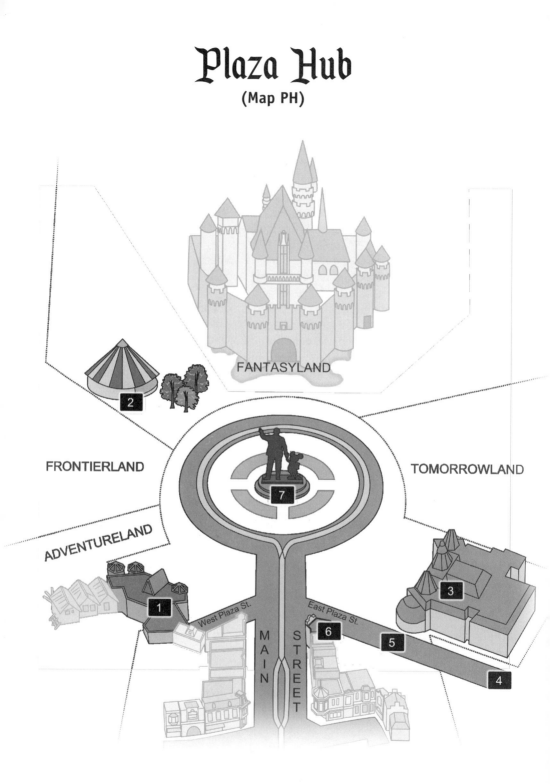

PH-1: Pin Trading Stations; Plaza Pavilion Restaurant, aka Stouffer's in Disneyland Plaza Pavillion

PH-2: Bandstand; Date Nite; Plaza Gardens, aka Carnation Plaza Gardens

PH-3: Red Wagon Inn, aka Plaza Inn

PH-4: Edison Square; First Aid and Lost Children

PH-5: Little Red Wagon

PH-6: Art Corner; Baby Station, aka Baby Center, aka Baby Care Center

PH-7: Dream Machine; Gift-Giver Extraordinaire Machine; *Partners*

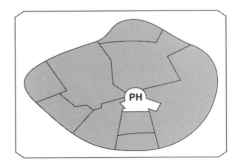

Adventureland

(Map A)

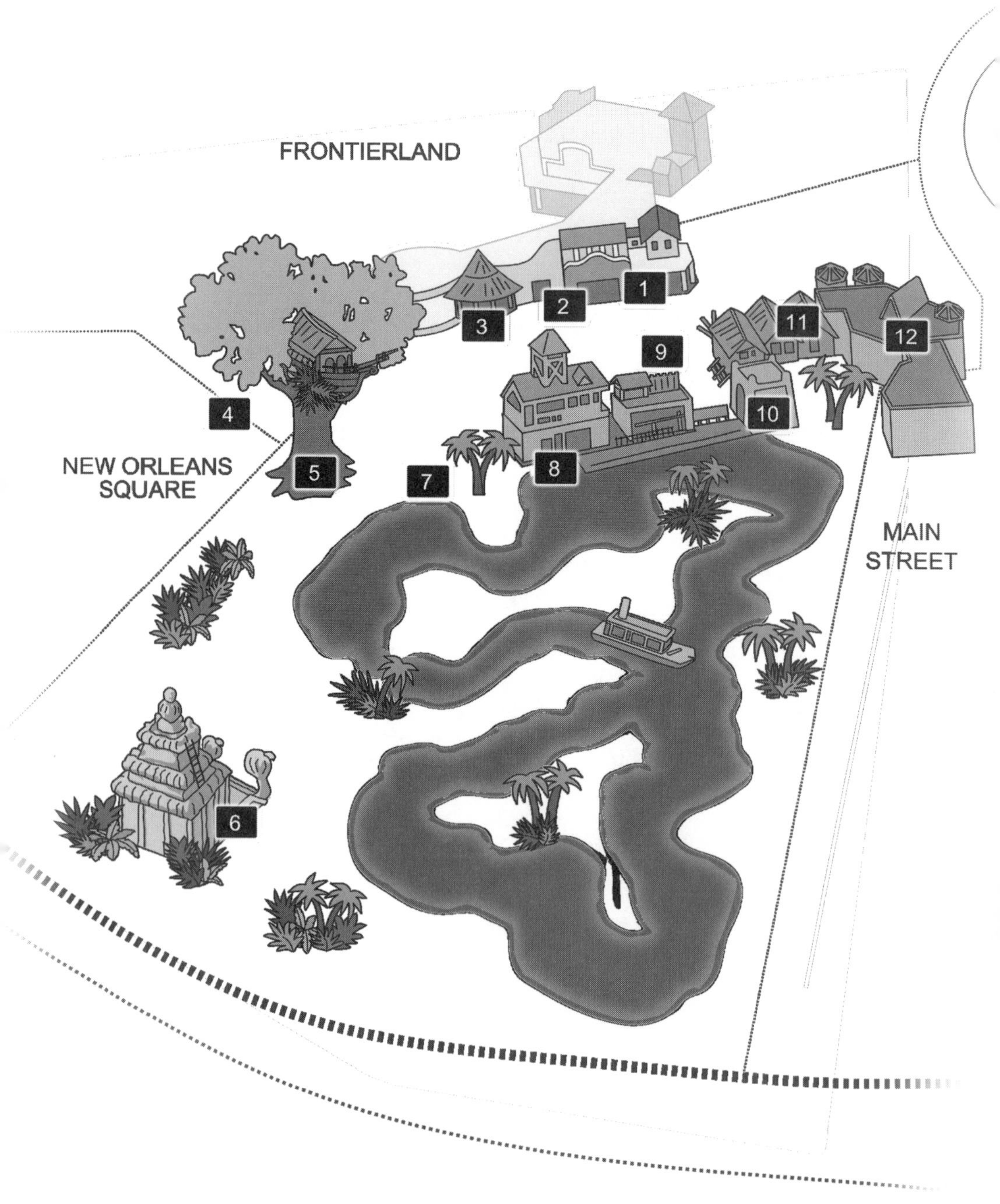

FRONTIERLAND

NEW ORLEANS
SQUARE

MAIN
STREET

1
2
3
4
5
6
7
8
9
10
11
12

A-1: Adventureland Bazaar

A-2: Big Game Safari Shooting Gallery; Indiana Jones Adventure Outpost; Safari Outpost; South Seas Traders

A-3: Bengal Barbecue; Sunkist, I Presume; Tropical Cantina, aka Adventureland Cantina

A-4: Magnolia Park

A-5: Swiss Family Treehouse; Tarzan's Treehouse

A-6: Indiana Jones Adventure

A-7: Indy Fruit Cart

A-8: Jungle Cruise

A-9: Tiki Tropical Traders, aka Tropical Imports

A-10: Aladdin's Oasis

A-11: Enchanted Tiki Room; Tiki Juice Bar

A-12: Tahitian Terrace, aka Stouffer's in Disneyland Tahitian Terrace

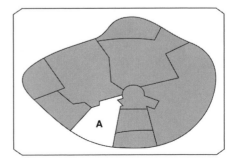

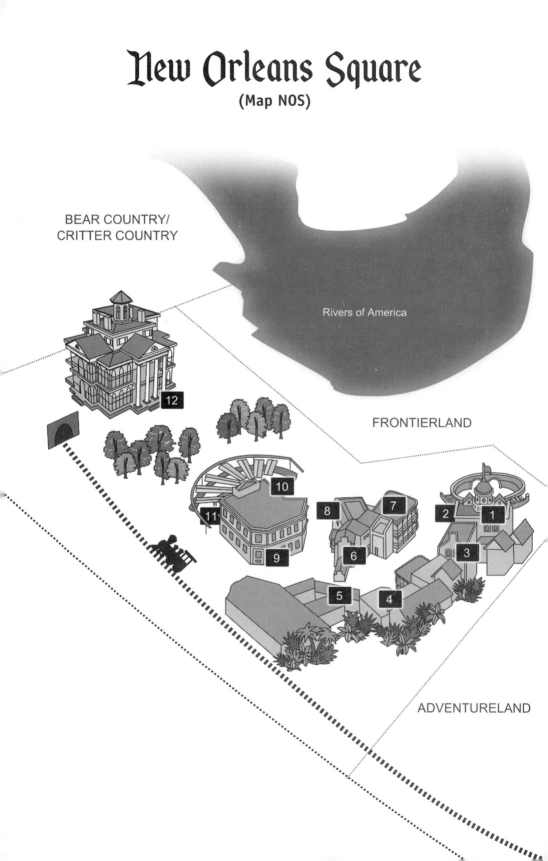

New Orleans Square
(Map NOS)

BEAR COUNTRY/
CRITTER COUNTRY

Rivers of America

FRONTIERLAND

ADVENTURELAND

NOS-1:   Apartments; Disney Gallery; Pirates of the Caribbean
NOS-2:   Royal Street Veranda
NOS-3:   Bookstand; Le Bat en Rouge; Le Gourmet, aka Le Gourmet Shop; One-of-a-Kind Shop; Pieces of Eight; Pirate's Arcade Museum; Port Royal
NOS-4:   Blue Bayou; Club 33
NOS-5:   Chocolate Collection, aka Chocolat Rue Royale; La Boutique de Noël; La Boutique d'Or; Le Bat en Rouge; Le Forgeron; Le Gourmet, aka Le Gourmet Shop; L'Ornement Magique; Port d'Orleans; Portrait Artists
NOS-6:   Cristal d'Orleans; Laffite's Silver Shop; Portrait Artists
NOS-7:   Candy Cart; Creole Café, aka Café Orleans; Royal Street Sweets
NOS-8:   Le Petite Patisserie
NOS-9:   Jewel of Orléans; La Mascarade d'Orléans; Le Chapeau; Marché aux Fleurs, Sacs et Mode; Mlle. Antoinette's Parfumerie
NOS-10: French Market; Parasol Cart
NOS-11: Mint Julep Bar
NOS-12: Haunted Mansion; Omnimover

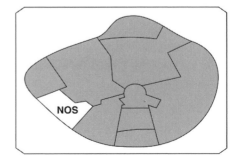

Frontierland

(Map Fr)

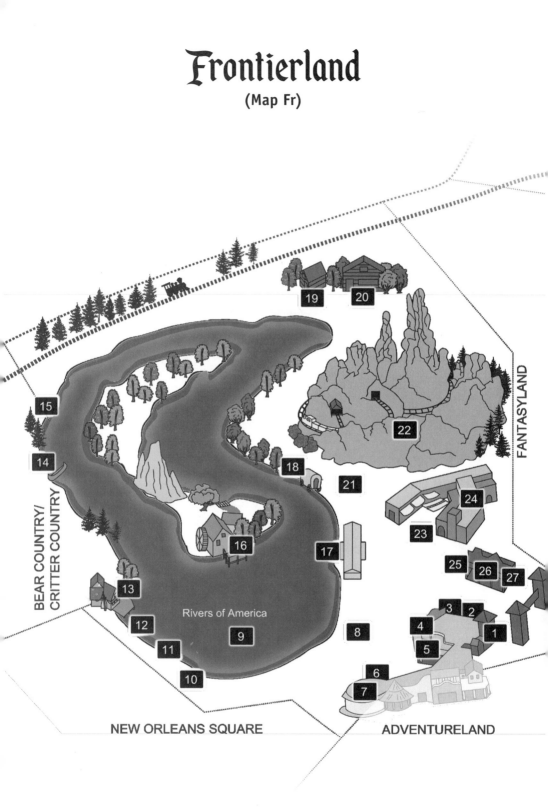

Fr-1: Bone Carving Shop; Davy Crockett Arcade, aka Davy Crockett Frontier Arcade; Davy Crockett Frontier Museum; Davy Crockett's Pioneer Mercantile, aka Pioneer Mercantile; Frontierland Miniature Museum; Leather Shop; Mexican Village; Reel-Ride

Fr-2: Bonanza Outfitters; Pendleton Woolen Mills Dry Goods Store

Fr-3: Silver Spur Supplies

Fr-4: American Rifle Exhibit and Frontier Gun Shop; Golden Horseshoe

Fr-5: Oaks Tavern; Stage Door Café

Fr-6: Don DeFore's Silver Banjo Barbecue; Malt Shop and Cone Shop; New Orleans Barbecue; Wheelhouse and Delta Banjo

Fr-7: Aunt Jemima's Pancake House, aka Aunt Jemima's Kitchen; Magnolia Tree Terrace; River Belle Terrace

Fr-8: Petrified Tree

Fr-9: Rivers of America

Fr-10: Chicken Plantation, aka Plantation House, aka Chicken Shack

Fr-11: Rafts to Tom Sawyer Island

Fr-12: Mike Fink Keel Boats

Fr-13: Fowler's Harbor, aka Fowler's Landing

Fr-14: Indian War Canoes, aka Davy Crockett's Explorer Canoes

Fr-15: Indian Trading Post; Indian Village

Fr-16: Fantasmic!; Tom Sawyer Island, aka Pirate's Lair on Tom Sawyer Island

Fr-17: *Mark Twain* Riverboat; Sailing Ship *Columbia*

Fr-18: Westward Ho Conestoga Wagon Fries

Fr-19: Big Thunder Ranch, aka Festival of Fools, aka Little Patch of Heaven

Fr-20: Big Thunder Barbecue, aka Festival of Foods; Santa's Reindeer Round-Up

Fr-21: Conestoga Wagons; Mule Pack, aka Rainbow Ridge Mule Pack, aka Pack Mules Through Nature's Wonderland; Rainbow Caverns Mine Train, aka Western Mine Train Through Nature's Wonderland; Stage Coach

Fr-22: Big Thunder Mountain Railroad; Discovery Bay; Nature's Wonderland; Painted Desert, aka Rainbow Desert

Fr-23: El Zocalo, aka El Zocalo Park

Fr-24: Casa de Fritos, aka Casa Mexicana; Mineral Hall; Rancho del Zocalo Restaurante

Fr-25: Marshal's Office; Miniature Horse Corral

Fr-26: Frontierland Shooting Gallery, aka Frontierland Shootin' Arcade, aka Frontierland Shootin' Exposition, aka Frontierland Shooting Exposition

Fr-27: Calico Kate's Pantry Shop; Frontier Trading Post; Westward Ho Trading Co.

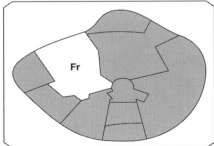

Bear Country/Critter Country
(Map B/C)

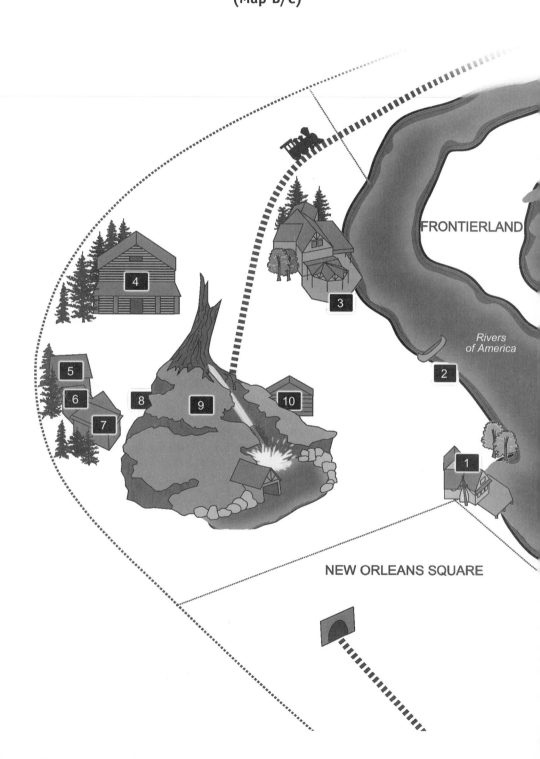

FRONTIERLAND

Rivers
of America

NEW ORLEANS SQUARE

B/C-1:   Harbour Galley
B/C-2:   Critter Country Fruit Cart
B/C-3:   Golden Bear Lodge, aka Hungry Bear Restaurant
B/C-4:   Country Bear Jamboree, aka Country Bear Playhouse;
         Many Adventures of Winnie the Pooh
B/C-5:   Brer Bar; Mile Long Bar; Pooh Corner
B/C-6:   Teddi Barra's Swingin' Arcade; Ursus H. Bear's Wilderness Outpost
B/C-7:   Crocodile Mercantile
B/C-8:   Professor Barnaby Owl's Photographic Art Studio
B/C-9:   Splash Mountain
B/C-10: Briar Patch; Critter Country Plush

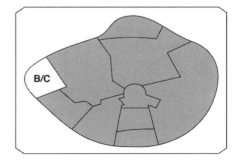

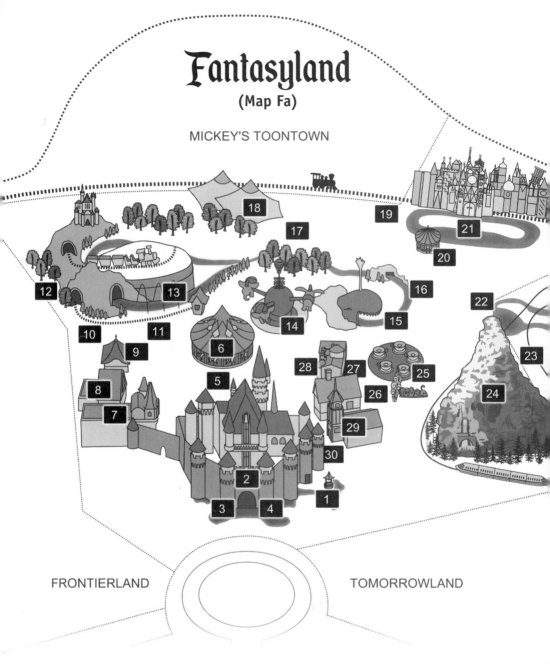

Fantasyland
(Map Fa)

MICKEY'S TOONTOWN

FRONTIERLAND

TOMORROWLAND

Fa-7: Tinker Bell Toy Shoppe, aka Once Upon a Time . . . the Disney Princess Shoppe

Fa-8: Snow White Adventures, aka Snow White's Scary Adventures

Fa-9: Fantasy Faire Gifts, aka Fantasy Shop, aka Fantasy Emporium, aka Fantasy Gift Faire; Geppetto's Arts & Crafts, aka Geppetto's Toys & Gifts, aka Geppetto's Holiday Workshop; Mickey Mouse Club Theater, aka Fantasyland Theater; Names Unraveled; Pinocchio's Daring Journey; Welch's Grape Juice Stand

Fa-10: Character Foods, aka Character Food Facilities; Stromboli's Wagon; Village Inn, aka Village Haus

Fa-11: Dumbo the Flying Elephant

Fa-12: Skyway to Fantasyland and Skyway to Tomorrowland

Fa-13: Casey Jr. Circus Train

Fa-14: Dumbo the Flying Elephant; Pirate Ship Restaurant, aka Chicken of the Sea Pirate Ship and Restaurant, aka Captain Hook's Galley; Skull Rock and Pirate's Cove, aka Skull Rock Cove

Fa-15: Canal Boats of the World; Rock Candy Mountain, aka Candy Mountain; Storybook Land Canal Boats

Fa-16: Fantasy Faire Gifts, aka Fantasy Shop, aka Fantasy Emporium, aka Fantasy Gift Faire; Midget Autopia

Fa-17: Enchanted Cottage Sweets & Treats; Yumz, aka Louie's, aka Meeko's, aka Fantasyland Theater Snacks, aka Troubadour Treats

Fa-18: Princess Fantasy Faire; Videopolis, aka Fantasyland Theater

Fa-19: Baloo's Dressing Room

Fa-20: It's a Small World Toy Shop

Fa-21: It's a Small World; Topiary Garden

Fa-22: Disney Afternoon Avenue; Fantasyland Autopia; Keller's Jungle Killers; Le Petit Chalet; Lilliputian Land; Mickey Mouse Club Circus; Motor Boat Cruise, aka Motor Boat Cruise to Gummi Glen

Fa-23: Fairytale Arts; Fantasia Gardens; Junior Autopia; Names Unraveled

Fa-24: Matterhorn Bobsleds; Matterhorn Mountain; Peter Pan Crocodile Aquarium

Fa-25: Mad Hatter's Mad Tea Party

Fa-26: Alice in Wonderland

Fa-27: Character Foods, aka Character Food Facilities; Mad Hatter of Fantasyland

Fa-28: Mr. Toad's Wild Ride

Fa-29: Peter Pan Flight, aka Peter Pan's Flight

Fa-30: Briar Rose Cottage; Disney Villains; Heraldry Shoppe, aka Castle Heraldry; Knight Shop; Merlin's Magic Shop; Mickey's Christmas Chalet; Quasimodo's Attic, aka Sanctuary of Quasimodo; Villain's Lair

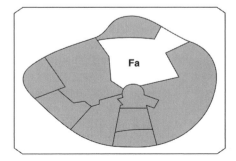

Mickey's Toontown
(Map MT)

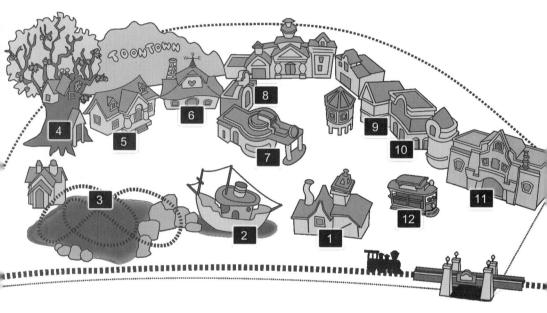

FANTASYLAND

MT-1:   Goofy's Bounce House, aka Goofy's Playhouse
MT-2:   Donald's Boat, aka *Miss Daisy*
MT-3:   Gadget's Go Coaster
MT-4:   Chip 'n Dale Tree House
MT-5:   Mickey's House
MT-6:   Minnie's House
MT-7:   Goofy's Gas Station; Toon Up Treats
MT-8:   Clarabelle's Frozen Yogurt; Daisy's Diner; Pluto's Dog House
MT-9:   Toontown Five & Dime
MT-10: Gag Factory
MT-11: Roger Rabbit's Car Toon Spin
MT-12: Jolly Trolley

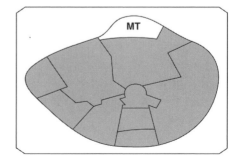

Tomorrowland

(Map T)

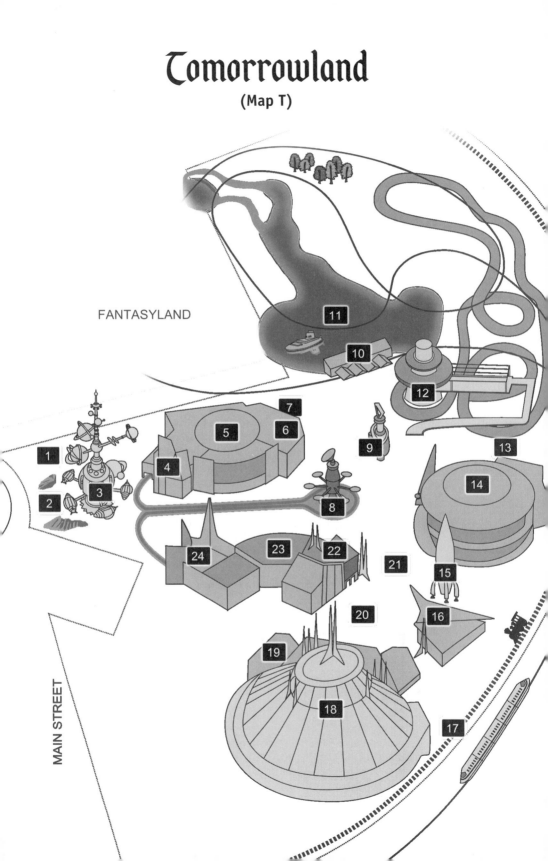

FANTASYLAND

MAIN STREET

T-1: Alpine Gardens; House of the Future; King Triton Gardens, aka Triton Gardens

T-2: Avenue of the Flags

T-3: Astro-Orbitor; Clock of the World, aka World Clock

T-4: Buzz Lightyear Astro Blasters; Omnimover

T-5: American Space Experience; Art of Animation; Bell Telephone Systems Phone Exhibits; Circarama, aka Circle-Vision, aka Circle-Vision 360, aka World Premiere Circle-Vision; Corridor of Murals; Space Station X-1, aka Satellite View of America

T-6: Art Corner; Little Green Men Store Command; Our Future in Colors, aka Color Gallery; Premiere Shop; World Beneath Us Exhibit

T-7: Yacht Club, aka Yacht Bar

T-8: Astro-Jets, aka Tomorrowland Jets, aka Rocket Jets; Court of Honor; Lunching Pad; Observatron; PeopleMover; Radio Disney Broadcast Booth; Rocket Rods; Space Bar; Tomorrowlanding

T-9: Club Buzz; Tomorrowland Terrace

T-10: Autopia Winner's Circle; Monorail, aka Disneyland-Alweg Monorail, aka Disneyland Monorail; Phantom Boats; Submarine Voyage, aka Finding Nemo Submarine Voyage; Viewliner; Yacht Club, aka Yacht Bar

T-11: Mermaids

T-12: Tomorrowland Autopia, aka Autopia, Presented by Chevron

T-13: Autopia Winner's Circle; Mad Hatter of Tomorrowland, aka Mod Hatter, aka Hatmosphere; Skyway to Fantasyland and Skyway to Tomorrowland

T-14: America Sings; Carousel of Progress; Innoventions; Space Bar

T-15: *Moonliner*; Spirit of Refreshment

T-16: Mission to Mars; Redd Rockett's Pizza Port; Rocket to the Moon, aka Flight to the Moon; Space Place; Toy Story Funhouse

T-17: Grand Canyon Diorama; Primeval World Diorama

T-18: Adventures in Science; Flying Saucers; Space Mountain, aka Rockin' Space Mountain

T-19: *Captain EO*; *Honey, I Shrunk the Audience*; Magic Eye Theater; Starcade; Tomorrowland Stage, aka Space Stage

T-20: Cosmic Waves; Hobbyland

T-21: Flight Circle, aka Thimble Drome Flight Circle

T-22: Bathroom of Tomorrow; Character Shop; Fun Fotos; Mad Hatter of Tomorrowland, aka Mod Hatter, aka Hatmosphere; Star Trader

T-23: American Dairy Association Exhibit, aka Dairy Bar; Corridor of Murals; Fashions and Fabrics Through the Ages; New York World's Fair Exhibit; 20,000 Leagues Under the Sea Exhibit

T-24: Adventure Thru Inner Space; Hall of Aluminum Fame; Hall of Chemistry; Omnimover; Star Tours

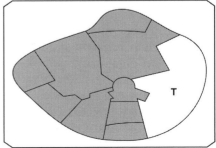

Adventureland

MAP: Park, P-11

CHRONOLOGY: July 17, 1955–ongoing

HISTORY: Guests are so used to finding Adventureland on the left side of the **Plaza Hub**, they might be surprised to know how Adventureland moved around in the early plans for Disneyland. One of the first color overhead illustrations of the park, drawn by **Marvin Davis** two years before **Opening Day**, placed Adventureland on the opposite side of the Plaza Hub, making it the first land to the lower *right* when guests walked north from **Main Street** towards **Sleeping Beauty Castle**. Adventureland ended up, of course, as the first land to the lower *left* from the Plaza Hub (the lower-right area that might've been Adventureland instead became a **Tomorrowland** expansion, essentially what is now the **Space Mountain** site).

Early on, what also changed was the name of the area—one cartographer would label it Adventureland, another would use True-Life Adventureland in reference to the popular *True-Life* documentaries the Disney Studios started releasing in 1949, with a total of eight by 1960. The exotic settings of these short films, especially *The African Lion*, which was in production as Disneyland was being designed, helped inspire the themes and textures of Adventureland, as did numerous Hollywood classics and great literary tales of exploration. Ultimately, however, the setting was generalized, with no one specific place pinpointed, no particular era identified. Adventureland was and is an amalgamation of African, Asian, and Polynesian influences that's more cinematic than real, more mysterious than overt.

Even though the Adventureland location, name, and source material varied, key Adventureland elements—a winding river with a boat ride, rows of stores and restaurants themed to remote locales—were always shown on the early maps. Artists like **Harper Goff** tried their best to pre-conceive it, but in truth some of Adventureland's details were literally made up on the spot during construction. The result was a meeting place between outposts of civilization and untamed nature. The main Adventureland entrance from the Plaza Hub is across a small pond (the same one that spreads under the **Frontierland** entrance) and through a tall bamboo gate topped by elephant tusks. The "street" ahead gently curves for about 300 feet towards Frontierland (and, as of 1966, towards **New Orleans Square**), with a two-story row of thatched shops and restaurants lining the right-hand side, and more shops and the landmark **Jungle Cruise** attraction on the left.

Massive in its scale and significance, the Jungle Cruise was Adventureland's only major attraction until the **Tahitian Terrace**, **Swiss Family Treehouse**, and **Big Game Safari Shooting Gallery** were added in 1962, to be followed a year later by the **Enchanted Tiki Room** and in 1995 by the **Indiana Jones Adventure**. That three-decade development gap between the Tiki Room and Indiana Jones has resulted in Adventureland being one of the park's least modified sections.

Though in its infancy it may have lacked multiple attractions, Adventureland has never lacked for verdant abundance. According to the park's **souvenir books**, Adventureland was intended to be a "wonderland of nature's own design." As such, it has always been the most densely planted of the lands, blending thousands of transplanted trees and bushes with old-growth trees saved from the original orchard that Disneyland was built upon. Even the trash cans, with their green paint and tiki patterns, look like they belong in the jungle. Attentive guests will notice that the resplendent natural images are supplemented with the sounds of chattering monkeys and chirping birds (all natural-sounding, but all prerecorded).

In 1955, an Adventureland plaque celebrating the spirit of "romance," "mystery," "tropical rivers," "the unbelievable splendor of exotic flowers," and "the eerie sounds of the jungle" was created but never installed. No matter—so exciting was Adventureland's concept, so detailed was its execution, and so universal is its appeal, it's doubtful any guests have ever needed to have the area explained to them.

Adventureland Bazaar

MAP: Adventureland, A-1

CHRONOLOGY: July 17, 1955–ongoing

HISTORY: As the park's **souvenir books** have long proclaimed, the Adventureland Bazaar has been selling "colorful wares imported from exotic lands" since **Opening Day.** The 1955 souvenir book specified "items from India, carvings from a Kenyan tribe in Africa," and "tropical ceramics" among the first "rarities" in a long line of toys, trinkets, imported clothes, odd furnishings, and unusual novelties that have filled the Bazaar over the decades.

In addition to the varied merchandise, the prime location has helped make the Adventureland Bazaar a perennial shopping favorite. It occupies the first right-hand building inside the **Adventureland** entrance, a high-traffic spot

**Disneyland's
Opening Day Attractions**
(July 17, 1955)

Adventureland
  Jungle Cruise
Fantasyland
  Canal Boats of the World
  King Arthur Carrousel
  Mad Hatter's Mad Tea Party
  Mr. Toad's Wild Ride
  Peter Pan Flight
  Snow White Adventures
Frontierland
  Golden Horseshoe Revue
  Mark Twain Riverboat
  Mule Pack
  Stage Coach
Main Street
  Main Street Cinema
  Main Street vehicles
  Santa Fe & Disneyland Railroad
Tomorrowland
  Space Station X-1
  Hall of Chemistry
  Tomorrowland Autopia

directly across from the **Enchanted Tiki Room**. Covering approximately 2,800 square feet, the Bazaar operates on the first floor of a two-story building that has always sported variations on adventure-themed décor, including an arched entryway, thatched awnings, and a weathered paint job. The 1955 souvenir book declared that the build-

ing conveyed "the savage beauty of the tropics" to "superlative degree," a lofty, even puzzling aspiration for a store more civilized than savage. Disney Legend **Rolly Crump** was one of the artists instrumental in creating an appealing exterior that hasn't changed much over the decades.

Inside, though, where many different shops selling unique imported merchandise have moved in and out, the Bazaar has sometimes been closer to a Bizarre. According to the souvenir books of the '50s and '60s, the building used to be subdivided into various individual businesses that offered non-Disney items from around the world. These interior shops, plus several small huts outside, seemingly included the Curio Hut (island-themed gifts), Here & There Imports, Far East Imports, Guatemalan Weavers, the Hawaiian Shop, India Magic Carpet, the Island Trade Store, the Mexican Mart, and Lee Brothers (imported Chinese gifts). These shops didn't all exist at the same time—in fact, some replaced others on the list (it's likely that Far East Imports took over for the Lee Brothers, for instance). The park's 1961 souvenir book listed seven of these under the heading "In the Bazaar."

In 1994, the store was temporarily closed for the **Adventureland** remodeling that brought extensive changes to the nearby **Jungle Cruise** line area. In the remodel, any remaining individual stores were absorbed into the one all-encompassing Adventureland Bazaar that exists today as a place seemingly filled with more plush animals than adventurous gifts. One unique recent addition is Aladdin's Other Lamp, a display along the back wall that dispenses "the wisdom of the genie" for a few coins and a quick rub.

Adventures in Science

MAP: Tomorrowland, T-18

CHRONOLOGY: Never built

HISTORY: Page 26 of the 1958 Disneyland **souvenir book** displayed a spellbinding painting of a new Space Age attraction for **Tomorrowland** called Adventures in Science. As seen in the painting, guests queued up under a large sloping roof and gazed through tall picture windows upon a tantalizing alien night. Outside were sharp lunar-like mountains and a large crater, with what looked like a domed observatory and giant protruding telescope standing off to the side. An immense ringed planet filled the distant sky, small moons hovered over the horizon, and stars spangled the blackness beyond. The view was more than tantalizing or beautiful—it was breathtaking, and it dramatically evoked the inspiring future that Tomorrowland represented.

That same year a huge parcel of Tomorrowland real estate was reserved for the coming Adventures in Science on the park's poster-size souvenir map. The location, had the attraction ever been built, was approximately where **Space Mountain** was to rise up in 1977. Adventures in Science would've begun with a "Powercade," a long covering that curved from the open Tomorrowland walkway and back towards a two- or three-story white building; under the Powercade covering were to be exhibited all manner of strange-looking futuristic gizmos. A walk along the length of the Powercade would've brought guests into the Adventures in Science building and onto some sort of transport for a trip through the universe (as some concept illustrations suggested) and/or a tour of scientific discoveries through the centuries.

Alas, by 1961, no Adventures in Science attraction was being shown in the souvenir books. In 1966, planning was already underway for a scientific tour that really would materialize a year later, albeit on a different site—**Adventure Thru Inner Space**.

Adventure Thru Inner Space

MAP: Tomorrowland, T-24

CHRONOLOGY: August 5, 1967–September 2, 1985

HISTORY: Adventure Thru Inner Space was a groundbreaking new attraction when it auspiciously debuted in the summer of 1967 as a key part of the extensive remodeling in **Tomorrowland**. From 1955 to 1966, the Inner Space building had housed, among other things, Monsanto's static **Hall of Chemistry** display, a walkthrough exhibit that showed off the wonders of chemical engineering. Identically sponsored and similarly science-influenced, Adventure Thru Inner Space was also intended to show chemical wonders, but these were to be viewed from a unique vantage point inside the atom.

Entered from the main walkway just inside the entrance to Tomorrowland, the Inner Space line area was a bustle of activity choreographed by **cast members** wearing futuristic yellow-and-black jump suits and white boots. The winding queue took guests past TV-size display terminals that previewed the amazing sights to come; guests also watched riders up ahead step into "Atomobiles," blue cocoon-shaped pods that then slid inside the 37-foot-long Mighty Microscope (in early 1967, Magic Microscope was one of the names considered for the whole attraction; Micro-World was another). This huge microscope "shrank" the Atomobiles and aimed them (eight-inch-tall replicas, actually) through a glass tube at a colorful illuminated snowflake. In addition to being seen by queuing guests, all of this was also being witnessed by curious passengers on the **PeopleMover**, since that attraction's track went right through the back of the room up near the ceiling.

Once they were out of view of the line area, "miniaturized" Atomobile riders heard the narration of the scientist who had already undertaken this journey (riders were informed that they were now hearing his "suspended . . . thought waves" of the experience). To create the illusion that the Atomobiles were continuing to shrink "beyond the limits of normal magnification-cation-cation" (according to the narrator), the approaching snowflakes got bigger and bigger until finally the Atomobiles actually entered them. More shrinking took Atomobiles into the domain of the water molecule and finally into one of the molecule's oxygen atoms, where speedy electrons whipped around on all sides and a glowing red nucleus pulsed.

Before the Atomobiles could enter the dangerous realm of the nucleus, they were gradually enlarged back to normal size, but not before some more drama was added when the original snowflakes melted, bringing unexpected motion to the Atomobiles and the surrounding molecules. The final return to normal size was monitored under the watchful blue eye of a scientist peering at riders through a giant microscope. Guests exited into a hallway of Monsanto and Disneyland displays, among them a delicate floor-to-ceiling sculpture of oil beads spiraling down thin wires.

When it was introduced in 1967, Adventure Thru Inner Space was one of Disneyland's most advanced attractions. Working closely with Monsanto engineers, Disney's own **Claude Coats** designed much of the journey, which lasted about six minutes and covered some 700 feet of displays. **Paul Frees**, who also spoke the baritone lines of the "ghost host" in the **Haunted Mansion**, voiced the scientist who had conducted, and was observing, this bold experiment; **X Atencio**, author of the **Pirates of the Caribbean** and Haunted Mansion scripts, also wrote Frees's Inner Space monologue. **Richard and Robert Sherman**, veterans of many other Disney attractions (**It's a Small World**) and movies (*Mary Poppins*), created the exhilarating "Miracles from Molecules" exit song, while **Buddy Baker**, who would later compose the Haunted Mansion's "Grim Grinning Ghosts" theme, penned the background music. **John Hench** drew up some of the initial concept sketches, which showed guests riding past sofa-sized protozoa inside an enlarged water droplet.

Thanks to Monsanto's support, the whole thing was a completely free attraction, needing no A-E ticket for entry; however, children had to use a special coupon from inside the **ticket books** to gain entry, thus limiting the number of times kids could ride unsupervised by parents. On December 15, 1972, the coupon system was abandoned, as was the free admission, and from then on a C ticket opened up Inner Space.

As exciting as the concept, sets, and effects were, the real breakthrough of Adventure Thru Inner Space was the Atomobile itself—it was the first Disneyland iteration of the innovative **Omnimover** ride system. In addition to efficiently conveying over 3,000 riders per hour through the attraction and cuing visual and sonic effects, the partially enclosed Atomobiles gave riders a sense of privacy and made Inner Space a prime rendezvous spot for amorous encounters. Even worse, the privacy seemed to provoke some riders into leaning out and damaging the sets. Hoping to curtail any in-the-dark intimacies or vandalism, supervisors installed closed-circuit TV cameras and then sped up the Atomobiles to help limit opportunities for misbehavior.

Sadly, its sets aging and its wait-time disappearing, Adventure Thru Inner Space closed in 1985 to make way for the new **Star Tours** attraction that would debut two years later. In tribute to the wonders of Inner Space, Star Tours for a time incorporated one of the small Atomobile replicas into its line-area exhibits; a miniature Mighty Microscope is visible in the hangar scene of the Star Tours film; and on the building across the way (formerly the home of the **Circarama** theater), snowflakes and molecules were included in an exterior mural to remind viewers of Tomorrowland's past glories.

Aladdin's Oasis

MAP: Adventureland, A-10

CHRONOLOGY: July 1, 1993–ongoing

HISTORY: Three months after the 31-year-old **Tahitian Terrace** in **Adventureland** closed, Aladdin's Oasis opened. While the location—tucked in a corner between the **Enchanted Tiki Room** and the **Jungle Cruise**—was the same, the architecture of the 300-square-foot building had drastically changed. Instead of Polynesian stylings, the new façade appropriated exotic elements of the *Arabian Nights*, in keeping

with the theme of *Aladdin*, Disney's hit movie of 1992. Whereas Tahitian Terrace guests enjoyed island cuisine and watched the *Polynesian Revue*, Aladdin's Oasis guests now enjoyed delicacies of the Middle East (shish kebabs, tabbouleh, chutney, etc.) and watched an Arabian-themed show featuring belly dancing, magic, and even a movie-inspired lamp and genie.

Even in its debut year Aladdin's Oasis wasn't open every day, and after two years the Arabian show wasn't open at all as the Oasis became solely a restaurant (albeit a nice restaurant with table service, not a buffet or informal counter service). Days of operation came with less frequency in 1996, and the building was often given over to private parties. Later that year the restaurant aspect of Aladdin's Oasis vanished, to be replaced by a new stage show called *Aladdin and Jasmine's Storytale Adventures*. The 25-minute presentation offered **cast members** dressed as *Aladdin* characters who retold (with the audience's help and some improvisation) tales from the *Arabian Nights*.

Though the building still has a sign identifying it as Aladdin's Oasis, in recent years it's been referred to as Aladdin and Jasmine at Aladdin's Oasis. The park now promotes the Oasis as a character-greeting area where guests can pose for photos with costumed cast members.

Milt Albright

CHRONOLOGY: 1916–ongoing

HISTORY: Born in 1916, this Missourian joined the Disney Studios in 1947 as a junior accountant. After getting to know **Walt Disney** personally, and after designing an unused-but-impressive car for the **Tomorrowland Autopia** attraction planned for Disneyland, Albright was transferred to the nascent park and given the title Manager of Accounting. In this role, one of his duties was to write and deliver paychecks to Disneyland brass, including Walt Disney.

Early in his park career Albright invented and ran the **Holidayland** picnic area in the late '50s, making him "the only manager of a land at Disneyland that failed" (according to his own description on the 2007 *Disneyland: Secrets, Stories & Magic* DVD). Later, while overseeing the Group Sales department, he founded two long-time staples of Disneyland history—the Magic Kingdom Club for neighboring businesses and frequent visitors (Albright was also listed as the editor of the club's quarterly magazine) and **Grad Nite** for celebrating teens. Albright eventually headed the Special Projects and Guest Communications departments and mentored many up-and-coming Disney executives, among them the future head of the Disney Studios, Richard Cook, before retiring in 1992. When Milt Albright was named a Disney Legend 13 years later, he was acknowledged as being the park's first-ever employee.

Alice in Wonderland

MAP: Fantasyland, Fa-26

CHRONOLOGY: June 14, 1958–ongoing

HISTORY: Themed to a popular Disney animated movie (just like **Peter Pan Flight**, **Snow White Adventures**, and many others), Alice in Wonderland is a long-standing indoor dark ride that places guests inside a colorful caterpillar-styled car and drops them into the bizarre world of Lewis Carroll's famous Victorian novel. The attraction was originally conceived of as a series of walk-through displays, ideally to be ready for **Opening Day** in 1955. Among the walk-through scenes were some tilty stairs to climb and a slide to ride down.

Unfortunately time and money were too tight for Imagineers to make the mid-July deadline, and in fact Alice in Wonderland wasn't ready until mid-June 1958. By then its location had been moved from the western **Fantasyland** row that held Snow White Adventures to the east side of **Sleeping Beauty Castle** opposite the **Matterhorn** (the **Mickey Mouse Club Theater** was built on the site Alice in Wonderland originally would've occupied; as of 1983 **Pinocchio's Daring Journey** has been on that spot). Alice in Wonderland shares part of its building with **Mr. Toad's Wild Ride**, and during the 700-foot trip through Wonderland, the caterpillar cars actually climb up to the second floor above Mr. Toad's layout. Alice required a D ticket for admission in the late '50s and a C in the '60s, but in 1971 it needed only a B ticket.

Twenty-five years after opening, Alice in Wonderland was late in arriving once again—when the rest of Fantasyland temporarily shut down for a massive renovation in time for a May 25, 1983 unveiling, Alice closed on September 6, 1982, and didn't reopen until April 14, 1984. Pre- and post-renovation, the attraction

has always been unique when compared to other Fantasyland indoor dark rides in that it takes guests outside its building, in this case for a gentle glide across the tops of over-size plants (a glide that lowers guests from the second to the ground floor and into a surprise "un-birthday" celebration finale that was added in 1984). Because of this outdoor stretch of track and the possibility of slippery situations, Alice in Wonderland occasionally closes when there's rain.

Inside the attraction the displays include familiar Carroll characters—Tweedle Dee and Tweedle Dum, the White Rabbit, the Mad Hatter, the Queen of Hearts, etc.—and incorporate the same surreal styles, kaleidoscopic colors, and buoyant music that had been in the 1951 Disney movie. Kathryn Beaumont, who voiced the movie's Alice character, reprised her vocals for the attraction, even updating them in 1984. Among the major changes that resulted from the 1984 renovation were the removal of the topsy-turvy Upside Down Room and the addition of about a minute of ride time, making it a more impressive four-minute attraction.

Disney Legend **Claude Coats**, who had worked on the *Alice in Wonderland* film, is credited as the attraction's main designer in its original iteration. The Imagineer who spearheaded the **Big Thunder Mountain Railroad** in the '70s, Tony Baxter, was in charge of bringing eye-popping new effects to the '84 renovation.

Alice in Wonderland, with its large butterflies, flowers, and mushrooms out front, has long presented an inviting view to guests riding on the nearby **Monorail** and **Matterhorn Bobsleds**. Attentive pedestrians will note one more nifty design element as they approach the attraction from the **Plaza Hub**: mounted in a rock wall along the walkway is a grinning Cheshire Cat. But there's one facet of the attraction that nobody can see because it was never realized—a proposed Alice in Wonderland Toy Shop that would've presented its wares within a Wonderland-style interior.

All American College Band

CHRONOLOGY: June 14, 1971–ongoing (seasonally)

HISTORY: Disneyland's All American College Band was born in 1971 as a part-time work-experience program for young musicians who were enrolled in a college or university. Dressed in snappy uniforms, the "vibrant, rhythmic musical aggregation" (so described in the park's 30th-anniversary **souvenir book**) still appears daily throughout the summer and throughout the park, often providing the music for each afternoon's **Town Square** flag retreat and adding special performances for special events (such as Disneyland's 45th birthday celebration in 2000).

By now over 2,500 members have graduated from the band. Of the musical directors, the longest-tenured has been Dr. Art Bartner, who led the band for over

25 years (Bartner is also the director of the band at USC). In mid-July of 2005, Disneyland threw a reunion for the band's alumni and welcomed back over 150 members for an afternoon performance in front of **Sleeping Beauty Castle**. The 2007 band was headed by Dr. Ron McCurdy from USC and featured musicians from over 16 universities across the country. The group performed from June 14th to August 13th in front of the castle, at **Tomorrowland Terrace**, at the **Main Street** train station, and at the **Plaza Gardens**, among other locations.

Less heralded has been the All American College Singers. This seemingly defunct spin-off group has rarely and barely been mentioned in Disneyland-related publications.

Alpine Gardens

MAP: Tomorrowland, T-1

CHRONOLOGY: December 1967–August 25, 1995

HISTORY: When the all-plastic **House of the Future** was demolished in 1967, the all-natural gardens surrounding it were retained. Rather than install another high-profile attraction in the area, Disney designers decided to save the space as a serene, largely undeveloped rest area.

Conveniently located just outside and to the left of the main **Tomorrowland** gates, the Alpine Gardens offered pedestrians a quiet, convenient stop halfway between Tomorrowland and **Fantasyland**. The appearance of a souvenir stand detracted from, but didn't ruin, the bucolic effect. The "alpine" in the name referred to the view of **Matterhorn Mountain**, which towered only 150 feet away to the northeast (although views of the **Plaza Hub** to the southwest and **Sleeping Beauty Castle** to the northwest were just as impressive). After closing in mid-1995, the area reopened in early 1996 as the more sophisticated **King Triton Gardens** with new landscaping and graceful new fountains.

American Dairy Association Exhibit, aka Dairy Bar

MAP: Tomorrowland, T-23

CHRONOLOGY: January 21, 1956–September 1, 1958

HISTORY: Six months after the park opened, the American Dairy Association brought some of its walk-through trade show displays into **Tomorrowland**. The building, second on the right just inside the Tomorrowland entrance, already housed the walk-through **20,000 Leagues Under the Sea Exhibit**.

Disneyland's **souvenir books** of the '50s described the ADA location as a not-so-tantalizing presentation of "future techniques in production and distribution of dairy products." Among other things, the room offered big plastic cows watching televisions while being milked; the large, sleek gauges and containers of modern milking machines; and a model of a milkman making a delivery in some kind of small jet-powered flying vehicle.

An interior barn-shaped Dairy Bar offered guests a folksy place to sit at tables and drink the obligatory glasses of cold milk in front of a sign that pro-claimed milk as "nature's most nearly perfect food." Many people referred to the entire exhibit as the Dairy Bar, but actually the Disneyland souvenir books listed the exhibit and the Dairy Bar as two separate entities, even though they shared the same sponsor and one naturally led to the other.

In 1958, the ADA was o-u-t when a Tomorrowland remodel preempted the site for **Fun Fotos** displays. All these buildings along this row of Tomorrowland would later undergo massive changes—within a decade all the walk-through exhibits were preempted in favor of major attractions and stores, most notably **Adventure Thru Inner Space** and the **Character Shop**.

American Egg House

MAP: Town Square, TS-7

CHRONOLOGY: July 14, 1978–September 30, 1983

HISTORY: The American Egg House was unusual because it is to this day one of the only Disneyland attractions, shops, or restaurants to be replaced by the very thing that it had replaced earlier. In 1976, the **Town Square Café** took over for the **Hills Bros. Coffee House and Coffee Garden** on **Main Street**; the site faced **Town Square** and was situated between the prominent **Disneyland Presents a Preview of Coming Attractions** and the **Mad Hatter** shop tucked away next to the **Opera House**.

After two years of being the Town Square Café, the American Egg House moved in and quickly became known as a great breakfast spot by virtue of its prime location as the first eatery visible to guests walking into the park each morning through the east tunnel. The Egg House also had the ideal morning menu—spon-sorship by the American Egg Board led to many egg-themed menu items, naturally, and in fact there's mention of some kind of "omelet record" being set at this Main Street location, though what that record was remains unclear and unverified. At the end of September in 1983, the American Egg House cracked its last shell and the Town Square Café returned the next day for a nine-year run.

American Rifle Exhibit and Frontier Gun Shop

MAP: Frontierland, Fr-4

CHRONOLOGY: 1956–ca. 1986

HISTORY: Actual weapons in Disneyland? Yes sir, and they were right at home in **Frontierland**, where there used to be staged "shoot-outs" between lawmen and villains, where there were realistic rifles in the **Tom Sawyer Island** fort, where the **Opening Day** celebration featured 16 Frontierland dancers cavorting with guns while singing about Davy Crockett's rifle "Ol' Betsy," where the **Sailing Ship** *Columbia* still blasts its cannon, and where a shooting gallery has been operating since 1957. For all the firearms, Frontierland has always been a little like Guntierland.

Details about a gun exhibit and shop are elusive. The park's '56 **souvenir book** listed an American Rifle Exhibit in Frontierland, and the '57 book listed both the exhibit and a Frontier Gun Shop, but neither book described what this pair was. Some maps of the park in the late 1950s showed a Gun Shop in the back of the **Davy Crockett Arcade** building, while contemporary photos placed a Frontier Gun Shop doorway next to the **Golden Horseshoe.**

The exhibit was a display of antique weapons from American history, including various muskets, Kentucky rifles, and Colt pistols. The Gun Shop, it's believed, sold replicas of those weapons, many of them, it's safe to speculate, to spirited rifle-ready kids wearing the Crockett-style coonskin caps made popular by gun-totin' Fess Parker on the hit *Disneyland* **TV series.** Some sundries were probably also available, as suggested by a sign on the door that read "Kodak Film."

As of 1958, the souvenir books deleted any references to the exhibit but retained the Frontier Gun Shop listing, even though the glass cases with the rifles were still present into the mid-'80s. In 1987, the whole Crockett Arcade, including the rifles, was remodeled and transformed into a large retail store called the **Pioneer Mercantile.**

American Space Experience

MAP: Tomorrowland, T-5

CHRONOLOGY: May 22, 1998–October 26, 2003

HISTORY: While other **Tomorrowland** exhibits have pointed to the future, the American Space Experience celebrated the recent past, specifically the last 40 years of NASA's achievements in outer space. Opened in 1998 along with new attractions in the remodeled Tomorrowland, this educational walk-through exhibit shared with **Rocket Rods** the large building just inside the Tomorrowland entrance that formerly housed the **Circarama** theater.

Because the space exhibit was sponsored by NASA, displays included an actual moon rock, Hubble Space Telescope photos, an Apollo spacesuit, and a live TV feed that showed NASA launches. A scale that revealed weights on other planets, models of future rockets, and a look at a bizarre Space Age material called aerogel were among the other displays that made this a fun-and-fascinating destination. On October 31, 2002, the exhibit added mock-ups of the Mars *Odyssey* spacecraft and one of the rovers that were set to explore the red planet in 2005 and 2006; a year after the mock-ups arrived, the Space Experience lost its space to a new **FastPass** area for **Buzz Lightyear Astro Blasters.**

America Sings

MAP: Tomorrowland, T-14

CHRONOLOGY: June 29, 1974–April 10, 1988

HISTORY: Located in the back corner of **Tomorrowland** near the **Tomorrowland Autopia**, the circular two-story Carousel Theater opened in the summer of 1967 as a three-quarter-acre cornerstone of the area's dramatic remodel. The innovative **Car-**

ousel of Progress was the building's first attraction; when its six-year spin ended in 1973 so it could move to Florida's Walt Disney World, the building was revitalized the following summer with a lively new attraction, this one arriving just in time for the Bicentennial festivities that would peak in 1976.

Though it revolved in the opposite direction, American Sings utilized the same rotating-theater format that the Carousel of Progress had used to slowly wheel the audience around a stationary hub. Whereas the Carousel of Progress had presented mini-plays with dialogue, America Sings was more like a six-part Carousel of Music. What was at the time the largest Disneyland assembly ever of **Audio-Animatronic** characters (114) saluted America's musical heritage with a 24-minute show that included a prologue, four lighthearted musical medleys, and an epilogue.

Overseeing the proceedings was a patriotic pair of Audio-Animatronic birds, an eagle named Sam and an owl named Ollie. A simple rendition of "Yankee Doodle Dandy" kicked off the show, followed by performances of more than three dozen classic American songs from, among others, a swamp of bullfrogs, a wailing possum, gospel-singing foxes, a chorus line of high-kicking birds, a guitar-playing turkey, an Old West bird quartet known as the Frontier Four, barbershop geese, grim vultures, storks on old-fashioned bicycles, and a modern long-haired rock band featuring a crane on lead guitar who invited the audience to join in for the rousing "Joy to the World" finale. Classic American costumes—cowboy hats, Gay '90s dresses, Jazz Age suits, etc.—and gentle humor boosted the feel-good tunes.

Some of the characters' voices probably sounded familiar to guests. Sam the Eagle was performed by amiable folk singer Burl Ives, and the pig who belted out "Bill Bailey, Won't You Please Come Home" was vocalized by **Betty Taylor**, the singer who starred as Sluefoot Sue over in the **Golden Horseshoe** in **Frontierland**. Many of the charming anthropomorphic animals were first drawn up by Disney Legend **Marc Davis**, whose illustrations in the '60s had added a comic flair to **Pirates of the Caribbean** and the **Haunted Mansion**.

The whole production was popular enough to be released later in 1974 as a Disneyland Records soundtrack LP with 39 songs. However, once the Bicentennial events gradually passed, so did the audiences for America Sings. With attendance in the Carousel Theater dwindling, the admission ticket was downgraded from an E to a D, and in 1988 the last song was finally sung. Offices occupied the building until **Innoventions** opened a decade later.

But while the America Sings show disappeared, its characters didn't. Most of the musical animals, still wearing their same hats and costumes, joined the zip-a-dee-doo-dah critters inside **Splash Mountain**, and the armatures of a couple of the geese were transformed into high-tech droids in the **Star Tours** line area.

Ken Anderson

CHRONOLOGY: March 17, 1909–January 13, 1993

HISTORY: Like many of the Disney Legends who helped create Disneyland, Ken Anderson worked on Disney's animated films for years before he started designing new park attractions. Born in Seattle, Washington in 1909, Anderson had been studying architecture and art when he was hired by **Walt Disney** in 1934 to work first on the *Silly Symphonies* cartoons and then on *Snow White and the Seven Dwarfs* (he's credited as the artist who, among other things, added Dopey's wiggling ears).

After contributing story ideas, art, and layouts to many more animated classics of the 1940s and '50s, Anderson sketched out the scenes of Norman Rockwell-style Americana that would've formed the miniature "Disneylandia" sets Walt Disney wanted to take on tour; when the tour idea proved to be unworkable, the Disneyland park concept coalesced. In the early '50s, Anderson joined the core Disneyland design team and became a major contributor to the attractions in **Fantasyland**, especially **Snow White Adventures**, **Peter Pan Flight**, the **Storybook Land Canal Boats**, and **Mr. Toad's Wild Ride.** Elsewhere in the park, Anderson worked on the **20,000 Leagues Under the Sea Exhibit** and the **Haunted Mansion**, among other attractions.

To other Imagineers, Anderson was more than just a brilliant artist—the book *Walt Disney Imagineering*, which was written by Anderson's peers, called him "the first Imagineer" because, long before Disneyland had even opened, he had taken on the challenge of developing a nine-inch-tall "dancing man," the earliest attempt at a Disney **Audio-Animatronic** figure. Ken Anderson was named a Disney Legend in 1991; two years later he died of a stroke in La Cañada Flintridge, California.

Apartments

MAP: Town Square, TS-5; New Orleans Square, NOS-1

CHRONOLOGY: July 1955–ongoing; ca. 1970–1987

HISTORY: The Disney Studios where **Walt Disney** usually worked are in Burbank, some 38 miles north of Disneyland. Since he frequently needed to be at the park, especially in its early days, he had a helipad built outside the **berm** in the **parking lot** area so he could easily helicopter back and forth between Anaheim and Burbank. And, to make his overnight stays at Disneyland even easier, he had an apartment built above the **Fire Department** on **Town Square.**

This apartment wasn't merely a VIP rest stop—it was an actual residence, a place where he and his family could stay overnight inside the park, for days at a time if necessary. Appropriately enough for this part of Disneyland, the posh apartment was decorated like something from the turn of the century with white columns, patterned wallpaper, red drapes, Victorian antique furniture and lamps, a Victrola phonograph that actually worked, and even an old-fashioned candlestick phone (a

big squat TV was one of the few conspicuous concessions to modern times). The apartment was small, though, just 500 square feet with a changing room, a cozy front room where the couches unfolded into beds, a bathroom, and a tiny kitchen area with a grill, refrigerator, and sink. A large outside lounge area stretching toward **City Hall** was decorated with white statues, plants, and wicker chairs.

From his front windows Disney could look out on the bustling activity of Town Square, with the **Santa Fe & Disneyland Railroad** train station to the right, the **Opera House** straight across, and the **Emporium** to his left. The public was never allowed inside, of course, and in fact the fire pole in the Fire Department below was blocked off to prevent anyone from shimmying up into the apartment (it's said that Disney himself used to slide down the pole occasionally). And so that the residents upstairs wouldn't be disturbed by people ringing the fire bell downstairs, the doors to the Fire Department were usually closed when the apartment was occupied.

No mention of the apartment was made in the Disneyland **souvenir books**, and no photos of the apartment were released until an exclusive shot of the Disney family relaxing in the main room ran in the August 1963 issue of *National Geographic* (the magazine dubbed the apartment "Disney's supersecret hideaway"). Relatives still occasionally use the apartment today, and it's also sometimes included as a stop on VIP tours. As a tribute to Walt Disney, a lamp, visible from Town Square, is always kept lit in the front window.

Meanwhile, in the '60s Disney decided that he needed another private apartment at the other end of the park for both himself and his brother **Roy Disney**. This bigger residence was above the **Pirates of the Caribbean** entrance in **New Orleans Square**, with bedrooms for grandchildren and a balcony that connected to the private dining rooms at **Club 33**. Unfortunately, Disney died before this second apartment was completed; when it was, it was used as offices by Disneyland staff until 1987, when the whole space was converted into the **Disney Gallery** with lavish décor to suggest what the apartment would have looked like. On the balcony outside the gallery's front door was an ornate iron railing with the initials of the apartment's intended occupants—WD and RD—woven into the design. In late 2007, the rooms were remodeled into a 2,600-square-foot Disneyland Dream Suite for the 2008 Disney Dreams Giveaway. The new guest quarters include a patio with "fireflies," a living room with French Provincial decor, two master bedrooms, two bathrooms, an electric train, a full-size carousel horse, vintage toys, and unique audio and visual effects.

Hideo Aramaki

CHRONOLOGY: 1915–2005

HISTORY: In the 1960s and '70s, guests who enjoyed fine meals in Disneyland had Hideo Aramaki to thank. He was the man in charge of the food at the park for almost two decades. Hawaii-born Aramaki, of Japanese descent but nicknamed Indian from childhood, came to Anaheim by way of Maui, Arizona, New York, and Chicago. After playing semi-pro ball in the 1930s, he began working in restaurant kitchens across the country in the '40s and moved to Southern California to run a Hawaiian-themed restaurant in the '50s.

In 1964, Aramaki was hired as the chef of the **Tahitian Terrace** in **Adventureland**; even though he had no formal culinary training, he was so successful that by 1967 he was the executive chef overseeing all of Disneyland's restaurants, standardizing the food quality and training the park's chefs (as well as personally preparing special meals for visiting dignitaries). After performing some of these same duties at Walt Disney World, Hideo Aramaki retired in 1985. He was named a Disney Legend 20 years later, the same year he died at age 90.

Art Corner

MAP: Plaza Hub, PH-6; Tomorrowland, T-6

CHRONOLOGY: October 1, 1955–September 6, 1966

HISTORY: During the summer of 1955, a temporary art show operated at the north end of **Main Street** under some canopies and a red-on-blue banner that announced "Disney Artists Exhibit." That October the exhibit relocated to a corner building about 200 feet inside **Tomorrowland**. The boxy Art Corner adjoined the round Satellite View of America building and stuck out towards the **Astro-Jets** some 50 feet away. To help make the gallery fit in with futuristic Tomorrowland, the Art Corner's exterior was painted up in colorful modern art motifs.

Inside was a French-themed setting for art supplies, Disney artworks (especially thousands of inexpensive—and now rare—cels from the animated movies), and many Disneyland postcards, among them sets that depicted Disney characters frolicking in the Art Corner itself. Animators were on hand to draw quick portraits of guests for only $1.50, and for convenience the shop offered framing, mailing, and even a mail-order catalog.

The comprehensive remodel that closed many attractions throughout Tomorrowland in 1966 made the art depart from the corner site, and a year later the building reemerged as part of the larger **Tomorrowland Terrace**. Though the attraction poster for the Art Corner listed only one location (the one in Tomorrowland), the park's **souvenir books** of the 1950s and '60s listed another Art Corner, selling "Pictures and Art Supplies," in **Fantasyland**; early maps pinpointed it as a small establishment northwest of the **Mickey Mouse Club Theater**, an area that was later remodeled into the **Village Inn** (now the Village Haus) restaurant.

Art of Animation

MAP: Tomorrowland, T-5

CHRONOLOGY: May 28, 1960–September 5, 1966

HISTORY: Like the **Art Corner**, the Art of Animation seemed slightly out of place in

Space Age **Tomorrowland**—both establishments basically celebrated the past, not the future. The Art of Animation sat in the big building that was to the right of the entrance into the **Circarama** theater. Previously the Satellite View of America had spun in this large round space, but by the end of the '50s, the novelty of looking at Earth from high altitude had worn off and audiences had all but disappeared, and finally so did the attraction in February of 1960.

Its replacement that spring, the Art of Animation, was a B-ticket exhibit promoting Disney's own movies. It was basically the same as several other Art of Animation exhibits that had already been touring the world to build excitement for *Sleeping Beauty*, the 1959 movie that was at the time the Disney Studios' most expensive production ever. The large attraction poster for the Art of Animation acknowledged the other touring exhibits: the burnt-orange background was decorated with sketches of three Disney characters (including one famous mouse) and text that touted the attraction as the "International Exhibit Direct from London—Paris—Tokyo."

Inside the room, the perimeter was lined with displays showing how animated movies were made. The center of the room was given over to arrangements of plastic chairs, potted plants, and ashtrays, enabling guests to sit, reflect, and smoke inside the exhibit. In the fall of '66, the Art of Animation followed the Satellite View of America onto the list of Disney's extinct attractions when the Circarama/Circle-Vision 360 theater building next door was expanded to become the World Premiere Circle-Vision theater with a new post-show area, all in conjunction with the "new Tomorrowland" that opened in 1967.

Arts and Crafts Shop

MAP: Fantasyland, Fa-3

CHRONOLOGY: Ca. 1958–ca. 1982

HISTORY: This intimate shop was located just inside the entrance to **Sleeping Beauty Castle** on the left-hand side. It didn't get mentioned in the Disneyland **souvenir books** until 1958, and even then it was no more than a simple name on a list of **Fantasyland** shops. In the mid-'60s, the **Clock Shop** replaced the Arts and Crafts Shop for a few years, but by the end of the decade the latter had replaced the former, according to a small Fantasyland map published in 1970. If true, the reappearance of Arts and Crafts was one of the few times that a closed Disneyland business reopened with the same name in the same location (the **Town Square Café** duplicated this feat in the '70s and '80s).

Delicate, expensive gifts were sold in the Arts and Crafts Shop, including ornate imported clocks and handblown glass sculptures. Sometime around 1982, with Fantasyland undergoing a major remodel, the shop closed for good; a year later a new glass shop, **Castle Arts**, opened in its place. The old arts and crafts theme still lived on, however, because another new store, **Geppetto's Arts & Crafts**, also debuted in '83, its location about 200 feet down the row in a spot adjacent to **Pinocchio's Daring Journey.**

Astro-Jets, aka Tomorrowland Jets, aka Rocket Jets

MAP: Tomorrowland, T-8

CHRONOLOGY: March 24, 1956–January 6, 1997

HISTORY: The basic Astro-Jet idea wasn't invented by Disney designers—rides with similar vehicles that whirled around a central pivot were already working in East Coast amusement parks before Disneyland even opened. The Disneyland spin on the spinners was to upgrade the theme with better detailing. Disney artist **John Hench** drew up a concept for a whirling-rocket attraction in 1955, dubbing it the "Saturn Patrol Ride Rocket." But Disneyland's first iteration, the Astro-Jets, didn't debut until the park had already been open for eight months, making this Disneyland's first major addition after **Opening Day.**

For the next four decades some variation of the Astro-Jets stood in the heart of **Tomorrowland** on the spot where the star-shaped **Court of Honor** had been (about 50 feet west of the Carousel Theater, the building that currently houses **Innoventions**). From 1956 to 1964, the attraction operated as the Astro-Jets, a

dozen stubby cylinders with thin wings, a headlight in the nose, and open cockpits barely big enough for two adults. Named after bright Milky Way stars, the jets were white with either red or blue trim and seemed a little more like contemporary Air Force aircraft than futuristic "astro" craft (indeed, honorary Air Force personnel were on hand when the attraction opened). Each jet was mounted on an arm extending about 20 feet from a central column that looked like an air-traffic control tower. Guests paid their C, later B, tickets, and entered the jets at ground level. Once the whirling began, pilots controlled their altitude with a lever inside each cockpit, raising the jets up to a height of about 36 feet.

On August 7, 1964, the name Tomorrowland Jets supplanted Astro-Jets to avoid any unintentional association with American Airlines, which had painted the words Astro-Jet on the side of its airliners. Two years later, the countdown to a much more dramatic change began. On September 5th of '66, the Tomorrowland Jets closed temporarily while a major remodel redefined all of Tomorrowland. When they reopened two days before Independence Day in 1967, the Jets had yet another first name, Rocket, and a new price, a D ticket, to match the attraction's dramatic restyling.

With America's space program in full swing, the decade-old winged cylinders were jettisoned in favor of new Apollo-style rockets. The sleek tubes were more bul-

Names of the Astro-Jets

Altair

Antares

Arcturus

Canopus

Capella

Castor

Procyon

Regulus

Rigel

Sirius

Spica

Vega

let-like with their sharper noses, prominent yellow headlights, and white-and-black livery reminiscent of NASA's latest spaceships. The redesigned central tower itself now looked like one of the imposing Saturn launchers seen regularly on TV thrusting astronauts into the Florida sky.

Even more impressively, the whole attraction had been lifted three stories off the ground to stand atop the main **PeopleMover** platform. With the center rocket topping out at about 85 feet, guests now rode an elevator (styled like the gantry alongside a NASA rocket) to reach the loading area. The fun factor zoomed when pilots pushed their vehicles to maximum altitude because they were now soaring some 70 feet above Tomorrowland pavement.

Soar they did in the beautiful photos shown in the park's **souvenir books**, especially in a full-page shot in the 1986 book. And soar they would until 1997, when the rockets were finally grounded on January 6th and replaced a year later by a spinning sculpture called the **Observatron**. Opening concurrently was a very different expression of the Astro/Tomorrowland/Rocket Jets idea, the **Astro-Orbitor**, with a new location about 250 feet away at the entrance into Tomorrowland.

Astro-Orbitor

MAP: Tomorrowland, T-3

CHRONOLOGY: May 22, 1998–ongoing

HISTORY: While variations of a whirling-jet attraction had been operating in Disneyland since 1956, the styling of the 1998 Astro-Orbitor actually came from Disneyland Paris, where it had originated as the Orbitron *Machine Volantes* (Orbitron Flying Machine), and Walt Disney World, where it had opened in 1994 as the Astro-Orbiter (with an "-er" suffix). When the latest "new **Tomorrowland**" was planned for Disneyland in the mid-'90s, designers basically re-created the Parisian and Floridian attractions, one of the few times a design emigrated from east to west instead of the reverse.

Instead of the uncomplicated white-with-trim **Astro-Jets**/Tomorrowland Jets/Rocket Jets that had orbited in Tomorrowland for four decades, the new Astro-Orbitor was a complex conglomeration of moving spheres and fanciful spaceships inspired, as Disneyland's own publications noted, by the works of Leonardo da Vinci. The color scheme was no longer stark and achromatic—vintage gold and brass tones, punctuated by strong blues, created the impression that this was an intricate mechanical whirligig built in some earlier century (or if not built, at least imagined in one of Jules Verne's 19th-century novels).

Not only was the look drastically different, so was the new location. The Astro-Orbitor stands about 250 away from the site deep inside Tomorrowland that had formerly been occupied by the Astro-/Tomorrowland/Rocket Jets. For the 21st century the 64-foot-tall Astro-Orbitor anchors Tomorrowland as the first attraction at the land's entrance. This new spot is just in front of the unused **PeopleMover** tracks and about 50 feet from the metallic gates (in the '50s this area had been part of the **Avenue of the Flags** that connected the **Plaza Hub** with Tomorrowland). At night the gleaming lights and shining metal turn the Astro-Orbitor into a kind of animated lighthouse that guides guests into Tomorrowland.

As with previous iterations of Disneyland's whirling-jets concept, there are 12 vehicles, the altitude of each vehicle is controlled by the pilot via an inboard handle, and the ride-time is about 90 seconds. One curiosity never explained is the spelling: the "-or" suffix has been said to be the result of a typo in original notes and plans, or perhaps it was intended to be a quick way to differentiate the two Florida and Anaheim attractions. The hyphen in the name seems to come and go capriciously in Disneyland's own literature.

X Atencio

CHRONOLOGY: 1920–ongoing

HISTORY: From classic movies to classic rides, X Atencio's Disney career paralleled Disney history from the 1930s to the '80s. Born in Colorado as Francis Xavier Atencio, he came to L.A. in 1937 as a teenager and began studying at a local art institute. A year later he was hired as a Disney animator, and a couple years after that he was working on *Fantasia*. Known simply as "X" around the company, he served in World War II and returned to Disney to work on some of the studio's most popular productions, including several Oscar-nominated and Oscar-winning shorts and acclaimed features like *The Parent Trap* and *Mary Poppins*.

In the '60s, Atencio moved to Disneyland projects that had him working all throughout the park. The August 1963 issue of *National Geographic* showed him programming an **Audio-Animatronic** bird for the **Enchanted Tiki Room**; he contributed to the **Grand Canyon** and **Primeval World Dioramas** on the **Santa Fe & Disneyland Railroad** line; he wrote the scientist's narration in **Adventure Thru Inner Space**; he created the script for the **Pirates of the Caribbean** characters and wrote the legendary "Yo Ho

(A Pirate's Life for Me)" lyrics (Atencio even performed the creepy voice for the talking pirate skull that prefaces the first waterfall); and at the end of the decade his work on the **Haunted Mansion** thrilled audiences—once again he wrote the narrator's script and penned the lyrics of the main theme song, in this case "Grim Grinning Ghosts" (the cemetery outside the mansion still pays tribute to Atencio's contributions with an honorary tombstone that reads, "REQUIESCAT FRANCIS XAVIER no time off for good behavior RIP").

When Disney expanded into Florida, Atencio was right alongside assisting on such major attractions as Space Mountain and EPCOT. He even helped with Tokyo Disneyland in the early '80s before finally retiring in 1984. A dozen years later X Atencio was named a Disney Legend.

Attraction Posters

MAP: Park, P-5

CHRONOLOGY: 1955–ongoing

HISTORY: Beautiful posters have adorned the Disneyland **entrance** since the mid-'50s. Most guests know the posters from their 16 positions inside the two main tunnels that lead from the ticket booths to **Town Square**, but the posters haven't always been there. In the '50s, they were placed along the low metal fence that surrounds the Mickey Mouse flower bed in front of the **Main Street** train station; additional posters have also appeared elsewhere in the park, such as along the **Avenue of the Flags**, upon the walls of the **Plaza Gardens**, and inside **Redd Rockett's Pizza Port**.

Wherever they've been, the posters have offered tantalizing glimpses of the park's highlights. The large size of the posters—three feet wide by four and a half feet tall—means that they can be seen from a distance, their 13.5 square feet of Disneyland excitement drawing guests towards them like moths to a thrilling flame. The posters aren't photographs, however; they're bold art images that capture the spirit of the attractions at the expense of literal renderings. Thus the Jungle River poster magnifies an elephant into a trumpeting goliath towering over the foliage, the **Skyway to Tomorrowland** poster raises its buckets hundreds of feet aloft, and the **Flying Saucers** poster shows saucers that actually work.

The simple designs make the posters easy to understand, a key requirement considering most of the viewers are distracted and on the move. Stenciled by hand, the posters usually present blocky shapes and

Attraction Poster Subjects

Adventureland
Enchanted Tiki Room
Jungle Cruise
Jungle River
Plaza Pavilion/Enchanted Tiki Room/
   Tahitian Terrace
Swiss Family Treehouse

Critter Country
Country Bear Jamboree
Splash Mountain

Main Street and Nearby
Disneyland Hotel
Great Moments with Mr. Lincoln
Primeval World
Red Wagon Inn
Santa Fe & Disneyland Railroad
Santa Fe & Disneyland Railroad/
   Grand Canyon Diorama

Fantasyland
Alice in Wonderland
Dumbo the Flying Elephant
It's a Small World
Mad Hatter's Mad Tea Party
Mad Tea Party/Dumbo/Carousel
Matterhorn Bobsleds
Mickey Mouse Club 3-D Theater
Peter Pan's Flight
Pinocchio's Daring Journey
Snow White's Scary Adventures
Storybook Land Canal Boats

Frontierland
Big Thunder Mountain Railroad
Casa de Fritos
Golden Horseshoe Revue
Mark Twain Riverboat
Mark Twain/Mike Fink Keel Boats/
   Indian War Canoes

Nature's Wonderland
Rainbow Caverns
Sailing Ship *Columbia*/
   Indian War Canoes
Stage Coach/Mine Train/
   Mule Pack
Tom Sawyer Island

New Orleans Square
Haunted Mansion
Pirates of the Caribbean
   (pirate with attraction scenes)
Pirates of the Caribbean
   (solo pirate with treasure chest)

Tomorrowland
Adventure Thru Inner Space
Art Corner
Art of Animation
Astro-Jets
American Journeys
America the Beautiful in Circarama
America the Beautiful in
   Circle-Vision 360
Carousel of Progress
Flying Saucers
Monorail
PeopleMover
PeopleMover and the
   Fantastic Superspeed Tunnel
Rocket Jets
Rocket to the Moon
Skyway to Fantasyland
Space Mountain
Space Station X-1
Star Tours
Submarine Voyage
Tomorrowland Autopia
20,000 Leagues Under the Sea
   Exhibit

strong colors instead of intricate details and subtle shading. Not always, though—the later **Jungle Cruise**, **Big Thunder Mountain Railroad**, and **Country Bear Jamboree** posters are all wonderfully ornate. Whenever guests are shown in the images, they're typically either small silhouettes (their diminutive size contrasting the immensity of something else on the poster) or flat, cartoony caricatures appreciating, but not distracting from, the main subject. No signatures appear on any of the posters, but several poster artists have been identified over the years, including Bjorn Aronson, **Mary Blair**, **Claude Coats**, **Rolly Crump**, Paul Hartley, and **John Hench**.

While the posters have usually advertised major attractions and exhibits, they have also occasionally promoted restaurants and businesses as well. **Casa de Fritos**, the **Red Wagon Inn**, the **Art Corner**, the **Art of Animation**, and the **Disneyland Hotel** have all had their own posters. Of the attractions, some have had two separate posters—the Jungle Cruise, **PeopleMover**, **Pirates of the Caribbean**, the *America the Beautiful* movie, and the **Enchanted Tiki Room** are among those that appear in multiple versions. Original posters mounted on fabric are collectors' items that sell for thousands of dollars. Relatively inexpensive productions have been sold in and out of the park for years in various formats and sizes; in 2007 Disneyland's own Art on Demand service offered customized presentations of 56 different posters.

Audio-Animatronics

CHRONOLOGY: 1961–ongoing

HISTORY: Much has been written about Disneyland's innovative Audio-Animatronics. The trademarked portmanteau word was coined by Disney Legend **Bill Cottrell** and eagerly appropriated by **Walt Disney** in 1961 as a descriptive name for the ambitious electromechanical figures his design team had built for Disneyland.

The seed for what would later blossom into **Great Moments with Mr. Lincoln** was planted on a vacation Walt Disney took in 1948. During the trip Disney was fascinated by, and purchased, a small mechanical bird, which inspired him to want to try to make something similar. Consequently, long before Disneyland was even

conceived, Walt Disney was already dreaming of a traveling exhibit with miniature sets and small mechanical figures. In '51, he even had several employees, notably **Ken Anderson** and **Roger Broggie**, create a small mechanical man who executed prerecorded dance moves (film of long-limbed song-and-dance man Buddy Ebsen helped the engineers work out the steps).

Once Disneyland was on the drawing boards, early plans called for talking Chinese characters and animals in an unrealized **Chinatown** area.

The first appearance in the park of early Audio-Animatronic figures came in 1960 in **Nature's Wonderland**, the **Frontierland** space toured by the **Mule Pack** and Western Mine Train. Hundreds of mechanical birds, reptiles, bears, and other wilderness animals made repeated motions that, while simple compared to later figures, seemed completely realistic from a distance. In 1963, the **Enchanted Tiki Room** brought Audio-Animatronics up close and center stage; there the cast of tropical birds and tiki sculptures performed a complex show filled with dialogue, song, and movement, all choreographed by a primitive (by today's standards) computer the size of a closet.

If audiences were delighted by this show, they were startled by the next developments in Audio-Animatronics, first unveiled at the 1964–1965 New York World's Fair. In Queens, **It's a Small World** immediately charmed audiences with its singing children and became a Disneyland fixture in 1966; towering dinosaurs squared off in an exhibit that became the **Primeval World Diorama** along the **Santa Fe & Disneyland Railroad** in 1966; Progressland presented 32 Audio-Animatronic family members in what Disneyland guests would know as 1967's **Carousel of Progress**; and, most ambitiously, a life-size President Lincoln stood up and delivered a speech to the amazement of anyone who saw the original figure at the World's Fair or the duplicate made for Disneyland's Great Moments with Mr. Lincoln in 1965.

With the hydraulics and electronics quickly improving, soon Audio-Animatronic figures populated every corner of the park. There were brainy Mission Control engineers talking to guests in Flight to the Moon, personable pirates cavorting through **Pirates of the Caribbean**, banjo-pickin' bears in the **Country Bear Jamboree**, bike-riding birds in **America Sings**, and so many more for so many years now that it's hard to remember a time when Audio-Animatronic figures *weren't* on display. By the time Indiana Jones swung through the **Indiana Jones Adventure** in 1995, the art and technology of Audio-Animatronics was so advanced that the truly lifelike figure didn't simply dazzle guests, he confused some of them into believing he was an actual person. Dazzlement, believability—two words that initially inspired the creation of Disneyland and then came to describe Disney's remarkable achievements with Audio-Animatronics.

Aunt Jemima's Pancake House, aka Aunt Jemima's Kitchen

MAP: Frontierland, Fr-7

CHRONOLOGY: August 9, 1955–1970

HISTORY: Back in the 1950s when **New Orleans Square** was still just a vague idea, Quaker Oats sponsored a restaurant that brought a "gracious 'Old South' setting" (according to an original place mat) to the western tip of **Frontierland**. Aunt Jemima's Pancake House opened a few weeks after the rest of the park did, its location about 75 feet from the nearest bank of the **Rivers of America** and another 75 from the spot where the base of the **Swiss Family Treehouse** would rise up in 1962.

Besides having a reputation for serving great pancakes and waffles with Aunt Jemima syrup, the restaurant was known for having Aunt Jemima herself on hand. Aunt Jemima was only a Quaker Oats character, of course, first played in public early in the century by a former slave who died in 1923. Seven women assumed the character over the decades, including Aylene Lewis, who portrayed her at Disneyland in the 1950s and '60s. As Aunt Jemima, Lewis would greet guests, visit tables, and, as declared on the place mats, "send you on your way with a cheerful 'You all come back!'"

In January of 1962, the restaurant temporarily closed, remodeled its way into the space next door where **Don DeFore's Silver Banjo Barbecue** had been, and reopened that July 17th as Aunt Jemima's Kitchen. Old photos show that there were two doorways into the restaurant, since it straddled the corner between Frontierland and **Adventureland**—one entrance was past umbrellas and outdoor tables and through plantation architecture on the Frontierland side, and the other entrance was underneath a thatched jungle-themed roof on the Adventureland side. Quaker Oats ended its participation at Disneyland in 1967, but the park sustained the Aunt Jemima theme until 1970, when the restaurant was remodeled and renamed the **Magnolia Tree Terrace**.

Autopia Winner's Circle

MAP: Tomorrowland, T-10, T-13

CHRONOLOGY: June 29, 2000–ongoing

HISTORY: Once again tying in a store with a nearby attraction, Disneyland opened the small Autopia Winner's Circle shop next to the 45-year-old **Tomorrowland Autopia** in 2000. The shop's opening was timed to the reopening of the Autopia, which had been remodeled to accommodate its new sponsor, Chevron. With its motoring souvenirs (including  models of the cute cars from Chevron's TV commercials) and an actual Autopia car on display, the store made for a nice pit stop for automotive fans. Guests could also get the photos for their Autopia Driver's Licenses taken here.

Previously this spot had been the site of lots of standing—it was the queue area for the **Submarine Voyage**, which closed in 1998. With the subs scheduled to resurface in mid-2007, and the Winner's Circle space slated to become a queue area once again, in late 2006 the Winner's Circle relocated across the walkway to a small space next to **Innoventions** where the **Mad Hatter of Tomorrowland**, aka Hatmosphere, had once set up shop.

Avenue of the Flags

MAP: Tomorrowland, T-2

CHRONOLOGY: Spring 1956–September 1966

HISTORY: On **Opening Day** flags from all the states in the union—there were only 48 in 1955—were flying on tall aluminum flagpoles in the star-shaped **Court of Honor** deep inside **Tomorrowland**. However, a year later the newly created **Astro-Jets** needed a home, so the flagpoles were uprooted, the Court was adjourned, and the Astro-Jets landed for four thrilling decades.

The flagpoles, meanwhile, were reinstalled in a prominent new location that needed some kind of dramatic statement—the 150-foot-long walkway that connected the **Plaza Hub** and the entrance to Tomorrowland. At one time a science-inspired sculpture rising up from the middle of a wide fountain had been planned for this walkway, but as construction invoices lengthened and deadlines shortened in the frantic spring of 1955, the sculpture concept was abandoned.

While not as imaginative as the sculpture-fountain combination, the flag-poles were a convenient and patriotic addition to the landscaped walkway that was

35 Movies That Inspired Attractions, Buildings, and Exhibits

The African Queen: Jungle Cruise

Aladdin: Aladdin's Oasis

Alice in Wonderland: Alice in Wonderland, Mad Hatter hat shops,
	Mad Hatter's Mad Tea Party

Babes in Toyland: Babes in Toyland Exhibit

Calamity Jane: Golden Horseshoe

Davy Crockett, King of the Wild Frontier: Davy Crockett Arcade, Davy Crockett
	Frontier Museum, Davy Crockett's Explorer Canoes, Mike Fink Keel Boats

Dumbo: Dumbo the Flying Elephant

Fantasia: Fantasia Gardens, Primeval World Diorama

Finding Nemo: Finding Nemo Submarine Voyage

Home on the Range: Big Thunder Ranch/Little Patch of Heaven

Honey, I Shrunk the Kids: Honey, I Shrunk the Audience

The Hunchback of Notre Dame: Festival of Foods, Festival of Fools,
	Quasimodo's Attic

Indiana Jones trilogy: Indiana Jones Adventure,
	Indiana Jones Adventure Outpost, Indy Fruit Cart

The Jungle Book: Baloo's Dressing Room

The Little Mermaid: King Triton Gardens

The Many Adventures of Winnie the Pooh: Many Adventures of Winnie the Pooh,
	Pooh Corner

soon dubbed the Avenue of the Flags. When they were installed in '56, the flags were placed in the numerical order in which their states had been admitted to the Union; three years later both Alaska and Hawaii were added to complete the 50. Mounted six feet up each flagpole was a black plaque identifying the state, its date of admission, its ordinal number among the states, and its motto. Crowning the Avenue of the Flags was Old Glory, flying at the Tomorrowland end of the walkway right in front of the **Clock of the World**; 250 feet behind the clock soared the majestic *Moonliner*, with the tantalizing Astro-Jets twirling nearby. In September of 1966, the flags were lowered and removed as construction began on the futuristic new Tomorrowland gates that would debut 10 months later.

Babes in Toyland Exhibit

MAP: Town Square, TS-9
CHRONOLOGY: December 17, 1961–September 30, 1963
HISTORY: *Babes in Toyland*, the Disney Studios' first big-budget live-action musical, hit the 1961 holiday season accompanied by lots of holiday hoop-la. With Annette

One Hundred and One Dalmatians: Dalmatian Celebration
Peter Pan: Peter Pan Flight, Tinker Bell & Friends, Tinker Bell Toy Shoppe
Pinocchio: Geppetto's Arts & Crafts, Pinocchio's Daring Adventure,
    Stromboli's Wagon
Pirates of the Caribbean: Port Royal
Sleeping Beauty: Sleeping Beauty Castle, Three Fairies Magic Crystals
Snow White and the Seven Dwarfs: Snow White Adventures
So Dear to My Heart: Frontierland train station
Song of the South: Briar Patch, Splash Mountain
Star Wars trilogy: Star Tours, Star Trader
Swiss Family Robinson: Swiss Family Treehouse
Switzerland: Matterhorn Bobsleds, Matterhorn Mountain
The Sword in the Stone: Merlin's Magic Shop,
    Sword in the Stone Ceremony
Tarzan: Tarzan's Treehouse
Third Man on the Mountain: Matterhorn Bobsleds,
    Matterhorn Mountain
Toy Story: Buzz Lightyear Astro Blasters, Club Buzz,
    Little Green Men Store Command, Toy Story Funhouse
True-Life Adventure documentaries: Grand Canyon Diorama, Jungle Cruise,
    Living Desert, Nature's Wonderland
20,000 Leagues Under the Sea: 20,000 Leagues Under the Sea Exhibit
Who Framed Roger Rabbit: Mickey's Toontown, Roger Rabbit's Car Toon Spin
The Wind in the Willows: Mr. Toad's Wild Ride

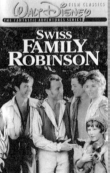

Funicello, America's sweetheart, starring alongside teen idol Tommy Sands and Disney mainstay Tommy Kirk, the picture was expected to be a blockbuster, and so a walk-through Babes in Toyland Exhibit was installed in the **Opera House** on **Town Square.**

This was the first public exposure to the Opera House's interior. From **Opening Day** onward for the next six and a half years, the Opera House doors were locked because the interior space was being used to store lumber for the park's construction projects. However, three days after *Babes in Toyland* opened in theaters, the Opera House's doors opened to guests. Inside the building were some of the actual sets and props from the movie, including the Mother Goose Village and the Forest of No Return, plus **cast members** dressed like Bo Peep, anthropomorphic trees, and other movie characters.

The exhibit proved to be only slightly more durable than the movie, which failed at the box office and wasn't rereleased as most Disney films usually were. There was no mention of the exhibit in any of the **souvenir books** of the early '60s, and within a year some of the sets were struck. Segments of *The Mickey Mouse Club* TV show were shot on what remained, but by October of '63 the last of the *Babes in Toyland* artifacts were gone, and the Opera House became home to the **Mickey Mouse Club Headquarters.**

Baby Station, aka Baby Center, aka Baby Care Center

MAP: Plaza Hub, PH-6

CHRONOLOGY: July 1957–ongoing

HISTORY: On the Fourth of July in 1979, out on a bench in the **Plaza Hub**, the first baby was born at Disneyland. Fortunately the park's official Baby Station was nearby. The Baby Station has always been located on East Plaza Street about 25

feet to the right of what was called the **Red Wagon Inn** back in 1955 and the Plaza Inn as of 1965. Anyone who was ever trying to find it could just look for all the baby strollers parked outside.

Though the Baby Station has a front that is only about 10 feet wide, the interior is about 50 feet deep. Inside the room parents can find all manner of helpful supplies and services, everything from pacifiers and baby bottles to diapers and a diaper-changing area (but no babysitters). The Mead Johnson Corporation, maker of Pablum baby cereal, was

the establishment's first sponsor, and thus this location sometimes incorporated Pablum into its name. The park's 1958 **souvenir book**, under the heading "Special Shows and Exhibits," listed the spot as the Pablum Baby Station, showed a drawing of a baby bottle and a safety pin, and described the site as "a facility for changing infants' diapers, preparing formulas, warming bottles and feeding babies. Pablum foods provided free of charge."

In the '61 souvenir book, Pablum was removed from the name and the site was simply the Baby Station. Subsequently it's been referred to as the Baby Center, Gerber Station, Gerber Baby Care Center, and Carnation Baby Care Center. In 2007, it was the Disneyland Baby Care Center, hosted by Nestlé, with an additional sign out front for Lost Children and a cordoned-off area for Lost Children in the main room. No matter the name, it's always had an adorable baby picture on the wall. The baby? None other than 10-month-old **Walt Disney**.

Buddy Baker

CHRONOLOGY: January 4, 1918–July 26, 2002

HISTORY: The rollicking "Grim Grinning Ghosts" theme music in the **Haunted Mansion**? That's the work of the prolific composer Buddy Baker, who wrote the music for hundreds of Disney attractions, movies, and TV shows. He was born Norman Dale Baker in Missouri in 1918. After earning a Ph.D. in music, he played with noted big bands and began composing music for television. Hired at the Disney Studios in 1954, he wrote and/or arranged music for *The Mickey Mouse Club* show, the later series *Walt Disney's Wonderful World of Color*, and dozens of Disney films, including *The Monkey's Uncle* and *Winnie the Pooh and the Blustery Day*.

At Disneyland, in addition to composing the Haunted Mansion music, Baker wrote the background music for **Great Moments with Mr. Lincoln**, the **Carousel of Progress**, the **Monorail**, **Adventure Thru Inner Space**, and **Innoventions**, as well as arranging a **Sherman** brothers' ditty for the multilingual **It's a Small World** cruise. And it was his "Swisskapolka," a composition for the film *Swiss Family Robinson*, that played inside the **Swiss Family Treehouse**. Later accomplishments included numerous compositions at Walt Disney World and Tokyo Disneyland. Having received an Oscar nomination and numerous prestigious music awards, Buddy Baker was named a Disney Legend in 1998. He died in Sherman Oaks, California, in 2002 at age 84.

Baloo's Dressing Room

MAP: Fantasyland, Fa-19

CHRONOLOGY: March 15, 1991–September 8, 1991

HISTORY: *Disney Afternoon*, the 1990s TV show, spawned **Disney Afternoon Avenue**, the 1991 temporary area. For a 400-foot stretch of **Fantasyland** walkway going north from the **Storybook Land Canal Boats** towards **It's a Small World**, guests could interact with popular cartoon characters throughout that summer of '91. One of these characters was Baloo, costar of 1967's *The Jungle Book* movie and the *Disney Afternoon TaleSpin* cartoons. The affable bear had his own hangout at the base of the train overpass at the back of Fantasyland.

Baloo's Dressing Room was a popular meet-and-greet site themed with *TaleSpin* décor. After six months Baloo and the rest of the Avenue regulars left as bigger plans were being made for the area. Two years later those plans were realized and Baloo's spot at the train tracks became the tunnel walkway into **Mickey's Toontown.**

Bandstand

MAP: Plaza Hub, PH-2

CHRONOLOGY: July 17, 1955–1962

HISTORY: Other than a pretty photo in the 1955 **souvenir book**, the bandstand got little mention in Disneyland's early literature. But the bandstand was a topic of much discussion in mid-'55. As he was re-creating small-town Midwestern America on **Main Street**, **Walt Disney** knew a traditional bandstand was a mandatory accessory.

Location was the issue. Before **Opening Day**, the bandstand, a cozy open-air gazebo where live music could be performed, sat in **Town Square** as one of the first structures incoming guests would see; unfortunately, that was the problem, since **Sleeping Beauty Castle** at the end of Main Street was obscured, and in fact the iconic castle couldn't even be seen from up on the platform of the Main Street train station. So, before any guests ever saw it in Town Square, a 65-foot flagpole was installed in the center of the square, and the bandstand was relocated to a spot alongside the **Plaza Hub** halfway between the entrances into **Frontierland** and **Fantasyland**. There it stood on Opening Day and into 1956, a little white wooden structure about 15 feet tall with a short staircase, a pastel roof, decorative railings and finials, and a flagpole on top.

The **Disneyland Band** played at the bandstand every day to audiences sitting on park benches and standing on the green lawn around the Plaza Hub. Realizing the bandstand was becoming increasingly popular, Disney had the area transformed in 1956 into the **Carnation Plaza Gardens** with a bigger stage and a dance area. Meanwhile, the bandstand was relocated again, this time to a Southern-styled rest area at the far tip of Adventureland called **Magnolia Park**. The bandstand played on for six more years until a 1962 expansion of the **Jungle Cruise** encroached into this part of Magnolia Park. Happily, the old bandstand was bought before it was dismantled, and today it lives on at a nursery in nearby Newport Beach called Roger's Gardens.

Bank of America,
aka Bank of Main Street, aka Annual Pass Center

MAP: Town Square, TS-10

CHRONOLOGY: July 17, 1955–ongoing

HISTORY: Walt Disney knew that guests would need lots of money to enjoy Disneyland to the fullest, so he wisely put a bank, not just anywhere, but as the very first building guests would encounter as they entered the park through the east tunnel under the **Santa Fe & Disneyland Railroad.** Located on the first floor of the handsome **Opera House** building, the 35-foot-long Bank of America in its early years had another serious organization, **Town Square Realty**, as its immediate neighbor to the north. Around the south corner is a nostalgic mural reminding bank customers that "a penny saved is a penny earned."

Inside the bank, the main room always felt like a traditional financial institution replete with teller windows and conservative décor; however, this particular B of A always functioned a little differently from other branches in that it was one

22 Sponsors of Multiple Locations

Arribas Brothers: Castle Arts, Cristal d'Orleans, Crystal Arts
Bank of America: Bank of America branch, It's a Small World
Brawny: Big Thunder Barbecue, Big Thunder Ranch
Carnation: Baby Station, Carnation Café, Carnation Ice Cream Parlor, Carnation Plaza Gardens
Coca-Cola: Refreshment Corner, Spirit of Refreshment, Tomorrowland Terrace
Dole: Enchanted Tiki Room, Tiki Juice Bar
Dreyer's: Gibson Girl Ice Cream Parlor, Main Street Cone Shop
Gibson Art Co.: Gibson Greeting Cards, Card Corner
Hills Bros.: Hills Bros. Coffee House and Coffee Garden, Market House
Kodak: Golden Horseshoe, Kodak Camera Center, Magic Eye Theater, Main Street Photo Supply Co.
McDonald's: Harbour Galley, Westward Ho Conestoga Wagon Fries
McDonnell Douglas: Flight to the Moon, Mission to Mars
Monsanto: Adventure Thru Inner Space, Fashions and Fabrics Through the Ages, Hall of Chemistry, House of the Future
National Car Rental: Main Street vehicles
Nestlé: Baby Care Center, Blue Ribbon Bakery, Chocolate Collection, Enchanted Cottage Sweets & Treats, Gibson Girl Ice Cream Parlor, Princess Fantasy Faire
Pepsi-Cola: Country Bear Jamboree, Golden Horseshoe
Richfield: Fantasyland Autopia, Tomorrowland Autopia
Santa Fe: Santa Fe & Disneyland Railroad, Viewliner
Stouffer's: French Market, Plaza Pavilion, Tahitian Terrace
Sunkist: River Belle Terrace; Sunkist Citrus House; Sunkist, I Presume
Swift: Chicken Plantation, Market House, Red Wagon Inn
TWA: *Moonliner*, Rocket to the Moon

of the few in America open on Sundays and holidays (and not many others required their customers to pay a steep park admission fee to gain access). Despite these differences, from **Opening Day** in 1955 until the summer of 1993, guests really could open a genuine B of A account inside, plus they could cash checks and get checks with Disneyland images on them.

After the Bank of America ended its participation at Disneyland in 1992 (the same year the bank stopped sponsoring **It's a Small World**), in late July of '93 the B of A became the B of MS for eight more years. The Bank of Main Street, though, wasn't a true bank with bank accounts; instead, it was more of an information center that also happened to exchange currency, cash checks up to $100, and offer access to an ATM.

In 2001, though it still looked like a bank with teller windows, and though it still sported the Bank of Main Street name out front, the room began focusing more on selling Annual Passports. In 2005, the room ceased all bank functions and now exists solely as the Annual Pass Center, the place where guests can buy the various year-long passes that offer frequent admission to the park at discounted prices (the prices depend on the number of times the passes can be used during the year). Unbeknownst to most pedestrians walking by, the curtained windows on the second floor front the sound rooms that generate the park's public-address announcements.

Bathroom of Tomorrow

MAP: Tomorrowland, T-22

CHRONOLOGY: April 5, 1956–August 30, 1960

HISTORY: One of the more unusual exhibits in Disneyland's history was born nine months after **Opening Day**. The location of the Bathroom of Tomorrow was at the end of the row of buildings on the right as guests entered **Tomorrowland**; this row already housed the science-and-industry displays in the **Hall of Chemistry** and the **Hall of Aluminum Fame**, so one more exhibit about life in the near future must've seemed appropriate.

What the Crane Plumbing Company installed was a 20-foot-wide bathroom that looked like something from an industrial trade show. From behind a railing guests inspected the bathroom and all its expected fixtures, all done in yellow and some plated with 24-karat gold. Flush with enthusiasm, Crane added to the excitement with separate laundry facilities and a kids' play area called Fun with Water (a colorful mobile, plus guest-controlled fountains and spigots).

While it's easy to joke in retrospect about an archaic exhibit called the Bathroom of Tomorrow, it was at least a serious attempt at showing how technology would impact the modern world, just as the **House of the Future** and the two nearby Halls were doing in the '50s. Disneyland, remember, wasn't built merely to entertain, it was also built to educate, even if the lessons did involve a posture-enhancing toilet seat. At the end of August in 1960, the Bathroom of Tomorrow became the Bathroom of Yesterday when it was replaced by more of the Fun Fotos displays that had moved into the Hall of Aluminum Fame the month before.

Bear Country

MAP: Park, P-14

CHRONOLOGY: March 24, 1972–November 23, 1988

HISTORY: Bear Country, the seventh major land in Disneyland, was added in 1972 after the plans for a Disney ski resort in California called Mineral King were abandoned in 1966. An elaborate show with singing **Audio-Animatronic** bears would've been performed in one of the Mineral King buildings, but when the ski dream ended, so did the show, at least for the next five years. In 1971, the **Country Bear Jamboree** opened in Walt Disney World, and that success prompted a whole new development, Bear Country, back in Anaheim.

Veteran guests recognized Bear Country as a familiar Disneyland name. Since 1960, there had been a small site called Bear Country in **Frontierland** along the route through **Nature's Wonderland** traversed by the Western Mine Train. This early Bear Country featured realistic bears fishing in a lake and lasted until 1977, when it was obliterated by the **Big Thunder Mountain Railroad** construction.

In the spring of '72, six years after **New Orleans Square** had opened next door, the "real" Bear Country opened on the land that had been home to the **Indian Village** from 1956 to 1971. Bear Country, however, extended beyond the borders of the Indian Village, which was defined by the **Rivers of America** to the east and the **Santa Fe & Disneyland Railroad** line to the west; in contrast, over half of Bear Country's 3.5 acres spread *under* the train tracks, pushing westward through Disneyland's perimeter **berm** into what had been an employee parking lot. One of the results of this expansion was Bear Country's entrance and exit—they were the same, so there was only one way in and out. Every other existing land (**Adventureland**, Frontierland, **Fantasyland**, **Tomorrowland**, **Main Street**, and New Orleans Square) had at least two pathways to neighboring areas. Bear Country uniquely rounded into a cul-de-sac that didn't lead anywhere else in the park.

Built for approximately $8,000,000, Bear Country cost almost half of what it cost to build all of Disneyland back in the mid-'50s. Disneyland's 1972 **souvenir book** played up Bear Country's arrival with a colorful back cover ("a whole new land . . . a wild new band") and a two-page spread that described the new area as "a lighthearted blend of the authentic with the fanciful." The 19th-century Pacific Northwest inspired Bear Country's rustic design—the buildings were made out of wood planks and exposed timbers, old-fashioned fonts decorated the store fronts, and newly planted forest trees grew thick and tall. The entrance into Bear Country was marked by a wooden sign, supposedly created by "J. Audubon Woodlore, Park Ranger," that declared this to be "a honey of a place" and then joked about the scratching, hibernating, tree-climbing residents (Woodlore, incidentally, was a character in several Disney cartoons of the '50s). Also to the left of the entrance was a cave, home to an ever-snoring but never-seen Rufus Bear.

When it opened, Bear Country had only one significant new attraction, the Country Bear Jamboree, which was, as it was in Florida, a musical extravaganza performed by almost two dozen Audio-Animatronic animals (most of them bears). Bear Country's other new establishments were **Teddi Barra's Swingin' Arcade**, **Ursus H. Bear's Wilderness Outpost**, the **Golden Bear Lodge**, and the **Mile Long Bar** (the lone holdovers from the Indian Village were the **Indian Trading Post** and the **Indian War Canoes**, which were renamed Davy Crockett's Explorer Canoes).

For some line-weary guests, the absence of high-profile attractions was welcome, because it meant Bear Country would stay a relatively quiet, rural, relaxing corner of the park. But the thin crowds concerned park officials, and after a decade they began working on a major new attraction. The arrival of **Splash Mountain** brought a name change to the whole area—since late 1988, Bear County has been known as **Critter Country**, with the mailbox out front for Rufus Bear changed to Brer Bear.

Bell Telephone Systems Phone Exhibits

MAP: Tomorrowland, T-5

CHRONOLOGY: 1960–ca. 1984

HISTORY: In 1960, Bell Telephone Systems started sponsoring the prominent **Circarama** theater in **Tomorrowland**. Quickly redesigning the pre- and post-show areas of the five-year-old theater, Bell installed an interactive promotional exhibit that fulfilled the Tomorrowland mission statement as printed in Disneyland's **souvenir books**: Tomorrowland was intended to offer a "living blueprint of our future."

For Bell in 1960, that blueprint included the wonders of dialing long distance. Thus the park's 1960 souvenir book introduced text announcing a new "demonstration of coast to coast Direct Distance Dialing. . . . Bell Telephone System representatives will dial cross country to local Weather Bureaus as a stop watch records the time necessary to complete the call." Also part of the theater's pre-show exhibit was "a dimensional mural" of movie screens that told the story of communications. In 1964, Bell added a Picture-Phone, which guests could witness but not actually try out themselves with personal calls (what friends could guests have called who had Picture-Phones in their homes?). The idea of seeing whom you're talking to may have seemed obvious and attractive at the time, and it was a moderately interesting spectacle to watch, but obviously the Picture-Phone did not find its way into every American home.

Later, possibly around 1967, Bell added something that guests really could use: small "phone rooms" called Chatterboxes. In a Chatterbox, a group sat in a booth in front of a large pay phone, dialed anyone anywhere who had any kind of phone, paid the charge via coins, and then talked conference-style to the dialee via a microphone mounted on the Chatterbox phone. Having a group conversation in a phone booth with no cumbersome handset to pass around was a fun novelty in the mid-'60s, and the speakerphone idea really did come to pass, albeit in offices more than in homes. One drawback to the Chatterbox was that the calls could only be made one way—a sign clearly announced that the phones did not accept incoming calls, which meant if one group wanted to tie up a Chatterbox for a long time, they'd be pumping lots of quarters into the slot.

Other options in the Bell exhibit included the Dial a Character wall, where guests could pick up phones and hear recordings of Disney characters talking on the other ends, and a phone that enabled listeners to hear what their own voices sounded like. Naturally, actual Bell phones that guests could buy for their homes were also on display. Presumably Bell hung up its Phone Exhibits in 1984 when it ended its sponsorship of the theater. In the late '90s, the **American Space Experience** landed here for five and a half years.

Bengal Barbecue

MAP: Adventureland, A-3

CHRONOLOGY: 1992–ongoing

HISTORY: The instantly popular Bengal Barbecue replaced **Sunkist, I Presume** in 1992. The location is in the heart of **Adventureland**, adjacent to the posh **River Belle Terrace** and directly across from the **Indiana Jones Adventure**.

Unlike the juices and snacks of the Sunkist eatery, the Bengal Barbecue has always offered something more substantial to hungry guests (the sign, which is clutched in the jaws of a large tiger's head, helps makes that point). The restaurant's highlight is the selection of marinated skewers—beef, chicken, and vegetables—that can be ordered with various sauces. Appropriating some Adventureland theming, the side dishes are called Extra Provisions and include a SSS-inamon Snake Twist and Tiger Tails (cinnamon twists and breadsticks, respectively). Also in keeping with the local color is the décor—the counter and tables are positioned under a thatched jungle roof. The Bengal may soon barbecue its last skewer if the River Belle Terrace is remodeled and expanded, as persistent rumors suggest.

Berm

MAP: Park, P—the railroad track around the park perimeter

CHRONOLOGY: July 17, 1955–ongoing

HISTORY: In order to enhance the illusion that Disneyland is a complete world unto itself, a tall earthen barrier, known as the berm, wraps around the perimeter of the park. "The terraced embankment which completely encloses Disneyland," explained the park's 1955 book *The Story of Disneyland*, "was designed to keep the outside world from intruding upon you." **Walt Disney**

knew how effective a berm could be—he'd already put one around his Disney Studios in Burbank and another around the large backyard of his home in Holmby Hills (near Beverly Hills).

A berm was always part of the plans for Disneyland—the famous concept drawing executed by **Herb Ryman** in 1953 showed an un-landscaped dirt wall as Disneyland's boundary. Subsequent

> ## Attractions and Lands "Beyond the Berm"
>
> "Show building" refers to a hidden structure outside the park where much of an attraction actually takes place, even if its façade and entrance are inside the park.
>
> Bear Country/Critter Country
> Haunted Mansion (show building)
> Holidayland
> Indiana Jones Adventure (show building)
> It's a Small World (show building)
> Mickey's Toontown
> Pirates of the Caribbean (show building)

construction over the decades (such as the additions of **Bear Country** and **Mickey's Toontown**) has pushed the berm outwards, so it no longer has its original shape or its original 1.3-mile length. But back when it did form the rounded triangle that was Disneyland's initial shape, the berm defined the park's actual boundaries and gave measuring points for the park's maximum distances. For instance, the maximum north-south distance of the original park (from the **Main Street** train station to a spot near the **Fantasyland** station before Mickey's Toontown was added) was about 1,900 feet, or just over 1/3 of a mile; the maximum east-west distance of the park (from the **Frontierland** berm near the extinct **Indian Village** to the **Tomorrowland** berm behind the **Tomorrowland Autopia**) was some 2,150 feet, approximately 2/5 of a mile. More than 50 football fields could've been laid out within the original berm.

Planted along the outside of the berm are stands of trees to help block outside distractions. While the trees and the 12-to-20-foot-high berm do keep pedestrians inside the park from seeing the world beyond, the berm hasn't ever been high enough to prevent guests on the **Matterhorn**, the extinct **Skyways to Fantasyland and Tomorrowland**, and other elevated attractions from seeing distant build-ings in Anaheim. And it hasn't always managed to keep nonpaying guests out—on **Opening Day,** bermcrashers found sneaky ways to get over it. But the berm has always successfully fulfilled one other important function: it's the support for the main train tracks circling the park.

Big Game Safari Shooting Gallery

MAP: Adventureland, A-2

CHRONOLOGY: June 1962–January 1982

HISTORY: Two shooting galleries already existed on **Main Street** and in **Frontierland** when another one opened in **Adventureland** for the summer of '62. The Adventureland version was the largest of the three shooting galleries and occupied a prominent space to the left of the **Adventureland Bazaar.**

The attraction went by several names during its two decades of existence, including Safari Shooting Gallery, Big Game Safari, and Big Game Shooting Gallery. It was themed for the jungle, naturally, and included a thatched roof, bamboo decorations, and elephant, rhino, hippo, snake, jungle cat, and other exotic targets along the watery bank of a jungle river. The park's 1962 **souvenir book** declared that the gallery "offered marksmen an opportunity to stalk and bring down a variety of game with their high-powered 'elephant rifles.'" No tickets were required to pick up a rifle—this was a "pay to play" attraction that cost a quarter for a tube full of lead pellets that were loaded by a **cast member.**

The guns were limited in their range of motion, of course, keeping the pellets in front of the guests. But the use of pellets meant that the target area had to be repainted every night to look fresh for the next day's shooters. Another pellet problem was the minute amount of toxic lead dust they generated, a gradually accumulating threat to the cast members who were breathing the gallery air for long spells. In 1982, the Big Game Gallery became the Game Over Gallery when a major remodel brought new shops and restaurants along this stretch of Adventureland.

Big Thunder Barbecue, aka Festival of Foods

MAP: Frontierland, Fr-20

CHRONOLOGY: December 14, 1986–January 21, 2001

HISTORY: Seven years after the wildly popular **Big Thunder Mountain Railroad** debuted, a rustic cafeteria-style restaurant called Big Thunder Barbecue opened directly north of the rowdy railroad and 150 feet west of the back entrance into **Fantasyland.** Formerly this section of **Frontierland** was designated the **Painted Desert**, a sunbleached territory explored by the **Mule Pack** and **Rainbow Caverns Mine Train.**

The restaurant was within an area known as **Big Thunder Ranch**; the restaurant, ranch, and railroad all shared the same Wild West theming that warranted inclusion under the unifying Big Thunder umbrella. Re-creating 19th-century American frontier life, the Big Thunder Barbecue offered alfresco dining on picnic tables arranged near old-fashioned chuck wagons and a fire pit. Barbecued ribs, chicken, turkey legs, a "Trail Boss Sampler" of meats, and even prime rib were all on the menu to satisfy the hungriest trail hand, with corn on the cob, beans and cornbread accompanying nearly every entrée.

From June 21, 1996, until April 18, 1998, the restaurant's name was changed to Festival of Foods and the theme was augmented with gypsy décor, appropriations from the 1996 animated movie *The Hunchback of Notre Dame.* Exactly why an outdoor barbecue restaurant in Frontierland was suddenly echo-

ing 15th-century France was never entirely clear.

Whatever the reasoning, at the end of May in 1998, the name and theme reverted back to the Big Thunder Barbecue, Brawny became the sponsor, and the food was temporarily supplemented by the musical stylings of Billy Hill & the Hillbillies on a small outdoor stage. In early 2001, the restaurant finally closed to the public for good, though it is still occasionally fired up for corporate functions and special picnics. Big Thunder Barbecue's farewell sign announced that "we have moved down the trail a bit . . . please visit us at our new hacienda, **Rancho del Zocalo**."

Big Thunder Mountain Railroad

MAP: Frontierland, Fr-22

CHRONOLOGY: September 2, 1979–ongoing

HISTORY: For several years in the 1970s, tantalizing conceptual art for a new Big Thunder Mountain Railroad attraction was shown in **Disneyland Presents a Preview of Coming Attractions** on **Main Street**. In the fall of 1979, the preview became a reality, which sadly can't be said of all the other ideas presented in that Coming Attractions room. Big Thunder was the third major mountain constructed in Disneyland after **Opening Day** (**Matterhorn Mountain** debuted in 1959, **Space Mountain** in 1977). Requiring some seven years to design and two years to construct, the E-ticket Big Thunder Mountain Railroad took longer to create than the entire park, and with a price tag approaching $16,000,000, it cost almost as much.

Fortunately, the attraction was heralded as an instant classic. The site was the large **Nature's Wonderland** area in **Frontierland** formerly traversed by, among other attractions, the gentle **Mule Pack**. Some of the old rocks, landscaping, and desert props from that earlier area were retained, but the dominant Big Thunder feature was brand new. Standing 104 feet high, the central Big Thunder mountain is about three-fourths as tall as Matterhorn Mountain and borrows the dramatic aesthetics of the soaring orange buttes in Utah's Bryce Canyon National Park (though the original plans called for big mesas from Monument Valley).

As a high-speed roller coaster, the Big Thunder Mountain Railroad was designed to compete with other Southern California theme parks that were wowing '70s teens with rapidly proliferating variations of highly kinetic roller coasters. The half-mile-long track is steep, tightly curved, and wet, thanks to a splash area similar to the one at the end of the **Matterhorn Bobsleds**. And the half-dozen runaway mine trains are rollicking, suitably noisy, and seemingly fast, justifying the **souvenir books'** claim that they put the "wild" in Wild West, even though the trains average only about 30 mph during their three-minute trip.

More than just thrills, though, Big Thunder has always offered humorous design details and imaginative Frontierland charm. Even before guests board the trains they can see in every direction some inspired Disneyland touches, such as the sign that touts Big Thunder as "the biggest little boom town in the West" with a population that has steadily decreased from 2015 down to 38; the genuine Old West antiques found in the queue area; the exposed wall of dinosaur bones; the miniature Rainbow Ridge town that once graced the loading area for the Western Mine Train Through Nature's Wonderland; and the little train engines named *U. B. Bold, I. M. Brave, U. R. Courageous, U. R. Daring, I. M. Fearless*, and *I. B. Hearty*. Along the track itself are some more creative touches, including a threatening rockslide, swarms of menacing bats, thunderous sounds at a tunnel exit, and assorted mechanical wildlife. Frontier flair, everywhere: an "old coot" is the attraction's narrator, and crashed into the back of the Big Thunder Mountain landscaping, visible from **Tom Sawyer Island**, is an old derelict train that's actually one of the original trains from the **Rainbow Caverns Mine Train**.

Several much-publicized accidents over the years have marred Big Thunder's reputation. But so durably popular is "the wildest ride in the wilderness" (as described on the **attraction poster**), variations have been installed in Disney's Orlando, Tokyo, and Paris parks, albeit with the Monument Valley-style landscaping that was originally intended for Disneyland.

Approximate Speeds of 12 Attractions

40 mph
Splash Mountain plunge

25–30 mph
Big Thunder Mountain Railroad
Monorail
Rocket Rods
Space Mountain
Viewliner

20 mph
Matterhorn Bobsleds

8–10 mph
Tomorrowland Autopia

4–6 mph
King Arthur Carrousel
Main Street vehicles
PeopleMover

1–2 mph
Finding Nemo Submarine Voyage

Big Thunder Ranch,
aka Festival of Fools, aka Little Patch of Heaven

MAP: Frontierland, Fr-19

CHRONOLOGY: June 27, 1986–ongoing

HISTORY: The unused area of **Frontierland** behind 1979's **Big Thunder Mountain**

Railroad was finally developed in 1986. Themed to match the noisy railroad nearby, the serene Big Thunder Ranch looked like a working frontier ranch from the 1880s, complete with log cabin, stables, farm animals, and what the sign called "the happiest horses on Earth." Of everything here, the most-photographed subject was probably Mickey Moo, a white cow with a natural black patch on its side that looked just like Mickey Mouse's head.

On June 21, 1996, the ranch got a new name based on the 1996 animated movie *The Hunchback of Notre Dame*. Festival of Fools was an acclaimed 28-minute pageant of music and effects that basically retold the *Hunchback* story; the elaborate multistage show lasted almost two years, and during this time the little log cabin was turned into a shop called Esmeralda's Cottage. The Big Thunder Ranch name and theme were restored on May 30, 1998.

On April 2, 2004, the sign above Big Thunder Ranch was modified to include the words Little Patch of Heaven, an announcement of some new theming appropriated from the 2004 animated movie *Home on the Range*. The log cabin, renamed Pearl's Cottage after one of the movie's characters, started offering "Crafts & Fun!" Less than two years later, however, the new Little Patch and Pearl's names were gone. The area is once again simply called Big Thunder Ranch, and the cabin is simply called the cabin. Brawny is the sponsor, just like at the Big Thunder Barbecue next door. The "Washin' Station" here not only stocks Brawny paper towels, it gives official directions on washin' up.

Incidentally, Big Thunder Ranch isn't the only close-up display of live animals ever placed in Frontierland; in the park's first two years of existence, a small **Miniature Horse Corral** offered up pettable Shetland ponies along Frontierland's main thoroughfare, and in recent years **Santa's Reindeer Round-Up** has brought live reindeer to the area over the holidays. Currently, the petting farm of goats, lambs, and other barnyard critters includes a warning sign that notifies guests of the possible minor chomps to be expected.

Mary Blair

CHRONOLOGY: October 21, 1911–July 26, 1978

HISTORY: It's a Small World, one of the most popular attractions in Disneyland's history, was given color and style by the prolific artist Mary Blair. Her imaginative art, which burst with shades and shapes that seemed childlike and simple but were actually sophisticated and subtle, was a perfect match for a fanciful cruise past the children of the world.

Blair was born Mary Robinson in 1911 in McAlester, Oklahoma, graduated from an L.A. art institute in 1933, and began working at MGM Studios in the animation department. Marriage in 1934 brought her the surname Blair. In 1940, she jumped to the animation department of the Disney Studios and over the next two decades worked on the color palettes of such classic cartoons as *The Three Caballeros* and the feature-length films *Song of the South, Cinderella, Alice in Wonderland*, and *Peter Pan*. She also contributed to movie sets and costume design before leaving the company in 1953 to start a career as a freelance illustrator for ads and children's books.

In the '60s, at the invitation of **Walt Disney**, Blair heavily influenced the creation of the It's a Small World attraction that was originally built for the 1964–1965 New York World's Fair and then moved to **Fantasyland** in 1966. Not only the colorful interior but the exuberant exterior was also inspired by her designs. Then, when the park's "new **Tomorrowland**" debuted in '67, the exterior walls of the main buildings were decorated with huge, beautiful tile murals of her joyous art, and the main Tomorrowland walkway was even designated the **Corridor of Murals** in tribute to her work. Blair's importance to the park was underscored when on January 3, 1965, she became one of the few artists to make an appearance on the *Walt Disney's Wonderful World of Color* TV show. She was shown, naturally, working on lighting effects for It's a Small World.

Later Blair brought her talents to bear on Walt Disney World in Florida, where she created an enormous mural for Disney's Contemporary Resort hotel. Mary Blair died in the summer of 1978 in Soquel, California, at age 66. Inducted as a Disney Legend in 1991, she was the subject of an appreciative biography called *The Art and Flair of Mary Blair* in 2003. And today guests can see a nice little tribute to Mary Blair inside It's a Small World—perched on the Eiffel Tower inside the attraction is a cheery balloon-holding doll dressed to look like her.

𝕭last to the 𝕻ast 𝕮elebration

MAP: Park, P-8, P-9, P-10, P-16, P-18

CHRONOLOGY: March 19, 1988–June 1989 (seasonally)

HISTORY: To jump-start the 1988 and 1989 summer seasons, Disneyland introduced an elaborate celebration called Blast to the Past. This springtime spectacular followed on the heels of the **Circus Fantasy** of 1986 and the **State Fair** of 1987 and 1988—of the three, Blast to the Past was probably the most popular, perhaps because it was the most timely. Blast to the Past celebrated recent, not distant, decades, and it was presented at a time when the 1950s were being showcased in the media (*Happy Days* was a TV hit as late as 1984, *Back to the Future* was a hit movie in 1985, and *Back to the Future Part II* was already in production).

With Blast to the Past, rockin' music, colorful costumes, special giveaways, and themed parades all helped evoke the innocent fun of the bygone days of poodle skirts and sock hops. The celebration even extended to the park's décor, which was dramatically changed. Blast to the Past signs were added over the **entrance** tunnels underneath the **Main Street** train station, an enormous jukebox joined the **Plaza Hub**, a palm-trees-and-sand beach scene appeared in front of **It's a Small World**, and a nostalgic name (Rainbow Diner) was given to the **Tomorrowland Terrace**.

Every day a parade of hot rods and classic motorcycles wended from **Fantasyland** to Main Street, and on weekends a "Main Street Hop" was thrown with legions of costumed dancers cavorting to a spiffy soundtrack while confetti showered them from above. What's more, hit bands from the '60s, including Herman's Hermits, the Turtles, and Paul Revere and the Raiders, performed on the **Videopolis** stage; the venerable **Dapper Dans** transformed themselves into the doo-wop group Danny and Dappers; and the park sold a special collection of songs from the era reworked for Disney characters (Donald's "Quackety Quack" instead of "Yackety Yak," for instance). There were plenty of prizes—the Guess-o-Rama offered an opportunity to win a car, and, thanks to a cross-promotion with McDonald's, guests could win discounted admission to the park. And there were lots of special events—the park set world records for mass hula-hooping and mass twisting. The whole festival peaked on May 20, 1989, when the TV special "Disneyland Blast to the Past" was aired just before the celebration itself became a thing of the past a month later.

Blue Bayou

MAP: New Orleans Square, NOS-4

CHRONOLOGY: March 18, 1967–ongoing

HISTORY: Though **New Orleans Square** was officially dedicated and opened to the public on July 24, 1966, its showpiece restaurant—indeed, the park's showpiece restaurant—didn't open for another eight months. When it did, it was instantly hailed as a landmark dining experience. For a while the Blue Bayou was the only restaurant of its kind anywhere—not until 1971 would another Disney restaurant (Walt Disney World's own Blue Bayou) be built directly inside of a large-scale major attraction.

The attraction, of course, in both California and Florida, is **Pirates of the Caribbean**, the revolutionary pirate-themed cruise that debuted in Disneyland the same day the Blue Bayou did. Entrance to the Blue Bayou is through a doorway on the south side of Royal Street between what was formerly **Le Gourmet** (later **La Boutique de Noël**) and the **Pirate's Arcade Museum** (later **Pieces of Eight**); also adjacent is the exit from Pirates of the Caribbean.

Inside the Blue Bayou building—and guests really are inside a building, no matter how things may appear—the illusionary setting is a terrace in front of a small Southern town situated along a quiet crepuscular riverbank. Here the ambience is always serene, the time is always twilight, and the delta moon is always shining, no matter what weather, season, or time of day exists out in the park. Nearby the crickets chirp, the fireflies meander, and shallow boats with passengers lazily float past; overhead, thin clouds drift slowly across an indigo sky that's punctuated several times a minute by shooting stars. For visual spectacle, the view Bayou can't be beat by any other indoor restaurant in Disneyland.

The Blue Bayou is special in other ways, too. For instance, it's the only restaurant in Disneyland that takes (and usually requires) reservations. Its menu is something of a collectible and can usually be taken home upon request. And the candlelit tables are welcome departures from all the quick-stop food counters found outside.

Over a million of the Blue Bayou's Le Spécial de Monte Cristo sandwiches have been sold, making it the most popular lunchtime entrée served here. Dinner entrées and desserts may include crab cakes, steak Diane, pork loin, baked salmon filet, prime rib, mahi mahi, Cajun gumbo, jamba-laya, Creole-style barbecue shrimp, pecan pie, and chocolate mousse cake. Unlike the food at nearly every other dining establishment in the park, these gourmet dishes aren't served buffet-style, they're brought to guests by **cast members**. Great scenery, food, and service—no wonder the Blue Bayou is still, as it's always been since it opened over 40 years ago, Disneyland's premier destination restaurant.

Blue Ribbon Bakery

MAP: Main Street, MS-6

CHRONOLOGY: April 6, 1990–ongoing

HISTORY: Guests who love the smell of sticky buns in the morning have always flocked to the Blue Ribbon Bakery. This bakery was the second one on **Main Street**. Previously, the **Puffin Bakery** had lived on this same west-side stretch next to the **Penny Arcade** in the '50s until the **Sunkist Citrus House** replaced it in 1960. When Sunkist departed the spot in 1989, the Blue Ribbon Bakery took over a year later. Then, on January 4, 1997, the bakery temporarily closed; when it reopened on March 21st of that year, it had acquired a new sponsor, Nestlé Toll House, and had traded places with the **Carnation Ice Cream Parlor**, jumping from the middle of the block to the corner of West Center Street and Main Street (the ice creamery switched to the space where the Blue Ribbon Bakery had been and reopened with a new name, the **Gibson Girl Ice Cream Parlor**).

No matter where it's been, the bakery has always been a popular breakfast destination, specializing in redolent baked temptations like fresh muffins, scones, croissants, "Cinnamon Apple Crumble Buns," biscotti, humongous cookies, and various bundt cakes. Later in the day the bakery whips up trendy sandwiches, too, plus specialty beverages for the holidays. The exotic coffees served here are made from beans roasted daily at the coffee roaster over in Disney's California Adventure.

Wally Boag

CHRONOLOGY: September 9, 1920–ongoing

HISTORY: Signed to a two-week contract at Disneyland in 1955, Wally Boag went

on to enjoy a record-setting career in **Frontierland** that lasted almost three decades. What kind of record did he set? A Guinness-verified world record. Boag was one of the stars of the longest-running stage show in history, the *Golden Horseshoe Revue*, which Boag helped write and then helped perform approximately 40,000 times from 1955 until he retired from the **Golden Horseshoe** after his last performance on January 28, 1982. Comedian Steve Martin has named Wally Boag as a major inspiration for his own career. According to Martin's memoir *Born Standing Up*, Boag "wowed every audience every time" as he "plied a hilarious trade of gags and offbeat skills such as gun twirling and balloon animals." Martin regularly attended Boag's zany shows and "tried to imitate his amiable casualness."

Born in Portland, Oregon, in 1920, Wally Boag learned his trade as a teenage dancer and comedian on American stages, even taking his talents to shows in prominent vaudeville theaters around the world. MGM Studios gave him small roles in several films, and then he auditioned in front of **Walt Disney** to work at Disneyland in 1955. Instantly popular as the show's balloon-bending, fake-teeth-spitting Traveling Salesman and Pecos Bill characters, the quick-witted, acrobatic Boag charmed audiences three times a day in the *Golden Horseshoe Revue*, guested on the TV shows *Disneyland* and *The Mickey Mouse Club*, and appeared in such Disney films as *The Absent-Minded Professor* and *The Love Bug*. Veteran parkgoers might recognize him as the voice of Jose the parrot in the **Enchanted Tiki Room** (he was also one of the main creative forces working on the **Chinatown** area that was planned in the late '50s but never built). Wally Boag and his two Golden Horseshoe costars, **Fulton Burley** and **Betty Taylor**, were all inducted as Disney Legends in 1995.

Bonanza Outfitters

MAP: Frontierland, Fr-2

CHRONOLOGY: June 29, 1990–ongoing

HISTORY: The **Pendleton Woolen Mills Dry Goods Store**, which had existed in **Frontierland** since July of 1955, finally closed after almost 35 years of meeting guests' flannel needs. Two months later, just in time for the 1990 summer season, Bonanza Outfitters opened in the same large location some 50 feet inside the Frontierland gates, with **Pioneer Mercantile** to the left and the **Leather Shop** and **Silver Spur Supplies** to the right.

The store still has the same wooden sidewalk out front and the same kind of rustic interior it had in its Pendleton days, and the clothes are still Frontierland-friendly, with the emphasis now on denim and leather. For a while cowboy boots, countrified kitchen supplies, and Western-themed gifts supplemented the expected Disney wares available here. But these days the merchandise seems to be all Western-style coats, sweatshirts, and hats. This is also a destination for pin traders looking to add to their collections.

Bone Carving Shop

MAP: Frontierland, Fr-1

CHRONOLOGY: Ca. 1956–ca. 1964

HISTORY: Other than what's recorded in the Disney Archives, little has ever been written about the little bone shop in **Frontierland**. It was listed as the Bone Carving Shop, Bone Jewelry, and Bone Craft in the park's **souvenir books** and maps of the '50s and early '60s. The shop was in the **Davy Crockett Arcade**, the first main building to the left as guests entered Frontierland; to the left of the Bone Carving Shop would've been the Leather Shop, to the right the **Pendleton Woolen Mills Dry Goods Store**. Crockett's arcade went through several remodels, and during one of them the Bone Carving Shop got remodeled out of existence as the building shifted and expanded on its way to becoming **Davy Crockett's Pioneer Mercantile**.

Bookstand

MAP: New Orleans Square, NOS-3

CHRONOLOGY: Ca. 1966–ca. 1973

HISTORY: Disneyland has always been populated with many small book- and postcard-selling establishments. One of them, simply called the Bookstand, stood in **New Orleans Square** on Royal Street near the exit of **Pirates of the Caribbean**. This location put it between the **One-of-a-Kind Shop** and what was then the **Pirate's Arcade Museum** (the Bookstand seems to have been in a corner of this latter building). The Bookstand wasn't listed or shown in the park's **souvenir books** (which the Bookstand sold), and only briefly did it turn up on some maps from 1966, the year New Orleans Square opened, until 1973, the year the Bookstand probably disappeared in a building renovation.

Chuck Boyajian

CHRONOLOGY: August 15, 1917–August 1, 2004

HISTORY: Guests have always admired and appreciated the immaculate cleanliness at Disneyland, which since **Opening Day** has earned a reputation as the tidiest, most sanitary park in the world. Indeed, cleanliness, as evidenced by this **Walt Disney** quote from *The Quotable Walt Disney*, was part of the Disneyland dream from the beginning: "When I started on Disneyland, my wife used to say, 'But why do you want to build an amusement park? They're so dirty.' I told her that was the point—mine wouldn't be." There was a motive to Disney's desire for cleanliness—he felt that a glistening park would inspire guests to try to keep it that way.

One man was in charge of establishing and maintaining the park's spotless reputation— Chuck Boyajian. Born in 1917, Boyajian grew up in Ohio and later served on a U.S. Navy aircraft carrier during World War II. He worked at Disneyland from Opening Day until 1981 as the Manager of Custodial Operations, creating procedures, setting standards, and training **cast members** so Disneyland would never look less than spotless.

To maintain Disneyland's radiant cleanliness even while it was packed with guests, Boyajian trained crews to work efficiently through the crowds and with as little fanfare as possible. In the early years, his crews had extra days for cleaning, because during the off-season the park was closed on Mondays, and sometimes on Tuesdays as well (Disneyland has been open seven days a week since 1986).

Some cleaning problems were anticipated—Walt Disney decreed that no peanuts in shells were to be sold in Disneyland, because he knew from his visits to other amusement parks that there would be pieces of broken shells everywhere. But other problems presented themselves after Opening Day and had to be solved on the fly—chewing gum, surprisingly, was one of the toughest, because it is difficult to remove quickly in the hot sun (eventually gum was added to the list of things not sold in the park). Diane Disney Miller, Walt Disney's daughter, named other problematical products in *The Story of Walt Disney*: candy with round sticks "because people might slip on those discarded sticks and fall," and "spun candy because children get it all over everything." And always the sheer volume of trash (about 20 tons on an average day, 40 on busy days) was an issue.

Ultimately, Boyajian met all his and Walt Disney's goals for cleanliness so successfully that he was brought on board to help set and meet the same standards in the Disney areas at the 1964–1965 New York World's Fair, at Walt Disney World in 1971, and at Tokyo Disneyland in 1983. Chuck Boyajian died at age 86 in 2004, one year before he was inducted as a Disney Legend.

Brer Bar

MAP: Bear Country/Critter Country, B/C-5
CHRONOLOGY: July 17, 1989–April 2003
HISTORY: When **Bear Country** was renamed **Critter Country** in 1989, many of the

establishments in the area were renamed too. The **Mile Long Bar** was one of them, taking a Brer name that echoed the *Song of the South* stylings of nearby **Splash Mountain**. The location, on the northern tip of the wide building that lined the back of Bear Country/Critter Country, didn't change. Nor did the food—like its predecessor, the Brer Bar was a quick-stop food spot for inexpensive hot dogs, cookies, Mickey Mouse-shaped pretzels, and drinks. In the spring of 2003, the Brer Bar was swallowed up by a remodel that left **Pooh Corner** in its place.

Briar Patch

MAP: Bear Country/Critter Country, B/C-10

CHRONOLOGY: December 1, 1988–February 1996; October 1996–ongoing

HISTORY: The **Indian Trading Post** was a long-time holdover from the days of the

old **Indian Village**. The rustic Trading Post cabin lasted from 1962 right through the '70s, when **Bear Country** was carved into this corner of **Frontierland**, and continued on up to the end of the '80s. Finally, in 1988, with **Critter Country** arriving to replace Bear Country, the Indian arts, crafts, and jewelry were moved out and the Briar Patch wares were moved in.

Like the nearby **Brer Bar**, the Briar Patch took its name from the zip-a-dee-doo-dah theme of **Splash Mountain**, the major attraction next door (it also took some décor—the cabin's roof has some of Brer Rabbit's carrots growing right down into the store's interior). In the Briar Patch, souvenirs and toys blended with clothes, sunglasses, and gifts on the shelves. Changes came in February of '96, when the store briefly changed its name to **Critter Country Plush** and filled up with new merchandise. Eight months later, the Briar Patch name was restored, though the plush toys stayed. In 2004, the store temporarily closed for yet another change, one that retained the Briar Patch name but replaced much of the plush with big hats.

Briar Rose Cottage

MAP: Fantasyland, Fa-30

CHRONOLOGY: May 29, 1987–July 15, 1991

HISTORY: In the late 1980s, guests who walked all the way through **Sleeping Beauty Castle** and into **Fantasyland** found an enchanting store on their immediate right. The name was appropriate, of course, since Briar Rose was the disguised movie character who was turned into a sleeping beauty by wicked Maleficent. Previously this choice location next to the **Peter Pan Flight** attraction had been the home of **Mickey's Christmas Chalet**, a charming spot selling holiday ornaments. The Briar

Rose Cottage was no less charming, its merchandise (Disney-themed figurines and collectibles) no less ornamental. In the summer of '91, evil conquered good when the **Disney Villains** store took over this spot.

Roger Broggie

CHRONOLOGY: October 22, 1908–November 4, 1991

HISTORY: The man known throughout the Disney Studios for his mechanical genius was born in Massachusetts in 1908. Roger Broggie then grew up in Illinois, learned how to work industrial tools and machines, and subsequently headed west to join the burgeoning film industry of the 1930s. In '39, Broggie landed at the Disney Studios in Burbank, where he developed special cameras and photographic equipment and eventually ran the company's machine shop. In between his days at the studio, he found time in the '40s to help **Walt Disney** create the elaborate miniature train, the famed Carolwood Pacific, in Disney's Holmby Hills backyard.

This train experience presaged Broggie's involvement with Disneyland as the park was being built. Broggie was instrumental in the development and construction of the original **Santa Fe & Disneyland Railroad**. That success propelled him to help develop other major attractions at the park, including the novel 360-degree films for the **Circarama** theater, the classic *Mark Twain* **Riverboat**, the sleek **Matterhorn Bobsleds**, the charming **Casey Jr. Circus Train**, the futuristic **Monorail**, and the groundbreaking **Great Moments with Mr. Lincoln**.

Other Disney credits include his contributions to the special effects for the film *20,000 Leagues Under the Sea* and his efforts at the new EPCOT Center in Florida in the early '70s before he finally retired in '75. Roger Broggie was named a Disney Legend in 1990, one year before he died in Los Angeles at age 91. In tribute to his long-time involvement with Disney theme parks, one of the train engines at Walt Disney World is named after him. *Walt Disney's Railroad Story*, a handsome book about Broggie and the various trains at Disneyland, was written by his son, Michael Broggie, in 1997.

George Bruns

CHRONOLOGY: July 3, 1914–May 23, 1983

HISTORY: Several of the most popular songs of the 20th century were composed by George Bruns for Disney projects. An Oregonian born in 1914, Bruns began taking piano lessons as a child, studied brass in high school, and ultimately was a master of more than a dozen different instruments. After playing with big bands in Oregon and working for Portland radio stations, in '34 Bruns went to L.A. to work first for Capitol Records and later for the Disney Studios.

For Disney, he was a prolific composer of film scores, among them three that garnered him Oscar nominations—*Sleeping Beauty*, *Babes in Toyland*, and *The Sword in the Stone* (he also shared an Oscar nod for a song in Disney's *Robin Hood*). His most famous screen composition, however, was the multimillion-selling "The Ballad of Davy Crockett" for the TV miniseries *Davy Crockett, King of the Wild Frontier*, which he soon followed with another million-seller, the theme from the *Zorro* series.

At Disneyland, Bruns is celebrated as the composer of one of the park's two most famous songs: "Yo Ho (A Pirate's Life for Me)" (the **Sherman** brothers' "It's a Small World" is its only rival). Not just a writer of music *for* the park, Bruns was also a performer *in* the park, playing tuba with the popular **Firehouse Five Plus Two** jazz band. After retiring from the Disney Studios in '75, Bruns went back to Oregon to teach and to continue to make music. In 1983, George Bruns died in Portland at age 68; he was inducted as a Disney Legend in 2001.

Fulton Burley

CHRONOLOGY: 1922–May 7, 2007

HISTORY: An Irishman raised in Canada, Fulton Burley was around lucky horseshoes for most of his long show-biz career. In 1943, having already appeared in several MGM films, he auditioned over the phone and got the lead in the *Diamond Horseshoe Revue* show on Broadway. Burley and actor **Wally Boag** both played fliers in the 1945 movie *Thrill of a Romance*; seventeen years later Boag invited Burley, who was appearing in Las Vegas, to come to Disneyland's **Golden Horseshoe**, where Boag was already starring in the successful *Golden Horseshoe Revue*.

At the Golden Horseshoe, Burley's rich tenor voice, his amiable comedy skills, and his Irish accent were a hit for the next 25 years in a show usually performed five times daily. In addition to costarring in the record-setting show, Burley appeared at special Disney functions and live shows, and he also provided the vocals for the parrot Michael in the **Enchanted Tiki Room** in **Adventureland**. Eight years after he retired from Disneyland, in 1995 Burley was inducted as a Disney Legend along with the two other stars of the *Golden Horseshoe Revue*, Wally Boag and **Betty Taylor**. In 2007, 84-year-old Fulton Burley died of heart failure in Carlsbad, California.

Harriet Burns

CHRONOLOGY: 1928–ongoing

HISTORY: Harriet Burns was born in Texas in 1928. After graduating with an art degree from Southern Methodist University, she continued her studies at the University of New Mexico before moving to Southern California in the early '50s. There she was employed by the company that helped design TV shows, Las Vegas hotels, and the Santa's Village park in the mountains east of L.A.

In '55, Burns started working for Disney Studios on the *The Mickey Mouse Club* TV show (she is credited as the designer of the show's actual clubhouse). Switching to Disneyland projects, she was a key contributor to **Sleeping Beauty Castle**, the **Storybook Land Canal Boats**, the **parades**, the **Enchanted Tiki Room**, **New Orleans Square**, the **Submarine Voyage**, the **Jungle Cruise**, **Great Moments with Mr. Lincoln**, **Pirates of the Caribbean**, and the **Carousel of Progress**, working on everything from models of the attractions to parade decorations, from Lincoln's head to pirate hair, from mermaid costumes to Tiki Room birds. Simultaneously, she was still contributing to such Disney films as *Darby O'Gill and the Little People* and *Babes in Toyland*.

Burns retired in 1986 and now lives in Santa Barbara, California. Today she is remembered, not just as a Disney Legend (she was inducted in 2000), but as something of a pioneer: Harriet Burns was Disney's first female Imagineer, and **Walt Disney** even introduced her to national TV audiences on several episodes of *Walt Disney's Wonderful World of Color*. "His enthusiasm," she wrote in *Disneyland . . . the Beginning*, "left us all inspired."

Buzz Lightyear Astro Blasters

MAP: Tomorrowland, T-4

CHRONOLOGY: March 17, 2005–ongoing

HISTORY: Needing a hit **Tomorrowland** attraction that would generate some positive buzz after the problematic **Rocket Rods** expired in 2001, Disneyland designers looked to other Disney theme parks for inspiration. Buzz Lightyear's SpaceRanger Spin at Walt Disney World and Buzz Lightyear's Astro Blasters at Tokyo Disneyland were already high-flying successes, so the next installation seemed obvious.

In Disneyland, the Buzz Lightyear Astro Blasters attraction zoomed into the former preshow and theater rooms of the old **Circarama**/Circle-Vision 360. What used to be a **Mary Blair**-designed tile mosaic on the curving exterior became a painted mural showing speeding rockets, floating Space Mountains, and fantastic planets. Inside, the attraction, just like its siblings in Florida and Japan, uses the cartoony characters and themes from the blockbuster *Toy Story* movies, all intensified with bright neon colors (Buzz himself is on view as a sophisticated **Audio-Animatronics** character). As described on the warning sign, the attraction "is an interactive adventure in which you travel aboard slow-moving spaceships that you can spin while helping Buzz Lightyear battle the evil Emperor Zurg." The Space Cruisers, a new iteration of the **Omnimover** system first developed in the '60s, are indeed slow, but as advertised they do spin 360 degrees under the guest's control.

What makes this four-and-a-half-minute ride popular enough to justify the **FastPass** ticket center outside is the interactive shoot-'em-up element. As they wend through the 10 different scenes inside the building, guests ("Space Rangers") aim and shoot their own "laser cannons" at different targets with various point values (distant triangular targets have the highest value, nearby circular targets the lowest). Point totals display digitally inside the cockpit, and rankings from Star Cadet to Galactic Hero are posted at the end. Talk about interactive— guests don't even have to be at the park to play, since they can blast away from home for free via the Internet and check daily scores at disneyland.com.

Calico Kate's Pantry Shop

MAP: Frontierland, Fr-27

CHRONOLOGY: 1965

HISTORY: This sounds like a charming store created by Disney designers, but actually Calico Kate's Pantry Shops already existed before one ever appeared in Disneyland. The first Calico Kate's was a countrified gift shop opened in Colorado in 1959, with an Arizona spin-off added a few years later. The business was begun and run by a couple whose daughter designed the Calico Kate character.

Disneyland's 1965 **souvenir book** listed a Calico Kate's Pantry Shop but gave no location or descriptive text; most likely it was in the same **Frontierland** row as the **Frontierland Shooting Gallery**. It's believed Calico Kate and her cute kitchen accessories career lasted only a year at Disneyland.

Canal Boats of the World

MAP: Fantasyland, Fa-15

CHRONOLOGY: July 17, 1955–September 16, 1955

HISTORY: Long before there was a Disneyland, **Walt Disney** loved and collected miniatures. Consequently, among his first ideas for new Disneyland attractions was one that set a little boat gliding quietly through an adorable setting decorated with cute miniature buildings. He'd already seen something similar while on vacation in Holland. Unfortunately the Disneyland version didn't live up to anyone's expectations, at least not at first.

For the Canal Boats of the World, the "Canal" in the title referred to the winding river dug into one acre at the back of **Fantasyland**; the "of the World" phrase alluded to the tiny, detailed buildings Walt Disney hoped would line the riverbanks; buildings that were to have been based on actual structures in international cities. Another scenery option turned up on early concept drawings that showed low-slung Northern European-style canal boats entering a garish mound called **Big Rock Candy Mountain**. In addition, a Bruce Bushman drawing executed in 1954 positioned Monstro the Whale at the end of the cruise so that boats could slide quickly out of his mouth for a splashdown near the unloading dock. But when the attraction debuted on **Opening Day**, no miniature buildings, no mountain made of sugar, and no Monstro slide were in place.

Disappointingly, the view from the eight boats as they wended through the narrow canals was basically of un-landscaped dirt banks and the charming **Casey Jr. Circus Train** that circled the same area. What's more, the primitive motors on the boats were so loud that they preempted the narration given by the skippers. Two months after opening, the Canal Boats of the World as guests knew it sank into history, but happily Walt Disney's idea survived. Nine months later the wonderfully remodeled **Storybook Land Canal Boats** opened with the quiet boats, the lavish landscaping, and the kind of adorable miniatures Disney had originally desired.

Names of the Original Canal Boats

Annie Oakley
Bold Lochinvar
Gretel
Lady Guinivere (sic)
Lady Katrina
Lady of the Lake
Lady of Shallot
Nellie Bly

Candle Shop

MAP: Main Street, MS-3

CHRONOLOGY: 1958–ca. 1975

HISTORY: Disneyland's Candle Shop stood in the back of the **Crystal Arcade** building on the left-hand side of **Main Street**. Just south of the Candle Shop, and also inside the Crystal Arcade, was Western Printing's **Story Book Shop**; to the north was West Center Street (which for two decades was filled with **Flower Mart** carts), with the **Upjohn Pharmacy** at the corner of West Center and Main Streets.

Starting with the 1958 edition, the park's **souvenir books** consistently played up the Candle Shop with large, prominent photos that made the interior look as colorful as a candy store. "A rainbow of color" filled the Candle Shop, according to the captions. A rainbow, indeed: colorful spiral candle displays hung from the ceilings, a broad spectrum of candles lined the walls, and candles of all shapes and sizes filled the shelves and display tables. Among the hundreds of different candles sold here were fun seasonal favorites (October pumpkins, November turkeys, etc.), food-shaped candles, exotically scented candles, twisted candles, tiki-head candles, plus all the long, simple tapers anyone could ask for.

Sometime at the end of the 1970s, the Candle Shop's flame flickered out and the store disappeared. This probably happened in '77 when the **Carnation Ice Cream Parlor** on the north corner of West Center and Main expanded into West Center, displacing the Flower Mart and remaking this side street for patio dining.

Candy Cart

MAP: New Orleans Square, NOS-7

CHRONOLOGY: Ca. 1966–ca. 1995

HISTORY: Disney-themed sweets were the treats at this little outdoor candy stand in **New Orleans Square** near the **Creole Café** (as it was called in the '60s before it became Café Orleans). In the mid-'90s, the cart got an expanded name, **Royal Street Sweets**, with an expanded list of merchandise.

Candy Palace, aka Candy Palace and Candy Kitchen

MAP: Main Street, MS-9

CHRONOLOGY: July 22, 1955–ongoing

HISTORY: Five days after Disneyland's **Opening Day**, the Candy Palace opened on the left-hand side of **Main Street**. Actually, when it opened, the Candy Palace was briefly called Candyland (the 1956 **souvenir book** listed both names). To the south of the Candyland/Candy Palace shop was the entrance to the **Penny Arcade**, and to the north was the **Refreshment Corner** run by Coca-Cola. In 1997, the old-fashioned Palace got renovated and renamed as the Candy Palace and Candy Kitchen.

Pedestrians cruising Main Street have always been tempted by the confections on display in the Candy Palace's windows. Today the ever-popular candy counters serve up lots of nostalgic treats like caramel apples, candy canes, and fudge as well as new creations made on-site, some right in the windows. Guests and some historians have long surmised that vents in front of the store pump candylicious scents like vanilla and peppermint into the Main Street air, but whether that was or is true has not been officially confirmed.

Captain EO

MAP: Tomorrowland, T-19

CHRONOLOGY: September 18, 1986–April 6, 1997

HISTORY: After successful screenings at Walt Disney World, the *Captain EO* film flew into the **Magic Eye Theater** in **Tomorrowland** in the fall of 1986. The film's credits were remarkable: Michael Jackson, at the time the world's most popular recording star, played the title character, who confronted the galaxy's Supreme Ruler, a wicked space queen played by Oscar-winner Anjelica Huston. Both of them were under the guidance of Oscar-winning director Francis Ford Coppola, and the whole thing was produced by the creator of *Star Wars*, George Lucas.

Jackson's weapons against his foe, and what transformed both her and her bleak world, were his singing and dancing, aided by a freaky alien crew with cuddly names like Idee, Odee, Hooter, Geex, Fuzzball, and Major and Minor Domo. Guests, wearing the requisite 3-D glasses, saw objects jump out at them and laser beams fire over their heads while Jackson's music filled the theater. Estimates place the production cost of this extravaganza at about $17 million, which works out to $1 million per minute of finished film.

Touting its exciting new attraction, Disney aired a making-of TV special called *"Captain EO* Backstage" in 1988. Additionally, for several years the park's **souvenir books** offered full-page photos and enthusiastic raves about the new "3-D musical spectacular with dazzling photography," the "hilarious crew," the "inimitable" Jackson, and the "legendary talents" who brought it all together.

Predictably, the big, overwhelmed crowds of the late '80s became small, underwhelmed crowds in the mid-'90s as the shine gradually came off Jackson's lustrous superstardom. In early '97, *Captain EO* was sent packing and another 3-D Florida import, **Honey, I Shrunk the Audience**, successfully jumped coasts.

Card Corner

MAP: Main Street, MS-14

CHRONOLOGY: June 14, 1985–October 1988

HISTORY: From 1956 until 1985, the prime corner location at the northeast tip of **Main Street** had been known as the **Carefree Corner** information center. In mid-'85, the spot became a card shop known as Card Corner, its sponsor the Gibson Art Co., makers of **Gibson Greeting Cards**. Gibson had already sponsored an eponymous card shop on Main Street from **Opening Day** until 1959 (that business had also been on a corner, that one halfway along Main at the East Center Street intersection).

Advertising signs for the Card Corner showed four old-time illustrations that exemplified what was inside the shop—gentle cards for Thanksgiving, Easter, Christmas, and Valentine's Day. Gibson's first Main Street shop lasted about four years; its second, the Card Corner, quit after about three and a quarter years. Gibson was later sold to American Greetings, and the Card Corner was replaced by Carefree Corner, back for another run that lasted into the mid-'90s.

Carefree Corner

MAP: Main Street, MS-12

CHRONOLOGY: August 22, 1956–spring 1985; November 1988–November 1994

HISTORY: For decades guests have used the name Carefree Corner to refer to the prominent corner location where the east side of **Main Street** runs into the **Plaza Hub**. The signage on that corner building supported the cheery reference, but technically this spot has served a slightly less carefree function as Disneyland's official information center. When it opened in the summer of '56, the site was hosted by the Insurance Companies of North America; the park's 1957 **souvenir book** stated that the "Information Center" was "located in the Plaza Apts. at the foot of Main," was "operated by the North America Companies," and offered "road maps, hotel-motel information, places of interest to see." Not until the 1958 souvenir book did the location start getting called Carefree Corner.

With INA continuing its sponsorship, the corner stayed carefree until 1974, at which time INA left and the site became known as the Hospitality Center. Then, in 1985, Gibson Greeting Cards moved in and added a new name, **Card Corner.** When Gibson left in '88, the Carefree Corner sign returned until it was replaced again in '94, this time by the current resident, the **Main Street Photo Supply Co.** The six-year Carefree Corner revival of the '80s and '90s marked one of the few times that an extinct Disneyland shop has been reopened in its original location with its original name.

Whenever the building was known as Carefree Corner, it was an open, uncluttered room that brought to mind a turn-of-the-century hotel lobby. Guests could relax on a round velvet banquette in the middle of the open room, they could get information about the park or the surrounding area from helpful **cast members** in old-fashioned costumes, and they could identify where they lived by signing an official registration book. For years INA gave away its own small park maps and brochures that today are collectors' items.

Disney Legend **John Hench** is usually credited as the designer of the building's impressive exterior, which offers three straight sides that angle around the corner to form an inviting entrance set back from the street. For years the upper floor had a large circular insignia that stated "Founded 1792," the year INA issued its first insurance policy. That upper floor is the site of official Disneyland offices.

Carnation Café

MAP: Main Street, MS-5

CHRONOLOGY: March 21, 1997–ongoing

HISTORY: When the venerable **Carnation Ice Cream Parlor** closed in January of 1997, it took three months for Carnation to open a new business on **Main Street**. When it did, ice cream parlor was taken out of the name, and café was put in. The Carnation Café's location, in West Center Street where the **Flower Mart** had once spread out its floral displays, was just a few steps south of where the Ice Cream Parlor had been. In fact, the Carnation Café took over the quaint outdoor tables that used to belong to the Ice Cream Parlor, making the remodeled dining area one of the best people-watching spots on Main Street.

The Carnation Café is also the only table-service restaurant on Main, and it has the most complete menu in the immediate area. Breakfasts feature huge sticky buns, exotic croissants, and Mickey Mouse-shaped waffles; lunches might be meatloaf, pasta, and gourmet sandwiches; and dinners include big sandwiches, soups, and fancy salads. Gone are the famous attraction-themed sundaes of the Carnation Ice Cream Parlor, but there are still some tempting desserts and gourmet coffee beverages here. One of the café's dinner cooks, Oscar Martinez, marked his 50th year with the park in 2006.

Carnation Ice Cream Parlor

MAP: Main Street, MS-6

CHRONOLOGY: July 17, 1955–January 4, 1997

HISTORY: Carnation, a milk-product company founded in 1899, has been associated with Disneyland for as long as the park's been open. Carnation's first enterprise at Disneyland was the much-loved Carnation Ice Cream Parlor on **Main Street**. The site was the northwest corner of Main and West Center Street in the same block as the **Penny Arcade**. For years the **Upjohn Pharmacy** was on the southwest corner of Main and West Center, and West Center was filled with the displays of the **Flower Mart**.

Like the **Market House**, which is still on the opposite diagonal corner across Main Street, the original Carnation building was (and still is) a three-story structure wrapped around the corner, with a mansard roof, dormer windows, and a widow's walk adding elegant flourishes. So picturesque was the turn-of-the-century interior, it was often featured with a prominent photo in the park's **souvenir books**. The same photo was used for years, one that showed a family, with one child wearing mouse ears, happily sitting at the counter while a female **cast member** in an old-time dress served them. Quipped the caption in the 1958 book, "In an 1890 setting, tempting 'modern' treats are mouth-watering at the Ice Cream Parlor."

In 1977, Carnation expanded into West Center Street, pushing the Flower Mart to the other side of Main and into East Center Street. The parlor's new outdoor patio area offered a great spot for people-watching and relaxing alfresco dining with table-side service. The menu had fancy salads, Mickey's Chicken Pot Pie, and various sandwiches among its options, but it's the indulgent dessert list that everyone recalls, especially the gigantic sundaes named after Disneyland attractions (the Big Thunder, the Matterhorn, the Star Tours, etc.). Some 20 years later, Carnation closed its Ice Cream Parlor and opened instead the **Carnation Café**, usurping the outdoor patio on West Center. At the same time the **Blue Ribbon Bakery** moved from the middle of the Penny Arcade block into the corner building where Carnation had served up its memorable ice cream treats for over 40 years.

Carousel of Progress

MAP: Tomorrowland, T-14

CHRONOLOGY: July 2, 1967–September 9, 1973

HISTORY: Disneyland's Carousel of Progress was an import from the 1964–1965 New York World's Fair. For the fair, **Walt Disney** had his Imagineers put together an ambitious stage show for General Electric called Progressland, which featured an auditorium that rotated around a stationary circular stage. On the stage were depictions of four different decades of American life populated with 32 **Audio-Animatronic** figures, all of them there to show how electricity (the sponsor was G.E., remember) had improved the domestic experience. Progressland was a crowd-pleasing hit in New York, so after the fair closed in October '65, Disney brought it to Disneyland.

Originally Progressland would've landed as a walk-through exhibit in **Edison Square**, a new land intended to go behind the eastern blocks of **Main Street**. When Edison Square failed to materialize, Progressland was installed as the Carousel of Progress in the newly constructed Carousel Theater. Built where the large **Space Bar** had stood on the eastern edge of **Tomorrowland**, the 200-foot-wide two-story Carousel Theater building looked like a stack of immense pancakes wrapped with a swooping ramp and adorned on the side with a thin sculpture that sported—what else?—the G.E. logo.

Inside the free attraction, **cast members** ushered guests into a 240-seat theater on the ground floor. The introduction to the show led off with an infectious theme song, "There's a Great Big Beautiful Tomorrow" by **Richard and Robert Sherman**. The theater, one of six on the perimeter around the stage "hub," then rotated to the first Audio-Animatronic scene featuring a typical family inside their home. The year was approximately 1890, and in the room were A-A parents, their two A-A children, an A-A cousin, A-A grandparents, an A-A dog (named Rover, Buster, and Sport throughout the show), and such turn-of-the-century devices as a gramophone, a hand-turned washing machine, and gas lamps. At the conclusion of their brief presentation, the theme song came up, the theater spun, and the audience moved ahead in time by just over three decades (meanwhile another audience, seated in another 240-seat theater one step back on the building's perimeter, wheeled into position to see the 1890s' scene). In the '20s, the same A-A family now had electric lights, an electric fan, an electric iron, and other electric gadgets. Cue the music, and the theater turned to the 1940s, when the scene was filled with small, handy appliances and Grandma wore a hearing aid. The late '60s were the setting for the next scene, offering a color TV with a "built-in video tape recorder," a self-cleaning oven, and subtle lighting.

While the final speech and the reprised theme music made the audience feel like this was the show's finale, actually there was one last act, this one up the Speedramp to the second floor. There guests walked past an elaborate, incredibly detailed model of Progress City, Walt Disney's dream of the ideal city of the future. At one time little ride vehicles were considered (and sketched by **John Hench**) that would've transported guests around the huge model. And it was indeed huge, covering almost a sixth of an acre and containing over 4,000 buildings, 20,000 miniature trees, thousands of individual vehicles, soaring skyscrapers, a climate-controlled downtown area, a **PeopleMover**, a **Monorail**, an airport, a theme park, a sports arena, and "a welcome neighbor"—a "G.E. nuclear power plant." Narration and lighting cues directed guests' attention to various parts of the model. Guests walked out of the building with the optimistic theme music playing in their ears and hopeful feelings swelling in their hearts.

Disney Legends **Roger Broggie**, **Marc and Alice Davis**, **Blaine Gibson**, **John Hench**, **Sam McKim**, **Wathel Rogers**, and **Herb Ryman** are usually identified as the main contributors to the Carousel of Progress. Surprisingly, the attraction, despite the huge commitment of space and energy required to create it, wasn't spotlighted in the park's **souvenir books**, which preferred to focus on more easily grasped Tomorrowland highlights such as the **Submarine Voyage** and **Tomorrowland Autopia**. The books showed a photo of the building's exterior but nothing from the carousel show, only the "model city of tomorrow."

Another surprise is that a show so complex, advanced, and confident barely lasted six years. After opening with the remodeled Tomorrowland in mid-1967, and after playing to 3,600 guests an hour at its peak, the Carousel of Progress was closed in the fall of 1973 and moved across the country once again. This trip took it to Walt Disney World, where Walt Disney's dream of Progress City was becoming the reality of EPCOT. The Carousel Theater didn't stay dark long, however—**America Sings** opened there the following June.

Carriage Place Clothing Co.

MAP: Main Street, MS-1

CHRONOLOGY: Ca. 1993–ongoing

HISTORY: This clothing store is attached to, and can be accessed from within, the big **Emporium** on **Main Street**. The Emporium dominates the left-hand corner where **Town Square** turns into Main, and the Carriage Place is away from Main Street towards the **Fire Department**.

The Carriage Place, "Clothiers of Distinction" according to the sign, is primarily a clothing shop selling higher-end Disney-themed sweatshirts, T-shirts, and other "fashions for the whole family." Occasionally special events, such as the release of new collectible clothes with Mouseketeers in attendance, have been held here.

Carrousel Candies

MAP: Fantasyland, Fa-5

CHRONOLOGY: Ca. 1983–ongoing

HISTORY: Operating infrequently in **Fantasyland** is a small blue candy cart called Carrousel Candies. It's visible as soon as guests walk north from the **Plaza Hub**, go across the drawbridge, and pass through **Sleeping Beauty Castle** into the castle's courtyard. When it's there, the cart is found on the left-hand side of the courtyard before guests reach the **King Arthur Carrousel** (hence the cart's name). Disney-themed specialty sweets made at "Goofy's Candy Factory" were originally available here, but now the cart leans more towards traditional candy, souvenirs, and film.

Casa de Fritos, aka Casa Mexicana

MAP: Frontierland, Fr-24

CHRONOLOGY: August 11, 1955–April 1, 2001

HISTORY: Three weeks after **Opening Day**, Casa de Fritos made its Disneyland debut, but not where it ended up for decades. Guests who are used to seeing a nice Mexican restaurant on the north side of **Frontierland** over by the **Big Thunder Mountain Railroad** may be surprised to know that the park's Casa Primera was located on the south side of Frontierland near the spot where the **River Belle Terrace** now stands. Back in '55, Big Thunder was the **Mule Pack** and **Stage Coach**, the River Belle Terrace was **Aunt Jemima's Pancake House**, and the small space next door to Aunt Jemima's in the direction of the **Golden Horseshoe** was Casa de Fritos. Just a year later, however, the thriving restaurant was looking to expand, so in mid-'56 it replaced the **Marshal's Office** at the end of the row along the right-hand side of Frontierland's main walkway; a year later, **Don DeFore's Silver Banjo Barbecue** moved into the old Fritos spot next to Aunt Jemima's.

Fritos, of course, was the fried snack made by Frito-Lay, making this the house of Fritos Corn Chips. And in a way, it was, because one of the most memorable features of the restaurant was a vending machine to the right of the entrance that looked like the Frito Kid, a cartoony cowboy who dispensed little bags of the fried tortilla pieces. To modern eyes, the old menu looks like relatively unimaginative Mexican fare, all the usual tacos, burritos, and enchiladas anyone would expect at any decent Mexican restaurant. But back in the '50s, Mexican food wasn't as commonplace as it now, and so a hacienda-style restaurant with lots of outdoor tables probably seemed fairly exotic, especially to guests who didn't live in the western U.S. or come from south of the border. The park's early **souvenir books** even had to spell out exactly what guests would find here: the establishment was identified as Frito House—Mexican Food.

Over the years the restaurant gradually expanded towards the **Mineral Hall**. Finally, after a brief closure in 1982, it reopened that October with a larger outdoor space, some more authentic-looking Mexican-themed architecture, a new name, Casa Mexicana, and a new sponsor, Lawry's. The name, décor, sponsor, and menu all got revised again when the restaurant became the **Rancho del Zocalo Restaurante** 19 years later.

Casey Jr. Circus Train

MAP: Fantasyland, Fa-13

CHRONOLOGY: July 31, 1955–ongoing

HISTORY: The sturdy little train from *Dumbo* almost got derailed before it got going at Disneyland. Initially planned as a slightly faster roller coaster-style attraction, early test runs through an acre of hills in the back of **Fantasyland** raised serious

safety questions. While the Casey Jr. Circus Train was indeed shown in the TV coverage of the park's **Opening Day** festivities, the train didn't really begin carrying passengers for two more weeks as workers flattened the track layout to make the three-and-a-half-minute trip smoother, slower, and safer.

When it did finally open to the public, Casey Jr. was a whimsical little train headed by a colorful engine and followed by a line of circus-themed cars. Disney Imagineers Bruce Bushman and **Roger Broggie** are credited with developing the two safe, charming trains that shared the track. In the first year the trip wasn't much, however, because the tracks passed across the barren dirt banks that lined the waterways of the **Canal Boats of the World**. Thus the park's 1956 **souvenir book** used descriptive text for Casey Jr. that focused more on the train than on the tour: "Casey Jr. huffs up hill and down with his cargo of carefree passengers." Once the remodeled **Storybook Land Canal Boats** attraction hit the water in the summer of '56

Major Attractions and Exhibits Added in the 1950s
(after Opening Day)

1955
Casey Jr. Circus Train; Circarama theater; Conestoga Wagons; Dumbo the Flying Elephant; Flight Circle; Mickey Mouse Club Theater; Mike Fink Keel Boats; Phantom Boats; 20,000 Leagues Under the Sea Exhibit

1956
Astro-Jets; Indian War Canoes; Junior Autopia; Rainbow Caverns Mine Train; Skyway to Fantasyland/Tomorrowland; Storybook Land Canal Boats; Tom Sawyer Island

1957
Frontierland Shooting Gallery; Holidayland; House of the Future; Motor Boat Cruise; Sleeping Beauty Castle Walk-Through

1958
Alice in Wonderland; Grand Canyon Diorama; Midget Autopia; Sailing Ship *Columbia*; Viewliner

1959
Fantasyland Autopia; Matterhorn Bobsleds; Monorail; Submarine Voyage

with a full complement of miniature buildings along the shores, the later souvenir books shifted readers' attention from the train to the scenery: Casey Jr., according to the text, was now a "colorful, gay circus train puffing up and down hills, with exciting view of Storybook Land."

Though it was never more than a B-ticket attraction, Casey Jr. has always had enough adorable detail to make it a Fantasyland favorite. Who isn't cheered up by the passenger car labeled Monkeys, for instance, or the beautiful sleigh-style cars transplanted from the original merry-go-round that became the **King Arthur Carrousel**? Who can't sing along to the swingin' song written by Frank Churchill (who had worked on *Snow White and the Seven Dwarfs*) and Ned Washington (*Pinocchio*)? Who isn't inspired by the audible "I think I can" mantra? This isn't just a train ride, it's therapy.

Veteran parkgoers might know that the whole track got replaced in 1989; careful observers might recognize that the propulsion for the Casey Jr. train is provided by the car *behind* the decorative engine, not the engine itself; and adults might lament the cramped cages more suitable for kids. But "carefree passengers" like those mentioned in the '56 souvenir book won't mind how it came to be, what is driving the train, or how tight the seating arrangements are, so enchanting is Casey's journey.

Castle Arts

MAP: Fantasyland, Fa-3

CHRONOLOGY: Ca. 1983–ca. 1987

HISTORY: The Arribas Brothers, Tomas and Alfonso, were master glass cutters who learned their craft in Spain. After meeting **Walt Disney** at the 1964–1965 New York World's Fair, they opened several shops in Disneyland, to be followed later by shops in Walt Disney World, Tokyo Disneyland, Disneyland Paris, and Hong Kong Disneyland.

One of their shops in Disneyland was inside **Sleeping Beauty Castle**, on the left-hand side of the entrance as guests walked from the drawbridge towards the castle's courtyard. Previously this had been the location of the **Arts and Crafts Shop**, and in the late '80s it would become the **Castle Christmas Shop** for a few years before transforming into the **Princess Boutique**. Beautiful glassware and cut-glass sculptures of Disney characters have long been an Arribas specialty.

Castle Candy Kitchen, aka Castle Candy Shoppe

MAP: Fantasyland, Fa-4
CHRONOLOGY: 1958–ca. 1967
HISTORY: Any shop immediately inside the well-traveled entrance to **Sleeping Beauty Castle** has to count itself fortunate. From 1958 until the mid-'60s, the Castle Candy Kitchen held down the right-hand side of that entrance, with the **Arts and Crafts Shop** across the way. The array of distinctive candies gave kids a chance to stock up before they hit all the attractions in the castle's courtyard. The word "Kitchen" in the name was replaced by "Shoppe" around 1967, and ultimately the whole store was replaced by the **Heraldry Shoppe**.

Castle Christmas Shop

MAP: Fantasyland, Fa-3
CHRONOLOGY: Ca. 1987–ca. 1996
HISTORY: This choice location on the left-hand side of the entrance to **Sleeping Beauty Castle** and **Fantasyland** belonged to the cozy **Castle Arts** store for much of the '80s. Around 1987, after the nearby **Mickey's Christmas Chalet** closed, the Castle Christmas Shop replaced Castle Arts to satisfy guests looking for holiday ornaments and decorations. A decade later the shop relocated to **New Orleans Square** as **La Boutique de Noël**, one of the two holiday stores in that area (**L'Ornement Magique** is the other). Meanwhile, back at the castle, the **Princess Boutique** filled the vacant space within the interior walkway.

Cast Members

CHRONOLOGY: July 17, 1955–ongoing
HISTORY: Cast members are the Disneyland employees who work in view of guests. They include ride operators, store cashiers, food servers, security personnel, parade performers, parking attendants, roving street sweepers, and costumed Disney characters. They have their own unions, their own parking lots, their own cafeterias in strategic locations behind (and sometime below) the scenes, their own in-park merchandise discounts of 20–35%, and even their own store, Company D, selling discounted Disney merchandise a few miles from Disneyland. Cast members who were  employed in 1955 even have their own club, Club 55, that throws its own golf tournament. The number of total cast members has swelled dramatically over the years from about 600 (some estimates double that number) on **Opening Day** to 6,200 in 1970 to over 13,000 at the turn of the millennium.

While they come from all around the world, most cast members are hired from a large pool of local applicants. Many of them are college-age kids from surrounding Orange County cities, though older adults and even retirees are also employed at the park. Because the supply of applicants has usually overwhelmed demand, Disneyland has nearly always been able to be selective in choosing people who are smart, attractive, personable, poised, and available for evening/weekend/holiday hours.

Of all the jobs in the park, the one usually considered the "coolest" is wise-cracking **Jungle Cruise** skipper. The most uncomfortable job is probably the one that puts a cast member inside a hot, cumbersome costume (such as Brer Bear or King Louie) and then places him or her in the path of over-friendly crowds. Bruises and abrasions are the badges frequently worn at the end of the day by these walk-around cast members (David Koenig's *Mouse Tales* books describe even more outrageous abuse, including stabbings and costumes set on fire). Many of the costumes, incidentally, are worn by dancers, and the Mickey and Pinocchio costumes are often worn by women.

Cast members have always had to adhere to the strict code of conduct and dress that's taught in a week-long "Traditions" orientation held in the "Disney University" offices behind **Space Mountain**. According to a decades-old manual, at one time cast members could be no shorter than 5' 2" and no taller than 5' 10", and among the things they couldn't have were dyed hair and gaudy jewelry. Women had to wear stockings and couldn't wear eyeshadow, eyeliner, fake eyelashes, or earrings in pierced ears; men couldn't have moustaches (even though **Walt Disney** had one) and had to wear black shoes and socks (some of these codes have relaxed over the years—moustaches were finally approved in 2000).

However, despite all the park's attempts at conformity, cast members do reveal their individual personalities. Stories are legion of pranks played upon one another, impulsive swims in one of the waterways, rearranged store merchandise that forms **Hidden Mickeys**, friendly group competitions, and playful nicknames for various attractions and characters (of the latter, cast members routinely refer to the **Fantasmic!** dragon as Bucky, the Jungle Cruise elephant spraying water as Bertha, and the **Matterhorn** yeti as Harold).

That employees are referred to as cast members is indicative of the park's intention to make the Disneyland experience something akin to seeing a show. Similarly, in the park's vocabulary the term "guest" has always been used in place of "customer," "costume" for "uniform," "backstage" for behind-the-scenes areas, and "on stage" for before-the-scenes areas. From 1955 until 1962, cast members wore name tags with impersonal numbers on them, but in subsequent years those name tags have included a first name for friendly identification (that name comes in handy for guests intent on critiquing—positively or negatively—a cast member's conduct, which they can do at **City Hall**). To honor their contributions to 50 years of Disneyland success, in 2005 The Walt Disney Company presented each cast member with a memory-filled 64-page book called *The Magic Begins with Me*.

The cast members seen during operating hours are not the only employees working at Disneyland, of course. After closing time, over 500 horticulturists, painters, welders, electricians, divers, and custodians hit the park to fix/clean/repaint/test everything for the next day. Every inch of the park is walked, all the waters are explored, every vehicle and track is closely inspected, and everything is cleaned, de-fingerprinted, hosed down, or sanitized. In addition, store shelves are restocked with clothes, hats, and souvenirs, restaurant kitchens are replenished with food and beverages, and many still-working light bulbs get changed before they have a chance to expire (something like a quarter-million Disneyland light bulbs get replaced every year). All of this work is done in an empty park so it won't have to be performed during the day in view of guests, thus maintaining Disneyland's carefully cultivated reputation of impeccable service, immaculate cleanliness, and undiminished illusion.

Character Foods, aka Character Food Facilities

MAP: Fantasyland, Fa-10, Fa-27
CHRONOLOGY: 1955–1981
HISTORY: For about a quarter-century, two **Fantasyland** fast-food huts shared the name Character Foods. One hut was in the small courtyard on the far northern side of the old **Mickey Mouse Club Theater**; the location would eventually be opened up to be the walkway to **Frontierland**. The other Character Foods hut was off to the east side of the main Fantasyland courtyard between **Mr. Toad's Wild Ride** and **Alice in Wonderland**, the approximate location of today's **Mad Hatter of Fantasyland** shop. Both stands were circular and roofed with a striped circus-style cone.

The "Character" in Character Foods referred to the snacky menu items, which were named after the stars of Disney animation. The park's early **souvenir books** never identified either of these facilities by name, instead grouping Fantasyland's casual eateries under the generic label "Food & Refreshment Stands." The Character Foods stand over towards Frontierland disappeared in 1979, and the one by Mr. Toad and Alice was lost to the Fantasyland remodel that lasted from 1981 to 1983.

Character Shop

MAP: Tomorrowland, T-22
CHRONOLOGY: Summer 1967–September 15, 1986
HISTORY: The massive remodel of **Tomorrowland** that began in 1966 brought an end to the **20,000 Leagues Under the Sea Exhibit** and the adjacent **Fun Fotos** displays. A year later, one of the largest stores in the park, the Character Shop, opened in their combined spaces. The size (only the **Emporium** on **Main Street** was bigger) and prime corner location made this an instant must-visit for guests in search of Disney-decorated clothes and gifts. For guests facing the doorway into

the Character Shop, next door to the right (towards the Tomorrowland entrance) was **Adventure Thru Inner Space**, while outside to the left was the **Tomorrowland Stage** and then, as of 1977, the ramp up to **Space Mountain.**

Inside the "Disney-themed toy and merchandise mart," as it was described in the park's 1969 *Walt Disney's Disneyland* book, was a floor filled with rows and rows of displays and a ceiling hung with futuristic abstract shapes. Giving the Character Shop even more character was the **PeopleMover**, which rode quietly through the back of the store about 10 feet above the floor, giving guests on that attraction a view of all the retail action below ("the modern way to window shop," explained *Walt Disney's Disneyland*).

Unfortunately, just as this store had appeared during a major Tomorrowland upheaval, so too did it disappear during another one. Late in 1986, only a few months before the heavily promoted **Star Tours** attraction was to open next door, the Character Shop was replaced by the space-themed **Star Traders** store.

Charles Dickens Carolers

CHRONOLOGY: 1956–ongoing (seasonally)

HISTORY: For five decades a group of singers called the Charles Dickens Carolers, or simply the Dickens Carolers, has enhanced holiday celebrations at Disneyland. Like some other musical groups at the park, the cast of singers continually changes to include new members. Typically the group presents four (two men, two women) or eight (four and four) performers at a time, all of them dressed in elegant 19th-century costumes: felt top hats, topcoats, and scarves for the men, long-sleeved hoop dresses, bonnets, and hand muffs for the women.

From mid-November to mid-January, the Dickens Carolers perform endlessly up and down **Main Street** and in front of the Christmas tree set up in **Town Square** (especially for the tree-lighting ceremonies), as well as in the Disney-owned hotels and restaurants outside Disneyland. The a cappella numbers favor traditional carols but also occasionally include more modern favorites like "Rockin' Around the Christmas Tree" and special requests from guests.

Chicken Plantation, aka Plantation House, aka Chicken Shack

MAP: Frontierland, Fr-10

CHRONOLOGY: July 17, 1955–January 8, 1962

HISTORY: On **Opening Day**, Swift, a meat-packing company that dated back to the 1850s, was sponsoring three locations in the park. Two, the **Market House** and the **Red Wagon Inn**, were on **Main Street**; the Chicken Plantation, sometimes also known as the Plantation House or simply the Plantation, was over near the far edge of **Frontierland.**

The Chicken Plantation occupied a distinguished two-story building overlooking the **Rivers of America**. Interestingly, the building was schizophrenic.

Viewed from the river to the east, the Chicken Plantation was like a white mansion, with dormer windows projecting from the roof, a decorative wooden balcony ringing the perimeter, and about 20 outdoor tables spreading across an expansive patio, all architecture that would've fit right in with the coming **New Orleans Square**. Conversely, when viewed from the west and the passing trains of the **Santa Fe & Disneyland Railroad**, the restaurant had a rough-timber façade more appropriate to the Frontierland wilderness. A fried chicken dinner for under $2 was the specialty here, and so popular was it that when the building was torn down in 1962 to make way for the **Haunted Mansion**, take-out meals were handed out to guests from a temporary Chicken Shack at the front of the construction site.

China Closet

MAP: Main Street, MS-13

CHRONOLOGY: Spring 1964–ongoing

HISTORY: Some form of china-selling shop has existed on the right-hand side of **Main Street** since **Opening Day**. Since 1964, the year **Ruggles China and Glass Shop** stopped operating, the sponsorless store has been called the China Closet. While the name changed, the location didn't—it's still one door north of the tiny **Silhouette Studio** and one door south of what's most commonly remembered as **Carefree Corner** and

10 Serene Hideaways
(quiet, often shaded places slightly off the beaten path)

Critter Country
Hungry Bear Restaurant's lower deck

Frontierland
Benches to the right of the Frontierland entrance
Big Thunder Trail opposite Big Thunder Barbecue
East-facing docks on Tom Sawyer Island
Riverfront walkway behind Fowler's Harbor
(see photo below)

Main Street
Porch in front of the China Closet

Mickey's Toontown
Toon Park

New Orleans Square
Inner courtyard where Royal and Orleans Streets merge

Plaza Hub
Garden in front of First Aid
Porch at the Plaza Pavilion

is now the **Main Street Photo Supply Co.** Inside, the room opens to both the photo store and **Crystal Arts**.

The China Closet sells porcelain and china decorated with Disney designs, plus an array of figurines and bronze statues. Lots of snow globes and delicate ornaments supplement the selection around the holidays.

Even guests not interested in the wares will be interested in the cozy porch out front. With its wooden chairs and bench, the porch is a serene spot for a quick rest. It's been spotlighted in several of the park's **souvenir books**, such as a 1986 shot that showed musicians entertaining from there.

Chinatown

MAP: Main Street, MS-17

CHRONOLOGY: Never built

HISTORY: East Center Street, the little lane just north of the **Market House** that divides **Main Street** into separate blocks, has been filled with flowers from the **Flower Mart** and the easels of portrait artists. Neither of these businesses would've existed on East Center if the 1959 Chinatown plans had come to fruition.

Unlike the rest of Main Street, which was built to echo turn-of-the-century American architecture, Chinatown, according to concept drawings executed by Disney Legend **Herb Ryman**, was going to look like it really was a Chinese section of town, with oriental shops and eateries lining the East Center cul-de-sac. An illustration under the heading "Dreaming" in the 1960 **souvenir book** showed a courtyard of two-story oriental buildings with only two signs legible on the store fronts—one read Fish, the other Arcade. As described in *Disneyland: The Nickel Tour*, Chinatown's main attraction was to be an **Audio-Animatronic** stage show in an elegant Chinese restaurant starring a philosophizing Confucius, a talking dragon, and singing birds, with much of the script written by **Wally Boag** from the **Golden Horseshoe**.

By the summer of 1960, the whole Chinatown idea was dead as attention focused on other developments in the park. The idea for singing Audio-Animatronic birds did survive, however, and flew over to **Adventureland** where it landed three years later in the **Enchanted Tiki Room**.

Chip 'n Dale Tree House

MAP: Mickey's Toontown, MT-4

CHRONOLOGY: January 24, 1993–ongoing

HISTORY: If **Mickey's Toontown** was created as a fun playland for youthful guests, the Chip 'n Dale Tree House (as the sign there spelled it) was created as a fun mini-playland for young children. The tree house was and still is a small, cute, architecturally askew exhibit built in a gnarled tree studded with oversize acorns. Winding kid-size stairs lead past Chip 'n Dale's mailbox, pass under a charming wood entranceway, and go up to the adorable house and balcony some 15 feet off the ground. Originally a Tree Slide enabled kids to scoot back down out of the tree house, and there was also an Acorn Ball Crawl at the bottom where kids under 48 inches tall could go nuts in a pit filled with acorn-shaped plastic balls.

In 1998, the slide and the pit were removed, leaving the tree house as basically a walk-through attraction with stairs leading out the back. Though the fun may be slightly reduced at the tree house site, at least there's no time limit on the amount of playing and viewing allowed, just like at the park's other two tree houses, the one in **Adventureland** formerly belonging to the **Swiss Family** and Tom & Huck's out on **Tom Sawyer Island**.

Chocolate Collection, aka Chocolat Rue Royale

MAP: New Orleans Square, NOS-5

CHRONOLOGY: Ca. 1980–ca. 1995

HISTORY: In the 1980s, the Chocolate Collection sold imported chocolate confections deep in the back of **New Orleans Square**. Formerly **Le Forgeron** and **La Boutique d'Or** had been in this spot at the back of Royal Street by **Le Gourmet**. The Chocolate Collection had Nestlé as its sponsor until the mid-'80s, at which point Nestlé left and the sponsorless business took the name Chocolat Rue Royale. Sometime in the mid-'90s the shop transformed into one of the small retailers currently selling decorative gifts.

Christmas

CHRONOLOGY: November 24, 1955–ongoing (seasonally)

HISTORY: Borrowing some words from *A Christmas Carol*, Disneyland has always managed to "keep Christmas well," and fans have responded to make the winter holidays one of the park's best-attended seasons of the year.

Since 1955, the centerpiece of the celebration has been a perfectly symmetrical, lavishly decorated, 60-foot-tall artificial tree that's been erected in **Town Square**. That first year, the park held a festival called Christmas at Disneyland from November 24th until January 8th of '56. The festival featured a special Christmas parade and a music concert held in an open space west of **Sleeping Beauty Castle** called the Christmas Bowl (in 1956 this site became home to the **Plaza Gardens**). This holiday concert was described in a 1955 promotional flyer: "Leading church and school choral groups from all over the West will provide Special Holiday Entertainment in the Christmas Bowl every day." The park's 1985 hardcover **souvenir book** remembered the Christmas Bowl with a black-and-white photograph and a caption that listed the musicians as "scores of local youth bands, choral groups and orches-tras as well as Disneyland's own **Charles Dickens Carolers**."

Christmas-season events have continually expanded over the decades to make it an all-park celebration. The 1980 hardcover souvenir book named some of the events that are typically held every year from mid-November to mid-January: "Christmas time at Disneyland has traditionally been highlighted by special holiday **parades**. Each year a magical procession of Christmas dreams 'comes to life' with the help of dozens of artists and technicians and more than 200 performers. The Park's Yuletide flavor is enhanced with bountiful holiday dressings, including a garland-draped **Main Street**."

That same book described the finale: "The most dramatic of all the Christ-mas festivities is, perhaps, the inspiring 'Candlelight Procession.' Premiering in 1958, this parade of carolers illuminates the Magic Kingdom with the glow of a thousand candles and the music of a thousand voices. Over the years, some of Holly-wood's most respected performers have participated in the finale of the 'Candlelight Procession'—the reading of the Christmas Story. These celebrities have included John Wayne, Henry Fonda, Cary Grant, Charlton Heston and Gregory Peck."

The Candlelight Procession and Massed Choir Ceremony have also included 16 lo-cal choirs, the Charles Dickens Carolers, an orchestra, and a Living Christmas Tree stacked with volunteer **cast members** who audition and then practice as a choir for half the year. In addition, from 1961 and into the mid-'70s, a sparkling 44,000-pound star, helicoptered into position and visible from the Santa Ana Freeway, topped the **Matterhorn** until energy concerns ended its long run. And there's been at least one TV special shot in the park for the holidays, the 1976 "Christmas in Disneyland with Art Carney."

The park's Christmas parades are among the most popular of all these spe-cial holiday events. In previous decades the parades would've been the Christmas in Many Lands Parade (1957–1964), Fantasy on Parade (1965–1976 and 1980–1985), and the Very Merry Christmas Parade (1977–1979 and 1987–ca. 2000). These parades have included such familiar favorites as marching toy soldiers, dancing gingerbread cookies, princesses like Cinderella and Sleeping Beauty with their princes, and strolling carolers.

It's the variety of events held in any given holiday season that ensures the park's popularity, because there's literally something special for everybody, no mat-ter the age or interest. Here's a partial list of the celebrations for one specific year, 2001: the Believe . . . in Holiday Magic Fireworks Spectacular, with "a magical snow fall at the finale"; the **Haunted Mansion** Holiday, with Jack Skellington from *The Nightmare Before Christmas* dressed as Sandy Claws; Minnie's Christmas Party at the Fantasyland Theater, performed up to six times a day; "fantastically festive foods," such as customized cookie decorating on Main Street; new holiday merchandise that included "seasonal gifts and collectibles"; a Christmas Fantasy Parade held twice a day; Santa Claus, available for visits eight hours a day; strolling Charles Dickens Carolers; and special decorations throughout the park (most elaborately on the **It's a Small World** façade). All that, just for six winter weeks of 2001. Even Charles Dickens' Scrooge would've been impressed.

Circarama, aka Circle-Vision, aka Circle-Vision 360, aka World Premiere Circle-Vision

MAP: Tomorrowland, T-5

CHRONOLOGY: July 18, 1955–September 8, 1997

HISTORY: In 1952, the non-Disney film *This Is Cinerama* introduced American audiences to the multiple-screen movie experience. The documentary, directed in part by one of the creators of *King Kong*, showed dramatic footage shot from the front of a roller coaster, from the cockpit of a swooping plane, and from other extremely visceral locations, all projected on three connected screens that partially wrapped around the audience. Within a few years numerous travel documentaries and major motion pictures (including the Oscar-nominated *How the West Was Won*) were utilizing the Cinerama three-screen projection system. An impressed **Walt Disney** decided that he would go Cinerama one better at Disneyland, and soon Disney Legend **John Hench** had drawn up a concept illustration that showed Grand Canyon images being displayed in the round.

Three years after *This Is Cinerama*, on the park's **Opening Day** Plus One, Disney's film *Circarama U.S.A.*, aka *A Tour of the West* debuted in the new Circarama building on the left-hand side of **Tomorrowland**. Instead of filming with three cameras, à la the Cinerama process, Imagineers employed 11 16-mm cameras and mounted them in a circle on top of an American Motors car (American Motors was one of the sponsors of the attraction). Disney Legend **Peter Ellenshaw** directed what was essentially a highlight compilation of a scenic drive from Beverly Hills to Monument Valley—the '56 **souvenir book** described it as "an exciting travel picture on a 360 degree movie screen."

Even though it was only 12 minutes long, the short movie was an instant hit. Audiences loved being at the center of a 360-degree movie that surrounded them with images. The seemingly unrelated displays lining the inside of the theater—cars made by American Motors and refrigerators made by another sponsor, Kelvinator—didn't exactly enhance the moviegoing experience, but they did establish a tradition of exhibits in the pre- and post-show areas that would be more fully developed later. Plus, since this was a free attraction requiring no A-B-C ticket, nobody was really complaining about extra things to see, no matter how superfluous those things were.

Five years later, a new 360-degree movie, the 16-minute *America the Beautiful*, expanded the tour to include aerial footage and shots from across the whole country. It proved to be even more popular than its predecessor. Bell Telephone Systems was the sole sponsor, adding fun **Bell Telephone Systems Exhibits** into the pre- and post-show areas. On November 8, 1964, the name Circle-Vision replaced Circarama as a way to avoid any confusion, and thus any legal entanglements, with Cinerama.

Three years later, a major remodel of the theater began on January 3, 1967, and lasted until June 25th. Once again the theater's name changed, this time to Circle-Vision 360, plus *America the Beautiful* was revised to include new footage, and the pre-show area was radically reworked. Guests now waited in a colorful room filled with upholstered blocks; above were flags with abstract representations of the initials of all 50 states. For about 15 minutes, a **cast member** conducted a playful identify-the-flags quiz with guests, a suitable participatory activity for a movie showcasing American landscapes. The female cast members wore patriotic outfits of red, white, and blue, featuring a blue skirt, red jacket, red tights, navy blue shoes in winter, white shoes in summer, and white gloves. Inspired by the patriotic vision and fun quiz, guests were eager to stand at railings inside the theater and enjoy the fire truck's crazy career through San Francisco, the nostalgic view from inside an old covered bridge, the wild ride through Waikiki surf, and more.

With Bell withdrawing its sponsorship in 1982, on January 3rd of '84 the theater closed again. For the July 4th reopening the theater again got a new name, and this time it got an all-new film. With the airline PSA on board, World Premiere Circle-Vision began showing a thematically correct eight-minute short called *All Because Man Wanted to Fly*, followed by *American Journeys*, a 21-minute documentary that showed further slices of American life. Later this longer film alternated with an import from Walt Disney World, *Wonders of China* (*China* for the morning shows, *Journeys* in the afternoons). Then, on July 16, 1989, PSA canceled its flight, but the next day another airline, Delta, took over sponsorship for seven years, with both movies still on the bill. Finally, on New Year's Day in 1996, Delta took off and World Premiere disappeared from the theater's name. In July, *America the Beautiful* was brought back for one last glorious sprint to the theater's finish line.

Circle-Vision and its signature film both closed forever on September 8, 1997, to be replaced by the short-lived **Rocket Rods**. Disney Legend **Roger Broggie** is usually credited as being the main architect of Disney's 360-degree filming process (with assists from **Ub Iwerks**, Eustace Lycett, and other masters of Disney cinema). Today, Circarama/Circle-Vision is fondly recalled as one of the best theater experiences in the park's history.

Circus Fantasy

MAP: Park, P-9, P-10, P-15, P-16

CHRONOLOGY: January 25, 1986–spring 1988 (seasonally)

HISTORY: Even before Circus Fantasy debuted in early 1986, circus themes had already been plentiful in Disneyland's history: Dumbo's Circusland and an Interplanetary Circus for **Tomorrowland** had been on the drawing boards for a while, **Dumbo the Flying Elephant** and the **Casey Jr. Circus Train** had been operating since the summer of 1955, the **Mickey Mouse Club Circus** had appeared in late 1955 for about six weeks, and that same year daily circus **parades** had frolicked down **Main Street**.

Like the **State Fair** and **Blast to the Past** promotions that followed it, Circus Fantasy was an attempt to speed up ticket sales during what were traditionally slow months of the year. For the winter and spring months of 1986–1988, Circus Fantasy filled Main Street and the **Plaza Hub** with actual circus acts, not merely enthusiastic shows put on by Disneyland **cast members**. There were elephants, clowns, a high-wire act across Main Street, stilt-walkers, a daredevil on a motorcycle, a man shot out of a cannon over in **Frontierland**—all the requisite attractions expected at a real circus. Every day Circus on Parade trumpeted down Main Street and a circus-themed show took over the **Videopolis** stage, with everything stopping for the summer when attendance naturally rose again. Some of the circus activities were shown on a TV special called "Disneyland's All-Star Comedy Circus" in 1988, the same year that Blast to the Past replaced Circus Fantasy as the new spring promotion.

City Hall

MAP: Town Square, TS-4

CHRONOLOGY: July 17, 1955–ongoing

HISTORY: Since **Opening Day** the regal City Hall has been proudly standing on the west side of **Town Square**. About 30 feet to the left (south) of the building is the **Police Station**, with a closed one-story row connecting it to City Hall; about 40 feet to the right (north) is the **Fire Department**, connected to City Hall by a one-story row of **restrooms**. These adjacent buildings differ significantly from those shown in a 1953 **Marvin Davis** concept illustration that placed a fire station and hospital to the left and a Hall of Records to the right.

Disney Legend **Harper Goff**, who designed City Hall, based the look on a structure in his Colorado hometown. Spreading approximately 45 feet wide, Disneyland's City Hall has three main stories crowned with a mansard roof and widow's walk, plus there's a central column that rises yet one more story. Sturdy red bricks and ornate white trim give the structure a handsome, dignified look, while the row of thin columns out front adds a graceful touch to the entryway. In the evening, white lights attractively define the upper stories. Decorating the inside of the City Hall lobby are displays of art, photos, and official proclamations.

In some ways, City Hall has indeed served as the park's official headquarters. The first **souvenir books**, which labeled the building both Town Hall and City Hall, identified it as the place to find lost children, the park's security officers, and First Aid. Eventually City Hall became home to **Guest Relations**, the information center for guests looking for foreign-currency exchanges, maps, Braille guidebooks, local phone directories, dinner reservations, entertainment schedules, answers to questions, and a place to lodge complaints. Behind the scenes, **Edward Meck**, the park's long-time publicity chief, also worked out of City Hall.

Football Fields as Units of Distance (100 yards = 1 FF)

City Hall to Opera House = .75 FF
Enchanted Tiki Room to Tarzan's Treehouse = 1 FF
Plaza Hub to Golden Horseshoe = 1 FF
Tom Sawyer Island Rafts to *Mark Twain* dock = 1 FF
Grand Canyon Diorama = 1 FF
Pirates of the Caribbean to Splash Mountain = 2 FF
Plaza Hub to Pirates of the Caribbean = 2 FF
Plaza Hub to Innoventions = 2 FF
Main Street train station to Plaza Hub = 2.5 FF
Tom Sawyer Island north to south = 2.5 FF

Rarely noticed by guests are the tall eucalyptus trees in back of the building. Happily, these were saved from the original groves that preceded Disneyland, making them, at about a century old, perhaps the oldest living things in the park.

Clarabelle's Frozen Yogurt

MAP: Mickey's Toontown, MT-8

CHRONOLOGY: January 24, 1993–ongoing

HISTORY: Clarabelle, the bucktoothed cow from Disney cartoons of the 1930s, got her own yogurt stand in 1993. Located in **Mickey's Toontown** next to **Pluto's Dog House**, the little blue building has a distinctive white awning speckled with irregular black spots. Clarabelle's counter offers a small menu of "udderly refreshing" yogurts, simple desserts, and soft drinks.

Clock of the World, aka World Clock

MAP: Tomorrowland, T-3

CHRONOLOGY: July 17, 1955–September 1966

HISTORY: Short on expensive, dramatic attractions for **Tomorrowland** in 1955, **Walt Disney** added some inexpensive spectacle with the futuristic Clock of the World. Standing inside a landscaped circle that was prominently placed at the entranceway to Tomorrowland, the clock was a 15-foot-tall cylinder with a middle pinched like an hourglass. The upper half of the hourglass was wrapped with a map of the world, while the bottom half was a bluish base. Around the top of the cylinder were the hours 1–24, and attached to the very top was a sphere that showed half of the sun facing a crescent moon.

The early **souvenir books**, which sometimes called it the World Clock,

played up the exhibit's presence with photos that showed fascinated guests pointing and staring at it. Their fascination, supposedly, was in the clock's ability to tell
the time, right to the minute, for any location on the planet. Evidently guests in
the 1950s and early '60s needed to know this information, but later guests didn't.
In 1966, time ran out for the Clock of the World, and it was dismantled for that
year's major remodeling of Tomorrowland.

Clock Shop

MAP: Fantasyland, Fa-3
CHRONOLOGY: 1963–ca. 1969
HISTORY: Few descriptions or photos are offered in any of the park's **souvenir
books** to help identify the old Clock Shop in **Fantasyland**. Its first reference was
a mention on the list of Fantasyland stores in the 1963 and '64 souvenir books.
The '68 book presented a nice color photo of a family surrounded by ornate cuckoo
clocks, plus the caption, "The Castle Clock Shop leaves no doubt about the time,
especially at the start of a new hour." Actually, the Clock Shop *did* seem to leave
doubt about the time, because of the dozen clocks in the photo with readable faces,
only two were set for the same time, which meant that a cuckoo clock was probably
cuckooing in the store every few minutes.

As to specific location, the 1962 souvenir book included on its list of Fantasyland stores the **Arts and Crafts Shop** inside the entrance to **Sleeping Beauty
Castle**, but that shop was missing from the '63 book, so it's likely the Clock Shop
replaced it. A small 1970 map of Fantasyland omitted the Clock Shop and restored
the Arts and Crafts Shop to its former position inside the castle arches.

Club Buzz

MAP: Tomorrowland, T-9
CHRONOLOGY: May 2001–November 2006
HISTORY: What had been the space-themed **Tomorrowland Terrace** since 1967 became the movie-themed Club Buzz in the spring of 2001. Borrowing names from
Toy Story and the nearby **Buzz Lightyear Astro Blasters** attraction, the eatery was
also called Club Buzz . . . Lightyear's Above the Rest. Club Buzz combined casual
dining and entertainment, just as the Terrace had in the previous century. The large
curving food counter away from the stage area offered a self-proclaimed "out-of-
this-world menu" of breakfast plates, sandwiches, fried chicken, salads, snacks,
and "the best burgers in the galaxy" (possibly true—this place served lunches to
thousands of guests per hour on its busiest days).

Meanwhile, a kid-friendly show, *Calling All Space Scouts: A Buzz Lightyear
Adventure*, was performed for several years on the Club Buzz stage. As with the old
Tomorrowland Terrace, this stage rose up from below ground level. Unlike the old
Tomorrowland Terrace stage, however, the top of the stage was decorated, not with
sleek, white planter boxes, but with an elaborate futuristic sculpture in blue, silver,

and purple. The new show was hosted by the heroic astronaut Buzz Lightyear and featured a confrontation with the evil Emperor Zurg. In 2007, when the new *Jedi Training Academy* zoomed in, Club Buzz reverted back to its original white design and former name, Tomorrowland Terrace.

Club 33

MAP: New Orleans Square, NOS-4

CHRONOLOGY: June 15, 1967–ongoing

HISTORY: One of the worst-kept secrets in Disneyland is the presence of a private restaurant on a second story in **New Orleans Square**. The name Club 33 has long been the subject of speculative guesses by fans who have generated a wide range of explanations, everything from 33 being the number of original Disneyland sponsors to 33 somehow representing Mickey Mouse's initials (or Mickey Mouse's ears) when the digits are turned sideways. According to official explanations, the name derives from the actual address, 33 Royal Street, on the ground-level doorway to the right of the entrance into the **Blue Bayou.**

Another private dining room used to exist in the back of the **Red Wagon Inn** on **Main Street**, but that one was much less elaborate than what now exists as Club 33. Originally the restaurant was going to be used by the Disney family as a VIP lounge in conjunction with the apartment above the **Pirates of the Caribbean** attraction nearby, but sadly **Walt Disney** died before the restaurant and the apartment were completed. When it did open, the restaurant was used for a while as a place for Disneyland executives to entertain VIPs and business associates. Within a few years it became a private club with a paid membership of just under 500 people. That membership was both expensive to purchase (an initiation fee in 2007 of almost $10,000 per individual, plus over $3,000 a year in annual dues) and hard to come by (the waiting list was so long it was finally cut off at 1,000). In 2007, Disneyland announced a small expansion that would take the number of members up to 500, but applicants can still expect to wait about a decade for membership.

The interior of Club 33 is reputed to be the most elegant and fascinating dining space in the park. Once members have been identified and admitted through the Club 33 door on Royal Street, a lift takes them upstairs where wooden floors, crystal chandeliers, antiques purchased by Walt and Lillian Disney, artifacts from Disney movies, and a gourmet buffet await. The floor plan wraps around the heart of New Orleans Square from the Blue Bayou area and across Royal Street into the space above yesterday's **Creole Café** and today's Café Orleans. There are two lavishly decorated dining rooms with balconies overlooking the **Rivers of America**. At one time some kind of interactive **Audio-Animatronics** arrange-

ment was going to be effected in the Trophy Room, and microphones were even placed in chandeliers for instant communication between staff and guests, but that plan never evolved past the experimental stage.

Besides the luxurious surroundings and magnificent views, Club 33 offers unique amenities that no other Disneyland restaurant does: it's the only one to serve alcohol; it gives its guests personalized items to help them remember their visits; and the impeccable service is provided by Disneyland's most highly trained food servers. There's never been a mention of Club 33 in any of the park's **souvenir books**, naturally, and while many people have heard of it, and even more have unknowingly walked right by the entrance, only a very few will ever be able to say they've been inside.

Claude Coats

CHRONOLOGY: January 17, 1913–January 9, 1992

HISTORY: A San Franciscan born in 1913, Claude Coats got a degree in architecture and fine arts at USC and then studied at an L.A. art institute. Hired at the Disney Studios in 1935, he developed a reputation as one of the company's most gifted artists, known especially

for his beautiful background paintings on such classic animated films as *Snow White and the Seven Dwarfs, Pinocchio, Fantasia, Cinderella*, and *Peter Pan*.

Switching to Disneyland projects in 1955, Coats was a key contributor to popular attractions all over the park. He helped paint the displays and backgrounds on early **Fantasyland** attractions like **Mr. Toad's Wild Ride** and **Snow White Adventures**; he designed almost everything in the original **Alice in Wonderland**; he created the Rainbow Caverns interiors for the **Rainbow Caverns Mine Train** in **Frontierland** and underwater scenes for the **Submarine Voyage** in **Tomorrowland**; he was in charge of the artwork for the **Grand Canyon Diorama**; and in the mid-'60s, he contributed interior designs to Tomorrowland's **Adventure Thru Inner Space** and two major additions to **New Orleans Square**, **Pirates of the Caribbean** and the **Haunted Mansion** (**Walt Disney** called Coats "the Imagineer in charge of the Pirates project" in a 1965 episode of *Walt Disney's Wonderful World of Color*).

Before he retired in 1989, Coats also helped with many attractions at Walt Disney World. Claude Coats died in 1992, a year after he was honored as a Disney Legend.

Coin Shop, aka Stamp and Coin Shop

MAP: Main Street, MS-15
CHRONOLOGY: Ca. 1957–ca. 1960
HISTORY: Narrow Center Street divides **Main Street** just past the big **Market House**.

Starting around 1957, a little Coin Shop briefly operated next to the **Pen Shop** in the East Center cul-de-sac. The park's 1957 **souvenir book** listed the Coin Shop but added no other information about it. The 1958 book omitted the Coin Shop entirely, and then the 1959 edition reintroduced it as the Stamp and Coin Shop. The 1960, and subsequent, souvenir books never mentioned any kind of coin, stamp, or coin-and-stamp store again. Presumably it was swallowed up in the 1960 remodel that brought the **Hallmark Card Shop** to the Main Street/East Center corner formerly occupied by **Gibson Greeting Cards**.

Cole of California Swimsuits

MAP: Main Street, MS-11

CHRONOLOGY: 1956–1957

HISTORY: Formerly a movie actor in the silent era, Fred Cole created his fashionable line of swimwear in 1923. After his suits became popular in the Hollywood community, in late 1955 or 1956 he opened a little shop on **Main Street** in the west-side block dominated by the **Refreshment Corner**, aka Coke Corner.

As enduring as the Cole line has been (Cole swimsuits are still made), the Disneyland sports spot was short-lived. The park's 1956 and '57 **souvenir books** listed the merchandise as "Swim Suits and Sports Wear" and then "Swimsuits & Sportswear." The 1958 book, though, didn't list Cole or anything swim-related at all, and it's likely that the first **Mad Hatter of Main Street** shop took over that same year.

Conestoga Wagons

MAP: Frontierland, Fr-21

CHRONOLOGY: August 1, 1955–September 13, 1959

HISTORY: The Conestoga Wagons were part of the old **Frontierland** that existed back when the **Painted Desert** was being explored by the **Mule Pack** and **Rainbow Caverns Mine Train**. The wooden wagons were replicas of the horse-drawn vehicles driven westward across America in the middle of the previous century. "Travel across the Rainbow Desert as pioneers did," read the text on the back of the 1959 **souvenir book**, "in Conestoga covered wagons of gold rush days."

In Frontierland those covered wagons were pulled by three-horse teams, held about a dozen guests, and, true to the pioneer spirit, had the words Westward Ho! roughly painted on their canvas tops. From the summer of 1955 until 1958, a ride in a Conestoga Wagon cost a B ticket, or 25 cents; in 1959, the price went up to a C ticket. Heading north to the desert and back, the trip roughly matched the route of the **Stage Coach**. What's more, the wagons and the stage expired on the same day and for the same reason—unreliable power plants. The horses, unfortunately, were sometimes startled by unexpected noises; though Disneyland tried to present this Frontierland area as a desert wilderness, it was actually part of a heavily traveled parkland filled with jubilant people, train whistles, popping balloons, amplified announcements, and other random sounds.

Fearful of spooked horses standing in front of a stalled wagon—or worse, panicked horses galloping off with a runaway wagon—the park quietly retired the Conestogas after the summer of '59. The Mule Pack and Mine Train stayed on to explore the new and improved **Nature's Wonderland** until everything was removed for the Big Thunder projects of the late '70s and '80s.

Corridor of Murals

MAP: Tomorrowland, T-5, T-23

CHRONOLOGY: 1967–1998

HISTORY: For three decades, beautiful tile mosaics greeted guests as soon as they passed through the metallic entrance into **Tomorrowland**. The mosaics adorned the **Circarama**/Circle-Vision 360 theater on the left and the **Adventure Thru Inner Space** building on the right, both of which were two-story structures that faced each other. On each building, hundreds of square feet of wall space was covered with one half of a large artwork called *The Spirit of Creative Energies Among Children*, thus giving this stretch of Tomorrowland the name Corridor of Murals.

Mary Blair, who had began working for Walt Disney in the 1940s as a designer and artist, was the creator of the murals. Blair had already helped in-vent the style and color palette of some of Dis-ney's animated movies (*Alice in Wonderland*) and attractions (**It's a Small World**). Here her mosaics depicted Small World-style children in international costumes frolicking in color-ful scenes, with a big smiling sun, an ocean, trees, long ribbons of color, and various

abstract shapes adding whimsical flourishes. The theme and execution might've seemed better suited to **Fantasyland** than Tomorrowland, but the murals did help humanize what otherwise might've seemed like cold, antiseptic buildings.

Unfortunately, neither section of the Corridor of Murals survived the cen-tury. The half on the Adventure Thru Inner Space building disappeared when **Star Tours** opened in 1987 with its own big artwork outside; the half on the Circle-Vision theater was lost to a 1998 remodel that filled the interior with the **Rocket Rods** and decorated the exterior with a new transportation-themed mural. As a small conso-lation, after dismantling Blair's work Disneyland sold off tile pieces to fans. And supposedly some of the tiles are still in place underneath the current murals. Even if her designs no longer fit in with Tomorrowland's future, they are still cherished reminders of Tomorrowland's past.

Cosmic Waves

MAP: Tomorrowland, T-20

CHRONOLOGY: June 1998–January 2002

HISTORY: The interactive fountain called Cosmic Waves must've seemed like a good idea when the Disneyland designers first drew it up. Who wouldn't have fun jumping among thin jets of water shooting up intermittently from the ground, especially on a blazing summer day? And who wouldn't want to try to spin a big wet marble sitting in the middle of all the action? Unfortunately the reality proved to less cosmic and more wavy than expected.

Cosmic Waves opened with the remodeled **Tomorrowland** in mid-1998, its location a 60-foot-wide circular plaza halfway between the *Moonliner* and the **Observatron**. The idea was for kids to run in between the fountain's five-foot-high spurting water jets without getting wet, and also for them to team up to rotate a giant 6.5-ton granite ball planted in the center of the jets. Kids, though, found that experiencing the water was more fun than avoiding the water, and so parents and the park were left with hordes of soaking-wet kids (and these were kids in their regular park clothes, not their bathing suits).

By the end of 2001, the wet kids were the only ones enjoying themselves, so with Cosmic Waves becoming more like a Cosmic Bath the park shut down the fountain at the beginning of the new year. Though the water jets are gone, the stone ball is still available for kids to take for a spin before they get to **Space Mountain**.

Bill Cottrell

CHRONOLOGY: November 19, 1906–December 22, 1995

HISTORY: Bill Cottrell was the first Disney employee to be recognized for 50 years of service. He came to California from South Bend, Indiana, where he'd been born in 1906. After graduating from Los Angeles's Occidental College and working briefly for the creator of the *Krazy Kat* comics, he took a job as a cameraman at the Disney Studios. Within a few years he was working on Disney's cartoons and animated movies, ultimately making major contributions to *Snow White and the Seven Dwarfs*, *Pinocchio*, *Alice in Wonderland*, and *Peter Pan*, among others.

As a key ally (and brother-in-law) of **Walt Disney**, Cottrell was instrumental in bringing Disney's Disneyland dream to life and was said to be his "right-hand man," helping him plan and build the park. In addition to overseeing many projects, Cottrell, who for a while had an office inside the park's **City Hall**, wrote scripts for some of the attractions and added important details, such as the names of the original **Jungle Cruise** boats and the term used for the electromechanical figures, **Audio-Animatronics**, that were first being developed in the '50s and '60s. He was later promoted to president of the company's design and development department (today's Imagineers) and was named a Disney Legend in 1994, a year before he died in L.A.

Country Bear Jamboree, aka Country Bear Playhouse

MAP: Bear Country/Critter Country, B/C-4

CHRONOLOGY: March 24, 1972–September 9, 2001

HISTORY: Like **Space Mountain** and the **Buzz Lightyear Astro Blasters**, the Country Bear Jamboree existed in Walt Disney World before it debuted in Disneyland. Actually, something like the Country Bear Jamboree would've appeared first in California's Sierra Nevada mountains had Disney's plans for a new resort called Mineral King not been scuttled in 1966.

When the Jamboree did finally open in Anaheim, it was the E-ticket showpiece of the new Bear Country area built in the western territory of **Frontierland**. While other Disney Legends worked on the attraction, the *brunneus* bruins and their distinctive personalities seem to have been the creation of artist **Marc Davis**, who drew up the original designs for the characters. Disney artist Al Bertino was the inspiration for the slow-singing Big Al character.

Dubbed "the wildest show in the wilderness" on the ornate **attraction poster**, and sponsored by Pepsi-Cola, the 15-minute Jamboree presented 18 **Audio-Animatronic** bears in various combinations to sing approximately a dozen short countrified songs on a gaudy stage. Among the tunes were the familiar "Ballad of Davy Crockett" and the heartbreaking "Tears Will Be the Chaser for My Wine," with such comical numbers as "My Woman Ain't Pretty But She Don't Swear None" and "He's Big Around the Middle and He's Broad Across the Rump" sprinkled into the mix. Henry, a friendly top-hatted bear with a starched collar and bow tie, was the putative emcee; "Zeke and Zed and Ted and Fred and a bear named Tennessee" formed the Bear Band; cute Teddi Barra swung down from the ceiling with her feather boa to knock out "Heart, We Did All That

Movies Based on Disneyland Attractions

The Country Bears (2002)
The Haunted Mansion (2003)
Pirates of the Caribbean: The Curse of the Black Pearl (2003)
Pirates of the Caribbean: Dead Man's Chest (2006)
Pirates of the Caribbean: At World's End (2007)

We Could"; Gomer played an upright piano topped with a honey pot; the Five Bear Rugs and the three Sun Bonnets added their own distinctive song stylings; Sammy the coonskin hat popped up to join in the fun; and a taciturn behemoth called Big Al stole the show with his languid rendition of "Blood on the Saddle." Adding to the festivities was a trio of talking trophy heads named Max, Melvin, and Buff mounted on the wall.

The park's 1972 **souvenir book** devoted an entire page to the Jamboree, calling it "a vaudeville-style free-for-all." Decades later, the 2000 book declared that "nobody hibernates through the rollicking, foot-stomping, paw-pounding country-western musical antics."

A small change arrived in '75 when Wonder Bread took over as the Jamboree's new sponsor. A bigger change came in 1984 when the bears performed the first Country Bear Christmas Show, which subsequently reappeared each holiday season (in that show a bear named Rufus was identified as the dimwitted stage manager—fans recognized him as the owner of the mailbox at the entrance to Bear Country). In February of '86, the bears staged a new show called Country Bear Vacation Hoedown. With the Jamboree gone, and with Wonder Bread also pulling out, the sponsorless theater was officially renamed the Country Bear Playhouse the following Independence Day.

The Hoedown held on for another 15 years, but ultimately the diminishing crowds were "unbearable" to park officials, and they closed the show in the fall of 2001. The replacement for the Country Bear attraction had a double irony—the **Many Adventures of Winnie the Pooh** attraction starred another bear, and he too was an import from Walt Disney World. Fans of the original bears got one more look at them in theaters when *The Country Bears*, a movie based on the Jamboree's characters, debuted in the summer of 2002.

Court of Honor

MAP: Tomorrowland, T-8

CHRONOLOGY: July 17, 1955–March 1956

HISTORY: The Court of Honor was a short-lived exhibit in the heart of **Tomorrowland**. Its location was in the plaza about 50 feet west of the spot where **Innoventions** currently innovates. The "court" was a large star-shaped flower box; the "honor" was represented by the 48 flags of all the states in the union (at the time,

Alaska and Hawaii had yet to be admitted). The flags waved from atop tall flag poles planted among the greenery, with six poles for each of the star's eight points and an even taller pole in the center displaying Old Glory.

What any of this had to do with Tomorrowland, which the 1956 **souvenir book** described as "a daring world of hopes and dreams" and "the realm of the unexplored," was unclear. While **Walt Disney** certainly loved to celebrate patriotism in the park, perhaps this tribute to America's past and present landed where it did only out of a desperate need to fill in empty Tomorrowland space for **Opening Day**. Anyway, in March of '56, the eight-month-old flags and poles were removed so they could be relocated to the newly constructed **Avenue of the Flags** at the Tomorrowland entrance. Within a few weeks the **Astro-Jets** touched down for a long stay right where the Court of Honor had been.

Creole Café, aka Café Orleans

MAP: New Orleans Square, NOS-7

CHRONOLOGY: July 24, 1966–ongoing

HISTORY: From the summer of 1966 until 1972, the Creole Café was a choice spot for **New Orleans Square** dining. Entered from Royal Street, the Creole was halfway between the **Pirates of the Caribbean** entrance and the **French Market** restaurant. Since it jutted out towards the **Rivers of America**, it was highly visible to anyone walking the main riverside thoroughfare from **Frontierland** towards the **Haunted Mansion**.

In 1972, the Sara Lee Corporation took over sponsorship and changed the name to the Sara Lee Café Orleans (also sometimes listed as Sara Lee's Café Orleans). Later the name was simplified to Café Orleans. In 1987, Marie Callender's, the pie company, briefly sponsored the restaurant. Over the years the relatively inexpensive meals have included sandwiches, crepes, chicken dishes, gumbo, and salads. Though the menu has often changed, and while days and hours of operation have varied, the riverside setting has never been less than picturesque. Café Orleans is serviced by the same giant underground kitchen facility that provides the food for the **Blue Bayou**, **Club 33**, and other New Orleans Square eateries.

Cristal d'Orleans

MAP: New Orleans Square, NOS-6

CHRONOLOGY: July 24, 1966–ongoing

HISTORY: In the heart of **New Orleans Square** is a beautiful crystal shop that is

as old as New Orleans Square itself. The sponsors are the Arribas Brothers, the same master craftsmen behind the current **Crystal Arts** on **Main Street** and the extinct **Castle Arts** shop that used to be in **Fantasyland**. Their Cristal d'Orleans has two doorways, one on Orleans Street across from **Jewel of Orléans** and the other on Royal Street across from **Le Bat en Rouge**. As in all Arribas shops, glassware, decanters, vases, jewelry, paperweights, and delicate Disney-themed sculptures are among the shimmering creations on display, with an engraving service available to personalize any item.

Critter Country

MAP: Park, P-14

CHRONOLOGY: November 23, 1988–ongoing

HISTORY: With **Bear Country** just eight months away from getting a dramatic new attraction, in late 1988 Disney officials decided to change the name of this corner of the park to Critter Country. The new name de-emphasized the bears, which still performed over in the Country Bear Playhouse, and threw the spotlight on all the various Southern critters of the soon-to-arrive **Splash Mountain**. The description of Critter Country in the 2000 **souvenir book** showed the new critters-over-bears priority: "Nestled in a lazy corner of the backwoods is Critter Country. Here amid shady trees and cool streams is a world where the rabbits, bears, opossums, foxes, alligators, owls, and frogs are just as social and neighborly as they can be. Keen eyes might spot wily Brer Rabbit outsmarting Brer Fox and Brer Bear atop Chickapin Hill. And keen ears will surely catch the applause and laughter drifting from the world-famous Country Bear Playhouse."

In addition to Splash Mountain, Critter Country is also home to another popular post-Bear Country attraction, the **Many Adventures of Winnie the Pooh**. What's more, several of the businesses have surrendered their old ursine identities to new critter-oriented names—**Ursus H. Bear's Wilderness Outpost** became **Crocodile Mercantile**, for instance. What hasn't changed from the Bear Country days is the lush vegetation, keeping Critter Country a quiet, rural contrast to its jazzy, urbane neighbor, **New Orleans Square**.

Critter Country Fruit Cart

MAP: Bear Country/Critter Country, B/C-2

CHRONOLOGY: Ca. 2000–ongoing

HISTORY: The third of the park's fruit carts is the most remote—it's located way back by **Splash Mountain** along the **Rivers of America** (guests snacking here have a splash-happy view of the zip-a-dee-doo-dah drop). Like the **Main Street Fruit Cart** and **Indy Fruit Cart**, the Critter Country Fruit Cart peddles simple, healthy snacks like fresh fruit, veggies, and juices. Guests needing quick calories can also rev up with muffins, cookies, and sodas.

Critter Country Plush

MAP: Bear Country/Critter Country, B/C-10

CHRONOLOGY: February 1996–October 1996

HISTORY: The **Briar Patch** and its rustic log cabin next to **Splash Mountain** have been **Critter Country** fixtures from 1988 until the present, with one major interruption. In February of '96, the store changed its stock from handcrafted gifts and clothes to modern plush toys, and it also changed its name.

Despite the ongoing popularity of the merchandise, the Critter Country Plush name didn't last from Valentine's Day to Halloween—by the end of October a sign announcing the return of the Briar Patch was already in place. The plush toys, however, endured to 2004, when many of them were removed in favor of souvenir hats.

Crocodile Mercantile

MAP: Bear Country/Critter Country, B/C-7

CHRONOLOGY: November 23, 1988–April 2003

HISTORY: The same day that **Critter Country** became the new name for **Bear Country**, Crocodile Mercantile became the new name for **Ursus H. Bear's Wilderness Outpost**. The location at the back of Critter Country was the same, as was much of the souvenir/T-shirt/toys merchandise. In 2003, this store, the **Brer Bar**, and **Teddi Barra's Swingin' Arcade** were all remodeled into a single new store, **Pooh Corner**.

Rolly Crump

CHRONOLOGY: February 27, 1930–ongoing

HISTORY: Born in 1930 near Pasadena, California, Rolly Crump started working at the Disney Studios 22 years later as a young artist contributing to animated films of the '50s, among them *Peter Pan* and *Sleeping Beauty*. During the '60s, he was a creative whirlwind who helped give life to numerous important attractions all around Disneyland, including the **Enchanted Tiki Room** (he sculpted most of the tiki gods), the **Haunted Mansion** (he added many of the comedic touches), the **Tomorrowland Terrace** (his abstract sculpture crowned the roof), and the **Adventureland Bazaar** (he came up with the overall design).

For the 1964–1965 New York World's Fair, he had a hand in seemingly everything Disney did. He's especially known for his major contribution to the **It's a Small World** building, where he designed some of the dolls that played inside and the 12-story *Tower of the Four Winds* that stood out front. When Small World moved to Anaheim in '66, Crump worked on the flamboyant façade and colorful interior, plus he created the oversize exterior clock that still marks each 15-minute period with a march of mechanical puppets. Among his other Disneyland efforts were stages and floats for some of the park's elaborate **parades**. Mid-'60s episode of *Walt Disney's Wonderful World of Color* presented Crump and his *Tower of the Four Winds* plus some of his creations for the Museum of the Weird (what would later become the **Haunted Mansion**). In the early '80s he was one of the leaders of the complex **Fantasyland** renovation.

Outside of Disneyland, Crump was a key designer at Walt Disney World, he helped develop theme projects for other companies, and eventually he formed his own design firm. Returning to Disney in '92, he helped remodel EPCOT before retiring in '96. Eight years later Rolly Crump was named a Disney Legend.

Crystal Arcade

MAP: Main Street, MS-3
CHRONOLOGY: July 17, 1955–ongoing
HISTORY: Since **Opening Day**, **Main Street** has had two arcades on its western side, but only one has kept generations of kids mesmerized for hours. Looming over the middle of the first, southerly block of Main are big, bright letters announcing the Crystal Arcade; one hundred and fifty feet north in the middle of Main's second block are the games, amusements, and old-time movie reels of the **Penny Arcade**.

For decades disappointed kids have probably asked **cast members** inside the Crystal Arcade where all the games are, because what they've found when they pass through the ground-floor doorway of the two-story building is a collection of shops, some of them art- or craft-related. An actual **Glass Blower** was a prominent inhabitant of the Crystal Arcade in its first decade. Other inner shops have included a **Candle Shop**, the **Story Book Shop**, and from '58–'62 a store just inside the entrance called Crystal Arcade Toys.

A remodel in '95 updated the interior so that it's more like an extension of the **Emporium** next door with its plush toys and souvenirs. The room, though, does still have glittering crystal chandeliers, making the "Crystal" in the name still relevant. A 2005 renovation revitalized the blue-green exterior. Somehow the flashy frontage missed the photographers' cameras for all of the park's early **souvenir books** until a wide photo put it behind the **Disneyland Band** in '68. The 2006 book showed the Crystal Arcade when it's at its best—evening, when the semicircular sign and the entrance glow with golden lights.

Crystal Arts

MAP: Main Street, MS-13

CHRONOLOGY: Ca. 1971–ongoing

HISTORY: After meeting and impressing **Walt Disney** at the 1964–1965 New York World's Fair, Tomas and Alfonso Arribas, two Spanish brothers who were master glass cutters, opened several shops in Disneyland. Their first shop was **Cristal d'Orleans** in New Orleans Square, and their second was Crystal Arts on **Main Street**. Later the brothers would open a third shop in Disneyland—**Castle Arts** in Fantasyland—as well as additional locations in Walt Disney World, Tokyo Disneyland, Disneyland Paris, and Hong Kong Disneyland.

On Main Street, the shop's location was in the second block on the right-hand side, a space that had formerly been home to Timex's **Watches & Clocks** shop. The **Silhouette Studio** was next door, and **Carefree Corner** was a couple of doors to the north. The Main Street shop is famous for its opulent crystal sculpture of **Sleeping Beauty Castle**, which sells for over $15,000 and takes months to create, and its dedicated craftsmen, who work in view of guests. An array of delicate crystal items, such as glassware, pitchers, Disney character figures, bells, vases, and lamps are on display here, with custom creations and free custom engraving also among the options.

Daisy's Diner

MAP: Mickey's Toontown, MT-8

CHRONOLOGY: January 24, 1993–ongoing

HISTORY: Miss Daisy, Donald Duck's girlfriend, has a boat named after her docked in Toon Lake; over by **Goofy's Gas Station** she's got her own diner, too. "Diner" is probably a misnomer for guests expecting a Blue Plate Special and old-fashioned banquettes. Daisy's Diner is a fast-and-cheap pizza counter serving simple pizzas, garden salads, and basic beverages to go, with outdoor tables conveniently located nearby.

Dalmatian Celebration

MAP: Town Square, TS-7

CHRONOLOGY: November 28, 1996–January 5, 1997

HISTORY: Disney's live-action version of *One Hundred and One Dalmatians* had its New York premiere on November 18, 1996; to help promote the new movie, 10 days later Disneyland opened the Dalmatian Celebration area. The spot for the spots was just to the right of the prominent **Disney Showcase** store, which sat on the corner where **Main Street** stretched northward from **Town Square**. Formerly the Dalmatian Celebration location had been utilized by various eateries, starting with the **Maxwell House Coffee Shop** in '55 and ending with the **Town Square Café** in '92.

Guests entering the park through the east tunnel couldn't miss the new area themed to Disney's biggest movie of the year. Inside they found lots of movie-related activities, including spots-on-the-face-painting, roll-around-on-the-floor dog tricks for kids, and photo opportunities with a menacing Cruella De Vil. The biggest surprise was the presence of actual puppies for guests to meet.

Once the holiday season passed, the six-week promotion concluded. The internal rooms became off-limits offices, the external space a character-greeting area. The Dalmatian Celebration wasn't the first occasion when Disneyland had gone to the dogs—from the late '50s to the mid-'60s, a one-day Kids Amateur Dog Show had been held every spring to recognize guests' pets and fetch a few more guests during the off-season.

Dapper Dans

CHRONOLOGY: 1959–ongoing

HISTORY: To many long-time Disneyland fans, **Main Street** wouldn't be Main Street without the Dapper Dans. This lighthearted all-male barbershop quartet has been performing in the park since 1959, though not always with the same singers. Dozens have performed as Dapper Dans over the years, either rotating into the group at Disneyland or singing in the quartets that perform at Walt Disney World and Hong Kong Disneyland.

The Dans' formula has changed only slightly since the late '50s: four smiling gentlemen in colorful striped suits who harmonize sentimental songs, usually a cappella, to evoke sweet memories of the turn of the century (the 20th, not the 21st). Well over 100 songs are in the Dans' repertoire, everything from barbershop classics like "Jeanie with the Light Brown Hair" and "In the Good Old Summertime" to Disney classics like "When You Wish Upon a Star" and "When I See an Elephant Fly" (the most-requested number dates from Disneyland's infancy but isn't a Disney song— "Lida Rose" from the 1957 musical *The Music Man*). A crowd-pleasing favorite is their performance while riding a bicycle built for four (wireless microphones project their voices through sidewalk speakers).

Popular as they were from the start, the Dans weren't shown in one of the park's **souvenir books** until 1968, when a small cropped photo showed them wearing white jackets, carrying straw boaters in hand, and riding their quadcycle with Goofy hitching a ride on the back. As recording artists, the Dapper Dans appeared on 1969's *Strike Up the Disneyland Band* vinyl LP, and their own *Shave and a Haircut* CD came out in 2000. On screen they've appeared in several Disney-produced TV shows and specials, such as a *Disneyland After Dark* episode in 1962 that showed the group entertaining a Main Street crowd with a humorous rendition of "Carry Me Back to Old Virginny." Fans of *The Simpsons* might recognize their vocals in the episode about Homer's group, the Be Sharps, and movie fans might remember the Dapper Dans' performance as the singing busts in Disney's *The Haunted Mansion*.

28 Long-Lasting Park Performers

Adventureland
Alturas
Trinidad & Tobago Showboat Steel Orchestra

Main Street
All American College Band
Charles Dickens Carolers
Coke Corner Pianist
Dapper Dans
Disneyland Band
Keystone Cops
Sax Quintet

Fantasyland
Make Believe Brass
Royal Jesters

Frontierland
Big Thunder Breakdown Boys
Billy Hill & the Hillbillies
Firehouse Five Plus Two
Laughing Stock & Co.
Strawhatters

Tomorrowland
Kids of the Kingdom
Krash
Trash Can Trio

New Orleans Square
Bayou Brass Band
Bilge Rats & Bootstrappers
Gloryland Brass Band
Jambalaya Jazz Band
Jolly Roger
Orleans Street Band
River Rascals
Royal Street Bachelors
Side Street Strutters

Date Nite

MAP: Plaza Hub, PH-2

CHRONOLOGY: Summer 1957–ca. 1964 (seasonally)

HISTORY: For several years in the park's early history, Date Nite was a pleasant and popular summer tradition. This musical event was held on Friday and Saturday evenings and lured young-adult couples who wanted to enjoy a sophisticated dance concert. The lovely outdoor **Plaza Gardens** in the northwest corner of the **Plaza Hub** provided the location, and the Date Niters (technically the Elliot Bros. Orchestra) provided the music. The orchestra, 10 musicians in red jackets and white pants, featured a half-dozen brass instruments, a stand-up bass, a piano, a drummer, and a vocalist. The group's 1958 album *Date Nite at Disneyland* showed off their repertoire of standards, including some Gershwin, Johnny Mercer, and Rogers and Hart numbers, with "Goodnight Sweetheart" a romantic coda.

Starting with the park's 1958 **souvenir book**, Date Nite was consistently featured in the **Main Street** section with a photo—well-dressed happy couples dancing in front of the orchestra—and an accompanying caption: "A gay twirl with your best girl to the dance rhythms of Disneyland's popular Date Niters orchestra is a Summertime evening favorite." And the Date Niters got to knock out a swingin' song for a national TV audience on a 1962 episode of *Walt Disney's Wonderful World of Color*. Two years later Date Nite made its last appearance in a souvenir book. Even though the Date Nite concept was abandoned, concerts did continue at the Plaza Gardens with such shows as the '60s' Cavalcade of Bands and the '80s' Big Bands at Disneyland series.

Marc and Alice Davis

CHRONOLOGY: March 30, 1913–January 12, 2000; 1929–ongoing

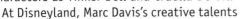

HISTORY: The husband-and-wife Davis team was instrumental in making Disneyland the beloved park it is. Marc Davis was one of the legendary "nine old men" (so nicknamed by an appreciative **Walt Disney**) whose art propelled Disney's classic animated films. Born in Bakersfield, California, in 1913, Davis studied at several art institutes before settling in at the Disney Studios in 1935. There he worked on many of the films from *Snow White and the Seven Dwarfs* in 1937 to *One Hundred and One Dalmatians* in '61, along the way creating such memorable movie characters as Tinker Bell and Cruella De Vil.

At Disneyland, Marc Davis's creative talents are still seen all over the park. He got his start writing jokes for the **Enchanted Tiki Room**, invented comic scenes for the **Jungle Cruise** and **It's a Small World**, added animals and settings to the **Nature's Wonderland** area in **Frontierland**, drew up the musical bruins for the **Country Bear Jamboree** and gave them all distinctive personalities, developed most of the characters and scenes for **America Sings**, and painted the humorous portraits in the "stretching room" of the **Haunted Mansion**.

His finest work may have been **Pirates of the Caribbean**, where he originated the concepts and designs that became the actual scenes still on view: the trio of jailed pirates trying to lure the dog holding the key; the pirate skeleton pinned to the wall by a sword, a seagull nested in his hat; the pirate who struggles under a mountain of hats and booty as he steps into a shaky launch; the drunk pirate who trips on a stack of explosive barrels while randomly shooting his pistol. On the 10th-anniversary episode of *Walt Disney's Wonderful World of Color* in 1965, Davis was introduced to a national TV audience along with highlights of the coming Pirates and Haunted Mansion attractions. Marc Davis officially retired in 1978 but stayed on to help with EPCOT and Tokyo Disneyland. Elected as a Disney Legend in 1989, he died in Southern California in 2000.

Meanwhile his wife, Alice Davis, also enjoyed a long Disney career. Born in 1929 in Escalon, California, she was a student at an art institute when she met her husband. After working as a fashion designer for most of the '50s, she was invited by her husband to work on costumes for Disney movies, which led to a job researching and designing hundreds of Velcro-lined costumes for the **Audio-Animatronic** kids of Disneyland's It's a Small World attraction. In '65, she began creating costumes for all the buccaneers in Pirates of the Caribbean, using Marc Davis's drawings for ideas. Later she worked on costumes for Flight to the Moon and the **Carousel of Progress**. Still affiliated with Disney, she's appeared at special events in recent years and continues on as a consultant. Alice Davis was named a Disney Legend in 2004.

Marvin Davis

CHRONOLOGY: December 21, 1910–March 8, 1998

HISTORY: When it came to creating Disneyland, Marvin Davis probably worked as closely with **Walt Disney** as any other Disney employee. Davis was right there in the inner circle as plans for the nascent park began to take shape, and he's often credited with drawing up the first layout of the park as we now recognize it. His 1953 illustration assigned the park a triangular shape, stretched **Main Street** from the **entrance** up to the **Plaza Hub**, and branched the lands from the center like spokes.

Like several other Disney Legends who contributed to Disneyland, Davis got his start working on movies. He was born in 1910 in New Mexico, was an award-winning architecture student at Los Angeles universities, and in 1935 got a job as an art director at 20th Century Fox. Two decades later, Disney brought him aboard the Disneyland design team.

In addition to helping determine the park's overall structure, Davis planned many specific areas and attractions over the next decade. He came up with over 100 variations of the main entrance into the park; he executed early designs of Main Street buildings (adding a residential area and a haunted house at the north end of the street); he worked on the design for **Sleeping Beauty Castle**; he translated Walt Disney's own rough sketch of **Tom Sawyer Island** into detailed plans for the island that was finally built; and he contributed to the designs of both **New Orleans Square** and the **Haunted Mansion.**

Throughout these years Davis was also directing Disney movies and TV shows, including *Babes in Toyland*, *Big Red*, *Zorro*, and *The Mickey Mouse Club*, picking up an Emmy in '62 for art direction and scenic design. In the late '60s and early '70s, Davis steered the planning and designing of Walt Disney World and its first resorts before he retired in 1975. Marvin Davis was named a Disney Legend in 1994, four years before he died in Santa Monica at age 87.

Davy Crockett Arcade, aka Davy Crockett Frontier Arcade

MAP: Frontierland, Fr-1

CHRONOLOGY: October 1955–1987

HISTORY: Sustaining the momentum of the Davy Crockett craze that was sweeping across the nation in 1955 (thanks to the three Crockett episodes on the ***Disneyland TV series***), the Davy Crockett Arcade took over for the **Davy Crockett Frontier Museum** in the fall of '55. The location—just inside the **Frontierland** gates, in the building to the immediate left—didn't change, and for a while not much else inside the arcade did either, since the museum's wax figures were still on display until the following June.

The Davy Crockett Arcade wasn't the games-playing room we think of today when we hear of an arcade (although it did have a coin-operated pistol shoot-out). Instead, Crockett's building ultimately became more of a collection of subdivided spaces occupied by retailers that changed over the years. Mexican Imports, the Frontier Rock Shop, Frontierland Hats, the Frontier Print Shop, a Souvenir Stand, the Western Emporium, the Squaw Shop, and the **Leather Shop** were among the businesses inside the building (according to the list on a small 1970 Frontierland map, the first five of these were all in the arcade that year).

The park's **souvenir books** didn't mention the Davy Crockett Arcade by name, but they often did show a photo of the sign out front. The interior looked like the inside of a 19th-century frontier building, with lots of pitted stucco and rough wood on view. The whole enterprise was renamed the Davy Crockett Frontier Arcade in 1985, and then two years later it was renamed again, this time to **Davy Crockett's Pioneer Mercantile.**

Davy Crockett Frontier Museum

MAP: Frontierland, Fr-1

CHRONOLOGY: July 17, 1955–October 1955

HISTORY: Capitalizing on the success of the three Davy Crockett episodes that ran on the ***Disneyland* TV series** in late 1954 and early 1955, Imagineers splashed the Davy Crockett theme all over **Frontierland** in the '50s. First up in the summer of '55 was the Davy Crockett Frontier Museum, a large space in the building to the immediate left of Frontierland's stockade gates. The museum showed off a collection of Crockett-themed displays, especially a detailed re-creation of a meeting between Crockett (who resembled TV's Fess Parker) and his sidekick George Russel (a Buddy Ebsen look-a-like) meeting Andrew Jackson (a dead ringer for Andrew Jackson) inside Jackson's headquarters. The full-size figures were done in wax and dressed in detailed frontier costumes. A row of rifles stood along the wall, historic art lined the rough-timber interior, and a period flag and wax sentry added authenticity.

       Elsewhere in the museum, a coin-guzzling pistol-shooting game and shops selling Crockett-related frontier items (coonskin caps, buckskins, souvenirs) competed for attention. The building was listed in the 1956 **souvenir book** as the Davy Crockett Museum, even though the photo clearly showed the exterior sign spelling out Davy Crockett Frontier Museum, but neither name was listed any year after that. About three months after opening, the museum was rebilled as the **Davy Crockett Arcade**, and eight months after that the wax figures were relocated to Fort Wilderness on **Tom Sawyer Island**.

Davy Crockett's Pioneer Mercantile,
aka Pioneer Mercantile

MAP: Frontierland, Fr-1

CHRONOLOGY: 1987–ongoing

HISTORY: What had been known for three decades as first the **Davy Crockett Frontier Museum** and then the **Davy Crockett Arcade** became Davy Crockett's Pioneer Mercantile in 1987. The Mercantile's location, a rough-timbered building on the left as guests entered **Frontierland**, was the same one occupied by its two predecessors.

       Unlike the adjacent **Pendleton Woolen Mills Dry Goods Store**, which was at the time primarily a clothing store, the new Mercantile offered a wide range of toys, videos, souvenirs, books, hats, polished rocks, and, yes, clothing too, most of it with frontier themes. Woody from *Toy Story* and Pocahontas from *Pocahontas* have been strong presences among the merchandise over the years, and when other Disney characters have been shown they're usually wearing their Western duds. The store itself evokes the pioneer spirit with a wood ceiling, rustic lighting fixtures, and a faux tree blended into the décor. Eventually Davy Crockett was dropped from the name, so the store exists today as simply Pioneer Mercantile, connecting through the interior to the store that replaced Pendleton, **Bonanza Outfitters**.

A Day at Disneyland

CHRONOLOGY: June 1982 (initial release)

HISTORY: In the tradition of previous Disney-produced documentaries like *Disneyland, U.S.A.* and *Gala Day at Disneyland*, *A Day at Disneyland* offered a state-of-the-park tour that celebrated favorite attractions and locations. But unlike the earlier two featurettes, both of which were released into theaters in pairings with Disney films, *A Day at Disneyland* was released on video in June of 1982 and was intended to be more of a souvenir keepsake.

Populating the 40-minute documentary were lots of Disney characters who frolicked in the park and on the attractions. Thus viewers watched Goofy riding on the **Jungle Cruise**, Hook and Smee touring **Pirates of the Caribbean**, Mickey cruising down **Main Street**, and more. Footage of already-extinct attractions like the **20,000 Leagues Under the Sea Exhibit** added a touch of nostalgia for viewers in the '80s, while footage of soon-to-be-extinct attractions like the **Skyway to Tomorrowland** added a touch of nostalgia for viewers in the 2000s. A rerelease a dozen years later incorporated new scenes of **Mickey's Toontown** and **Fantasmic!**, both of which were, in '94, recent additions to the park.

Discovery Bay

MAP: Frontierland, Fr-22

CHRONOLOGY: Never built

HISTORY: During the '70s, **Disneyland Presents a Preview of Coming Attractions**, the **Main Street** exhibit that showed attractions hopefully to come, presented artwork that suggested a whole new area was heading to the park. Discovery Bay, as it was called, would've been styled like a 19th-century San Francisco dock alongside a new body of water located somewhere between **Fantasyland** and **Frontierland**, possibly in the area later given to the **Big Thunder Mountain Railroad**. Small waterfront buildings would've evoked the spirit of the Barbary Coast, while in and around the harbor the submarine *Nautilus* would've evoked the spirit of a classic Disney movie (*20,000 Leagues Under the Sea*).

Dominating the Discovery Bay imagery was a giant hangar set back from the shore. From its open door the sleek 200-foot airship *Hyperion* from the 1974 Disney movie *Island at the Top of the World* looked like it was emerging for some unexplained purpose. Was it a walk-through exhibit? Some kind of balloon-ride attraction? And the "looping upside-down on a magnetic roller-coaster" experience mentioned in the book *Walt Disney Imagineering*, where and what was that attraction? Unfortunately, the public never got to find out. The *Island* movie was a disappointment at the box office, and Discovery Bay was never built, though elements did turn up later at Disneyland Paris.

Disney Afternoon Avenue

MAP: Fantasyland, Fa-22

CHRONOLOGY: March 15, 1991–November 10, 1991

HISTORY: The success of the *Disney Afternoon* TV series led to a new Disneyland area called Disney Afternoon Avenue. This temporary exhibit went up along Small World Way, the name for the walkway between **Matterhorn Mountain** and **It's a Small World** in **Fantasyland**.

      The cartoony structures along the 400-foot-long avenue evoked a brightly colored small town, sort of an early version of **Mickey's Toontown**. As with Toontown, which would open two years later, guests could visit cute buildings themed to specific characters—Duckburg City Hall, for instance—and could meet with Disney characters, including Scrooge McDuck, King Louie, and Baloo (who had his very own **Baloo's Dressing Room** at the far end of the avenue). Nearby several other attractions—**Fantasyland Autopia**, **Videopolis**, and the **Motor Boat Cruise**—joined in on the *Disney Afternoon* theming. The whole enterprise peaked with the airing of a TV special, "Disney Afternoon Live! at Disneyland," on September 14th of '91. Never intended to be a long-term presence in the park, Disney Afternoon Avenue closed two months later.

Disneyana

MAP: Main Street, MS-4, MS-19

CHRONOLOGY: January 9, 1976–ongoing

HISTORY: Recognizing that rare Disney collectibles were hot commodities, Disneyland opened its own memorabilia shop early in 1976. Originally Disneyana was where the **Hurricane Lamp Shop** had been, a small location in the building on the left-hand side of the first block of **Main Street** (the old **Upjohn Pharmacy** had been on the adjacent corner). The Disneyana shop did indeed sell rare vintage pieces, but eventually the line of merchandise expanded to become mostly limited-edition contemporary pieces.

      Needing more room, on May 30, 1986, Disneyana jumped to the east side of the street and switched places with the **Jewelry Shop**, placing it between the **Main Street Cinema** and the **Market House**. Meanwhile the jeweler, aka Rings 'n' Things, took Disneyana's place on the west side of Main. Today Disneyana is still a fascinating visit for Disneyphiles interested in animation cels, statues in bronze or pewter, and other collectibles.

Disney Clothiers, Ltd.

MAP: Main Street, MS-14

CHRONOLOGY: March 23, 1985–ongoing

HISTORY: For a quarter-century the **Hallmark Card Shop** occupied the large space on **Main Street** across from the **Carnation Ice Cream Parlor** and the **Sunkist Citrus House**. In 1985, Disney Cloth-iers, Ltd., "where good style is always in fashion," moved into this prime retail spot on the corner of East Center Street and Main. The clothes selection has varied from infant wear, souvenir T-shirts, and jeans to fashionable sweaters, dress shirts, jackets, and dresses, all adorned with Disney themes. At dif-ferent times vintage styles and even bath products and linens have appeared on the shelves, even though the sign out front announces: "Clothing with character—a Main Street tradition since 1905."

In recent years two ornamental signs outside have helped identify different rooms within the store: Castle Brothers ("collegiate fashions") fronting Main Street and Chester Drawers ("togs for toddlers") in the back. Antique sports and hobby equipment, such as old golf clubs, skis, and sewing kits hang in Castle Brothers, while Chester Drawers looks like a baby's nursery. All the rooms are connected to each other, and Castle and Chester both open to **Crystal Arts** next door to the north.

Disney Dollars

CHRONOLOGY: May 5, 1987–ongoing

HISTORY: Scrooge McDuck was on hand when Disneyland's Disney Dollars debuted. Created by **Jack Lindquist**, the marketing whiz who would become president of the park in 1990, the new currency generated fun for guests and bolstered the notion that Disneyland really was its own self-contained world. The results were immedi-ate and impressive—so popular were the bills, they were soon found at Walt Disney World and at Disney Stores across America, and today they're available at virtually ev-ery store in Disneyland.

Since that 1987 debut, guests have bought and used the bills just like they're real money, which in a sense they are—they can be used throughout the park for purchases, and at any time they can be exchanged for cash at full monetary value. The bills themselves have undergone many revisions. The first series of Disney Dollars came in two denominations, a $1 Mickey bill backed with **Sleeping Beauty Castle**, and a $5 Goofy bill backed with the *Mark Twain*. Two years later, a $10 Minnie Mouse bill was added that featured several Disneyland attractions on the back.

Revisions came in 1993, when **Mickey's Toontown** imagery was added, and again in 1997, when Mickey took on his *Fantasia* costume, Goofy got a tuxedo, and Simba (of *The Lion King* fame) replaced Minnie, all backed with images of Walt Disney World attractions (the Florida park was in the midst of its 25th-anniversary celebration at the time). Redesigns continued in the 21st century, too—in 2000, Mickey was dressed up for a millennium New Year's party; in 2002, he became the whistler from *Steamboat Willie*; and in 2005, he was temporarily replaced by Chicken Little. In 2007, the park began offering singles themed to the *Pirates of the Caribbean* movies (complete with a skull on the front and a pirate ship on the back), plus singles, fives, and tens with Ariel, Aurora, and Cinderella, respectively. A small drawing of Tinker Bell has always been shown on the front of the each bill.

Fun as they may be, the bills aren't play money. They're created with sophisticated engraving and printing processes that rival those used on actual U.S. currency. The bills have anti-counterfeiting security symbols worked into their art, and the serial numbers on them are real (numbers begin with an A if the bills are from Disneyland, with a D if they're from Walt Disney World). Oh, and the signature on all the bills? The Treasurer, Scrooge McDuck.

Disney Gallery

MAP: New Orleans Square, NOS-1

CHRONOLOGY: July 11, 1987–July 31, 2007

HISTORY: What had been intended in the mid-'60s to be a private **apartment** in **New Orleans Square** for **Walt Disney** and his family was finally opened to the public two decades later as the Disney Gallery. Originally this area was dubbed the Royal Suite because of the discreet entrance on Royal Street that the Disney family was going to use.

For two decades, entry was via sweeping stairways that led up to the second-floor gallery, a dramatic entrance built when the walkway to the ground-floor **Pirates of the Caribbean** was remodeled in early 1987. Upstairs, the ornate iron railing added outside the art rooms still has the initials WD and RD curled into the filigree as a tribute to Walt and his brother Roy Disney. The Disney Gallery interior spread out over various quiet rooms and short hallways that bent around a small patio. The luxurious furnishings, elegant moldings, and parquet floors all approximated the 3,000-square-foot apartment as it would have looked had it been finished.

But it was the art, not the architecture, that compelled frequent repeat visits. On the walls were changing displays of Disneyland-related paintings and drawings, while mounted in glass cases were detailed models of Disneyland buildings and attractions. Typically the artworks represented a specific theme, such as the inaugural "The Art of Disneyland 1953–1986" exhibit, 1997's "A Look at the Future—Tomorrowland: 1955–1998" installation, 2002's display of Mickey Mouse imagery, and 2007's "Inspired by Disneyland" show.

The room to the immediate right of the gallery entrance was known as the Disney Gallery Collector's Room and was filled with Disneyland-inspired books, prints, and note cards for sale. Art on Demand consoles enabled guests to select and frame art that could be mailed home or picked up later. Special events, such as book signings or new releases of limited-edition art, were also occasionally held in the Disney Gallery. Furthermore, the **cast members** here took evening reservations for the balcony outside, enabling guests to sample desserts and enjoy an uncrowded view of that night's **Fantasmic!** presentation.

With little notice the Disney Gallery, just after it celebrated its 20th anniversary, permanently closed at the end of July in 2007. That fall, a thorough remodel converted the historic space into an overnight suite for 2008's **Year of a Million Dreams** promotion.

Disneyland Band

CHRONOLOGY: July 17, 1955–ongoing

HISTORY: Since **Opening Day**, the Disneyland Band has been helping to evoke the feeling of small-town America on **Main Street**. Uniformed marching bands have a long tradition in popular culture, of course, and in 1957 they got a boost when *The Music Man*, a nostalgic tale of a small Iowa town starting up its own marching band, became a Broadway hit (five years later, it became a Hollywood hit, too).

At Disneyland the band is 16 instruments strong, including lots of brass and a big bass drum. The uniforms vary but usually feature bright red or white jackets with ornate trim; pants that are white, black, or red with gold stripes down the sides; and sturdy brimmed hats adorned with flashes.

Players have rotated in and out over the years. Usually about 20 are available at a time, and some of the band's members have occasionally dressed up in costumes to play in Disneyland combos like the Keystone Cops and the **Strawhatters**. However, the bandleaders have rarely changed. The first one lasted for the first 15 years of Disneyland's history—**Vesey Walker**, usually clad in white. Later bandmasters have included Jim Barngrover, James Christensen, and Stanford Freese.

From its inception, the Disneyland Band has been a picturesque target for the park's official photographers and cameramen. The 1956 **souvenir book** showed a wide photo of Walker and the band, complemented by this descriptive text: "The harum-pa-pa of marching music quickens the steps and widens the smiles of Disneyland guests as the Disneyland Band parades up Main Street." In the back of that book, a "Disneyland Data" page claimed that the band gave "1460 concerts annually" (that's about four a day, every day of the year). Later souvenir books showed off even bigger photos with new text that noted "the ever-popular home town parade led by the marching Disneyland Band" might include "Sousa marches, even state songs." In the 1956 featurette *Disneyland, U.S.A.*, band members were shown playing their instruments while riding the spinning teacups of the **Mad Hatter's Mad Tea Party**.

In addition to marching in parades, the band used to perform concerts in the long-gone **bandstand**, plus they've appeared at the park's **entrance**, at special park events, and at the late-afternoon flag-lowering ceremonies on **Town Square**. The band has also released several albums over the years: *Strike Up the Disneyland Band* (1969) and *I Love a Parade* (1974), in addition to appearing on collections like *Walt Takes You to Disneyland* (1958) and *The Official Album of Disneyland/Walt Disney World* (1980). Not surprisingly, the "Mickey Mouse March" is the band's most-performed song, though the band's broad repertoire includes everything from those aforementioned Sousa standards and state songs to polkas and waltzes. Durably popular, the Disneyland Band delivered performance number 50,000 in the summer of 1982.

Disneyland: The First 50 Magical Years

MAP: Town Square, TS-9

CHRONOLOGY: May 5, 2005–ongoing

HISTORY: Disney Legend Steve Martin starred with Donald Duck in this celebratory film released in May 2005 to coincide with Disneyland's 50th anniversary. Martin, who in decades past worked in **Frontierland** and the **Main Street Magic Shop**, brought both humor and affection to his narration of the 17-minute film, which included footage of **Walt Disney**, the park's construction, and long-extinct attractions. Supplementing the film were historical displays and rare artworks from the park's past, all on view in the pre-show lobby area.

Disneyland: The First 50 Magical Years played in the **Opera House** on **Main Street** in the theater usually reserved for **Great Moments with Mr. Lincoln**. That attraction was due to return in November of 2006, but the film's successful 18-month run was extended into 2007.

Disneyland Presents a Preview of Coming Attractions

MAP: Main Street, MS-20

CHRONOLOGY: 1973–July 22, 1989

HISTORY: Originally the **Wurlitzer Music Hall**, and later the **Legacy of Walt Disney**, occupied the highly visible corner on the right-hand side of the first block on **Main Street**. But from 1973 until 1989, the large room was given over to a fascinating, closely studied exhibit called Disneyland Presents a Preview of Coming Attractions. Inside the handsome room were detailed models, concept illustrations, and even videos depicting proposed developments for the park. Among the tantalizing plans were some that were fully realized (**Space Mountain** and **Big Thunder Mountain Railroad**), and some that never materialized (**Discovery Bay** and a new area near **Dumbo the Flying Elephant** called Dumbo's Circusland).

Ultimately, this well-trafficked location, which all guests walked past on their way up Main Street to the **Plaza Hub**, proved to be too tempting for business-minded Disney officials. In July 1989, they closed the space for three months so it could be converted into a large retail store called **Disney Showcase**. Some of what had been shown in the Coming Attractions room later appeared in the **Disney Gallery** in **New Orleans Square**.

Disneyland TU Series

CHRONOLOGY: October 27, 1954 (initial broadcast)

HISTORY: Television was the great ally to **Walt Disney** as he ramped up the work on Disneyland in 1954. Disney's weekly *Disneyland* show not only promoted the coming park but financed it—the network presenting the series, ABC, also presented a loan that went towards the park's construction.

That Walt Disney, a successful movie producer, even deigned to venture into television was unique for the times. Rival studio heads disdainfully ignored the new medium, but Disney embraced it. His success on the smaller screen presaged the later TV successes of movie moguls like Irwin Allen, Steven Spielberg, and George Lucas.

After debuting with several holiday specials in the early '50s, Disney launched his first regular primetime show, *Disneyland*, in 1954's fall season on Wednesday nights. The show lasted for a record 29 years, won seven Emmy Awards, eventually played on all three major networks, switched from Wednesday to Sunday nights, and amplified Davy Crockett into a national merchandising craze. It also changed names five times to *Walt Disney Presents* (1958–1961), *Walt Disney's Wonderful World of Color* (1961–1969), *The Wonderful World of Disney* (1969–1979), *Disney's Wonderful World* (1979–1981), and *Walt Disney* (1981–1983).

Throughout its long history, the show, in addition to presenting popular miniseries and theatrical films, frequently presented episodes devoted to Disneyland. Walt Disney first presented the Disneyland concept—and that's all it was at the time, since nothing had really been built yet—just before Halloween in 1954. On the premiere episode, called "The Disneyland Story," he showed maps, models, and illustrations, and he described his goals for the park: "We hope it'll be unlike anything else on this Earth. A fair, an amusement park, an exhibition, a city from *Arabian Nights*, a metropolis from the future. In fact, a place of hopes and dreams, facts and fancy, all in one. . . . A place of knowledge and happiness."

The list of Disneyland-themed episodes includes:

October 27, 1954	"The Disneyland Story," the premiere episode that presented maps, illustrations, and models of the coming park (though much of the hour was given over to unrelated cartoons).
February 9, 1955	"A Progress Report/Nature's Half Acre," an aerial tour of the park seven months into its construction.
July 13, 1955	"A Pre-Opening Report from Disneyland," aka "A Further Report on Disneyland," shown four days before **Opening Day** to build excitement.
February 29, 1956	"A Trip Through Adventureland/Water Birds," spotlighting the **Jungle Cruise**.
April 3, 1957	"Disneyland the Park/Pecos Bill," an aerial tour of Disneyland.
April 9, 1958	"An Adventure in the Magic Kingdom," a guided tour of the park led by an animated Tinker Bell.
May 28, 1961	"Disneyland '61/Olympic Elk," showing recent park additions.
April 15, 1962	"Disneyland After Dark," spotlighting nighttime music (Louis Armstrong, the four Osmond Brothers making their TV debut, and more) and **fireworks**.
September 23, 1962	*Golden Horseshoe Revue*," the popular show in **Frontierland** celebrated its 10,000th performance.
December 23, 1962	"Holiday Time at Disneyland," a tour of the holiday-themed park by Walt Disney.
May 17, 1964	"Disneyland Goes to the World's Fair," a preview of Disney attractions at the 1964–1965 New York World's Fair.
January 3, 1965	"Disneyland's Tenth Anniversary," with Julie Reihm ("**Miss Disneyland**") helping to show off the coming **Pirates of the Caribbean** and **Haunted Mansion** attractions.
December 18, 1966	"Disneyland Around the Seasons," highlighting the newly opened **New Orleans Square** and **It's a Small World**.
January 21, 1968	"Disneyland—From the Pirates of the Caribbean to the World of Tomorrow," a preview of the changes in **Tomorrowland**.
March 22, 1970	"Disneyland Showtime," a celebration of the new Haunted Mansion with the Osmond Brothers and Kurt Russell.

Outside of the weekly show, many Disney-produced TV specials showcased the park, among them:

July 17, 1955	"Dateline: Disneyland," a live presentation of Opening Day festivities hosted by Bob Cummings, Art Linkletter, and Ronald Reagan (an estimated 90,000,000 viewers).
June 15, 1959	"Disneyland '59," aka "Kodak Presents Disneyland '59," a live salute to the new **Matterhorn Mountain**, **Matterhorn Bobsleds**, **Monorail**, **Motor Boat Cruise**, **Fantasyland Autopia**, and **Submarine Voyage** attractions.
June 9, 1962	*Meet Me at Disneyland*, a series of specials that lasted until September 8, 1962, and featured appearances by the Osmond Brothers.
April 10, 1974	"Sandy in Disneyland," starring Sandy Duncan.
July 11, 1974	"Herbie Day at Disneyland," Bob Crane, Helen Hayes, and Volkswagen promoting the film *Herbie Rides Again*.
December 6, 1976	"Christmas in Disneyland with Art Carney," featuring Sandy Duncan and Glen Campbell.
March 6, 1980	"Kraft Salutes Disneyland's 25th Anniversary," starring Danny Kaye.
June 28, 1984	"Big Bands at Disneyland," the first of 12 music shows airing on the Disney Channel.
February 18, 1985	"Disneyland's 30th Anniversary Celebration," starring Drew Barrymore and John Forsythe.
May 23, 1986	"Disneyland's Summer Vacation Party," featuring comedians Jay Leno and Jerry Seinfeld.
September 20, 1986	"Disney's *Captain EO* Grand Opening," starring Patrick Duffy, Justine Bateman, and the Moody Blues.
February 12, 1988	"Disney's Magic in the Magic Kingdom," featuring George Burns and the disappearing **Sleeping Beauty Castle** trick.
November 13, 1988	"Mickey's 60th Birthday," featuring John Ritter, Carl Reiner, and a party in the park.
December 11, 1988	"Disneyland's All-Star Comedy Circus," featuring circus stars performing at Disneyland.
February 4, 1990	"Disneyland's 35th Anniversary Celebration," starring Tony Danza and the Muppets.
September 14, 1991	"Disney Afternoon Live! at Disneyland," spotlighting **Splash Mountain**.
July 10, 1993	"Disneyland Presents: Tales of Toontown," showing off the new **Mickey's Toontown**.
March 4, 1995	"40 Years of Adventure," hosted by Wil Shriner, debuting the new **Indiana Jones Adventure** attraction.
May 23, 1997	"Light Magic: A Spectacular Journey," celebrating the new parade.
February 1, 2000	"Disneyland 2000: 45 Years of Magic," an anniversary special hosted by Ryan Seacrest.
October 14, 2003	"Disneyland Resort: Behind the Scenes," airing on the Travel Channel.

While many park traditions were shown on the *Disneyland* TV series over the decades, at least one tradition was initiated by the show itself. From the premiere episode onward, the show began with an animated Tinker Bell splashing sparks with her wand; the public expectations for just such a sight at Disneyland led to the appearance of an actual **Tinker Bell** character who soared above Fantasyland on summer nights beginning in 1961.

Disneyland, U.S.A.

CHRONOLOGY: December 20, 1956 (initial release)

HISTORY: Released into movie theaters for the 1956 holidays alongside *Westward Ho the Wagons!*, this Cinemascope featurette was essentially a 42-minute advertisement for Disneyland. It began by showing off the park from the air via spectacular helicopter footage, ventured to the grounds of the new Disneyland Hotel, and then trammed over to the park for a walking tour of **Main Street** and all the lands.

Extensive scenes of extinct attractions (such as the old-fashioned transportation systems in **Frontierland** and the **Skyway to Fantasyland/Tomorrowland**), plus long looks at areas that have been much-modified over the decades (the **Jungle Cruise** back when the skipper's spiel was serious, **Fantasyland** with its original medieval décor), make this essential viewing for Disneyland fans. Winston Hibler, who also wrote the words on the dedication plaque in **Town Square**, cowrote and narrated the film's text. In 2007 *Disneyland, U.S.A.* was included on a compilation DVD called *Walt Disney Treasures: Disneyland: Secrets, Stories & Magic*.

Roy O. Disney

CHRONOLOGY: June 24, 1893–December 19, 1971

HISTORY: Without the advice and efforts of his older brother Roy, **Walt Disney** never would have been able to make his Disneyland dream a reality.

Roy Oliver Disney was born in Chicago in 1893, about eight years ahead of Walt. Several years before Walt would hold the same job, teenage Roy worked as a "news butcher" selling items on trains. In 1923, the brothers cofounded an animation company, with their roles generally divided between Roy's financial wizardry and Walt's creative genius. Staunchly loyal to his brother's goals, Roy served as CEO of the company (which eventually became Walt Disney Productions and then The Walt Disney Company) for over 40 years and as president for over 25. During his career Roy supervised merchandise licensing, negotiated the contract that brought the company its own *Disneyland* **TV series** in the '50s, and in the fall of '53 he found and won over the investors who backed the construction of Disneyland. Significantly, Roy Disney was the first person to buy a Disneyland admission ticket, ticket #000001, which he purchased for $1

(91 cents for the ticket price plus nine cents tax).

After Walt Disney's death in '66, Roy assumed leadership of the coming Walt Disney World and guided that immensely complex project from its construction to its 1971 opening. He died of a cerebral hemorrhage just two months later. Several Disney tributes honor him: his initials were in the balcony at Disneyland's **Disney Gallery** (see photo, previous page), a building at the Disney Studios and a train engine at Walt Disney World are named after him, and a statue in the Florida park's Town Square shows him sitting on a bench next to Minnie Mouse. His son Roy E. Disney is a top Disney executive who was named a Disney Legend in 1998.

ꭰisney Showcase

MAP: Main Street, MS-20

CHRONOLOGY: October 27, 1989–ongoing

HISTORY: This eminent store welcomes guests to the eastern side of **Main Street.** Placed right where the street begins to stretch northward from **Town Square** towards the **Plaza Hub**, its corner is a busy conduit of pedestrian traffic and has always hosted high-profile occupants.

In 1955, the **Wurlitzer Music Hall** sold piano rolls here. Later the space presented the **Legacy of Walt Disney** tribute and then, up until the summer of 1989, the exhibits of **Disneyland Presents a Preview of Coming Attractions.** Just before the holidays in 1989, it became an attractive retail store with an ornate sign above the door. The Disney Showcase endures today as a popular destination for movie- and Disneyland-themed clothes, sportswear with team logos, plus pins and gifts.

ꭰisney ꮙillains

MAP: Fantasyland, Fa-30

CHRONOLOGY: July 16, 1991–June 21, 1996

HISTORY: One day after the sweet **Fantasyland** store known as the **Briar Rose Cottage** closed, the sinister Disney Villains store opened. The location was the same—just through the **Sleeping Beauty Castle** entrance and to the right in the castle's courtyard—but the theme was completely inverted to showcase the wicked characters from the Disney film canon. The beauty-obsessed queen who tormented Snow White, malevolent Maleficent from *Sleeping Beauty*, Pan-chasing Captain Hook, and puppy-chasing Cruella De Vil all got clothing and gifts decorated with their faces.

Five years after it opened, the Disney Villains shop was replaced by **Quasimodo's Attic**, a celebration of that year's *Hunchback of Notre Dame* movie. Some of the villain merchandise returned for the **Villains Lair** shop in 1998 and eventually found its way to other stores in the park, among them **Le Bat en Rouge** in **New Orleans Square.**

Walt Disney

CHRONOLOGY: December 5, 1901–December 15, 1966

HISTORY: Walt Disney was a man of contrasts. His peripatetic youth was dominated by a joyless, penurious father and drained by struggle, but when he memorialized his childhood it manifested as Disneyland's sweet, happy **Main Street**. A high school dropout, he later aggressively promoted education and was a prime mover in the development of the California Institute of the Arts. He had a nostalgic love of American folklore and history, but he eagerly embraced a utopian future humming with high-tech gadgets and sleek new transportation. Stridently patriotic, he also championed global "small world" unity. He was an extravagant traveler who toured South America, took frequent vacations to Europe, and late in life flew by private jet, but if given his choice, his preferred meal might've been a can of beans and his preferred activity might've been riding his miniature train around his backyard. The movies he produced were often about making and keeping friends, but he himself remained distant from long-time associates and rarely socialized. The affable exterior he displayed in public belied the gruff, sometimes truculent personality known to his employees. The same man who demanded intense loyalty also made ruthless business decisions that cut loose long-time employees once they'd worn out their usefulness. The wise, kindly, wholesome image he cultivated as the world's fairy tale-loving uncle was offset by the private man who had a short temper, enjoyed nightly cocktails, and chain-smoked. He banned employee mustaches, but he himself wore one. Urban myth said he was cryogenically frozen before he died so he could be revived when there was a cure for the cancer that was killing him, but  cremation, not freezing, consumed him upon his death in 1966. He's remembered by many as being conventional and old-fashioned, but actually many of his business and creative decisions were daring and bold. While his company was making millions and earning 30 Oscar nominations in the '30s and '40s, it never got out of serious debt until the '50s. And while Disney promoted himself as one of the common people, during his lifetime he was bestowed with hundreds of major international honors, his name was on one of the world's biggest entertainment companies and the world's most famous theme park, and upon his death he was extolled as few people in history have ever been.

Many of these contrasts came into play as Walt Disney invented Disneyland. He'd been thinking about amusement parks since before World War II and making notes in the late '40s for a plan to develop the seven-acre plot next to his movie studio in Burbank. Those early ideas included a village based on Marceline, Missouri, his Midwestern hometown, plus a railroad station, an opera house, a movie theater, a farm, an Indian village, carnival rides, ponies, and a merry-go-round. The ideas were still modest, and so were his descriptions of them—"I had a little dream," he'd later say when recalling the first notions for "a three-dimensional thing that people could come and visit." At this stage it was still just a "magical little park," an "amusement area," an "amusement enterprise."

Finances were a pressing concern for something so experimental and expensive. Millions would be needed, just to get a firm start. And Walt Disney wasn't exactly flush—his track record at theater box offices had been dreadful in the '40s when *Fantasia, Pinocchio,* and other labor-intensive films were costly flops. So, rather than risk his studio, he risked himself. As his daughter, Diane Disney Miller, wrote in *The Story of Walt Disney*, "In the end he put his own money into it, not the studio's money. He hocked his life insurance and raised $100,000 and when his day-dreaming reached the point of drawing up plans, he paid a draftsman out of his own pocket to lay out what he'd planned." Disney even sold his just-finished Palm Springs vacation home, and he borrowed from friends and employees to keep the project advancing. Eventually, major corporate sponsors were recruited, and, most importantly, **Roy Disney**, Walt's older brother, negotiated a TV deal that brought ABC in as an investor and gave Walt Disney a chance to promote his park with his own show. It debuted in '54 with the simple title *Disneyland* and quickly became ABC's top-rated program.

Progress at the park accelerated quickly. By the spring of '51, Disney had

Harper Goff visiting amusement parks in Europe, and by the end of that year Goff was drawing plans for Disneylandia, a much larger Burbank park with double-digit acreage that included an island in a lake. At the end of '51, Disney installed Owen and Dolly Pope in a trailer at the Disney Studios to start building Western-style carriages and gather animals for the coming park. A year later, Disney was starting to hire architects to work on what he'd begun calling Disneyland, a park that included a rocket, a submarine, and canal boats. He formed WED Enterprises (his initials) to assemble his core design team, recruiting as members some of the animators and art directors from his movie studio—**Bill Cottrell**, art director **Richard Irvine**, art director **Marvin Davis**, layout artist Goff, layout artist **John Hench**, and more. These were the pioneers who would revolutionize amusement parks and amusement park rides.

On March 27, 1952, Burbank's *Daily Review* newspaper broke the story about the Burbank park with the headline, "Walt Disney Make-Believe Land Project Planned Here—$1.5 million dreamland to rise on site in Burbank." But that plan soon changed. Within a year, Disney knew that the Burbank plot was too limiting for his ambitious dreams, so in the summer of '53 he hired **Harrison Price** from the Stanford Research Institute to pinpoint Southern California's best site. Price found it 38 miles south of Burbank: Anaheim, where weather, freeway access, cheap land, and a population about to soar from 14,000 were favorable variables in his formula for success. Disney first saw the Disneyland site in the fall of '53 and soon began spending around $750,000 to acquire 160 acres of Anaheim orchards previously owned by 17 different farmers. Moving with alacrity on his unified assemblage, in the spring of '54 Disney removed 12,000 orange trees, had the telephone poles cleared and their lines buried, designated 100 acres for the **parking lot**, and prepared to build his park. Anaheim's *Bulletin* newspaper officially announced the switch to Orange County on May 1, 1954.

Meanwhile, realizing that his own designers could execute his ideas better than any outsiders, Disney released the architectural firm he'd hired and sent Goff back out to amusement parks, fairs, and tourist areas around the country for more ideas. Long brainstorming sessions with the group he later called his Imagineers ensued throughout '53 and '54. To observers, Disney was in his element, happily working off his nervous energy with an all-consuming new project that demanded tenacious focus (something similar had happened in the early days of the Disney Studios when he and his galvanized artists cranked out short cartoons and created the first full-length animated feature, *Snow White and the Seven Dwarfs*).

25 Landmark Disneyland Dates

July 12 or 16, 1954: Ground is broken for the construction of Disneyland.

July 17, 1955: Opening Day

September 8, 1955: Guest number 1,000,000 enters the park.

June 14, 1959: Matterhorn, Monorail, Submarine Voyage, and E tickets all officially debut.

June 10, 1960: Nature's Wonderland opens.

June 23, 1963: Enchanted Tiki Room opens.

May 28, 1966: It's a Small World opens.

July 24, 1966: New Orleans Square opens.

December 15, 1966: Walt Disney dies.

March 18, 1967: Pirates of the Caribbean opens.

July-August 1967: Remodeled Tomorrowland opens.

August 9, 1969: Haunted Mansion opens.

June 17, 1971: Guest number 100,000,000 enters the park.

March 24, 1972: Bear Country opens.

May 4, 1977: Space Mountain opens.

May 25, 1983: Remodeled Fantasyland opens.

August 24, 1985: Guest number 250,000,000 enters the park.

January 9, 1987: Star Tours opens.

November 23, 1988: Critter Country opens.

July 17, 1989: Splash Mountain opens.

January 24, 1993: Mickey's Toontown opens.

March 3, 1995: Indiana Jones Adventure opens.

November 19, 1999: FastPass tickets debut.

February 8, 2001: Disney's California Adventure and Downtown Disney open.

January 9, 2004: Guest number 500,000,000 enters the park.

Disney personally made more scout trips to other parks (among them nearby Knott's Berry Farm) to watch the crowds and step off measurements of park geography. He also consulted with numerous "experts" from the amusement industry, several of whom derisively predicted failure and harrumphed their standard rules for success: sell alcohol, add a Ferris wheel and simple carnival games, don't waste money on landscaping and non-revenue-producing structures like **Sleeping Beauty Castle**, don't stay open more than four months a year, etc. To these unimaginative disbelievers, real and ideal were trains on perpendicular tracks.

Disregarding the unsettling advice, Walt Disney finally broke ground on his Anaheim park in mid-July of '54. Unlike nearly every subsequent event in Disneyland's history, there was no fanfare, no initial spade-turning ceremony. Thus the start date is disputed—Neal Gabler's biography says July 12, 1954, other writers claim July 16th, and Walt's daughter, Diane Disney Miller, stated in *Disneyland . . . the Beginning* that it was July 17th. But the deadline was indisputable, because TV commitments soon placed the finish line at July 17, 1955. For the next year, work progressed steadily, then hurriedly, and finally frantically, especially in the last months. Even Walt Disney's wife Lillian picked up a broom to sweep off the decks of the *Mark Twain* **Riverboat** in the final days.

Incredibly, despite spiraling costs that drove the price over $17 million, despite labor strikes and bad weather and daily construction problems, despite being told by his own staff that he needed to postpone the opening until the fall, the park was finished on time. Well, if not completely finished, at least finished enough to *look* finished, even if it really wasn't. Some of the attractions, including the **Casey Jr. Circus Train** and **Rocket to the Moon**, were ready only for viewing, not for riding. And **Tomorrowland** had to be swathed in balloons and bunting to camouflage its empty buildings. Still, the great park was open for business right when Walt Disney said it would be, and an instantly seduced America quickly set the turnstiles spinning at a record-setting pace.

Meanwhile, Disney himself was a creative whirlwind stirring multiple pots. During the mid-'50s, when he was so deeply immersed in detailed Disneyland planning and construction that he was actually living in an **apartment** at the park much of the time, he also oversaw ongoing production on his studio's most ambitious animated movie yet, *Sleeping Beauty*; completed the 1953–'56 films *Peter Pan, 20,000 Leagues Under the Sea*, and *Lady and the Tramp*; produced numerous documentaries and dozens of cartoons; and created his new TV show with its landmark miniseries *Davy Crockett*. Busy as he and his company were, there was no drop-off in quality—the Disney features and short films completed in the full-speed Disneyland years from '53 to '56 earned 13 Oscar nominations.

Obviously Walt Disney wasn't doing it all single-handedly, but he was deeply, some said obsessively, involved in everything his company did, and he routinely worked all day and late into the evening. "Get a good idea and stay with it. Dog it and work at it until it's done, and done right," he advised, not exactly the mantra of a free-spirited creative artist but certainly one of a fiercely determined entrepreneur. When he did neglect something and let others run with it—the '51 film *Alice in Wonderland*, for instance—it was usually derided by critics as one of the studio's lesser efforts.

With Disneyland, the arc of Disney's career, from small to big, from simple to sophisticated, from drawing to movie to life, was finally complete. He'd begun with unrefined humorous sketches and transitioned first to silent black-and-white cartoons and then singing color cartoons; he'd leaped to full-length animated features and live-action movies and *True-Life* documentaries; and he'd culminated with the real-life world of Disneyland. Actually, it wasn't merely a real-life world—Disneyland was an improvement upon real life. When Disneyland opened in mid-'55, it was the cleanest, safest, most orderly, most thematically unified, and most totally immersive park anyone had ever seen.

And easily the most imaginative. The 60-acre triangle was bursting with archetypal imagery from Disney's own movies and every kid's dreams—pirates and princesses, cowboys and stagecoaches, rockets and rivers, majestic castles and quaint towns, cool little cars and cozy little boats, whirling teacups and flying elephants—with enough added exhibits, parades, and live music to enable everyone to find something to enchant/entice/entertain them no matter their age or disposition. The conspicuous presence of dozens of respected sponsors like Coca-Cola and TWA eased concerns about quality and helped make the untried park a little more familiar.

Everything seemed safe and family-friendly. Many attractions appeared to relate to American heritage or timeless fairy tales, most espoused traditional values even while celebrating wonderful new technology, and everything was either fun, patriotic, or educational, or all three. Even the revolutionary queues, cleverly snaking back and forth and offering eye candy to sweeten the line-waiting experience, seemed entertaining, even comforting, and thus another expression of Walt Disney's people-pleasing philosophy. "All I want you to think about," Disney told his designers, "is that when people walk through or ride through or have access to anything that you design, I want them, when they leave, to have smiles on their faces. Just remember that; it's all I ask of you as a designer." A smile. Ultimately, what he sought wasn't the most thrilling, or the most educational, or even the most fun park in history—his kingdom, he famously declared, was to be "the happiest place on Earth."

What daughter Diane Disney Miller called his "insatiable, omnivorous curiosity" drove Disney to nurture Disneyland for all the rest of his days ("to plus" the park was his own invented verb). Miller quoted him: "The way I see it, my park will never be finished. It's something I can keep developing and adding to. A movie is different. Once I've wrapped it up and have turned it over to Technicolor to be processed, I'm through with it. As far as I'm concerned the picture I've finished a few weeks ago is done. There may be things in it I don't like, but if there are I can't do anything about them. I've always wanted to work on something alive, something that keeps growing. I've got that in Disneyland. Even the trees will grow and be more beautiful every year." Thus, even in his last months Disney was still tinkering—in mid-'66, near the end of his life, he approved the designs for two of his most ambitious attractions yet, **Pirates of the Caribbean** and **Adventure Thru Inner Space**, while simultaneously pushing forward the long-gestating **Haunted Mansion** and Walt Disney World projects, announcing plans for a new ski resort in

California (Mineral King, never built), and overseeing production on his last major films, *The Jungle Book* and *The Happiest Millionaire*. All this, even as he lived with constant pain and failing health.

Not everyone has accepted the park with equal glee, of course. Some critics deride the artifice and saccharine sweetness, others the rampant merchandising and sky-high prices. The adjective "Disneyfied" is used pejoratively, and accusations that Disney was a calculating phony with his ear eagerly cocked to the silvered sirens of the marketplace are often supported with Disneyland as Exhibit A.

Fortunately, most of the public, for whom Disney truly built the park, loved it from **Opening Day** and made it an instant and lasting financial success. Walt Disney's teetering pre-Disneyland company was soon in the black after the park opened; within a decade of opening his park was making more money than his movies; and today, 50+ years after it opened, Disneyland still draws around 14 million visitors annually (some 35,000 people every single day of the year). "I'm not interested in pleasing the critics," Walt Disney once said. "I'll take my chances pleasing the audiences." Yet another contrast, one that worked for him in movie theaters and again in Anaheim, and one that has kept Walt Disney in the rarified pantheon of beloved geniuses. Ultimately, the words on the dedication plaque in **Town Square**—"a source of joy and inspiration to all the world"—apply as much to the revered man who spoke them as they do to the wondrous park he was describing.

Dixieland at Disneyland

CHRONOLOGY: October 1, 1960–1970

HISTORY: One of the most fondly remembered musical events of Disneyland's first decades was the series of Dixieland at Disneyland evening concerts held each fall from 1960 to 1970. Requiring a special ticket that included admission to the park and its attractions, Dixieland at Disneyland featured an all-star team of world-renowned jazz combos and music superstars, including Louis Armstrong, Kid Ory, Al Hirt, Bob Crosby and the Bob Cats, and Teddy Buckner, plus Disney's own groups the **Firehouse Five Plus Two** (which included well-known Disney animators) and the **Strawhatters**.

For the first five years the shows were held at the **Rivers of America** in **Frontierland**, with crowds lining the banks and the musicians playing on the southern tip of **Tom Sawyer Island** or floating past on the island's log rafts and the **Mike Fink Keel Boats**. The grand finale involved **fireworks** and the *Mark Twain* wheeling past the cheering audience while the jazz musicians and a 200-person choir on board wailed through "When the Saints Go Marching In." A **parade** ensued that carried musicians throughout the park for more celebratory music.

In '63, the show was updated to include a three-acre stage, Mardi Gras-style floats, singers, and dancers. For the last half of the '60s, the show moved to **Main Street**, where the bands performed on wagons and then embarked on a park-touring parade. The undeniable star of any show was Louis Armstrong, who first performed at Disneyland in 1961 and totaled a half-dozen park engagements during the '60s. The king of jazz's raft was specially designed with a huge crown on top, and Satchmo himself would wear a crown while leading the festivities.

Donald's Boat, aka Miss Daisy

MAP: Mickey's Toontown, MT-2

CHRONOLOGY: January 24, 1993–ongoing

HISTORY: Maximum play, minimum complexity. That seems to be the philosophy behind many attractions in **Mickey's Toontown**, including Donald's Boat. Named for Donald Duck's girl-friend, the *Miss Daisy* sits in little Toon Lake like a big colorful duck. Entry via a walkway takes guests past Donald's mailbox and into the hull. Once inside, the boat reveals itself as a simple walk-through, or more accurately a simple play-through, attraction. Guests can see charming interior reminders of who supposedly owns this craft and can then take a rope ladder or a spiral staircase up to the decks where there's more room to run around and explore and make noise.

Nifty details abound to quack up the young clientele: Donald's sailor suit hanging on the laundry line between the masts, a speaker shaped like a duck bill, etc. No minimum height requirement makes this a ducky spot for young children to burn up excessive energy while parents rest in the shady area nearby.

Don DeFore's Silver Banjo Barbecue

MAP: Frontierland, Fr-6

CHRONOLOGY: June 15, 1957–September 1961

HISTORY: Almost two years after **Opening Day**, the self-proclaimed "finest bar-becue this side of the Missisippi" opened next door to **Aunt Jemima's Pancake House** in **Frontierland**. Previously, this ground-floor space underneath a pair of balconies was the site of **Casa de Fritos**, which had already vacated in favor of a more prominent location.

Ribs, chicken, pork, and even fish were on the Silver Banjo's menu, all of it barbecued on the premises in a kitchen so small it was chided by fire marshals for code violations. The "Don DeFore" of the restaurant's name referred to the popular 1950s actor best known as Thorny, neighbor to the Nelsons, on *The Adventures of Ozzie and Harriet*. The "Silver Banjo" name referred to one of DeFore's prized per-sonal possessions, which seemed to fit in with Frontierland imagery (a fortunate choice, since another name he considered for his eatery was Don DeFore's Bean Palace). DeFore himself was the chef, with his brother Verne the manager.

After four years, the Silver Banjo finally closed in 1961. Most of the interior space was engulfed in the expansion that transformed Aunt Jemima's Pancake House into Aunt Jemima's Kitchen, while the front areas became the **Malt Shop and Cone Shop**.

Dream Machine

MAP: Plaza Hub, PH-7

CHRONOLOGY: 1990

HISTORY: Always ready to celebrate any anniversary divisible by the number five, Disneyland cranked up the Dream Machine 35 years after opening. Guests entering the park that year received a special ticket that granted them a pull on the lever at the Dream Machine.

Stationed at the **Plaza Hub**, the Dream Machine looked like a wildly decorated giant cake but worked like a slot machine. The tickets were decorated with smiling Disney characters, among them Dopey, Brer Rabbit, Pluto, Goofy, and Snow White (there were 24 such character tickets in all). Usually the prizes were for free food treats and beverages, but occasionally a guest won something bigger, such as videos, toys, or watches. Once in a while the prizes were even heftier—airline tickets to any location in America, for instance—and once a day the prize was a new Chevy. Guests who won the car watched it rise up from inside the cake before their very eyes as Mickey danced around them and confetti dropped on the scene; the car, though, was only a duplicate of the actual prize, as guests had to go pick theirs up from a dealer later on.

Duck Bumps

MAP: Fantasyland, Fa-6

CHRONOLOGY: Never built

HISTORY: As shown on **Bill Martin's** color illustration in 1954, Duck Bumps was to be located behind the **King Arthur Carrousel** in **Fantasyland** (that same illustration showed a "Canal Boat Ride" where the **Alice in Wonderland** attraction was actually built, while Alice in Wonderland was placed at the left side of Fantasyland adjoining **Snow White Adventures**). The Duck Bumps placed 11 ring-shaped boats in a pool for "bumper-car" maneuvering. A Donald Duck head was mounted on a tall pole attached to each boat. Adjacent to this attraction was a 20-foot windmill called "The Old Mill," after the landmark 1937 cartoon, but neither the Bumps nor the Mill ever made it past the drawing tables.

Dumbo the Flying Elephant

MAP: Fantasyland, Fa-11, Fa-14

CHRONOLOGY: August 16, 1955–ongoing

HISTORY: An attraction based on *Dumbo*, Disney's hit film from 1941, was present in early plans for the park. And that attraction was always intended to be something with spinning pachyderms. However, there was a considerable difference between what appeared on the first concept drawings and what finally appeared in **Fantasyland** in mid-1955.

Originally the elephants were pink, representing the pink elephants parading through the movie's hallucination sequence (none of these pink elephants was Dumbo himself, which meant Dumbo would've been on the attraction's sign but not actually part of the attraction itself). What's more, the big ears were going to flap, Timothy Mouse was slated to stand atop a circus-themed column in the middle, and

ultimately the whole attraction was supposed to be in operation on **Opening Day**. New designs, and problems with time, budget, and a flawed prototype, brought not only a different attraction but a delayed one as well. Almost a full month after the rest of the park opened, Dumbo the Flying Elephant finally debuted 10 gray elephants, all of them Dumbo, all of them with collars and colored hats, and no flapping ears or Timothy in sight.

For the next 27 years, Dumbo spun happily as a minute-and-a-half B-ticket attraction in the rear-left corner of Fantasyland. This was back when there was no connecting walkway to **Frontierland**, making the Dumbo corner more of a Dumbo cul-de-sac. Kids especially loved the elephants because they could control their own altitude with the same kind of cockpit-lever system used to elevate the **Astro-Jets** in **Tomorrowland**.

The early **souvenir books** routinely featured big photos of flying Dumbos that needed very little explanation, and so captions usually were as simple as "Flying with Dumbo is fun for Disneyland guests of all ages." The beautiful **attraction poster** was a little more poetic and included this rhyme: "Whirling and twirling way up in the blue . . . elephants fly, and so can you!" One guest who wouldn't whirl and twirl was former President Truman, a Democrat who visited Disneyland in 1957 but refused to board and be photographed on an attraction that evoked Republican Party symbolism.

Two years later, changes started to come to the aerodynamic elephants. In 1959, the year the ticket price went from B to C, the souvenir books started labeling the attraction Dumbo's Flying Elephants. At some point Timothy was added, wielding his whip and standing on top of a shiny silver ball mounted atop a circus platform. And in the '70s, plans for something called Dumbo's Circusland with its own new, unexplained attractions were announced with a display inside **Disneyland Presents a Preview of Coming Attractions** over on **Main Street**.

While Circusland never happened, Dumbo did make an important move—a move about 75 feet to the northeast. In 1982, Dumbo, and most of the other attractions in Fantasyland, were closed for a major year-long remodeling. When the new Fantasyland reopened in May of 1983, the **Pirate Ship Restaurant** (aka Captain Hook's Galley) and **Skull Rock and Pirate's Cove** had all disappeared, and Dumbo was now spinning where they'd been (Dumbo's former cul-de-sac was opened up to become the shortcut to Frontierland). Dumbo now had his own vintage band organ, too, a refurbished antique that pumped out Disney classics.

Another important change came in 1990, when the whole attraction was dramatically refurbished. Instead of 10 elephants, there were now 16 (originally built for Disneyland Paris, they were brought to Anaheim first and Paris got its own elephants later). Timothy lost his silver-ball platform but found a colorful hot-air balloon to stand on, and the central column lost its circus theme but gained a glittering-toy theme, as shown off in big beautiful color photos in some of the park's later souvenir books. The whole attraction now sits in a lovely fountain setting where the charming elephants whirl and twirl more attractively than ever.

Don Edgren

CHRONOLOGY: September 11, 1923–December 28, 2006

HISTORY: Don Edgren figured out how **Matterhorn Mountain** could carry bobsleds, he put streaking rockets inside **Space Mountain**, and he took **Pirates of the Caribbean** underground. What **Walt Disney** and his Imagineers dreamed up, Edgren, leader of the park's engineering team, got built.

Edgren was born in Los Angeles in 1923. After graduating high school, he joined the Army Air Forces and flew 45 combat missions during World War II. Returning to Southern California, he started working at an engineering firm while simultaneously earning his civil engineering degree from USC. The company he was with helped ready Disneyland for **Opening Day**, and Edgren worked as a field engineer at the busy construction site. A few years later, Edgren, still not a Disney employee, had a major role in constructing the Matterhorn and managed to incorporate the **Matterhorn Bobsleds** and the **Skyway to Fantasyland/Tomorrowland** into the unusually shaped structure.

In '61, Edgren was lured away to work full-time for Disney alongside the company's Imagineers. Assembling his core engineering staff, Edgren erected the **Swiss Family Treehouse** and **New Orleans Square**; in the latter, Pirates of the Caribbean was perhaps the biggest challenge because partway through the planning it went from being a walk-through exhibit to a subterranean boat ride that necessitated elaborate waterways and eventually a new "show building" beyond the park's perimeter **berm**.

Working outside of Disneyland, at the 1964–1965 New York World's Fair

Edgren supervised the Ford Motor Company exhibit, which put visitors inside cars and toured them past dinosaurs and other displays. In 1966, Edgren shifted his efforts to Walt Disney World, where he was a chief engineer and team leader of 1975's Space Mountain project. Late in the '70s, he moved to Japan to help build Tokyo Disneyland. After retiring to California in '87, Don Edgren was named a Disney Legend in 2006, just a few months before the 83-year-old grandfather died of a stroke while visiting relatives in Oregon.

Edison Square

MAP: Plaza Hub, PH-4

CHRONOLOGY: Never built

HISTORY: The same large 1958 park map that laid out a detailed plan of **Liberty Street**, an area never built at Disneyland, also showed another spin-off from **Main Street** that was intended to open in 1959 but never made it beyond the drafting table. Whereas Liberty Street was supposed to run roughly parallel to Main Street, designers imagined another new side street, but this one would've extended from the north end of Main Street and gone perpendicular to the right for two blocks. As shown on the '58 map, Edison Square was to start from an entrance next to the **Red Wagon Inn** on the **Plaza Hub**, continue as a narrow street for a block, and then end in a cul-de-sac behind the **20,000 Leagues Under the Sea Exhibit** building in **Tomorrowland** (Liberty Street would've been just to the south of Edison Square). The theme of this new area was to be American progress as propelled by Thomas Edison—in fact, a statue of Edison would've graced Edison Square's center, and his life story would've been told with a series of dioramas around the statue, culminating with his invention of the incandescent light bulb.

Unlike Main Street, which was a commercial area of colorful shops and eateries, Edison Square looked more like a mature residential neighborhood of attractive two-story buildings. Each building in the neighborhood was actually going to be a theater that led guests through decades of electronic progress. According to the map, the four theaters were labeled American Home: Pre-Electricity; American Home: Advent of Electricity; Contemporary Living; and The Electronic Age (this last theater was to conclude with interplanetary travel). **Audio-Animatronic** figures would've populated the four stages, but unfortunately the technology needed to pull everything off wouldn't be perfected until the mid-'60s. By then Edison Square had become Edison Nowhere in the park's plans. However, veteran visitors might recognize the theme of electronic progress, the sponsor (General Electric), and the Audio-Animatronic Americans as the cornerstones of the **Carousel of Progress** that eventually spun in Tomorrowland in 1967.

Several Disneyland-history books have explored the Edison Square plans. *Disneyland: The Nickel Tour* gave alternative names for the Edison Square theaters, but the theatrical presentation was basically the same; *Disneyland: Then, Now, and Forever* showed concept illustrations by **Sam McKim** and **John Hench** that detailed some of the exhibits.

Ellen's Gift Shop

MAP: Main Street, MS-13

CHRONOLOGY: 1955–1956

HISTORY: In the '50s, standing one door north of the **Gibson Greeting Cards** shop on the right-hand side of **Main Street** was a little store called Ellen's. The 1956 and '57 **souvenir books** made passing mentions of it, calling it Ellen's Gift Shop, and Gifts, Ellens, and in one reference simply Gift Shop. The contents were summarized as metal and wood gifts. In '58, the souvenir book replaced Ellen with something undefined called Art Corner Gallery, but a year later that too was gone. Today, the big **Disney Clothiers, Ltd.** store engulfs the corner formerly held by Gibson and Ellen.

Peter Ellenshaw

CHRONOLOGY: May 24, 1913–February 12, 2007

HISTORY: The man who painted both beautiful movie backgrounds and extraordinary Disneyland artworks was a Londoner born in 1913. While working as a teen in a car garage, Peter Ellenshaw also pursued his early love of art and managed to land a job painting sets for various English films of the 1930s.

A 1947 meeting with **Walt Disney**, who was in England to start work on his first live-action movie, *Treasure Island*, brought Ellenshaw an invitation to create detailed background paintings for that movie as well as for *20,000 Leagues Under the Sea* a few years later. For the former movie, Ellenshaw painted English coastlines and dock areas that were shown behind the main action; for the latter, he depicted Vulcania, the secret island shown behind the submarine; in both movies his work looked more like realistic photographs than paintings. Following these early successes, Ellenshaw enjoyed a long Disney career as a matte artist and production designer for such classics as *Swiss Family Robinson*, *The Absent-Minded Professor*, and *The Love Bug*. He won an Oscar for his memorable cityscapes in *Mary Poppins* and contributed to Disney movies as late as 1979 (that year's *The Black Hole* earned him his fourth Oscar nomination).

Meanwhile, back before Disneyland was built, Ellenshaw painted one of the park's original maps, a majestic four-by-eight-foot overhead view that showed the overall triangular shape with lands spreading out from the **Plaza Hub** (it also included some details that were never realized, such as a hot-air balloon ride near **Fantasyland** and a **Liberty Street** area parallel to **Main Street**). This important image was shown on the *Disneyland* TV series (with Walt Disney pointing out its highlights), plus it was used on the first-ever Disneyland postcard and on the cover of the 1955 **souvenir book.** For **Tomorrowland**, Ellenshaw created the detailed backdrop for **Space Station X-1**, an **Opening Day** attraction that offered a view of

Earth from outer space, and a couple of years later he directed *A Tour of the West*, the first film for the new **Circarama** theater.

Peter Ellenshaw was elected a Disney Legend in 1993; three years later, a book of his art, *The Garden Within*, was published. He died in 2007 in Santa Barbara, California at age 93. His son, Harrison Ellenshaw, is an Oscar-nominated visual effects artist who has worked on several *Star Wars* films.

El Zocalo, aka El Zocalo Park

MAP: Frontierland, Fr-23

CHRONOLOGY: 1958–1963

HISTORY: From 1958 to 1963, Disneyland's **souvenir books** showed a small circular plaza in **Frontierland**. This little space was named El Zocalo, a traditional name in Mexico for a town square (the grandest Zocalo is probably the one in Mexico City). The reference wasn't accidental—the site really was trying to emulate historic California and Mexico. More specifically, the site was trying to evoke Zorro. When Disneyland was in its

infancy, Zorro was one of the Disney Studio's most popular characters, thanks to the Friday-night TV series that ran from 1957 to 1959, starred Guy Williams, had Spanish California as a setting, and used rural California as an outdoor filming location.

El Zocalo covered about a fifth of an acre near the landing for the *Mark Twain*. There were no major attractions in El Zocalo, but there were certainly some nearby. From this convenient Frontierland spot, guests in the late '50s would've had easy access to such frontier transportation as the **Mule Pack**, **Conestoga Wagons**, and **Stage Coach**. What's more, they could've shopped at Mexican Imports, a short-lived Southwestern-themed store nearby, and dined at **Casa de Fritos**, a long-lived Mexican restaurant that moved to the eastern edge of El Zocalo from another Frontierland location in 1956.

Any mention of El Zocalo disappeared from the '64 and subsequent souvenir books, but in recent years the name has enjoyed something of a resurgence. The Casa de Fritos restaurant, later Casa Mexicana, reopened in 2001 as the **Rancho del Zocalo Restaurante**, and later a small stage for character greetings opened up near where El Zocalo had been some five decades earlier. The flag-decorated sign above the stage reads, "El Zocalo Park, dedicated 55," an affectionate tribute to Disneyland's own history.

Emporium, aka Disneyland Emporium

MAP: Main Street, MS-2

CHRONOLOGY: July 17, 1955–ongoing

HISTORY: Just as a small American town's main street probably has a big department store on it, so too does Disneyland's **Main Street** have its big Emporium. The

signage on the exterior of this beautiful building actually reads both Emporium (on the Main Street side) and Disneyland Emporium (on the **Town Square** side). Inside is the park's biggest (at well over 4,000 square feet) retail display space, filled with classic and new souvenirs, toys, hats, coffee mugs, picture frames, books, figurines, jewelry, maps, pens, and more. Everything is on view in an open space given even more character by the deep-brown woodwork along the walls. For added interest, up by the ceiling the balconies use old-fashioned artifacts and figures to show such nostalgic scenes as a barber with a kid and a lady in a milliner's shop.

The Emporium's main entrance, 800 feet south of **Sleeping Beauty Castle** on the corner of Main and Town Square, represents perfect product placement, as this is the last major store guests walk past on their way to the exits and so is their final chance to splurge on whatever they don't already have with whatever money they haven't already spent. Half the time guests probably don't even realize they're in the Emporium, since the original room now stretches northward all the way through the block to the **Carnation Café**, where a toy train circles on a 100-foot-long track above a final toy-selling area.

Curiously, such an important and prominent building has rarely snuck into any of the park's **souvenir books**, not even in the backgrounds of **parade** photos. The Emporium did make it into the 2006 book with a captionless full-frontal photo showing the Main Street signage for Books, Gifts and Emporium outside, with a white balcony over the main entrance and handsome mansard-style upper stories dotted with heavily ornamented circular windows. Windows in particular are a favorite at the Emporium, as those on the ground floor have been filled, not with the expected merchandise and mannequins, but with imaginative dioramas depicting characters and settings of recent Disney films. This tradition began in 1969 to promote a rerelease of *Peter Pan*; since then, dozens of movies have been retold with detailed artwork and puppets, giving the Emporium the best window-shopping in Disneyland.

Enchanted Cottage Sweets & Treats

MAP: Fantasyland, Fa-17
CHRONOLOGY: 2004–ongoing
HISTORY: It's not all that enchanted, nor is it really a cottage, but the Enchanted

Cottage snack stand does get a lot of business, probably because of its location just outside the **Videopolis**/Fantasyland Theater stage show. Previously, this eatery had been known as **Yumz**, Meeko's, Louie's, Fantasyland Theater Snacks, and Troubadour Treats, with the theming changing to match whatever theatrical presentation was being performed next door. But no matter the name, the place had always been a quick stop for fast food.

When *Snow White—An Enchanting Musical* opened in the Fantasyland Theater in the spring of 2004, the woodsy Enchanted Cottage was born and adorned with an ornamental sign that announced "sweets & treats," sponsored by Nestlé. The new Bavarian menu was themed to match the Snow White story, with sausages, pretzels, German chocolate cake, and dessert treats and drinks getting names like Diamond Mine Delight, Magic Wishing Apple, and Charmed Beverages. Outdoor patio seating, specialty coffee drinks, and souvenir containers all add to the

enchantment. Even though the **Princess Fantasy Faire** replaced the *Snow White* show in 2006, the cottage has continued on with no retheming and no name change.

Enchanted Tiki Room

MAP: Adventureland, A-11

CHRONOLOGY: June 23, 1963–ongoing

HISTORY: In June of 1963, some kind of history was made inside the first left-hand building within the **Adventureland** gates. That's where the debut of the Enchanted Tiki Room ratcheted up Disneyland's achievements in **Audio-Animatronic** characters.

Previously, the park had displayed moving animals on the **Jungle Cruise** and in the **Nature's Wonderland** area, but those had been simple, repetitive motions viewed at a distance. In the Tiki Room the A-A characters sang and moved with sophisticated subtlety just a few feet from over 200 studious guests. The 17-minute show (later tightened to about 15) showcased 225 moving birds, drumming tiki figures, chanting tiki masks, and singing orchids and birds-of-paradise blossoms inside a tropical hut where fountains rose and fell, a rain storm raged outside, and an elaborate "birdmobile" descended from the ceiling. The songs included "Hawaiian War Chant," "Barcarole," and the sing-along finale "Let's All Sing Like the Birdies Sing." Hosting the festivities were Fritz, José, Michael, and Pierre, four wisecracking A-A macaws of international heritage.

The birds themselves have always appeared incredibly lifelike, thanks to their varied movements and the real feathers covering their plastic bodies. And the lively presentation has always drawn compliments, especially in its first decades. In August 1963, *National Geographic* declared the Tiki Room to be "a tremendous show" and gave it over two pages and three big photos (the magazine also estimated that it was a million-dollar-plus attraction). The park's own **souvenir books** also lavished praise over Disneyland's unique creation. The '63 souvenir book christened it "a new dimension in entertainment," with a photo showing the room, guests, and two tiki hostesses with island clothes, flower leis, and floral headgear. The '68 book called it "a musical fantasy recalling legends of the South Seas," while the 35th-anniversary hardcover book described it as "a whole new era" and "a magnificent obsession . . . overflowing with the color and spirit of the islands."

Surprisingly, all the fuss was being made over a scaled-down version of what had been originally planned. Early in the discussions, the Tiki Room designers envisioned a restaurant followed by an after-dinner singing-bird show, but when the plan proved to be unworkable the entertainment was enhanced to become the entire attraction. The **attraction poster** even made a reference to what might have been: "Tiki talk say 'better go! Wondrous food! Wondrous show!'" Another curiosity was the ticket pricing: early on, guests needed, not the usual A-E tickets, but instead a separate 75-cent tiki ticket (by about 1966 a normal E ticket was the admission price).

For **Walt Disney**, of course, the rave reviews only inspired him to sprint ahead to his next Audio-Animatronic leaps—the 1964–1965 New York World's Fair exhibits that included a talking Lincoln, large dinosaurs, **It's a Small World** children, and **Carousel of Progress** families. Meanwhile, back at Disneyland United Airlines took over sponsorship of the Enchanted Tiki Room from 1964 to 1973, followed by Dole Pineapple from 1976 onward (Dole added a pre-show video about

Major Attractions and Exhibits Added in the 1960s

1960
Pack Mules Through Nature's Wonderland; Skull Rock and Pirate's Cove; Western Mine Train Through Nature's Wonderland

1961
Babes in Toyland Exhibit; Flying Saucers

1962
Big Game Safari Shooting Gallery; Swiss Family Treehouse

1963
Enchanted Tiki Room

1965
Great Moments with Mr. Lincoln

1966
It's a Small World; Primeval World Diorama

1967
Adventure Thru Inner Space; Carousel of Progress; PeopleMover; Pirates of the Caribbean

1969
Haunted Mansion

Hawaii and pineapples and also began sponsoring the **Tiki Juice Bar** next door). After years of neglect, a major renovation in 2005 upgraded the room's interior and exterior.

Many Disney Legends are now credited as having contributed to the Tiki Room's longevity. **Rolly Crump** and **Marc Davis** worked on the whole project from the start; **John Hench** drew up colorful design sketches and invented the rising-fountain concept; **Wally Boag** from the **Golden Horseshoe** wrote the script and voiced both José the macaw and the bird that used to talk out in front of the building; **Fulton Burley**, also a Golden Horseshoe regular, did the vocals for the Irish macaw, Michael; **Thurl Ravenscroft**, later a prominent **Haunted Mansion** presence, vocalized Fritz, the German macaw; the **Sherman** brothers wrote the infectious theme song (the one that goes, "In the tiki tiki tiki tiki tiki room . . ."); and **Harriet Burns** created the intricate plumage for the birds. While the Enchanted Tiki Room may seem tame and corny to 21st audiences, its reputation is assured among long-time guests who recognize its significance and enjoy its gentle pleasures.

Entrance

MAP: Park, P-5

CHRONOLOGY: July 17, 1955–ongoing

HISTORY: "Walt understood the function of an entranceway, or threshold," said **John Hench** in the book *Remembering Walt*. "The threshold is supposed to embrace you. It's where you feel like you're entering some very special place." This architectural philosophy wasn't new in 1955, but Disneyland's distinctive entrance sure was.

Against the advice of seasoned operators of fairs and parks around the country, **Walt Disney** opened Disneyland with only one entrance. Whereas many "experts" thought there needed to be a variety of convenient ways to get into the park, Disney reckoned that he'd be better able to control a guest's initial Disneyland experience if he welcomed them through a single portal.

The result was the wide entrance at the southern tip of the park. For decades guests naturally walked to this point from the huge **parking lot** to the south or on the footpaths to the west and east. Painted freestanding ticket booths are still scattered across this clean, open plaza in front of the turnstiles; the **Monorail** still glides some 25 feet above; and the **Main Street** train station still beckons ahead to the north. Stretching 200 feet to the left of the turnstiles are one-story buildings that house a **Newsstand**, Guest Services, a small room with lockers, and **restrooms**; to the right is a shorter row with the **Guest Relations** office and the park's pet kennels.

Having bought their admission tickets, guests stream into Disneyland through 32 covered turnstiles arranged in a slight semicircle. Once through the turnstiles, guests are 75 feet from a face-to-face encounter with Mickey Mouse, whose famous likeness has been carefully formed in a colorful 25-foot-wide parterre. Park photographers and characters are often milling about this highly photogenic area. So are parents as they angle towards the popular **Stroller Shop** at the far right. For decades the smooth concrete here was red, which many observers have speculated was Disney's way of extending an inviting "red carpet" to his guests. Today, reddish pavers greet feet.

Even at this stage, when guests have paid their way in and passed through turnstiles, the park is still not clearly visible. Revelation comes once guests walk through one of the two tunnels that are on either side of the manicured Mickey garden. These arched tunnels are both decorated on the inside with eight beautiful **attraction posters** and are both topped with plaques that render Walt Disney's declaration about the wonders just ahead: "Here you leave today and enter the worlds of yesterday, tomorrow and fantasy." The tunnels lead guests under the tracks of the **Santa Fe & Disneyland Railroad**, through the park's perimeter **berm**, and into **Town Square** where **Main Street vehicles**, the **flagpole**, and Disneyland's first two-story buildings await.

Thankfully, Disneyland has nearly always been able to keep its posted hours, so guests can rely on the entrance gates being open as scheduled. There have been about a dozen unscheduled closures in Disneyland history, however. Most of these have resulted from extreme winter weather conditions. One sudden closure resulted from a death—not Walt Disney's passing in 1966, as some might expect, but John F. Kennedy's assassination in 1963. Park officials also closed the park on September 11, 2001, in response to that morning's terrorist attacks on the East Coast.

Morgan "Bill" Evans

CHRONOLOGY: June 10, 1910–August 10, 2002

HISTORY: Many guests love Disneyland's exotic landscaping, imaginative topiaries, and ornamental flower gardens as much as they love the attractions. Those guests can thank Morgan "Bill" Evans, the man who first planted the plants.

Gardening and landscaping were always in Evans's blood. He was born in 1910 into a family that owned a huge Santa Monica garden filled with exotic plants. Upon returning from the Merchant Marine in the late '20s, he studied geology in college. Then in 1934, Evans helped turn the family garden into a thriving West L.A. business that supplied rare plants to the growing Hollywood community, including such luminaries as Gable and Garbo. In '52, **Walt Disney** invited Bill Evans to do the landscaping around Disney's large home near Beverly Hills (this was the house that had the Carolwood Pacific miniature railroad in the backyard). Two years later, an impressed Disney invited Bill and his brother Jack Evans to be the chief landscape architects in charge of planting Disneyland.

For the next year, the pair, using about a half-million dollars and input from other notable Southern California landscapers like Ruth Shellhorn, worked to turn the bulldozed orange groves into a verdant, beautifully manicured park. The brothers also had to meet all the special landscaping requirements for the park's unique attractions. One story had them intentionally planting trees upside-down along the riverbanks of the **Jungle Cruise** to reveal their twisted, exotic-looking roots. Another tale, related in the Bob Thomas biography *Walt Disney: An American Original,* described their last frantic days before the opening when they were running out of time, money, and plants; with some of the berm behind **Fantasyland** still bare, Walt Disney told Bill Evans to put little signs with long Latin names in front of the weeds, thus disguising the weeds as desirable specimens.

Ultimately, Bill and Jack Evans filled Disneyland with so many varieties of plants, only 10% of what was in the finished park was native to California. The park's '56 **souvenir book** boasted about the brothers' Disneyland accomplishments, especially their **Adventureland** exotica: "The vegetation in Adventureland represents most of the tropical areas of the world. Among the trees in this fascinating wonderland are Gunnera plants, Bod plants, Black stem trees of New Zealand, and a Bo-tree (Ficus Religiosa), a native of India, whose history goes back some 2500 years."

Bill Evans continued supervising Disney landscaping and training the company's landscape architects for years, working on Walt Disney World, Tokyo Disneyland, Disneyland Paris, Disney's California Adventure, Disney's Animal Kingdom, and Hong Kong Disneyland (so valuable was his knowledge, he was asked to help with some of these parks even after he retired in 1975). He wrote a book about his Disneyland experiences called *Disneyland: World of Flowers.* Bill Evans was named a Disney Legend in 1992, 10 years before he died at age 92.

Fairytale Arts

MAP: Fantasyland, Fa-23

CHRONOLOGY: December 2006–ongoing

HISTORY: Fairytale Arts is a collection of open booths stretching alongside the **Fantasyland** waters formerly toured by the **Motor Boat Cruise**. Decorative plants of the extinct **Fantasia Gardens** still grow along these riverbanks north of the **Matterhorn Bobsleds** queue area.

The Fairytale Arts booths cover about 60 feet of walkway. The arts available would fit right into a Renaissance faire—old-fashioned calligraphy of personal names and exotic face-painting. To the right of the arts is Fantasia Freeze, a cart dedicated to cooling off hot guests with tart Slurpee-style ice drinks.

Fantasia Gardens

MAP: Fantasyland, Fa-23

CHRONOLOGY: January 1993–2006

HISTORY: Nearly every major animated movie produced by the Disney Studios in the '30s, '40s, and '50s has been represented by an attraction at Disneyland. *Snow White and the Seven Dwarfs*, *Pinocchio*, *Song of the South*, *Alice in Wonderland*, *Peter Pan*, and *Sleeping Beauty* all have attractions based on their characters and settings. Missing from that list are *Bambi*, *Cinderella*, and, for the park's first 38 years, *Fantasia*. In '93, this last film finally found a home in the park on the right side of Small World Way, the walkway from the **Matterhorn** to **It's a Small World** in **Fantasyland**. The **Motor Boat Cruise** had formerly putted around this area, and at one time a miniature ice cream train had been parked on the grounds to vend orange popsicles and ice cream bars.

But soon after the last motor boat sailed in January of '93, the landscaping and fountains of Fantasia Gardens filled in what had been the boats' loading area. Like the **Topiary Garden** in front of It's a Small World, some of the bushes here formed recognizable shapes, in this case the hippo and crocodile characters from *Fantasia*. A snack stand nearby made this a convenient rest stop until everything was closed off in 2006. **Fairytale Arts** and a temporary designated smoking area set up here in late 2006.

Fantasmic!

MAP: Frontierland, Fr-16

CHRONOLOGY: May 13, 1992–ongoing (seasonally)

HISTORY: "Some imagination, huh?" So concludes Mickey Mouse at the end of Fantasmic!, and it's doubtful any viewer could disagree. Fantasmic!, originally intended to be called either Imagination or Phantasmagoria, is a state-of-the-art outdoor music and pyrotechnic entertainment that almost defies definition, simply because it has so many ingredients.

To install the stage and special effects in 1992, the **Rivers of America** waterway in **Frontierland** was drained, the southern tip of **Tom Sawyer Island** was rebuilt, and the island's Mill was relocated. After the first year proved to be overwhelmingly successful (but also overwhelmingly crowded), terraced walkways were added back towards Frontierland and **New Orleans Square** to accommodate the 16,000+ guests who still gather along the riverbanks each night to witness the mesmerizing 22-minute show.

Fantasmic! has evolved over the years, but the basic presentation has stayed consistent. It has usually included over 50 **cast members**, most in multiple roles; thrilling music, voices, and sound effects; thousands of gallons of water that create huge water screens 30 feet tall by 50 feet wide by 4 inches thick; colorful animated images that are projected on those screens; 30-foot-tall spotlight towers; 125 fiery effects that can generate 6-foot flames; 11 floating watercraft; a dragon nearly 50 feet tall; a 100-foot-long snake; a crocodile 25 feet wide by 17 feet tall; a 20-foot-tall Ursula from *The Little Mermaid*; an appearance by the **Mark Twain** or the **Columbia**; and an assortment of smoke machines, lasers, black lights, fire, **fireworks**, and water cannons. The plot of the show pits Mickey in his sorcerer's costume against various Disney villains, resulting in a tour of classic Disney movies, everything from *Snow White and the Seven Dwarfs, Fantasia, Pinocchio,* and *Dumbo* to *Peter Pan, Sleeping Beauty, The Jungle Book,* and *Beauty and the Beast*. The one possible drawback: Fantasmic! is a seasonal presentation, and even in the summer it is occasionally canceled in inclement weather (high winds would soak the audience with water from the water screens). The best possible view: from a balcony outside the nearby **Disney Gallery**, where reservations claimed a special vantage point and a dessert buffet.

The park's **souvenir books** have justifiably touted the one-of-a-kind Fantasmic! experience. According to the 2000 souvenir book, it is "one of the most complex and technically advanced shows ever presented at Disneyland Park"; added the 2006 book, it's "a pioneer in its own right of multimedia entertainment." Just as the **Main Street Electrical Parade** reinvented nighttime entertainment in the '70s, so too did Fantasmic! reinvent it in the '90s to become one of the best, and certainly one of the most elaborate, large-scale nightly shows ever presented.

Fantasy Faire Gifts, aka Fantasy Shop, aka Fantasy Emporium, aka Fantasy Gift Faire

MAP: Fantasyland, Fa-9, Fa-16

CHRONOLOGY: Ca. 1955–ca. 1981; ca. 1996–ongoing

HISTORY: In the park's early decades, Fantasy Faire Gifts shared a building with the **Mickey Mouse Club Theater** in **Fantasyland**. This small castle-themed shop lasted until the major 1981–'83 renovation that brought in Pinocchio themes and the **Village Inn** restaurant. At various times, in various souvenir books and on various maps, the shop was also called the Fantasy Shop (as in a 1956 book), Fantasyland Emporium (on a 1958 map), and Fantasy Gift Faire (a 1970 map).

After disappearing in the early '80s, the shop was reborn in the mid-'90s. Today, standing way in the back of Fantasyland near **It's a Small World**, is a freestanding hut called Fantasy Faire Gifts. Less a gift shop than a convenient open-air quickie mart, Fantasy Faire stocks film, postcards, candy, spray bottles, and other essentials a guest might need. As for what a guest might *want*, there are hats, plush toys, pins, and souvenirs, too, justifying the word "Gifts" in the Fantasy Faire name.

Fantasyland

MAP: Park, P-16
CHRONOLOGY: July 17, 1955–ongoing
HISTORY: Fans of Fantasyland might be surprised to know how fortress-like this most charming of Disneyland areas looked at its inception. In 1953, 10 months before construction began, **Herb Ryman** drew up a detailed sketch of the park as it was envisioned by **Walt Disney**, who was coaching him through the two-day creative process. That landmark drawing showed Fantasyland standing imperiously atop a high plateau. Imposing walls, turrets, and battlements ringed an enormous

vertical castle in the center, making Fantasyland look more like something that should've been called Fantasyempire. A crooked moat wended its way completely around the plateau's perimeter, isolating it from the rest of Disneyland. Other details were less formidable and only slightly less unexpected, such as the carousel that spun in *front* of the castle, not behind it, and the lagoon out back where a large sailing ship was parked.

Later, still months before the park was built, Disney artists created a smaller study of a circular "Fantasy Land" that looked a bit more like what today's guests see. The area stretched from a familiar-looking castle up to a big lagoon with an island in the middle. Sharing the lagoon were a "Pirate Ship" and "Nemo's Sub," the latter obviously a reference to the movie *20,000 Leagues Under the Sea*. Two wings angled from the castle, as they do now, but these had only two labels—"Snow White Ride Thru" on the left, and "Peter Pan Fly Thru" on the right. In the northwest space between Snow White and the lagoon was something called "Mother Goose Fun Thru," and on the opposite northeast side between Peter Pan and the lagoon was the "Alice in Wonderland Walk Thru." In the center of Fantasy Land were a carousel and the undefined buildings of "Pinocchio Square." While some of these attractions did end up in locations approximating the drawing (especially **Sleeping Beauty Castle**, **Snow White Adventures**, the **Peter Pan Flight**,

Alice in Wonderland, the **King Arthur Carrousel**, and the **Pirate Ship Restaurant**), new attractions were shown (Mother Goose, the sub, the island, the square) that were never built, and many actual **Opening Day** or soon-after-Opening Day attractions weren't shown at all, including **Canal Boats of the World**, the **Mad Hatter's Mad Tea Party, Mr. Toad's Wild Ride, Dumbo the Flying Elephant**, the **Casey Jr. Circus Train**, and the **Mickey Mouse Club Theater**.

Clearly Fantasyland went through many changes before the end of 1955, and in nearly every case the change was a move towards a Disney animated movie. More than any other area in the park, Fantasyland opened as a celebration of Disney's film classics, and thus within a few years two *Dumbo* attractions (the airborne elephants and Casey Jr.), two *Alice in Wonderland* attractions (Alice and the Tea Party), Toad's cars from the '49 film *The Adventures of Ichabod and Mr. Toad*, and a theater for cartoon favorites had replaced Mother Goose, Nemo, the big lagoon, and Pinocchio Square.

Walt Disney probably had several strategies in mind as he was infusing Fantasyland with his movies. Certainly the buildings and attractions would be marvelous ways to promote his films, including those like *Snow White*, *Pinocchio* and *Dumbo* that were already over a decade old, and those like *Peter Pan* and *Sleeping Beauty* that were either brand new or were on the drawing board. Even Fantasyland plans that never materialized, such as Bruce Bushman's 1954 concept drawing of a Ferris wheel attraction, were steeped in classic Disney animation (Bushman's attraction

FastPass Attractions

The Nine Attractions with FastPass in 2001
Adventureland: Indiana Jones Adventure
Critter Country: Splash Mountain
Frontierland: Big Thunder Mountain Railroad
Mickey's Toontown: Roger Rabbit's Car Toon Spin
New Orleans Square: Haunted Mansion; Pirates of the Caribbean
Tomorrowland: Autopia, Presented by Chevron; Space Mountain; Star Tours

The Seven Attractions with FastPass in 2007
Adventureland: Indiana Jones Adventure
Critter Country: Splash Mountain
Frontierland: Big Thunder Mountain Railroad
Mickey's Toontown: Roger Rabbit's Car Toon Spin
Tomorrowland: Autopia, Presented by Chevron;
Buzz Lightyear Astro Blasters; Space Mountain

was made to look like the '37 cartoon *The Old Mill*).

More importantly, with so much in Disneyland that was unusual and overwhelming to 1955 guests who had never been in a theme park before, Walt Disney perhaps sensed that there would be comfort in seeing some friendly film faces in Fantasyland to help ease guests towards areas as strange as **Adventureland** and **Tomorrowland.** The same general strategy probably helped him decide to lead off the park with a stroll down a gentle, recognizable **Main Street** instead of an immediate confrontation with something dramatic and different. Give guests the familiar first, he seemed to be saying, acclimate them, orient them, comfort them, and then lead them to the unfamiliar.

In addition to connecting to movies, Fantasyland connects to idyllic, dreamy memories shared by anyone who was, or used to be, a kid. Disneyland literature emphasizes this collective memory—the park's '56 **souvenir book** called Fantasyland "the happiest kingdom of them all" and "a magic land that takes you back to childhood." The '58 book summarized the area as the place "where dreams could actually come true. . . . The classic stories from childhood have become actual realities for you to participate in. . . . The time you spend in the gay and carefree kingdom will be a dream come true—for everyone who is young in heart." When introducing Fantasyland to a TV audience on the premiere episode of the *Disneyland* TV show, Walt Disney himself said that here you can do "anything your heart desires, because in this land hopes and dreams are all that matter." That's a lot of happiness, magic, dreams, childhood memories, hope, and heart for a little six-acre section of the original 60-acre park, but that's how Fantasyland was conceived, and that's how it is generally thought of by guests today.

Unfortunately, decades would pass before the Fantasyland Walt Disney wanted would actually be built. With Opening Day approaching, time pressures and budget problems forced Disney to abandon his idea of uniting the Fantasyland attractions with old-time village architecture, so instead he had his artists paint up some medieval-style boards for the fronts of the attractions. These façades, plus banners and pennants installed along the roofs, gave Fantasyland the atmosphere of an ancient European fair or tournament. The overall medieval look would last for decades, but within a year of opening some major changes were already in place. The delightful **Storybook Land Canal Boats** replaced the dreary Canal Boats of the World, a scenic **Skyway to Tomorrowland** drifted high in the sky, and a **Junior Autopia** cranked up on the east side of Fantasyland. A year later, in 1957, the passageway to the **Sleeping Beauty Castle Walk-Through** opened and a smaller set of cars at the **Midget Autopia** began motoring. Next, 1959 welcomed the addition of the tallest structure in the park, **Matterhorn Mountain**, which flanked Fantasyland to the east near the new **Fantasyland Autopia.** Seven years later, Fantasyland dramatically expanded northward when **It's a Small**

World pushed past the train tracks and the park's perimeter **berm**.

And then came the massive $50 million remodel of 1983, the one that remade the heart of Fantasyland into what Walt Disney had first visualized. Some old attractions were retired (the Pirate Ship Restaurant, **Skull Rock and Pirate's Cove**, the Fantasyland Theater), others were relocated (Dumbo, the Mad Tea Party, the King Arthur Carrousel), tired attractions got refreshed (Snow White, Peter Pan, Alice), and a new one was added (**Pinocchio's Daring Journey**). Most impressively, everything within the castle courtyard got village architecture to approximate the movies the attractions were based upon. Consequently, the exterior of Mr. Toad's Wild Ride really looked like Mr. Toad's wild home, the Pinocchio building evoked Geppetto's alpine village, etc. It had taken 28 years, but Walt Disney's Fantasyland visions had come to life. He must've believed they eventually would; after all, the Fantasyland dedication plaque he created (but never placed in view) read, in part: "Fantasyland is dedicated . . . to those who believe that when you wish upon a star, your dreams come true."

Fantasyland Autopia, aka Rescue Rangers Raceway

MAP: Fantasyland, Fa-22

CHRONOLOGY: June 1959–1999

HISTORY: So popular was the **Tomorrowland Autopia**, which had been a hit since **Opening Day**, that Disneyland opened three subsequent Autopia attractions. After the small **Junior Autopia** and **Midget Autopia** were built for younger drivers, the expansive Fantasyland Autopia opened in 1959 in the park's northeast corner. Previously, this area was partially covered by track from the Junior Autopia until that attraction was towed away in September of 1958. The new Fantasyland Autopia entrance was on the main walkway behind the **Matterhorn** and between the **Motor Boat Cruise** and the **Submarine Voyage**.

The Fantasyland Autopia first appeared in the park's **souvenir books** in 1960, where it was labeled both the Super Autopia Freeway and the Fantasyland Autopia with "the latest Mark V cars." Mark V was a reference to the fifth iteration of Autopia car design and matched what was running concurrently over in the Tomorrowland Autopia. In fact, from '59 until '91, the Fantasyland and Tomorrowland Autopias were almost identical in many ways, sharing sponsorship (Richfield Oil Corporation), similar track design (the two tracks overlapped and were side-by-side in some places), simultaneous car redesigns by **Bob Gurr**, and price (both were C-ticket attractions for most of their existence).

The biggest difference between the two Autopias came on March 15, 1991, when the Fantasyland version was briefly renamed the Rescue Rangers Raceway in accordance with the temporary re-theming that brought **Disney Afternoon Avenue** to **Fantasyland**. The Fantasyland Autopia name was restored on November 10th of that year and lasted until 1999, at which point this attraction was closed so it could be merged into Tomorrowland's heavily remodeled Autopia, Presented by Chevron for the new millennium.

Fashions and Fabrics Through the Ages

MAP: Tomorrowland, T-23

CHRONOLOGY: March 1965–December 1965

HISTORY: To keep up with the styles of the future, guests need to understand the styles of the past. Or so it seemed in 1965, when **Tomorrowland** welcomed a fashion exhibit, of all things, into its pantheon of unusual displays. Like its neighbors the **Bathroom of Tomorrow** and the **Hall of Aluminum Fame**, Fashions and Fabrics Through the Ages was an industrial show added to promote a needed sponsor, in this case Monsanto, the multibillion-dollar chemical company founded in 1901.

Lasting only nine months in 1965, and listed in only one of the park's **souvenir books** (the '65 edition), Fashions and Fabrics was the shortest-lived of the four Disneyland attractions and exhibits sponsored by Monsanto (the others, with their opening years—the **Hall of Chemistry**, 1955; the **House of the Future**, 1957; and **Adventure Thru Inner Space**, 1967). Monsanto set up the exhibit adjacent to its Hall of Chemistry in the first right-hand building inside the Tomorrowland entrance.

The fashions on view were all women's garments, most of them historical, shown in wall displays or on mannequins. The exhibit began with the ragged animal skins worn by cavewomen, continued on from the exotic attire of Ancient Egypt and Renaissance Europe to the fine dresses of the 18th, 19th, and 20th centuries, and culminated with synthetic space wear (the synthetic angle dovetailed nicely with the chemical advances being showcased in the Monsanto hall next door). At the end of '65, the Monsanto fashions were out, and during '66 the entire building was gutted for the construction of what would be, in '67, Adventure Thru Inner Space.

FastPass

CHRONOLOGY: November 19, 1999–ongoing

HISTORY: Already a triumph in Walt Disney World and Disneyland Paris, the FastPass ticketing system came to Disneyland for the 1999 holiday season. The first attraction to get a FastPass ticket-distribution machine placed outside its building was **It's a Small World**. Soon many of Disneyland's other top attractions—the **Indiana Jones Adventure**, **Big Thunder Mountain Railroad**, **Space Mountain**, **Splash Mountain**, etc.—had their own FastPass machines, and guests were happily spending extra hours walking around the park instead of standing in lines.

Anyone who's ever waited 90 minutes for a busy attraction can appreciate how simple and advantageous FastPass reservations are: a guest can show up at a popular park attraction, acquire a free FastPass ticket by inserting her park admission ticket into a FastPass machine near the attraction's entrance, and then return to the attraction at the time indicated on the FastPass ticket (usually an hour or two later). Once she shows up at her appointed time, the guest doesn't have to wait in line and is instead ushered up to the front for almost immediate boarding.

To some guests, however, the system isn't flawless. Theoretically there should be little wait for FastPass ticket holders, but occasionally they end up waiting anyway if the loading bogs down and renders their ticket SlowPass. Also, since the FastPass return time is precisely designated and carefully enforced, guests aren't completely free to wander at will because they have a small window of opportunity for using their FastPass tickets; thus, even if a terrific **parade** starts up or some other attraction beckons as a temptation, the FastPass-holding guest must abandon it to claim the FastPass reservation at the appointed time or else forego that reservation altogether. A final issue is the one-FastPass limit. Guests can't stock up on FastPass tickets and then use them consecutively with a flurry of dashes from attraction to attraction; rather, each guest can get only one ticket at a time and must wait to use the one he has (or wait for the designated time to pass) before getting another one somewhere else.

Ultimately, however, these complaints seem pretty feeble when compared to the huge advantage of jumping past a long hot line right to the front of a cool attraction. And Disney executives have realized an advantage too, as many of those guests who were formerly standing still in queues are now FastPass ticket holders actively shopping and dining before their reservation times arrive. So successful has the FastPass system been in Disney's parks, the amusement park industry lauded it with a Breakthrough Innovation award in 2001.

50th Anniversary Shop

MAP: Fantasyland, Fa-3

CHRONOLOGY: May 2005–November 2006

HISTORY: In conjunction with all the celebrations mounted for Disneyland's 50th birthday, for over a year the **Princess Boutique** in **Fantasyland** was transformed into the 50th Anniversary Shop. The location was the same—inside the **Sleeping Beauty Castle** entrance, on the left-hand side—but the merchandise switched from princess accoutrements to 50th-anniversary souvenirs and collectibles, including some sold exclusively in the shop. After all the long anniversary partying was over, the shop glittered anew as the **Tinker Bell & Friends** fairy shop in late 2006.

Fine Tobacco

MAP: Main Street, MS-19

CHRONOLOGY: July 17, 1955–June 3, 1990

HISTORY: From **Opening Day** and for the next 35 years, Disneyland had a little tobacco shop on **Main Street**. Its location was in the first right-hand block, sandwiched tight in between the **Magic Shop** and the **Main Street Cinema**. The ornamental sign out front proclaimed it as Fine Tobacco, and the park's early **souvenir books**, while never showing a photo of it, listed the store as both the Tobacconist and the Tobacco Shop.

Such a store, complete with its wooden Indian out front, would've been a natural on a small-town street at the turn of the century, making it an authentic addition to Disneyland. And **Walt Disney**, himself a long-time smoker, seemed to have had no qualms about selling cigarettes, cigars, pipes, and smoking accessories in his park. In a nod to tradition, the shop handed out complimentary matchbooks. Some of these matchbooks showed the store's exterior, others put an old-fashioned Main Street lamppost on the front and the cigar-store Indian on the back.

Come the politically correct '90s, however, and tobacco's days were numbered at Disneyland. Fine Tobacco closed at the beginning of the decade, to be replaced by the **Patented Pastimes** collectibles shop and later the **20th Century Music Company** store. Sales of tobacco elsewhere in the park concluded at the end of the decade, and within a few years there were only a handful of places in the park designated as smoking areas. As a remembrance of things past, Fine Tobacco's wooden Indian still stands watch in his usual place along Main Street, just as he has since 1955.

Fire Department, aka Fire Station

MAP: Town Square, TS-5

CHRONOLOGY: July 17, 1955–ongoing

HISTORY: An attractive two-story brick building outlined in white stone, the Fire Department (or Fire Station) has stood proudly to the right (north) of **City Hall** since **Opening Day**. The park's **souvenir books** have rarely given the Fire Department much coverage, for decades showing it only in long-distance shots at the back of **Town Square**. Finally, the 2006 souvenir book flaunted a big color photo of the building and a fireman, with a Mickey Mouse flag and an old-time fire bell atop the upper balustrade.

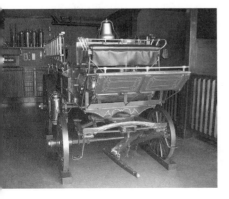

What did get mentioned in many of the souvenir books was the horse-drawn "fire engine" (as it was called in the '56 souvenir book, which also dubbed it "an old-time hose and chemical wagon"). This beautifully appointed red wagon was one of the original **Main Street vehicles** that cost only an A ticket for a ride down **Main Street** to the **Plaza Hub**. From '59 to '61, the park's souvenir books humorously touted the fire wagon with a tiny illustration of the horses, the wagon, and clinging firemen racing down the street.

In the summer of 1960, the horse-drawn wagon was withdrawn from service and was permanently parked inside the Fire Department, where it has been on view, along with displays of actual fire-fighting equipment, a potbelly stove, antique fire extinguishers, and a wall-mounted checkerboard, ever since. Kids can't play with all the accoutrements, but they're encouraged to climb on the fire wagon. The horses that pulled the wagon were moved to the park's **Pony Farm**, but their stalls in the building were kept intact and are still adorned with the names Bess and Jess, the Fire Department's first equine employees.

Upstairs and off-limits to the public is the private **apartment** that was frequently occupied by **Walt Disney** and his family. Also off-limits is the park's real fire department. The Fire Department building familiar to guests only looks like an actual fire-fighting service; the park's true fire-fighting equipment is in an unseen building in back of the **Opera House** on the opposite side of Town Square.

Firehouse Five Plus Two

CHRONOLOGY: 1949–1971

HISTORY: The rollicking septet known as the Firehouse Five Plus Two was a summertime staple at Disneyland for 15 years. The group was all over the park, playing in front of the **Fire Department** on **Town Square**, inside the **Golden Horseshoe** in **Frontierland**, on the streets of **New Orleans Square**, while riding in **parades**, and even aboard the **Santa Fe & Disneyland Railroad** on **Opening Day**. Their signature look was a fireman's outfit—bright red shirt, white suspenders, and authentic fire helmet—and their signature sound was fan-friendly Dixieland jazz punctuated by bells, whistles, and sirens.

As with the **Dapper Dans** and **Disneyland Band**, membership varied during the group's career. Most of the players worked at the Disney Studios in some capacity. Among the long-time players were Danny Alguire (cornet), **George Bruns** (tuba), **Harper Goff** (banjo), Ward Kimball (trombone, and the band's leader), Johnny Lucas (trumpet), Clarke Mallery (clarinet), Monte Mountjoy (drums), Erdman Penner (tuba), George Probert (saxophone), Dick Roberts (banjo), and Frank Thomas (piano). Kimball and Thomas were two of the famed "nine old men," the influential animation team nicknamed by Walt Disney.

The FF5+2 actually began as a lunchtime, after-work, and weekend hobby for a few Disney animators and technicians in the late 1940s. For their early performances at parties, they went by the names Huggajeedy Eight and then the San Gabriel Valley Blue Blowers. In 1949, the group developed its good-time firehouse theme, complete with an old fire engine for photos. In the '50s, they performed live on TV variety shows, on radio shows, and in nightclubs. The group also got airtime on the 1955 "Dateline: Disneyland" special that welcomed the nation to the newly completed park.

Additionally, throughout the 1950s and '60s the group recorded a dozen albums. One of them, 1962's *At Disneyland,* was recorded live at the Golden Horseshoe. The songs included numerous popular stomps and rags, and the cover showed the boys hamming it up while sitting in the **Fantasyland** teacups. After recording their last album in 1970, the FF5+2 disbanded a year later.

Fireworks

MAP: Fantasyland, Fa-2

CHRONOLOGY: Summer 1957–ongoing

HISTORY: The *Disneyland* **TV series** began with an animation of fireworks exploding over the park in 1954, but Disneyland itself didn't actually have these pyrotechnics until 1957. According to *Disneyland: The Nickel Tour,* the fireworks "began when **Tommy Walker** convinced Walt to invest in a nightly fireworks show as a way of encouraging guests to stay for dinner—at the Park's restaurants of course."

The first fireworks show was called Fantasy in the Sky, with pyrotechnicians launching them from an area north of the perimeter **berm** where **Mickey's Toontown** would eventually be built. At the time, the beautiful bursts of kaleidoscopic chrysanthemums, synchronized to music that played throughout the park and visible from Anaheim neighborhoods, were the state of the fireworker's art, and the park's **souvenir books** were quick to show it off. The '58 book was the first to show a photo of the colorful display, adding a caption that boasted how "Disneyland's brilliant 'Fantasy in the Sky' fireworks burst over the Fantasyland Castle every Summer evening."

In '65, the souvenir book splashed two pages with bursting fireworks, showed a new photo of the illuminated castle being showered with fiery sprays, and changed the text: "Every Summer evening at 9, fireworks cascade a shower of color over Disneyland. At that hour, Tinker Bell 'flies' across the Magic Kingdom—down from the Matterhorn and high over Fantasyland—drawing the curtain on daytime fun . . . and shining the footlights on nighttime magic." **Tinker Bell**, actually a 71-year-old circus aerialist named Tiny Kline, joined the fireworks show in 1961. The best fireworks photos of the first two decades appeared in the park's hardcover books from 1964 and 1969 called *Walt Disney's Disneyland*—full-page shots of the fireworks graced the first and last pages, and even a back cover, of those handsome books. Souvenir books over the next decades mentioned the fireworks to varying degrees until the early '90s, when the nighttime pyrotechnic show being spotlighted was the new **Fantasmic!** presentation in **Frontierland**.

In the 21st century, the fireworks got re-themed and renamed with ever-present ellipses: Believe . . . There's Magic in the Stars (2000), Believe . . . in Holiday Magic (2001), Imagine . . . a Fantasy in the Sky (2004), and Remember . . . Dreams Come True (2005), these later shows adding narration, new moves for Tinker Bell, and the most complex, most expensive pyrotechnics yet. In a nostalgic nod to the glory of the park's original fireworks show, Fantasy in the Sky returned briefly in 2005 and 2006 for several special events. The Fantasy in the Sky music made it onto the album *Walt Disney Records: The Official Album* (1997), while the music of the 21st-century fireworks shows appeared on later CD collections of park-related songs. No matter the show, the schedule has stayed fairly uniform: lasting about a half-hour, fireworks have usually launched every night of the summer and weekend nights the rest of the year.

First Aid and Lost Children

MAP: Town Square, TS-4; Plaza Hub, PH-4

CHRONOLOGY: Ca. 1958–ongoing

HISTORY: On **Opening Day**, facilities for First Aid and Lost Children were both headquartered in **City Hall**. A free map handed out in the summer of '55 pinpointed the specific **Town Square** location and offered descriptions of the two services: "A doctor and registered nurses are always in attendance" for the former, and "experienced attendants . . . maintain a special playground" for the latter.

Since about 1958, when it was first mentioned in one of the park's **souvenir books**, rooms for First Aid and Lost Children have existed north of **Main Street** on the right-hand-side of the **Plaza Hub.** To alleviate guest concerns about emergency situations, an early sign directing guests to First Aid showed a cartoon Alice, wearing a nurse's hat, and the White Rabbit attending to guests, with Pluto looking on; the sign for Lost Children showed various Disney characters safely leading kids by the hand. These days the First Aid sign is simply sedate text and a red cross without any cute graphics, and the Lost Children area is announced with just those two words.

First Aid is in its own building a little further back from the Plaza Hub near the Plaza Inn. Next door used to be the Lost Children area, but now that room is called the Wish Lounge for kids being served by the Make-a-Wish Foundation. Meanwhile, inside First Aid are registered nurses who treat injuries, dispense free aspirin, and offer anti-nausea remedies. There are also rooms with beds for a short rest and refrigerators where guests can store their medications. Most medical matters are pretty routine, thankfully—blisters are still the number one malady.

The Lost Children area is now actually a subsection of the **Baby Station**, aka Baby Care Center, a conspicuous space on the Plaza Hub next to the **Main Street Photo Supply Co.** In the Baby Station, the children have an attractive waiting room where they're tended to by entertaining **cast members** and shown Disney books and movies to help pass the time.

Flagpole

MAP: Town Square, TS-6

CHRONOLOGY: July 17, 1955–ongoing

HISTORY: Since **Opening Day**, a flagpole has risen from the center of **Town Square**. But that wasn't the original plan. **Walt Disney** intended to have an old-fashioned **bandstand** in that spot, and in fact one was installed there. However, just days before the park officially opened, he realized that the gazebo-like structure blocked the view of **Sleeping Beauty Castle** to guests entering the park, and so he relocated the bandstand to the other end of **Main Street** and had a stately flagpole erected in its place. A photo in the park's '56 **souvenir book**, and a larger full-page photo in

the '64 hardcover *Walt Disney's Disneyland* book, showed the 65-foot flagpole standing inside a circular flower bed about 25 feet across.

The flags of the United States and California fly from the top and are occasionally lowered to half-mast—for September 11th observances, for example. Interesting details add some colorful history to the flagpole area. For instance, the ornate base is said to have been rescued by a Disney employee from under an electric light pole that was knocked down in an L.A. car accident.

Two authentic 19th-century French army cannons are positioned 40 feet from the flagpole and 90 feet from each other; one is aimed at the **Opera House**, the other at **City Hall**. Seating around the flagpole is provided by old restored park benches from San Francisco. A respectful, patriotic flag-lowering ceremony usually attended by the **Disneyland Band** or **Dapper Dans** is held daily around dusk (the specific time is available in City Hall). And Disney characters are frequently in this immediate area for meet-and-greet visits with guests.

Most importantly, the flagpole marks the site of the plaque that spells out Walt Disney's Opening Day dedication speech (presented here as it's punctuated on the plaque):

—DISNEYLAND—TO ALL WHO COME TO THIS HAPPY PLACE:—WELCOME—DISNEYLAND IS YOUR LAND. HERE AGE RELIVES FOND MEMORIES OF THE PAST . . . AND HERE YOUTH MAY SAVOR THE CHALLENGE AND PROMISE OF THE FUTURE. DISNEYLAND IS DEDICATED TO THE IDEALS, THE DREAMS, AND THE HARD FACTS WHICH HAVE CREATED AMERICA . . . WITH THE HOPE THAT IT WILL BE A SOURCE OF JOY AND INSPIRATION TO ALL THE WORLD. JULY 17, 1955.

Incidentally, this isn't the only flagpole erected at Disneyland. In the 1950s, flags for every state decorated the **Court of Honor** and the **Avenue of the Flags**. Currently another flagpole stands inside the entrance to **Frontierland**.

Flight Circle, aka Thimble Drome Flight Circle

MAP: Tomorrowland, T-21

CHRONOLOGY: September 1955–January 1966

HISTORY: A free exhibit called the Flight Circle was shown in a big photo of **Tomorrowland** in Disneyland's 1956 **souvenir book**, but there was no text identifying or describing what exactly the Flight Circle was. The Flight Circle opened about two months after the rest of the park, in the plaza area in front of the *Moonliner* rocket. The exhibit's paved circle was about 75 feet in diameter, had the four compass points marked in the center, and was ringed on the perimeter with a chain-link fence. Guests stood behind the fence to watch demonstrations of . . . ta da! . . . motorized model planes, cars, and boats.

Most of the planes were the kind that got whirled around in a circle by an operator holding a long cable. Cox Manufacturing, a 10-year-old company that made a line of Thimble Drome model vehicles with Baby Bee motors that burned Thimble Drome "glow fuel," assumed sponsorship in '57 and renamed the exhibit the Thimble Drome Flight Circle (the boats motored around a small pond). The sole mention of the site in any later souvenir books came in '58, when a close-up photo showed hard-hatted operators attending to an array of vehicles.

Anyone who heard the loud, droning model planes can attest to the annoying noise they produced, but somehow the models proved themselves popular enough for Cox and the Thimble Drome Flight Circle to keep flying, driving, and boating for over a decade. An illustrious moment came in the holiday season of 1965, when the **Rocket Man** took off from this spot on his jet pack. However, starting in September of '66, this real estate, like most of Tomorrowland, was heavily remodeled. Eventually some of the area became a walkway, and some became the loading area for the **PeopleMover**.

Flower Mart, aka Flower Market

MAP: Main Street, MS-5, MS-17

CHRONOLOGY: 1957–ca. 1995

HISTORY: Fresh-cut real flowers wouldn't have lasted long in the Southern California sunshine or made it through a whirl on the **King Arthur Carrousel**. Fortunately, artificial flowers could do both. Thus in 1957, **Walt Disney** added a beautiful little Flower Mart, or Flower Market, to his idealized **Main Street**. The park's **souvenir books** didn't mention any floral store on Main Street until 1961, when that year's book touted these as "the world's finest natural flowers not grown by nature."

Sold on open-air wheeled carts and from large flower pots, the flowers were mobile and so, like several other establishments on Main Street (the **Blue**

Ribbon Bakery, for instance), the Flower Mart switched locations. Originally it was halfway down the left side of Main Street, filling the middle of the small, intersecting West Center Street (the original neighbors were the **Upjohn Pharmacy** to the south and the **Carnation Ice Cream Parlor** to the north). The plastic posies stayed there until a Carnation expansion in 1977 took over West Center Street, sending the Flower Mart carts across the way to the open area on East Center Street, the former home of the Main Street **portrait artists**. Here the new neighbors were the **Market House** to the south and the **Hallmark Card Shop** to the north until the Flower Mart quietly vanished sometime in the '90s. During the Flower Mart's heyday, over a dozen different blooms were even available through the mail.

Flying Saucers

MAP: Tomorrowland, T-18

CHRONOLOGY: August 6, 1961–September 5, 1966

HISTORY: Showing more ambition than practicality, Disneyland opened its unique version of Space Age bumper cars in early August of 1961. Appropriately enough for **Tomorrowland**, what bumped in the Flying Saucers attraction weren't cars at all. Flying saucers had been a hot topic throughout the '50s, of course, when sightings headlined newspapers and bug-eyed saucermen invaded drive-in movie screens across the country. Thus the time seemed right for saucers to invade Disneyland.

The park's promotional literature certainly made the saucer concept sound appealing. "Fly Your Own Flying Saucer" at the "Space Terminal," touted the **attraction poster**; "each guest pilots his own ship in free flight, above the ground," announced the park's 1961 **souvenir book**; "space travel" at a "space station," captioned the '62 book for its Flying Saucers photo; "choose a 'flight pattern,' shift your weight and away you go," explained the '65 book. All intriguing descriptions, to be sure.

In reality, Disneyland's Flying Saucers probably should've been called the Hovering Saucers. Operating on a circular open-air platform that covered a third of an acre next to the **Rocket to the Moon** attraction (approximately where the **Magic Eye Theater** now sits), the **Bob Gurr**-designed saucers were small one-person hovercraft about five feet in diameter, topped with a center seat and bottomed with a ring of red shock absorber. The saucers got airborne thanks to high-powered jets of air thrust upwards by large motors under the floor. When they hovered successfully, the 64 saucers (in two fleets of 32) could lift a few inches off the ground and could be steered independently by guests, who only had to lean to dip their saucers in any direction, even into other saucers for some bumper-bashing.

Unfortunately, persistent problems with the air jets led to lots of ground time for the E-ticket attraction. Big guests couldn't get off the ground, small guests couldn't get their saucers to dip anywhere, crashing guests occasionally turned their saucers completely over, and too often no guests could go anywhere when the whole system shut itself down. Some five million pilots did give the saucers a test flight, but after five years of headaches, Disney designers finally grounded the troublesome craft for good in 1966 and remade the whole area as the **Tomorrowland Stage** in 1967.

Joe Fowler

CHRONOLOGY: July 9, 1894–December 3, 1993

HISTORY: Joe Fowler, the man entrusted by **Walt Disney** to construct Disneyland, was born in Maine in 1894. After graduating from both the Naval Academy and M.I.T., Fowler worked as a naval architect, designed the World War II aircraft carriers *Lexington* and *Saratoga*, and was in charge of two-dozen naval shipyards in the '40s. He retired from the U.S. Navy a rear admiral in 1948, but an introduction to Walt Disney brought him an invitation to oversee construction of Disney's new park project in Anaheim. Fowler joined the Disneyland team in April 1954, he began construction three months later, and in a year he had the park ready for the already announced **Opening Day.**

Once Disneyland opened, Fowler supervised operations into the next decade and had a hand in every attraction and building project in the park. Within a few years, Fowler was leading the way on several new, and exceedingly complex, Disneyland developments—the **Matterhorn**, the **Submarine Voyage**, and the **Monorail**. In the '60s, Fowler got **New Orleans Square**, sophisticated attractions like the **Haunted Mansion** and **Pirates of the Caribbean**, and the heavily remodeled **Tomorrowland** all built while the park was still open for business, and all while he was helping plan the coming Florida park.

In the late '60s, Fowler was in charge of construction at Walt Disney World and served as a senior VP at Walt Disney Productions. He also ran the whole Imagineering department that designed new attractions and areas for Disney parks before he finally managed to retire for good in 1978. Joe Fowler, nicknamed "Can Do" Fowler for his optimism, was inducted as a Disney Legend in 1990, three years before his death in Florida at age 99. At Disneyland, **Fowler's Harbor** along the **Rivers of America** in **Frontierland** is named after him.

Fowler's Harbor, aka Fowler's Landing

MAP: Frontierland, Fr-13

CHRONOLOGY: June 14, 1958–ongoing

HISTORY: The dock along the southwest side of **Rivers of America** where the **Sailing Ship *Columbia*** is often parked is officially named Fowler's Harbor. Years ago the **Mike Fink Keel Boats** launched just south of this dock, and the **Indian War Canoes** launched just north.

The Fowler's Harbor name is a tribute to **Joe Fowler**, the Navy admiral who

in 1954 and '55 supervised the construction of Disneyland and stayed on as a top Disney executive for decades. In 1955 the little dock area was an informal, unnamed place for servicing the *Mark Twain*. However, when the *Columbia* started berthing here in June of '58, it had the official name of Fowler's Harbor (or Fowler's Landing, as it has occasionally been called). Small workshops at the harbor are still decorated with **Frontierland** theming, including one façade that reads Fowler's Inn. For a while, a sign at Fowler's Harbor promoted a nonexistent restaurant called Maurie's Lobster House, named after Joe Fowler's wife. The 100-foot-long path that winds behind Fowler's Harbor towards **Critter Country** is a wonderful hidden area offering picturesque views of **Tom Sawyer Island** and, better still, some serenity.

Van Arsdale France

CHRONOLOGY: October 3, 1912–October 13, 1999

HISTORY: Guests have long appreciated the extraordinary service provided by Disneyland's smiling **cast members**. Van Arsdale France was the man who first schooled the park's employees, and along the way he created many of the training techniques still used in Disney parks and throughout corporate America.

France was born in Seattle in 1912, got a college degree in liberal arts 22 years later, and then held numerous jobs before establishing himself as a labor-relations expert in the '40s. Beginning his Disneyland career four months before the park opened, he and his assistant, **Dick Nunis**, who would later become the president of Walt Disney Attractions, fixed up an abandoned house near the Disneyland construction site and converted it into a training center called the Personnel Annex (the Disneyland Hotel was later built on the property). France had been given the task of making all Disneyland employees the most helpful, most efficient, most congenial employees anywhere. Just as a clean park would inspire guests to avoid littering, polite, helpful employees, **Walt Disney** believed, would inspire guests to be on their best behavior. "You can design, create, and build the most wonderful place in the world," he once said, "but it takes people to make the dream a reality."

To accomplish Disney's ambitious goals for Disneyland's employees, Van France established what would became known as the Disney University, convened first in small trailers and then in an office building near the **Primeval World** tunnel in the park's southeastern corner. There France wrote the manuals that set procedures and attitudes for decades to come. These manuals, with names like "You'll Create Happiness," "You're on Stage at Disneyland," "The Traditions of Walt Disney at Disneyland," and "The Spirit of Disneyland," taught Disney philosophy first and specific job skills second. Employees came to believe in the overriding goal of creating happiness before they learned how to serve food or park cars. France reinvented employees as actors and actresses in an elaborate show where all customers, not just the famous ones, were treated as special guests.

Among his other duties in the park's first decade, France briefly supervised **Tomorrowland**, helped resolve traffic issues on the nearby streets, worked with labor unions, smoothed relations with the community, put together *Backstage Disneyland* (the first magazine for cast members), and set up the Disneyland Alumni Club. Though he officially retired in 1978, France stayed on as a consultant and spokesman. His autobiography, *Window on Main Street*, was published in 1991. Named a Disney Legend three years later, Van France died in Newport Beach in 1999.

Paul Frees

CHRONOLOGY: June 22, 1920–November 2, 1986

HISTORY: Guests may not know the name Paul Frees, but they certainly know his voice. Born in Chicago in 1920, Frees was a D-Day veteran who did thousands of radio, TV, and movie voices in a career that stretched from the '40s to the mid-'80s. Sci-fi fans recognize him as the narrator of *The War of the Worlds* ('53) and as the talking rings in *The Time Machine* ('60). Fans of Disney movies might recall his vocals from *One Hundred and One Dalmatians* and *The Absent-Minded Professor*, among others. In the '60s, he gave voices to many memorable cartoon characters, including John and George on the Beatles' cartoon show, Boris Badenov, Professor Ludwig von Drake, and the Thing on *The Fantastic Four*. He also voiced several famous characters in TV commercials, among them the Pillsbury Doughboy, Toucan Sam for Froot Loops, and the elf who got the Jolly Green Giant to say ho-ho-ho.

Many more movies and cartoons followed into the '70s and '80s, but it was at Disneyland where he found his biggest audience. Since the late '60s, Frees has been heard by hundreds of millions of visitors on a variety of landmark attractions—his is the voice of the Ghost Host in the **Haunted Mansion**, several buccaneers in **Pirates of the Caribbean**, the shrinking scientist in the fondly remembered **Adventure Thru Inner Space**, and the original narrator for **Great Moments with Mr. Lincoln**. Paul Frees died of heart failure in 1986; two decades later he was named a Disney Legend.

French Market

MAP: New Orleans Square, NOS-10

CHRONOLOGY: July 24, 1966–ongoing

HISTORY: The French Market has been an attractive dining destination since **New**

Orleans Square opened in July of 1966. Located near the **Frontierland**/New Orleans Square Train Station and the **Haunted Mansion**, the restaurant has always offered alfresco tables in front of a stage populated by jazz musicians, with views of the **Rivers of America** an added attraction.

Curiously, the park's **souvenir books** never mentioned or showed the French Market, and when it did get a line in the 1969 hardcover *Walt Disney's Disneyland* book it was for the décor: "The brick-walled French Market attracts diners with two tile murals depicting early New Orleans." The menu has changed considerably over the years from the open-faced turkey-on-white-bread sandwiches of the late '60s to the more sophisticated buffet-style Creole cuisine served today at lunch and dinner. French dip sandwiches, jambalaya, pastas, fried chicken, beef stew served in a sourdough bread bowl, and big cake slices are some of the favorites on the menu. Stouffer's, the frozen-food company that has also sponsored the **Plaza Pavilion** and the **Tahitian Terrace**, is the sponsor here.

Frontierland

MAP: Park, P-15

CHRONOLOGY: July 17, 1955–ongoing

HISTORY: Covering some 20 acres and about 33% of 1950s Disneyland, the original Frontierland was the largest of the park's first five lands. Even after **New Orleans Square** and **Bear Country** carved into Frontierland in the '60s and '70s, it was still bigger than **Tomorrowland**, bigger than **Adventureland**, and bigger than the combined **Town Square**/**Main Street**/**Plaza Hub** (in fact, Frontierland has always been bigger than Adventureland plus the Town/Main/Plaza conglomerate). Much of this vast Frontierland acreage was and is accessible only by boat, mule, or train, since the **Rivers of America**, **Tom Sawyer Island**, the **Painted Desert**, and **Nature's Wonderland** have sprawled over large portions of the territory.

Early in the planning stages, **Walt Disney** decreed that one of the park's lands would be inspired by "America's frontiers." The park's **souvenir books** added temporal boundaries, declaring these to be the frontiers "from Revolutionary days to the great southwest settlement" where guests would "experience the high adventure of our forefathers who shaped our glorious history." True to that frontier spirit, the "downtown" Frontierland walkway leading from the entry gates straight ahead to the *Mark Twain* landing is only about 300 feet long, leaving vast regions of Frontierland seemingly undeveloped. Only "seemingly," since that "wilderness" has been carefully constructed, of course, and plenty of attractions over the decades have transformed this part of Frontierland into Funtierland.

Like Adventureland, the neighbor with an entrance only 30 feet to the south, Frontierland has an entrance from the Plaza Hub that spans a shallow pond and goes through a thematic portal, here built with real logs to look like the gates of a frontier stockade. Pre-opening concept drawings by both Bruce Bushman and **Herb Ryman** showed guests passing teepees *before* they entered the gates of the fort, but in reality the teepees were relocated to the far-west edge of Frontierland and into the **Indian Village**.

Once they're under the stockade gates, guests are 40 feet from a wood flag-pole bearing a plaque presented to Walt Disney by the American Humane Association in 1955. Guests then walk towards what looks like a small 19th-century Western town that has wood sidewalks, small, colorful shops, an exuberant saloon, and a shooting gallery. Prints from cowboy boots and horse shoes are stamped into the pavement, and Western music drifts through the air. Even the brown metal trash cans, painted to look like they've been made out of planks, contribute to the theme.

At the Rivers of America, more stores and restaurants bend around the walkway to the left, Tom Sawyer Island spreads out straight ahead, and an expansive wilderness area stretches to the right (north). An array of watercraft ply the river's waters, among them the grand *Mark Twain*, the stately **Sailing Ship Columbia**, the **Rafts to Tom Sawyer Island**, **Indian War/Davy Crockett's Explorer Canoes**, and, in the old days, the **Mike Fink Keel Boats**. In the '50s, hoping to give Frontierland some authenticity, a **Marshal's Office** stood along the main walkway, a **Miniature Horse Corral** preceded the **Frontierland Shooting Gallery**, and that wilderness to the north was explored by the horse-drawn **Stage Coach**, the lumbering **Mule Pack**, the rustic **Conestoga Wagons**, and the old-fashioned **Rainbow Caverns**/Western Mine Train. Further Old West realism materialized every day in the mid-'50s in the form of a staged "shoot-out" between Sheriff Lucky and Black Bart on the Frontierland streets in front of the **Golden Horseshoe**.

While the basic building architecture has stayed the same over the decades, massive changes have uprooted the relatively simple, serene pleasures offered by the Indian Village and the archaic low-capacity transportation that had plodded through the desert wilderness since 1955. The biggest modifications began in 1979 when a sweeping Big Thunder renovation added the high-speed, high-capacity, high-tech **Big Thunder Mountain Railroad** to the Nature's Wonderland area, followed a few years later by the **Big Thunder Barbecue** and **Big Thunder Ranch** (as well as a new pedestrian path into the back of **Fantasyland**). The stockade at the front gates has been remodeled twice, first in 1980 and then a dozen years later, and the outdoor music has graduated from the early '60s **Dixieland at Disneyland** jazz concerts on the river to the elaborate **Fantasmic!** show installed in 1992.

Even with all the modernization, Frontierland has stayed faithful to Walt Disney's original vision for this part of the park. His inspirational articulation of that vision would've been shown on the land's 1955 dedication plaque, had it ever been installed: "Frontierland is a tribute to the faith, courage, and ingenuity of the pioneers who blazed the trails across America." Five decades on, the old frontiers of the past are still thrilling and pleasing guests on the side of the park directly across from Tomorrowland's new frontiers of the future.

Frontierland Miniature Museum

MAP: Frontierland, Fr-1

CHRONOLOGY: Never built

HISTORY: Walt Disney's love of miniatures, most obviously manifested with the **Storybook Land Canal Boats** over in **Fantasyland**, almost found expression in **Frontierland**. The Miniature Museum would've been located just inside the stockade gates and on the left as guests entered Frontierland from the **Plaza Hub**. According to some early concept drawings, the museum and stockade entrance would've shared the same hewn-log architecture, with an old-fashioned display font announcing the Miniature Museum painted on the front.

Inside the museum, guests would've found displays of miniature towns, houses, and people, plus a small dancing mechanical man that foreshadowed the later **Audio-Animatronic** figures of the '60s. Many of these displays, and the mechanical man, actually existed, and in fact, back before a Disneyland plan was even being seriously discussed, Walt Disney intended to send them on tour around the country until logistics intervened. Ultimately, a museum did open in this space, but its theme was something that mid-'50s TV audiences could more easily relate to— the King of the Wild Frontier. In July of '55, the **Davy Crockett Frontier Museum** opened where guests will now find the **Pioneer Mercantile**.

Frontierland Shooting Gallery,
aka Frontierland Shootin' Arcade, aka Frontierland Shootin' Exposition, aka Frontierland Shooting Exposition

MAP: Frontierland, Fr-26

CHRONOLOGY: July 12, 1957–ongoing

HISTORY: Two years after the park opened, the success of the **Main Street Shooting Gallery** prompted Disneyland executives to add a rootin' tootin' rifle range to **Frontierland**. The Frontierland Shooting Gallery opened along the right-hand side of the first row of Frontierland buildings, a 45-foot-wide spot where the **Miniature Horse**

Corral had been. The rifles in Frontierland fired lead pellets at frontier-themed metal targets that had to be laboriously repainted each night. To keep the guns from being aimed too far from the targets, they were held in a cradle, although the sheer weight of the rifles was enough to keep young kids from whipping them around. As with the later **Big Game Safari Shooting Gallery** in **Adventureland**, visits to the Frontierland Shooting Gallery required quarters, not admission tickets.

In the spring of 1985, concerned with the hazardous lead dust generated by the pellets and the high maintenance of the gallery, Imagineers installed 18 new electronic rifles that fired infrared beams and new targets that produced humorous motions and sound effects. The gallery got a new name, too—Frontierland Shootin' Arcade, which was later revised to replace the apostrophe with the original "g." The name and effects were updated once more with the debut of the Frontierland Shootin' Exposition in 1996. The mining town of Boot Hill was the new target, and the effects included a cell door that popped open when guests hit the jail and a skeleton that popped up when guests hit a graveyard shovel. Some of the Boot Hill tombstones on view have playful epitaphs reminiscent of those at the **Haunted Mansion**: "An arrow shot straight n' true/made its mark on Little Lou." Bunting out front adds festive color, and frontier signs add lighthearted reassurances: "Our rifles shoot straight, guaranteed."

Frontier Trading Post

MAP: Frontierland, Fr-27

CHRONOLOGY: July 17, 1955–1987

HISTORY: From **Opening Day** until the late 1980s, guests who walked from the **Plaza Hub** through the **Frontierland** stockade gates found the Frontier Trading Post on their immediate right (this shop is not to be confused with the similarly named **Indian Trading Post**, which existed over in the **Indian Village** from '62 until '88). The Frontier Trading Post had a rustic wood-plank design that fit right in with this stretch of the main Frontierland walkway; to the left (west) was the **Miniature Horse Corral**, which was later replaced by the rowdy **Frontierland Shooting Gallery**.

From its small space the Trading Post sold frontier souvenirs, many that were related to the *Davy Crockett* miniseries that overwhelmed TV audiences in the mid-'50s. The park's **souvenir books** of the 1980s often showed a nice photo of the entrance with a wooden Indian standing outside, but by the fall of 1987, the Frontier Trading Post had been traded in for the **Westward Ho Trading Company**.

Fun Fotos

MAP: Tomorrowland, T-22

CHRONOLOGY: 1960–1966

HISTORY: In Disneyland's first decade, whenever vacancies opened up inside the exhibit buildings along the right-hand side of **Tomorrowland**, Fun Fotos were installed as temporary, inexpensive space fillers. The **American Dairy Association Exhibit**, **Bathroom of Tomorrow** and **Hall of Aluminum Fame** all left their spaces in the late '50s/early '60s, and all got replaced at one time or another by Fun Fotos.

      The fun of the fotos was two-fold: guests got their pictures taken in front of painted Disneyland-themed backgrounds, and those Polaroids were then developed "while you wait" (quick-developing photos were still a novelty back then). All these Fun Fotos displays disappeared around 1966, when the buildings were completely remade for 1967's **Adventure Thru Inner Space** and **Character Shop**.

Gadget's Go Coaster

MAP: Mickey's Toontown, MT-3

CHRONOLOGY: January 24, 1993–ongoing

HISTORY: Just as **Mickey's Toontown** has its own scaled-down version of **Tarzan's Treehouse** (the **Chip 'n Dale Tree House**) and the **Main Street vehicles** (the **Jolly Trolley**), this cartoony land also has its own small version of an outdoor **Big Thunder Mountain Railroad**-style roller coaster. Gadget's Go Coaster is located at the west end of Toontown near the Chip 'n Dale Tree House, with part of the track venturing over a small pond.

      Intended as an attraction for young kids, the Go Coaster is a quick-moving ride along a rolling, turning track. The Gadget in the title refers to Gadget Hackwrench, the mouse inventor from the *Chip 'n Dale Rescue Rangers* TV show. The roller coaster is supposed to be one of her clever inventions, and it's also supposed to represent the world from a mouse-eye view. Consequently, it places guests inside big acorns for a trip on what looks like a Tinker Toy-supported track past oversize displays like gigantic pencils, combs, spools of thread, soup cans, matchbooks, and more.

      Lasting just under a minute, the brief 700-foot-long trip is perhaps the shortest ride in the park. But it's a popular one. Unfortunately, with only two trains on the track (one off coastering while the other is loading), and with each train holding a maximum of only 16 guests at a time, lines can get long here. Appropriately enough for an attrac-

tion targeted to young children, the sponsor is a company that helps parents clean up messes, Sparkle paper towels.

Gag Factory

MAP: Mickey's Toontown, MT-10
CHRONOLOGY: January 24, 1993–ongoing
HISTORY: Cynics might suggest that something named the Gag Factory probably sells

Approximate Ride Times of Disneyland Attractions

1 Minute or Less
Gadget's Go Coaster, Rafts to Tom Sawyer Island

90 Seconds–Under 3 Minutes
Jolly Trolley, King Arthur Carrousel, Mad Hatter's Mad Tea Party, Matterhorn Bobsleds, Mr. Toad's Wild Ride, Peter Pan Flight, Snow White Adventures

3–5 Minutes
Alice in Wonderland, Big Thunder Mountain Railroad, Buzz Lightyear Astro Blasters, Casey Jr. Circus Train, Indiana Jones Adventure, Many Adventures of Winnie the Pooh, Pinocchio's Daring Journey, Rocket Rods, Roger Rabbit's Car Toon Spin, Space Mountain

6–9 Minutes
Adventure Thru Inner Space, Haunted Mansion, Jungle Cruise, Skyway to Fantasyland/Tomorrowland (round trip), Splash Mountain, Star Tours, Storybook Land Canal Boats, Submarine Voyage, Tomorrowland Autopia, Western Mine Train Through Nature's Wonderland

10–15 Minutes
Country Bear Jamboree, Great Moments with Mr. Lincoln, Indian War Canoes/Davy Crockett's Explorer Canoes, Finding Nemo Submarine Voyage, It's a Small World, *Mark Twain* Riverboat, Mike Fink Keel Boats, Mission to Mars, Mule Pack, Rocket/Flight to the Moon, Sailing Ship *Columbia*, *A Tour of the West* film

16–20 Minutes
America the Beautiful film, *Captain EO* film, Enchanted Tiki Room, *Honey, I Shrunk the Audience* film, *Magic Journeys* film, PeopleMover, Pirates of the Caribbean

21+ Minutes
American Journeys film, America Sings, Fantasmic!, Festival of Fools, Santa Fe & Disneyland Railroad

really bad fast food, but actually this is a clever retail store in the downtown section of **Mickey's Toontown**. The factory décor includes a brick interior and gears on the walls. The gags include a talking mailbox and bendable jail bars out front, a painted interior wall that reads "Do not paint on this wall," and the motto *Carpe Gag 'Em* above the door.

The shelves here used to be full of crazy toys, practical jokes, and magic tricks, the latter a consolation for fans of the late, lamented **Merlin's Magic Shop** in **Fantasyland**. However, recently the merchandise has shifted to less-jokey jewelry, mugs, clothes, and hats. The Gag Factory added the first-ever Disney dime-press machine in 2005, some two decades after the first Disney penny-press machine was installed on **Main Street**. This store connects to the adjacent **Toontown Five & Dime**, making this block a funtastic shopping destination.

Gala Day at Disneyland

CHRONOLOGY: January 21, 1960 (initial release)

HISTORY: This 27-minute documentary was released into movie theaters on January 21, 1960. Like an earlier Disney featurette, 1956's *Disneyland, U.S.A.*, *Gala Day at Disneyland* was essentially a well-developed commercial for the park's newest attractions. Key among these were the **Monorail**, **Matterhorn Bobsleds**, and **Submarine Voyage**, all of which had debuted the previous summer as Disneyland's first E-ticket attractions. **Parades**, **fireworks**, and an appearance by Vice President Nixon were also part of the footage.

Gallen-Kamp Stores Co.

MAP: Main Street, MS-13

CHRONOLOGY: July 17, 1955–early 1957

HISTORY: Listed in only one **souvenir book**, the 1956 edition, was a **Main Street** shop with the unwieldy name Shoe Store, Gallen-Kamp Stores Co. Gallen-Kamp was located in the second right-hand block between **Carefree Corner** and the **Intimate Apparel** shop. Two additional names of shoe stores, Shoe Corp's Shoe Store (run by Shoe Corporation of America) and Bluebird Shoes (a sister store of Gallen-Kamp), also got listings in small complimentary booklets handed out at Disneyland in 1955, but there were no further details.

While a Gallen-Kamp store selling shoes might've seemed like a good fit for Main Street, it's likely that guests, especially young guests, were too distracted by everything else going on at the park to want to spend time shoe shopping. Accordingly, stores devoted exclusively to footwear made early exits from Disneyland history.

Geppetto's Arts & Crafts, aka Geppetto's Toys & Gifts, aka Geppetto's Holiday Workshop

MAP: Fantasyland, Fa-9

CHRONOLOGY: May 25, 1983–2007

HISTORY: The village architecture that surrounds **Pinocchio's Daring Journey** once embraced a Pinocchio-themed gift shop as well. Tucked in right next to the attrac-

tion's exit out to **Fantasyland** was a store named after Pinocchio's toy-making father. Dense with charming Old World details, Geppetto's Arts & Crafts was designed to look just like the cozy toy shop in the classic movie. In its first incarnation, lots of marionettes, figurines, and old-fashioned cuckoo clocks (reminiscent of the **Clock Shop** that used to be inside **Sleeping Beauty Castle**) dominated Geppetto's place.

Sometime around 1995, Geppetto's switched to Toys & Gifts and focused more on plush toys and dolls, with same-day custom-made dolls a specialty. Geppetto's was also the site of special toy-related events and frequent appearances by Disney princesses. Around 2004, the toy maker and his toys moved out and **Names Unraveled**, formerly a cart that operated elsewhere in Fantasyland, moved in. In 2006, Geppetto's Holiday Workshop was the new sign above the door, but early in 2007 the store was closed again. A nice photo of Geppetto's old shop ran in the park's 2006 **souvenir book**.

Blaine Gibson

CHRONOLOGY: February 11, 1918–ongoing

HISTORY: Blaine Gibson's childhood hobby was sculpting. Eventually his hobby became his career.

Born in Colorado in 1918, Gibson started at the Disney Studios in 1939 in the animation department, and he's listed in the credits of many of the company's classic films and cartoons from the '40s to the early '60s, including *Song of the South*, *Peter Pan*, *Sleeping Beauty*, and *One Hundred and One Dalmatians*. Even as he was working on these films by day, he was continuing to take sculpting classes at night, and in 1954 **Walt Disney** invited him to start making models for Disneyland attractions.

Over the next three decades, Gibson supervised the sculpture department and created hundreds of sculptures that were transformed into the **Audio-Animatronic** characters in such diverse attractions as the **Enchanted Tiki Room**, **Great Moments with Mr. Lincoln**, and the **Haunted Mansion**. His Timothy Mouse rode the top of **Dumbo the Flying Elephant**, his fair maiden graced the bow of the **Sailing Ship *Columbia***, his coy mermaids floated underwater in the submarine lagoon, and his little demons lined Hell at the end of **Mr. Toad's Wild Ride.** In 1965, he appeared on *Walt Disney's Wonderful World of Color* alongside some of his pirate sculptures for **Pirates of the Caribbean.** Later, Gibson sculpted all the chief executives for the Hall of Presidents at Walt Disney World, and later still, after he'd retired in 1983, he created *Partners*, the ineluctable bronze statue of Walt Disney and Mickey Mouse that was installed in Disneyland's **Plaza Hub** in 1993. That same year, Blaine Gibson was named a Disney Legend in celebration of his four decades as one of the company's master artists.

Gibson Girl Ice Cream Parlor

MAP: Main Street, MS-7

CHRONOLOGY: March 21, 1997–ongoing

HISTORY: The 1997 shuffle of ice cream parlors and bakeries on the second left-hand block of **Main Street** brought a new dessert spot, the Gibson Girl Ice Cream Parlor, next to the **Penny Arcade.**

At one time the **Puffin Bakery** and the **Sunkist Citrus House** had been here, followed by the **Blue Ribbon Bakery** until early '97. When Blue Ribbon moved to the corner space where the **Carnation Ice Cream Parlor** had been, the Gibson Girl strutted into the vacant space in the middle of the block.

Gibson Girls, of course, were the curvy pinups created by American illustrator Charles Dana Gibson in the early 20th century. While the curvy-pinup part didn't get re-created inside the ice cream parlor (except for a few discreet drawings), the early-20th-century part sure did. From the ornate display fonts and striped awning outside to the old-fashioned lighting fixtures and soda fountain inside, this is a place where the time travel is as enticing as the desserts. A five-foot-long, four-foot-tall glass elephant imported from Disneyland Paris makes for an interesting conversation piece in the back dining room.

Most of the people who pack the interior throughout the day are probably focused strictly on the sweets, however. Unlike the old Carnation Ice Cream Parlor, which was famous for its elaborate Disneyland-themed desserts, the Gibson Girl offers simpler treats. "Old-fashioned hand scooped ice cream," touts the sign outside, which means lots of sundaes, cones, frozen yogurts, root beer floats, sodas, and lemonade. There aren't a lot of ice cream flavors, but what they've got is certainly served up in generous portions—something like 600 gallons of ice cream a week are scooped out of here (vanilla is still the most-requested flavor). Special creations for the holidays are big hits, as are the homemade waffle cones year-round. Not surprisingly, two ice cream companies, Nestlé and Dreyer's, have been the sponsors.

Gibson Greeting Cards

MAP: Main Street, MS-14

CHRONOLOGY: July 17, 1955–1959

HISTORY: Gibson stores sold charming cards and postcards printed by an Ohio-based company that had been started in 1850 by four Scottish brothers. The Gibsons began their business printing up labels and business cards, but in the 1880s they added a new product, Christmas cards, to their line and established themselves as one of the country's biggest card companies well into the next century.

At Disneyland, the Gibson Art Co. has had two stores with two names in two **Main Street** locations (neither store was in any way related to the **Gibson Girl Ice Cream Parlor**). The first store, Gibson Greeting Cards, debuted on **Opening Day** and lasted until 1959. This initial location was at the corner of Main Street and East Center Street where **Disney Clothiers, Ltd.** now sits. The **Hallmark Card Shop** took over for Gibson in 1960, and Gibson disappeared from Main Street until mid-June of 1985, when its **Card Corner** filled the spot up by the **Plaza Hub** that had formerly been known as **Carefree Corner**. Disney Legend **John Hench**, one of the most influential shapers of the park's original look, designed the first Gibson location.

Gift-Giver Extraordinaire Machine

MAP: Plaza Hub, PH-7

CHRONOLOGY: 1985

HISTORY: To celebrate its 30th anniversary, in 1985 Disneyland displayed a running tally of ticket sales in anticipation of the arrival of guest number 250,000,000. Out in front of the park stood the "Incredible Countdown Clock," designed with gears shaped like Mickey's ears and a counter that had nine digits. What's more, throughout the year every 30th guest who walked through the gates won an instant prize, which for some winners was a chance to take home a new car.

That chance came with a spin of the Gift-Giver Extraordinaire Machine back on the **Plaza Hub**. This showy device was similar to the **Dream Machine**, the slot-machine cake created for the park's 35th birthday five years later. As it worked out, every 30,000th guest got a new car (about a car a day), and the 3,000,000th guest got a new Cadillac (there were over 12,000,000 guests that year, which meant over 400 cars and four Caddies). Winners collected their prizes at the Prize Redemption Center next to the **Opera House** doorway.

The idea for all this beneficence is credited to the park's long-time marketing chief, Disney Legend **Jack Lindquist**. Lindquist's goal was to spark 1985 attendance after a disappointing 1984 (that year's L.A. Olympics had kept many guests away from the park). After months of generous giveaways, celebratory confetti, and even a February TV special, Disneyland attendance jumped over the previous year's tally, and that 250,000,000th guest finally walked through the gates on August 24, 1985.

The Gift-Giver Machine didn't stop giving, however, and in fact it continued into September of '86. Prizes that year included a round-trip airline ticket on PSA, VCR cassettes, watches, cameras, color TVs, and even "the official car of Disneyland '86," a 1986 Pontiac Firebird. The most bizarre aspect of the promotion was this puzzling fine print: "Canadian winners will be required to take a test of skill."

Glass Blower

MAP: Main Street, MS-3

CHRONOLOGY: 1955–1966

HISTORY: Starting sometime in 1955, Disneyland had a glass blower in his own shop. He was Bill Rasmussen, and he leased a space on the first left-hand block of **Main Street** in the rear of the **Crystal Arcade**. Rasmussen worked there sculpting delicate, whimsical glass figurines in full view of guests. In fact, he worked in full view of the whole nation when he appeared on an episode of *The Mickey Mouse Club*.

Rasmussen left in 1966 and moved to a series of shops that he opened in San Francisco, Boston, Honolulu, and other American cities (he called the shop in Hawaii the Little Glass Shack). Meanwhile, back on Main Street, other glass blowers replaced Rasmussen in his Crystal Arcade spot, as shown on small park maps into the '70s.

Harper Goff

CHRONOLOGY: March 16, 1911–March 3, 1993

HISTORY: Movie fans know Harper Goff's *Nautilus*—both the distinctive steel exterior and the luxurious interior—from a memorable Disney film; Disneyland fans know his widespread designs all over the park, from the charming buildings on **Main Street** to the wild jungles of **Adventureland**. And fans of jazz music might know his contributions as the banjo player in the **Firehouse Five Plus Two** combo.

The multi-talented Harper Goff was born in 1911. His Fort Collins, Colorado upbringing ultimately found its way into Disneyland, as several of the buildings he designed for the park, including **City Hall**, were based on actual buildings in his hometown. After going to art school in L.A., Goff moved to New York and in the '30s drew illustrations for popular magazines like *National Geographic* and *Esquire*. Back in Hollywood in the '40s, he became a set designer at Warner Bros. and worked on *Casablanca* and *Captain Blood*, among other favorites. Moving to the Disney Studios in the '50s, he was instrumental in establishing the story and creating the design and special effects that made *20,000 Leagues Under the Sea* an Oscar-winning classic.

Goff was also involved with the nascent Disneyland project from the beginning, even before Anaheim was set as the park's location. At **Walt Disney's** behest, he took several trips around the country to gather information from other amusement parks, fairs, and museums, and it was his research that informed the earliest plans for Disneyland. As one of the first illustrators on the project, in '51 he drew up concept art for a 16-acre somewhat-rectangular park that would've been located in Burbank; in his drawing are boats on a lake, an island, a circus tent, something that looks like an autopia track, a frontier town, and a train ride. That year he also rendered drawings of Main Street buildings and a rickety haunted house that would one day be transformed into the **Haunted Mansion.**

As Anaheim plans were coming to fruition, Goff designed and oversaw construction on the **Jungle Cruise**, and he created the interior for the **Golden Horseshoe** in **Frontierland**, in addition to making countless other contributions. A decade later, when Walt Disney built new exhibits for the 1964–1965 New York World's Fair, it was Goff who designed the symbol for the whole exposition, the Unisphere globe encircled by orbiting metal ribbons. A decade after that, he helped create EPCOT in Florida, and he was still consulting on Disney theme parks into the early 1990s. Named a Disney Legend in 1993, 81-year-old Harper Goff died that same year in Los Angeles. He's memorialized in Disneyland with a window, not on Main Street with other artists, but alone in Adventureland on a second story next to **South Seas Traders**.

Golden Bear Lodge, aka Hungry Bear Restaurant

MAP: Bear Country/Critter Country, B/C-3

CHRONOLOGY: September 24, 1972–ongoing

HISTORY: The only real dining in **Bear Country/Critter Country**, and some of the most serene dining in the park, began life in 1972 as the Golden Bear Lodge. It was found just inside the entrance to Bear Country on the right-hand side, a large plot adjacent to the **Country Bear Jamboree**. Since the big two-story wooden restaurant was positioned along the **Rivers of America**, its upper and lower terraces offered scenic views of **Tom Sawyer Island** and the passing river traffic. The Golden Bear

Lodge got two inviting photos in the 1972 **souvenir book**, the one that welcomed the recently finished Bear Country to the park. "To dine on the porch of the Golden Bear Lodge and look out across the Rivers of America," read the accompanying text, "is to imagine another time, and other places, in a world that was."

By 1977, the lodge had a new name. That year's souvenir book showed the same exact photos and text, but this time the name on the sign and in the text was Hungry Bear Restaurant, and in fact a large sculpture of a bear now greeted guests as they entered. The restaurant has always been a counter-service establishment just a few notches up from a fast-food eatery. Today, hosted by the company that makes Dixie cups, the Hungry Bear serves burgers, hearty sandwiches, salads, and desserts. It's still on the river, and it's still a fun place to feed the approaching ducks, but now the attraction next door isn't anything Country Bearish, it's the **Many Adventures of Winnie the Pooh.**

Golden Horseshoe

MAP: Frontierland, Fr-4

CHRONOLOGY: July 17, 1955–ongoing

HISTORY: The beautiful Golden Horseshoe has been delighting guests since **Opening Day.** Technically, the name Golden Horseshoe only applies to the building, even though people frequently attach those two words to whatever show is being performed inside. Situated on a prominent **Frontierland** corner that juts towards the **Rivers of America**, the Golden Horseshoe is a shining two-story structure all in white with gold trim. The decorative finials on the roof and the long balcony with a turned balustrade add timeless elegance, while the wooden sidewalk out front grounds the building in frontier history.

Disney Legend **Harper Goff** created the glamorous interior, basing his designs on the saloon set he had already drawn up for the 1953 Doris Day film *Calamity Jane*. The approximately 2500-square-foot room features a curtained stage flanked by private boxes, a main floor with dining tables, and a curling balcony that forms a horseshoe shape (there's also a prominent golden horseshoe mounted above the stage, its arms extending upwards for luck). The bar along the right-hand side serves up burgers, chili, snacks, and elaborate desserts that guests carry back to their tables. While the food is contemporary, the building's architectural details and atmosphere make it the closest thing Disneyland has to the idyllic Old West.

Several shows and sponsors have been involved with the Golden Horseshoe over the decades. The famed *Golden Horseshoe Revue*, a lighthearted presentation that required reservations but no admission ticket, began running on July 17, 1955, and continued until October 12, 1986, with Pepsi-Cola the sponsor for all but the last four of those years. After Eastman Kodak took over sponsorship from '82 to '84, the sponsorless revue continued deep into 1986. On November 1,

1986, the *Golden Horseshoe Jam-boree* began an eight-year run, the last four sponsored by Wonder Bread. As of December 18, 1994, various acts and special presentations have appeared on the Golden Horseshoe's stage, including *Woody's Roundup* (a *Toy Story*-themed show) in 1999, the *Golden Horseshoe Variety Show* in 2000, and the zany music-and-comedy combo of rotating musicians known collectively as Billy Hill & the Hillbillies.

But it's the original *Golden Horseshoe Revue* that established the building's golden reputation. It was "the Grandest Show in the West" and "Dazzlin' Rootin' Tootin' Fun" on the **attraction poster**, "the most scintillating shows in Disneyland" in the 1955 **souvenir book**, and "the world's longest-running live stage show" in the *Guinness Book of World Records*. The show's original 1955 stars were singers Judy Marsh and Donald Novis and comedian **Wally Boag**. Marsh, playing Sluefoot Sue, who was noted on the sign out front as the building's owner, was soon replaced by spunky **Betty Taylor**; Irish tenor **Fulton Burley** took over for an ill Novis from '64 until '86; and the durable Boag stayed with the show as Sue's boyfriend Pecos Bill from its inception until 1982 (the trio of Taylor, Burley and Boag would all be named Disney Legends in 1995). Supporting them was a small live band; joining them on

---

10 Official and Unofficial Streets Inside Disneyland

East Center Street/West Center Street
(intersects Main Street at the Market House)
East Plaza Street/West Plaza Street
(separates the Plaza Hub from Main Street)
Esplanade (diagonal walkway between New Orleans Square and
the Rivers of America)
Front Street (north-south alley on west side of New Orleans Square)
Main Street (north-south connector between Town Square and Plaza Hub)
Matterhorn Way (north-south walkway between Alice in Wonderland and
Matterhorn Mountain)
New Orleans Street (east-west walkway between the Golden Horseshoe and
the River Belle Terrace)
Orleans Street (diagonal street in center of New Orleans Square)
Royal Street (southernmost street in New Orleans Square)
Small World Way (wide walkway from Storybook Land Canal Boats
to It's a Small World)

stage, and getting most of the photos in the park's souvenir books over the decades, was a changing lineup of high-kicking can-can girls sporting gaudy dresses, colorful headwear, and black garters.

So popular was the *Golden Horseshoe Revue*, it was spotlighted on a 1962 episode of *Walt Disney's Wonderful World of Color* in honor of its 10,000th performance, and ultimately its 50,000+ performances rated a listing in the *Guinness Book*. **Walt Disney** was a fan, frequently catching the show from his private box adjacent to the stage (today's guests can use that same box). Later Golden Horseshoe shows—the *Jamboree*, the *Variety Show*, Billy Hill—have been popular, but it's likely nothing will last as long on stage or in fans' memories as the original *Golden Horseshoe Revue*.

Goofy's Bounce House, aka Goofy's Playhouse

MAP: Mickey's Toontown, MT-1

CHRONOLOGY: January 24, 1993–ongoing

HISTORY: No adults, no shoes, and no frowns are allowed in this interactive structure. Located near the entrance to **Mickey's Toontown**, Goofy's Bounce House launched with the rest of Toontown in January 1993. Designed to look, uh, goofy, the Bounce House is, from the outside, a wildly discombobulated residence where all the angles are askew and Goofy has crashed his own car into the bent mailbox. Inside, the building is a crazy playpen for toddlers. To ensure that it is for only the youngest kids, there's a height maximum of 4' 4" tall, making this one of the few attractions that puts an *upper* limit on a guest's height.

Within the structure, a **cast member** supervises the kids who are literally bouncing off the walls. And the floor. And the furniture, since everything is inflated and made for play. The charming décor (a kite inside the house, a nutty piano) and the wacky noises add to the silly fun.

After temporarily closing on January 7, 2005, on March 5, 2006, the Bounce House reopened as Goofy's Playhouse, supplemented by an additional play area outside where parents could be with their children. Everything out in the yard is still screwy, suggesting the builder is a klutz, but now the garden grows pre-carved pumpkins, bell peppers that are actual bells, and ears of popcorn, suggesting the gardener is a genius. After bouncing, climbing, crawling, and sliding all over the property, kids can cool off with icy beverages from Goofy's Free-Z Time, a trailer with flat tires always parked out front but only occasionally open.

Goofy's Gas Station

MAP: Mickey's Toontown, MT-7

CHRONOLOGY: January 24, 1993–ongoing

HISTORY: This toontastic rest stop in the heart of **Mickey's Toontown** offers bathrooms, water fountains, phones, quick snacks at **Toon Up Treats** around the back, a playful car to sit in out front, and frequent chances to meet the Goof himself. As with everything else in Mickey's Toontown, the real fun is discovering all the humorous details worked into the design and the décor—the fish inside the gas pumps, the water fountains that talk to guests as they get a drink, the sign out front that reads, "Did we goof up your car today?" A list posted outside the station identifies the Goofy Water on tap here, everything from Whacky Water and Liquid Water to Wet Water and High Water.

Yale Gracey

CHRONOLOGY: September 3, 1910–September 5, 1983

HISTORY: It's no coincidence that in the 2003 Disney film *The Haunted Mansion* one of the main characters is named Master Gracey, and in fact the whole eerie building carries the Gracey name. Yale Gracey was one of the key contributors to the long-gestating **Haunted Mansion** at Disneyland, and he's credited now as the creator of many of the spooky special effects, such as the singing busts in the graveyard.

Before he helped develop major Disneyland projects, Gracey grew up in Shanghai, China and studied art in L.A. His Disney career began at the Disney Studios in 1939. Gracey worked as an art director and layout artist on over 60 Disney films and cartoons stretching from *Fantasia* in 1941 to *Babes in Toyland* 20 years later.

Throughout the '40s and '50s, he supplemented his hours in the art department with hours spent devising homemade gadgets and models. An impressed **Walt Disney** invited him to bring his gadget-making talents to new attractions at Disneyland. During the '60s, Gracey added special effects to the **Carousel of Progress**, **Space Mountain**, and the **Pirates of the Caribbean** attractions, among others (one specific example of his ingenuity is the fiery Pirates finale when the town is seemingly torched by the realistic flames Gracey created).

Though he retired in 1975, Yale Gracey continued to consult on special effects at Walt Disney World. In 1983, he died in Los Angeles at age 73, and 16 years later he was inducted as a Disney Legend.

Grad Nite

CHRONOLOGY: June 15, 1961–ongoing (seasonally)

HISTORY: The long-running party known as Grad Nite was a new marketing concept created in the early '60s by Disney Legend **Milt Albright**. The idea was to invite graduating high school seniors from the L.A. area to the park in the late spring, charge the students a special fee, keep the park open to them exclusively all night long, and sell them special photos and souvenirs. Obviously, filling a late-night park full of jubilant teenagers was a recipe for disruption, so to ensure proper conduct Disneyland had several strictly enforced rules, in addition to the usual no-drinking, no-bad-behavior, no-overly-amorous-displays rules. Teenage guests had to arrive on school buses with chaperones; guys had to wear sports coats; shorts and T-shirts weren't allowed; nobody could leave before dawn; and nobody could nap in the park. However, as Disneyland officials soon discovered, rules were made to be broken.

The inaugural Grad Nite was held on June 15, 1961, for over 8,000 local students. Within a few years, tens of thousands of students were coming from all over the country to party at Grad Nite. Within two decades, over 150,000 were joining the fun, a number so high that the event was spread out over several different nights.

Unfortunately, the kids were enjoying the party much more than the park's **cast members** and security personnel were. Alcohol consumption, mischievous pranks, minor vandalism, and extremely affectionate couples were persistent problems that kept all adults, be they chaperones, employees, or parents, on continual alert. Park officials tried various solutions to keep things running smoothly and safely. They subjected teens to a "friendly frisk" at the entrance, they tried shutting down dark attractions such as **Adventure Thru Inner Space**, they stationed extra personnel inside attractions to watch for suspicious activity, and they regularly swept through theaters to clear out half-dressed or drowsy teens. Even so, each night hundreds of teens would still get in enough trouble to warrant either a stay in a holding area or removal from the park. Many more teens would conk out early and try to sleep on benches or curbs.

But on goes Grad Nite. Changes, though, have come to the nightly program. New additions include a Blast Off pre-party before the main party begins, special **fireworks** shows, new dance areas with deejays, big-name musicians, and new themes for existing attractions (**Space Mountain** has become Rock It Mountain). Even though the list of rules (including no gum or camera cases) and dress codes (including no hats or beanies) is longer than ever, the event continues to be a popular tradition. For many American teens, the high school experience isn't complete until they've graduated Grad Nite.

Grand Canyon Diorama

MAP: Tomorrowland, T-17

CHRONOLOGY: March 31, 1958–ongoing

HISTORY: While the park's **souvenir books** have always located this attraction in the **Main Street** section of their pages, and while the images and animals seem like something more suited to **Frontierland**, the beautiful Grand Canyon Diorama is actually situated in **Tomorrowland** behind the old **Rocket to the Moon/Mission to Mars** building. The diorama lines one interior wall of a long tunnel along the **Santa Fe &**

Disneyland Railroad track just before the train reaches the Main Street station. Back in the 1950s, when a 100-acre **parking lot** wrapped around the **entrance** to Disneyland, the area in the parking lot nearest this tunnel was the site of a heliport used by **Walt Disney**.

Like many other attractions in the park, the Grand Canyon Diorama was inspired by a Disney movie, in this case the Oscar-winning 1958 documentary *Grand Canyon*. As in that documentary, the diorama pairs visually stunning images with the clip-clopping "On the Trail" passage from Ferde Grofé's *Grand Canyon Suite*. The Grand Canyon Diorama presents a 90-second pass along one rim of the immense canyon. The view includes a sunrise, ancient cliff-dweller ruins, a storm, a 180-degree rainbow, and a sunset, with a glass wall separating the displays from the train.

Combining a detailed 300-foot-wide, 34-foot-tall background painting with dozens of foreground animals and hundreds of rocks, bushes, and other props, the diorama was touted for years as the world's longest, and with a price tag estimated to be about $375,000 back in '58, it was also probably one of the world's most expensive. Certainly it is still one of the world's most realistic. Disney Legend **Claude Coats** was its primary creator and painter, while the cougar, eagles, skunks, mule deer, snakes, and other desert animals were the products of a taxidermist (none of them are **Audio-Animatronic** machines). A 1968 issue of *Vacationland* magazine proclaimed that creating the Grand Canyon canvas took 4,800 man-hours and 300 gallons of paint.

At the official opening in the spring of '58, a band, park officials, and Native Americans in their native dress dedicated the new D-ticket attraction with a blessing-of-the-trains ceremony. For the next decade the souvenir books ran the same colorful photo and caption: "Sure-footed desert mountain sheep are viewed atop a rock formation in the foreground of Disneyland's Grand Canyon Diorama." The spectacular **attraction poster** presented the canyon and a handful of animals in shades of lavender, a silhouetted train (with standing passengers) riding past.

Happily, the Grand Canyon exhibit has changed little over the decades. However, it got a mighty supplement in 1966 when the new **Primeval World Diorama** and its impressive Audio-Animatronic dinosaurs were added onto the next section of train track, thus intensifying the diorama drama.

Grandma's Baby Shop

MAP: Main Street, MS-13

CHRONOLOGY: July 17, 1955–September 1955

HISTORY: A charming shop for infant clothes and accessories opened along with the park on July 17, 1955. Unfortunately, the shop, itself still an infant at barely two months old, would be the first one on **Main Street** to fold ("fold" as in "close," since other clothing shops continued to do lots of folding). About three months after **Opening Day**, the **Silhouette Shop** was ensconced in Grandma's little spot on the east side of Main Street halfway between East Center Street and East Plaza Street.

Great Moments with Mr. Lincoln

MAP: Town Square, TS-9

CHRONOLOGY: July 18, 1965–spring 2005

HISTORY: A decade of advances in **Audio-Animatronic** technology culminated in 1964 with the creation of a mechanical Abraham Lincoln. Lincoln was originally planned for the Hall of Presidents in the **Liberty Street** area that never came to be at Disneyland (Liberty Square and the Hall of Presidents would exist later at Walt Disney World). When it did appear for the first time in public, the A-A Lincoln was used by the state of Illinois in its pavilion for the 1964–1965 New York World's Fair.

The life-size electronic effigy incorporated everything Disney designers had learned from earlier mechanical animals made for the **Nature's Wonderland** section of **Frontierland** and the **Enchanted Tiki Room** in **Adventureland**. Lincoln, however, was by far the most ambitious Audio-Animatronic project yet. Not only did he look and sound exactly like a very famous, very dignified public figure (Lincoln's life mask was the model for the face), he had a wide range of complex motions. Mid-1960s viewers, expecting a sitting Lincoln figure that would merely swivel its head and perhaps blink, must have been utterly astonished to see the Great Emancipator stand up, move his arms, and deliver an impassioned speech that utilized hand gestures and remarkably subtle facial movements. In August '63, *National Geographic* called the Lincoln illusion "alarming" in its realism while giving a two-page preview that detailed the 16 air lines in his head, the 14 hydraulic lines in his body, and the 15 expressions in his face. Some members of the press were so amazed they invented their own details about what Lincoln could do, crediting the seemingly sentient figure with walking around and shaking hands with front-row guests.

While the robotic Lincoln couldn't do all that, getting him to do what he actually did was an extreme challenge for Disney's Imagineers. Over two years of development went into the project, yet even in final testing Lincoln was still capable of flattening a chair when he sat on it.

After an overwhelmingly positive reception at the fair, **Walt Disney** had an even more sophisticated Lincoln rushed into Disneyland's **Opera House** on **Town Square** for the 1965 10th-anniversary "Tencennial" celebrations. There the 13-minute show began with a short biographical film, featured a dramatic monologue that blended excerpts from four of Lincoln's speeches, and ended with a 50-foot post-show mural that celebrated American freedom (Walt Disney himself was among the portraits shown). The **attraction poster** for Great Moments with Mr. Lincoln proclaimed it as "The Amazing Audio Animatronic Show Acclaimed by Press and Public," and noted that it was "Presented by Lincoln Savings & Loan Association."

Initially, Great Moments was an E-ticket attraction, though anyone under 17 years old could get in free thanks to a special coupon in kids' ticket books. The show closed on New Year's Day in 1973 when the **Walt Disney Story** moved into the Opera House, but fans were so insistent about bringing the president back that the Mr. Lincoln exhibit was returned on June 12, 1975, generating the longest title for any attraction: The Walt Disney Story, Featuring Great Moments with Mr. Lincoln. Updates in 1984 and 2001 enhanced the presentation with new special effects and better sound. In the early years of the 21st century, the best Lincoln figure ever still delivered his inspiring speech, with a flag, white columns, an ornate chair with red upholstery, the Capitol Building, and a star-spangled sky all behind him. Starting in 2005 the celebratory movie *Disneyland: The First 50 Magical Years* replaced Lincoln while the park celebrated its 50th anniversary.

Lincoln's voice was performed by Royal Dano, a character actor with a long career in movies and TV shows, many of them Westerns. Dano, who was 42 when he first recorded his Lincoln vocals, died in '94 of a heart attack at age 71. **Paul Frees** provided the original narration, **Buddy Baker** the heart-swelling music (both men would later gain fame for their contributions to the **Haunted Mansion**). As for the mechanical president, Disney Legends **Roger Broggie**, **Harriet Burns**, **Marc Davis**, **Blaine Gibson**, **Bob Gurr**, and **Wathel Rogers** were among those who made Great Moments great.

Guest Relations

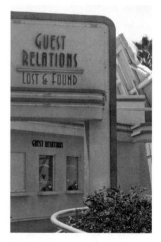

MAP: Town Square, TS-4; Park, P-7

CHRONOLOGY: 1955–ongoing

HISTORY: The park's 1956 **souvenir book** was the first one to note the existence of Guest Relations inside the **City Hall** building on **Main Street**. It's still there as an information center for Disneyland guests who have questions, are looking to lodge a complaint or a compliment about a **cast member**, require maps (of the park or the surrounding area), or need to speak to a Disneyland official for any reason. Disney Legend **Robert Jani** was the first person in charge of Guest Relations, with another Disney Legend, **Cicely Rigdon**, running it in the '60s.

Outside the park, a second Guest Relations office has existed since at least the mid-'80s for visitors who have not yet walked through the gates. This office, shown on the free brochures handed out at the turnstiles, was originally maintained in a small building between the main **entrance** and the kennels to the right. Here, anyone who was picking up free passes, members of the press who had appointments, and anybody else who needed attention or answers before entering the park could get help. Today these functions are handled in a new Guest Relations office near the main entrance to Disney's California Adventure.

Not all of the problems solved by Guest Relations are routine. The single most controversial guest issue, at least in the park's early years, concerned the possible arrival of Soviet Premier Nikita Khrushchev. His request to visit Disneyland while on a visit to America in September 1959 was denied by government officials (not park officials) for security reasons. The incident drew international attention when an irate Khrushchev complained about the rejection and wondered aloud what the park had to hide (his wild guesses included cholera, "rocket-launching pads," and "gangsters"). **Walt Disney** later said he'd been looking forward to showing off his new submarine fleet to the Communist leader. In the '60s his studio briefly considered developing a movie about the whole affair, a comedy to be called *Khrushchev in Disneyland* starring Peter Ustinov.

Bob Gurr

CHRONOLOGY: 1931–ongoing

HISTORY: Any guest who's ever ridden in any of Disneyland's **Main Street vehicles**, trains, bobsleds, or Autopia cars knows Bob Gurr's work. Gurr is the Disney Legend who created and developed the transportation in the park. Born in L.A. around 1931, Gurr grew up fascinated with machines and automobiles. After graduating from college in 1952 with a degree in industrial design, he promptly started his own company and soon found himself consulting on the cars for the new **Tomorrowland Autopia** attraction at Disneyland.

Soon Gurr was not only consulting on the cars, he was designing and mechanically engineering them. From then on he was a full-time Disney Imagineer who made real the elaborate vehicles dreamed up by **Walt Disney**, including such diverse devices as the hovercraft for the **Flying Saucers** in **Tomorrowland** and the old-time cars and omnibuses that have cruised **Main Street**. Gurr transformed an actual car into the modern **Viewliner** train of the late '50s; he redesigned the boxy Alweg monorail train in Germany into the sleek, futuristic **Monorail** in Disneyland (Gurr piloted the Monorail's first test-drive); he drew up the original passenger coaches for the **Santa Fe & Disneyland Railroad**; he designed the 1959 locomotive called the *Ernest S. Marsh*; he worked on the **Omnimover** pods for **Adventure Thru Inner Space** and the **Haunted Mansion**; he made **Mr. Toad's** wild cars; and he built the bobsleds on **Matterhorn Mountain**. In the early '60s Gurr was one of the wizards who brought Abraham Lincoln to life for **Great Moments with Mr. Lincoln.**

Retiring from Disney in '81, he worked on creations for other theme parks and special events, among them the King Kong attraction at Universal Studios and the UFO at the '84 Summer Olympics. Still a consultant on Disney attractions, Bob Gurr was named a Disney Legend in 2004.

Hallmark Card Shop

MAP: Main Street, MS-14

CHRONOLOGY: June 15, 1960–January 6, 1985

HISTORY: Three businesses have operated out of the attractive **John Hench**-designed building on the northeast corner of Main Street and East Center Street. Two of those businesses were card shops, starting with **Gibson Greeting Cards** from **Opening Day** until sometime in 1959. When Gibson bid farewell, the Hallmark Card Shop bid hello in June of 1960.

It was probably only a matter of time before Hallmark showed up at the park. Founded in 1910, the company had been making Disney-themed greeting cards as early as 1931, and its headquarters were in Kansas City, the Missouri town where **Walt Disney** had spent some of his childhood and later started his Laugh-O-Gram animation company. Even without any photos or descriptive text in any of the park's **souvenir books**, the Hallmark Card Shop continued for almost a quarter of a century, closing in early 1985 so a big new retailer, **Disney Clothiers, Ltd.**, could open that spring.

Hall of Aluminum Fame

MAP: Tomorrowland, T-24

CHRONOLOGY: December 1955–July 1960

HISTORY: In Disneyland's first year, **Walt Disney** was in need of some **Tomorrowland** sponsors that could provide their own exhibits, thus allowing him to concentrate his time and money on other aspects of the park. Some five months after Disneyland's **Opening Day**, the Kaiser Aluminum & Chemical Corporation debuted the Hall of Aluminum Fame in the same educational-exhibit building that already housed Monsanto's **Hall of Chemistry**. This building, prime Tomorrowland real estate just inside and to the right of the Tomorrowland entrance, would be transformed into the **Adventure Thru Inner Space** attraction in 1967 and into **Star Tours** 20 years after that. In 1955, however, such exciting prospects weren't even thought of, and it was enough to have a shiny and slightly futuristic walk-through exhibit filling what might've otherwise been empty space.

"Aluminum in Our Future" was how the Kaiser exhibit was dubbed in Disneyland's **souvenir books** of the 1950s, with supplementary text describing it as an "entertaining exhibit" of "Today's and Tomorrow's uses of the vital metal." Guests entering the Hall of Aluminum Fame first encountered a sign announcing "the brightest star in the world of metals" next to a 40-foot slanting aluminum cylinder that looked like a giant telescope, complete with oversize dials and two narrow finder scopes mounted along the top. The telescope was actually the entrance into the Hall—guests walked through the base and entered a room lined with displays showing the history and uses of aluminum. A six-foot-wide "time sphere" in the center of the room presented images of men using, and even wearing, aluminum. Above the room a cascade of aluminum stars streaked overhead, but with no ceiling on the room the rafters and steel beams of the building were clearly visible.

Enjoying the proceedings from a pedestal near a wall was a three-foot-tall grinning aluminum pig named Kap. With his work clothes and wrench, Kap was a cute mascot, but he was not a Disney character; "Kap" was an acronym for Kaiser Aluminum Pig, "pig" being the term used to describe the impure base alumina that is refined into pure aluminum. Like the Hall itself, Kap was a strained attempt at making science and industry entertaining to kids and laypeople.

Five years after opening, the lights dimmed on the brightest metal's exhibit in favor of less cerebral **Fun Fotos** displays. Some Disneyland historians claim that the 37-foot-long Mighty Microscope of Adventure Thru Inner Space stood in the late '60s exactly where the Kaiser Aluminum telescope had stood in the late '50s, a nice bridge between Disneyland decades if true.

Hall of Chemistry

MAP: Tomorrowland, T-24

CHRONOLOGY: July 17, 1955–September 19, 1966

HISTORY: Of the four Monsanto attractions that existed in **Tomorrowland** in the '50s and '60s, the Hall of Chemistry was the only one to debut on **Opening Day** (the **House of the Future** opened two years later, followed by **Fashions and Fabrics Through the Ages** in '65, and **Adventure Thru Inner Space** two years after that). The Hall's big rectangular building, the first one on the right-hand side within the Tomorrowland entrance, was adorned on the outside with the red Monsanto logo and Space Age atoms.

Inside, the Hall of Chemistry was a free walk-through exhibit that featured informational displays demonstrating how the modern world benefited from chemical engineering ("Chemistry's part in future living" and "Chemistry Contributes to Tomorrow's Living," according to the photoless descriptive text in the park's 1956 **souvenir book**). Large test tubes, oversize beakers, electrified wall displays, a globe, and a metaphorical arm reaching across the ceiling all contributed to the educational experience. "Carpet makes it home" was a pitch for the synthetic Monsanto fibers in modern floor coverings.

As pedestrian as the Hall of Chemistry sounds today, it did last for over 11 years and must've educated millions of visitors. It finally gave way when a sweeping renovation of Tomorrowland in 1966 completely remade this building, which reopened in '67 as Monsanto's more dramatic Inner Space attraction. Today's guests will find **Star Tours** where chemistry was shown and inner space was explored.

Halloween Time

CHRONOLOGY: September 29, 2006–ongoing (seasonally)

HISTORY: While other Southern California parks began celebrating Halloween with month-long activities as far back as 1973, Disneyland didn't do any park-wide Hal-

loweening during the 20th century. However, come the 21st and Disneyland inaugurated Halloween Time, a month of spooky events that was intended to spark ticket sales during what was otherwise a relatively slow time of year. This same strategy of setting up long-term special events in the off-season had been tried several times in the 1980s with the **Circus Fantasy**, **State Fair**, and **Blast to the Past** celebrations. Realizing that October attendance jumped at other local theme parks that offered Halloween events, Disney executives could no longer ignore the public's affection for big Halloween parties, and so on the last weekend of September in 2006 it was finally time for Halloween Time.

The Disney difference was the target audience: whereas other parks aimed their Halloween at teens, and thus offered intense thrills and chills, Disneyland captured the family audience with gentler activities that were as fun as they were frightening. Those activities included spooky characters along **Main Street**, scary shows at the temporary Woody's Halloween Roundup in **Frontierland**, and the playful restyling of Haunted Mansion Holiday (continuing a **Haunted Mansion** tradition begun in 2001). Pumpkins were everywhere, beginning with a 16-foot Mickey-shaped jack-o'-lantern out on Main Street between the **Disney Showcase** store and the **Emporium** on Main Street, and continuing with hundreds of smaller pumpkins placed in every corner of the park. In addition, windows and lampposts were adorned with Halloween décor, and stores were stocked with suitably seasonal items.

In 2006, Halloween Time ran out on the last night of October, leaving a month to transform the park with elaborate new decorations for the upcoming holidays. So popular was this first Halloween Time, in 2007 it began even earlier, September 21st, and the Haunted Mansion was closed from the 4th to the 20th for two weeks of extra-spooky decorating.

Harbour Galley

MAP: Bear Country/Critter Country, B/C-1

CHRONOLOGY: 1989–ongoing

HISTORY: In 1989, a riverfront restaurant called the Harbour Galley opened near the **Haunted Mansion**. The walkway where the restaurant was located was named Mill View Lane, a reference to both Disney Legend **Joe Fowler** (this was supposedly the street he lived on in Florida) and the Old Mill over on **Tom Sawyer Island**.

As the maritime sign out front announced, the Harbour Galley offered

"delectable seafood specialties." The menu featured Cajun popcorn shrimp, chowder, fish and chips, and Mickey-shaped mozzarella sticks. Unfortunately, business was often so slow at the Harbour Galley that it was frequently closed. In the summer of 2001, the Harbour Galley, while retaining its name, changed to become a McDonald's outlet, though all it served were McDonald's fries and beverages (an abbreviated menu similar to the one in **Westward Ho Conestoga Wagon Fries** on the other side of the river).

Haunted Mansion

MAP: New Orleans Square, NOS-12

CHRONOLOGY: August 9, 1969–ongoing

HISTORY: After the thrilling buildup to **Opening Day**, the next day in Disneyland history to be anticipated with high-pitched excitement was the long-awaited debut of the Haunted Mansion in **New Orleans Square**. Certainly the arrival of the **Pirates of the Caribbean** attraction was eagerly awaited in 1967, but that one opened in

March, the off-season, and guests really didn't know what to expect. The Haunted Mansion, however, opened at the height of the summer tourist season, and the legion of fans who had already sailed with the Pirates were dying to see what Disneyland would do with a haunted house. What's more, guests at the park had been hearing about the Haunted Mansion since 1961 and had been staring at its gleaming exterior since 1963.

Tentative plans for some kind of haunted house actually preceded Disneyland itself—the 1951 concept drawings of the park by **Harper Goff** showed a haunted mansion on a hill, and two years later **Marvin Davis** placed a rickety haunted house near the **Plaza Hub** in his illustration of what **Main Street** might look like. Once

The Haunted Mansion's
Main Outdoor Cemetery in 2007

Interred in the Wall

Theo Later

U.R. Gone

Ray N. Carnation

Dustin T. Dust

Levi Tation

I.M. Mortal

G.I. Missyou

I. Trudy Departed

I.L. Beback

Rustin Peece

M.T. Tomb

Pets with Tombstones

Bat: "Freddie the Bat, We'll Miss You, 1847"

Dog: "Buddy, Our friend until the end"

Fish: "October 10, 1867"

Frog: "Old Flybait, He Croaked, August 9, 1869"

Pig: "Rosie, She was a poor little Pig, But she bought the Farm, 1849"

Rat: "In Memory of My Rat Whom I Loved,
Now He Resides in the Realms Up Above"

Snake: "Here lies my snake whose fatal mistake was frightening
the gardener who carried a rake"

Spider: "Here lies long-legged Jeb, got tangled up in his own web"

Squirrel: "Beloved Lilac, Long on Curiosity . . .
Short on Common Scents—1847"

Disneyland opened in 1955, initial work began on a haunted attraction in 1957 when **Ken Anderson** was asked to come up with a basic design and a story to go with it. Expecting a New Orleans section to be built at some point, Anderson drew up a Southern mansion and invented a plot that included the Headless Horseman and a murderous sea captain who ended up hanging himself (most of this plot would be abandoned, but some individual elements would endure, such as the hanging man still seen soon after the guests are inside the building).

One of the variations on the design was a dilapidated mansion reminiscent of the creepy haunted houses in films, but **Walt Disney** quickly rejected that plan because he didn't want any Disneyland structure to look rundown and neglected. In 1961, he announced that the Haunted Mansion would open within two years, and in fact an elegant three-story antebellum mansion with four stately columns was built in 1963 where **Holidayland** had once stood, a spot halfway between **Adventureland** and the **Indian Village**. Guests were tantalized, and all decade long the park's **souvenir books** touted the attraction's imminent arrival with an eerie painting by **Sam McKim**.

In reality, work had stopped on the Haunted Mansion. Dedicating himself and his design team to creating four new attractions for the 1964–1965 New York World's Fair, Disney put the Haunted Mansion on indefinite hold. He did stir up excitement once again when he re-announced it in 1965 on an episode of his *Wonderful World of Color* TV show, and he even mentioned specifics to expect, such as a Museum of the Weird (which was never built).

Finally, the real Mansion work was underway and accelerating in 1967, using ideas okayed by Walt Disney before he passed away late in 1966. An all-star team of future Disney Legends was all over the project: **John Hench** was credited as the overall supervisor; **Bill Justice** developed the **Audio-Animatronic** corpses; **Fred Joerger** made the plaster models; **Rolly Crump**, **Bill Martin**, and **Yale Gracey** designed most of the scary special effects; **Marc Davis** added whimsical touches; **Claude Coats** designed the building's spooky interiors; and **Buddy Baker** and **X Atencio** wrote the "Grim Grinning Ghost" theme song sung by **Thurl Ravenscroft** and the Mello Men (Atencio also penned the Ghost Host's script).

From the time it was first drawn up to its actual debut, the Haunted Mansion underwent two major changes. The first came when it gradually transformed from being a completely frightening to a half-frightening/half-funny "happy haunt" attraction. The second came when it went from being a series of walk-through exhibits narrated by a maid or butler to an **Omnimover** attraction. The Omnimover system, basically little semi-enclosed pods on a conveyor belt, had already proven itself as a safe, efficient way to move thousands of people per hour through the popular **Adventure Thru Inner Space** attraction over in **Tomorrowland**. Realizing that pedestrians would move too slowly through the large mansion interiors (especially if those pedestrians were frightened or fascinated), designers decided to convey them via Omnimover "Doom Buggy" pods that would swivel on preprogrammed command.

And large those mansion interiors indeed are. Once inside the building, guests are lowered by elevator in the "stretching room" to a 90-foot walkway inside a portrait gallery. Besides showing off clever intaglioed sculptures and double-image paintings, what the gallery is really doing is leading guests under the park's railroad track and outside the **berm**, effectively taking them beyond the perimeter of the park's original layout to a one-acre "show building" next door. There a chain of 131 Doom Buggies carries guests through haunted hallways, past the haunted attic and haunted ballroom, into a haunted cemetery, and back to an exit ramp. Next to Pirates of the Caribbean, the Haunted Mansion was the most ambitious and complex attraction of its time.

Just before the Haunted Mansion opened to the public in August of 1969, the excitement was so intense that legends circulated about viewers who had died of fright while inside the building on preview tours. When it did open, guests were met by elegantly dressed **cast members** who intensified the suspense with their uniformly somber demeanor (indeed, they are still the only employees encouraged *not* to smile). Quickly, the Haunted Mansion became the park's most popular attraction—on August 16, 1969, one week after officially opening, a record 82,516 guests roamed Disneyland, all of them, it seemed, there to line up for hours to get scared by eight minutes of Haunted Mansion horrors (that attendance record lasted for almost two decades; though Disneyland stopped giving attendance figures in 1984, it's believed that the record was finally eclipsed in 1987 when **Star Tours** debuted).

Over the years, a large group of loyal fans has unearthed and disclosed some of the Haunted Mansion's secrets: Walt Disney himself considered doing the narration later performed by **Paul Frees**; the Madame Leota floating-head illusion is the face of Leota Toombs, a Disney Imagineer (the voice is provided by veteran actress Eleanor Audley, who added her vocals to the films *Cinderella* and *Sleeping Beauty*); the organ in the ballroom is the one used in the film *20,000 Leagues Under the Sea*; the humorous tombstones formerly in the cemetery out front referred to actual Imagineers; in addition to the main cemetery in the queue area to the left of the building, there's a small hidden cemetery to the right with tombstones and epitaphs for departed pets; the singing busts have names—Cousin Algernon, Ned Nub, Phineas P. Pock, Uncle Theodore, Rollo Rumkin (Walt Disney's visage is not on a broken bust, as rumored; that's actually singer Thurl Ravenscroft); the cake on the banquet table has 13 candles; the maritime weathervane atop the Haunted Mansion is a reference to the original, but barely used, murderous-mariner story line; and at one time live cast members in costume (including a suit of armor) would jump out at guests to enliven the experience for repeat visitors (one "secret" that's been long-rumored but is untrue concerns the horse-drawn hearse out front—it's not the one used for Brigham Young's funeral).

The Haunted Mansion has become a staple of other Disney theme parks, although Disneyland is the only one to place it in New Orleans Square (Walt Disney World=Liberty Square, Disneyland Paris=Frontierland, Tokyo Disneyland=Fantasyland). And the venerable Disneyland original still gets revised occasionally. In 2001, the Haunted Mansion Holiday first dressed it with décor from *The Nightmare Before Christmas* (Leota Toombs's daughter is shown reading tarot cards during this special winter event). In recent years, the building has been the endpoint for a Disney's Mysteries, Myths & Legends tour held during the winter, and in 2006 high-tech updates in the attic caused portraits to vanish before guests' eyes. What's more, Madame Leota's head now floats around the room, and the soundtrack has been revised.

No matter how it changes, and no matter what other attractions are developed elsewhere, the Haunted Mansion continues to exert an irresistible pull on guests. Millions of them still "hurry ba-ack, hurry ba-ack," just as the Little Leota figure near the exit has beckoned them to do for over three decades.

John Hench

CHRONOLOGY: June 29, 1908–February 5, 2004

HISTORY: Many historians have decided that no person, other than the man Disneyland was named after, had more influence on Disney theme parks, or understood them better, than John Hench. And no one appreciated Disneyland more than this erudite polymath did. "Disneyland is our greatest achievement," Hench wrote in his book *Designing Disney*. "Disneyland was first and set the pattern for others to follow."

An Iowan born in 1908, Hench studied at art institutes in New York, San Francisco, and Los Angeles before joining the Disney Studios in 1939. There he worked as an artist and story editor for almost 20 years on animation classics like *Fantasia*, *Dumbo*, *Cinderella*, and *Peter Pan*. Hench also helped with the Oscar-winning special effects on 1954's *20,000 Leagues Under the Sea*.

That same year, he switched over to designing Disneyland projects and shaping the park's aesthetics, which meant that everything from attraction layout to landscaping to color schemes was within his purview. **Tomorrowland**, the **Moonliner**, and the **Rocket to the Moon** were among his first achievements. Other specific park locations Hench worked on included **Main Street**, where he designed many of the buildings; **Sleeping Beauty Castle**, where he added the **Snow White Wishing Well and Grotto**; the **Monorail**, where he drew up concept illustrations and designed the flashy **attraction poster**; the **House of the Future**, where he picked and designed the verdant Tomorrowland site; and **New Orleans Square**, where he was chief planner. He was also a leading Imagineer on the **Skyway to Fantasyland and Skyway to Tomorrowland** and the **Carousel of Progress** attractions, plus he supervised the 1967 remodel of Tomorrowland and the design of the

Haunted Mansion. Cast member costumes, queue areas, and even **restrooms** were sketched by John Hench. The nation got a glimpse of him working on **Plaza Inn** interiors on a 1965 episode of *Walt Disney's Wonderful World of Color.*

Hench was quick to point out that Walt Disney was the real designer of all these lands and attractions, however. "By the time you got your ideas back from Walt," Hench said in the book *Remembering Walt,* "you wouldn't recognize them as your own. He absorbed and digested everything. In the end, the production was all his."

Outside the park, Hench was **Walt Disney's** right-hand man as Disney was developing the opening and closing ceremonies of the 1960 Olympic Games (Hench designed the Tower of Nations and an array of snow sculptures). He also helped with the new exhibits for the 1964–1965 New York World's Fair. In later decades, Hench was one of those in charge of the plans for Walt Disney World, and he was a key contributor to Tokyo Disneyland, Disney's California Adventure, and Animal Kingdom. He was also Mickey Mouse's official portrait artist, creating new commemorative paintings for the star's 25th, 50th, 60th, and 70th birthdays.

Named a Disney Legend in 1990, John Hench was long respected as the wise mentor to younger Imagineers who followed his guidance as they developed new attractions for Disneyland. In 1999, the park's great theorist celebrated a 60-year Disney career, and in 2003 he eloquently summarized what he'd learned in a retrospective book called *Designing Disney.* The following year John Hench died in Burbank at age 95. Today fans can find him listed as Capt. J. Hench on a doorway inside **Space Mountain** (see photo, previous page).

Heraldry Shoppe, aka Castle Heraldry

MAP: Fantasyland, Fa-4, Fa-30

CHRONOLOGY: Ca. 1995–ongoing

HISTORY: For years **Fantasyland** has offered guests several genealogical resources. In addition to the now-absent **Names Unraveled**, which researched proper nouns, the durable Heraldry Shoppe enables guests to look up their family history. Also sometimes called Castle Heraldry because of its first location, the Heraldry Shoppe was inside the passageway to **Sleeping Beauty Castle**, directly across from the **Princess Boutique** in the spot formerly occupied by the **Castle Candy Kitchen.** In 2006, it moved to the prominent store next to **Peter Pan Flight**. Once upon a time, this well-themed room had housed **Merlin's Magic Shop. Three Fairies Magic Crystals**, meanwhile, replaced the Heraldry Shoppe inside the castle.

Heraldry started in the Middle Ages as a way for English families to trace their heritage, establish their ruling status, and define their coats of arms. At Disneyland guests can investigate the geographical and historical origins of their family name, check out the family crest, and buy attractive hard copies of all the pertinent information. Also available are souvenir coats of arms, $150 swords, personalized plaques, and more, all sold in the presence of a real suit of armor. Kids might soon get bored by this regal shop, but adults should be fascinated.

Hidden Mickeys

CHRONOLOGY: 1970s-ongoing

HISTORY: The term "Hidden Mickey" is something of a misnomer, because the Mickey that's supposedly hidden is actually in plain sight. A Hidden Mickey is primarily a three-circled shape that's patterned after Mickey Mouse's silhouetted head and round ears. However, simple mouse ears placed on an attraction's character, or the appearance of Mickey's oversized gloves or shoes, can also qualify as Hidden Mickeys.

The Hidden Mickey concept probably started on a small scale at Disneyland in the 1970s when Disney Imagineers planted a few Hidden Mickeys for their own amusement. But as interest in Disneyland trivia intensified over the decades, the Imagineers began incorporating Hidden Mickeys into Disneyland's architecture and

attractions with increasing frequency, placing the little symbols as fun, challenging details to be discovered by enthusiastic guests. By now there are now dozens of subtle Hidden Mickeys of varying sizes and shapes scattered throughout the park. On the Internet, several unofficial fan sites attempt to catalogue the Hidden Mickeys and take reports when new ones appear.

Hidden Mickeys are to be distinguished from "actual" Mickeys that have been obviously worked into

10 Hidden Mickeys

Big Thunder Trail, cacti
Buzz Lightyear Astro Blasters, continent on planet Ska-densii in queue-area mural
Clarabelle's Frozen Yogurt, pattern on closed metal shutter
Entrance, end supports on ticket-area benches (see photo, left)
Entrance, supports underneath ticket-area shelves
Haunted Mansion, arrangement of dinner plates in ballroom
Indiana Jones Adventure, queue-area hieroglyphics
King Arthur Carrousel, the flank of the horse with bells
Mickey's House, sheet music in the Mouseway player piano
Pirates of the Caribbean, hanging barrels near end

décor or design (the Mickey Mouse-shaped parterre at the **entrance**) or that constitute the shape of a product (a Mickey Mouse-shaped lollipop). A true Hidden Mickey usually takes careful observation and even repeat visits for confirmation. For Disneyland's golden anniversary in 2005, an additional 50 Hidden Mickeys in gold and blue were placed in plain sight. These Mickeys were much more conspicuous than their traditional hidden brethren, and in fact **City Hall** even provided a list of their locations to help guests find them all.

Hills Bros. Coffee House and Coffee Garden

MAP: Town Square, TS-7

CHRONOLOGY: June 13, 1958–December 1976

HISTORY: Eight months after the **Maxwell House Coffee Shop** closed on **Town Square**, Hills Bros., the San Francisco coffee company founded in the early 1900s, reopened it. An expanded outdoor area warranted an addition to the original name, and so the park's **souvenir books** called the new spot the Hills Bros. Coffee House and Coffee Garden.

The location was ideal for a morning-coffee business, since it faced guests as they entered the park through the east tunnel and crossed **Town Square** to head up Main Street. After almost two decades of caffeinating incoming guests, the Bros. headed for the **Market House**, and the **Town Square Café** took over this spot as a full-service sit-down restaurant.

Hobbyland

MAP: Tomorrowland, T-20

CHRONOLOGY: September 4, 1955–January 1966

HISTORY: For over 10 years, the open area south of the **Flight Circle** in **Tomorrowland** was the site of a freestanding retail area known as Hobbyland. If Hobbyland were in place today, it would begin outside the **Star Traders** store and extend across the **Cosmic Waves** area.

Hobbyland didn't get much respect in the park's **souvenir books**, which offered no photos of it and from 1956 to 1964 listed it as Hobbies and Toys. Perhaps the reason for the snub was Hobbyland's lackluster design, which even in the late '50s certainly wouldn't have qualified for any honors, especially in futuristic Tomorrowland. Hobbyland was nothing more than about a dozen countertops separated by aluminum struts that supported temporary fiberglass roofs.

What justified its existence, however, was the treasure mined by guests who studiously sifted through the countertop displays. Hobbyland's jewels were model kits, a comprehensive collection that included everything from cars and ships to rockets and dinosaurs, plus some of the motorized vehicles that were being spun around the nearby Flight Circle. By the spring of '66, this whole area was closed off for the extensive Tomorrowland remodeling that would put the **PeopleMover** and new walkways where Hobbyland's simple booths had once dazzled model-makers.

Holidayland

MAP: Park, P-13

CHRONOLOGY: June 16, 1957–September 1961

HISTORY: One of Disneyland's most curious land developments ever wasn't actually in the park. Originally slated for the **parking lot** area behind **Tomorrowland**, Holidayland ended up outside the park's perimeter **berm** in a nine-acre field west of the train tracks behind **Frontierland.**

      The minimally landscaped terrain out here was devoted to simple, inexpensive outdoor family fun. Holidayland offered picnic tables, a baseball field, volleyball, tug of war, a children's playground, horseshoe pits, square dancing, basic refreshment stands, and picnic baskets sold by Swift, the same company that already sponsored the **Market House** and **Red Wagon Inn** on **Main Street** and the **Chicken Plantation** in Frontierland (among the contents of Swift's picnic baskets was, surprisingly, beer). Dominating Holidayland was a traditional red-striped circus tent, where special events, ranging from bingo to performances by the Mouseketeers, could be held. This tent was the same one used for the short-lived **Mickey Mouse Club Circus** in **Fantasyland.**

      Holidayland was intended to attract big family reunions, or, ideally, corporations that would buy up to 7,000 tickets for their employees and then bring them all together for a day-long company picnic. Admission to Holidayland, unfortunately, did not include admission to Disneyland; it did, however, include access to a special Disneyland entrance where a park-admission ticket could be purchased and then a path could be taken under the berm into what would now be the back of **New Orleans Square.** This was the only time in Disneyland's history when guests could enter the park any place other than through the front gates or via the **Monorail** station in **Tomorrowland.**

      Disney Legend **Milt Albright**, who would later devise more successful group-sales strategies, supervised Holidayland in its early years. Ticket sales for this isolated, unshaded area were always a challenge, and so in the fall of 1961, the circus tent already destroyed in a storm, Holidayland became Permanentlyclosedland. Guests still visit the old Holidayland acreage, though they aren't aware of it, because this is where the "show buildings" for the **Haunted Mansion** and **Pirates of the Caribbean** are hidden.

Honey, I Shrunk the Audience

MAP: Tomorrowland, T-19

CHRONOLOGY: May 22, 1998–ongoing

HISTORY: Taking over for the decommissioned *Captain EO* in the **Magic Eye Theater** was *Honey, I Shrunk the Audience*, a Kodak-hosted 3-D movie that debuted with the rest of remodeled **Tomorrowland** in May of 1998. Like *EO, Honey* had been shown in Florida before it was brought west to Anaheim.

      During the film's 18 minutes guests, wearing the obligatory 3-D glasses, meet emcee Dr. Nigel Channing, played by Eric Idle of *Monty Python's Flying Circus*. Channing then brings on the Inventor of the Year, Professor Wayne Szalinski, played by Rick Moranis in a reprise of his role from the *Honey, I Shrunk the Kids/Honey, I Blew Up the Kid* movies of the late '80s/early '90s. Soon the nutty but well-intentioned Szalinski accidentally miniaturizes the theater to lunchbox size, and merriment ensues as the audience views everything in the film—the cast, the props, a dog, a lunging snake—as if it were gigantic.

Improving over *Captain EO*, this film is synchronized with several impressive special effects in the theater itself, such as jets under the seats that squirt air to simulate scurrying mice. The park's 2000 **souvenir book** merrily gave the show the full-page treatment and called *Honey* "hilarious," ironically the same adjective the souvenir books had used in the write-up for *Captain EO*.

House of the Future

MAP: Tomorrowland, T-1

CHRONOLOGY: June 12, 1957–December 1, 1967

HISTORY: In *The Graduate*, Benjamin Braddock (played by Dustin Hoffman) received one key word of advice as he considered his coming career: plastics. Anyone who saw Disneyland's House of the Future might've summarized modern living the same way.

The second Monsanto-sponsored attraction at Disneyland (the **Hall of Chemistry** preceded it, **Fashions and Fabrics Through the Ages** and **Adventure Thru Inner Space** followed), the House of the Future was a free walk-through exhibit located outside the entrance to **Tomorrowland**. Guests in the **Plaza Hub** who gazed at the house would've seen **Sleeping Beauty Castle** to the left and, after 1959, **Matterhorn Mountain** rising up behind. The House of the Future stood on a raised 256-square-foot platform surrounded by landscaped gardens and a winding pool that collectively covered about a quarter of an acre.

From above, the 1,280-square-foot, three-bedroom, two-bath home was shaped like a graceful plus sign, its four compartmentalized modules spreading from a central core and extending over open air. These modules, guests were told, could be supplemented with additional modules to accommodate the expanding family. An optional rotating platform enabled inhabitants to spin their house to face any direction.

During its decade-long existence, the House of the Future got two redecorations and welcomed some 20,000,000 guests (more than the entire population of California at the time). Viewers saw, not a Disney-designed fun attraction, but a serious mass-produced tract home designed by M.I.T. and Monsanto engineers to show off technological advances from Monsanto's Plastics Division. One of the strengths of the house was, in fact, its strength: when it came time to dismantle the entire structure in 1967, engineers discovered that the four extending wings of the house had drooped less than a quarter-inch despite all the heavy traffic, and demolition had to be done by hand with crowbars and saws because the wrecking ball that was brought in to bring down the house merely bounced off the sides.

Prerecorded narration inside the home bragged that nearly everything on view was artificial and adjustable. Fixtures in the bathroom and shelves in the cabinets could be raised or lowered at the push of a button; the climate-controlled air could be instantly warmed, cooled, purified, or scented; the futuristic communications included an intercom, push-button speaker phones, picture phones, a sound system in the shower, and a large wall-mounted TV screen; floor-to-ceiling windows covered most of the exterior walls, with interior illumination provided by "panalescent fixtures," "trans-ceiling polarized panels," and mobile lights that could "bathe each room with the glow of natural sunlight"; sleek furniture was made from vinyl and urethane, drapes from nylon; and the kitchen highlights were appliances called an "ultrasonic dishwasher" and a microwave oven.

The house got big showings in the **souvenir books** of the late '50s and early '60s, sometimes with two photos and several paragraphs of text describing the "all plastic," "ultra modern" wonders within. While the House of the Future may seem silly or dated now, at the time it was an ambitious attempt to make the spirit of the Space Age real and practical, which is what **Walt Disney** also tried to do with the

Monorail, the **Skyway to Fantasyland**, the **PeopleMover**, even the **Hall of Chemistry** and the **Bathroom of Tomorrow**. The **Astro-Jets**, **Tomorrowland Autopia**, and other Tomorrowland attractions entertained as fanciful futuristic rides, but the House of the Future educated as a true, working vision of what the future could be.

After the House of the Future became the House of the Past in late 1967, the **Alpine Gardens** were established over the landscaped grounds, and a souvenir stand incorporated part of what had once been the patio of tomorrow. However, the seeds planted by the House of the Future later blossomed into the Progress City model that would fill the upper floor of the **Carousel of Progress**. What's more, in mid-2008 a new 5,000-square-foot technologically enhanced version of the House of the Future opened inside the **Innoventions** building. Walt Disney's urban dreams, of course, flourished on an even larger scale as EPCOT in Florida.

Hurricane Lamp Shop

MAP: Main Street, MS-4

CHRONOLOGY: Ca. 1972–ca. 1976

HISTORY: Sometime in 1971 or '72, a **Main Street** room that had formerly been part of the corner **Upjohn Pharmacy** became home to the Hurricane Lamp Shop. Victorian hurricane lamps with glass chimneys and oil-burning wicks might've seemed like appealing items for turn-of-the-century Main Street, but guests would "glow" out of them in a few years. In early 1976, the **Disneyana** shop replaced the non-Disney lamps with Disney collectibles.

Indiana Jones Adventure

MAP: Adventureland, A-6

CHRONOLOGY: March 3, 1995–ongoing

HISTORY: Arriving in the spring of 1995, the Indiana Jones Adventure was the first major new attraction to open in **Adventureland** since the **Enchanted Tiki Room** had debuted in 1963. As with **Captain EO** and **Star Tours**, the Indiana Jones Adventure represents a fruitful pairing with movie giant George Lucas.

Planning for what turned out to be the most exciting new attraction of the '90s actually began in the mid-'80s, back when the second Lucas-produced Indiana Jones movie, *Indiana Jones and the Temple of Doom,* was busy establishing itself as a huge hit in theaters. Various Disney designers had a crack at incorporating elements from that movie and Lucas's previous Indy blockbuster, *Raiders of the Lost Ark,* into some kind of Disneyland adventure. Some of the early concept drawings showed battered vehicles careening along a cliff above a lava-filled ravine, with the vehicle leaning over the edge; others attempted to include the **Jungle Cruise** boats, the **Santa Fe & Disneyland Railroad**, and a roller coaster-style mine-car chase; and still other illustrations had queuing guests lined up through the "spike room" from *Temple of Doom.* Nearly all the early plans found a place for the rolling-boulder sequence from *Raiders.*

When the Indiana Jones Adventure finally arrived in 1995, it did so with the highest price tag for any Disneyland attraction ever (most estimates are over $100,000,000, about six times the total cost to build the entire Disneyland park in the mid-'50s). For construction to begin in 1993, designers first reshaped the adjacent Jungle Cruise river to make room for the three-story temple structure (some of it underground) and the elaborate queue area. At over a quarter-mile long, this would be the longest, and most densely detailed, queue area in Disneyland history.

The real achievement, however, wasn't the construction of the building as much as it was the engineering of the cars, which are the most complex vehicles in the park. Created to look like well-used jeep-style jungle trucks from 1935, each of the 16 vehicles dips, swerves, shakes, tilts, accelerates and brakes all along the 2,500-foot track, making the ride crazy and unpredictable. What's more, each vehicle carries its own computer that generates random bumps, fire flashes, and other effects throughout the trip to create 160,000 possible variations of the experience.

Once they leave from the archaeological dig at the beginning of the ride, the trucks speed up to 13 mph and whip guests through a perilous three-and-a-half-minute journey inside the Temple of the Forbidden Eye. Snakes, fire, rats, bugs, blow guns, a collapsing bridge, that famous rolling stone, and sophisticated **Audio-Animatronic** Indiana Jones figures await. Pumping through the on-board audio systems are realistic sound effects, Indy's voice, screaming mummies, and the familiar movie music, all propelling the excitement to unprecedented heights.

After years of building up expectations, the Indiana Jones Adventure was an instant hit, drawing the biggest crowds (and lines) to Disneyland since the 1987 Star Tours opening. A 1995 TV special called "40 Years of Adventure" spotlighted the new attraction and further amped up that year's crowds. Fortunately, **FastPass** tickets can expedite today's wait times.

Fans have always loved the delightful details that add to the authenticity and the fun. Among them: Sallah (a character in the Indy movies) delivers the pre-boarding instructions; the queue area displays coded symbols deciphered via special decoder cards (no longer handed out to every guest, but still available at the **Indiana Jones Adventure Outpost**); one of the queue-area crates is addressed to Obi Wan, a character in another Lucas movie; a tempting lever in the queue area brings an unexpected response; the jungle trucks don't really go in reverse, even though an illusion suggests they do; often a skeleton named Bones sports mouse ears in the finest **Hidden Mickeys** tradition; and one of the old magazines on view is a 1938 issue of *Life* with Mickey Mouse on the cover. These and many, many other surprises make this one of the best, most thrilling, most inventive additions to the park in a generation. To paraphrase one of the movie ads upon which it is based, if adventure has a name, it must be the Indiana Jones Adventure.

Indiana Jones Adventure Outpost

MAP: Adventureland, A-2

CHRONOLOGY: Spring 1995–ongoing

HISTORY: Capitalizing on the massive attention brought to the west end of **Adventureland** when the **Indiana Jones Adventure** opened, the Indiana Jones Adventure Outpost debuted across from the attraction's entrance in that same spring

of 1995. Indy's Outpost replaced the **Safari Outpost**, which had been selling khaki safari gear for almost 10 years from this spot next to the **Sunkist, I Presume** (now **Bengal Barbecue**) eatery.

The Outpost's interior is about 45 feet wide and 20 feet deep, and it opens to **South Seas Traders** next door to the right. Since Indy made it his, the Outpost has sported lots of classic fedoras, maps, and archaeological artifacts. Shirts, pins, jewelry, and additional attraction-related souvenirs also fill the shelves. An unexpected surprise: in the far left corner stands a very cool, very playable Indiana Jones pinball machine.

Indian Trading Post

MAP: Frontierland, Fr-15

CHRONOLOGY: July 4, 1962–December 1, 1988

HISTORY: The store known as the Indian Trading Post joined the seven-year-old **Indian Village** in **Frontierland** on 1962's Independence Day. The rustic little building had a great location near the **Rivers of America** and the launch site of the **Indian War Canoes**. From this site guests would've had a swell view of boats on the water and kids on **Tom Sawyer Island**.

Inside the Trading Post were authentic Indian crafts, such as turquoise jewelry, clothing, and pottery. Despite the 1972 remodeling in this area that replaced the Indian Village with **Bear Country**, the Indian Trading Post was left untouched, its Indian theming still appropriate for the new land that was supposedly set in the Pacific Northwest woods of the previous century. Unfortunately, the Indian Trading Post didn't survive the 1988 remodel that replaced Bear Country with **Critter Country**—a week after the critters arrived, the Trading Post became the equally rustic but more Disneyish **Briar Patch**.

Indian Village

MAP: Frontierland, Fr-15

CHRONOLOGY: July 1955–October 1971

HISTORY: In mid-1955, a realistic Indian Village opened just a tomahawk's throw from the **Chicken Plantation** restaurant at the western edge of **Frontierland**. From here guests could see the southern tip of what would soon be called **Tom Sawyer Island**. For the first few months, the Indian Village was a small collection of a few teepees and simple wooden structures that re-created the dwellings of various 19th-century Plains Indians. Unlike most of the rest of Disneyland, the village had dusty dirt paths, not paved sidewalks, winding through it.

In the Indian Village actual Native Americans demonstrated ceremonial dances such as the Eagle and the Mountain Spirit and showed off their customs. The result was a touch of frontier authenticity in an area of the park that was otherwise only an imitation of the frontier experience (the park's 1985 hardcover **souvenir**

book proudly noted that the "authentic dances from such tribes as the Apache, Navajo, Comanche and Pawnee" were "performed with the permission of the respective tribal councils and the U.S. Bureau of Indian Affairs").

Within a year, with developments such as the new **Rafts to Tom Sawyer Island** being added to the southern shores of the **Rivers of America**, the Indian Village was relocated farther north along the river's west bank, a spot opposite the middle of Tom Sawyer Island. This was a larger space for the village, and there was more development here, including a more ornate dance circle, additional teepees, lodges, a burial ground, and the D-ticket **Indian War Canoes** (even though it was bigger, the rustic village was still a free attraction). Demonstrations of archery and more displays of arts and crafts added to the colorful fun. A 1962 remodel of the village expanded the location and brought in the waterfront **Indian Trading Post**.

Most years the park's souvenir books showed photos of "full-blooded Indians" performing "tribal dances," or Chief Shooting Star in his elaborate native garb, or canoes paddling past the painted teepees. In one happy photo, a gray-suited **Walt Disney** wore a ceremonial headdress while smiling in front of a tribal drum. Everything was showcased on a 1970 episode of *The Wonderful World of Disney*, but the village's days were numbered. In the fall of 1971, the Indian Village was dismantled so that this corner of Frontierland could be transformed into **Bear Country**.

Indian War Canoes, aka Davy Crockett's Explorer Canoes

MAP: Frontierland, Fr-14

CHRONOLOGY: July 4, 1956–ongoing

HISTORY: Of all the many cars, trolleys, boats, ships, trains, and vehicles guests can ride in at Disneyland, only one has required its passengers to help with the actual propulsion. But that's what the Indian War Canoes in **Frontierland** asked of its guests, starting on Independence Day of 1956.

As with the **Mike Fink Keel Boats**, the *Mark Twain*, and the *Columbia*, the D-ticket canoes made an approximately 12-minute trip around **Tom Sawyer Island**, though the canoes gave a view from just above water level (they also deferred right-of-way to all those other bigger, less mobile watercraft). The canoes launched from the northernmost dock along the western bank of the **Rivers of America**, a spot near the **Indian Village** and opposite the central section of Tom Sawyer Island; to the south were **Fowler's Harbor**, the dock for the keelboats, and the landing for the **Rafts to Tom Sawyer Island**.

Unlike other Disneyland boats, the canoes weren't made by Disney designers, instead coming from a canoe-building company in Maine. The 35-foot-long canoes originally had small motors to supplement the paddlers, but these were soon eliminated and all power came from the dozen guests and two strong-armed **cast members**. Occasionally the photos in the park's **souvenir books** showed full canoes with Native Americans fore and aft: "Hardy braves 'paddle their own canoe,'" read the captions, while a small illustration on the back of the books offered a canoe and the text, "Indian guides help 'pioneers' paddle on the Frontierland river."

On May 19th of '71, some five months before the adjacent Indian Village was disbanded, the Indian War Canoes got a more politically correct name, though Davy Crockett's Explorer Canoes was basically the same attraction. They've operated irregularly because of weather concerns, and there was some talk that they'd be permanently retired in the late '90s, but today the canoes still exist as rustic throwbacks to the park's earlier, simpler years.

Indy Fruit Cart

MAP: Adventureland, A-7

CHRONOLOGY: Ca. 1995–2006

HISTORY: Of the temporary fruit carts that have been stationed throughout Disneyland over the years, the most prominent and durable was the Indy Fruit Cart parked at the west end of **Adventureland**. Themed to the nearby **Indiana Jones Adventure** and **Indiana Jones Adventure Outpost**, the cart looked like a battered World War II jeep, complete with dings, faded paint, and an old tire mounted on the hood. The menus lodged into the steering wheel and chained to the body announced the various fresh fruit selections that were supplemented with nuts, chips, and juices. Unfortunately, this healthy haven seems to have been towed away in 2006.

Innoventions

MAP: Tomorrowland, T-14

CHRONOLOGY: July 3, 1998–ongoing

HISTORY: A quarter of a century after the **Carousel of Progress** show had stopped spinning, and a decade after **America Sings** had sung its last song, Innoventions was installed into the big round Carousel Theater at the back of **Tomorrowland**. Innoventions wasn't a daring risk for Disneyland—it had already been a success at Walt Disney World for about four years before it came to Anaheim.

Unlike the Carousel of Progress's earlier shows, which barely changed once

they were put in place, Innoventions continues to be an ever-changing multifaceted presentation of innovative edutainment. And unlike its two predecessors, Innoventions doesn't spend most of its time looking back into America's past in order to spring slightly forward in time. Innoventions has always focused on the future—not the distant future, but the future nonetheless, even if that future sometimes seems like it's only about 10 minutes away.

Spread out across 30,000 square feet and two big floors are displays of up-to-the-minute or soon-to-arrive gadgets, games, and technology. Subdivided zones pertaining to modern living—entertainment, home, transportation, information, and sports/recreation—group exhibits together thematically, with each zone sponsored by a major company such as Yamaha, Compaq, Hewlett-Packard, Pioneer, AT&T, etc. What's in the zones gets frequently updated, making each Innoventions visit a new experience. Typically, there is a ring of exhibits around the slowly rotating perimeter that are demonstrated by **cast members** (one complete revolution takes about 18 minutes), and then in the central hub are hands-on games, quizzes, gadgets, and computers for guests to linger over. The upstairs floor offers more exhibits, corporate displays, and the exits.

In Innoventions, guests might see voice-activated appliances, the latest PlayStation games, an imaging program that ages a just-taken photograph, a tree made out of circuit boards, **fireworks**-generating software, a futuristic car, and virtual-reality exercycles. What they won't see are **restrooms** inside the huge structure, as evidently those haven't been innovented yet.

The Carousel Theater has usually been filled with **Audio-Animatronic** figures (over 100 for America Sings); but now only one prominent A-A character is on view in Innoventions. He's a doozy, though. Hosting the proceedings is Tom Morrow, a wisecracking robot with Nathan Lane's voice, transparent skin, and a see-through lab coat (his is thought to be the same A-A skeleton used for the Flight Director in the old Flight to the Moon attraction, who was also named Tom Mor-

A Disneyland Dozen Imported from Walt Disney World

Astro-Orbitor
Buzz Lightyear Astro Blasters
Captain EO film
Country Bear Jamboree
FastPass
Honey, I Shrunk the Audience film
Innoventions
Magic Journeys film
Many Adventures of Winnie the Pooh
Mile Long Bar
Space Mountain
Wonders of China film

row). The latest Tom is often the featured photo when the park's **souvenir books** tout Innoventions, as they did with a big two-page splash in 2000.

There are a couple of other nostalgic nods to the past, too. The Sherman brothers' familiar "There's a Great, Big Beautiful Tomorrow" tune, bolstered with some new lyrics, still plays inside the building. And while the Carousel Theater's interior celebrates the future, its exterior salutes the past with a half-dozen banners showing old Tomorrowland attractions, a nice reminder that innovating is nothing new at Disneyland.

International Street

MAP: Town Square, TS-7

CHRONOLOGY: Never built

HISTORY: From 1956 to 1958, a tall wooden wall near the **Opera House** on **Town Square** carried a sign that announced a new area, International Street, was under construction and was due to open soon. Behind the sign, and visible to curious guests through small viewing holes, were photographs of what the street would look like. Supposedly the new street was being built parallel to the eastern row of buildings along **Main Street**. International Street was to be lined with architecture inspired by a half-dozen European countries, plus Japan, with themed shops and stores just like those found elsewhere in the park.

Actually, what guests were seeing was a scaled-down version of something called International Land that would've ended up out in Disneyland's northeast corner between **Tomorrowland** and **Fantasyland**. Roughly triangular in shape, International Land, as shown in the 2005 book *Disneyland: Then, Now, and Forever*, was surrounded by water and connected to the rest of the park by three bridges. Some kind of transportation system curled across the five-acre triangle, and several large buildings sat in the interior.

While neither International Street nor International Land was built, similar concepts did find expression some two decades later and over 3,000 miles away in Florida's Walt Disney World. In Disneyland, plans and announcement for a coming International Street were replaced in 1958 by plans and announcements for a coming **Liberty Street**, but those too would soon pass.

Intimate Apparel, aka Corset Shop

MAP: Main Street, MS-13

CHRONOLOGY: 1955–December 1956

HISTORY: Ever since Disneyland opened, one of the best places to sit on **Main Street** has been on the elevated porch along the right-hand side of the street near the **Plaza Hub**. Modern guests who take a rest on the bench and chairs here probably don't realize that this little porch, only about 18 feet wide and five feet deep, originally belonged to the Intimate Apparel shop (also called the Corset Shop in the park's 1956 **souvenir book**).

In case the euphemistic Intimate Apparel name didn't register with 1950s guests, the sign above the porch back then clearly spelled out what was available inside—"Brassieres" and "Torso-lettes." The sponsor was the H-M Company, better known at the time as Hollywood-Maxwell or "the Wizard of Bras." H-M had created, and was selling in Disneyland, the "strapless Whirlpool bra" that "makes the most of you." Not only that, Intimate Apparel even told the history of women's undergarments via an in-store exhibit.

Some experts have speculated that the porch was built as a buffer to set the window displays back from Main Street a few feet and away from innocent eyes; others have suggested that the porch was intended as a seating area for gentlemen while their ladies shopped for unmentionables inside. Whatever the motive, H-M abandoned the porch and Disneyland in late 1956, at which point the **Ruggles China and Glass** shop next door spread into the vacant room.

𝕽ichard 𝕴rvine

CHRONOLOGY: April 5, 1910–March 30, 1976

HISTORY: Imagineers have led the way to new Disneyland attractions; Richard Irvine led the Imagineers. He was born in 1910 in Salt Lake City, but a dozen years later his family moved to California. Irvine attended Stanford University, USC, and a prominent art institute before getting a job in the young film industry of the 1930s. Working as an art director for the next two decades, he contributed to such notable films as *Miracle on 34th Street*, Disney's *The Three Caballeros*, and *Sundown*, the latter bringing him an Oscar nomination.

Lured away from 20th Century Fox in 1952 by **Walt Disney**, Irvine was initially charged with helping outside architects design Disneyland. However, Irvine soon realized that the best people to design a park that was to incorporate strategies from stage and screen were the people already working on Disney films. Accordingly, Walt Disney gathered many of his top animators, artists, set designers, and craftspeople into his own newly formed design department, what would eventually be called Imagineering. Richard Irvine headed this key department.

For the next 20 years, Irvine was point man in the creation of every Disneyland attraction, including such sophisticated classics as **Pirates of the Caribbean**. In addition, he supervised all the Disney attractions for the 1964–1965 New York World's Fair, among them the beloved **It's a Small World** cruise. At the end of the '60s, Irvine focused on attractions for Walt Disney World, where one of the old-fashioned steamboats is now named after him. Richard Irvine retired in 1973 and died three years later in Los Angeles. He was named a Disney Legend in 1990.

It's a Small World

MAP: Fantasyland, Fa-21

CHRONOLOGY: May 28, 1966–ongoing

HISTORY: It's a Small World was launched on a large stage—the 1964–1965 New York World's Fair, where over 10,000,000 visitors joined "the happiest cruise that ever sailed 'round the world." However, what those visitors saw wasn't what was originally planned, because the happy cruise went through a major change before it ever sailed.

A charismatic boat ride past hundreds of singing **Audio-Animatronic** dolls from six continents was always the main concept. But initially the international dolls were going to sing all the various national anthems on all those continents. This would've resulted in a disharmonious jumble to guests who were still hearing the previous anthems even as they were approaching the next. Instead of a multitude of melodies, a single Disneyland anthem written by **Richard and Robert Sherman** in 1963 filled the entire trip with a 15-minute reminder that it was indeed a small world after all.

What's more, the building's exterior in New York was vastly different from what ended up in Anaheim. For the fair, It's a Small World was in the Pepsi-Cola pavilion, where the relatively bland exterior was dressed up with signage and an elaborate 120-foot-tall, 100-ton art piece out front. This structure, called the *Tower of the Four Winds*, had mobile elements that expressed "the boundless energy of youth," according to its designer, Disney Legend **Rolly Crump**. At Disneyland, the new acre-and-a-half Small World building supplanted the train depot at the back of **Fantasyland** and extended well beyond the perimeter **berm**. The Small World exterior lost Crump's huge tower but gained an intricate, smile-inducing collage of moving, whirling, rocking shapes that evoked grand monuments—the Taj Mahal, the Eiffel Tower, etc.—from around the world. In recent years, the *Tower of the Four Winds* has been echoed in an arcing sign out front.

Wonderful and whimsical, Disneyland's It's a Small World isn't architecture, it's high-spirited *lark*-itecture. Designed by several Disney Legends, among them **Mary Blair**, this imaginative façade has gone through several paint revisions that have taken it from white-and-gold and white-and-blue color schemes to a sweet rainbow of candy pastels. The gold touches are done in actual 22-karat gold leafing, and some of the elaborate front decorations are enlarged duplications of personal jewelry owned by the designers. A lavish **Topiary Garden**, an elaborate cuckoo clock that chimes with marching toy soldiers every 15 minutes, and even the **Santa Fe & Disneyland Railroad**, which passes right through the building's layered frontage from west to east, all add to the fanciful fun. As charming as the cruise is, the trip itself is almost unnecessary because there's so much to see outside.

Inside the building, the winding 1,400-foot river, laid out by Disney Legend

Claude Coats, meanders past over 500 singing dolls and kinetic effects. The dolls and effects are scattered across dozens of **Marc Davis**-created scenarios to illustrate how happiness is a global emotion, whether it's being experienced by island kids on surfboards, Dutch girls clacking their wooden shoes, giggling hyenas and native

children, skating Scandinavians, a snake-charming Indian boy, a Chilean flautist, or all-American frontier kids (in 2007, the American cowgirl twirled a lariat and the boy wore a Native American headdress). **Alice Davis's** adorable doll costumes put the fun in functional—they're fastened with Velcro so they can be opened in the back whenever interior mechanisms need repair.

Veteran riders may remember the multilingual hello and goodbye signs at the entrance and exit, and also the sponsor's own final message—no matter where in the world guests went, Bank of America would be there, according to the cheery text. B of A, which had been a participant in Disney projects dating back to the *Snow White and the Seven Dwarfs* film in'37, sponsored It's a Small World until '92, when Mattel took over (in 2007, there was no sponsor at all). Other changes came with the arrival of special decorations and carols for It's a Small World Holiday in '97.

A hit from its New York debut in '64 and its Disneyland debut in '66, It's a Small World had its own mid-'60s soundtrack album complete with a colorful 10-page booklet, probably the first Disneyland attraction so honored. It also had one of the most inspired opening tributes ever for a park attraction—as dreamed up by Disney Legend **Jack Lindquist**, **Walt Disney** and some international chil-

dren ceremoniously poured water from each of the world's oceans into the Small World river while press photographers merrily clicked away (this after an elaborate opening **parade** with over 500 kids). In another promotional move, the park's 1965 **souvenir book** showed off the coming E-ticket spectacular with two big pages and nine colorful photos, this a year *before* the attraction opened. The text described the exterior as a "symphony in light" and the cruise as "a musical fantasy where *all* the world is a colorful, carefree stage . . . proving there is no world like a child's." In 1999, It's a Small World became the first Disneyland attraction to get the new **FastPass** ticket-distribution system, a significant sign that "the happiest cruise" is still as adored and adorable as ever.

It's a Small World Toy Shop

MAP: Fantasyland, Fa-20

CHRONOLOGY: December 18, 1992–ongoing

HISTORY: To cash in on the high volume of pedestrian traffic emerging from **It's a Small World**, two stores sit near the exit of the famous attraction. The smaller store slightly farther away is **Fantasy Faire Gifts**, and the larger one right in the path of departing guests is the It's a Small World Toy Shop.

For most of its history, the Toy Shop was sponsored by Mattel, the toy giant that also sponsored It's a Small World. This meant the toy store was typically filled with lots of Mattel toys, not all of them Disney-related. Hot Wheels cars, games, and collectible Barbie dolls populated the shelves. Today there are still plenty of Disney dolls, statues, and toys for tots filling the store. The building's fanciful design makes it look like one of the playful scenes displayed along the banks of the It's a Small World cruise.

Ub Iwerks

CHRONOLOGY: March 24, 1901–July 7, 1971

HISTORY: One of the great Disney animators was also a key creative force behind several major Disneyland attractions. Ubbe "Ub" Iwerks was born in Missouri in 1901, the same year as **Walt Disney**. Working at an art studio in Kansas City, the teenage Iwerks met Disney, a fellow employee, and together they started up their own Iwerks-Disney commercial-art business. The short-lived company led to a bigger one, Laugh-O-Gram Films, in 1922, with Iwerks on board as the chief animator.

A few years later, both men reunited in Hollywood at the new Disney Brothers Cartoon Studio, where Iwerks worked on the *Alice Comedies*, became the first person to draw Mickey Mouse, and single-handedly animated Mickey's first cartoon, *Plane Crazy*. After pioneering the *Silly Symphonies* of the late '20s, Iwerks left Disney's company during the '30s to create his own cartoons, but his Flip the Frog and other characters weren't as successful as those he'd created with Disney, and so he returned in the early '40s.

Heading the studio's research and development team, Iwerks devised new cinematic advances that propelled imaginative live-action/animation combinations. These special effects would memorably flourish in *Song of the South* and *Mary Poppins* and win him two Oscars for his technical achievements. Iwerks is listed in the credits of dozens of Disney classics, among them *Cinderella*, *20,000 Leagues Under the Sea*, *Sleeping Beauty*, and *One Hundred and One Dalmatians*, plus Alfred Hitchcock's *The Birds*.

At Disneyland, Iwerks brought his technological expertise to three of the biggest new attractions of the mid-'60s: the Circle-Vision 360 theater in **Tomorrowland**, **Great Moments with Mr. Lincoln** on **Main Street**, and **It's a Small World** in **Fantasyland**. In the **Haunted Mansion**, the illuminated floating head in the séance room and the singing busts in the graveyard are based on a projection system Iwerks devised. After working on the Hall of Presidents for Walt Disney World, Ub Iwerks died in 1971 at age 70 of a heart attack. He was inducted as a Disney Legend, along with the first fleet of great Disney animators, 18 years later.

Robert Jani

CHRONOLOGY: 1934–1989

HISTORY: Disneyland's long-time entertainment specialist devised imaginative productions that redefined the **parade** concept for hundreds of millions of delighted guests. Robert Jani was born in 1934 in L.A. and graduated from USC two decades later. In 1955, he started working at Disneyland as the first person to lead **Guest Relations**, an all-purpose information and problem-solving department based in the park's **City Hall**. Jani then served two years in the army; upon returning, he worked at USC and then formed his own production company, Pacific Pageants. In '67, Jani rejoined Disney as the company's director of entertainment in charge of creating and staging live shows, parades, and special events.

At Disneyland, his two most famous creations were the legendary **Main Street Electrical Parade**, which ran from 1972 for over two decades, and America on Parade, the patriotic spectacular of the mid-'70s. Jani's Electrical Parade was probably the most popular parade in the park's history, though initially it was a tough sell to Disney execs when he first pitched the unique nighttime concept (this according to Jani himself on the 2007 *Disneyland: Secrets, Stories & Magic* DVD). In addition to these Disneyland events, Jani and his company produced several prominent non-Disney events, including Super Bowl halftimes, New York's Bicentennial Celebration of 1976, massive Christmas shows at Radio City Music Hall and Orange County's Crystal Cathedral, and numerous TV specials.

Though he retired in 1978, he stayed on to consult on the plans for Disneyland Paris and Disney-MGM Studios. After fighting Lou Gehrig's disease, Bob Jani died in Los Angeles in 1989 at age 55. He was named a Disney Legend in 2005.

Jemrock Shop

MAP: Main Street, MS-13

CHRONOLOGY: Ca. 1955–ca. 1957

HISTORY: Listed among the earliest stores on **Main Street** was something small and undefined called the Jemrock Shop. From 1956 to 1957, the park's **souvenir books** also used the name Jemrocks and Gem Shop in their listings, with no indication of a precise Main Street location. Possibly it was in the cluttered second east-side block of small stores, or perhaps it was in the **Crystal Arcade** across the street. This latter location would've been appropriate for what was presumably some kind of lapidary store. By the time the 1958 souvenir book came out, any mention of Jemrock(s) on Main was gone.

Jewel of Orléans

MAP: New Orleans Square, NOS-9

CHRONOLOGY: 1997–ongoing

HISTORY: Any survey of the prettiest shops in the park would have to include a mention of Jewel of Orléans. Sparkly chandeliers, a decorative ceiling, ornate wall details, exquisitely decorated mirrors, a tile floor, and lace curtains all combine to evoke a Parisian setting, perhaps even a room at Versailles (an appropriate reference, given that the former long-time occupant of this space was **Mlle. Antoinette's Parfumerie**).

Jewel of Orléans is located adjacent to the **French Market** restaurant in New Orleans Square, an easy-to-find, easy-to-linger-over corner location. This isn't the only Jewel of Orléans in California—the original has been charming San Franciscans since 1989. The Jacobs family, owners of a jewelry business called Dianne's Estate Jewelry, owns and runs both shops. Antique jewelry is their specialty, as announced by the sign out front: "One of a kind fine estate sellers." This broad category includes Victorian bangles and cameos, vintage pocket watches, Edwardian pendants and necklaces, exquisite rings in velvet boxes, Art Deco trinkets, rare gems, and even some Disneyland-related pieces of recent decades.

To study the historic, dazzling displays here is to feel like Jewel of Orléans is more museum than shop, especially since some of the items here can run into the tens of thousands of dollars. The Disneyland location works with the one in San Francisco to procure special requests, and no-interest layaway plans are available.

Jewelry Shop, aka Rings 'n' Things

MAP: Main Street, MS-19

CHRONOLOGY: Ca. 1957–1986

HISTORY: Starting in 1957, the park's **souvenir books** gave the names Jewelry and Jewelry Shop to a small space on the right-hand side of the first block of **Main**

Street. This was not the **Jemrock Shop**, which had a separate listing in those same books. The Jewelry Shop's neighbors in the '50s and early '60s would've been the **Main Street Cinema** to the south and the **Yale & Towne Lock Shop** one door northward towards the **Plaza Hub**. Not shown in photos or described in detail in any souvenir books, the Jewelry Shop is almost completely lost to Disneyland lore.

It's likely that in 1966 or '67, the Jewelry Shop absorbed the adjacent space that had been the Lock Shop. The store got new signage as the slightly more specific Rings 'n' Things around 1970. Then in 1986, Rings 'n' Things switched locations with the **Disneyana** shop across the street. The new location was the corner building that had once been the **Upjohn Pharmacy**; the new name was (and still is) **New Century**, an umbrella title applied to both New Century Jewelry and New Century Timepieces next door.

Jimmy Starr's Show Business Souvenirs

MAP: Town Square, TS-8

CHRONOLOGY: March 23, 1956–September 20, 1959

HISTORY: Nicknamed Stage Door Jimmy, Jimmy Starr was a long-time Hollywood insider who started working in the movies in the 1920s and eventually had careers as a newspaper gossip columnist, publicist, press agent, novelist, screenwriter, and minor actor. From the spring of '56 to the fall of '59, a collection of his Hollywood memorabilia filled a leased space located to the left (north) of the **Opera House** on **Town Square**.

The park's **souvenir books**, evidently figuring that guests might not know who Jimmy Starr was, listed his shop as Show Business, as Show Business Souvenirs, and as Motion Picture Souvenirs, with no reference to Starr at all. Inside the store guests could view some movie props and buy photos, autographs, and other collectibles. No retail super Starr, the shop closed after three years to become the Disney-owned **Wonderland Music** in 1960. Some 30 years later, Jimmy Starr died at age 84.

Fred Joerger

CHRONOLOGY: December 21, 1913–August 26, 2005

HISTORY: Designers and architects made two-dimensional drawings of new Disneyland attractions and buildings. Fred Joerger turned those drawings into intricate 3-D models.

Joerger was born in 1913 in Illinois and graduated in 1937 with a fine arts degree from the University of Illinois. Moving to Los Angeles, he started building models at Warner Brothers Studios, and in 1953 he joined Disneyland's model-making team, which included two other Disney Legends,

Wathel Rogers and **Harriet Burns**.

Among Joerger's first creations was a model of the *Mark Twain* **Riverboat**, followed quickly by elaborate miniatures of **Main Street** buildings, the **Jungle Cruise**, **Sleeping Beauty Castle**, the **Storybook Land Canal Boats** villages and palaces, and many more early attractions, all before any of them were built. In the late '50s, his 3-D **Matterhorn** rendering rose as the park's tallest structure, and in the early '60s his **Haunted Mansion** model was translated into the park's most eagerly awaited attraction. Meanwhile, Joerger was also contributing models of movie sets to the Disney Studios, among them detailed miniatures of the **Harper Goff**-designed submarine for *20,000 Leagues Under the Sea*.

In addition to building models, Joerger was also an expert at sculpting the faux rocks that added realistic atmosphere to Disneyland attractions, among them **Tom Sawyer Island**, the **Jungle Cruise**, the **Big Thunder Mountain Railroad**, and **Pirates of the Caribbean**. His rock work was acknowledged on a Haunted Mansion tombstone that reads, "Here lies Good Old Fred, a great big rock fell on his head."

After working on Walt Disney World, Joerger retired in '79, though he later consulted on EPCOT and Tokyo Disneyland. He was named a Disney Legend in 2001, four years before he died in Los Angeles at age 91.

Jolly Trolley

MAP: Mickey's Toontown, MT-12

CHRONOLOGY: January 24, 1993–ongoing

HISTORY: In **Mickey's Toontown**, public transportation is provided by the wacky Jolly Trolley. "It's clean! It's fun! It bounces a lot!" reads this attraction's sign, and few guests could disagree.

Looking like little toy versions of the beautiful horse-drawn street cars that have roamed **Main Street** since 1955, these happy trolleys are built with soft curves, have bright red paint with gold trim, and sport cartoony wind-up keys on the top. About 10 guests at a time can fit inside for the scenic fountain-to-fountain ramble across Toontown. What puts the jolly in the trolley is the series of gentle jiggles, dips, and bumps as it weaves along its 800-foot track.

Appropriately enough for this joyous ride, **cast members** here wear bright blue conductor uniforms with big yellow buttons, red bow ties, and snappy multi-colored hats. The park's **souvenir books** of the '90s and 2000s nearly always showcased the photogenic Jolly Trolley, which seems incapable of taking a bad picture.

Mary Jones

CHRONOLOGY: Unknown-ongoing

HISTORY: The woman in charge of Disneyland Community Relations first started working at the park in 1962 as a secretary. Within a few months of being hired for her clerical skills, Mary Jones was heading Community Relations, a department that worked with local leaders to assure Disneyland's happy coexistence with its neighbors. She began by administering awards for community service. Later, Jones implemented her plans for the Community Action Team (which established volunteer programs and assistance for nonprofit organizations) and Operation Christmas (a community-outreach program that brought Christmas celebrations to children's hospitals).

Jones also worked as the liaison with consulates and the State Department to bring visiting foreign dignitaries and royals safely and successfully into the park, leading to many impressive photo opportunities that broadened Disneyland's international appeal. She retired from Disneyland in 1986 but stayed on with the local government to set up and run the Orange County Office of Protocol, continuing there the community work she'd pioneered for almost 25 years at the county's most-visited destination. Mary Jones was inducted as a Disney Legend in 2005.

Jungle Cruise

MAP: Adventureland, A-8

CHRONOLOGY: July 17, 1955–ongoing

HISTORY: Arguably the most important attraction during Disneyland's first decade was the Jungle Cruise. From 1955 until the 1962 arrival of the nearby **Swiss Family Treehouse**, it was the only major attraction in all of **Adventureland**. What's more, with its land and water covering approximately three southwest acres of the park, the Jungle Cruise has always been one of Disneyland's largest single attractions. And it has also been one of the most heavily promoted. Even before the park opened, the ***Disneyland* TV series** previewed the coming cruise—in one episode **Walt Disney** even drove a car through the unfilled river while touting the wonders to come.

Once the park opened, the early **souvenir books** devoted more space and photos to the Jungle Cruise than any other attraction. Calling the attraction the Explorer Boat Ride, the River Boat Ride, the Jungle River Boat Ride, the Jungle River Boat Safari, and finally (in 1959) the Jungle Cruise, the souvenir books of the '50s liberally sprinkled colorful photos of the boats and colorful adjectives about the scenery found along the nine-minute E-ticket ride. The enthusiastic text described how "adventure lurks at every bend" of this "jungle wonder world" filled with "thrills and excitement" and flowers "ablaze with color." The 1969 hardcover *Walt Disney's*

Disneyland souvenir book opened and closed with four full-page photos of hippos and a boat and then devoted two and a half interior pages to a detailed description of what it suggested was "Disneyland's finest achievement." If **Sleeping Beauty Castle** was the park's iconic building, the Jungle Cruise was its signature attraction.

As with the **Painted Desert** area of **Frontierland**, the Jungle Cruise incorporated themes and images from Disney's *True-Life Adventure* films of the '50s, in this case the 75-minute documentary *The African Lion*. The original **attraction poster** for the Jungle Cruise italicized this connection with the words "For true life *adventure*, ride the Jungle River," though what the imaginative art showed—a colossal elephant towering over the jungle and guests who were *standing* in a boat—wasn't exactly "true life." Disney Legend **Harper Goff** laid out the four-foot-deep river and drew some of the first concept sketches of the scenery along its teeming banks, taking some of his ideas from another '50s movie, the 1951 Oscar-winning classic *The African Queen*. Africa, though, isn't the only setting for the Jungle Cruise. Scenes along the waterway actually suggest different international rivers, including the Amazon, the Mekong, the Congo, and the Nile. Landscaper **Morgan "Bill" Evans** made creative use of exotic plants as he planted the dense foliage that soon filled in like real jungles of the world.

Early plans called for real animals to populate the jungle and the river, but that idea was quickly scotched when designers realized that jungle wildlife usually sleeps out of view all day, and even those beasts not sleeping would probably be hiding from noisy, intrusive boats. Eventually, dozens of realistic mechanical animals and natives went on display, among them majestic elephants, curling snakes, charging hippos, munching giraffes, half-submerged crocodiles, and dancing headhunters. Though their motions were relatively simple and repetitive, these machines were, in the '50s, considered advanced special effects and gave the Jungle Cruise its unique thrills; more sophisticated **Audio-Animatronic** mechanicals wouldn't appear until the singing birds debuted in 1963's **Enchanted Tiki Room**.

Since 1955, there have been at least 10 updates to the Jungle Cruise. Veteran jungle cruisers may recall that at one time the Jungle Cruise river and Frontierland's **Rivers of America** were linked by a small canal, which was soon closed off. In '62, the playful elephants and their bathing pool were added. The African Veldt, **Marc Davis's** "lost safari" climbing up out of range of a rhino, and the Cambodian ruins all joined the fun by '64, and then a dozen years later the gorillas started playing in the abandoned camp. In 1994, with the **Indiana Jones Adventure** under construction next door, Imagineers rerouted part of the river and built a wonderfully themed two-story queue area at the dock. This wooden structure, made to look old and abandoned, intentionally sags to suggest that nature is reclaiming what man has encroached upon. Guests waiting inside will hear old-time music and see period artifacts that evoke the 1930s.

At some point in its infancy, the attraction went from being a daylight-only cruise to one that could be taken at night, thanks to spotlights on the boats. Those gas-powered vessels have undergone other stylistic changes over the years. The first versions were gleaming white with red-and-white striped roofs, while current versions are brown, canvas-covered, and suitably dingy to evoke Humphrey Bogart's much-traveled movie *Queen*. The 27-foot boats have always held about 32 passengers and have always been guided by unseen rails.

One key aspect of the Jungle Cruise that separates it from other Disneyland attractions is the jokey patter spoken by the wisecracking boat skippers. Initially, these **cast members**, wearing safari garb and brandishing blanks-loaded pistols, delivered serious narration about the cruise and its dangerous inhabitants, but after a few years that narration, with the blessing of park officials, was played for laughs. The purpose, perhaps, was to deflate the menace of the realistic spiders, jungle beasts, and savages with bursts of humor. Eventually, however, the cruise became a nonstop joke-fest that begins before guests are even in their seats.

By now most guests can recite one or two of the corny puns and gags that have been repeated thousands of times over the decades—the safari member who will surely get the rhino's point in the end; the crocs looking for a hand-out; the rare view of the back side of water; Trader Sam, the attraction's mascot, who will trade two of his shrunken heads for one of yours; and the most dangerous part of the trip, the return to civilization. Much of this is scripted, but skippers have a long tradition of ad-libbing new material, especially on the last run of the night. Kevin Costner, Robin Williams, and Nixon's press secretary Ron Ziegler are all said to have been Jungle Cruise skippers in their youth. These might be fanciful legends to go along with the entertaining stories of boats that have sunk, the leeches that have supposedly been found on their hulls, the Mickey Mouse doll half-hidden in the bushes, and the skippers who swung from ropes in the trees, but they reveal the fascination guests have always had with this beloved Disneyland classic.

Names of the Jungle Cruise Boats
(*denotes an original 1955 boat)

*Amazon Belle**
*Congo Queen**
*Ganges Gal**
Hondo Hattie
*Irrawaddi Woman**
Kissimmee Kate
Magdalena Maiden
*Mekong Maiden**
*Nile Princess**
Orinoco Adventuress
*Swanee Lady**
Ucayali Una
Yangtze Lotus
Zambesi Miss

Junior Autopia

MAP: Fantasyland, Fa-23

CHRONOLOGY: July 23, 1956–September 15, 1958

HISTORY: Of the four Autopia attractions that have chugged through Disneyland's history (the **Tomorrowland Autopia**, **Fantasyland Autopia**, and **Midget Autopia** are the others), the Junior Autopia came and went the quickest. It was the second Autopia to debut, following the Tomorrowland Autopia by a year and preceding the Midget Autopia by nine months.

To capitalize on the popularity of the Tomorrowland Autopia, Disneyland opened the Junior Autopia to accommodate younger, shorter drivers who weren't able to handle the Tomorrowland Autopia cars. The Junior Autopia site was a little farther north of its Tomorrowland predecessor, which put this Autopia in **Fantasyland** instead of **Tomorrowland**; formerly the short-lived **Mickey Mouse Club Circus** had operated in this northeast corner.

The track design for the Junior Autopia was not as elaborate as the track for the Tomorrowland Autopia, and it was safer, too—unlike the early version of the Tomorrowland Autopia, the Junior track included a center guide rail to help novice drivers keep their cars in line. The cars of the Junior and Tomorrowland Autopias were basically identical (sleek **Bob Gurr**-designed sports cars with fiberglass bodies) except for extended gas pedals and higher seats in the former, both intended to make the cars more child-friendly.

About 26 months after opening, the Junior Autopia closed for a major remodel. The site reopened in 1959 as the larger Fantasyland Autopia, with some of the land filled in by the waters of the **Motor Boat Cruise**.

Bill Justice

CHRONOLOGY: February 9, 1914–ongoing

HISTORY: Animator, programmer, **parade** designer, Imagineer—Bill Justice wore many hats as a key Disney employee for over four decades. An Ohioan born in 1914, Justice was raised in Indiana and graduated from an Indiana art institute in 1935. Two years later, he was living in Southern California and starting a long career with the Disney Studios.

Working on animated films, he contributed memorable scenes and characters to such classics as *Fantasia*, *Bambi*, *Alice in Wonderland* and *Peter Pan*. Along the way he directed the opening animation for *The Mickey Mouse Club* TV show; he co-created the special opening titles for such popular Disney films as *The Shaggy Dog*, *The Parent Trap*, and *The Misadventures of Merlin Jones*; and he designed the nursery sequence in *Mary Poppins*.

In 1965, Justice moved over to Disneyland attractions, especially those involving sophisticated **Audio-Animatronic** figures like **Great Moments with Mr. Lincoln**, **Pirates of the Caribbean**, the **Haunted Mansion**, **Mission to Mars**, **America Sings**, and the **Country Bear Jamboree**. Rounding out his great Disney career, Justice contributed costumes and floats for Disneyland's elaborate parades, and he helped develop the famous **Main Street Electrical Parade**.

Finally, after working on projects for Walt Disney World and Tokyo Disneyland, he retired in 1979. *Justice for Disney*, published in 1992, was his autobiographical book that discussed his 42-year Disney career in depth. Bill Justice was inducted as a Disney Legend in 1996.

Keller's Jungle Killers

MAP: Fantasyland, Fa-22

CHRONOLOGY: February 19, 1956–September 7, 1956

HISTORY: Killers, in **Fantasyland**? Well, sure. If an **American Rifle Exhibit** could exist in **Frontierland**, and if real guns could be fired in the **Main Street Shooting Gallery**, why not show some dangerous animals east of the **Storybook Land Canal Boats**? The only real surprise is that Keller's Jungle Killers wasn't over in the jungle-themed **Adventureland**.

When the short-lived **Mickey Mouse Club Circus** bailed from Fantasyland in January of 1956, one of the circus attractions, Keller's Jungle Killers, stayed on for that next spring and summer. George Keller's B-ticket attraction featured, not costumed **cast members** or mechanical replicas, but actual animals in a big cage. They were indeed killers, albeit sedated and declawed ones.

Wearing sparkly outfits, Keller himself would interact with the leopards, lions, and tigers. The most famous part of his act came when he put his head inside of a lion's mouth. Prior to arriving in Disneyland, Keller had already performed his shows at circuses and fairs across the country, and after departing Disneyland, he briefly joined the Ringling Bros. Barnum & Bailey spectacular in 1959 before he was felled by a heart attack a year later.

Back in Fantasyland, meanwhile, the site of the Mickey Mouse Club Circus and Keller's Jungle Killers was extensively remodeled from 1956 to 1959. The **Junior Autopia** drove in as the area's first new attraction.

Ken-L Land Pet Motel, aka Kennel Club, aka Pet Care Kennel

MAP: Park, P-7

CHRONOLOGY: January 18, 1958–ongoing

HISTORY: In an effort to accommodate pet owners who might otherwise leave their animals sitting in sun-baked cars in the uncovered **parking lot**, Disneyland added a pet-care facility in 1958. Conveniently, the location was outside the park, butted up against the **berm** about 100 feet from the east tunnel into **Town Square**. While

pets couldn't be left overnight, they could be left for the entire day in "airy, individual enclosures" for modest fees (for years that daily fee was under $1, including food, but in early 2008 the service was $20). Over the years, everything from lizard to pig has stayed in one of the 100+ cages.

When it first appeared, early **souvenir books** labeled the building a "Main Street Service" and gave it the name Ken-L Land Dog and Cat "Hotel," even though the actual flag-topped sign at the site clearly spelled out Ken-L Land Pet Motel. Five different pet-food companies have hosted and remodeled the kennel service over the decades. Ken-L Ration sponsored its Pet Motel from 1958 to 1967; Kal Kan created the Kennel Club from 1968 to 1977; after a sponsorless period in which the service was called simply the Kennel, Gaines renamed it the Pet Care Kennel from 1986 to 1991; Friskies restored the Kennel Club name in 1993; Purina took over in 2002 and kept the Kennel Club signage.

Kids of the Kingdom

CHRONOLOGY: Ca. 1967–ca. 1977

HISTORY: The Kids of the Kingdom was the name of an energetic musical ensemble that performed in Disneyland from the late '60s to the late '70s. The Kids weren't exactly kids in the manner of the preteen Mouseketeers; these Kids were college-age singers and dancers. Primarily they performed in **Tomorrowland** on the large **Tomorrowland Stage**, which had replaced the **Flying Saucers** in 1967. However, they also appeared at special events in other park locations, such as the **Plaza Hub**.

Wearing colorful matching outfits, the coed Kids belted out upbeat, choreographed versions of Disney classics, show tunes, and other popular songs, reminding many guests of the clean-cut Osmond Brothers. The Kids of the Kingdom cut an eponymous album in 1968 on Vista Records. Subtitled *Young Singing Stars of Disneyland*, that album showed 14 well-groomed, white-sweatered performers, half of them holding Mickey balloons, all of them smiling in front of **Sleeping Beauty Castle**. Two years later, the Kids got introduced to a national audience on a 1970 episode of *The Wonderful World of Disney* TV show. On that "Disneyland Showtime" episode, actor Kurt Russell, the barbershop harmonists the **Dapper Dans**, and, yes, those same Osmonds all celebrated the new **Haunted Mansion** and other recent additions to the park.

While accurate chronology isn't known, it's believed the Kids of the Kingdom lasted in Disneyland at least until 1977, the year the Tomorrowland Stage was remodeled into the **Space Stage** (a Florida branch of the Kids of the Kingdom continued at Walt Disney World for years). The Kids were certainly gone by the time construction began in 1985 to transform the outdoor Space Stage into the indoor movie stage called the **Magic Eye Theater**.

King Arthur Carrousel

MAP: Fantasyland, Fa-5, Fa-6

CHRONOLOGY: July 17, 1955–ongoing

HISTORY: The beautiful King Arthur Carrousel is near the center, not just of Disneyland, but of the Disneyland story. **Walt Disney** always maintained that some of his ideas for a new kind of amusement park came while he was sitting near

a carnival merry-go-round that his daughters were riding (that merry-go-round anecdote was detailed in one of the park's official anniversary books, *Disneyland: The First Thirty Years*).

When it finally came time to build his own park, Disney placed his carousel in a most telling place. Not only is it in the middle of the **Sleeping Beauty Castle** courtyard, where it pumps out gaiety, music, and color as if it were **Fantasyland's** beating heart, but it is in a conspicuous location where it can be seen from hundreds of

feet away. Guests at **Town Square** can look northward up **Main Street** and across the **Plaza Hub** to see the whirling lights of the King Arthur Carrousel through the castle's archway. The alluring sight has helped draw hundreds of millions of cautious, novice guests into the core of the park, away from their modern reality and toward Disneyland's fairy-tale fantasy.

Regarding carousel history, two points need clarification. While many Fantasyland attractions are based on Disney movies, and while the King Arthur Carrousel's name derives from the same Arthurian legend that was the basis of Disney's *The Sword in the Stone*, there's no other connection or imagery shared by the 1955 attraction and that 1963 movie. Also, while the King Arthur Carrousel uses an old spelling variation of the more familiar "carousel" in

Six Disneyland Attractions That Moved to New Locations

1. Bandstand (Plaza Hub to Adventureland)
2. Astro-Jets (Tomorrowland)
3. Dumbo the Flying Elephant (Fantasyland)
4. Indian Village (Frontierland)
5. King Arthur Carrousel (Fantasyland)
6. Mad Hatter's Mad Tea Party (Fantasyland)

its name, the meaning—a whirling ride with moving horses—is identical. Whether the machine is a carrousel or carousel, neither one is a merry-go-round, which is the same type of attraction but one with all kinds of animals and benches on it, plus some of the horses won't move up and down.

Ironically, before it got to Disneyland, the carousel was originally a merry-go-round. It was built in 1875 and was located in Toronto, Canada, when Walt Disney bought it. After he transported it to his new park, and after Disneyland designers took off the non-equine animals and seats, they added over two dozen horses purchased from Coney Island (some of those removed seats, by the way, were added onto the cars of the **Casey Jr. Circus Train**). Ultimately, the Disneyland carousel opened with 72 hand-carved, hand-painted antique wooden horses arrayed in 18 rows of four (guests in 2007 found 68 horses in 17 rows of four, plus a bench). All the horses now look to be leaping, an effect Disney designers created when they attached new legs to some of the horses that previously had four on the floor. And all the prancing steeds are now a gleaming white, a result of the new paint applied

over the previous shades of black, tan, cream, and brown. Distinctive color variations are provided by the brightly colored saddle, trim and jewels that distinguish each horse.

As noted in the Disneyland Data page of the 1956 **souvenir book**, "ten shields on the spears supporting the covering canopy of the carousel represent ten of the founding Knights of the Round Table. Among those represented: Sir Lancelot, Galahad, Perceval, Tristan, Gawain and Gareth, Bedevere, Lionel and Bors." In addition, the nine panels displayed around the carousel's central hub are, appropriately enough for an attraction just a few feet from Sleeping Beauty Castle, hand-painted scenes from *Sleeping Beauty*. For the first three decades, a calliope provided the rollicking music. In its first three decades it also only cost an A ticket to take the carousel for a two-minute four-mph spin.

In the early '80s, the King Arthur Carrousel was remodeled right along with the rest of Fantasyland. First, Imagineers moved the carousel north about 20 yards to open up the congested area near the castle. This move put the carousel, which had formerly been near **Peter Pan Flight**, closer to **Mr. Toad's Wild Ride**; it also precipitated the relocation of the **Mad Hatter's Mad Tea Party** attraction to a spot outside **Alice in Wonderland**. Next, the music changed when the Disney classics playing next door for **Dumbo the Flying Elephant** became the same soundtrack for the carousel.

What hasn't changed in over 50 years is the affection guests have for the King Arthur Carrousel. It is still shown off in today's souvenir books as prominently as it was in books of the '50s. It still gleams, thanks to six hours of polishing on the brass poles every single night and frequent touch-ups of the horses. And it still warms hearts with its traditional pleasures, its regal style, and its timeless beauty, making it the perfect centerpiece for Fantasyland's rich buffet.

King Triton Gardens, aka Triton Gardens

MAP: Tomorrowland, T-1

CHRONOLOGY: February 1996–ongoing

HISTORY: What had formerly been the grounds for the **House of the Future** and then the serene **Alpine Gardens** got re-landscaped into the splashy King Triton Gardens in 1996. Also called simply the Triton Gardens, the beautiful area is named after the monarch from the 1989 Disney movie *The Little Mermaid*.

Located just off the **Plaza Hub** and to the left of the **Tomorrowland** gates, the Triton Gardens sport several statues to let guests know just whose gardens these are—the water-spouting king himself is out in the middle of the pond, and a smiling Ariel is perched on a rock. Kids love the fountain jets that shoot playful streams of water over the walkway (at night the lights make the gardens and the waters especially lovely). Parents appreciate the quiet 300-foot walkway that leads around the pond. In a small clam-shaped area at the northern edge called Ariel's Grotto, a **cast member** dressed as the lovely red-haired, long-tailed Ariel is often on hand to sign autographs and pose for photos.

Knight Shop

MAP: Fantasyland, Fa-30

CHRONOLOGY: August 16, 1997–October 3, 1998

HISTORY: This Middle Ages-themed store took over for **Quasimodo's Attic**/Sanctuary of Quasimodo after the excitement over 1996's *The Hunchback of Notre Dame* movie died down. The Knight's location was the same as Quasimodo's, greeting guests as the first shop on the right-hand side of the **Sleeping Beauty Castle** courtyard, with **Peter Pan's Flight** one stop northward. The merchandise inside included daggers, swords, and armor accoutrements.

Disneyland planners must've thought the Knight Shop would've been a successful pairing with the **Princess Boutique** nearby. But within a year, the Knights had gone to the dark side and become the **Villains Lair**, a return of the Disney bad guys who had been here in the **Disney Villains** store of the early '90s.

Kodak Camera Center, aka GAF Photo Salon, aka Polaroid Camera Center

MAP: Main Street, MS-13

CHRONOLOGY: July 17, 1955–November 1994

HISTORY: From day one, Disneyland has had a camera store on **Main Street**. The allure for camera and film companies has been obvious—most guests, it seems, are always walking around with cameras. Or they wish they were walking around with cameras and so need to buy them. Or they lose the one they had (every day **cast members** find dozens after closing time) and need to replace what's gone. Plus, with all the photogenic subjects to shoot in Disneyland, those insatiable cameras gulp film, film that needs to be replenished immediately.

Ergo, the Kodak Camera Center, meeting all these camera and film needs as of **Opening Day** from a space in the middle of Main Street's second right-hand block. Not only did the store sell still and movie cameras, it rented them too. And, to inspire even more picture-taking and film-buying, Kodak posted helpful signs around the park to prompt especially scenic photographs, such as a nicely framed view of the **Submarine Voyage** with the **Matterhorn** towering in the background.

Sometime around 1970, the General Aniline Film Corporation (GAF) replaced Kodak as the sponsoring company, so for most of the '70s the shop operated as the GAF Photo Salon. Polaroid got into the picture at the end of the decade and renamed the business the Polaroid Camera Center. Finally, in a new development that yanked the camera saga back to its origins, Kodak reappeared as the sponsor from 1984 until November of 1994, at which time the whole operation got a new name (**Main Street Photo Supply Co.**) and a new location—to the building that had been known for decades as **Carefree Corner.**

La Boutique de Noël

MAP: New Orleans Square, NOS-5

CHRONOLOGY: Ca. 1998–March 2006

HISTORY: The larger of the two Christmas shops that existed simultaneously in **New Orleans Square**, La Boutique de Noël was full of holiday cheer and Christmas trees all year long. Formerly **Le Gourmet** had been in this spot along Royal Street between the **Blue Bayou** and the hidden little courtyard where **portrait artists** work.

While it may have seemed a little anachronistic to be browsing for colored lights, little wooden soldiers, ornaments, and stocking holders in the middle of summer, for guests who couldn't come in the winter, La Boutique de Noël did give a nice approximation of the kind of glittering Disney things that usually fill the whole park when it really is the holiday season. Great deals were available in the off-season, but unfortunately this shop entered its own permanent off-season in the spring of 2006. Later that year **Le Bat en Rouge** moved from the other end of Royal Street (the end near **Pirates of the Caribbean**) into this space at the back of New Orleans Square.

La Boutique d'Or

MAP: New Orleans Square, NOS-5

CHRONOLOGY: Ca. 1974–ca. 1980

HISTORY: In the mid-'70s, La Boutique d'Or sold bold gold across from **Le Gourmet** at the back of **New Orleans Square**. Jewelry and home décor, all stamped with karats, made this a glittering stop along Royal Street. The metal merchandise of **Le Forgeron** preceded the golden goods of La Boutique d'Or, and a different kind of indulgence followed when the **Chocolate Collection** moved in around 1980.

Laffite's Silver Shop

MAP: New Orleans Square, NOS-6
CHRONOLOGY: Ca. 1966–1988
HISTORY: Jean Laffite has a tribute inside the **Pirates of the Caribbean** attraction, where Laffite's Landing is the launching dock for the attraction's shallow boats. He's also remembered out on the remodeled **Tom Sawyer Island**, though there his name is spelled Lafitte. Additionally, for about two decades the early-19th-century privateer also had his own namesake shop in **New Orleans Square**.

Tucked in behind what was then the **Creole Café**, and across Royal Street from the **Blue Bayou**, Laffite's Silver Shop offered a wide array of silver items, all of them ready for engraving right on the premises. Laffite la-left when the Creole Café, renamed Café Orleans, expanded into its space in 1988.

La Mascarade d'Orléans

MAP: New Orleans Square, NOS-9
CHRONOLOGY: Ca. 1985–ongoing
HISTORY: From its corner behind the **French Market** at the back of **New Orleans Square**, La Mascarade d'Orléans beckons like a fine, fanciful Parisian confection. After it replaced **Marché aux Fleurs, Sacs et Mode** in the mid-'80s, La Mascarade introduced elaborate Mardi Gras masks as the store's specialty.

A 1999 makeover made La Mascarade into something of an antique store, supplementing the masks with some vintage and artistic items, including beautiful candles and, later, regal princess hats. In recent years, the glittering shop has become a center for modern pin traders who come to gape at displays of limited-edition pins, lanyards, and accessories. But to remind guests of the history here, "Sacs et Mode" is still painted on the outside of the building.

Leather Shop

MAP: Frontierland, Fr-1
CHRONOLOGY: Ca. 2000–ongoing
HISTORY: A Leather Shop was first listed in the park's 1957 **souvenir book** as one of

the businesses operating in or around the **Davy Crockett Arcade** just inside the **Frontierland** gates. That original Leather Shop was remodeled out of existence years ago, but in recent times another station for leather goods has appeared in roughly the same location.

Operating from a small space along the sidewalk to the right of the **Davy Crockett's Pioneer Mercantile** and to the left of **Bonanza Outfitters**, today's Leather Shop draws a steady flow of pedestrians. Shoppers pause to peruse the custom leather items on display, especially the stylish key chains and bracelets. Belts, luggage tags, and other useful leather items are supplemented by pewter and silver objects, and everything can be personalized right here.

Le Bat en Rouge

MAP: New Orleans Square, NOS-3, NOS-5

CHRONOLOGY: October 2002–ongoing

HISTORY: Le Bat en Rouge is a retail spin-off of the popular Haunted Mansion Holiday that transforms the **Haunted Mansion** with *The Nightmare Before Christmas* theming. In 2001, the first year of that holiday celebration, a cart outside the Haunted Mansion sold *Nightmare* souvenirs, but in 2002 the cart disappeared and the souvenirs

flew over to a scary-looking shop on the left-hand side of Royal Street near the **Royal Street Veranda**. Formerly the **One-of-a-Kind Shop** and then **Le Gourmet** had been in this space.

Le Bat en Rouge, of course, is a playful take on Baton Rouge, the Louisiana city within 100 miles of New Orleans and thus a suitable identity for a space in New Orleans Square. Jack Skellington is the store's star, but there are lots of other creepy Halloween-appropriate books, posters, clothes, figurines, skeletons, and skulls on display. Some of the merchandise on view here used to be in the **Villains Lair** store in **Fantasyland** until that one closed around 2002. In 2006, Le Bat flew to the other end of Royal Street and into the space to the right of the **Blue Bayou** and **Club 33** that was formerly occupied by **La Boutique de Noël**.

Le Chapeau

MAP: New Orleans Square, NOS-9

CHRONOLOGY: 1966–ca. 1974

HISTORY: Disneyland has never wanted for hat shops. Most of them have been dominated by the usual Disney souvenir hats and mouse ears, but not the elegant Le Chapeau in **New Orleans Square.** The women's hats on view here on the corner behind the **French Market** were mostly fine, feathered, frilly creations suitable for Mardi Gras. For men, there were derbies, top hats, boaters, and other handsome styles. Some of the expected Disney hats were on hand, but they weren't as prominent as the expensive merchandise. Around 1975, Le Chapeau became another French-themed store, **Marché aux Fleurs, Sacs et Mode.**

Le Forgeron

MAP: New Orleans Square, NOS-5
CHRONOLOGY: 1966–ca. 1974
HISTORY: Early in the history of **New Orleans Square**, Le Forgeron occupied a spot at the end of Royal Street. Named after the French word for "blacksmith," the shop offered sturdy, old-fashioned metal and leaded-glass objects for the home. Paired with **Le Gourmet** across the street, Le Forgeron made it possible for a guest's home and kitchen to be decorated with authentic-looking styles evoking the French countryside. A shop evoking a glittery French jewelry store, **La Boutique d'Or**, replaced Le Forgeron in the mid-'70s.

Legacy of Walt Disney

MAP: Main Street, MS-20
CHRONOLOGY: January 15, 1970–February 11, 1973
HISTORY: For the first three years of the 1970s, the prominent **Main Street** corner that had formerly been occupied by the **Wurlitzer Music Hall** became a celebration of the life and achievements of **Walt Disney.** The Legacy of Walt Disney offered biographical information about the man Disneyland was named after, and it also showed many of the awards, tributes, and honors Disney had received in his lifetime.

In 1973, the awards and honors were moved to the **Opera House** on **Town Square**, where they became the centerpieces of a new presentation called the **Walt Disney Story.** Back on Main Street, the Legacy corner became **Disneyland Presents a Preview of Coming Attractions**, a showcase for new park ideas. Today, the **Disney Showcase** store is in this high-profile spot.

Le Gourmet, aka Le Gourmet Shop

MAP: New Orleans Square, NOS-5, NOS-3
CHRONOLOGY: 1966–ca. 1998
HISTORY: Le Gourmet, also sometimes referred to as Le Gourmet Shop, filled a large space at the end of Royal Street one stop past the **Blue Bayou.** A small photo in the park's 1968 **souvenir book** showed the Old World interior with studious shop-

---

Major Attractions and Exhibits Added in the 1970s

1970
Legacy of Walt Disney

1972
Country Bear Jamboree

1973
Disneyland Presents a Preview of Coming Attractions; Walt Disney Story

1974
America Sings

1975
Mission to Mars;
Walt Disney Story, Featuring Great Moments with Mr. Lincoln

1977
Space Mountain

1979
Big Thunder Mountain Railroad

---

pers examining "rare culinary items." Ten years later, a small photo in the park's '78 book showed Le Gourmet's exterior, which was dominated by racks of iron pots and wooden casks.

Le Gourmet sold all the fine kitchen tools and stylish accessories a connoisseur could want, everything from copper pots, potholders, and chef hats to wooden utensils, colorful dish towels, and Aunt Sally's Creole Pralines. Many of these items were adorned with Disneyland or New Orleans Square logos.

After about three decades, part of this space ceased to be a mecca for gourmands and instead became a mecca for holiday decorators when **La Boutique de Noël** moved in; **Port d'Orleans** took over the rest of the space with gourmet sauces and coffees. Meanwhile, for a couple more years Le Gourmet lived at the other end of this street, back next to the **Royal Street Veranda** where the **One-of-a-Kind Shop** had been from 1966 until 1996. **Le Bat en Rouge** started haunting this spot around 2002.

Le Petit Chalet

MAP: Fantasyland, Fa-22

CHRONOLOGY: 1997–ongoing

HISTORY: Themed to the adjacent **Matterhorn**, the Swiss-styled Le Petit Chalet gift shop is definitely petite. Actually, it's not much more than several open counters un-

der a well-themed alpine roof. The gifts are small items like Disneyland-themed dolls (including an Abominable Snowman from the mountain next door), pens, hats, T-shirts, autograph books, and the obligatory princess-related merchandise that has swept through **Fantasyland** in the 21st century. Disposable cameras, film and other necessities make this a handy stop before heading off to **It's a Small World.**

Le Petite Patisserie

MAP: New Orleans Square, NOS-8

CHRONOLOGY: 1988–ca. 2004

HISTORY: One of the best hidden jewels of **New Orleans Square** was Le Petite Patisserie, a hard-to-find spot that wasn't always open but was always satisfying. More of a countertop

in an open window than a true dining location, "the little pastry shop" was tucked in behind the Café Orleans and faced the **Jewel of Orléans.**

Le Petite Patisserie was famous for cooking up four different kinds of waffles and serving them on a stick. The waffle variations ranged from the simple Royal (sprinkled with powdered sugar) to the decadent Mascarade (coated in dark and white chocolate). Nonalcoholic daiquiri slushies and well-made cappuccinos made this an indulgent stop for those guests lucky enough to find it, and find it open. In recent years, all trace of the window has been removed and the space along Orleans Street has been given over to tables and potted plants.

Liberty Street

MAP: Town Square, TS-7

CHRONOLOGY: Never built

HISTORY: First announced in 1958 with a sign on **Town Square**, Liberty Street was a coming attraction that would've expressed Walt Disney's unabashed patriotism. Originally, **International Street** had been announced on the sign, but when enthusiasm for that idea cooled, the Liberty Street concept heated up.

According to a large 1958 park map, Liberty Street would've run roughly parallel to **Main Street**. It would've started from the upper-right corner of Town Square, a spot halfway between the **Wurlitzer Music Hall** and the **Opera House** where the **Maxwell House Coffee Shop** operated. From Town Square, Liberty Street would've angled northeast towards the **Edison Square** area that was also never built (an imaginary line extended from Liberty Street would've ended at the back of the circular **20,000 Leagues Under the Sea Exhibit** building in **Tomorrowland**).

The '58 park map showed Liberty Street laid out as a quaint small-town street that doglegged to the right. There were no spinning rides, no little cars or cute boats, just a dignified, historically accurate presentation of what would've really existed in an American colony in the late 1700s. Listed on the map, counterclockwise from the right, were these structures: U.S. Capitol in Miniature, Colonial Shoppes, Hall of Presidents, Declaration of Independence Diorama, Boston Observer Print Shoppe, Paul Revere's Silver Shop, Griffin's Wharf, Glass Shoppe, and Blacksmith. Griffin's Wharf was at the dogleg intersection and appeared to be a small dock where several sailing ships were tied up. What looked like a prominent church steeple stood at the entrance to Liberty Street, and an even more imposing building called Liberty Hall, which fronted the twin auditoriums for the Hall of Presidents and the Declaration of Independence Diorama, towered over the cobblestone-paved cul-de-sac at the back end (supposedly a Liberty Bell would've tolled from the top of Liberty Hall). A color illustration in the 1958, '59, and '60 **souvenir books** (the only souvenir books to mention Liberty Street as a coming attraction) labeled that cul-de-sac as Liberty Square, with a Liberty Tree and Liberty Hall as the two dominant features.

While the full Liberty Street area never blossomed as intended, some of its seeds did disperse elsewhere into the park. The U.S. Capitol model actually exists, and in fact it has been a fixture in the **Walt Disney Story** exhibit in the Opera House since the mid-'70s. The **Audio-Animatronic** technology didn't exist in the late '50s to create the Hall of Presidents, but by the mid-'60s a solitary Abraham Lincoln figure was up and talking, first at the 1964–1965 New York World's Fair and then in Disneyland in the **Great Moments with Mr. Lincoln** exhibit. The Hall of Presidents would later exist in the Liberty Square area of Walt Disney World. The *Disney Insider Yearbook: 2005 Year in Review* and *Disneyland: The Nickel Tour* both showed several concept drawings and gave detailed descriptions of the Liberty Street that was carefully imagined but never built.

Lilliputian Land

MAP: Fantasyland, Fa-22

CHRONOLOGY: Never built

HISTORY: Before there were any plans for a **Canal Boats of the World** cruise past tiny buildings in **Fantasyland**, **Walt Disney** wanted to build an entire land devoted to miniatures. Named after Lilliput, the tiny kingdom in *Gulliver's Travels*, Lilliputian Land appeared on a park map drawn by **Marvin Davis** in September of 1953, some 22 months before Disneyland opened. Davis's rendering of what the park might look like showed Lilliputian Land as a two-and-a-half-acre rounded triangle sandwiched in between Fantasyland and **Tomorrowland**. The area had its own entrance from the **Plaza Hub**, a curling track for a small railroad, a winding river for canal boats, and plenty of small hills and trees.

Later that month, **Roy Disney** took a similar drawing executed by **Herb**

Ryman, plus some descriptive text, to New York to pitch the Disneyland concept to potential investors. Ryman's map also showed a Lilliputian Land with a train and canal boats to the right of Fantasyland; the descriptive text included a line that said Lilliputian Land would have "an Erie Canal barge ride through the famous canals of the world, passing miniature towns with nine-inch people."

Unfortunately, once Walt Disney decided to enlarge those nine-inch people and hopefully make them move electronically, he realized the **Audio-Animatronic** technology he needed was still years away, so the Lilliputian Land idea was scrubbed. Instead, a smaller, less ambitious attraction, the Canal Boats of the World, debuted inside Fantasyland on **Opening Day**. Within five years, the **Matterhorn** would rise, the **Submarine Voyage** would navigate, and the **Fantasyland Autopia** would drive upon some of the acreage at one time reserved for Lilliputian Land.

Jack Lindquist

CHRONOLOGY: March 15, 1927–ongoing

HISTORY: According to the tribute listed on one of the **Main Street windows**, Jack Lindquist is the park's "Honorary Mayor." But according to the book *Remembering Walt*, Walt Disney had another name for him: "Looks like a Bob to me," said Disney when explaining why he always called Jack Lindquist Bob.

Before he worked at Disneyland as either Jack, Bob, or the Mayor, Lindquist was a child actor. Born in Chicago in the roaring '20s, Lindquist's family headed west, and young Jack landed roles in several of the *Our Gang* comedies of the early '30s. Two decades later, he was serving in the Air Force and then attending USC.

Lindquist started at Disneyland in 1955 as the park's advertising manager, later heading the marketing department and eventually serving as the park's president. As a top executive, he championed some of Disneyland's signature promotions, concepts, and expansions, among them the E-ticket **ticket books**, **Disney Dollars**, **Grad Nite**, the college bowl game known as the Disneyland Pigskin Classic, the **Gift-Giver Extraordinaire Machine** for the park's 30th anniversary, **Mickey's Toontown**, and Disney's California Adventure. During his decades at Disneyland, virtually every corner of the park was improved or promoted by one of his ideas or decisions. As testament to Lindquist's significance, Charles Ridgway's book *Spinning Disney's World* identifies him as one of the passengers in the very first boat to take the new **It's a Small World** cruise in 1966.

In the '70s and '80s, Lindquist was a key contributor to the marketing and promotional plans for Walt Disney World, Tokyo Disneyland, and Disneyland Paris. A year after he retired in 1993, Jack Lindquist was named a Disney Legend. A tribute to Lindquist in the form of a grinning pumpkin still sits outside **Goofy's Bounce House** in Mickey's Toontown.

Little Green Men Store Command

MAP: Tomorrowland, T-6

CHRONOLOGY: March 2005–ongoing

HISTORY: Aliens have arrived, and they've set up their own store in the heart of **Tomorrowland**. The Little Green Men live next to the exit of the **Buzz Lightyear Astro Blasters** attraction, an appropriate home for a store with a *Toy Story* theme. During the park's golden anniversary, a large photo collage of Buzz hung outside the shop. The store's name, of course, is a takeoff on Buzz's Star Command.

Formerly, the **Premiere Shop** had filled this space, and like its predecessor Little Green Men Store Command still exhibits spaceships from Tomorrowland's extinct Rocket Jets attraction (formerly black and white, the two on display are colorfully re-painted and used as display cases). Light fixtures look like Saturn, and wall murals show legions of smiling three-eyed aliens. The draw for galactic pin traders is the large pin selection, including all the attendant lanyards, cases, and other accessories. Buzz Lightyear fans will also find plenty of toys, figures, and clothes to remind them of their out-of-this-world hero and the movie that introduced him.

Little Red Wagon

MAP: Plaza Hub, PH-5

CHRONOLOGY: Ca. 1995–ongoing

HISTORY: This movable snack stand isn't the kind of wagon that is towed around by a horse or a child—it's a drivable food wagon more like an old-fashioned catering truck. Usually it's parked in the southeast corner of the **Plaza Hub** near the Plaza Inn, a location that has some historical wagon-related signifi-cance. Originally, the adjacent Plaza Inn was called the **Red Wagon Inn**, sponsored by Swift, the meat-packing company with a logo that incorporated a red wagon.

Today the Little Red Wagon serves a menu about as simple as that found on another wagon in the park, the **Westward Ho Conestoga Wagon Fries** over in **Frontierland**. Here in the hub, Little Red's menu has hand-dipped corn dogs, chips, sodas, and other quick impulse items for guests heading off to nearby **Tomorrowland**.

Locker Area, aka Main Street Lockers & Storage

MAP: Main Street, MS-1; Park, P-3; Main Street, MS-16

CHRONOLOGY: July 17, 1955–ongoing

HISTORY: A locker area has been available in the park since **Opening Day**, but it's

changed locations and names several times. The first location was a small building on **Town Square** to the right of (but not attached to) the **Fire Department** and to the immediate left of the **Emporium**. This original locker area was labeled the Bekins Van & Storage Locker Area and the Bekins Locker Service in the park's early **souvenir books**. In May of 1963, another moving company moved in and the site became known in the souvenir books as the Global Van Lines Locker Area and the Global Locker Service (even though the signs on the building read Lost & Found and Parcels). This lasted until 1979, to be followed on June 1, 1980, by the National Car Rental Locker Area for the rest of the '80s, ending January 2, 1990.

At some point during these decades a second locker area for suitcases and large items was built outside the park near a picnic area about 150 feet to the left of the **entrance** and the west tunnel; formerly a small bus terminal sat on the spot. Then, when the Emporium was remodeled and expanded to include the **Carriage Place Clothing Co.**, the Town Square locker area closed and reopened adjacent to the **Lost and Found** at the end of East Center Street, the short road that bisects **Main Street** just after the **Market House**.

The formal name of this locker area is now Main Street Lockers & Storage, with a big gold key planted in a lock above the door and displays of antique luggage mounted on the shelves inside. There's something unexpected outside—the upstairs rooms near the locker area belong to a dentist, according to the signage on the window, and the realistic sounds of a dental office can be heard from the street.

Lockers have always been available on a first-come, first-served basis, with nominal daily fees for different size lockers (small lockers were $7 in 2007). Today's Main Street Lockers room offers four islands lined with lockers, plus walls of more lockers, for a total of 2,759 lockers (according to the math, which lists the first locker as #1100 and the last one as #3859). Phones, phone card machines, and postcard machines are also available. For guests who need lockers when they're already deep inside Disneyland, yet another locker area appeared in the 1990s, this one near the **Fantasyland Theater** at the back of **Fantasyland**.

L'Ornement Magique

MAP: New Orleans Square, NOS-5

CHRONOLOGY: October 10, 1998–ongoing

HISTORY: Open since 1998, L'Ornement Magique helps fill the old **Le Gourmet** location where Royal Street and Orleans Street touch at the back of **New Orleans Square**. For most of its existence, the shop next door was **La Boutique de Noël**, which like L'Ornement Magique sold holiday decorations all year long.

L'Ornement specializes in the elaborate handcrafted ornaments created by New York-based artist Christopher Radko. Radko is famous for his delicate glasswork—the *New York Times* dubbed him the "Czar of Christmas Present." At Disneyland, much of his work is themed to Disney characters, and many of the ornaments on view have been created exclusively for the park. Budget-minded tree-trimmers will find that prices tend to drop in the off-season.

Lost and Found

MAP: Town Square, TS-9; Main Street, MS-16, MS-1; Park, P-2

CHRONOLOGY: July 17, 1955–ongoing

HISTORY: Lost and Found just might be the most peripatetic office in Disneyland. Over the decades, at least five locations have been used for this important function.

The park's 1956 **souvenir book** listed Lost and Found as "Above **Opera House**, **Town Square**," a direction that pointed to a conspicuous building but an unclear final destination. The '57 book instructed guests looking for Lost and Found to "Inquire Security Office" but didn't identify where that office was (the **Police Station** in Town Square would've been a guest's best guess, but large park

maps showed the **Security Office** and Lost and Found just off **Main Street** on East Center Street, around the corner from the **Market House**). For the next decade there was not a single mention of the Lost and Found in the souvenir books.

In reality, in the early '60s Lost and Found, as announced by a sign on the building, had been relocated to the **locker area** in the northwest corner of Town Square, with Global Van Lines as the sponsor. The park's 1968 souvenir book finally acknowledged this location as Lost and Found, but subsequent souvenir books gave no mention of it. Sometime in the '90s, Lost and Found was relocated once again, this time back to East Center Street, where it was shown on the small, free maps that are handed out to guests as they enter the park. The park's official Web site now lists Lost and Found as being located outside Disneyland in the plaza area closer to Disney's California Adventure.

No matter where it's been located, the office has stayed busy. Something like 400 items a day are turned in to Lost and Found, everything from umbrellas, sunglasses, and wallets to medication, expensive jewelry, iPods, and cell phones (on average, a phone is turned in every 20 minutes). In addition to matching up lost items with owners, the office matches them up with finders, too—guests who find an item can bring it to Lost and Found, fill out a form, and claim the item if it isn't picked up within two months.

Love Bug Day

MAP: Park, P-2, P-8, P-9, P-10, P-16

CHRONOLOGY: March 23, 1969; June 30, 1974

HISTORY: DVDs of Disney's *The Love Bug* include brief snippets of film showing an unusual day in Disneyland history. Love Bug Day was first held on March 23, 1969, to celebrate the box-office triumph of *The Love Bug*, which had debuted late in '68 but gone into wide release in March of '69. The event had two main parts. The first, held out in the **parking lot**, involved a contest whereby guests decorated their own VW Beetles in order to win a new one. Some of these vehicles were so heavily laden with giant ears, noses, legs, eyes, signs, and multicolored paint that they looked more like weird alien creatures or psychedelic hallucinations than popular cars.

The second part of Love Bug Day was a **parade** with the **Disneyland Band** and all the wildly disguised Beetles. Since the cars had been out in the parking lot, this parade began in **Town Square**, cruised northward up **Main Street**, and ended deep inside **Fantasyland** (thus it traveled in the opposite direction of most Disneyland parades). In front of the **It's a Small World** building, the movie's star, Dean Jones, presented the winning Beetle decorator with the keys to a new car. This wasn't the first time cars had overrun Main Street, by the way—in 1956 the Antique Automobile Parade (aka the Old Fashioned Automobile Parade) had sent a line of old Model T's chugging from the **Plaza Hub** to Town Square.

Five years later, with *Herbie Rides Again* in theaters as of June 4th, Disneyland held a second Love Bug Day on June 30, 1974, again with a contest and a parade. Two weeks later, this one turned up on a TV special called "Herbie Day at Disneyland," featuring lots of Volkswagens and one of the film's stars, Helen Hayes. While there were no more Love Bug Days, there were four more *Love Bug* movies, plus a 1982 TV series.

Lunching Pad

MAP: Tomorrowland, T-8

CHRONOLOGY: 1977–1998

HISTORY: Starting around 1977, a small snack bar with a Space Age theme settled in beneath the main second-story loading area for the **PeopleMover**. Though it wasn't always open, the Lunching Pad was usually a handy hot dog/popcorn/soda spot for guests on the go. Previously a small snack stand called the **Space Bar** had been here (a larger Space Bar had existed elsewhere from '55 to '66, and a downsized Space Bar had existed in this site at the base of the PeopleMover since '67). The Lunching Pad lasted about two decades, but with the extensive remodel of **Tomorrowland** in 1998, it blasted off for good, to be replaced by the broadcast station for **Radio Disney**.

Mad Hatter of Fantasyland

MAP: Fantasyland, Fa-27

CHRONOLOGY: 1956–ongoing

HISTORY: Three separate Disneyland areas—**Fantasyland**, **Main Street**, and **Tomorrowland**—have had Mad Hatter hat shops. Though they didn't all start at the same time, the shops all operated simultaneously from the late 1950s into the 21st century.

The first Mad Hatter to open was the one in Fantasyland in 1956. The shop, identified simply as Mad Hatter in the 1957 **souvenir book** with no descriptive text, was tucked into a corner of the building that held **Mr. Toad's Wild Ride**. This location put the Mad Hatter within about 75 feet of its namesake attraction, the **Mad Hatter's Mad Tea Party**, which had been twirling away since **Opening Day** out in the **Sleeping Beauty Castle** courtyard to the west. In 1958, another related attraction, **Alice in Wonderland**, opened about 75 feet to the east of the Mad Hatter's spot, giving this section of Fantasyland three Alice-related establishments within easy walking distance, but not quite in sight of each other.

Visual proximity would come in 1983, when the three establishments were pulled together to make a little "Aliceland" area. The Mad Hatter's Mad Tea Party was moved over to the walkway next to Alice in Wonderland, and the Mad Hatter hat shop was swung around from the castle courtyard to a wraparound garden and cottage next to Alice, making this an all-Alice corner. Underscoring the connection is one of the Tea Party teacups in the hat store's front garden.

Hats, of course, are the Mad Hatter's specialty, everything from adorable princess hats and baseball caps to the famous Mickey and Minnie ears that can be embroidered with names. And yes, they have the signature Mad Hatter hat with the "10/6" shillings/pence price on the outside. The interior's second story displays lots of antique hats, and the sales counter displays a pretty nifty trick—periodically the mirror on the wall reveals a grinning Cheshire Cat.

Mad Hatter of Main Street

MAP: Main Street, MS-11; Town Square, TS-8

CHRONOLOGY: June 1958–ongoing

HISTORY: A Mad Hatter hat shop has existed on **Main Street** since 1958, but not always in the same location. The first Mad Hatter, which opened two years after the **Mad Hatter of Fantasyland**, was at the far north end of Main Street by the **Plaza Hub**. Also sometimes called Mad Hatter Hats, the shop was around the bend from Coke's **Refreshment Corner** on the little side street called West Plaza Street. This shop offered the classic Disney-themed hats—the pirate hats, Donald Duck hats, and mouse ears—that are still sold around the park.

In the fall of 1963, a remodel of this Main Street building meant the hat shop had to go, and go it did, to a more prominent location along the row where the **Opera House** stands on **Town Square**. It's still there today, presenting guests with their first chance inside the park to try on some zany headwear, such as a Goofy-eared hat or a crazy jester's hat with bells.

𝔐ad 𝔥atter of 𝔗omorrowland, aka 𝔐od 𝔥atter, aka 𝔥atmosphere

MAP: Tomorrowland, T-22, T-13

CHRONOLOGY: 1958–December 2006

HISTORY: A 1958 park map suggested that the Mad Hatter hat shop in **Tomorrowland** was situated in, or just outside of, the exhibit building that held the **Bathroom of Tomorrow** and the **American Dairy Association Exhibit**. This was the third Mad Hatter in Disneyland, following the original in **Fantasyland** and the second one on **Main Street** (chronologies aren't entirely clear, so it's possible the Tomorrowland location opened *before* the Main Street shop).

When Tomorrowland underwent its extensive remodeling in 1966–1967, the Mad Hatter emerged in a showy new place with a hip new name. The new freestanding building was next to the massive **Carousel of Progress** structure back by the **Tomorrowland Autopia**, and the new name was, appropriately enough for the psychedelic '60s, the Mod Hatter. As cool as it sounded, the merchandise wasn't much different from that found in the other two Mad Hatter locations, basically offering all the Disney-themed headwear anyone could want.

Sometime in the '80s, possibly coinciding with the arrival of **Star Tours** in 1987, the name went less mod and more spacey as the revised Hatmosphere. Mickey's sorcerer hats, whimsical sun hats, and of course the ubiquitous mouse ears were among the many hats 'n' caps still on view until 2006. That year the **Autopia Winner's Circle** relocated from across the walkway into this space so that the previous Winner's Circle area could be used as the queue for 2007's updated **Submarine Voyage**. While a few hats are still available among the car-related items, the move brought to a close almost 50 years of Tomorrowland hat history.

𝔐ad 𝔥atter's 𝔐ad 𝔗ea 𝔓arty

MAP: Fantasyland, Fa-6, Fa-25

CHRONOLOGY: July 17, 1955–ongoing

HISTORY: One of the original **Fantasyland** attractions that debuted on **Opening Day**, the Mad Hatter's Mad Tea Party has undergone very few changes since 1955. In fact, even before the park opened, the early Mad Tea Party concept drawings showed basically what guests see now, a whirl of teacups themed to Disney's 1951 *Alice in Wonderland* movie. The most conspicuous stylistic differences between what was drawn and what was built concerned the track layout and the attraction's centerpiece. According to one early illustration, 20 teacups circled a central hub like they were on a racetrack with banked curves, and that hub displayed the movie's eccentric tea party.

When it opened, the Mad Tea Party and its colorful teacups were positioned in the **Sleeping Beauty Castle** courtyard to the west of **Mr. Toad's Wild Ride**, a location now occupied by the **King Arthur Carrousel**. Originally, the main platter upon which the cups spun was gray; later that platter was painted with a psychedelic red-and-orange spiral. Guests instantly took to the crazy cups, liking the price (initially only a B ticket) and the control wheel in the center that enabled riders to spin the cups faster or slower, clockwise or counterclockwise. So frantic is the spinning, guests probably don't even realize that the Mad Tea Party, at only 90 seconds long, is one of the shortest rides in the park.

Promoting the Mad Tea Party has always been pretty easy for Disneyland publicists—the attraction is easy to understand and basically sells itself. An early **attraction poster** showed Mickey and Minnie in a teacup, plus the Alice characters in cups of their own, with a helpful tagline informing guests they could "spin into the fun-filled world of Wonderland at the Mad Tea Party." The park's early **souvenir books** showed off the teacups with large colorful photos of twirling people who always seemed to be laughing. Interestingly, the souvenir books didn't know what to call the attraction, listing it as the Mad Tea Party, the Mad Hatter's Tea Party, the Mad Hatter Tea Party Ride, and the Mad Hatter Tea Cup Ride.

The books sure knew how to describe it, though, using text like "a merry whirl in spinning cups, twirling saucers" and "whirl and spin at a dizzy pace." One of the legends that's grown over the years is that the "dizzy pace" is dizzier in some cups than it is in others; guests are constantly testing out the spin rates of the different cups to determine which color is the fastest (of today's 18 cups, purple and orange seem to get the most votes). Something that isn't a legend is the frequency with which guests stumble out and get sick after a vertiginous reel—the park's Web site cautions riders that it's "best to eat after you spin" and "guests who are prone to motion sickness should not ride." Also, guests should note that the Mad Tea Party shuts down in the rain so they won't slip on a wet surface as they stagger away from their cups.

In early 1982, Disney designers shut down the Mad Tea Party for over a year so it could be relocated, appropriately enough, about 150 feet to the east to a spot near the **Alice in Wonderland** attraction. The King Arthur Carrousel, which had already been in the castle courtyard, moved north to fill the Mad Tea Party's former location, and the Mad Tea Party filled what had been an empty walkway. New party lights were strung above the cups, and the "Very Merry Un-Birthday" song from the movie was pumped up to enhance the theme.

One thing the attraction doesn't have is something that exists at other Disney parks—a teapot at the center of the whirling platform. Most guests, though, don't notice or care. While it may seem like a stomach-churning attraction of perplexing appeal to some older guests, younger ones who attend the Mad Tea Party still find the same thrills that has kept this particular party going for over five decades.

Magic Eye Theater

MAP: Tomorrowland, T-19

CHRONOLOGY: May 1986–ongoing

HISTORY: The big outdoor site that had hosted the **Flying Saucers**, the **Tomorrowland Stage**, and the Space Stage finally went indoors in 1986 when the 575-seat Magic Eye Theater opened. This new building, located to the right of **Space Mountain**, was one of the first major Disneyland projects completed under the Michael Eisner regime that began in 1984.

**Major Attractions
and Exhibits
Added in the 1980s**

1983
Pinocchio's Daring Journey

1985
Magic Eye Theater; Videopolis

1986
Big Thunder Ranch; *Captain EO*

1987
Disney Gallery; Star Tours

1989
Splash Mountain

While most guests could name the biggest attractions that have played inside the Magic Eye, few could name the initial offering. *Magic Journeys* was a Kodak-sponsored 3-D movie that had been imported from Walt Disney World in 1984 for a two-year run, first on the Space Stage and then for four months at the Magic Eye. Billed as "a 3-D Film Fantasy" on the **attraction poster**, the 16-minute film enabled guests, especially children, to "soar on the wings of imagination."

But at the Magic Eye, *Magic Journeys* was really just a placeholder until the star attraction was ready for his 3-D close-up. *Captain EO*, another Florida import, debuted in September of '86 with a whirlwind of publicity and excitement, thanks to the superstar talent involved—singer Michael Jackson, producer George Lucas, and director Francis Ford Coppola. A decade later, with audiences dwindling, *EO* had to flee-o and another popular film, ***Honey, I Shrunk the Audience***, jetted in from Orlando. While the Magic Eye Theater itself hasn't gotten much play in the park's **souvenir books**, the theater's shows sure have—*EO* and *Honey* routinely received a full page of text and photos that spotlighted the cast and the effects while barely mentioning the building they were shown in.

The Magic of Disneyland

CHRONOLOGY: October 1969 (initial release)

HISTORY: Released in the fall of 1969, this 16-mm color documentary gave an overview of Disneyland history and then focused on recent developments at the park, including the **PeopleMover, Pirates of the Caribbean**, and especially the **Haunted Mansion**, which had just opened that summer. The film's music was created by **Richard and Robert Sherman**. Footage from the film—a few aerial shots and a look inside the Haunted Mansion—is included among the special features on *The Love Bug* DVD.

Magnolia Park

MAP: Adventureland, A-4

CHRONOLOGY: July 17, 1955–1962

HISTORY: In Disneyland's early years, a small, serene rest area known as Magnolia Park existed on the far western edge of **Adventureland**. Guests strolling through Magnolia Park had the **Rivers of America** to the north and the **Jungle Cruise** to the south, with the **Indian Village** ahead to the northwest. Strolling was the operative verb here, supplemented with sitting, as trees, benches, and quiet paths were, initially, all that Magnolia Park offered.

The closest thing to a permanent attraction Magnolia Park ever had was the decorative little **bandstand** that landed here in 1956 after it had been removed from the perimeter of the **Plaza Hub**. In 1958, a series of special outdoor shows was performed in Magnolia Park; these were promotions for Disney's popular *Zorro* TV show and starred some of the actual TV stars.

Four years later, Magnolia Park disappeared as redevelopments supplanted this valuable real estate. First, a Jungle Cruise expansion pushed a new elephants' bathing pool into what had been the southern part of Magnolia Park. By the end of '62, the new **Swiss Family Treehouse** was dominating this southern section. Next came **New Orleans Square**, which in '63 overwhelmed the area westward with major excavations and construction.

In what might be seen as a tribute to the long-lost little park area, the restaurant at the western tip of the Adventureland buildings, **Aunt Jemima's Pancake House** (aka Aunt Jemima's Kitchen), changed its name to **Magnolia Tree Terrace** in 1970.

Magnolia Tree Terrace

MAP: Frontierland, Fr-7

CHRONOLOGY: 1970–1971

HISTORY: As the '60s turned into the '70s, one prominent **Frontierland** restaurant underwent a quick succession of name changes. Quaker Oats sponsored **Aunt Jemima's Pancake House**/Aunt Jemima's Kitchen in the '50s and '60s, and Oscar Meyer began sponsoring the same restaurant with the new name **River Belle Terrace** in 1971. But for a year in between these two eras, the building was the unsponsored, upscale Magnolia Tree Terrace.

The pretty name was a reference to **Magnolia Park**, which is what the area off the tip of Frontierland and **Adventureland** had been called before **New Orleans Square** came along in 1966. The restaurant's location has always been conspicuous and attractive, situated as it is on the corner where Frontierland turns towards Adventureland, with the **Rivers of America** only about 75 feet away.

𝕸ain 𝕾treet

MAP: Park, P-9

CHRONOLOGY: July 17, 1955–ongoing

HISTORY: The term "Main Street" is often used as an all-inclusive heading for three identifiable areas in the southern half of Disneyland. In fact, many people automatically assume that Main Street is everything from the park's **entrance** tunnels up to the **Sleeping Beauty Castle** drawbridge about 1,000 feet to the north. Certainly the park's **souvenir books** have supported this notion that **Town Square** and the **Plaza Hub** are on Main Street, as their photos and descriptions have always been gathered together under a single Main Street heading. However, to throw a fuller spotlight on each separate area, we've defined Main Street as only the two-block-long business district *between* the rectangular Town Square and the circular Plaza Hub. This smaller, more manageable Main Street begins at the **Emporium** and ends at the **Refreshment Corner** 350 feet away.

Within this concentrated Main Street area are two distinct intersecting streets. Iconic Main Street, about 32 feet from curb to curb and lined with candy-colored buildings, is divided in half by narrow Center Street. Center itself is bifurcated into West Center (separating the old **Upjohn Pharmacy** from the **Carnation Ice Cream Parlor/Blue Ribbon Bakery**) and East Center (separating the **Market House** from **Gibson Greeting Cards/Disney Clothiers, Ltd.**). In addition to Main and Center, a third street, Plaza, runs from west to east across the north end of Main. Plaza Street divides the Main Street district from the Plaza Hub and is within the latter's domain.

The two blocks of Main Street constitute the most densely developed acreage in the park. With no large attractions or plazas filling up space, there are far more doorways and businesses here than anywhere else. And, visually at least, this is also the least changed area of the park. Dozens of businesses have opened and closed, or opened and relocated, on Main Street over the decades, yet the exterior architecture remains basically what it's been since **Opening Day**. The same can't be said of **Adventureland**, **Frontierland**, **Fantasyland**, and **Tomorrowland**, all of which have undergone massive remodelings and expansions.

Even in the first stages of planning his park, **Walt Disney** knew that he wanted to create a long entranceway that funneled guests through a charming re-creation of a turn-of-the-century small American town. This strategy, he felt, would help orient guests and ease them into the stranger, more chimerical lands that waited ahead. If the guests themselves didn't live in a small town, thought Disney, surely their relatives did, or their ancestors had, or they'd seen one in popular movies or '50s family-oriented TV shows. Thus they'd be comforted to walk into one at Disneyland. Theoretically, the same small-town sweetness that had made Andy Hardy one of the most durable film characters of the '40s would work in Anaheim in the '50s and beyond.

And so the early concept drawings for the park always showed something called Main Street. But just what that Main Street looked like varied considerably. For one thing, two additional major streets were almost built in the Main Street area. **International Street** and **Liberty Street** both would've branched off from Main Street, but designers abandoned both ideas by the early '60s. Also, some early designs called for full-size buildings along Main Street, while others placed residential homes at the northern end. The famous **Herb Ryman** drawing of the 45-acre park as Walt Disney envisioned it in 1953 showed what looked like an enormous high-steepled church along Main Street, and the **Marvin Davis** sketch from that same year put open-air courtyards inside some of the Main Street buildings. One 1956 concept drawing put a "Disneyland Dog Pound" on Main Street, something that would've been a comical photo opportunity styled like the dog-catcher's cart in *Lady and the Tramp*.

Unlike other lands in the park that derive from Disney movies and TV shows—think of how *Davy Crockett* shaped Frontierland and all the animated classics spread across Fantasyland—Main Street ultimately sprung from Walt Disney's own life. In the end, what he built was a charming evocation of the Midwest town where he grew up, Marceline, Missouri. The Disneyland version, however, is more generic. It's not Main Street, Marceline, it's Main Street, U.S.A., a place that everybody, not just Missourians, can identify with. "Here is the America of 1890–1910," read the introductory text in the park's early souvenir books. Not "Here is the Marceline of 1890–1910."

In its five decades of history, Main Street has had in its blocks most of the features that would've been found in any small town's commercial center in the years bracketing the fin de siècle—an apothecary, a tobacconist, a movie theater, a **Penny Arcade**, candy stores, bakeries, a **Flower Mart**, an **Emporium**, jewelers, horse-drawn surreys, horseless carriages, etc. But Disney didn't merely re-create what he remembered—he improved upon it. At its best, everything sparkles, runs perfectly, stays fresh. In fact, so idealized, polite, and beautiful is Disneyland's Main Street, it's more like a gentle Disney movie of what a turn-of-the-century town would have been like had all the defects and blemishes of the real world been expunged. Indeed, like a detailed movie set, the impeccable façades suggest individual buildings and storefronts, but in reality the interiors of the buildings are all connected and open to each other, making it possible to walk north to south hundreds of feet from one shop to the next and the next without venturing outside.

On Main Street, the buildings feel safer and cozier than real buildings because the architects designed them that way. The original Disneyland Imagineers, remember, were art directors borrowed from the Disney Studios, so they employed visual tricks from the movies as they planned out the park, including Main Street. Just as the **Santa Fe & Disneyland Railroad** was built at 5/8 the size of a real train, and just as Sleeping Beauty Castle has larger blocks at the bottom than at the top to give the illusion of towering height, so too do the multistory buildings on Main Street play with perspective. All along the street the ground floors were constructed at approximately 90% of full size to make doorways slightly less intimidating and shops a little more inviting to anxious guests. Next, the second floors were all constructed at about 90% the size of the ground floors, making them about 80% of full size. While none of these second stories can be entered by guests, the illusion is visible from the street. Finally, third floors were built at about 80% the size of the second floors, making them about 60% full-size and giving the whole Main Street area a snug, comfortable atmosphere. A small town? Indeed, in more ways than one.

Adding to the warm feeling along Main Street is the bright paint on the buildings, none of which have just one color, all of which are frequently retouched to keep everything looking rejuvenated. In addition, wonderful old-fashioned architectural elements are everywhere—no matter where guests look they'll see beautifully adorned upper-story windows, decorative mansard roofs, striped awnings, turned finials, and ornate iron railings, all of it put there after designers studied thousands of old books, photos, and historic sites to get the details just right.

Main Street is a place for sights, and smells, and sensations. There are rounded trees, but not so big they block the view. There are century-old gas lamps purchased from St. Louis and Baltimore, and new **Main Street vehicles** made to look like vintage buggies and trolleys. There are old-time musicians, fragrant scents, and, happily, the joyous rewards of slow, unhurried exploration (no whirling rides or fast-moving cars here). Studious guests can take their time trying to decipher the proprietors identified on the upper-story **Main Street windows**, or they can linger over the Emporium's wonderful window displays. And at night, the white trim lights that have been outlining all the buildings since 1956 create an atmosphere that is pure delight. Walt Disney declared that his favorite time of day at Disneyland was dusk, when the skies were darkening and the lights were all coming up; anyone seeing Main Street by twilight would find it hard to disagree with him.

As if all that weren't enough, Main Street is filled several times a day with buoyant **parades**. In addition, special events occasionally fill Main Street with unique fun. From 1957 until 1964, for example, Main Street hosted the California State Pancake Races. This friendly competition was an inexpensive entertainment that supported Quaker Oats, sponsor of **Aunt Jemima's Pancake House** in Frontierland. For the pancake race, two dozen housewives sprinted from the Plaza Hub to Town Square while flipping pancakes over raised ribbons that draped the street. The winner won $100, a plaque, and a gift basket. So popular were these races, celebrity judges, marching bands, and Disney characters eventually joined the festivities. Later special events have included ice skating on a synthetic Main Street pond for a 1974 TV audience and a 2002 swimming demonstration by Olympic athletes in a full-length Main Street pool.

While some of these activities probably sound corny to today's iPod-listening, cell-phone-dialing crowds, it's typical of the old-fashioned fun that has distinguished this old-fashioned area. Main Street may be just a nostalgic fantasy, but for many guests it's the best one in Disneyland

Main Street Cinema

MAP: Main Street, MS-19

CHRONOLOGY: July 17, 1955–ongoing

HISTORY: Since **Opening Day**, the Main Street Cinema has presented short films in a stylish brick building in the middle of the first right-hand block of **Main Street**. In the '50s, the movie house had **Fine Tobacco** to the south and the **Jewelry Shop** to the north. Also to the north is a locked doorway that's supposedly the home of the Disneyland Casting Agency, where "It takes People to Make the Dream a Reality" and Walter Elias Disney has been "Founder & Director Emeritus . . . since 1955."

The Main Street Cinema's Programs

Six Silent Films

A Dash Through the Clouds (a 1912 Mack Sennett drama about biplanes)
Dealing for Daisy (a 1915 William S. Hart Western)
Fatima's Dance (year uncertain, a risqué belly dance sequence by Fatima)
Gertie the Dinosaur (Winsor McCay's 1914 cartoon, one of the first ever made)
The Noise of Bombs (a 1914 Keystone Kops comedy)
Shifting Sands (a 1918 Gloria Swanson melodrama)

Six Disney Cartoons

The Dognapper (1934)
Mickey's Polo Team (1936)
The Moose Hunt (1931)
Plane Crazy (1928)
Steamboat Willie (1928)
Traffic Troubles (1931)

A prominent marquee out front still announces the movie building and its shows. Those movies and cartoons are shown on six small screens inside one wood-paneled room, with an oval riser in the center helping kids to get a clear view. Like another movie theater that used to exist in the park, the **Circarama** in **Tomorrowland**, the Main Street Cinema doesn't have seats, only railings that standing guests can lean upon. Back when Disneyland used ticket books, admission to the Main Street Cinema initially cost only an A ticket (the price rose to a B in 1960).

For the first three decades the program offered black-and-white silent movies, each lasting only 10 or 15 minutes, each dating to the earliest years of film history. Old newsreels added authenticity to the proceedings. Sometime in the '80s the selection changed to a collection of early Disney animation, including *Steamboat Willie*, the 1928 cartoon that made Mickey Mouse a star.

Main Street Cone Shop

MAP: Main Street, MS-16

CHRONOLOGY: Ca. 2000–ongoing

HISTORY: Halfway down **Main Street**, in the little side street called East Center where the **locker area** is found, hides this little Dreyer's-sponsored delight. The Main Street Cone Shop isn't always open, but when it is (usually on the hottest, busiest afternoons) it serves up cold, tempting summertime treats. The ice cream bars here are shaped liked Mickey, the sundaes come with an assortment of toppings, and the root beer floats are served in souvenir cups. Umbrellas offer shade for the outdoor seating. The upstairs offices of E.S. Bitz, D.D.S., offer the humorous sounds of the "painless dentist."

Main Street Electrical Parade

MAP: Park, P-16, P-10, P-9, P-8

CHRONOLOGY: June 17, 1972–November 25, 1996

HISTORY: It's hard to describe the Main Street Electrical Parade to anyone who never saw it. Yes, it did have floats, but with no marching bands or synchronized performers it was far from a traditional **parade**. The recorded narration enthusiastically described it as a "spectacular festival pageant of nighttime magic and imagination in thousands of sparkling lights and electro-syntho-magnetic musical sounds." Close, but in truth, still not enough.

The Electrical Parade was the brainchild of **Robert Jani**, for years Disneyland's director of entertainment. Jani produced many of the parades and special events that are now treasured memories for millions of guests, but the Electrical Parade was his signature creation. His inspiration was a display that had helped inaugurate Walt Disney World in 1971. That display was a series of electrified scenes towed across a lake. For Disneyland, Jani put elaborate 3-D scenes on unseen motorized carts, outlined everything with a half-million lights, and had hidden **cast members** drive the glittering vehicles down a darkened **Main Street** towards **Town Square**.

Another Disney Legend, **Bill Justice**, designed many of the mechanical floats in the parade. These included a train, scenes from Disney classics like *Alice in Wonderland*, *Cinderella*, *Dumbo*, *Pinocchio*, and *Snow White and the Seven Dwarfs*, plus the spectacular title character from the more recent *Pete's Dragon* and a rousing patriotic finale. The memorable electronic music that played through the loudspeakers was a non-Disney composition from 1967 called "Baroque Hoedown," supplemented with snippets of other songs, all of it played on the futuristic Moog synthesizer.

While the Main Street Electrical Parade began on the park's 27th birthday and ended two dozen years later, its career was twice interrupted. In 1975 and '76, a special America on Parade celebration commemorated the Bicentennial, and in '83 and '84, the Flights of Fantasy parade took over Main Street to coincide with the Summer Olympics. Over the Electrical Parade's 24-year run, several of the floats were retired, among them the ones for **It's a Small World**, the movie *Return to Oz*, and the birthday cake for Mickey's 60th in 1988.

When Disneyland officials announced that the last performance of the Main Street Electrical Parade would come in mid-October of 1996, fan response was so strong, the surge in attendance so great, that the parade got extended to Thanksgiving. Even then the Main Street Electrical Parade lingered on—for the next few months some of the bulbs from the floats were sold off to benefit charity. Replacing the Electrical Parade the following spring was Light Magic, a hugely promoted but ultimately disappointing four-month "streetacular" that had enormous stages, 4,500 miles of fiber optics, confetti cannons, and over 100 performers who interacted with guests. In 2001, a modified version of the Main Street Electrical Parade did reappear in Anaheim, but not at Disneyland (hence the name change). Disney's Electrical Parade cruised past Paradise Bay over at Disney's California Adventure to help spark attendance at the new park.

Main Street Fruit Cart

MAP: Main Street, MS-17

CHRONOLOGY: Ca. 2000–ongoing

HISTORY: Parked in the intersection of **Main Street** and East Center Street, a busy spot right between the **Market House** and **Disney Clothiers, Ltd.**, is the highly visible, highly tempting Main Street Fruit Cart. Here strolling guests can get healthy snacks to go, especially pieces of fresh fruit and fruit juice, all arrayed on 20 feet of shaded displays. Right behind the Fruit Cart are the equally tempting, but slightly more sinful, ice cream treats of the **Main Street Cone Shop**.

Main Street Magic Shop

MAP: Main Street, MS-19

CHRONOLOGY: 1957–ongoing

HISTORY: The Magic Kingdom's most enduring magic store is tucked into a cozy spot just past the corner building on the first right-hand block of **Main Street**. When it opened in 1957, the Main Street Magic Shop had as its neighbors the **Wurlitzer Music Hall** on the corner to the south and **Fine Tobacco** to the north, with the **Main Street Cinema** two doors northward. This is the second magic-supply store in the park's history—the first, **Merlin's Magic Shop** in **Fantasyland**, was two years older, but it pulled the disappearing-store trick in 1983.

At night the Magic Shop's sign stands out along Main Street—while nearly every other sign is outlined in pretty white lights, this one is outlined in garish blue and yellow, and it's the only one on the block that flashes. And though that sign announces "MAGIC," there's more here than meets the eye. Scar makeup, disguises, toys, and gag gifts offer additional amusements.

Still, it's the prestidigitation that offers a genuinely magical experience. Right before a guest's very eyes skillful **cast members** can demonstrate card tricks, coin tricks, and other sleight-of-hand illusions, and while they don't explain the tricks, the magicians will point out the how-to books that do. As shown in the 50th-anniversary movie ***Disneyland: The First 50 Magical Years***, in the '60s Disney Legend Steve Martin worked the Main Street Magic Shop counter, demonstrating tricks and developing a rudimentary magic act that would lead to his professional career (in Martin's memoir, *Born Standing Up*, he noted that he split time between this location and Merlin's Magic Shop).

Main Street Photo Supply Co.

MAP: Main Street, MS-12

CHRONOLOGY: November 19, 1994–ongoing

HISTORY: At the far northeast end of **Main Street**, the prominent building formerly known as **Carefree Corner** has been the Kodak-sponsored Main Street Photo Supply Co. since the fall of 1994. As the sign above the door announces, "a picture is worth a thousand words" in this shop. Whether guests are shooting still photos or making movies, this is the best-developed photography center in Disneyland.

That "Photo Supply" in the name doesn't begin to suggest the wide range of photo-related products here, everything from disposable cameras, abundant film types, and various camera batteries to View-Master reels, Disney-themed frames, and souvenir photo books. In addition, the shop offers cameras to rent, film-processing services, camera repair, and battery chargers. Finally, this is where the photos taken of guests by park photographers—such as the portraits taken with the mouse himself inside **Mickey's House** or with Ariel over in **King Triton Gardens**—can be picked up.

Main Street Shooting Gallery

MAP: Main Street, MS-8

CHRONOLOGY: July 17, 1955–January 1962

HISTORY: The first, and shortest-lived, of the three major shooting galleries that have existed in the park, the Main Street Shooting Gallery debuted on **Opening Day** (the **Frontierland Shooting Gallery** opened two years later, the **Big Game Safari Shooting Gallery** five years after that). On **Main Street**, the shooting gallery's location was inside the **Penny Arcade** halfway down the second left-hand block. Today it seems like an odd place to put a rifle range—after all, most of the park's **souvenir books** have opened with a quote from **Walt Disney** that Main Street represents "carefree times" in "the heartline of America." Evidently those carefree times involved actual .22-caliber weapons, since that's what guests fired.

Disneyland publicists weren't shy about promoting the Main Street Shooting Gallery—from 1959 to '62, the souvenir book had a small illustration on the back cover that showed a smiling adult handing a rifle to a gleeful little boy, with accompanying text that read, "Empty rapid-firing rifles at moving or motionless targets." By early 1962, with a popular shooting gallery well-established in **Frontierland** and another one coming soon to **Adventureland**, the live ammo was finally discharged from Main Street in favor of the more urbane pleasures of the remodeled Penny Arcade and its associated shops.

Main Street Vehicles

MAP: Park, P-8, P-9, P-10

CHRONOLOGY: July 17, 1955–ongoing

HISTORY: Adding immeasurably to the atmosphere on **Main Street** are the various Main Street vehicles that have been in operation since the park opened. Six varieties of vehicles have traveled up and down Main Street from **Town Square** to the **Plaza Hub**, all of them moving at three to four mph, all of them costing only an A ticket back when ticket books were in use, all of them shown off with abundant big photos in the park's **souvenir books**. No matter the vehicle, pick-ups and drop-offs are made at either end of the route, and all the rides are one-way.

Only three types of conveyances were in service on **Opening Day**, and all of them were towed by horses. The three types were the horse-drawn fire wagon, streetcar, and surrey. The gleaming red fire wagon, or fire engine as it was called in the park's 1956 souvenir book, was "an old-time hose and chemical wagon" pulled by two horses. There was only one fire wagon, and of all the Main Street vehicles, it had the shortest career. After only five years of service, it was retired in mid-1960 to the **Fire Department** on Town Square, where it has been on display ever since.

The second Main Street vehicle available on Opening Day was the horse-drawn surrey. This small cart with tall wooden wheels was pulled by two horses and carried 8 to 10 passengers spread out over three bench seats. It was retired in early 1971, after about 15 years of service.

The third horse-powered vehicle dating back to 1955 is the beautiful street-car, which continues to run to this day. Two streetcars can operate at a time, their wheels spinning in the metal tracks that are grooved into Main Street (the street

has two sets of these tracks to enable the streetcars to pass each other). As big as these vehicles are— and they are big, each holding up to 30 passengers and weighing up to two tons—each one is pulled by just a single horse, usually a Percheron or a Belgian. Observant guests will find the names of the horses on their bridles.

Horsepower of a different kind was introduced to Main Street on May 12, 1956. That's when a shiny red horseless carriage, the first of two, began to make the one-way Town Square-Plaza Hub trip. Seven months later, a second horseless carriage with bright yellow paint also chugged along the route. While both motor cars were meticulously created to look like antiques from about 1903, they're actually newfangled cars built by Disney Legend **Bob Gurr.** Each has a fringed top, toots a bulbous "ah-oo-gah" horn, and carries a half-dozen passengers on two bench seats.

In the summer of '56, a huge green double-decker bus, called the omnibus, was added to the roster of Main Street vehicles. It was supplemented with a second omnibus on Christmas Day in 1957. Built, like the horseless carriages, by Bob Gurr, a Disneyland omnibus looks old but isn't, and in fact the only true antique on it is the old-fashioned horn. Though it's modeled after the big buses that toured Manhattan in the '30s, the omnibus is fully capable of today's freeway speeds. This gentle giant isn't always in service, but when it is it offers one of the best views of the Main Street area for up to 45 passengers at a time.

The last vintage vehicle to appear was another Gurr creation, the motorized fire truck that began carrying small groups of guests on August 16, 1958. To deliver his creation to the park, Gurr actually drove it for almost an hour down the freeway from the Disney Studios where it was built to Anaheim. Inspired by turn-of-the-century fire engines, the fire truck carries lengths of hose along its sides and has a bell mounted at the rear (the expected siren has been replaced by a horn, though).

Now over 50 years old, all the motorized vehicles are still running at Disneyland, and as of 2006 all of them—the horseless carriages, omnibuses, and fire truck—are sponsored by National Car Rental. While these aren't the fastest vehicles guests will ride at the park, they are among the most charming and historically significant.

Main Street Windows

MAP: Park, P-9
CHRONOLOGY: July 17, 1955–ongoing
HISTORY: Many fans have known for a long time that the names on the upper-story

Names on the Main Street Windows

New names are occasionally added to the windows, so the following alphabetical list may not be up-to-the-minute accurate, but it does identify most of the Main Street names and their actual Disneyland-related occupations. Some of this information came from the Web site LaughingPlace.com.

Milt Albright, accountant/manager
Charles Alexander, construction supervisor
W. Fred Allen, executive at Upjohn Pharmacy, an early sponsor
Hideo Amemiya, Disneyland Hotel executive
Ken Anderson, artist
X Atencio, artist/writer
Renie Bardeau, official park photographer
H. Draegart Barnard, Walt Disney's doctor
Wally Boag, comedian
Chuck Boyajian, janitorial superintendent
Charles Boyer, artist
C. Randy Bright, designer/engineer
Harriet Burns, model maker
Bruce Bushman, artist
Cast members, honoring the long history of park employees
John Louis Catone, Communications Services Department
Royal Clark, treasurer
Claude Coats, artist
Renie Conley, costume designer
Ray Conway, construction
Jim Cora, executive
Bill Cottrell, planner/designer
Don DaGradi, writer
Marc Davis, artist
Marvin Davis, architect/designer
Elias Disney, father of Walt Disney
Ron Dominguez, executive/lived on property bought up for Disneyland
Peter Ellenshaw, artist
Greg Emmer, executive
Morgan "Bill" Evans, landscape architect
Orlando Ferrante, executive

Van Arsdale France, guest services
Blaine Gibson, sculptor
Donald S. Gilmore, chairman of Upjohn Pharmacy, an early sponsor
Bob Gurr, engineer
Jacob Samuel Hamel, engineer
John Hench, artist
Alexander Irvine, doctor, father of Richard Irvine
Richard Irvine, art director/designer
Robert F. Jani, created Main Street Electrical Parade
Fred Joerger, model maker
Emile Kuri, decorator
Leopold (first name unknown), lawyer
Gunther R. Lessing, lawyer
Jack Lindquist, publicist
Mary Anne Mang, public relations
Bill Martin, art director/designer
Ivan Martin, prop maker
Sam McKim, artist
Edward T. Meck, publicist
Christopher D. Miller, Walt Disney's grandson
George Mills, carpenter
Seb Morey, taxidermist
Dick Nunis, executive
George Patrick, art director
C.V. Patterson, executive at Upjohn Pharmacy, an early sponsor
Bob Penfield, cast member from Opening Day to mid-1997
Cicely Rigdon, supervisor of Guest Relations
Wathel Rogers, engineer
Jack Rorex, construction
L.H. Roth, construction
Wade B. Rubottom, art director
Herb Ryman, artist
Gabriel Scognamillo, art director
Cash Shockey, paint department
E.G. Upjohn, president of Upjohn Pharmacy, an early sponsor
Ray Van De Warker, office manager
Frank Wells, executive
William T. Wheeler, engineer
George Whitney, designer/manager
Ed Winger, supervisor of paint department
John Wise, engineer
Robert Wiskey, supervisor
Gordon Youngman, lawyer

windows along **Main Street** pay tribute to real people, most of them Disney employees who contributed to Disneyland in some significant way. Typically the windows identify a "proprietor" and then give a brief description of a fictional business supposedly operating behind the window. That descriptive text is usually a clue as to what the person did at the park. For instance, the window for **Wally Boag**, the long-time comedian at the **Golden Horseshoe**, states that his business is "Golden Vaudeville Routines"; for **X Atencio**, "The Musical Quill—Lyrics and Librettos" suggests his musical contributions to the **Haunted Mansion**, **Pirates of the Caribbean**, and other attractions; and "Evans Gardens—Exotic & Rare Species" honors the landscaping artistry of **Morgan "Bill" Evans**. Photos of tribute windows accompany 22 entries in this encyclopedia.

Not all of the windows on Main Street have names on them—some have no text at all, and some identify a fictional business (Piano Lessons, Fine Food Chinese Restaurant, Massage Parlor) without naming a specific proprietor. Two of the windows are given to relatives of **Walt Disney**: his father, Elias, who died 14 years before Disneyland opened, and his grandson, Christopher Miller, who was born in late '54 while Disneyland was being built. Walt Disney himself does not have a Main Street window, but he does have a window in **Mickey's Toontown** at the library: "Laugh-O-Gram Films, Inc. W.E. Disney, Directing Animator."

Malt Shop and Cone Shop

MAP: Frontierland, Fr-6

CHRONOLOGY: Ca. 1958–ca. 1970

HISTORY: A Malt Shop and Cone Shop tandem seems now like it would've been natural for **Main Street**, but actually this pair, according to the park's **souvenir books**, existed for about a decade over in **Frontierland**. The small, adjacent locations were between the **Oaks Tavern** and **Aunt Jemima's Pancake House**, fronting the space occupied from 1957 to 1961 by **Don DeFore's Silver Banjo Barbecue**.

Both the Malt Shop and Cone Shop were fast-food counters. The Malt Shop cooked up dogs and burgers along with the malts, and the Cone Shop served up ice cream to go. A remodel sometime around 1970 replaced these two eateries with another pair, the equally small and fast **Wheelhouse and Delta Banjo**.

Many Adventures of Winnie the Pooh

MAP: Bear Country/Critter Country, B/C-4

CHRONOLOGY: April 11, 2003–ongoing

HISTORY: After almost 30 years on the job, the ursine entertainers of the **Country Bear Jamboree** finally retired in 2001. Replacing them was another bear, this one

A. A. Milne's whimsical literary creation who had been starring in Disney animated films since 1966.

Like the Country Bear Jamboree, the Many Adventures of Winnie the Pooh originated in Florida, where it had replaced Mr. Toad's Wild Ride. When fans protested the threatened removal of **Mr. Toad's Wild Ride** from Disneyland, Pooh found a place just inside the entrance to **Critter Country** on the right-hand side. There

the attraction was set up as an indoor dark ride with an outdoor line.

To experience the Many Adventures, guests sit in adorable beehive-shaped "beehicles"—each with its own name—and venture for three and a half minutes into the serene, verdant Hundred-Acre Wood. Along the way are visits with all of Pooh's animal friends, including Tigger, Rabbit, and Eeyore, plus a "blustery day" experience, the inevitable search for "hunny," a Heffalump-and-Woozle dream, and a party.

Designed primarily as a visual treat for young children, the attraction is filled with bright colors, gentle bounces, friendly faces, heartwarming sentiments, and delightful **Richard and Robert Sherman** music. Fans of the old Country Bears will be happy to glimpse the three **Audio-Animatronic** heads of Max the deer, Melvin the moose, and Buff the buffalo still mounted on a darkened wall (they're behind and above guests as they leave the Woozles). What's more, Pooh's balloon ride is accomplished via the same mechanism that once carried Teddi Barra, one of the singing Country Bears, aloft on her swing.

𝕸arché aux 𝕱leurs, 𝕾acs et 𝕸ode

MAP: New Orleans Square, NOS-9

CHRONOLOGY: 1975–ca. 1985

HISTORY: "Flower Market, Stylish Bags" was a shop located for over a decade at the back of **New Orleans Square** behind the **French Market**. Previously, **Le Chapeau** had been on this corner. The merchandise was just as French and frilly as the hats that had previously lined the shelves, and indeed hats were still sold here. Fancy handbags were also on view, plus fashion accessories and even handy supplies for anyone who'd gotten deep into New Orleans Square without any film. The Mardi Gras masks of **La Mascarade d'Orléans** replaced the handbags sometime in the mid-'80s.

𝕸arket 𝕳ouse

MAP: Main Street, MS-18

CHRONOLOGY: July 17, 1955–ongoing

HISTORY: The nostalgic Market House has been a **Main Street** staple since **Open-**

ing Day. Located on the southeast corner of Main and East Center Street, the Market House stands to the left (north) of, and opens into, what used to be the **Yale & Towne Lock Shop**. The exterior has three street-facing sides—two of brick, one of wood—that wrap around the corner, plus it has four stories topped with a mansard roof and a widow's walk, making it one of the most imposing structures on Main Street.

The Market House was identified in a 1954 concept drawing as a combination "grocery store" and "meat market," and it was designed as a handsome 1890s general store. The ground-floor interior has always been a fascinating room to explore and is in some ways more like a museum than a retail space. An ornate potbellied stove invites guests to relax over a game of checkers; swirling candy sticks stand in decorative jars; pickle barrels are scattered around the hardwood floors; kitchen supplies, gourmet foods, and a huge selection of mugs line the shelves; cocoa and coffee drinks are served by costumed women in long old-fashioned dresses; a row of bins displays selections of coffee beans; and, in a delightful touch added in 1974, the antique phones here, when picked up, convey gossipy party-line conversations.

Swift & Company, the meat packager, was the first sponsor, though this wasn't their first participation in Disneyland, as Swift also sponsored two Opening Day restaurants, the **Red Wagon Inn** and the **Chicken Plantation**. Swift's name was prominently displayed outside, and in the park's 1956 and '57 **souvenir books** the building was called Swift's Market House, with the added description "meats and groceries" (just how many groceries were purchased and lugged around the park is debatable). The part of the building to the right of the front door is where the meat shop existed. By 1958, the souvenir book listed the Swiftless appellation Market House on the park map, but, under the "Special Shows and Exhibits" heading in the back, there was a description of Swift's Market House—"The old-fashioned General Store of Grandfather's day"—illustrated with a drawing of the big potbellied stove.

In 1970, a small park map identified three modern entities within the turn-of-the-century Market House, though no text or photos were offered in any of the park's larger souvenir books. The three concerns mentioned on the map: Burry's Cookies (Burry's, makers of Scooter Pies, was a division of Quaker Oats, the company that sponsored **Aunt Jemima's Pancake House** in **Frontierland** in the '50s and '60s); the C&H Sugar Corner (C&H—short for California and Hawaii—was the famous sugar refiner, making this a sweets spot in all likelihood); and Sunsweet Growers (the California-based dried-fruit company).

Currently, the dignified signs out front proclaim the Market House's wares as Canned Fruits and Vegetables, Coffee, Candy, Preserves, Coffee again, and Canned Goods and Spices. As always, thanks to the absence of Disney-themed T-shirts, hats, and obligatory souvenirs, this is still one of the most genuine old-timey locations in the park.

𝕴𝖑𝖆𝖗𝖐 𝕿𝖜𝖆𝖎𝖓 𝕽𝖎𝖛𝖊𝖗𝖇𝖔𝖆𝖙

MAP: Frontierland, Fr-17

CHRONOLOGY: July 17, 1955–ongoing

HISTORY: Nearly every write-up of the *Mark Twain* includes the adjectives "stately" and "majestic." The gracious white ship is certainly both. As the first large paddle wheeler built in America since the early 20th century, it's also historic. And at 105 feet long, 150 tons, it rivals the magnificent **Sailing Ship *Columbia*** as the single most imposing watercraft in Disneyland.

    Walt Disney wanted a resplendent riverboat in his park long before the park was built—early concept drawings of Disneyland always included something that looked like the *Mark Twain* circling waters that looked like the **Rivers of America**. Tellingly, when the ship's landing was built, it was placed in a highly visible location at the end of the main **Frontierland** street so that guests would be able to see the docked, dazzling *Mark Twain* from the **Plaza Hub**. The tempting vision drew many a timid newcomer deep into

Disneyland's Watercraft
(with years of operation)

Attached to Rails
Canal Boats of the World (1955)
Jungle Cruise (1955–ongoing)
Mark Twain Riverboat (1955–ongoing)
Motor Boat Cruise (1957–'93)
Sailing Ship *Columbia* (1958–ongoing)
Storybook Land Canal Boats (1956–ongoing)
Submarine Voyage/Finding Nemo Submarine Voyage
(1959–'98/2007–ongoing)

Free-Floating
Indian War Canoes/Davy Crockett's Explorer Canoes (1956–ongoing)
It's a Small World (1966–ongoing)
Mike Fink Keel Boats (1955–'97)
Phantom Boats (1955–'56)
Pirates of the Caribbean (1967–ongoing)
Rafts to Tom Sawyer Island (1956–ongoing)
Splash Mountain (1989–ongoing)

Stationary
Donald's Boat, aka *Miss Daisy* (1993–ongoing)
Pirate Ship Restaurant (1955–'82)

the wild frontier.

The ship's illustrious history began with the steel hull, built at shipyards in nearby Long Beach. Meanwhile, the wooden decks and ornate superstructure were constructed at the Disney Studios in Burbank, trucked down to Anaheim, and then added to the hull inside the park. While the twin-smokestack *Mark Twain* is an authentic-looking replica of the larger sternwheelers that plied the Mississippi in the 19th century, it isn't architecturally perfect—some parts were built proportionally to a smaller scale than other parts, in accordance with the specific safety and maritime needs at Disneyland. The ship can hold over 350 passengers, though when it debuted there was no official loading capacity. Thus there are old tales of **cast members** accidentally overloading the boat to the point that it almost capsized when all the guests shifted to one side to catch a sight along the riverbank.

On July 13, 1955, the *Mark Twain* made a prominent trial voyage at a party thrown by Walt Disney and his wife to celebrate their 30th wedding anniversary. Four days later, actress Irene Dunne christened the ship during televised **Opening Day** ceremonies. From then on it has endured as one of Disneyland's iconic attractions. Strangely, in its first three decades the *Mark Twain* swung back and forth from being a C, D, and even briefly an E attraction.

Its lovely, serene trip, however, hasn't changed significantly. Powered by steam and propelled by its stern paddle wheel, it travels on a submerged track around, appropriately enough, the island named after one of Mark Twain's greatest literary creations, Tom Sawyer. On its 12–14-minute journey, the ship travels about a half-mile and takes in panoramic views of the **Big Thunder Mountain Railroad**, the **Golden Horseshoe**, **New Orleans Square**, the **Haunted Mansion**, **Splash Mountain**, and the wilderness at the back of **Tom Sawyer Island**. Sharp-eyed guests keep watch for **Audio-Animatronic** animals along the water's edge, one of the unused **Mike Fink Keel Boats**, and wreckage from the old **Rainbow Caverns Mine Train**.

The *Mark Twain* has always been a star attraction in the park's **souvenir books**, naturally, frequently getting spotlighted with full-page photos. And it's often been the star attraction for special events. In its 50+ years and 260,000+ miles, the *Mark Twain* has been specially decorated for holidays, it's paraded jazz combos and the **Disneyland Band** in front of shoreline guests, and it's been worked into the **Fantasmic!** show. At one time it even sold mint juleps on board. Occasionally a few lucky guests are invited to visit the captain's wheelhouse to control the ship for a few moments. But most guests don't need anything special to enliven their trip—on a hot day, a quiet voyage on cool waters aboard the stately, majestic *Mark Twain* is plenty special enough.

Marquee

MAP: Park, P-1

CHRONOLOGY: 1958–ongoing

HISTORY: For over 40 years, a magnificent marquee graced the automobile entrance to the Disneyland **parking lot.** Surprisingly, there was no big sign there on **Opening Day**, and in fact the first true marquee didn't get installed along Harbor Boulevard until 1958.

When it did go up, the marquee offered a friendly and memorable welcome to drivers. The sign was in three parts. The top section spelled out the name Disneyland, with each blue letter mounted separately in a differently sized white rectangle and spelled out in a fantasy-style font. Underneath was a wide horizontal section that read "The happiest place on Earth," and underneath that was a board with manually placed letters that spelled out the park's hours and that day's special events. Stretching skyward from the sign was a row of flagpoles festooned with stiff banners.

After some 30 years, a new marquee went up in the same spot on October 6, 1989. This one was essentially the same as the original, save for the new electronic billboard in the bottom third that announced hours and events. This sign was replaced in 1996 with a dazzling new sign with all-new components. The name Disneyland was now spelled out in white letters on a blue background. While the letters were still written in the same fantasy font, and while they were still mounted in separate rectangles, those rectangles were now all approximately 14-feet high, giving the sign a more uniform look. Underneath, a white-on-pink sign reprised the "happiest place on Earth" tag line, and below that a new computerized billboard offered flashier announcements. Crowning the whole sign were six small pink, yellow, and blue banners and, in the center, an 18-foot-tall gold castle in a blue circle. From the street to the top of the gold castle, the marquee stood about six stories tall. For a few years in the '90s, customers ordering out of the Disney Store catalog could temporarily rent the electronic billboard for a private message, which would be shown briefly and photographed as a keepsake.

On June 14, 1999, this large marquee flashed its last announcement, as the whole thing was removed the next day in anticipation of the construction that would replace Disneyland's 100-acre parking lot with Disney's California Adventure. The marquee didn't completely disappear, however. After it was dismantled into separate pieces, the Disneyland letters, the "happiest place" section, and the gold castle were auctioned off on eBay. Actor John Stamos purchased the Disneyland letters in 2000 with a closing bid of $30,700.

Two less imposing marquees now greet guests along Harbor Boulevard. The east-side walkway into Disneyland is marked by a 20-foot-wide, 15-foot-tall blue aluminum banner adorned with fabric fairy wings and the phrase "where dreams come true." On the reverse is a "thank you for visiting" sign. Of note to fans is the star for Walt Disney in the sidewalk here. Placed in 2006, this was the inaugural star on the new Anaheim/Orange County Walk of Stars. Spanning Disney Way some 200 yards to the south is a second marquee, this one wide and yellow. It has a more perfunctory look as it guides cars into the core of the resort area without attempting to communicate the meaning or magic of what waits ahead.

Marshal's Office

MAP: Frontierland, Fr-25

CHRONOLOGY: July 1955–July 1956

HISTORY: Adding a touch of authenticity to **Frontierland**, a small one-story Marshal's Office once stood on the right-hand side of Frontierland's main street. The little wooden building was at the far end of the row of Western-themed structures; immediately to the east (heading back towards the **Plaza Hub**) was the **Miniature Horse Corral** (later the **Frontierland Shooting Gallery**), and to the west was the open **El Zocalo** plaza and the dock for the *Mark Twain*.

The Marshal's Office lasted only a year—in the summer of '56 the nearby Mexican restaurant **Casa de Fritos**, which had been situated around the corner to the south towards **Aunt Jemima's Pancake House**, relocated into this spot with a newer, bigger building. The only **souvenir book** to make mention of the marshal or his office was the '58 edition, which showed a photo and caption of the misspelled Marshall Lucky getting held up by a pistol-packin' child on the walkway out in front of the **Golden Horseshoe**.

Decorated with small flags along the roof, the office wasn't really a workplace of any kind and was there more as a backdrop for photos with the costumed marshal. The sign on top of the slanted roof read, "Willard P. Bounds, Blacksmith and U.S. Marshal." *Disneyland: The Nickel Tour* identified Bounds as a specific real-life frontier marshal **Walt Disney** actually knew—his father-in-law.

Bill Martin

CHRONOLOGY: June 15, 1917–ongoing

HISTORY: Many of the original Disneyland designers were moviemakers recruited from the Disney Studios; Bill Martin was a moviemaker recruited from 20th Century Fox, where he'd worked before and after World War II as a set designer. Martin was an Iowan born in 1917. When his family moved to Southern California, he studied architecture and design at local colleges and art institutes until he got hired to work as a Hollywood art director. After serving in the Air Force, and after continuing his career at Fox, in '53 he joined the Imagineers who were planning out Disneyland.

It's said that Martin had a hand in everything at the park. One of his tasks was to create the original **Fantasyland**—its layout, its look, its attractions.

Working with other Disney Legends like **Ken Anderson**, Martin designed most of the major attractions that are still favorites today, including **Peter Pan Flight**, **Mr. Toad's Wild Ride**, and **Snow White Adventures**. A few years later, he was in on the creation of the **Nature's Wonderland** area in **Frontierland**, the **Fantasyland Autopia**, and the **Submarine Voyage** in **Tomorrowland**, and he also laid out the long looping path of the **Monorail**. In the '60s, Martin was a key architect of **New Orleans Square** and its two landmark attractions, the **Haunted Mansion** and **Pirates of the Caribbean**. Unbeknownst to guests, he also helped design the private apartment that **Walt Disney** wanted in New Orleans Square, a decorous space that later became the **Disney Gallery**.

Martin rose to the position of VP of design for the company in '71 and supervised the plans for the Magic Kingdom at Walt Disney World. He also contributed designs for specific attractions and boats at the Florida park, including the riverboats and Cinderella Castle. Though he formally retired in 1977, he stayed on as a consultant and helped plan Tokyo Disneyland, among other projects. Bill Martin was named a Disney Legend in 1994.

𝔐atterhorn 𝔅obsleds

MAP: Fantasyland, Fa-24

CHRONOLOGY: June 14, 1959–ongoing

HISTORY: Nowadays, guests appreciate the fun and aesthetics of the thrilling Matterhorn Bobsleds, but few people realize how innovative this attraction was when it debuted in mid-June of 1959. Up until then, all roller coaster-style rides had put long trains on clackety wooden tracks that had wide looping curves. In contrast, Disneyland's attraction, its first true thrill ride, put small, sleek bobsleds, not on wooden tracks, but on hollow metal tubes that were both quieter and smoother, making for a better ride. And a wilder one, as well, since the metal tubes could be bent into tighter curves.

Furthermore, the Imagineers created this as the first attraction to put more than one vehicle at a time on a track, an important strategy for cutting down on wait times (when the single bobsleds were later doubled up into pairs, the Swiss-costumed **cast members** could get over 1,500 guests per hour through the attraction). Disney Legend **Bob Gurr** is credited as the main designer of the little blue-and-yellow (later red-and-white) bobsled and its track, while another Disney Legend, **Fred Joerger**, made numerous models of the mountains with various track layouts. The result of their efforts was a revolution in ride design and the very definition of an E-ticket attraction.

The bobsleds run on two tracks that climb up through the inside of the Matterhorn to a point about two-thirds of the way to the top. They then glide down quickly around and through the mountain, a total distance of about 2,100 feet. For decades guests have tested their theories that one track yields a faster ride than the other, but ultimately the speed has more to do with the load inside the sleds than it does with the tracks. During the two-and-a-quarter-minute trip, the sleds on both tracks travel at an average speed of barely 20 mph. Speeds sure *seem* faster, though, and riders can grab only quick glimpses of the spectacular Disneyland scenery below.

When it opened, the bobsleds quickly got famous as the park's hottest vehicles, and they held that reputation for almost two decades. Until **Space Mountain** opened in 1977, there was simply no other speedy roller coaster ride in Disneyland. So special were they, on the day they debuted **Walt Disney**, his family, and Vice President Richard Nixon rode the first bobsleds down the Matterhorn. The park's **souvenir books** have always played the attraction up big with exhilarating photos, though they've been unsure of the location, sometimes putting the bobsleds in the section for **Fantasyland** and other times in **Tomorrowland.**

One of the special touches that has made the trip distinctive is its climax, a sudden, splashy swoop through a "glacier lake" (as the souvenir books dubbed it). No other ride anywhere had an effect like this in the late '50s. The splashdown not only creates a great visual effect for riders and pedestrians but also serves to slow down the speeding sleds (before the lake was in place, pre-opening test rides culminated in sandbags and bales of hay). At the end of the trip the prerecorded voice of **Jack Wagner** tells riders to "remain seated please"—fans of the band No Doubt will recognize that request as the 11-second introduction to the song "Tragic Kingdom."

𝕸atterhorn 𝕸ountain

MAP: Fantasyland, Fa-24

CHRONOLOGY: June 14, 1959–ongoing

HISTORY: For many guests arriving via the Santa Ana Freeway, their first view of Disneyland has often been a quick glimpse of the Matterhorn's peak, caught from a moving car. The Matterhorn has been a Disneyland icon since 1959, when it opened after less than a year of construction. The Matterhorn was one of that year's three major additions to the eastern half of the park (the **Monorail** and **Submarine Voyage** were the others).

Like dozens of other Disneyland locations, the mountain was inspired by a Disney movie, in this case two—a 1955 documentary called *Switzerland* and a 1958 feature called *Third Man on the Mountain*. In addition, **Walt Disney** had already made several trips to the actual Matterhorn and been enchanted by it, so when the idea for a snow-capped hill with a toboggan ride occurred to him in late 1956, by 1957 that idea had evolved into a taller snow-capped mountain with some kind of roller coaster ride, and by late 1958, it had grown into the majestic Matterhorn with its revolutionary **Matterhorn Bobsleds**. The name evolved right along with the plan—as noted in *Disneyland: The Nickel Tour*, what began as Snow Hill became Snow Mountain, then Mount Disneyland, Disneyland Mountain, Sorcerer's Mountain, Magic Mountain, Fantasy Mountain, Echo Mountain, the Valterhorn (adapting Walt's name), and finally Matterhorn Mountain.

Matterhorn Mountain rose on a barely used, barely landscaped picnic mound called Holiday Hill. This hill, straddling the **Fantasyland/Tomorrowland** border, was built up with dirt excavated from the **Sleeping Beauty Castle** moat. The location makes the European mountain clearly visible from all-American **Main Street**, a potentially jarring sight that bothered some of the designers but never Walt Disney. The location also places the mountain in the middle of lots of park traffic. Not including the bobsleds, five different vehicles have passed close by over the years—the **Motor Boat Cruise** to the north, the **Fantasyland Autopia** to the northeast, the Submarine Voyage to the east and south, the **Alice in Wonderland** caterpillar cars to the west, and the curving Monorail to the north, west, and south. Additionally, the trams of the old **Skyway to Fantasyland and Skyway to Tomorrowland** actually passed through, not around, the mountain.

During the planning phase, Disney Legend **Fred Joerger** made many models of the mountain to get its shape correct from all perspectives. As it rose, the construction project gobbled up over

The 15 Tallest Structures in Disneyland History
(measurements in feet)

1. Matterhorn Mountain (147)
2. Space Mountain (118)
3. Big Thunder Mountain (104) (see photo below)
4. Splash Mountain (87)
5. Rocket Jets tower (85)
6. Skyway to Tomorrowland tower (85)
7. Sailing Ship *Columbia* (84)
8. Pirate Ship Restaurant (80, estimated)
9. Sleeping Beauty Castle (77)
10. Original *Moonliner* rocket (76)
11. Swiss Family Treehouse (70)
12. Flagpole in Town Square (65)
13. Astro-Orbitor (64)
14. Christmas tree (60)
15. 1998 *Moonliner* rocket (53)

2,000 steel girders for the frame, with no two girders identical in size and shape. The finished mountain, its landscaped grounds, and its alpine-themed loading area created a circular park footprint of about one and a half acres. The mountain stands precisely 147 feet tall, which is 1/100th the height of the actual Matterhorn. Not only is it still the tallest structure in Disneyland, for a while Disneyland's Matterhorn was the tallest structure in the county until a building boom in the '60s raised the surrounding skyline. Forced perspective, the same moviemaking technique that causes Sleeping Beauty Castle to look taller than it really is, also makes the Matterhorn seem to stretch higher than it really does—here the trick is in the trees, which are large at the mountain's base and small closer to the peak.

The mountain has many unique features. For one thing, its placement between two lands has meant that it has at times been listed in the park's **souvenir books** in Tomorrowland (for its first nine years) and at other times in Fantasyland (its designated position in the 1968 and subsequent souvenir books). Also, the mountain is regularly ascended by a team of 14 trained alpine climbers. According to the August 1963 edition of *National Geographic*, members of that team scale the Matterhorn eight times a day (on a 1965 episode of *Walt Disney's Wonderful World of Color*, Walt Disney said the climbing only took place "in the vacation months"). Occasionally, those climbers even make their ascent dressed as Mickey or Goofy. They can take any of 30 routes to the summit, where they command views of Catalina Island and, on the clearest days, the Hollywood sign some 40 miles away (a climber wearing sunglasses was spotlighted in a photo in the 2000 souvenir book).

Today's bobsled riders may not realize that in the '60s and '70s riders clearly saw the support beams inside the Matterhorn. A 1978 remodel added new "ice cave" features that blocked off the exposed beams, and it also introduced the Abominable Snowman creature as a scary presence that can still be heard and occasionally glimpsed throughout the ride. Another aesthetic improvement came when the Skyway trams were shut down and their mountain openings were sealed off in 1994. Also, at some point two slender spires were added to the summit to serve as a lightning rod and a beacon to aircraft.

A no-longer-hidden secret about the climbers is that they have their own small basketball court about 100 feet up inside the Matterhorn. It's not a full-size court, just a flat surface with a mounted hoop that serves as a break area so the climbers don't have to descend all the way back down to the park between ascents. At least one local radio station has broadcast its show from the basketball court inside the mountain. However, the court may no longer exist, as some unconfirmed stories suggest that it's been removed in recent years.

Another distinctive feature of the Matterhorn is its interior elevator. Besides carrying maintenance workers, this elevator lifts **Tinker Bell** to her platform for her summertime glide across the park. Tink's flight isn't the only nighttime event to feature the Matterhorn—from 1961 until the mid-'70s, a 22-ton sparkling star, visible from the nearby freeway and neighborhoods, adorned the apex over the **Christmas** holidays.

Finally, fittingly, the Matterhorn is unique in the history of Disney parks. Unlike other Disneyland mountains such as **Splash**, **Space**, and **Big Thunder**, which have all been built in other Disney parks around the world, the mighty Matterhorn has never been duplicated, an appropriate tribute to the first, and some say still the most beautiful, Disney pinnacle.

Maxwell House Coffee Shop

MAP: Town Square, TS-7

CHRONOLOGY: December 1, 1955–October 8, 1957

HISTORY: Almost five months after the park opened, the Maxwell House Coffee Shop debuted on **Town Square**. Its location was just to the right of the **Wurlitzer Music Hall** on the corner and to the left of the **Opera House** building. A charming coffeehouse facing guests as they entered the park through the east tunnel in the morning must have seemed like the perfect blend of location and timing. So perfect that after Maxwell House left in 1957, **Hills Bros.** stepped in eight months later.

George McGinnis

CHRONOLOGY: Unknown-ongoing

HISTORY: Futuristic vehicles may have been George McGinnis's specialty, but he also contributed to some of the old-style attractions at the park. After studying engineering and design in college in the early '60s, this Pennsylvanian was invited to work on some of the new projects being developed for the **Tomorrowland** remodel of 1966–'67. McGinnis began with the tiny transportation systems shown on the large model of Progress City above the **Carousel of Progress**. Still working in Tomorrowland, he designed the whirling vehicles that updated the old **Astro-Jets** into the new Rocket Jets attraction, and he created the Mighty Microscope that greeted guests inside **Adventure Thru Inner Space**.

Moving to Walt Disney World projects, McGinnis designed that park's PeopleMover in the late '60s. Back at Disneyland, he was one of the key designers of the massive new **Space Mountain** that rose up to become one of the park's signature attractions in 1977. A decade later, his redesigned purple **Monorail** train, the sleek and luxurious Mark V, began running at Disneyland. During this time, McGinnis also joined Disney moviemakers on the production of *The Black Hole*, and his four robot characters are seen in that sci-fi classic.

Throughout the '80s and '90s, McGinnis continued to help with a wide variety of significant attractions at Disney parks throughout the world: Disneyland's new **Snow White Adventures** vehicles, old-style jungle trucks for the **Indiana Jones Adventure**, and the state-of-the-art **Rocket Rods**; a new monorail and exhibits at Walt Disney World; trams at Disney-MGM Studios; boats for Splash Mountain at Tokyo Disneyland; boats/cars/trains at Disney's Animal Kingdom; river rafts at Disney's California Adventure, and more. George McGinnis was elected to the National Inventors Hall of Fame in 2001.

Sam McKim

CHRONOLOGY: December 20, 1924–July 9, 2004

HISTORY: One of the best souvenirs a guest can take home from Disneyland is a large, beautifully illustrated park map. Artist Sam McKim drew the first of these maps in 1958 and continued his cartography until 1964. Veteran guests may also recall his smaller map of **Tom Sawyer Island**, which was offered as a free **Frontierland** handout until 1976. Over the decades McKim also drew many, many detailed concept drawings for other attractions and buildings that eventually found their way into the park.

A Canadian born in 1924, McKim and his family moved to Southern California in 1935. Related to an MGM casting agent, he was soon getting jobs as a child actor in numerous Westerns, even landing a contract with Republic Pictures and a recurring role in the *Three Mesquiteers* series (as an actor he was listed in film credits as Sammy McKim).

After serving in World War II, after studying at L.A. art colleges, and after winning medals for his bravery during the Korean War, Sam McKim became an artist in Hollywood. In the mid-'50s he drew set sketches for 20th Century Fox until a layoff sent him over to the Disney Studios, where he was hired by **Marvin Davis** for a few months to draw sketches of upcoming Disneyland attractions. McKim ended up staying with the company for the next three decades.

During this time, McKim worked closely with **Walt Disney** to make Disney's visions for Disneyland a reality. Today, McKim's drawings of Frontierland, the **Golden Horseshoe**, **Main Street**, **Great Moments with Mr. Lincoln**, **It's a Small World**, the **Monorail**, **New Orleans Square**, **Pirates of the Caribbean**, the **Haunted Mansion**, the **Carousel of Progress**, and more still inspire Disney designers and artists.

Outside of Disneyland, McKim worked on numerous live-action Disney films of the '50s and '60s as a storyboard artist; he also drew concept illustrations for the 1964–1965 New York World's Fair and several Walt Disney World attractions. Though he retired in '87, five years later he drew a lavish park map for the debut of Disneyland Paris. Sam McKim was elected a Disney Legend in 1996, eight years before he died of heart failure at age 79.

Edward Meck

CHRONOLOGY: 1899–1973

HISTORY: Eddie Meck was working in publicity and promotion long before he became the publicist for Disneyland. Born in 1899 in Wisconsin, Meck started with Pathé Frères, an early film company that made pre-'20s dramas, the *Perils of Pauline* serials, and the Harold Lloyd comedies. After promoting those movies for most of the 1920s, he jumped to Columbia Pictures in the '30s and helped promote Frank Capra's films to Oscar-winning success.

Meck joined the Disneyland team in the spring of 1955 and helped build up the pre-**Opening Day** excitement to a fever pitch. He did it, not with the fantastic stunts and invented publicity gimmicks that heralded other big premieres and events of the '40s and '50s, but with simplicity, letting the beauty and diversity of the park speak for themselves. Throughout his Disney career, his idea was to invite the press from all over the world (flying them in when necessary) and let them each find their own stories to write about. There were plenty of subjects, after all, and plenty of unique ways to enjoy the park, so he let every writer discover those pleasures for himself. The result was a flood of gushing travel articles in national newspapers and magazines, and quickly Disneyland surged to its long-standing position as the top tourist attraction in the West.

Working out of **City Hall**, Meck befriended reporters and photographers, and he and his staff regularly hand-delivered news items to newspaper offices in Southern California. Meck also invited lots of celebrities to come share in the fun, leading to plenty of well-publicized photos. In 1971, Meck's soft-sell approach was used to introduce the media to Walt Disney World, where Meck himself set up the new publicity department. Edward Meck died in 1973 at age 74, and he was inducted as a Disney Legend 22 years later.

Merlin's Magic Shop

MAP: Fantasyland, Fa-30

CHRONOLOGY: July 17, 1955–January 16, 1983

HISTORY: The first of Disneyland's two magic shops, Merlin's in **Fantasyland** was ready on **Opening Day**, about two years before the **Main Street Magic Shop**. But whereas the shop on **Main Street** has never closed down, the one in Fantasyland was replaced after 27 years.

Merlin's occupied a great location in the **Sleeping Beauty Castle** courtyard right next to the popular **Peter Pan Flight** attraction. The shop had a half-timbered, peak-roofed, European-village exterior like something from an old fairy tale, a look suitable both for something attached to the castle and for something that was themed to the wizard from *The Sword in the Stone*. Inside the large room were magic tricks, how-to books, and practical jokes, with enthusiastic **cast members** ready to demonstrate sleight-of-hand illusions right at the counter.

As fun and venerable as Merlin's Magic Shop was, it didn't survive the huge Fantasyland renovation of the early '80s. It was replaced in 1983 by a new retail space called **Mickey's Christmas Chalet**.

Mermaids

MAP: Tomorrowland, T-11

CHRONOLOGY: Summer 1959; summer 1965–summer 1967 (seasonally)

HISTORY: For decades the beautiful **attraction poster** for the **Submarine Voyage** showed a looming lavender sub with lithe, long-haired mermaids swimming underneath it. Veteran visitors will recall that there were three summers in the mid-'60s when lithe, long-haired mermaids really did splash around in the submarines' lagoon.

Originally these sirens, attractive local swimmers wearing ocean-themed halter tops and long, svelte mermaid tails, had been part of the celebratory festivities promoting the new Submarine Voyage attraction when it launched in mid-June of '59. Entertainment specialist **Tommy Walker** is usually credited with coming up with the mermaid idea. Some six years later, after conducting auditions in the Disneyland Hotel pool, Disneyland officials brought back the mermaids to frolic in the **Tomorrowland** waters and stretch out on the surrounding rocks for four hours a day. Unfortunately, extensive exposure to the lagoon's chlorine became a concern, and when some of the male guests found the mermaids so irresistible they had to jump in after them, Disney officials whistled everyone out of the pool in 1967.

Mexican Village

MAP: Frontierland, Fr-1

CHRONOLOGY: Ca. 1957–ca. 1964

HISTORY: From 1957 to 1964, the park's **souvenir books** listed something called the Mexican Village under the Shops and Stores category for **Frontierland**. Placement of the listing in the souvenir books suggested that it was in the retail area near the entrance to the Frontierland stockade, though which side it was on and what it sold were never explained. The Mexican Village is not to be confused with **El Zocalo**, a plaza area with a well-recalled location at the western end of Frontierland's main street.

Mickey Mouse Club Circus

MAP: Fantasyland, Fa-22

CHRONOLOGY: November 24, 1955–January 8, 1956

HISTORY: While many new, wondrous attractions that debuted in 1955 thrived at the park for decades, a few of the early ideas were out and out flops that quickly expired. One of these was the Mickey Mouse Club Circus, which on paper must've been an appealing attraction to **Walt Disney**, a long-time circus-lover.

In early November of '55, two circus tents went up in the northeast corner of **Fantasyland**, an area that would later be filled with the junior freeway of the **Junior Autopia**. The official circus opened on Thanksgiving Day with a parade down

Main Street, an hour-and-a-quarter show in heated tents, and a special 50-cent admission charge.

Theoretically, fans of *The Mickey Mouse Club* TV show should've been fans of the circus acts—Jimmie Dodd, the TV host, was the ringmaster, and the young Mouseketeers, "clowning, riding elephants, and in an Aerial Ballet" (according to a promotional flyer) were among the stars. Additionally, a dozen professional acts presented 150 animals and performers,

> ## Attractions and Exhibits Permanently Closed within One Year of Debuting
> (in chronological order)
>
> 1. Canal Boats of the World (7/55–9/55)
> 2. Davy Crockett Frontier Museum (7/55–10/55)
> 3. Court of Honor (7/55–3/56)
> 4. Marshal's Office (7/55–7/56)
> 5. Phantom Boats (8/55–1/56)
> 6. Mickey Mouse Club Circus (11/55–1/56)
> 7. Keller's Jungle Killers (2/56–9/56)
> 8. Fashions and Fabrics Through the Ages (3/65–12/65)
> 9. Disney Afternoon Avenue (3/91–9/91)
> 10. Toy Story Funhouse (1/96–5/96)
> 11. Dalmatian Celebration (11/96–1/97)

including camels, ponies, trained seals, dogs, trapeze artists, equestrians, Bob-O the Disneyland Clown, and Professor Keller's ferocious jungle cats. There were also appearances by Disney characters and a tent-filling 40-foot "magic Christmas tree" that rose up at the finale.

Unfortunately, the circus stands, which could've held 2,500 guests, were rarely full and more often were barely occupied at all. Disneyland guests, it turned out, wanted to see the one-of-a-kind park, not a run-of-the-mill circus that they had probably already seen back in their own hometown. Besides, if they were looking for something with a circus theme, there was already the charming **Casey Jr. Circus Train** nearby. What's more, several of the animal acts were problematical (some actually escaped at one point), and a few of those professional circus performers weren't exactly consistent with the wholesome Disney image.

After only six weeks of daily parades and "death-defying" circus acts, the Mickey Mouse Club Circus was dismantled. However, some of its elements did linger at the park for a while. Professor Keller stayed on with a scaled-down circus attraction called **Keller's Jungle Killers**, and the main tent was relocated to the picnic grounds of **Holidayland** just outside of **Frontierland**.

Mickey Mouse Club Headquarters,
aka Mickey Mouse Club Shop

MAP: Town Square, TS-9
CHRONOLOGY: Fall 1963–1964
HISTORY: After the **Babes in Toyland Exhibit** left **Town Square** in the fall of '63,

the Mickey Mouse Club Headquarters set up shop. And it really was a shop, selling Mouseketeer photos and souvenirs in addition to serving as club headquarters where new club members could enroll and get membership cards. The location was where Babes had been, a guest-friendly spot near the park **entrance** on the ground floor of the beautiful **Opera House.**

The timing for a Mickey Mouse Club Headquarters might've seemed a little off to many guests—after all, *The Mickey Mouse Club* TV show had been canceled in 1959, and the only episodes being seen on TV in 1963 were reruns. The headquarters itself got canceled in 1964, and the next year this space was finally filled by something that would last—**Great Moments with Mr. Lincoln.**

Mickey Mouse Club Theater, aka Fantasyland Theater

MAP: Fantasyland, Fa-9

CHRONOLOGY: August 27, 1955–December 20, 1981

HISTORY: *The Mickey Mouse Club* TV show was still about 10 weeks away from airing when the Mickey Mouse Club Theater opened in **Fantasyland**. The theater covered about 5,000 square feet of the northwest wing that extends from **Sleeping Beauty Castle. Pinocchio's Daring Journey** is in this spot today.

On **Opening Day**, the theater made it into national TV coverage, not for anything going on inside, but for the debut of the Mouseketeers being held outside. Guests and viewers saw that the exterior of the theater carried the same medieval-festival theme common to all the structures in the castle courtyard in the '50s. Inside, the air-conditioned 400-seat theater showed cartoons, but no live Mouseketeers, for the price of a B ticket. The park's 1956 **souvenir book** specified the program as "thirty-minute cartoons running continuously from 11 A.M. until closing." Starting on June 16, 1956, a half-hour show called *3D Jamboree* included 3-D glasses, a 3-D Mouseketeer movie, and 3-D cartoons. The promo poster declared the show was "all in color~all in music~all in fun." Behind the scenes, the theater was also used to hold official meetings and training sessions.

By 1964, new episodes of the original *Mickey Mouse Club* show hadn't been made for five years, and there was another location for club activities, the **Mickey Mouse Club Headquarters**, open over on **Town Square**. Subsequently, the Mickey Mouse Club Theater got a new name. Rechristened the Fantasyland Theater in '64, it continued showing cartoons on a varying schedule until December 20, 1981, when it was closed permanently for the construction that would bring in Pinocchio's Daring Journey. The Fantasyland Theater name would live on, however—on June 23, 1995, it became the new name of **Videopolis** over by **It's a Small World.**

Mickey's Christmas Chalet

MAP: Fantasyland, Fa-30

CHRONOLOGY: May 25, 1983–May 17, 1987

HISTORY: When **Fantasyland** was extensively remodeled in early '83, several venerable attractions and shops were replaced. In addition to the **Pirate Ship Restaurant** (aka Captain Hook's Galley) and the **Mickey Mouse Club Theater** (aka the Fantasyland Theater), **Merlin's Magic Shop** also disappeared, leaving the **Main Street Magic Shop** as the park's only supplier of magic tricks.

Merlin's had existed for almost three decades next to the **Peter Pan Flight** attraction along the right-hand side of the **Sleeping Beauty Castle** courtyard. Replacing the magic of Merlin was the magic of Christmas. Mickey's Christmas Chalet was a year-round holiday-themed store filled with decorations and ornaments (not all of them adorned with Disney characters). The park's 1986 **souvenir book** showed off an exterior that had been refurbished with fresh paint, flower boxes, and trimmed shrubs. In '87, the holiday merchandise got relocated to a nearby space within the castle's entryway, the **Castle Christmas Shop**. Moving into Mickey's spot next to Pan was another attractive store, the charming **Briar Rose Cottage**

Mickey's House

MAP: Mickey's Toontown, MT-5

CHRONOLOGY: January 24, 1993–ongoing

HISTORY: For decades, many guests wondered where Mickey Mouse lived and where they could meet him. They found out in early 1993 when the mouse who started it all got his own fascinating home at 1 Neighborhood Lane in the brand-new **Mickey's Toontown** section of Disneyland.

It turns out that Mickey lives in a bright yellow bungalow that's got bulbous columns, white and green trim, peaked dormer windows, curving walls, and sloping roof lines. Inside, Mickey has splurged on beautiful hardwood floors. Outside, his garden is beautifully cared for and is outlined with a white picket fence.

Throughout Mickey's House are clever architectural flourishes and design details that leave no doubt as to whose home this is (Imagineers must have been laughing steadily as they came up with all the delightful gags and puns that are found at every turn). There's a cartoony car parked outside; a garage for the star's sports equipment, tools, and garbage cans; famous books revamped with mouse-related titles (*Toons Along the Mohawk*, *Random Mouse Dictionary*, *Mice Station Zebra*, etc.) in the crooked bookshelves; a Mouseway player piano with **Hidden Mickeys** in the music; movie scripts from his cartoons; a smiling old-time radio and a TV that plays cartoons; Mickey's actual passport with Disney-related stamps in a glass case; Pluto's bed and water bowl; photos of Mickey with **Walt Disney**; and tons more artifacts and souvenirs spread across a kitchen, living room, laundry room, stairway, den, and greenhouse.

The walk-through mouse house is actually a lead-in to this attraction's signature event. Out back is the Movie Barn, a rustic prop-filled building where cartoons are supposedly still being made. A small stand-up theater runs Mickey's highlights, and old posters line the walls. To the delight of kids, the main mouse, dressed in a natty tux, is available in his dressing room all day long for greetings and photos (photos taken here by **cast members** are available later that same day at the **Main Street Photo Supply Co.**). To the delight of adults and Disney fans, Mickey's House is a wonderfully imaginative, amazingly detailed museum worthy of careful study.

Mickey's Toontown

MAP: Park, P-17

CHRONOLOGY: January 24, 1993–ongoing

HISTORY: Since the early '90s, the park's **souvenir books** have spent many colorful pages enticing guests to explore the land in the park's distant north. How distant? Mickey's Toontown exists completely outside of the **berm** that encloses Disneyland's original perimeter. Formerly this area beyond **Fantasyland** was the site of a narrow road, the park's **pony farm**, and storage facilities. A new tunnel through the berm provides the gateway into Toontown. A population counter above the tunnel pretends to keep track of incoming guests, but the wacky digits include blanks and question marks and random spinning. Making it perfect for Toontown.

Toontown was the first entirely new themed land added to the park since **Bear Country** had opened in 1972 (Bear Country was renamed **Critter Country** about three years before Mickey's Toontown debuted). It's also the smallest of the park's lands: Toontown measures only 200 feet from the back of southern Toon Park up to the door of the Third Little Piggy Bank, and 500 feet from behind the **Chip 'n Dale Tree House** in the west to behind Roger's fountain in the east, an area totaling under three acres.

Originally called Mickeyland when it was in the early planning stages, Toontown derives from a small character-greeting area that had been successful at Walt Disney World. The concept was greatly expanded at Disneyland to include themes, designs, and gags from the blockbuster Disney movie of 1988, *Who Framed Roger Rabbit*. It stands today as the least changed land in the park—whereas dozens of stores have moved in and out of **Main Street** (some stores left in the very first summer), and while dozens of attractions have come and gone in **Tomorrowland**, **Adventureland**, etc., Toontown exists today almost exactly as it did when it was first built.

When it opened in early 1993 with a special ceremony attended by Disney CEO Michael Eisner and comedian Harry Anderson, guests learned that the hilarious little Toontown village had supposedly existed for over 50 years but was only now being opened up to visitors. As an animation destination, everything in Mickey's

Toontown is designed primarily for kids (like most cartoons) but can be appreciated by adults (like the best cartoons). And as in cartoons, buildings here don't have right angles or straight lines and instead look swollen or inflatable. What's more, ordinary objects get whimsical touches,  and silly sounds and sights can pop up at any moment. **Walt Disney** would've loved it all, presumably; curious guests will want to seek out the window tribute to him above Toontown's Library.

Many of the locations in Toontown are scaled-down versions of places that exist elsewhere in Disneyland. For instance, Toontown has its own City Hall and Fire Department, a walk-through treehouse, a roller coaster-style attraction, a car-driving attraction, and a large boat, plus inexpensive snack stands and souvenir stores, just like Disneyland itself does. Like other small towns, Toontown is divided into a downtown district (to the east) and a residential neighborhood (to the west), with mass transit (the **Jolly Trolley**) connecting the two. Downtown includes stores, fast-food eateries, and kid-friendly attractions like **Roger Rabbit's Car Toon Spin**, while the star-studded neighborhood boasts wacky homes for Mickey, Minnie, Goofy, and Chip 'n Dale, all of them looking appropriate for their owners but none of them copied from specific Disney cartoons. Two fountains provide centerpieces for the plazas, and the rolling Toontown Hills (adorned with a Hollywood-style sign) provide the backdrop.

Toontown's many wonderful surprises invite guests to touch, try, and interact with literally everything. Stand on a manhole cover near the **Toontown Five & Dime** and weasel voices will call out. Drink from a water fountain and it will utter wisecracks. The plunger at the Fireworks Factory, the doorbells at the Electric Company, the Dalmatian pup occasionally peering out of the firehouse, the interactive mailboxes, the street sign announcing "Wrong Turn O.K.," the blank sign announcing that it is merely a "Blank Sign" with no message on it, the humorous window signs advertising such inside-joke businesses as "P.L. Pete, Prosthetic Devices"—like the rest of Disneyland, there are so many delights to discover in Toontown, it really is a place that warrants, and rewards, deliberate exploration by each individual guest.

⟨Midget Autopia⟩

MAP: Fantasyland, Fa-16

CHRONOLOGY: April 23, 1957–April 3, 1966

HISTORY: Following in the slipstreams of the popular **Tomorrowland Autopia** (opened in 1955) and the **Junior Autopia** (1956), the Midget Autopia debuted in the spring of '57 as a destination for the youngest drivers of all—preschoolers. The Midget's track was laid out around the corner past the **Storybook Land Canal Boats** in **Fantasyland**; formerly a relatively undeveloped eating area, this location would be eliminated in favor of wide walkways when the much-anticipated **It's a Small World** appeared in 1966.

Whereas the two other Autopias banned the smallest guests from driving the cars, the Midget Autopia actually invited them to take the wheel (in fact, adults weren't even allowed on the attraction). In contrast to the sleek Tomorrowland and

Junior Autopia sports cars, the Midget Autopia bodies were rounder and friendlier, like cartoon cars with two steering wheels side by side. And unlike the other Autopias, which touted their tracks as freeways, the Midget Autopia track was a gentle, winding road that at one point crept through a little rural building.

After the attraction was dismantled in the spring of '66, the cars and displays were donated to Marceline, Missouri, the hometown of **Walt Disney**. In Marceline's Walt Disney Park, the cars ran as a kiddie ride until they were eventually removed from service. One of the Midget Autopia cars is still on view in Marceline's Walt Disney Hometown Museum. Another Midget Autopia car is mounted on a pedestal alongside the track in today's Tomorrowland Autopia, giving 21st-century guests a glimpse at 1950s fun.

𝕸ike 𝕱ink 𝕶eel 𝕭oats

MAP: Frontierland, Fr-12

CHRONOLOGY: December 25, 1955–May 17, 1997

HISTORY: For over 40 years two keelboats operated in **Frontierland** waters. Many modern guests wouldn't know what a keelboat is unless they've seen the episode called "Davy Crockett's Keel Boat Race" on the old **Disneyland TV series**. In the late '50s, however, everyone would've recognized a keelboat as being something like a small, old-fashioned wooden houseboat, since that much-seen TV episode was part of the Davy Crockett craze that swept the nation. On the show, tough guy Mike Fink raced his ramshackle *Gullywhumper* against Davy and his boat, the *Bertha Mae*, down the mighty Mississipp'. To the vanquished went the spoils, because Mike, the loser in the race, got a long-running attraction at Disneyland.

The *Gullywhumper* began operating on Christmas Day in 1955, to be followed three months later by the *Bertha Mae*. Both boats were the actual crafts used on the TV show, both were powered by modern diesel engines, and both sailed freely without any submerged guide rails. About 30 guests, sitting inside and on the roof, could take the 11-minute, C-ticket tour of the **Rivers of America**. By '58, the wooden originals had been replaced by fiberglass replicas that could better stand the constant wear and tear (they also had six, not four open windows). Throughout all these

first years the keelboats were always given at least one photo, plus "rollicking" descriptions, in the park's **souvenir books**.

The boats' route around **Tom Sawyer Island** was basically the same one taken by the big ships on the river—the *Mark Twain* and, as of mid-'58, the *Columbia*—but the keelboats launched on the opposite side of the river from where the big boats launched. Home for the keelboats was a rugged dock on the southwestern riverbank over by **Fowler's Harbor**. The keelboats kept an irregular schedule, operating mostly during the summers and on the busiest days. Things got really irregular when the two boats were temporarily pulled from service in the fall of '94.

Unfortunately, after returning on March 30, 1996, a near disaster led to their abrupt demise. In May of '97, a possibly overloaded *Gullywhumper* capsized suddenly, dumping frightened guests into the water and sending several to the hospital with minor injuries. Both boats were immediately shut down, and eventually the attraction was quietly and permanently closed. In 2001, Disney auctioned off the *Bertha Mae* for $15,000, and two years later the *Gullywhumper* was installed along the river as stationary scenery near Big Thunder Mountain.

Mile Long Bar

MAP: Bear Country/Critter Country, B/C-5

CHRONOLOGY: March 24, 1972–July 17, 1989

HISTORY: Debuting with the rest of **Bear Country** in the spring of 1972 was this unique eatery that served up dogs, chips, and other lightweight snackables. Like other Bear Country elements, the Mile Long Bar had already been successfully tried out at Walt Disney World before it opened in Disneyland right next to **Teddi Barra's Swingin' Arcade**.

The brown, two-story exterior was shown in the park's **souvenir books** of the '70s, but it was so hidden behind foliage nobody could tell from the photos what they were looking at. What would've made a great photo was the interior, which, thanks to an arrangement of mirrors, created the "mile long" illusion referred to in the name. In '89, that name got a zip-a-dee-doo-dah revision to the **Brer Bar** to match its new zip-a-dee-doo-dah neighbor, **Splash Mountain**.

Mineral Hall

MAP: Frontierland, Fr-24

CHRONOLOGY: July 30, 1956–December 1962

HISTORY: In the late '50s, guests who walked through the **Frontierland** gates, continued down the main thoroughfare past the **Frontierland Shooting Gallery**, and turned right into **El Zocalo** would've found a dignified two-story white building at the back of the square. The Mineral Hall showed and sold exotic rocks and minerals, highlighting the merchandise with black lights to draw out the spectacular colors. So impressive was this display, dazzled guests could even buy the lights along with their mineralogical wonders so they could re-create the whole show at home.

  After the Mineral Hall closed in late '62, gradually the restaurant next door, **Casa de Fritos**, expanded onto the right-hand side of the property. Eventually the rest of the old hall became offices closed off to the public. The only remnant left for today's guests is a Mineral Hall sign at the back of today's **Rancho del Zocalo Restaurante**.

Miniature Horse Corral

MAP: Frontierland, Fr-25

CHRONOLOGY: July 1955–July 1957

HISTORY: Never mentioned or shown in any of the **souvenir books**, the Miniature Horse Corral was an early, inexpensive exhibit in **Frontierland**. The ponies, donkeys, and miniature horses behind the rough-hewn wooden fences were for viewing and petting, not for riding, making this area a precursor of the petting zoo that later appeared in Frontierland's **Big Thunder Ranch**. The quiet corral was closed in July 1957, and quickly replaced by the noisier, rowdier **Frontierland Shooting Gallery**.

Minnie's House

MAP: Mickey's Toontown, MT-6

CHRONOLOGY: January 24, 1993–ongoing

HISTORY: Appropriately enough, Mickey Mouse's girlfriend has her own adorable walk-through exhibit right next to his residence in **Mickey's Toontown**. Like other homes in the neighborhood, Minnie's House is a bungalow-style structure with curved rooflines, a stone chimney, rounded columns, and a white picket fence. But whereas **Mickey's House** is a sunny

**Eight Books
on Minnie's Shelves**

*Ben Fur
Cat on a Hot Toon Roof
Cheese Louise
Cheese and Remembrance
A Doll's Mouse
Five Cheesy Pieces
From Ear to Eternity
Little Mouse on the Prairie*

yellow and definitely belongs to a male, hers is a more romantic lavender and is decidedly feminine, with hearts and frills adorning walls and furnishings.

As with everything else in Toontown, Minnie's place invites interactivity by offering an array of gizmos to touch and gags to discover. Knock out a tune on the pans on the stove, explore all the cheeses in the Cheesemore fridge and the cookies in the kitchen, check Minnie's e-mails on her heart-shaped computer with an eight-key keyboard, play at her makeup table, try to find the Elvis book on the shelves, check out her magazines (*Mademouselle*)—kids will have fun, and adults will have laughs. Out back is a special wishing well that generates a familiar voice, and Minnie herself is usually on the premises for photos and autographs.

𝕸int 𝕵ulep 𝕭ar

MAP: New Orleans Square, NOS-11

CHRONOLOGY: July 24, 1966–ongoing

HISTORY: Guests may come to the Mint Julep Bar for the juleps, but they'll probably stay for the fritters. This little snack counter tucked away on the back of the **French Market** restaurant in **New Orleans Square** has been offering some of the park's tastiest baked goods, especially fresh-baked sugar-coated fritters with fruit dipping sauce, for over 40 years.

As the bar's name suggests, mint juleps are the famous specialty, and they are indeed cool, tasty concoctions with mint and flavoring, but purists will decry the absence of bourbon (only one restaurant inside Disneyland serves alcohol, and it's not open to the public—the nearby **Club 33**). Perhaps the Mint Julep Bar's virgin version is more historically accurate anyway. After all, the name julep derives from *julab*, the Persian word for "rose water," not "hard liquor." Supplementing the fritters and juleps are other baked goods, ice cream treats, and fancy coffee drinks, all of them quick and delicious to-go items that make it easy to wait for the arrival of the train at the nearby New Orleans Square/Frontierland Train Station.

Miss Disneyland, aka Disneyland Ambassador to the World

CHRONOLOGY: January 1, 1965–ongoing

HISTORY: Starting in 1965, Disneyland established a position for **cast members** called, for the first few years, Miss Disneyland; later this title was changed to Disneyland Ambassador to the World. From 1965 until 1994, the position was given only to women, who were selected on the basis of their appearance, personality, and poise. Each year the new Miss Disneyland/Ambassador to the World would represent the park in parades, on TV shows, and at special events.

The first Miss Disneyland, selected in 1964 but serving in 1965, was a Texan named Julie Reihm. Reihm was a Long Beach college student who had been a Disneyland **Tour Guide** for two years before she assumed her new role. On January 3, 1965, she costarred on the *Walt Disney's Wonderful World of Color* TV series. For the episode called "The Disneyland Tenth Anniversary Show," Reihm helped preview the coming **Pirates of the Caribbean** and **Haunted Mansion** attractions by commenting on models and displays alongside **Walt Disney**. She was wearing the standard Tour Guide uniform of plaid skirt, white long-sleeved blouse buttoned at the neck, plus a vest, with a riding crop and a black equestrian-style hat as accessories. During the show, Walt Disney reinforced the equestrian connection by calling Reihm and the Tour Guides "guest jockeys."

Connie Swanson, another Tour Guide, was the second Miss Disneyland. While she didn't appear on the *Wonderful World of Color*, she did travel extensively on behalf of the park. Melissa Taylor, the Disneyland Ambassador for 1985, circled the globe on a 30-day flight with Mickey Mouse to celebrate the park's 30th anniversary.

In 1995, the Ambassador title went plural, and since then an Ambassador to the World team, not just a single Ambassador, has been selected, with men also included in the mix. Actress Julie Andrews was named an honorary Disney Ambassador to the World in 2005 as part of Disneyland's 50th-anniversary celebration.

Mission to Mars

MAP: Tomorrowland, T-16

CHRONOLOGY: March 21, 1975–November 2, 1992

HISTORY: Once man landed on the moon in July of 1969, Disneyland's Flight to the Moon attraction started to seem like Flight to the Mundane. Been there, done that, the aloof crowds in **Tomorrowland** seemed to be saying. So how you gonna keep 'em down in their seats, once they've seen the Sea of Tranquility?

Helped by NASA, Disneyland's designers did what America's space program would eventually do—target a new heavenly body. Thus, in the spring of '75, an upgraded, enlarged flight-simulation attraction, this one the Mission to Mars, debuted in the same space where the lunar flight had launched, a low building slung to the right of the **Carousel of Progress** theater and, as of 1977, to the left of **Space Mountain**.

Considering how different Mars is from the moon, the two flights were surprisingly similar. The sponsor was the same, the McDonnell Douglas aerospace company, and so was the price, a D-ticket. The pre-show Mission Control area for the Mars mission looked and operated the same way it did for the Flight to the Moon—in fact, during the late '70s the park's **souvenir books** used the exact same photo for the Mars mission that they'd used to promote the earlier lunar expedition, a picture that showed banks of computers and TV monitors that were being closely watched by official-looking **Audio-Animatronic** figures wearing headsets. Supervising these mission controllers was Mr. Johnson (no longer Tom Morrow from the lunar mission), a dignified scientist with a headset, glasses, tie, lab coat, and clipboard. Johnson discussed space travel and the Mars vehicle, played the incoming-bird gag that Tom Morrow had used before the moon flight, and then excused everyone for boarding.

As with the Flight to the Moon, over 100 guests sat in a circular theater and watched two screens, one on the floor and one on the ceiling, to show them where they'd been and where they were going. Small screens ringing the theater provided additional views of the 15-minute journey. After lift off, which was felt through the seats with a lowering/raising effect, and after getting the moon in view on the overhead screen, a speedy jump through hyperspace brought the Red Planet quickly into range. Camera probes beamed back surface details of the Martian canyons and mountains until a sudden meteor shower impelled the main ship to dash back to Earth.

While the visuals were still exciting, and while the seats still did a nice job of simulating G-forces, by the mid-'70s guests were probably underwhelmed by the whole space-travel experience. After all, they'd been watching real Gemini and Apollo missions on TV since the early '60s, and those TV audiences had become so small and uninterested that some of the later flights weren't even televised. In 1992, Tomorrowland's last Mars mission returned home for good, and the building stayed vacant for the next six years.

At one point in the '90s, a dramatic attraction called Alien Encounter was targeted for the space, but it was deemed too big and ambitious for this location and so ended up in Walt Disney World instead. In early '96, the **Toy Story Funhouse** temporarily went up at the Mission site, but that quick spring fling came down by summer. Finally, with the big remodel of Tomorrowland in '98, the old Mission to Mars building reopened, this time serving up lunch instead of interstellar space flight. **Redd Rockett's Pizza Port** still operates here in the shadow of **Innoventions**.

Mlle. Antoinette's Parfumerie

MAP: New Orleans Square, NOS-9

CHRONOLOGY: 1967–1997

HISTORY: As shown with a photo in the park's 1968 **souvenir book**, this elegant little shop had a beautiful interior that was heavily French, boasting such features as a sparkling chandelier, ornate mirrors, and display cases lined with delicate bottles. It fit right in with the neighbors—this same block towards the back of **New Orleans Square** already had the prominent **French Market** out front and the stylish **Le Chapeau** next door.

In Mlle. Antoinette's, "ladies," as specified in the souvenir book, "blend their own exclusive perfumes," aided by trained perfumers who could mix customized fragrances. Famous-name perfumes were also sold here. Some 30 years after it opened, the Parfumerie was replaced by an equally luxurious jewelry store, **Jewel of Orléans**.

Monorail, aka Disneyland-Alweg Monorail, aka Disneyland Monorail

MAP: Tomorrowland, T-10

CHRONOLOGY: June 14, 1959–ongoing

HISTORY: The magnificent Monorail debuted in mid-June of 1959, an auspicious moment in Disneyland history. Of the three new vehicles that began running that month (the **Matterhorn Bobsleds** and the **Submarine Voyage** were the others), the Monorail was the only one that was intended to be a serious advance in American transportation. The other two attractions were wonderful, but the Monorail was significant. So significant, in fact, that Vice President Nixon was on hand for the ribbon-cutting honors. So significant that it was awarded a special plaque by  the American Society of Mechanical Engineers in 1986. So significant that, unlike every other vehicle in the park that either stayed on its original course or was eventually shut down à la the **PeopleMover**, the Monorail had its service *expanded* to cover more than three times its original length. Other vehicles made memories; the Monorail made history.

Walt Disney and his staff didn't invent the monorail-on-an-elevated-track concept. That was done in Germany by Dr. Axel Lennart Wenner-Gren, whose initials formed the name of his design company. But when Walt Disney saw the boxy train run on a rural test track in '57, he quickly partnered with Alweg to create a new, sleeker version for Disneyland. Disney Legend **Bob Gurr**, who designed most of the vehicles at the park, came up with a tapered, futuristic version. Working from Gurr's pencil drawings, another Disney Legend, **John Hench**, enhanced them with color and effects to make the Monorail look like a horizontal rocket ship. **Roger Broggie** and his engineering team built the first Monorail at the Disney Studios, and **Bill Martin** laid out the track about where the **Viewliner** had been. For all of them, the ambitious goal wasn't merely to create a Disneyland-Alweg Monorail for fun, stylish sightseeing; it was to create a meaningful alternative to public transportation, an all-electric train that would smoothly, silently glide along an elevated "highway in the sky" to convey guests into and out of the park's interior.

Not that it started out that way. When it opened as one of the first E-ticket attractions, there was only one three-car train, *Monorail Red* (the trains have always been known by their colors), and there was only one stop, which was next to the Submarine Voyage in **Tomorrowland**. That meant 82 passengers, not hundreds at a time, were starting and stopping at the same point. From the Tomorrowland station guests looped for eight-tenths of a mile around the submarine lagoon, the **Fantasyland Autopia**, the **Tomorrowland Autopia**, and **Matterhorn Mountain** (the view even took in some of the surrounding Anaheim area). It was a scenic journey but not a vital one.

The traveling was splendid. Speeds were usually in the 20–35 mph range, though the Monorail could've easily doubled those numbers had its drivers been allowed to cut loose. As impressive as the smooth speed was the elevated track, which rose from about 12 feet above the Autopia road to about 20 feet above **Fantasyland** walkways. And everybody loved the low, booming horn. With crowds quickly at capacity, a second train, *Monorail Blue*, joined the route three weeks after the debut of *Monorail Red*. But still the world's first daily-operating public monorail was a Tomorrowland-only ride.

Expansion plans, however, were soon in the works. On April 10, 1961, the Monorail was temporarily shut down so the track could be dramatically extended to the Disneyland Hotel outside the park. Reopening on June 1st, the Monorail now made two-and-a-half-minute one-way trips on a 2.3-mile-long track that left Tomorrowland, ventured along Harbor Boulevard. and over the **parking lot**, crossed a public street (West Avenue), and reached a new monorail station at the hotel, where the train picked up and dropped off guests for a return journey back into the park. The new route added elevation to the ride as it rose to about 25 feet above the park's **entrance**. The new route also added meaning—by delivering guests from one station to another, the Monorail had become the real mass-transit system Walt Disney always intended it to be.

Not only was the route different, so was the vehicle. Another passenger car, upping capacity to 108 guests, joined the train, and a new train, *Monorail Gold*, joined the line. These Mark II trains also had a nifty new design feature: the little bubble canopies on the first cars. More revisions were to come—the Mark III Monorail debuted in 1968 with a fifth passenger car (for 127 total riders), larger windows, and bucket seats instead of benches. Plus there was a fourth train, *Monorail Green* (not all the trains operated simultaneously, instead subbing for each other during the frequent maintenance periods).

Everything associated with the Monorail was cool. **Cast members** on the attraction dressed like pilots and stewardesses. The breathtaking **attraction poster** showed *Monorail Red*, the lagoon, the *Moonliner*, and the Matterhorn all at once, adding up to one of Disneyland's best promotional images ever. And for years the **souvenir books** lavished on the Monorail colorful photos and proud text about "the future in city mass transportation," a declaration that made this one of the boldest additions ever to the original park.

Always advancing, the Imagineers kept the changes coming. The Mark IV Monorail never made it to Disneyland, settling in Orlando instead, but the Mark Vs came to Anaheim in April of 1987 with a new shape created by **George McGinnis**; a new color, *Monorail Purple*; new features, such as automatic sliding doors and air-conditioning; and a new Alweg-less name—it was now simply the Disneyland Monorail (Alweg had run into financial problems in the '60s and been taken over by another company). In 2001, concurrent with the arrival of Disney's California Adventure, an updated monorail station in Downtown Disney replaced the one that had been at the Disneyland Hotel. Next, the entire Monorail line ceased operations on August 21, 2006, and for the next four months to accommodate the extensive remodel of the old submarine attraction into the new Finding Nemo Submarine Voyage. Once the subs resurfaced in mid-2007, one of the Monorail trains was painted bright yellow and decorated with portholes and text to help draw attention to the lagoon. All-new monorails that hearken back to earlier, sleeker designs went into service in the spring of 2008. These Rhode Island-built/Vancouver-assembled trains sport new colors and window-facing bench seats that offer panoramic park views.

Unfortunately, the urban revolution that Walt Disney hoped his 1959 Monorail augured never arrived. While several other Alweg monorails went into service, notably one in Seattle, other major cities, most disappointingly Los Angeles, never adopted them, which makes the one in Disneyland even more special. The first one built in America, the longest-lasting of its kind, and always a majestic sight anytime it streams into view, Disneyland's Monorail is still a grand, well-functioning symbol of an optimistic future.

𝕸oonliner

MAP: Tomorrowland, T-15

CHRONOLOGY: July 17, 1955–ongoing

HISTORY: Just as **Sleeping Beauty Castle** draws guests northward up **Main Street** and the *Mark Twain* draws them westward into **Frontierland**, so too did the original *Moonliner* rocket, visible from the **Plaza Hub**, compel pedestrians to venture eastward into **Tomorrowland**. The *Moonliner* wasn't a ticketed attraction, and guests couldn't go inside it, but by its very design and placement it was a dramatic invitation to come explore the world of the future.

Most of the early concept drawings that rendered aerial views of the proposed park had a rocket standing tall in the eastern section of Disneyland. In 1954, **Herb Ryman** drew a close-up of a spindly rocket that looked a lot like the

elegant design that **John Hench** eventually came up with. When its pieces were assembled in the heart of Tomorrowland just a few weeks before **Opening Day**, the *Moonliner* towered an imposing 76 feet high right in front of the low-slung **Rocket to the Moon** attraction, with the big **Flight Circle** plaza nearby.

Unlike the actual moon rockets that fired from the Florida coast in the '60s, the *Moonliner* had no separate stages, no capsule, and no cluster of engines at the bottom. It also had no adjacent support gantry and instead stood on its own legs. What it did have was a slender tapered shape, a cockpit near the top, two rings of portholes, horizontal red stripes on its white hull, and a corporate sponsor, TWA, which billed itself as "the Official Airline to Disneyland." While the *Moonliner* technically wasn't what moon rockets turned out to be, it sure looked like what everyone in the '50s imagined a cool rocket *should* look like.

What's more, theoretically it was going to do more than what actual rockets of the '60s did. The *Moonliner* wasn't supposed to be just a one-time disposable vehicle that visited the moon for a quick scientific visit and returned as a single tiny capsule on parachutes. This was a *liner*, a futuristic ship that conveyed travelers back and forth between the earth and the moon, with lunar bases awaiting at one end, reusable launch pads at the other, and the ultimate frequent-flyer miles in between.

Something so sleek and optimistic perfectly symbolized Tomorrowland, as the early **souvenir books** pointed out: "Looking down on all Tomorrowland, TWA's tall rocket pylon symbolizes Disneyland's dream world of the future" (1958). Thus it was frequently shown in photos and **attraction posters**, especially the one for the Rocket to the Moon, where the *Moonliner* rose proud and tall in the foreground, its needle nose already in the stars.

Somehow, such an important symbol barely lasted a decade. On June 8, 1962, Douglas Aircraft took over sponsorship, painted its name vertically down the side, and replaced the horizontal red stripes with blue stripes that went up and down the hull. Incredibly, four years later the beautiful *Moonliner* was deemed expendable during the major remodel of Tomorrowland, and in the fall of '66 it was dismantled. The rocket's site was assumed by the sprawling **Carousel of Progress** building (Douglas, meanwhile, was acquired by McDonnell to become the McDonnell Douglas that sponsored 1967's Flight to the Moon).

Veteran guests happily welcomed back a replica of the *Moonliner* 32 years later. At 53 feet tall, this 1998 version, however, was only about two-thirds the size of its classic predecessor. The small size of the new rocket isn't readily apparent because of its new location about 20 yards from its previous spot. The rocket now sits on top of the roof of a snack stand called the **Spirit of Refreshment**. Since the snack stand is sponsored by Coca-Cola, the red stripes have returned to the *Moon-liner* to echo the red-and-white livery of Coke cans. While it's not the awe-inspiring spectacle it once was, most Disneyland fans will agree that a stunted *Moonliner* being used to advertise cola is still better than no *Moonliner* at all.

Motor Boat Cruise, aka Motor Boat Cruise to Gummi Glen

MAP: Fantasyland, Fa-22

CHRONOLOGY: June 1957–January 11, 1993

HISTORY: After unending maintenance problems finally sank the infamous **Phantom Boats** in the fall of 1956, a new boat ride opened at the start of summer in 1957. Whereas the Phantom Boats had toured the big broad lagoon in **Tomorrowland**, the Motor Boat Cruise crept along a new waterway in **Fantasyland** where the **Mickey Mouse Club Circus** had formerly operated. In its first year, the Motor Boat Cruise's neighbors were the **Junior Autopia** and the **Viewliner**; two years later both of those attractions were replaced by, respectively, the new **Fantasyland Autopia** and **Mono-rail**, with their new pylons and overpasses carrying them above the cruise's waters.

Even though its boats looked like sleek little speedsters, all of them with aerodynamic shapes, open cockpits, brightly colored hulls, and white decks, the Motor Boat Cruise was to boating what the Autopia cars were to driving. The boats operated on a submerged guide rail and so offered limited returns no matter how much effort was put into cranking the wheel. In addition, the gas pedal had little effect on the whole experience (some have suggested that all it did was increase engine volume). Young guests probably enjoyed the illusion of control, while older guests could relax, peruse the rocky river and the disparate vehicles in the vicinity, and take comfort in knowing that they'd only spent a B ticket for this attraction. For years photos in the park's **souvenir books** showed boats easing past big boulders in gentle waters. In the accompanying caption—"Steering through rapids is fun on the Motor Boat Cruise"—"rapids" was undoubtedly a technical term meaning "leisurelies."

Somehow, with Disneyland moving to new high-tech, high-speed, high-profile attractions like

Oldest Attractions to Be Retired

42 years: Circarama/Circle-Vision theater (1955–'97)
41: Astro-Jets/Tomorrowland Jets/Rocket Jets (1956–'97)
40: Fantasyland Autopia (1959–'99)
39: Submarine Voyage (1959–'98)
38: Skyway to Fantasyland/Tomorrowland (1956–'94)
37: Swiss Family Treehouse (1962–'99)
36: Motor Boat Cruise (1957–'93)
29: Country Bear Jamboree/Playhouse (1972–2001)
28: PeopleMover (1967–'95)
20: Rocket to the Moon/Flight to the Moon (1955–'75)

Space Mountain, Big Thunder Mountain, and Splash Mountain in the '70s and '80s, the gentle Motor Boat Cruise hung on into the '90s. Just before the end came, the boats got a major change from March 15th to November 10th of 1991. When Disney Afternoon Avenue took over part of Fantasyland from the spring to the fall of that year, the Motor Boat Cruise took on a new name—Motor Boat Cruise to Gummi Glen—and some new scenery—painted plywood images of Gummi Bears— all to offer eight months of support to the Gummis' TV show. By Thanksgiving the attraction had been rechristened simply the Motor Boat Cruise, and by February of '93 the boats and the waterway had been replaced for good by the lush landscaping of Fantasia Gardens.

Mr. Toad's Wild Ride

MAP: Fantasyland, Fa-28

CHRONOLOGY: July 17, 1955–ongoing

HISTORY: Whereas the purpose of the other two original **Fantasyland** indoor dark rides was either to enchant with wondrous airborne views (**Peter Pan Flight**) or effectively reduce a classic story to its most emotional elements (**Snow White Adventures**), Mr. Toad's Wild Ride had one simple goal: make guests laugh. The early **souvenir books** emphasized this intention with its Wild Ride photos—two older ladies, or a parent and child, in an antique motorcar, everyone laughing. The jaunty captions explained how "the hilarious misadventures of Mr. Toad in Fantasyland bring fun and laughter to everyone," it's "a hilarious adventure for the young in heart of all ages," and it offers "a hilarious race through the quaint streets of Old London Town." The Wild Ride was only a C-ticket attraction, but it might've been the jolliest attraction in the park.

The Wild Ride is housed in a rectangular building at the far right end of **Sleeping Beauty Castle**. Toad shares this building with **Alice in Wonderland**, and in fact Alice's caterpillar vehicles crawl up onto the second floor above Toad's tracks. A whirling ride has always been out in the courtyard near Toad—from '55 to '63 that ride was the **Mad Hatter's Mad Tea Party**, and since '83 it's been the **King Arthur Carrousel**.

The theme came from Disney's half-hour 1949 animated movie *The Wind in the Willows*, based on the classic Kenneth Grahame book. Though the attraction doesn't really retell that movie plot, movie elements are reprised throughout: the cars are named after key characters (Mr. Toad, Ratty, Moley, MacBadger, Weasel, Winky the barkeep, Cyril the horse); most of those characters actually make an appearance along the two-minute trip; Toad's own home is the ride's preliminary racetrack; and Toad's madcap energy propels the whole adventure.

After winding through the arbor-covered queue past a statue of J. Thaddeus Toad, Esq., "Master of Toad Hall & Incurable Adventurer," guests approach

Toad's house. A colorful mural in the loading area foretells some of the hijinks to come. Boarding a stylish but uncontrollable little antique car, riders immediately careen and crash their way through the hallways, then tear off across the English countryside. Their destination—Nowhere in Particular; their goal—unbridled merriment.

The most astonishing part of the tour is the non-Disney ending. After the rollicking romp through London's streets, after making it through the TNT-filled warehouse and bashing through Winky's pub, after the police chase and the courtroom trial and the prison getaway, after the whole frantic escapade is brought to a sudden crashing halt by the scary approach of a noisy train, guests wind up . . . in Hell. Literally, a fiery, demon-populated Hell. No other Disneyland attraction veers so far from the movie that inspired it (the movie ends with Toad happily soaring off in a flying machine) or ends so calamitously (the **Haunted Mansion** sends guests home with a hitchhiking ghost, but that's nothing compared to the eternal torment that culminates the Wild Ride). It's this kind of unexpected nuttiness that makes Toad's attraction such a fan favorite.

When it was first being planned, Mr. Toad's Wild Ride was possibly going to be Mr. Toad's Wild roller coaster-style Ride, but that idea was reined in to make it essentially the same simple, glorious gambol it's been for over 50 years. A Disney Legends team was there at the core of creation—architect **Bill Martin** laid out the basic ride, **Claude Coats** drew illustrations of potential interiors, **Ken Anderson** designed the sets, and **Bob Gurr** built the eight vehicles.

An update in 1961 improved some of the interior's flat wooden boards that had been quickly painted up for **Opening Day**. More significantly, a major renovation in 1983 brought new effects to both the interior and exterior. Inside, new areas and gags filled out the escapade. Outside, a stunning new mansion design replaced the medieval-tournament façade that had been common to all of Fantasyland but which had made far more sense for the King Arthur Carrousel than it did for Toad's Edwardian-era automobile adventures. Toad Hall is now one of the area's architectural stars, a wonderful multi-chimneyed structure that is as fun as it is fascinating (it also matches the miniature Toad Hall that's shown along the banks of the **Storybook Land Canal Boats**).

As beloved as it is, park designers almost eliminated Mr. Toad's Wild Ride in the '90s when they talked about bringing the **Many Adventures of Winnie the Pooh** into Fantasyland. Fortunately, Toad was saved, and Pooh wound up in **Critter Country**. Toad's survival brought a sigh of relief to fans and gave generations of new guests fresh chances to decipher the fractured Latin of Toad's family motto, to giggle at all the cleverly titled books (*Toadman of Alcatraz, Twice Toad Tales, For Whom the Toad Croaks*, etc.) on the bookshelves, to watch for the Sherlock Holmes silhouette in the upstairs window, to take the Toadster's roadster on a rowdy road trip, and finally to experience the surprise of Infernoland for themselves.

Walt Disney himself acknowledged the importance of the attraction. According to the book *Remembering Walt*, when a park waitress addressed him as Mr.

Disney, he reminded her that he was Walt. "There's only one 'mister' in Disneyland," he told her, "and that's *Mr.* Toad."

Mule Pack, aka Rainbow Ridge Mule Pack, aka Pack Mules Through Nature's Wonderland

MAP: Frontierland, Fr-21

CHRONOLOGY: July 17, 1955–February 1, 1973

HISTORY: The Mule Pack debuted in **Frontierland** on **Opening Day** and enjoyed a surprisingly long run through the Disneyland decades. While it's easy to dismiss it as an unsophisticated artifact of the '50s, in actuality some form of this attraction survived into the early '70s. This was not the only time live animals were used at Disneyland—other animal attractions included the **Stage Coach**, the **Conestoga Wagons**, the horse-drawn vehicles on **Main Street**, the **Miniature Horse Corral**, the **Mickey Mouse Club Circus**, **Keller's Jungle Killers**, the petting zoo at **Big Thunder Ranch**, and the **Dalmatian Celebration**. The Mule Pack was, however, the only time guests got to actually *ride* on live animals.

    The mules operated from a Frontierland loading area that sent guests and their mighty steeds charging . . . uh, guests and their little mules clomping along dusty wilderness trails. The mules operated in sight of other, rowdier forms

of transportation that included the Stage Coach and the Conestoga Wagons. Usually nine mules at a time were strung together in a long line, headed by a cowboy-costumed **cast member** on a lead horse. Kids were the target audience, with younger, lighter children getting belted into their saddles. Bought for $50 apiece, the mules were kept at night in the park's **pony farm.**

    Changes came quickly. In early '56, the attraction temporarily closed so the wilderness area could be updated and reinvigorated with more landscaping, simple mechanical creatures, and the new train tracks of the **Rainbow Caverns Mine Train.** When the mules returned on June 26th of that year, they'd gone from being a C-ticket to a D-ticket attraction and had acquired a new name, the Rainbow Ridge Mule Pack. This lasted until October 2, 1959, when again the attraction temporarily shut down so the desert area could be remodeled. The new Pack Mules Through Nature's Wonderland opened on June 10, 1960, now cost an E ticket to board, and included a cool display of dinosaur fossils along the journey.

    After that, the attraction didn't change much until the Pack Mules finally packed it up in early 1973. By then there were many stories of problems along the trail. Recalcitrant mules had been startled by the sudden train noises, boat whistles, and other sounds of Frontierland. The animals had sometimes nipped guests, and occasionally they'd stopped in their tracks altogether, at times turning what should've been a 10-minute trip into a long, frustrating ordeal.

Naturally the park's **souvenir books** from the '50s to the '70s showed smiling kids when they depicted the mule ride, and the captions usually bragged how "young cowpokes delight in a trip across the Desert on a mule 'train.'" The mules in those photos, however, always looked pretty serious. Six years after closing, the trails where the little mules had once ambled reopened as the thrilling **Big Thunder Mountain Railroad** attraction. Rainbow Ridge, the miniature town which served as a backdrop to the mule attraction, still exists near the Big Thunder queue area (see photo, previous page).

Names Unraveled

MAP: Fantasyland, Fa-23, Fa-4, Fa-9

CHRONOLOGY: Ca. 1995–ca. 2005

HISTORY: Names Unraveled could be called Names Well-Traveled, since this little specialty service had three locations in its decade-long existence. It started as a cart parked in **Fantasyland** over on the northern side of **Matterhorn Mountain**, a place filled at different times by the **Mickey Mouse Club Circus** and the **Junior Autopia**. From there it moved indoors, taking over one of the rooms inside the entrance to **Sleeping Beauty Castle** in the late '90s. Then, after a few years, Names changed again, this time to the shop that had formerly been **Geppetto's Toys & Gifts** over by **Pinocchio's Daring Journey**.

No matter where it's been, Names Unraveled has always done the same thing—investigate the derivations and definitions of first and middle names, and then offer guests ways to take that information, or just stylishly printed versions of the names, home as keepsakes. Hard copy, stationery, plaques, glasses, key chains, and more items were available until Names Unraveled became Names Unavailable sometime around 2005.

Nature's Wonderland

MAP: Frontierland, Fr-22

CHRONOLOGY: May 28, 1960–January 2, 1977

HISTORY: The biggest change to hit **Frontierland** during the 1960s arrived in the decade's very first year. Nature's Wonderland was a huge new $2.5-million remodel in Frontierland's desert area.

Formerly this barren landscape had been mostly unnamed except for an acre-and-a-half section in the north called the **Painted Desert**. Beginning in 1955, three old-fashioned modes of transportation had left tracks back here—the **Mule Pack**, **Stage Coach**, and **Conestoga Wagons**—and as of 1956 the **Rainbow Caverns Mine Train** had chugged through on its way to the luminous Rainbow Caverns. All four of these attractions were shut down in 1959 so the wilderness through which they ventured could be transformed into Nature's Wonderland.

When the Mine Train resumed service on May 28th of 1960, Nature's Wonderland presented guests with a seven-acre area that blended unspoiled American backcountry with the latest in **Audio-Animatronic** technology. To the west, overlooking the **Rivers of America** and **Tom Sawyer Island**, was a new snow-capped five-story mountain called Cascade Peak. Across the center of Nature's Wonderland was a T-shaped body of water: the upper horizontal part of the T was Bear Country, and the stem was Beaver Valley (this Bear Country is not to be confused with the **Bear Country** that opened on the other side of the Rivers of America in 1972). To the northeast was the Living, formerly the Painted, Desert. Gone for good were the Stage Coach and Conestoga Wagons, but back for long runs were the mules and the train, both of which would survive into the '70s, albeit as the renamed Pack Mules Through Nature's Wonderland and the Western Mine Train Through Nature's Wonderland.

Like the **Jungle Cruise** and the original Painted Desert, Nature's Wonderland took its imagery from the *True-Life Adventure* films the Disney Studios had made in the '50s. Here the four inspirations were *Bear Country*, *Beaver Valley*, *The Living Desert*, and *The Olympic Elk*, all of them half-hour-long documentaries, the first three winning Oscars as Best Short Subject. Populating Nature's Wonderland were over 200 new Audio-Animatronic animals, everything from snakes, rodents, and birds to beavers, bobcats, and bears. As viewed from the train, the landscape offered stunning new views of waterfalls splashing down Cascade Peak, wildlife splashing in the rivers, and Old Unfaithful Geyser splashing 70 feet above the desert.

So proud was **Walt Disney** of the new area that he himself had sketched out for his designers, he gave it a special wraparound cover on the outside of the park's 1960 **souvenir book**. Called "The Story of Nature's Wonderland," this unique outsert detailed the attractions that awaited: "Here, in a primitive setting that duplicates the remote wilderness country, you may watch beavers, busy as always, on home-building and tree-cutting chores; coyotes and mountain lions; clown-like bears, romping without a care in the world; Olympic Elk engaged in a battle for survival, just as it is enacted daily in the natural wilderness." A colorful full-page map laid out the entire Nature's Wonderland acreage and spotlighted "exciting wilderness scenes" like two elk butting heads, a bear using a tree as a back-scratcher, a beaver gnawing on a fallen tree, a moose drinking from a river, a cougar about to pounce, and an eagle with its wings spread.

In addition, Disney even gave Nature's Wonderland its own rustic **attraction poster**. Divided into four sections that were circumnavigated by train tracks, the poster reinforced the movie connection by labeling its quadrants Bear Country, Beaver Valley, Living Desert, and Olympic Elk. Representative animals and majestic backgrounds were silk-screened into each section.

Despite all the hullabaloo, by the early '70s work was already underway to undo Nature's Wonderland. The mules were led away in '73, the train was gone in '77, and the **Big Thunder Mountain Railroad** was roaring across the dramatically redesigned landscape by the fall of '79. Some of the old Nature's Wonderland elements could still be found, however for the next three decades. Hollow Cascade Peak, gradually deteriorating from within, didn't give way to demolition until 1998; a few of the A-A animals are still on view from the speeding Big Thunder trains; and the miniature ghost town of Rainbow Ridge, which in the '50s was the backdrop for the Mine Train's loading area, has hung on to be the backdrop for Big Thunder's loading area.

New Century Watches & Clocks,
aka New Century Timepieces and New Century Jewelry

MAP: Main Street, MS-4

CHRONOLOGY: Ca. 1972–ongoing

HISTORY: The **Main Street** corner that had been the **Upjohn Pharmacy** since 1955 became a clock shop called New Century around 1972. At the time it seemed to have been called New Century Watches & Clocks, based on the sign out front that bracketed the words New Century with "Watches" on one side and "Clocks" on the other. Elgin was the sponsor until around 1986, when Lorus took over and the store became more formally known as New Century Timepieces.

That same year, the Rings 'n' Things store across the street moved in next door to New Century Timepieces, where there was a small space vacated by the **Disneyana** shop. The new vertical signage declared this space to be New Century Jewelry. Even though the jewelry shop and the adjacent clock shop share the New Century name, they're still listed separately as New Century Jewelry and New Century Timepieces in Disneyland's free brochures and at the park's official Web site. From the outside, the businesses look separate and have different paint jobs.

Inside the building, however, are two rooms wide open to each other, and really they seem more like two halves of one big store. The prominent corner room offers what the sign announces as "Disney traditions in time," which means lots of vintage-style Disney-character watches and Disney-themed clocks from famous-name manufacturers. The jewelry cases in the room to the south show off sparkling pieces of fine and costume rings, earrings, and bracelets, plus gold charms. One unique specialty is on the timepiece side, where an artisan often sits painting $300–$500 customized watch faces in view of guests.

New Orleans Barbecue

MAP: Frontierland, Fr-6

CHRONOLOGY: August 1956–June 1957

HISTORY: Listed just once in a **souvenir book** was New Orleans Barbecue, which appeared under the **Frontierland** heading in the 1957 edition. No location or description was offered, though it was probably along the row of eateries that included the **Oaks Tavern** and **Aunt Jemima's Pancake House.**

It's likely that New Orleans Barbecue was a temporary placeholder for the small space that had been **Casa de Fritos** until mid-'56 and became **Don DeFore's Silver Banjo Barbecue** in mid-'57. The New Orleans name would've fit in with this Southern-style walkway that led to Southern-style **Magnolia Park** at the western tip of Frontierland.

New Orleans Square

MAP: Park, P-12

CHRONOLOGY: July 24, 1966–ongoing

HISTORY: Walt Disney had long been a fan of the city known as the Queen of the Delta, and he believed that a small, graceful replica of New Orleans's famous French Quarter would fit in nicely at his park. Conceptually, it would be historic and pretty, like **Main Street**; economically, it would enable lots of French-themed shops and restaurants to find their way into Disneyland.

Actually, years before New Orleans Square ever opened, Disney had already worked some Southern theming in and around **Frontierland**, particularly in the riverfront area to the west. The *Mark Twain* steamed along the nearby **Rivers of America**

as of **Opening Day**, **Magnolia Park** and the **Chicken Plantation** restaurant were both on view in the '50s, until the early '60s Dixieland music was played in a little waterfront gazebo opposite a New Orleans-styled walkway, and the empty shell of the antebellum-style **Haunted Mansion** was erected in 1963. New Orleans Square would consolidate Disney's Delta dreams into one marvelous neighborhood. Those dreams wouldn't be cheap—the price for New Orleans Square, according to Walt Disney on the 2007 *Disneyland: Secrets, Stories & Magic* DVD, was about $15,000,000, almost 90% of what it had cost to build all of Disneyland a decade before.

Imagineers began sketching ideas for a New Orleans area in 1957, just two years after Disneyland opened. The park's **souvenir books** began showing preview illustrations of "Old New Orleans" in 1961, adding a line of text that described just a single New Orleans-style street. Early construction began on a more complex New Orleans Square in 1961, but in 1963 work stopped because of the sudden urgency to create new high-profile attractions for the 1964–1965 New York World's Fair.

In 1965, a full year before New Orleans Square debuted, public excitement about the new land began to surge. The park's '65 souvenir book devoted a full page of drawings and descriptions to the coming area, showing off the ambitious blocks and buildings: "In atmosphere and architecture, it will recall the Crescent City of

a century ago. Along winding streets and in sheltered courtyards, guests will find fine shops that add a new dimension to Disneyland, offering unusual merchandise for the antique collector as well as the souvenir hunter. The French and Creole traditions of New Orleans will spice the area's restaurants."

When it opened in mid-1966 with a special ceremony attended by Walt Disney and the mayor of New Orleans, New Orleans Square was the first permanent new land added to the park's original roster of Main Street, **Adventureland**, Frontierland, **Fantasyland**, and **Tomorrowland**. It was also the only land at the time not directly connected to the **Plaza Hub**. And it was the last major Disneyland project dedicated during Walt Disney's lifetime. Three days after Disney's death, and a week before Christmas in 1966, an episode of *Walt Disney's Wonderful World of Color* put his version of New Orleans before a national TV audience.

That audience saw a compressed idealization of what everyone still imagines a few perfect blocks of New Orleans should look like. But there's far more going on here than meets the eye, because the geography of New Orleans Square isn't as readily apparent as, say, straight Main Street or open **Town Square**. Unlike the actual New Orleans, which has streets crisscrossing in a grid pattern, New Orleans Square isn't really square. Three separate blocks angle through the main neighborhood: to the south, a large east-west block that houses **Pirates of the Caribbean** and the **Blue Bayou**; north of that, a smaller diagonal block, the one with Café Orleans, that extends southwest to northeast and points towards the **Rivers of America**; and on the west side, a third block that has the **French Market** at its northern end and aims up at the Haunted Mansion about 150 feet away.

Between the three blocks are two narrow asymmetrical streets, each only about 15 feet wide. Royal Street separates the Pirates of the Caribbean block from the diagonal Café Orleans block, and Orleans Street separates the Café Orleans block from the north-south French Market block. Bordering New Orleans Square to the west and south is 75-foot-long Front Street and the track of the **Santa Fe & Disneyland Railroad**; to the east is Adventureland; to the northeast, the Esplanade and the Rivers of America; to the north, what used to be Frontierland but later became **Bear Country** (and later still, **Critter Country**).

A Dozen New Orleans Square Establishments with French Names

Cristal d'Orleans
Le Bat en Rouge
La Boutique de Noël
La Boutique d'Or
La Mascarade d'Orléans
Le Chapeau
Le Forgeron
Le Gourmet
Le Petite Patisserie
L'Ornement Magique
Marché aux Fleurs, Sacs et Mode
Port d'Orleans

New Orleans Square's diminutive scale keeps everything intimate. The main neighborhood, not including the separate Haunted Mansion, covers only about three acres. Not only are the blocks compact, they're short, too, reaching only two and three stories tall. To make the buildings seem bigger than they are, architects have incorporated the same "forced perspective" design they first applied to Main Street (upper stories are scaled smaller than lower stories).

Compressed though they may be, the buildings *feel* right. Appreciated more by strolling adults than fast-moving kids, the fascinating shops and cafés are adorned with authentic design details such as hanging plants, French doors, cozy verandas, and lacy wrought-iron railings. The buildings are intimate, perfectly suited for sophisticated purposes. Appropriately, New Orleans Square has no noisy, whirling rides like those spinning in Fantasyland and Tomorrowland. No huge **Emporium**-style stores, no wide Frontierland-like expanses, no towering mountains to rival **Big Thunder** or the **Matterhorn**. Instead, the focus here is on architecture and music, on shopping and dining. Relaxing, not riding, has always been the area's raison d'être.

Guests still marvel at the wonderful variety of sights and sounds that evoke the New Orleans spirit. Since the Crescent City itself was named after French royalty (Philippe II, Duke of Orléans) and was once a French colony, many of the businesses in New Orleans Square have had either French names (**Le Petite Patisserie**, **Le Chapeau**, etc.) or been named after famous French figures (**Mlle. Antoinette's Parfumerie**, **Laffite's Silver Shop**). And since New Orleans, as the birthplace of Dixieland, is a world-renowned jazz capital, the New Orleans Square air is often sweetened with the sounds of jazz combos, either playing on the streets or at the French Market. Just as New Orleans hosts Mardi Gras, so too does New Orleans Square feel like the best place in the park to party (after all, it has the park's best restaurant, the Blue Bayou; it has an eatery named after a cocktail, the **Mint Julep Bar**; and it's got the only restaurant in Disneyland that serves alcohol, **Club 33**). Realistic prerecorded sounds drift down from the upper windows, just as they do on Main Street, though here those sounds include a voodoo priestess preparing spells.

More pleasing than the accurate New Orleans touches are the nice surprises that are pure Disney. A small entranceway opens into the vast indoor Blue Bayou, and the magnificent Pirates of the Caribbean cruise begins as a calm drift toward dark subterranean caves. Walk around a corner and guests will find a quiet courtyard where **portrait artists** practice their craft and potted plants climb the curving staircase; tucked behind a building, a hidden counter sells delicious baked goods; wander a street, and there's a mysterious doorway marked 33. Look up, and some of the buildings are topped with maritime sails, put there to hide lights; if guests could go below ground they'd find a subterranean level honeycombed with tunnels, storerooms, kitchens that serve the area's main restaurants, offices, a cafeteria for **cast members**, and elevators. As famous, familiar, and photographed as it is, New Orleans Square is still a place for personal discovery.

Newsstand

MAP: Park, P-4

CHRONOLOGY: July 17, 1955–ongoing

HISTORY: Guests get their first and last looks at Disneyland souvenirs right at the entry gates. In fact, thanks to the Newsstand just outside the park's **entrance** and west tunnel, guests don't even have to buy an admission ticket to snag some Disney-themed memorabilia.

In addition to postcards, **souvenir books**, shirts, and small gift items, the Newsstand sells film, disposable cameras, and other necessities for a day in Disneyland. The sign above the little freestanding building reads both "Newsstand" and "Information": in addition to handling sales, **cast members** here can answer questions about the park, will help locate larger items not on display on their shelves, and are able to hold Package Express items purchased inside the park for convenient pick-up on the way out. An even smaller newsstand, sans any signage, sells the same kind of merchandise to guests walking through the other entrance tunnel about 200 feet to the east.

New Year's Eve Party

CHRONOLOGY: December 31, 1958–ongoing (seasonally)

HISTORY: Every year the holiday celebrations that begin with **Christmas** festivities include an all-park New Year's Eve Party. The New Year's tradition was inaugurated in 1958 with a relatively modest late-night party. Since then the annual event has been expanded to include special **parades** (often a preview of bands from the next day's Rose Parade in Pasadena), creative light shows projected onto **Sleeping Beauty Castle**, music, a dramatic countdown, and unique **fireworks**.

Over the years, special events like these have drawn bigger and bigger crowds to New Year's Eve night in the park. What began with about 7,500 partygoers in 1958 has often drawn crowds 10 times that size. The biggest New Year's Eve gathering ever was probably the one that showed up at the end of 1999, when well over 80,000 guests came to the huge once-in-a-lifetime millennium celebration.

New York World's Fair Exhibit

MAP: Tomorrowland, T-23

CHRONOLOGY: 1963–1964

HISTORY: In 1963, **Walt Disney** suddenly pulled his Imagineers off of in-the-works Disneyland projects, including **Pirates of the Caribbean** and the **Haunted Mansion**, to create four big new attractions for the 1964–1965 New York World's Fair. For Disney, the fair gave him the opportunity to explore new ideas while not having to pay for them himself, since each attraction was being sponsored by a major corporation and was being installed in a building that Disney himself didn't have to construct. Additionally, once they proved themselves to New York audiences, Disney planned to import the attractions, or some of their elements, to Disneyland. In a sense, then, the two-year New York World's Fair was like a free Disneyland research laboratory.

With all four New York attractions on the drawing boards, in 1963 a free preview called the New York World's Fair Exhibit was installed in Disneyland. This exhibit, listed in the park's 1963 and '64 **souvenir books**, was installed at the end of the first right-hand row of buildings in **Tomorrowland**, a spot where the **American Dairy Association Exhibit** had been. The four new developments it showed off were the Wonder Rotunda's Magic Skyway, sponsored by the Ford Motor Co. (this attraction's dinosaurs would appear at Disneyland as the **Primeval World Diorama** in 1966, and the vehicles would be modified into Tomorrowland's **PeopleMover** in 1967); General Electric's Progressland (what would become Tomorrowland's **Carousel of Progress** in 1967); **It's a Small World** for Pepsi-Cola (the cruise came to an elaborate new **Fantasyland** building in 1966); and **Great Moments with Mr. Lincoln** in the state of Illinois's pavilion (a duplicate Lincoln opened in the **Opera House** in 1965).

For Walt Disney, the Tomorrowland exhibit of the New York attractions served two purposes: it helped him gauge the public's interest in his upcoming attractions, and it stirred up excitement for Disneyland guests who saw what was in the park's immediate future. As they almost always were, Disney's instincts were on target—his new attractions were among the most-visited in New York, and when they arrived in Anaheim they were quickly among the most-visited in Disneyland.

In '65, with the New York attractions either already in Anaheim or due to arrive soon, the Tomorrowland World's Fair Exhibit was taken down. A year later, the massive remodeling of Tomorrowland would eventually bring the big **Character Shop** into the exhibit's former space. Back in New York, the fair organizers invited Disney to build an East Coast version of Disneyland where the World's Fair had been held. Disney declined, his vision already fixed on Florida for his next park location.

Dick Nunis

CHRONOLOGY: 1932–ongoing

HISTORY: A Georgian born in 1932, Dick Nunis was an Academic All-American football player at USC in the early '50s. Upon graduating in '55, he applied to work at Disneyland two months before **Opening Day.** Hired by **Van Arsdale France**, who was in charge of training all new employees, Nunis

started as a $1.80-per-hour orientation trainer for the park's first class of **cast members**. Later he was made head of the mail room, supervisor of **Adventureland** and **Frontierland**, and, ironically, Van France's boss in 1962.

Working with France, Nunis developed the park's employee manuals. According to the book *Remembering Walt*, after **Walt Disney** died in 1966 France and Nunis decided to shift the theme of those manuals towards a "traditions" concept "so that Walt's words, traditions and philosophies would go on forever."

Later promotions elevated Nunis to positions as Disneyland's director of operations (it was Nunis who pushed Disney Imagineers to create a new Disneyland water ride, which finally opened as **Splash Mountain** in 1989) and executive vice president for both Disneyland and Walt Disney World (he oversaw final construction to get the mammoth Florida park open on time). In the '80s, he was put in charge of EPCOT, and in the '90s, Disney-MGM Studios. After exactly 44 years of helping to shape the philosophy, growth, and legacy of Disney theme parks, Dick Nunis retired in 1999 as one of the company's top executives. He was named a Disney Legend that same year.

Oaks Tavern

MAP: Frontierland, Fr-5

CHRONOLOGY: 1956–summer 1978

HISTORY: A saloon on the corner (the **Golden Horseshoe**), and a tavern a little farther down the row towards **Don DeFore's Silver Banjo Barbecue**—in the '50s, these were the businesses that put the wild in Wild West, right? In **Frontierland**, not so much. The Oaks Tavern was merely a fast-food operation that cooked up chili, burgers, sandwiches, and snacks. At least the patio tables overlooked the **Rivers of America** for some scenic dining. Last call came to the Oaks Tavern in 1978 when the space got recast as the **Stage Door Café**.

Observatron

MAP: Tomorrowland, T-8

CHRONOLOGY: May 22, 1998–ongoing

HISTORY: The Observatron is one of the eye-catching creations that opened in the spring of 1998. While it was a new addition to Disneyland, it wasn't a new addition to the Disney canon—a similar device had already been operating at Disneyland Paris. A futuristic kinetic sculpture that looks like a screwdriver mounted on top of dish antennas, the Observatron sits above the old **PeopleMover** loading area in the heart of **Tomorrowland**. For its first few years, **Rocket Rods** attempted to operate out of that loading area until they were withdrawn in 2001.

The park's 2000 **souvenir book** showed off the Observatron with a full-page photo and text that explained how it worked: "Sitting majestically atop the Rocket Rods loading platform, Observatron signals the quarter hour with an impressive array of movements, lights, and vibrant music." As an elaborate timepiece, then, the Observatron is akin to the mechanical toy-soldier clock that charms **It's a Small World** guests every 15 minutes. Exactly how guests are able to divine the current time from the whirling Observatron and its elevating antennas isn't clear, but it does make for a fascinating sight, especially at night.

Jack Olsen

CHRONOLOGY: 1923–1980

HISTORY: Many '60s items that are now valuable Disney collectibles were first brought into the park's stores by Jack Olsen. Olsen enjoyed a two-decade career as a key Disneyland executive.

He was born in Salt Lake City in 1923 but was raised in California. In the early '40s, Olsen went to Penn State before he became a medal-winning G.I. in World War II. Returning stateside he pursued his art-making hobbies while operating L.A. art galleries.

Olsen began working for the Disney Company in 1955, first as an artist at the Disney Studios and then as a store manager at Disneyland. In his book *Window on Main Street*, **Van Arsdale France**, whom Olsen mentored in these early Disney years, called Olsen "a brilliant artist" with a "brilliant mind and great talent."

From 1960 until 1970, Olsen supervised the company's Merchandising Division, bringing cool new T-shirts, hats, toys, gifts, novelties, and more onto store shelves. It was also his idea to bring **portrait artists** to **Main Street** to draw caricatures of guests. During the '70s, Olsen helped with the merchandising at Walt Disney World, where a Main Street window still identifies him as "the Merchant Prince." He retired in '77, and after several years of ill health he died in 1980 at age 56. Jack Olsen was named a Disney Legend in 2005.

Omnimover

MAP: Tomorrowland, T-24, T-4; New Orleans Square, NOS-12

CHRONOLOGY: August 5, 1967–ongoing

HISTORY: Well-known and much-celebrated are the advances made by Disney Imagineers in the 1960s as they designed breakthrough new attractions like **Pirates of the Caribbean** and the **PeopleMover**. What's less conspicuous now is the significance of the new Omnimover vehicle system that debuted in Disneyland in 1967.

Before the Omnimover system was invented and implemented, ride vehicles were variations on little miniature cars, trains, boats, and whirling teacup-like enclosures. As fun as these vehicles were, they were limiting in several ways. Sitting in open vehicles, guests could freely look ahead to see other parts of the attraction, or even look behind them to see structural elements they weren't meant to see. Music and narration were blared through loudspeakers to many vehicles at once, causing either confusion (when guests had already passed what the narration was about) or a cacophony (when guests heard sounds from other parts of the attraction). What's more, some of these attractions were notoriously slow-loading, since the whole ride had to stop in order to get guests into vehicles (think of the **Mad Hat-**

ter's Mad Tea Party). In the '60s, as Imagineers realized that exciting, and extremely long, attractions like the **Haunted Mansion** would be handling thousands of guests per hour, they knew they had to come up with some new way of both improving the experience and moving large numbers of guests through the ride efficiently.

Their solution was the Omnimover. The Omnimover actually derived from the vehicles that were first tried at the 1964–1965 New York World's Fair. There the General Motors pavilion and the Disney-designed Ford Magic Skyway both incorporated long trains of vehicles that formed continuous loops, like a closed necklace of little cars. Guests boarded the vehicles from a moving platform alongside, which meant the rides didn't have to stop to load and unload their passengers. The Disney vehicles were otherwise fairly primitive—they didn't move independently, and they didn't have their own individual sound systems. But they soon would.

After a year of development, the park's first iteration of the Omnimover ride system was the Atomobile in **Adventure Thru Inner Space**, a major new attraction that opened in **Tomorrowland** on August 5, 1967. As with the New York vehicles, the continuous chain of blue, pod-like Atomobiles had a moving conveyor belt next to it in the loading and unloading areas, and each pod had a self-closing metal bar that helped secure its pair of passengers. To the delight of waiting guests, over 3,000 passengers per hour could be transported through the world of the molecule.

What's more, Disney Imagineers, particularly **Bob Gurr**, **Roger Broggie**, and **John Hench** added important new wrinkles to the Omnimover's movement (*omni*, the Latin word for "all" or "abundant," suggested the new range of motion). First, the Atomobiles could spin in any direction on computer command, thus directing the rider's attention to particular sights. In addition, the pods could tilt backward or forward, which meant riders could be kept level as the pods went up and down hills. The tilting effect also meant that riders could be relaxed back into their seats when the pods leaned backwards and showed them something up near the ceiling. Plus, with an on-board speaker delivering the narration and music, sound did not have to be blasted through an entire room from large speakers and could instead travel with each individual Omnimover vehicle, to be played at appropriate moments. A memorable example of how these options all came together occurred at the end of the Inner Space journey when the pods sprung a nifty joke: while moving forward, the pods suddenly swiveled and bent back to direct attention up at a microscope in the corner, where a giant eye was looking back at riders. At that moment the narrator's voice inside the Atomobile announced, "We have you on visual."

The next Disneyland attraction to use the Omnimover system was the Haunted Mansion (see photo, previous page) two years later. There, black Doom Buggies still convey guests up inclines and down slopes, aim guests sideways and backwards, and create an effect that has often been described as cinematic. In *The Art of Walt Disney*, Christopher Finch explained how the Doom Buggy "is used exactly like a movie camera. The rider is traveling through a programmed show which unfolds in time. The choice of where to look is not his to make—it has already been made by the designer, who determines what will be seen, just as a director determines what the movie patron will see." And just as all viewers see the same movie, so do all riders see the same attraction and get the same experience (unless they lean out of the Omnimover pods to sneak looks where they're not supposed to). Just as Inner Space had a cool closing joke provided by the Omnimover, so too did the Haunted Mansion—at the very end of the attraction, the Doom Buggies swivel toward a mirror just as the on-board speaker cautions guests to "beware hitchhiking ghosts!"

A third Omnimover attraction opened at Disneyland in 2005. **Buzz Lightyear Astro Blasters** added yet one more dimension—rider control. Guests could now point their vehicles in different directions as they tried to shoot at dozens of different targets during their trip. It was the latest improvement to what was a great technological advancement made at the park, one so important it was awarded its own patent in 1971.

One-of-a-Kind Shop

MAP: New Orleans Square, NOS-3

CHRONOLOGY: July 24, 1966–May 1996

HISTORY: The fascinating One-of-a-Kind Shop opened with the rest of **New Orleans Square** in July of 1966. The small store, located at the front of Royal Street just past the entrance to **Pirates of the Caribbean** and the **Royal Street Veranda**, was the first retail space guests encountered upon entering this new area of the park.

Unlike other Disneyland stores that sold replicas of antiques, the One-of-a-Kind Shop sold the real deal, actual antiques that were sometimes priced at thousands of dollars. The publicity photo and caption in the park's 1968 **souvenir book** confirmed the store's serious intent: the photo showed, not smiling kids, but a mature couple in suits standing underneath ornate chandeliers, with text that noted the "imported antiques." It's said that the store was suggested, or at least inspired by, the wife of **Walt Disney**, Lillian Disney, whose love of antiques had already led to the old-fashioned décor inside their **apartment** above the **Fire Department** on **Town Square**. Inside the One-of-a-Kind Shop were items that were, if not truly unique to Southern California or the world at large, certainly unique to Disneyland—large spinning wheels, Victorian music boxes, dolls in elegant baby carriages, objets d'art, vintage jewelry, and old clocks, all of them authentic antiques.

How many people walked into Disneyland hoping to walk out with a valuable spinning wheel is debatable, but the store did thrive for three decades. In 1995, the merchandise expanded to include reproductions and more generic gift items.

By the summer of '96, the One-of-a-Kind Shop was the gone-of-a-kind shop, to be replaced in '98 by **Le Gourmet** and four years after that by **Le Bat en Rouge**.

Opening Day

CHRONOLOGY: July 17, 1955

HISTORY: Disneyland's Opening Day has nearly always been declared a failure. Certainly that's how it was reported by some of the press the next day, and throughout his lifetime **Walt Disney** himself nicknamed it Black Sunday. For decades the many small crises that occurred July 17, 1955 have been well-chronicled, the park's early flaws and deficiencies well-documented, the failure of Opening Day generally accepted.

In truth, the real failure would have been if nobody had shown up and nothing had happened at all. Nearly all the crises, flaws, and deficiencies resulted

from a sudden, overwhelming number of guests who came to the infant park even when they were told not to (the official count put the number at 28,154 people, while unofficial tallies claimed over 30,000). What some call failure others could call success—the success Walt Disney had in building something so alluring that the public had to see it sooner rather than later. Too few visitors, not too many, would have been the real failure, as proven by the ignored advertisements for thousands of embarrassing Broadway openings, forgotten film premieres, and other dead-on-arrival events that litter the fast-moving highway of entertainment history.

Disneyland in mid-1955 was not the Disneyland guests see now, of course. The entire park had been built on an undeveloped agricultural parcel in less than a year, still an astonishing feat to contemplate. The run-up to Opening Day had been a frantic sprint to get most of the park functioning, or if not functioning, at least well-disguised. Out of plants, landscape architect **Morgan "Bill" Evans** resorted to decorating existing weeds with little signs adorned with important-sounding Latin names. Out of time, designers put the **Rocket to the Moon** and **Casey Jr. Circus Train** on view but not in operation. And out of money, **Tomorrowland** was left undone, its incompletion covered up by balloons and bunting. Workers were still applying paint to some of the buildings just hours before the first guests were due.

When they did arrive, those guests arrived en masse. Attendance that first sunny Sunday was supposed to be 10,000, all of them dignitaries, celebrities, reporters, Disney employees, and Disneyland sponsors holding special invitations for a 2 P.M. entrance into the park. Alerts were posted in the newspapers that nobody else should come to Disneyland on July 17th, but evidently some 20,000 additional members of the general public didn't get the word. Despite the traffic being jammed for miles around, a huge vanguard of unsolicited guests managed to get to the park, there to present counterfeit invitations or to sneak in over the perimeter **berm**. By mid-afternoon, the huge crowd working its way up **Main Street** and streaming off to the different lands was walking shoulder to shoulder.

With attendance suddenly triple what it was supposed to be, the inexperienced **cast members** were immediately confronted with food and beverage shortages and an inadequate number of **restrooms** and trash cans. Some attraction lines quickly bunched up into chaos; some attractions were sent out overloaded with guests. At least one of the watercraft came close to catastrophe—the *Mark Twain* was so weighted down with extra guests that water splashed onto the decks.

What predicaments the high attendance didn't cause, bad luck did. The intense summer sun caused some of the newly poured cement to soften and trap the high heels of some of the women who had dressed up for the opening. With frustrated crowds waiting, a few of the indoor ride vehicles stopped working altogether. **Van Arsdale France** wrote in *Window on Main Street* that the doors into **Sleeping Beauty Castle** were inadvertently left unlocked, allowing curious guests to roam through the unfinished interior.

The hourly dilemmas were all new for everyone. Awestruck guests were as perplexed as they were dazzled, and dewy employees were on the front lines trying to solve problems they'd never been trained for. Back then, remember, not a single person in the world had any familiarity with the practical workings of a huge theme park.

Compounding the inexperience of the cast members was the inexperience of the TV crews on hand to film everything. There were 29 TV cameras scattered around the park for a live coast-to-coast show, the most ambitious broadcast ever attempted. Nobody had ever televised anything so big, so spread out and so complex before, and it showed. Cues were missed, stars were in the wrong places, and cameras caught activity they weren't supposed to

Then and Now at 1313 Harbor Blvd.

1955

Hours: 10 A.M. to 10 P.M., open daily all summer,
closed Mondays the rest of the year
Admission: $1 for adults, 50¢ for children
(plus additional charges for attractions)
Number of lands: Five (Adventureland, Fantasyland, Frontierland, Main Street, Tomorrowland)
Number of main attractions: 18

2007

Hours: Varied, often from 8 or 9 A.M. to 10 P.M.
or midnight, open daily.
Admission: $66 for adults, $56 for children 3–9
(no additional charges for attractions)
Number of lands: Eight (original five plus Critter Country, Mickey's Toontown, New Orleans Square)
Number of main attractions: 60+

(like actor Bob Cummings spontaneously smooching a dancer). At a time when the total U.S. population was only about 165 million, 90 million Americans tuned in to see what was a humorous, confusing, spontaneous, but ultimately triumphant spectacle of unprecedented proportions.

Celebrities were everywhere that day, either being interviewed, walking in **parades**, or enjoying the attractions. Art Linkletter, Ronald Reagan, and Bob Cummings served as jovial hosts, while Alan Young, Jerry Colonna, Danny Thomas, Frank Sinatra, Sammy Davis Jr., Kirk Douglas, Charlton Heston, Maureen O'Hara, Jerry Lewis, Debbie Reynolds, Eddie Fisher, Fess Parker, Buddy Ebsen, Irene Dunne, Roy Rogers, Dale Evans, Hedda Hopper, California governor Goodwin Knight, Santa Fe Railroad president Fred Gurley, Annette Funicello and the rest of the Mouseketeers were on hand to celebrate. A laughing Sammy chased Frank on the **Tomorrowland Autopia**, Fess and Buddy wore their costumes from the *Davy Crockett* TV miniseries and sang, Irene christened the *Mark Twain,* Colonna was the highballin' engineer on the Casey Jr. train, and Walt Disney roamed the park to make televised speeches.

As on every Disneyland day since, free entertainment was abundant. The park's first parade wound northward from **Town Square** and up Main Street towards the **Plaza Hub**. The procession included soldiers wearing uniforms from the Revolutionary War, horse-drawn buckboards, a stagecoach, Cinderella's pumpkin coach, Tomorrowland Autopia cars, Disney characters, the **Disneyland Band**, the Mouseketeers wearing cowboy gear and hobby-horse costumes, and, bringing up the rear, a Carnation milk truck. During the day the **Firehouse Five Plus Two** jazz band, after walking in the parade, played atop the **Santa Fe & Disneyland Railroad**. That night's **fireworks** rocketed above Sleeping Beauty Castle while a jubilant Walt Disney watched from his **apartment** on Town Square. Neal Gabler's *Walt Disney: The Triumph of the American Imagination* summarized the day as "the longest and quite possibly the best of Walt Disney's life."

The next day, Monday the 18th, Disneyland officially opened to the public. Thousands of guests began queuing up before dawn, and the parking lot was virtually full by the time the turnstiles began twirling at 10 A.M. A 22-year-old college student who'd been waiting out front since 2 A.M. was the first guest to buy a ticket. Walt Disney personally greeted the first children in line. For all the high spirits, though, bad luck continued to plague the park when a gas leak forced **Fantasyland** to close early (some sources claim that leak occurred on the 17th, not on the 18th).

On that first Monday morning, several major newspapers published praising reviews of the previous day's special Opening Day events. "Dream Realized—Disneyland Opens," read the July 18th headline in the *L.A. Times*, supplemented with lots of big photos and enthusiastic text that called the park "once-upon-a-time land," a "land of magical fantasy and faraway places," and a "dream come true."

However, when several columnists published excoriating critiques, Walt

Disney immediately assembled his top lieutenants to address the writers' issues. Here he was only one day into Disneyland's history, and already Disney was changing his park. This was the first of thousands of attempts to improve Disneyland after it opened, to put into effect one of the principles that has guided the park's eternally ongoing creation: "Disneyland is like a piece of clay," Disney declared, "if there is something I don't like, I'm not stuck with it. I can reshape and revamp."

Revamp his team did, working feverishly to solve the traffic problems in the streets, in the restaurants, and on the attractions. Workers quickly attended to the construction that had been left unfinished, the landscaping that had been left unplanted. And over the next few weeks Disney himself courted the press with special invitations and events, always showing up in person to offer apologies for the Opening Day mishaps.

Hardly anyone could miss the sign above the Main Street train station (see photo) that on Opening Day was optimistically announcing Disneyland's population as 5,000,000 people. Critics would have wagered that "Disney's Folly" wouldn't ever draw a tenth of that number and would close by Christmas, but Disneyland didn't merely survive, it thrived. Attendance, as it had been on Opening Day, was higher for the next weeks and months than anyone expected. According to the Disneyland Data page in the park's 1956 souvenir book, guest number 5,000,000 walked through the gates on October 4, 1956, less than 15 months after Black Sunday.

Opera House

MAP: Town Square, TS-9

CHRONOLOGY: July 17, 1955–ongoing

HISTORY: Like **Adventureland**, the Opera House jumped from one side of the park to the other while it was in the planning stages. When it appeared on an early concept drawing—in this case, the large detailed map of Disneyland drawn up by **Herb Ryman** in 1953—the Opera House was clearly shown and labeled on the left-hand (western) side of **Town Square**. The imposing two-story building, of course, ended up on the right-hand side of Town Square, making it one of the first structures guests encounter as they walk into Disneyland through the east tunnel.

What they find upon entering the park is a long square block that spreads ahead of them about 180 feet from south to north. The Opera House dominates this block and extends about 125 feet back to the east, giving the Opera House a total area of about a third of an acre. The actual entrance into the Opera House is in the center of the block and stretches about 35 feet along Town Square, with several ground-floor businesses and window displays surrounding the entrance.

With all the buildings going up in the months leading to **Opening Day**, something had to be finished first, and the Opera House turned out to be that something. Perhaps the main reason it needed to be completed so quickly was because of the way it was going to be utilized, at least in its early years. Though **Walt Disney** originally intended it to be a large, opulent theater, from 1955 until mid-1961, the Opera House was really a working lumber mill, its warehouse-like interior filled with wood and carpentry projects destined for other Disneyland locations.

Starting in '61 and continuing throughout the '60s, the Opera House was put to a variety of uses, none of them having to do with opera. First it was the location for the **Babes in Toyland Exhibit**, next a temporary TV studio for *The Mickey Mouse Club* scenes, then the site of the **Mickey Mouse Club Headquarters**, and finally home to **Great Moments with Mr. Lincoln**. Lincoln moved in during the summer of '65, at which point the Opera House really was functioning like the theater it was meant to be, and stayed until early 1973, when the **Walt Disney Story** temporarily replaced him. Two years later the Great Emancipator returned for the joint Disney/Lincoln exhibit that continued for the next 30 years. Finally, in 2005 the Opera House became the site of a special exhibit honoring the park's golden anniversary, complete with a model of the park in mid-1955 (see photo on page 310) and the tribute film *Disneyland: The First 50 Magical Years*.

No matter what has filled the interior of the building, the exterior has always stayed dignified and regal, its roof crowned by curling classical ornamentation that makes the Opera House look one full story taller than it is. Somehow the Opera House has rarely made it into the park's **souvenir books**, which instead have focused on the nearby train station, **City Hall**, and the **Fire Department** when they've shown Town Square buildings. However, it was much-observed by one key fan: the Opera House is the building directly across from the front windows of Walt Disney's **apartment**.

Our Future in Colors, aka Color Gallery

MAP: Tomorrowland, T-6

CHRONOLOGY: March 1956–January 1963

HISTORY: For the first two years of its existence, this exhibit was listed in the park's **souvenir books** as the Dutch Boy Exhibit, Our Future in Colors. Then, from 1958 to 1963, the souvenir books named it simply the Color Gallery. Either way, it had just one location, in the back of the rectangular **Tomorrowland** building that housed the **Art Corner** and Richfield's **World Beneath Us Exhibit**.

Dutch Boy was a brand name and logo owned by the National Lead Company, a paint manufacturer that was an early Disneyland sponsor. Throughout the summer and fall of 1955, the exhibit's future site was marked by a Dutch Boy statue until construction began that winter for a spring opening.

What finally appeared was pretty docile, even by the standards of the calm child-friendly technical exhibits found elsewhere in Tomorrowland in the '50s. Surrounded by color swatches, guests spun color wheels into new shades. Musical tones accompanied the activity to encourage or discourage possible color combinations. Not surprisingly, no fun-filled photos or inviting text ever appeared in any of the souvenir books. In '63, this spot got absorbed into the **Circarama** remodel that would produce a newer, bigger Circle-Vision 360 theater.

Painted Desert, aka Rainbow Desert

MAP: Frontierland, Fr-22

CHRONOLOGY: July 17, 1955–October 11, 1959

HISTORY: In the 1950s, just as **Adventureland** had its **Jungle Cruise** area inspired by one of the Disney Studios' *True-Life Adventure* films, so too did **Frontierland** have its own *True-Life* area. The Painted Desert, loosely themed after the Oscar-winning 1953 documentary *The Living Desert,* was an acre-and-a-half spread in the northeast corner of Frontierland. The park's **souvenir books** of the '50s also referred to this acreage as Rainbow Desert for its panoply of colors.

    The desert being emulated here wasn't an Arabian bleached-sand desert with dunes swelling like ocean waves; Disneyland's desert was styled after the rocky, cactus-studded landscape of Arizona. Previewing what the **Big Thunder Mountain Railroad** would speed through in 1979, the Painted Desert had pale orange rock formations crowned with balancing boulders and rough fields of sagebrush. Some bubbling paint pots added bright hues, and anthropomorphic saguaro cacti posed into expressive positions added humor. There weren't lots of **Audio-Animatronic** animals on display yet—any moving creatures on view were actual birds and lizards that had stopped in for a visit.

    From 1956 until 1959, the **Rainbow Caverns Mine Train** slowly traversed the Painted Desert on its way to the spectacular Rainbow Caverns. The Painted Desert and the train both closed in mid-October of '59, but both reopened the following summer. The desert was reborn as the more animated Living Desert section of the much bigger, much more Audio-Animatronic **Nature's Wonderland**, and the train returned as the Western Mine Train Through Nature's Wonderland.

Parades

MAP: Park, P-16, P-10, P-9, P-8

CHRONOLOGY: July 17, 1955–ongoing

HISTORY: As discussed in Bob Thomas's *Walt Disney: An American Original,* **Walt Disney** had to convince his own staff that extravagant, expensive parades were a vital part of the Disneyland experience: "We can't be satisfied," said Disney, "we've always got to give 'em a little more. It'll be worth the investment. If they ever stop coming, it'll cost ten times that much to get 'em back."

    But there was more than just a financial concern that drove Walt Disney's passion for parades; he'd loved them since boyhood and closely observed them whenever one passed down the streets of Marceline, Missouri. He transferred that love to Disneyland, where parades have been a daily ritual ever since the first one on **Opening Day.** So popular are the parades, the rest of the park often empties out as guests crowd the parade route, making parade-time a no-line-time at some attractions.

Disneyland parades typically (but not always) begin near **It's a Small World** in **Fantasyland**, come past **Matterhorn Mountain** and **Sleeping Beauty Castle** to

A Chronological List of 38 Disneyland Parades

1955: Opening Day Parade, Mickey Mouse Club Circus Parade, Christmas Show Parade

1956: Antique Automobile Parade (aka Old Fashioned Automobile Parade)

1957–1964: Christmas in Many Lands Parade

1958–ongoing: Candlelight Procession

1960: Mickey at the Movies Parade, Parade of Toys

1965–1976, 1980–1985: Fantasy on Parade

1965: Tencennial Parade

1967: Easter Parade

1968: Valentine's Day Party, St. Patrick's Day Parade, Cinco de Mayo Fiesta

1969, 1974: Love Bug Day

1972–1975, 1977–1983, 1985–1996: Main Street Electrical Parade

1975: America on Parade

1977–1979, 1987–2000: Very Merry Christmas Parade

1980: Family Reunion Parade

1983: Flights of Fantasy Parade

1984: Donald Duck's 50th Birthday Parade

1986: Totally Minnie Parade

1986–1988: Circus on Parade

1987–1988: Come to the Fair Parade

1988: Mickey Mouse's 60th Birthday Parade

1990: Party Gras Parade

1991: Celebration U.S.A. Parade

1992: World According to Goofy Parade

1993: Aladdin's Royal Caravan Parade

1994: Lion King Celebration

1997: Hercules Victory Parade

1997: Light Magic

1998: Mulan Parade

2000: Parade of the Stars, 45 Years of Magic Parade

2001: Christmas Fantasy Parade

2004: Mickey Mouse's Birthday Parade, Mickey's Shining Star Cavalcade Parade

2005: Walt Disney's Parade of Dreams

the **Plaza Hub**, and then bend south down **Main Street**, leaving the public's view through an exit near the **Opera House** on **Town Square**. Parades usually last about a half-hour and often culminate with an appearance by a waving Mickey Mouse.

In addition to the daily hometown parades that have been performed most frequently, special parades have celebrated everything from park anniversaries and character birthdays to national holidays and new Disney movies. Any given parade might include vehicles, horses, circus acts, floats, raised stages with performers, Disney characters, the **Disneyland Band**, street performers who interact with the crowd, celebrities, and anything else the Imagineers can dream up. The **Main Street Electrical Parade**, the only parade identified on a **Main Street window**, is probably the most famous of the park's parades; the Candlelight Procession, born in 1958 and still running every **Christmas** season, is the longest-lasting. Disney Legends **Robert Jani**, **Bill Justice**, and **Tommy Walker** are usually named as the pioneers of the park's parades.

Parasol Cart

MAP: New Orleans Square, NOS-10

CHRONOLOGY: Ca. 1990–ongoing

HISTORY: Near the entrance to the **French Market** restaurant in **New Orleans Square** sits this pretty, two-wheeled cart that sells frilly parasols. While not the sturdiest thing to have as a guest strolls around the busy park and rides on fast-paced attractions, a parasol is still a lightweight, sophisticated shelter from the blazing summer sun (and a sweet gift for a Disney princess).

The cart is operated by Rubio Arts, a company that places artists in different art-related concessions around the park (the nearby **portrait artists** are also from Rubio). For under $20, the artists at the parasol cart hand-paint flowers, animals, and other happy patterns (plus names as well) onto the colorful fabric panels of the parasols. Guests who order customized parasols can pick them up a couple of hours later after the paint has dried.

Parking Lot

MAP: Park, P-2

CHRONOLOGY: July 17, 1955–January 22, 1998

HISTORY: If the park's parking lot seemed big, it was—in fact, with an area of 100 acres, it was 40 acres bigger than Disneyland itself. When it was first built, the parking lot's capacity was 12,175 cars, all of which entered from Harbor Boulevard on Disneyland's east side, crossed the 2,000-foot-wide lot, and exited onto West Street. Most of the parking lot wasn't paved, which is perhaps why it cost only 25 cents to park in it back in 1955. Other

than a couple of areas closest to the entrance, the original parking lot was all dirt, with parking spaces marked off by chalk.

After a "remodel" and complete paving, the lot was divided into over 15,000 marked spaces. To help guests remember where they left their cars, the parking lot was divided into smaller themed sections that were labeled with character names and pictures. The names were arranged alphabetically, with Alice designated as the first parking area in the northeast corner (near Harbor Boulevard) and Winnie the Pooh as the last in the southwest corner (near the West Street/Katella Avenue intersection). The Mickey, Minnie, and Sleepy sections were closest to the main auto entrance on Harbor; the Bambi section was closest to the ticket booths at the **entrance** to the park; motor homes parked in Eeyore, and a 10-minute handicapped zone was in Donald. **Walt Disney** himself didn't park his car in any of these sections—he had a private spot behind the west side of **Town Square**, close to his **apartment** above the **Fire Department**.

For four decades, the tantalizing views of Disneyland from the parking lot—especially of the elevated **Santa Fe & Disneyland Railroad** and the **Monorail**, both of which pass near the ticket booths—inspired quick dashes from the cars to the park's entrance. While everybody could dash (or walk) through the parking lot if they wanted to, convenient trams continually circulated to scoop up pedestrians. Requiring no ticket for boarding, these trams were the only free Disneyland vehicles on the entire property. The trams saved footwear, but they didn't always save time, since they took a circuitous route to get to the tram stop up near the ticket booths.

One big drawback to the uncovered, unlandscaped parking lot was its lack of shade over any of its spaces. Some experts have speculated that the parking lot was designed to be intentionally drab and treeless so as to throw the color and excitement of Disneyland into high relief. That thought was small consolation to anyone who returned to a car during the day and discovered that what they'd parked under the searing Southern California sun wasn't a car but was actually a metal furnace on wheels.

After 43 years of service, the parking lot was demolished in 1998 to accommodate Disney's California Adventure, the Grand California Hotel, and Downtown Disney. During the new construction, the ominous towers that carried high-tension power cables across the parking lot were relocated and made less conspicuous. These days most drivers avail themselves of the Mickey and Friends parking structure to the northwest of Disneyland (see photo, previous page). This massive edifice, featuring six levels and spaces for over 10,000 cars, is one of the largest of its kind in the world and offers something other parking structures don't—a rooftop view of Disneyland's **fireworks** (some visitors favor this viewing location because it puts them near their cars for a quick getaway ahead of the exiting crowds). Three smaller parking lots with character names—Pinocchio, Pumbaa, and Timon—supplement Mickey and Friends with additional spaces to the west and south of the park.

Partners

MAP: Plaza Hub, PH-7

CHRONOLOGY: November 18, 1993–ongoing

HISTORY: Disney artist **Blaine Gibson** came out of retirement to sculpt the heralded *Partners* statue that now serves as the centerpiece of the **Plaza Hub**. The inspiring bronze statue was installed at Disneyland in a special ceremony overseen by **Roy Disney** and **Jack Lindquist**, both top Disney executives and future Disney Legends. The date of the installation, November 18, 1993, wasn't chosen capriciously: exactly 65 years earlier, *Steamboat Willie*, Mickey Mouse's cartoon sensation, had debuted, making this the company's official birth date for their superstar. Eight years later, a rededication ceremony was held on December 5th, what would've been the 100th birthday of the company's founder.

From the moment it was unveiled, *Partners* instantly became one of the most photographed locations in the park, thanks in part to its location in front of **Sleeping Beauty Castle**, but also thanks to its consequential subjects. The statue's two figures are a smiling **Walt Disney**, who stands at full-size, and Mickey Mouse, who is presented at half of Disney's size. Disney's left hand holds Mickey's right, and Disney's upraised right arm points southward towards **Main Street**. While Disney wears his readily identifiable business suit, playful Mickey wears his trademark short pants with big front buttons, plus shoes and gloves. Showing on Disney's tie are the letters "STR," which were the initials of his Smoke Tree Ranch in Palm Springs (Disney had sold the vacation home to help pay for the construction of the park, but he re-purchased it later).

The pair stand on a three-foot-tall cylindrical pedestal that's surrounded by a 30-foot-wide circular planter bursting with flowers. On the southern side of the pedestal is a plaque with this inscription: "I think most of all what I want Disneyland to be is a happy place where parents and children can have fun together," followed by Walt Disney's signature. After *Partners* went up at Disneyland, similar statues were installed at other Disney theme parks.

Passports

CHRONOLOGY: June 1982–ongoing

HISTORY: From **Opening Day** up until early 1982, the full Disneyland experience required guests to make at least two purchases. One was for admission into the park, and the other was for supplemental tickets to go on the attractions. For most of these years, these tickets were gathered into convenient **ticket books**. But because these ticket books were *optional*, for 27 years it was possible for a guest to walk around Disneyland just for the modest admission price, which started out at $1 and for decades was only a few dollars.

However, in the '70s another theme park about 60 miles away, Magic Mountain, introduced a one-price $5 admission ticket that included both entry into the park and unlimited use of all the rides. The advantages were instantly apparent: for the park, all guests paid a higher price to get in; for the customers, there were no unwieldy, expensive single-ride tickets that had to be carefully husbanded during the day. The only guests left out of this equation were those who wanted to pay for admission only, not ride tickets. Those guests must not have constituted a very large group, because by the end of the '70s Disneyland was experimenting with its own all-inclusive, unlimited-attraction admission policy patterned after the one at Magic Mountain.

Originally, the only guests to be offered all-inclusive admission tickets were the members of the Disneyland's Magic Kingdom Club. Then, in the summer of '82, all adult guests at Disneyland found themselves paying a single price for a one-day unlimited-attraction passport (young children were free, as they are now). The adult price stayed in the teens through the '80s, passed $20 in '87, and has continued to surge past significant price points every half-decade or so—past $30 in '94, $40 in 2000, $50 in 2005, $60 in 2007.

Over the years, Disneyland has introduced ways for guests to reduce the cost of admission, among them annual passes, multi-day discounts, "park hopper" passports that offer combined admission to both Disneyland and Disney's California Adventure at less than what each park's admission would cost separately, and lower prices for seniors and local residents (lately the park has phased out the word "passports" in favor of "tickets" or "passes"). Meanwhile, guests holding old tickets from the pre-1982 ticket books have always been able to cash them in towards the cost of admission. Since these individual A-E tickets usually have printed values of less than $1, they're often more valuable as nostalgic collectibles than they are as currency at the ticket booth.

Patented Pastimes, aka Great American Pastimes

MAP: Main Street, MS-19

CHRONOLOGY: June 15, 1990–1999

HISTORY: Since **Opening Day** the **Fine Tobacco** shop had been wedged between the **Main Street Cinema** and the **Main Street Magic Shop** in the first right-hand block of **Main Street**. That changed at the beginning of summer in 1990 when Patented Pastimes, a shop specializing in vintage toys and other collectibles, opened in this small space.

Nine months later, the store's name changed to Great American Pastimes, and its merchandise expanded to include nostalgic sports items ("great American pastime" is a description often applied to baseball). In 1999, the approach of a new century saw the arrival of a new replacement, the **20th Century Music Company**, for this location.

Pendleton Woolen Mills Dry Goods Store

MAP: Frontierland, Fr-2

CHRONOLOGY: July 18, 1955–April 29, 1990

HISTORY: Missing **Opening Day** by 24 hours, the Pendleton store in **Frontierland** stood for the next 35 years as one of the longest-lasting sponsored stores in the park. The location was about 50 feet within the Frontierland gates on the left side—guests heading to the **Golden Horseshoe** on the corner got there by walking past Pendleton's door. The sidewalk out front was wooden and the exterior was appropriately rustic, as if guests were going to hitch up their horses before shopping inside. The interior continued the area's Old West theme with frontier décor and merchandise.

At the time its Disneyland store debuted, Pendleton had already been operating for over 40 years as a respected manufacturer of woolen fabrics and blankets, with men's and women's clothes supplementing the line mid-century. In the Disneyland store, flannel shirts, which would be popular with '60s surfers (the Beach Boys wore them in their first iteration as the Pendletones), were especially prominent. In 1990, Pendleton finally left and the store became **Bonanza Outfitters**, another retailer of Frontierland fashions.

Penny Arcade

MAP: Main Street, MS-8

CHRONOLOGY: July 17, 1955–ongoing

HISTORY: Staying true to his desire to re-create what locals would've found in their small American towns in the early 1900s, **Walt Disney** put a Penny Arcade along Disneyland's **Main Street**. Observant guests would know it was the Penny Arcade even if there weren't an illuminated sign out front, because an oversized Indian-head penny, dated 1901, is mounted over the doorway (see photo, next page). The arcade fills most of the street's second left-hand block, its big open entrance gaping with tantalizing sights and sounds that invite curious pedestrians to step inside. This is

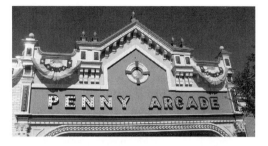

the same block that for years had the **Carnation Ice Cream Parlor** and the **Refreshment Corner** at either end.

Page seven of the 1957 **souvenir book** listed the Penny Arcade in the "rides" category, but the closest thing the building ever had to a major attraction was the **Main Street Shooting Gallery** that was in the back of the arcade from **Opening Day** until 1962. Most of the Penny Arcade has always been given over to old-fashioned family fun—simple (and inexpensive) games, hand-cranked silent movies starring Charlie Chaplin and other stars, and bizarre gizmos that were neither games nor movies. Of these latter devices, guests may recall (and still look forward to) encounters with the Electricity Is Life device that hooks guests up to a battery and enables them to see how much pain they can take, the grip-tester that extends Uncle Sam's right hand for guests to shake, the souvenir penny-pressers, and the beautiful Esmeralda's fortune-telling machine (Esmeralda is popular enough to have her own cloisonné tribute pin).

A 1998 remodel replaced some of the old machines with new video games and space for a candy counter. Unchanged is the classic Orchestron, a century-old mechanical "Welte-style" brass and wood music-maker from Germany that Walt Disney bought before the park opened. Also unchanged is the Penny Arcade's glittering appeal at night, when it seems to burst forth onto the street with bright lights and exuberant activity.

Pen Shop

MAP: Main Street, MS-15

CHRONOLOGY: July 17, 1955–1959

HISTORY: For the second half of the 1950s, a small store for pens operated on East Center Street. East Center is the east-west street that cuts across **Main Street** to separate the **Market House** from what was then the **Gibson Greeting Cards** store. The Pen Shop, as it was listed in the **souvenir books**, was behind Gibson and open to the East Center cul-de-sac.

Writing instruments were the main items for sale, but there was more to the shop than retailing—it also displayed replicas of historical documents and offered handwriting analysis. The Pen Shop and **Coin Shop** both got written off in the 1960 expansion that transformed the Gibson store into the **Hallmark Card Shop**.

PeopleMover

MAP: Tomorrowland, T-8

CHRONOLOGY: July 2, 1967–August 21, 1995

HISTORY: "Tomorrow's transportation . . . today!" declared the PeopleMover's **attraction poster.** For 40 years, that optimistic description seemed prophetic.

Fondly remembered as one of the coolest little vehicles in Disneyland history, the popular PeopleMover debuted in the summer of 1967 along with the rest of the newly remodeled **Tomorrowland.** It was certainly one of the most visible of that year's new attractions—the little blue, red, green, and yellow cars rode an elevated track that took them across the Tomorrowland entrance, into the **Adventure Thru Inner Space** queue area where they could be seen by waiting guests, past the shoppers in the **Character Shop**, in and out of the **Carousel of Progress** building, near the **Submarine Voyage** lagoon and the **Monorail**, through the waiting area of the **Circarama**/Circle-Vision 360 theater, and, as of the late '70s, inside **Space Mountain**. For the price of a D ticket, guests got a quiet, scenic, 16-minute tour of most of Tomorrowland.

The PeopleMover was truly different from any other futuristic transportation in the park. The book *Walt Disney's Disneyland* pointed out that whereas the Monorail was "an old idea in a new showcase, the PeopleMover was a new concept developed by Disney engineers and introduced for the first time, anywhere, in Tomorrowland." Those Disney engineers had first experimented with PeopleMover technology in their Magic Skyway ride at the 1964–1965 New York World's Fair. There the new propulsion concept was used to push unpowered vehicles along a track like they were unfinished factory cars being moved down an assembly line. According to his book *Designing Disney*, Disney Imagineer **John Hench** actually got the idea from a Ford plant where he watched steel for car bodies being moved on tracks from area to area.

At Disneyland two years later, a similar system propelled the PeopleMover. Unlike the Monorail, the **Viewliner**, the **Santa Fe & Disneyland Railroad**, and the **Casey Jr. Circus Train**, the PeopleMover trains themselves weren't motorized—the track was. Rubber tires (of course, since Goodyear was the sponsor) were mounted every nine feet along the mile-long track and were powered by electricity to push the PeopleMover gently along at walking speed, an average of six miles per hour. About four people at a time could fit comfortably on the bench seats inside one of the cars, which had white canopies to shield the sun. With the four-car trains running nonstop, and with guests stepping directly into their seats from a moving walkway, well over 4,000 passengers per hour could be moved through the attraction.

Regrettable milestones marred the PeopleMover's three-decade run at Disneyland. Tragically, reckless guests trying to move from car to car caused two fatalities in the '60s and '80s. In addition, the attraction got what many people considered to be unnecessary makeovers in '77 and '82 when a "superspeed tunnel" and effects from the movie *Tron* were incorporated into the

trip. Ultimately, the slow-moving trains were derailed in the late '90s by the decision to replace them with the ill-fated **Rocket Rods**.

Happily, a ride similar to the PeopleMover still exists at Walt Disney World; even better, in the 21st century there's been talk of the PeopleMover being revived with an *Incredibles* theme at Disneyland, where the unused tracks still gracefully arc across Tomorrowland. Ideally, **Walt Disney** wanted his PeopleMover to be adopted by cities for urban transit, and the system was indeed studied by engineers and city planners. However, except for a single airport, nobody wanted it, and the PeopleMover exists today merely as a memory of one of the most ambitious eras in Disneyland history.

Peter Pan Crocodile Aquarium

MAP: Fantasyland, Fa-6, Fa-24

CHRONOLOGY: Never built

HISTORY: Had Bruce Bushman's color concept art of 1953 come to be, a large aquarium themed to the movie *Peter Pan* would've been built somewhere in **Fantasyland**. Possibly the location would've been the courtyard where the **Mad Hatter's Mad Tea Party** and **King Arthur Carrousel** were eventually installed, or perhaps over in the open area where the **Matterhorn** eventually went up. A Pan-themed aquarium would've given Fantasyland three Peter Pan attractions (**Peter Pan Flight** and the **Pirate Ship Restaurant** both debuted in the summer of '55).

Bushman's art for the Peter Pan Crocodile Aquarium showed a large crocodile stretched out in a pool, the croc's head and tail sticking out at the ends. Guests would've walked through the gaping jaws and down below the waterline to an aquarium area where they would've gazed at live fish through at least four large round windows. The closest Disneyland ever actually got to an aquarium was the **Submarine Voyage** lagoon, which was filled with mechanical marine life. Like the art for the **Reel-Ride**, Bushman's illustration was among the exhibits in the Behind the Magic: 50 Years of Disneyland show held at the Oakland Museum of California in 2006.

Peter Pan Flight, aka Peter Pan's Flight

MAP: Fantasyland, Fa-29

CHRONOLOGY: July 17, 1955–ongoing

HISTORY: Many guests count Peter Pan Flight among their favorite attractions of all time. Indeed, as an enchanting flight over Victorian London to a fantasy island, it offers one of the prettiest views in the park, and for most of its years it only cost a C ticket. However, many guests also count Peter Pan Flight among Disneyland's most frustrating attractions. Even when park attendance is low Peter

Pan always seems to have long, slow-moving lines. And though the under-three-minute ride time approximates that of other **Fantasyland** rides, it still feels too short by half. Having waited 45 minutes for the privilege, guests are whisked quickly away from the scenic Never Land vistas before they can really study them. Frustrated Pan fans are like sleepers roused prematurely from a beautiful dream.

Peter Pan Flight (as the signage outside called it on **Opening Day** and for the first three decades) was one of the three original indoor "dark" rides in Fantasyland. Like **Mr. Toad's Wild Ride** and **Snow White Adventures**, it sends guests into fantasy worlds on small vehicles that are attached to a track. The Pan innovation is the position of that track—rather than winding along the ground, the track hangs from the ceiling. With the vehicles, in this case small pirate ships, suspended from the track, guests get the sensation of flying (the same principle is given a high-tech treatment in the Soarin' Over California attraction at Disney's California Adventure).

The exquisite **attraction poster** summarizes the voyage: "Sail Over Moonlit London to Never Land in a Pirate Galleon." The lovely mural in the queue area piques interest, and the gilded galleons beckon like jewel boxes. Peter's famous cry of "C'mon everybody, here we go!" leads pairs of guests forward, and quickly everybody's swooping out the Darlings' nursery window. Guests then float seven feet above an enchanting London that's so detailed it has lighted traffic moving along its roads. At the "second star on the right," the ships fly to Never Land, where the bird's-eye view reveals Skull Rock, Captain Hook's ship anchored in the lagoon, and teepees on one of the bluffs. All along the movie's soundtrack is the flight's soundtrack, encouraging guests to "think of a wonderful thought." After 90 wondrous seconds, the rest of the ride features a colorful, action-packed encounter with Hook and the rescue of Tiger Lily.

Much of the attraction was enhanced in 1961, and the second half with Captain Hook was dramatically remodeled in 1983, the same year the rest of Fantasyland was remade. The '83 Pan improvements added 3-D figures, brighter colors, some pieces off the old **Pirate Ship Restaurant**, and the addition of Peter himself, who formerly had been represented only by his shadow; outside, a majestic new clock tower marked the entrance, and a respelled sign announced that this was now Peter Pan's Flight.

Throughout this attraction, fun details are sprinkled like pixie dust, everything from the children's blocks that spell famous names to the bubbling lava inside the volcano to the thematic weathervane above the clock tower. Photos of smiling guests in galleons or the attraction's colorful interiors have turned up in nearly every **souvenir book**, every photo reminding veteran riders how divine the Peter Pan dream is.

Petrified Tree

MAP: Frontierland, Fr-8

CHRONOLOGY: September 1957–ongoing

HISTORY: Guests love finding new surprises at Disneyland. Guests arriving in the fall of '57 found an *old* surprise in **Frontierland**—a 70-million-year-old surprise, to be exact. That September the park began to display an authentic petrified tree along the southern tip of the **Rivers of America** near **Aunt Jemima's Pancake House**.

Twice this tree has been given away. The first time, **Walt Disney** presented it to his wife Lillian in 1956. They'd found the unique item together while on vacation in the Pike's Peak area of Colorado. Walt Disney bought it on the spot from a private seller and had it sent to California as a gift to his wife for their 31st wedding anniversary. Mrs. Disney realized Disneyland could exhibit it better than she could, so a year later she donated the petrified tree—more accurately, a mineralized sequoia stump—to the park, where it's been an imposing presence ever since. Surrounded by a low metal fence and supported by a metal brace, the white, stony-looking wood stands ten feet tall and weighs five tons. A plaque at the site explains the ancient history of the stump in detail and names Mrs. Disney as the donor.

Phantom Boats

MAP: Tomorrowland, T-10

CHRONOLOGY: August 16, 1955–October 1956

HISTORY: The Phantom Boats have two interesting distinctions—they were the first attraction ever removed from Disneyland, and they're one of the only attractions ever brought back from total extinction (in this latter regard, the scaled-down *Moonliner* and the revived **Great Moments with Mr. Lincoln** would also qualify).

In mid-August of 1955, the Phantom Boats took over for the temporary Tomorrowland Boats that had been cruising for about three weeks. Styled like their immediate predecessors, the odd-looking Phantom Boats were slightly futuristic fiberglass speedboats with pointy noses, inboard motors, and huge fins (fins being the decade's fab design feature, whether they adorned rockets, big cars, movie monsters, or boats). "Speedboat" was really a misnomer—they looked fast but drove slow. The 14 boats came in two great '50s colors: pink or aqua. The "phantom" in their name had no basis in any backstory told to guests—supposedly the name just sounded alluring.

Amazingly, guests piloted themselves, sans an on-board **cast member** and with no guide rails or track, around the lagoon in Tomorrowland where the **Subma-**

rine Voyage would start operating in 1959. Unfortunately, the boats were so hard to keep running that guests often stalled their boats out on the water (perhaps this is why the attraction only cost a B ticket). So frustrated were park officials with the boats' performance (or lack of it) and their maintenance requirements (which were almost nightly), they added a cast member as a backseat skipper for each boat to ensure guests would make it back safely, or at least that same afternoon.

On January 15th of the following year, only five months after debuting, the Phantom Boats were pulled from the lagoon permanently. Or so it was thought. Unfortunately, their successors, an Everglades-type shallow-draft "airboat" pushed by a large airplane prop mounted out of the water, never made it past the test stages. The following July, with the lagoon still empty of watercraft, the Phantom Boats were resurrected from the dead for one last troublesome summer, but there was no illusion that the return would last long. By Halloween the Phantom Boats had became phantoms once again. In June of '57, the nearby **Motor Boat Cruise** made a successful debut as Tomorrowland's new boat attraction.

Photo Collages

CHRONOLOGY: May 2005–September 2006

HISTORY: To help personalize Disneyland's mammoth golden-anniversary celebration, in 2005 and 2006 the park prominently displayed unique artworks that required the participation of guests. These artworks were large photo collages comprised of thousands of guest photos.

The collage concept was announced on Disneyland's 49th anniversary. According to the plan, from July 17th to December 31st of 2004, anyone could submit Disney vacation photos that would be integrated with thousands of other photos into oversize images depicting Disney-related scenes. These collages would then be installed in the park beginning in May of 2005. Guests whose photos were accepted even got e-mail notification as to the location of the collage that incorporated their photos. Kiosks at the park also identified photo and collage locations.

Dubbed "The Happiest Faces on Earth . . . A Disney Family Album," the collages proved to be enormously successful. Hundreds of thousand of photos were sent in, and the completed collages were constantly surrounded by clusters of guests looking for recognizable faces. The collages varied from enormous wall-size murals (most ambitiously, the glorious *20,000 Leagues Under the Sea* squid-and-submarine display in **Tomorrowland**) to smaller poster-size works. One of the images, which showing a scene from *Steamboat Willie*, even included a second collage within the main collage.

The collages included characters from 18 different Disney movies (*Sleeping Beauty* was represented three times, *Toy Story* twice), two different Mickey cartoons (*Steamboat Willie*, *Mickey's Trailer*), and four different Disneyland attractions (**It's a Small World**, the **Many Adventures of Winnie the Pooh**, the **Haunted Mansion**, and **Fantasmic!**). **Walt Disney** himself shared a collage with Mickey Mouse (see a close-up of this collage on page 141).

Photo Collages (and Disneyland locations)

Alice in Wonderland (Mad Hatter's Mad Tea Party)
Beauty and the Beast (Fantasyland walkway)
Cinderella (Fantasyland walkway
Donald Duck (Mickey's Toontown)
Fantasmic! dragon (French Market)
Hercules (Fantasyland walkway)
Hitchhiking ghosts (Haunted Mansion)
It's a Small World children (It's a Small World Toy Shop)
The Jungle Book (Tarzan's Treehouse)
Lady and the Tramp (Plaza Pavilion)
Lilo & Stitch (Redd Rockett's Pizza Port)
The Lion King (Jungle Cruise)
The Little Mermaid (Fantasyland walkway)
Mickey Mouse (Mickey's Toontown)
Mickey Mouse and Walt Disney (Opera House)
Mickey's Trailer (Mickey's Toontown)
Mulan (Fantasyland walkway)
Pocahontas (Fantasyland walkway)
Sleeping Beauty dragon (Sleeping Beauty Castle)
Sleeping Beauty prince and princess (Sleeping Beauty Castle)
Sleeping Beauty villainess (Sleeping Beauty Castle)
Snow White and the Seven Dwarfs (Mickey's Toontown)
Steamboat Willie (Disneyland Showcase)
Toy Story (Golden Horseshoe)
Toy Story (Little Green Men Store Command)
Toy Story 2 (Golden Horseshoe)
20,000 Leagues Under the Sea (Club Buzz)
Winnie the Pooh with balloon (Many Adventures of Winnie the Pooh)

Typically the collages were posted in areas with thematic connections: *The Lion King* was mounted outside the **Jungle Cruise**, Fantasmic! was posted in **New Orleans Square**, the trio of ghosts thumbed a ride at the Haunted Mansion, the three *Sleeping Beauty* collages decorated different walls of **Sleeping Beauty Castle**, the Alice portrait hung outside the **Mad Hatter's Mad Tea Party**, Buzz Lightyear towered above **Little Green Men Store Command**, etc.

In all, 28 photo collages went up at the park for about 18 months, with another six within or outside of Disney's California Adventure. In 2007, guests could still see a semblance of the anniversary collages inside the **Opera House** lobby, where a single 10-foot-wide, eight-foot-tall collage of Walt Disney and Mickey Mouse, based on a 1966 photo, was created from tiny photos of the park.

Pieces of Eight

MAP: New Orleans Square, NOS-3

CHRONOLOGY: Ca. 1980–ongoing

HISTORY: Conveniently enough, exhilarated guests still humming "Yo Ho (A Pirate's Life for Me)" can walk straight out of **Pirates of the Caribbean** and say "ahoy matey" to Pieces of Eight, a well-decorated store filled with the pirates' cursed treasure. Well, if not exactly cursed treasure, then at least pirate skulls, pirate shirts, pirate weapons, pirate hats, and other bone-decorated merchandise ready to be plundered. There are no buried pirate chests to dig up, but there are open bins filled with glittering gems ready to be scooped out by the handfuls.

Named after the much-coveted Spanish coin of the 1700s, Pieces of Eight is in the same space where the **Pirate's Arcade Museum** used to be, and as a tribute to that **New Orleans Square** fave, the newer store still has some of the museum's old machines. Notable among these are the metal-stamper, which cranks out personalized pieces of eight, and the **Audio-Animatronic** fortune-telling pirate named Fortune Red, who delivers small cards with jaunty sayings.

Pinocchio's Daring Journey

MAP: Fantasyland, Fa-9

CHRONOLOGY: May 25, 1983–ongoing

HISTORY: The major 1982–'83 remodel of **Fantasyland** brought extensive changes to existing attractions and the addition of one new one—Pinocchio's Daring Journey. On the northerly spot where the old **Mickey Mouse Club Theater** (aka Fantasyland Theater) had once been now rises a captivating Tyrolean exterior complete with cobblestone walkways out front, a steeply sloping alpine roof, and a half-timbered façade with a puppet show above the doorway.

Inside is a richly colored three-minute adventure that retells the familiar tale of the wooden boy, the wood-carving Geppetto, Pleasure Island, Tobacco Road, and more. An entire page of the 2000 **souvenir book** offered photos and detailed descriptive text: "Guests follow little Pinocchio and his faithful conscience Jiminy Cricket as they attempt to avoid fateful encounters with the wily Foulfellow and Gideon, the Coachman, and Monstro the Whale. Guided by the 'wishing star,' guests meet the lovely Blue Fairy and ultimately share in Pinocchio's happy ending."

Pinocchio's Daring Journey was new to Disneyland in 1983 but not to Disney theme parks—the original version had opened a month earlier at Tokyo Disneyland. The attraction incorporates a colorful exterior mural, little wooden vehicles, meticulously crafted 3-D figures, and state-of-the-art ride elements to deliver the animated movie's key plot points. Some of the special effects come from other attractions (the effect for the Blue Fairy is the same one used to produce ghosts in the **Haunted Mansion**), and some of the charming architectural details are borrowed from other buildings (the themed weathervane outside is reminiscent of the one on **Peter Pan Flight** across the way). But there's at least one new technical achievement along the journey: the first appearance in a Disneyland attraction of a hologram, used here to transform boys into donkeys.

While not a major breakthrough, Pinocchio's Daring Journey is a compellingly attractive one worthy of the classic film upon which it's based. The lovely **attraction poster** got it right: "Wish Upon a Star and Relive Fantastic Adventures!"

Pin Trading Stations

MAP: Plaza Hub, PH-1

CHRONOLOGY: April 2000–ongoing

HISTORY: To support fans who were already buying and trading souvenir pins, Disneyland inaugurated a pin program in April of 2000. Soon park officials had scattered various Pin Trading Stations (usually colorful carts or display cases within existing stores) into every land. Conveniently, a large, conspicuous headquarters for pin traders is found in front of the **Plaza Pavilion Restaurant** in the **Plaza Hub**.

At all locations knowledgeable **cast members** are on hand to effect trades with pin pals, offer encouragement and suggestions, and sell accessories like cases and lanyards. Nearby, Downtown Disney has its own central location called Disney's Pin Traders to supplement the park's pin activity. A special promotion called Mickey's Pin Festival of Dreams ran from June 18th to August 12th in 2007 and brought with it some new limited-edition pins.

Disneyland's Pin Trading Stations in 2007

(and locations)

Adventureland Bazaar (Adventureland)
Bonanza Outfitters (Frontierland)
Emporium (Main Street)
Fantasy Faire Gifts (Fantasyland)
Gag Factory (Mickey's Toontown)
La Mascarade d'Orléans (New Orleans Square)
Little Green Men Store Command (Tomorrowland)
Plaza Pavilion (Plaza Hub)
Pooh Corner (Critter Country)

Pirate's Arcade Museum

MAP: New Orleans Square, NOS-3

CHRONOLOGY: February 14, 1967–ca. 1980

HISTORY: The Pirate's Arcade Museum opened a few weeks before its famous neighbor, **Pirates of the Caribbean**, made its auspicious debut. Once they were both open, dazzled guests who were in mid-saunter away from the landmark attraction back out to **New Orleans Square** found themselves exiting right past the tempting pirate-themed Arcade Museum, a room that was much more the former than it was the latter.

Most of the arcade games that filled the Pirate's Arcade Museum had pirate imagery worked into their game play and exterior design. Freebooter Shooter, for instance, required guests to blast away at tipsy pirates. A one-dimensional challenge, to be sure, but all arcade games were simpler back then, and they cost only a dime to play. Elsewhere in the Pirate's Arcade Museum, current fans of classic Disney art would love to get their coins into the old postcard machine that sold the **Marc Davis** concept illustrations for Pirates of the Caribbean. Also available was a metal-stamping machine that personalized antique-looking pieces of eight.

Fortune Red, a pirate who dispensed fortune-telling cards, proved to be one of the most durable of the room's amusements. As shown in the Behind the Magic: 50 Years of Disneyland show at the Oakland Museum of California in 2006, originally Fortune Red was intended to be a full-size, full-body pirate with one leg and a parrot, just like Long John Silver from *Treasure Island*; he ended up as just the upper half of a pirate with a red beard and no parrot. Along with the metal-stamper, he's survived into the 21st century as one of the cornerstones of **Pieces of Eight**, the pirate-themed store that took over this space around 1980.

Pirate Ship Restaurant, aka Chicken of the Sea Pirate Ship and Restaurant, aka Captain Hook's Galley

MAP: Fantasyland, Fa-14

CHRONOLOGY: August 29, 1955–August 29, 1982

HISTORY: This nautical restaurant was usually called the Pirate Ship Restaurant in the **souvenir books** of the '50s and '60s, but because of its sponsor it was also known back then as the Chicken of the Sea Pirate Ship and Restaurant. Movie fans who recall the pusillanimous Captain Hook from *Peter Pan* have to smile at a restaurant themed to the cowardly captain and named Chicken of the Sea.

The actual Chicken of the Sea, of course, is StarKist Tuna, the staple of the "light meals and snacks" menu presented here. Seemingly everything—the burgers, sandwiches, pot pies—had tuna in it. Food was ordered and served at a counter within the ship's hull. Guests then ate at wooden-keg tables on an outdoor patio facing creepy **Skull Rock**. Actually, the rock and its landscaped setting, Pirate Cove, weren't built until 1960—up till then, the ship sat in a plain pond, and guests sat on benches on an ordinary concrete patio.

The real fun, though, was the ship itself, which was built to look like an elegant, fully rigged frigate with a black hull, red-striped sails, and well-appointed decks that guests could tour. From waterline to the tip of the main mast the colorful ship towered approximately 80 feet, a height about equal to the **Sailing Ship Columbia** over in **Frontierland**.

The waterside eatery was a **Fantasyland** landmark from six weeks after **Opening Day** in 1955 until the closing in 1982, though not always with the same name: in 1969, the restaurant was rechristened Captain Hook's Galley. In the early '80s, there was talk of moving the Galley, Skull Rock, and Pirate's Cove over to the **It's a Small World** area, but unfortunately the ship's wooden hull was found to have water damage, and so during the Fantasyland remodel of '82–'83 it was finally dismantled (some pieces from the ship did end up inside the remodeled **Peter Pan Flight**). The place where the ship, rock, and cove had been was filled in and given to the relocated **Dumbo the Flying Elephant** attraction. Captain Hook himself, however, has never really left Fantasyland, as he's long been part of the Peter Pan Flight interior.

Pirates of the Caribbean

MAP: New Orleans Square, NOS-1

CHRONOLOGY: March 18, 1967–ongoing

HISTORY: Often regarded as the best attraction in Disneyland (or if not the best, certainly one of the top two or three), Pirates of the Caribbean was one of the last attractions **Walt Disney** worked on. It was also the first major attraction to open after he died at the end of 1966.

Discussions about some kind of pirate museum actually began in the late '50s, and in fact the park's 1958 poster-size map even placed an unbuilt "Wax Museum" approximately where the later boat ride would be built. According to Charles Ridgway's book *Spinning Disney's World*, in 1960 Walt Disney made his first public announcement of the new attraction at the opening ceremonies for **Nature's Wonderland**. A year later, the name Pirates of the Caribbean was used for a preview in the park's **souvenir book**. These early hints suggested that the attraction would be a walk-through exhibit called the Rogues Gallery, "composed of famous pirates of the Spanish Main" who were shown in a crude drawing of drunken buccaneers in a tavern.

Construction on something pirate-ish began in 1961, but the project was interrupted for at least three years so the company could concentrate on Disney exhibits for the 1964–1965 New York World's Fair. Disneyland's 1963 souvenir book then mentioned an upgraded Pirates of the Caribbean "presentation" featuring a "Bayou voyage" past "famous and infamous pirates who once terrorized the Caribbean." A shadowy painting of pirates studying a treasure map conveyed mood but nothing about the actual ride experience.

Two years later, the 1965 souvenir book raised expectations by describing how **Audio-Animatronic** pirates would "come to life" and "attack, burn and loot a city" in what "promises to be Disneyland's longest and most action-packed attraction." That same year, Walt Disney further fueled excitement by showing off the coming attraction to a national TV audience on *Walt Disney's Wonderful World of Color*. While **New Orleans Square** technically opened in mid-1966, everyone was primed for the arrival of the Pirates of the Caribbean the following spring. And they weren't disappointed.

Heralded by an official opening that featured the nearby **Sailing Ship *Columbia*** decked out with a Jolly Roger, the E-ticket Pirates attraction represented the summit of creative and technological achievement in ride design up to that time. No other park in the world had anything nearly as sophisticated; for that matter, neither did Disneyland. For the first time, Imagineers implemented Audio-Animatronic humans on a grand scale—previously their A-A figures had been either relatively primitive mechanical animals (as in the **Enchanted Tiki Room**) or a single person viewed from a distance (**Great Moments with Mr. Lincoln**). Now, though, there were over 60 A-A humans and another 50 or so A-A pigs, donkeys, chickens, and dogs cavorting through realistic settings that included a trip through the bayou; a plunge down two 21-degree waterfalls; a raging storm; a life-size pirate ship called the *Wicked Wench* and a fort lobbing cannonballs at each other as guests drifted between them; a town engulfed in flames; and a trip back *up* a waterfall. All of it was viewed from only a few yards away, and, even more incredibly, all of it was presented indoors.

The attraction was a tour de force of imagination and engineering. No longer did park rides have to be short and compact—this one was slow (about 16 minutes long) and covered 1,800 feet of canals that held 750,000 gallons of water. The 46 shallow bateaux traversed three levels in two big new buildings, one of them built across what was formerly **Magnolia Park**, the other built outside the park's perimeter **berm**, with both buildings together covering over 2.5 acres. The cost to create such an elaborate attraction in the mid-'60s? Some $8,000,000, almost half of what it had cost to build the entire park a decade before.

The press and public immediately recognized the magnitude of Disney's monumental achievement. Disney souvenir books played up the revolutionary Pirates with lavish photos and descriptive text; Pirates was also one of only two attractions (**It's a Small World** was the other) to get its own lengthy souvenir booklet in the '60s and '70s; and Walt Disney again tantalized TV audiences with more views

in 1968, making visitors who'd already seen it eager to experience it all again.

Fortunately, the attraction rewards repeat visits, because it was designed with a scrupulous attention to detail. Precise detail was born out of necessity, of course, since about 18 guests per bateau are drifting, not racing, along and are thus carefully analyzing everything from the jeweled display in the queue area to the pirate garb on the **cast members** in the Laffite's Landing launch site, from the moving clouds in the bayou section to the artwork mounted on the back walls of the main scenes, and on and on until the last walk past the last dancing fireflies by the exit.

While the pirate behavior on view has always seemed un-Disneylike, what with all the pillaging, the wench-auctioning, and the heavy drinking, and while these colorful rascals have little in common with the savage cutthroats who are their historical counterparts, the attraction's rollicking spirit and good humor have negated any serious complaints. That spirit and humor were created by a roster of designers and artists that reads now like a who's who of Disney's fabled Imagineers: artist **Marc Davis** generated hundreds of whimsical ideas and concept drawings; his wife **Alice Davis** did the costumes; **Richard Irvine** and **Claude Coats** oversaw the art direction and general design; sculptor **Blaine Gibson** made the models; **Roger Broggie**, **Fred Joerger**, and **Wathel Rogers** were the mechanical wizards behind the A-A swashbucklers; **Bill Martin** and **Yale Gracey** invented many of the special effects; **George Bruns** and **X Atencio** created the instantly hummable "Yo Ho (A Pirate's Life for Me)" theme song (Atencio also wrote the attraction's script); and **Thurl Ravenscroft** and **Paul Frees** were among the vocal performers.

So revered is the attraction, long-time fans have greeted changes warily. The entrance was modified in 1987, and then everything was closed from January 6, 1997, to March 7, 1997, for an update that replaced the pirates-chasing-women scenes with pirates-chasing-food scenes. This '90s remodel also added a re-dedication plaque honoring "the original" to the outside queue area. Everything was shut down again in the spring of 2006 for a June 26, 2006 reopening that revealed a re-mixed soundtrack and lifelike characters from the block-buster *Pirates of the Caribbean* movies among the motley crew. Of these movie characters, Jack Sparrow is now seen three times, Davy Jones once, and Barbossa is the vociferous commander of the *Wicked Wench*.

Celebrated over the years in books and films and exhibits, duplicated in Disney's Orlando, Tokyo, and Paris parks, enjoyed and appreciated by hundreds of millions of people, the cherished Pirates of the Caribbean is still thriving as a supreme example of what intelligent theme park entertainment can be.

Plaza Gardens, aka Carnation Plaza Gardens

MAP: Plaza Hub, PH-2

CHRONOLOGY: August 18, 1956–ongoing

HISTORY: Dining and dancing are at their swingin'est at the Plaza Gardens. Located in the northwest corner of the **Plaza Hub** just to the left of **Sleeping Beauty Castle**, this spacious half-acre site is also called the Carnation Plaza Gardens in deference to the sponsor (on nearby **Main Street**, Carnation has also sponsored two eateries, the venerable **Carnation Ice Cream Parlor** and the more recent **Carnation Café**, plus the **Baby Station**).

While it has a long history, the Plaza Gardens doesn't date back to **Opening Day**. That honor goes to the old **bandstand**, which was situated on this site among landscaped gardens from July of '55 until the following summer. As the bandstand concerts got more popular that first year, **Walt Disney** decided to relocate it over to the far end of **Frontierland** and build a big new dance pavilion to help keep guests staying and playing after dark.

The result was an old-fashioned wooden building painted a gleaming white. The structure is open to the Plaza Hub and on the sides to make the entertainment more visible and inviting to passers-by. Guests enter the Plaza Gardens by crossing a small pond on a footbridge, with paths leading from both the Plaza Hub and Sleeping Beauty Castle's side entrance. Guests then face a seating area, a stage, and, when it's open, a doorway at the back that leads to Frontierland. The food, served at a counter to the side, has always been fun and nostalgic with lots of cheeseburgers, fries, and enormous ice cream desserts. Occasionally some special items have made it onto the menu to coincide with special events, such as the I Scream sundaes that were offered in August of 1969 to commemorate the opening of the **Haunted Mansion**.

More memorable than the Plaza Gardens' menu, however, is its entertainment legacy. Many distinctive music events here have livened up Disneyland's nights and been spotlighted in the Disneyland After Dark pages of the **souvenir books.** Classic swing bands have been the traditional performers here ("tried and true favorites for Mom and Dad," boasted the park's 1965 souvenir book). Other shows have included **Date Nite** concerts with the Date Niters in the late '50s-early '60s, the Cavalcade of Bands concerts starting in 1963, and the televised Big Bands at Disneyland shows of 1984 with, among others, the Glenn Miller and Count Basie Orchestras. The Donny-less Osmond Brothers also made a splashy debut here in 1961.

Recent years have brought some updates. The once-white building is now striped red and gold, for instance. In the '90s, the Plaza Gardens began hosting small stage shows, including *The Enchanted Book Shoppe* (1991–1992) and *The Little Mermaid and Her Secret Grotto* (1997–1998). After the summer of '98, the Plaza Gardens closed for a year for remodeling. It reopened with a wall of **attraction posters** in the back and a new dance show, the Jump, Jive, Boogie Swing Party that is sometimes held four times a night on holidays and summer weekends. Small live concerts, often featuring school bands and choirs, are also still held here many afternoons. Though it's now over 50 years old, the stylish Plaza Gardens continues to deliver stylin' entertainment.

Plaza Hub, aka the Hub, aka Central Plaza

MAP: Park, P-10

CHRONOLOGY: July 17, 1955–ongoing

HISTORY: All the earliest concept drawings of the full-size Anaheim park showed something called the Plaza Hub or Hub as an organizing principle for the overall layout. **Walt Disney** wanted his guests to walk into a cozy, familiar setting—**Main Street**—before they ventured into his unknown lands. Once past Main Street, guests would arrive at the park's chief terminal, from which all other areas could be accessed. Situated 800 feet north of the Main Street train station and the **entrance** tunnels, this terminal, the park's nucleus, Disneyland's Grand Central Station, is the Plaza Hub.

As it always has, the Plaza Hub, or Central Plaza as it's now sometimes called, serves as both a departure point and a meeting point for guests. Radiating from the Plaza Hub like spokes around a wheel are six main walkways that lead guests south to Main Street, west to **Adventureland** and **Frontierland**, north into and around **Sleeping Beauty Castle** towards **Fantasyland**, and east to **Tomorrowland**. Smaller walkways also lead to the main restaurants on view from the Plaza Hub: the **Plaza Pavilion** to the southwest, the **Plaza Gardens** to the northwest, and what was the **Red Wagon Inn** (now the Plaza Inn) to the southeast. It's not impossible, but it's very unlikely that a guest can avoid crossing the Plaza Hub circle at least once during a visit.

Few guests, however, *want* to avoid the Plaza Hub. The circular expanse covers about 35,000 square feet (four-fifths of an acre), and it's beautifully landscaped with trees, shrubs, flowers, and benches. The views from here make this one of the park's best spots for watching people, enjoying **fireworks**, and admiring vehicles (the **Main Street vehicles** round the Hub on their trips back up to **Town Square**).

In addition, popcorn carts, cappuccino stands, and character greetings are usually available along the sidewalks. A helpful information board outside the Plaza Pavilion offers up-to-the-hour information about upcoming parades and live entertainment, closed attractions, and current queue lengths. Along the southern border of the Plaza Hub are West and East Plaza Street, home to the **Refreshment Corner** piano player and the **Baby Station**, among other important sites.

Finally, as of 1993, *Partners*, the **Blaine Gibson** statue of **Walt Disney** and Mickey Mouse, has stood in the Plaza Hub. The placement is significant. This digni-fied tribute to the park's origins wasn't installed in Town Square, or at the highly visible entrance by the turnstiles, or in Fantasyland (reputed to be Walt Disney's favorite area), or in **New Orleans Square** (the last area Disney worked on before he died), or in any of the other key locations around the park. *Partners* is at the heart of the Hub, and thus at the very heart of Disneyland itself.

𝕻laza 𝕻avilion 𝕽estaurant,
aka 𝕾touffer's in 𝕯isneyland 𝕻laza 𝕻avillion

MAP: Plaza Hub, PH-1

CHRONOLOGY: July 17, 1955–July 1998

HISTORY: The lovely Victorian-style Plaza Pavil-ion is today an underused gem in the southwest corner of the **Plaza Hub.** In the '50s, the Plaza Pavilion was identified more with **Adventure-land** than the Plaza Hub, and in fact it was list-ed in the early **souvenir books** as the Pavillion (with a double consonant) in the Adventureland section. The reason was the patio. Guests did indeed enter from the Plaza Hub side, but they carried their pasta, classy sandwiches, and big salads on cafeteria-style trays through the res-taurant and out the other side to a patio situ-ated above the banks of the **Jungle Cruise.**

In 1962 the restaurant got an unwieldy new name, Stouffer's in Disneyland Plaza Pavillion, and the back patio became the Stouffer's in Disneyland Tahitian Terrace. By '65, when the restaurant got a nice photo in the souvenir book, the Stouffer's reference had been dropped and Plaza Pavilion had been respelled (Stouffer's moved over to **New Orleans Square** to sponsor the **French Market**). Interestingly, the two exterior décors still meet in the middle of the roof, so depending on the viewing angle guests see either turn-of-the-century cut shingles or tropical thatch (see photo below).

In the 21st century, the restaurant has been closed so often and for so long that it barely registers with modern guests, and when it does register it probably isn't as a dining destination. Lately the Pavilion has been the site of the Junior Chef Baking Experience in which kids get to don toques and bake their own Nestlé Toll House cook-ies. The porch facing the Plaza Hub frequently has

a ragtime piano player borrowed from Coke's **Refreshment Corner** next door, and the outside dining area on the Plaza is now a large **Pin Trading Station**. The walkway out front hosts the information board where guests can see which rides are closed, what the lines are like, when parades are due, and more. None of these functions, unfortunately, tap into the full potential of what was, and could be again, a memorable dining experience.

Pluto's Dog House

MAP: Mickey's Toontown, MT-8

CHRONOLOGY: January 24, 1993–ongoing

HISTORY: Several restaurants in Disneyland history have had humorous names—**Lunching Pad** and **Toon Up Treats**, for instance. The niftiest play on words might be Pluto's Dog House, a little snack counter in the heart of **Mickey's Toontown** that serves up—what else?—hot dogs. The dogs are foot-longs for adults and mini-size for kids, plus there are the usual extras like chili, chips, and sodas. Combos, a dog-shaped dessert, and alfresco dining will help on-the-go guests develop a case of puppy love.

Police Station

MAP: Town Square, TS-3

CHRONOLOGY: July 17, 1955–ongoing

HISTORY: Rarely noted or shown in the park's **souvenir books**, the Police Station is the first brick building guests will encounter, and the last they'll go past, when they enter and exit through the park's west tunnel. The Police Station is one of three "official city buildings" that line up along the left-hand side of **Town Square**; next door is **City Hall**, and two doors northward is the **Fire Department**. The one-story Police building is the smallest along the row, but it's just as handsome as the others, constructed of red brick and decorated with a yellow balustrade on top and cream-colored columns that bracket the doorway.

Despite its name, the Police Station hasn't ever been the headquarters for the park's own security personnel. A free map handed out to guests in the summer of '55 located Security Headquarters in City Hall on Town Square. According to the Disneyland Data page in the 1956 souvenir book, this City Hall headquarters was home base to "45 Security Officers" who were "employed on a full-time basis at Disneyland with eight others on call to protect the Park and its guests." Within a few years the security people were moved out of City Hall to another building behind Town Square and out of the public's eye (guests with security concerns were still directed to City Hall).

The Police Station, meanwhile, was actually home to the Publicity Department, which needed to be near the park's entrance to greet reporters and photographers. At one time the front of the building also served as the designated rendezvous for lost guests and their groups. A 2001 brochure handed out at the park identified a kiosk just south of the Police Station as the American Automobile Association's "Touring & Travel Services Center" where guests could get AAA maps, info, free towing, and flat-tire repair. Today that pretty little kiosk is where guided tours are booked, and the flower-filled area is informally known as Guided Tour Garden, the spot where **Tour Guides** gather their guests. The closed-off Police Station, according to the **cast members** here, is now a VIP lounge.

Pony Farm, aka Circle D Corral

MAP: Park, P-17

CHRONOLOGY: July 17, 1955–ongoing

HISTORY: All those horses, mules, and ponies that have been worked, ridden, or paraded through Disneyland over the years have grown up and gotten their educations at the park's Pony Farm, aka the Circle D Corral. The Pony Farm used to be located at the back of **Frontierland**, directly behind the perimeter **berm** on acreage that was later incorporated into **Mickey's Toontown**. In addition to stables for the horses, the Pony Farm also had a barn and a carpentry shop on the property.

In 1980, the Pony Farm got renamed as the Circle D Corral. A decade later, in anticipation of the construction for Mickey's Toontown, the Circle D got relocated farther west, still close to the park but no longer directly behind Frontierland.

The current Circle D is smaller than the original Pony Farm, which had to prepare for more horse-related attractions than exist now. This was especially true in the park's first decade, when there were horses pulling **Conestoga Wagons**, the **Stage Coach**, and several **Main Street vehicles**. What's more, there were Shetland ponies on view in the **Miniature Horse Corral** and a whole train of mules trekking the trails of the **Mule Pack** attraction. While most of these attractions closed within a few years, a few horses are still seen every day at Disneyland, especially on **Main Street** where the horse-drawn streetcar continues to be the same beautiful and popular mode of transportation it's been since **Opening Day**.

Even when there were lots of park attractions that needed horses, no horses ever had more than part-time employment. According to the Disneyland Data page of the 1956 **souvenir book**, "Disneyland horses punch time cards. No horse is allowed to work over four hours per day or six days a week, and each is signed 'in' and 'out' by the timekeeper." These days, the six-day workweek is probably more like a four-day workweek (the horses, evidently, have a pretty strong union). Some of the horses are rarely used at all—the Lipizzans, for instance, are presented mainly at Christmas and for special wedding events.

Not only four-legged animals have lived at the Pony Farm/Circle D. So have their handlers. Originally, the horses were raised by two people who were the only full-time live-in residents at the park (the Disneys also had a private residence at Disneyland, but their **apartment** was only used part-time). The Popes, Owen and Dolly, were horse trainers who began working for **Walt Disney** in the early '50s. Back then they were building Western-style carriages and acquiring the horses Disney thought he'd need for the small park he was planning for the lot next to his Burbank movie studios.

When the Popes moved their 200 animals onto the Pony Farm the week before Disneyland opened, they found that one of their main challenges was to get their charges used to distractions. Sudden loud noises, anything from popping **Jungle Cruise** gunfire to shrieking *Mark Twain* whistles, are still heard without warning throughout the day. To acclimate the animals to the park, the Popes played tapes of shouting voices, a shooting gallery, and other loud noises. Furthermore, they trained the horses to handle the over-friendly crowds that still rush up close for photographs (veteran parkgoers know that polite photo requests made to the operators first are nearly always accommodated).

In addition to training the horses to deal with unusual situations, the Popes also kept the swans that swam daily in front of **Sleeping Beauty Castle**, and they built several of the old-fashioned frontier vehicles used in the park, including the Conestoga Wagons. After getting the Pony Farm started and running successfully, the Popes later left to perform the same function at Walt Disney World.

Pooh Corner

MAP: Bear Country/Critter Country, B/C-5

CHRONOLOGY: April 11, 2003–ongoing

HISTORY: Guests fresh off the **Many Adventures of Winnie the Pooh** attraction and eager to buy the bear necessities should head straight to Pooh Corner, the park's Winnie the Pooh headquarters. This 120-foot-long **Critter Country** shop fills the large building where the **Mile Long Bar** and **Teddi Barra's Swingin' Arcade** used to be back when the neighborhood was called **Bear Country.**

Since 2003, Pooh Corner has sold all the plush toys, shirts, pins, mugs, cookie jars, and infant clothes any Pooh fan could want (plus lots of candy in a room to the right). With its adorable interior and "hunny" pots on display, the store is decorated like something out of the Hundred-Acre Wood. Outside is Pooh's Thotful Spot character-greeting area for photos with the bear himself (see photo above).

Port d'Orleans

MAP: New Orleans Square, NOS-5

CHRONOLOGY: Ca. 1995–2002

HISTORY: Some of what used to be the old **Le Gourmet** shop at the back of **New Orleans Square** became a smaller cooking-related shop in the mid-'90s. The park's 2000 **souvenir book** called Port d'Orleans "a lively mart that features items imported directly from Louisiana, such as a variety of spicy Cajun sauces, beignet mixes, and coffees with chicory."

A minor remodel in 1999 supplemented the coffees and sauces with lots of souvenirs from nearby attractions like the **Haunted Mansion**, **Pirates of the Caribbean**, and **Fantasmic! Le Bat en Rouge** took over this space in 2002.

Portrait Artists

MAP: New Orleans Square, NOS-5, NOS-6

CHRONOLOGY: Ca. 1986–ongoing

HISTORY: In the past portrait artists have graced Center Street on **Main Street**, the **Opera House** in **Town Square**, and the **Art Corner** in **Tomorrowland**. **Van Arsdale France** wrote in *Window on Main Street* that **Jack Olsen** had the original idea to bring in artists to draw quick, lucrative caricatures of guests.

Today portrait artists add a serene, graceful touch to **New Orleans Square**. The artists usually sit in or near a charming courtyard behind the **French Market**, a spot close to the walkway that leads from Royal Street up to the local train station. Sometimes artists can also be found part of the way down Royal in a little enclave across from the **Blue Bayou.**

Depending on the artist, guests can sit for a profile or a face-on portrait, in pastels or watercolors, either representational art or a caricature. Scenes from New Orleans Square are usually in the backgrounds of the portraits. The management for these artists is Rubio Arts, the same company that handles the nearby **Parasol Cart** artists.

Port Royal

MAP: New Orleans Square, NOS-3

CHRONOLOGY: 2006–ongoing

HISTORY: In 2006, the spot next to the **Royal Street Veranda** that had once been **Le Gourmet** and then **Le Bat en Rouge** became Port Royal, a name referring both

to the street outside and to a location popularized in the *Pirates of the Caribbean* movies. Historically, Port Royal was the Jamaican home of many 17th-century buccaneers and earned a reputation as being the world's wickedest town.

At Disneyland, Port Royal's merchandise, spelled out above the doorway as "curios and curiosities," is piratical and souvenir-ish, just like many other establishments in **New Orleans Square**. In addition to offering lots of pirate clothes, hats, and jewelry, the room sometimes has a popular doubloon-pressing machine, though it's frequently inoperative.

Premiere Shop

MAP: Tomorrowland, T-6

CHRONOLOGY: 1963–2005

HISTORY: The Premiere Shop saw a lot of history go by during its four decades in the center of all the **Tomorrowland** action. When the Premiere Shop debuted back in the '60s, nearby was the exit of the **Circarama**/Circle-Vision 360 theater and the Chatterbox speakerphones from the **Bell Telephone Systems Phone Exhibits**. Later the theater was conquered by the **Rocket Rods** and the **Buzz Lightyear Astro Blasters**, the phones gave way to the **American Space Experience**, and eventually the Premiere Shop itself surrendered to **Little Green Men Store Command**.

While not as big as the **Character Shop/Star Trader** across the way, the Premiere Shop was still an appealing shopping destination. For years it sold California- and sports-themed merchandise, and then in the '90s its shelves were filled with Disneyland-related clothes and gifts.

In the 21st century, the Premiere Shop became more of a pin-and-lanyard headquarters, supplemented by several cool kiosks. Called Disneyland Forever, these kiosks enabled guests to burn their own 10-track CDs from a broad selection of Disney songs, sound bites from Disneyland attractions, and other auditory gems. At the Art on Demand kiosks guests could print customized Disney art (the **Disney Gallery** was another source for this service). While the kiosks aren't here anymore, pin collectors will be happy to know that the pins live on in the Little Green Men store that landed in 2005.

Harrison Price

CHRONOLOGY: Ca. 1921–ongoing

HISTORY: Back when Disneyland was still just a drawing on paper, **Walt Disney** was scrutinizing locations to find a suitable construction site. He knew it should be in

Greater Los Angeles somewhere—the region boasted warm weather, its five-county population was huge, and his movie studio was already there—but exactly where in those 4,000 square miles he should start building his park was still unclear. Harrison Price, a top business consultant whom Disney treated with "paternal affection" according to the book *Remembering Walt,* is the man who found Anaheim for him.

Price also looked at other potential locations for Disneyland, among them the west San Fernando Valley (deemed too hot), downtown L.A. (too expensive), and Palos Verdes and the beach communities (too inaccessible). He narrowed his search to 150 square miles between L.A. and Orange County, and then he identified the 10 best available parcels in that area. A 160-acre spread in Anaheim got the top ranking.

At the time, Anaheim wasn't an obvious choice to anyone. Back then it was a sleepy agricultural area, nothing like the crowded city it is now, and it seemed impossibly far from glamorous Hollywood and downtown L.A. Yet after careful study, Price declared that within a few decades a map of Southern California's spreading population would show Anaheim at the center (an amazing prediction—the actual center ended up being in Fullerton, just one town over and only four miles away). Growth in Orange County, Price felt, would continue as it had in the '40s and early '50s, when its population had almost doubled.

What's more, Price knew that a massive north-south freeway project, the Santa Ana (Interstate 5), was already underway and would eventually cross right through Anaheim, putting the town within easy reach of millions of drivers. He learned that Anaheim's climate was dryer than L.A. County's, and he found plenty of land that was still undeveloped and relatively cheap at under $5,000 per acre. And so, in 1953, Harrison Price recommended to Walt Disney that he build his park in freeway-close, financially friendly Anaheim. History, of course, soon proved Price right.

Harrison "Buzz" Price was born in 1922 in Oregon, raised in San Diego, and educated at the California Institute of Technology in Pasadena. After serving in the Air Force and working in Peru in the late '40s for three years, Price returned to California to get his graduate degree from Stanford. In '52, he became a member of the Stanford Research Institute, and soon he was consulting on key Disneyland decisions, especially its location.

Three years later, with Disneyland established as a stunning success, Price formed his own consulting company, ERA (Economics Research Associates), and continued doing research for various Disney projects. In the '60s, he hand-picked the Florida site for Walt Disney World; evaluated the Mineral King ski resort in California that was eventually abandoned (the "number one disappointment" of his career, he claimed); he made recommendations for one of Walt Disney's pet projects, the CalArts campus in Southern California; and he even advised Disney to buy a company plane to expedite his many travels.

After selling ERA, Price formed another company in 1978, HPC (Harrison Price Company), and for the next two decades continued to research new business developments. Among the thousands of clients he's served over his long career are the Six Flags parks, Knott's Berry Farm, Universal Studios, IMAX theaters, the World's Fairs in Seattle and New York, NASA, famous restaurant chains, major aquariums, and Las Vegas mega-hotels. Price's autobiography, *Walt's Revolution! By the Numbers*, came out in 2003, the same year he was inducted as a Disney Legend.

Primeval World Diorama

MAP: Tomorrowland, T-17

CHRONOLOGY: July 1, 1966–ongoing

HISTORY: About eight years after the **Grand Canyon Diorama** joined the **Santa Fe & Disneyland Railroad** line, the Primeval World Diorama was added in the same general geographical area of the park. Both dioramas get listed as **Main Street** attractions, but both are technically on the southeastern edge of **Tomorrowland**.

The Primeval World follows the Grand Canyon along the route. Whereas the first diorama is behind the **Rocket to the Moon/Mission to Mars** building, the second is behind **Space Mountain** and ends in back of the **Opera House** about 300 feet from the Main Street train depot. Both dioramas are enclosed in long tunnels—the second tunnel for the Primeval World is about 500 feet long, a little longer than the Grand Canyon's tunnel. The combined tunnel experience lasts about 3.5 minutes.

If the first diorama transports train guests to another location, the second transports them to another time. For the Primeval World Diorama, that time is the age of dinosaurs as it's depicted in the dramatic "Rite of Spring" sequence from *Fantasia*. At slow speed, the train crawls past almost four dozen extinct creatures, some 15 feet tall, living in a prehistoric world. Gigantic brontosaurus necks rise up from a swamp, mouths munching on vegetation. A pterodactyl watches from atop a rock. Raptor-looking reptiles sip from a pond. Triceratops babies wriggle out of their eggs. Interestingly, the stirring music in the background isn't Stravinsky's—it's Bernard Herrmann's and comes from his score for *Mysterious Island*, a 1961 adventure film made by Columbia Pictures.

The most memorable encounter, and the one shown on the **attraction poster** and in big photos in the **souvenir books**, comes when the towering tyrannosaurus rex attacks a stegosaurus, a powerful scene re-created from *Fantasia*. Not shown anywhere are cavemen, who weren't in *Fantasia* either. They were, however, part of this attraction when Disney designers first created it for the Ford pavilion at the 1964–1965 New York World's Fair. **Walt Disney** deemed the fair's **Audio-Animatronic** humanoids too rudimentary in their design and execution for inclusion at Disneyland, especially since he had much more sophisticated A-A humans coming soon to **Pirates of the Caribbean** (cavemen wouldn't have been historically accurate, either, since their appearance followed the extinction of the dinosaurs by tens of millions of years).

Savvy guests long on interest but short on time know a simple trick for catching this attraction at the last minute. Rather than hopping on board a train at the Main Street station for the long run around the park, they'll catch a quick ride in nearby Tomorrowland, immediately venture back to the primeval past, and zip back to the future a few minutes later at Main Street. Invigorated by the time travel and dazzled by the dinosaurs, they emerge ready to brave the modern world beyond the turnstiles.

Princess Boutique

MAP: Fantasyland, Fa-3

CHRONOLOGY: Ca. 1997–2005

HISTORY: In the last decade guests have had several chances to shop in **Fantasyland** for the princesses in their lives. For about eight years, one prime opportunity came on the left-hand side of the entrance into **Sleeping Beauty Castle**. Also inside the entrance, just across the walkway, was the **Heraldry Shoppe**, with the drawbridge a few steps south and the castle's courtyard a few steps to the north.

Like most of the clientele giddily shopping here, the Princess Boutique was small, pretty, and princessy. Lots of pink, lots of irresistible dresses, and lots of costume jewelry were on display. In 2005 this shop was turned into the **50th Anniversary Shop** for Disneyland's golden anniversary celebration.

Princess Fantasy Faire

MAP: Fantasyland, Fa-18

CHRONOLOGY: November 2006–ongoing

HISTORY: After *Snow White—An Enchanting Musical* closed at the **Videopolis**/Fantasyland Theater in 2006, the large performance space at the back of **Fantasyland** was transformed into a Nestlé-sponsored character-greeting area "where happily ever after happens every day." Under a tent roof that displays a starry scene, and on a stage decorated as a castle, throne, and forest, a steady stream of Disney royalty moved in as the new tenants.

Five different activities are presented on the grounds. In the Royal Crafts area, guests can get their hair braided and faces painted. There's also shopping for princess merchandise, storytelling with Disney Princesses, and a Royal Coronation Ceremony. Most popular of all is the Disney Princess Royal Walk, where guests linger with the young beauties "and other royal visitors along an enchanted pathway." The happy photo opportunities generate long lines of youthful princesses and their camera-clicking parents throughout the day.

Professor Barnaby Owl's Photographic Art Studio

MAP: Bear Country/Critter Country, B/C-8

CHRONOLOGY: January 31, 1992–ongoing

HISTORY: Many guests stop to look at the photos on view here at the back of **Critter Country**, but few guests know Professor Barnaby Owl's legacy. He was the knowledgeable character in two classic *Adventures in Music* cartoons of the '50s, *Melody* and the Oscar-winning *Toot, Whistle, Plunk and Boom* (plus many Disney Sing-Along-Songs videos of the '80s and '90s). As for the photos in the good professor's Art Studio, they're the action shots snapped of guests just as they're beginning their plunge down the **Splash Mountain** log flume. The sudden realization of what's about to happen—a 52-foot drop towards a briar patch—usually puts expressions of surprise, terror, or a combination of both on guests' faces.

The Art Studio displays all the photos snapped in the last few minutes and then offers them for immediate sale in a cardboard frame. In recent years the Art Studio got some notoriety when photos started appearing of women with their shirts open or lifted up, for a while giving Splash Mountain the nickname Flash Mountain.

Puffin Bakery, aka Puffin Bake Shop

MAP: Main Street, MS-6

CHRONOLOGY: July 18, 1955–June 3, 1960

HISTORY: Had it opened one day earlier, the Puffin Bakery would have been one of the charter businesses that debuted when Disneyland did. Even if it missed **Opening Day**, the Puffin Bakery did enjoy almost a five-year run that briefly carried it into the '60s.

For some reason the **souvenir books** of those years listed the name as both the Puffin Bakery and the Puffin Bake Shop. However it was known, its location was along the left-hand side of **Main Street** in the middle of the second block. Immediately to the south of the bakery was **Sunny-View Farms Jams & Jellies**, and to the north was the showy **Penny Arcade**.

When the baked goods finally went flat in 1960, the **Sunkist Citrus House** poured into the combined space of both the bakery and the swimsuit shop. Later the spot reverted to what it had been in the '50s when the **Blue Ribbon Bakery** moved in for most of the '90s.

Quasimodo's Attic, aka Sanctuary of Quasimodo

MAP: Fantasyland, Fa-30

CHRONOLOGY: June 21, 1996–February 1997

HISTORY: In the summer of 1996, the new Quasimodo's Attic replaced the five-year-old **Disney Villains** shop in **Fantasyland**. This prominent location in the **Sleeping Beauty Castle** courtyard next to the **Peter Pan Flight** attraction was given to Quasimodo merchandise to help promote that year's *The Hunchback of Notre Dame*. Simultaneously, two other *Hunchback*-themed locations opened elsewhere in **Frontierland—Big Thunder Barbecue** became the Festival of Foods, and **Big Thunder Ranch** became the Festival of Fools.

By the end of the summer, Quasimodo's Attic had changed its name to Sanctuary of Quasimodo. And by the end of the winter, with the *Hunchback* juggernaut subsiding, the Quasimodo shop closed permanently, its location to be filled by another medieval store, the **Knight Shop**, six months later.

Radio Disney Broadcast Booth

MAP: Tomorrowland, T-8

CHRONOLOGY: March 1999–December 2002

HISTORY: For a couple of years at the turn of the millennium, Radio Disney operated out of a small glass-walled booth in the middle of **Tomorrowland**. Deejays and broadcast electronics occupied a space underneath the old **PeopleMover** loading platform that had formerly been used by the **Lunching Pad**. The park's 2000 **souvenir book** explained: "Under the **Observatron** is the official Disneyland home of Radio Disney. Through soundproof glass, guests can view Radio Disney's state-of-the-art radio studio and watch daily live broadcasts carried across the nation on 'the radio network just for kids.'"

While Radio Disney is still on the air, the Radio Disney Broadcast Booth went silent in the winter of 2002. In 2006, **Tomorrowlanding** landed where the booth had been.

Rafts to Tom Sawyer Island

MAP: Frontierland, Fr-11

CHRONOLOGY: June 16, 1956–ongoing

HISTORY: Guests could see **Tom Sawyer Island** on **Opening Day** in 1955, but they couldn't access it until the summer of '56. That's when the D-ticket Rafts to Tom Sawyer Island began their regular service between a dock on the southern riverbank of **Frontierland** and a dock on the southern end of the island about 100 feet away. The following summer a second dock in Frontierland, this one close to the **Indian Village**, opened up to accommodate more guests. As shown on the free island maps handed out dockside, this second dock connected to the island's midsection, deliv-

ering guests nearer to Fort
Wilderness until the dock
closed in 1971.

No matter which
location guests used, the
service was about the same,
with some 40 or so passengers at a time making the
one-minute trip at about
four mph. The trip is made
only during daylight hours,
because the rafts have al-
ways stopped running when the sun goes down and the island is closed.

The rafts and their promotional materials are designed to look roughly
made. The hand-painted sign at the dock, for instance, has some of its letters
printed backwards to announce "no strollers or smoking permitted on rafts." The
Tom Sawyer Island **attraction poster** shows off an old log raft reminiscent of the
one used for the Mississippi River escape in *The Adventures of Huckleberry Finn*. The
illustration's raft has an unfurled, breeze-filled sail, a pirate flag flying high, and
pole-power pushing it toward the island; in reality, the sails are kept wrapped up,
for years the flags were more like red rags, and propulsion has always been provided
by diesel engines.

Like the canoes and the old **Mike Fink Keel Boats**, the rafts do not run on
underwater tracks and are instead carefully steered by **cast members**. And as with
everything else associated with this attraction, these cast members, in their rustic
Tom-and-Huck adventure clothes, looked like throwbacks to the 19th century. More
allusions to Mark Twain's literary creations were made by the names on the rafts
themselves—they're called the *Huck Finn*, *Injun Joe*, *Becky Thatcher*, and *Tom Sawyer*.
In the spring of 2006, the *Huck*, *Joe*, and *Becky* rafts got renamed *Blackbeard*, *Anne
Bonny*, and *Captain Kidd* to match the new pirate theming out on Tom Sawyer Island.

Rainbow Caverns Mine Train,
aka Western Mine Train Through Nature's Wonderland

MAP: Frontierland, Fr-21

CHRONOLOGY: July 2, 1956–January 2, 1977

HISTORY: About a year after 1955's **Opening Day**, the first of several railroad attractions began chuffing through the wilderness territory of **Frontierland**. Ultimately
this land would be traversed by the high-speed **Big Thunder Mountain Railroad**, but
back in the '50s it was explored at the more sedate speeds of the Rainbow Caverns
Mine Train. Before it opened, the park's 1956 **souvenir book** called it the "Mine
Ride"; the '57 book used the name Rainbow Mountain Mining & Exploration Company
Mine Train in a caption for a photo of the little engine and six green cars navigating
through "weird cactus formations" of the **Painted Desert**.

Approximate Train Distances

2.3 miles: Monorail
1.3 miles: Santa Fe & Disneyland Railroad
1 mile: PeopleMover, Viewliner
.5 mile: Big Thunder Mountain Railroad
.3 mile: Casey Jr. Circus Train, Western Mine Train Through Nature's Wonderland

Built for under a half-million dollars, the Rainbow Caverns Mine Train was closer in size and spirit to the cozy **Casey Jr. Circus Train** over in **Fantasyland** than it was to a full-size railroad. At 30 inches wide, the track was six inches narrower than the 36-gauge track of the **Santa Fe & Disneyland Railroad**. Guests sat in open cargo cars behind a small old-fashioned engine run by an electric motor. Anywhere along the quarter-mile journey the sights might have included the **Conestoga Wagons**, **Stage Coach**, or **Mule Pack**, since they also served this same dusty territory.

The highlight of the whole trip, however, and what gave the Mine Train its name, was exclusive to train passengers. Shown frequently in souvenir books, Rainbow Caverns was a beautiful, natural-looking cave illuminated by black lights and glowing with neon-colored waterfalls and pools of luminescent water. **Claude Coats** and **John Hench** are acknowledged as the Imagineers behind the caverns. According to the Disneyland Data page of the park's 1957 souvenir book, "approximately 270,000 gallons of water per hour are circulated to create the seven multi-colored waterfalls seen in the Rainbow Caverns."

The complex visual effects, accompanied by choral mood music, were impressive enough to survive the makeover that hit the rest of the attraction at the turn of the decade. After closing down for six months from October 11, 1959, to May 28, 1960, the line reopened as the Western Mine Train Through Nature's Wonderland (sometimes simplified without the "Western"). **Nature's Wonderland** was an extensive re-landscaping of what had been arid land to accommodate over 200 new **Audio-Animatronic** animals in river and mountain settings. The nine-minute D-ticket train ride now went over trestles and operated without the Conestoga Wagons or Stage Coach in sight, as neither of those attractions made it out of the '50s.

As with other Disneyland railroads, **Walt Disney** was actively involved in the design of this one, in both its iterations. **Roger Broggie** was the Imagineer in charge of building the train sets. In 1977, the Mine Train was finally pulled from service as the era of fast roller coasters, which had already put **Space**

Mountain in **Tomorrowland**, brought Big Thunder Mountain to the Western wilderness. A relic of the old days is still on view, however, from **Tom Sawyer Island**—one of the Mine Train locomotives, with a couple of cars askew behind it, is crashed in the wilderness near Big Thunder Mountain (see photo, previous page).

Rancho del Zocalo Restaurante

MAP: Frontierland, Fr-24

CHRONOLOGY: February 5, 2001–ongoing

HISTORY: Casa Mexicana, the well-themed Mexican restaurant in **Frontierland** that had begun operating in 1982, underwent some *cambios grandes* in 2001. Ortega, the chile and salsa company, was the new sponsor, and Rancho del Zocalo was the new name, though a sign outside reading "*mi casa es su casa*" honored the previous establishment. Zocalo itself is an allusion to the name applied in the '50s to this section of Frontierland, **El Zocalo** ("the square").

The new menu, while mainly serving cafeteria-style Mexican cuisine to be eaten on an outdoor patio near the **Big Thunder Mountain Railroad**, was augmented to include some of the barbecue flavors from the extinct **Big Thunder Barbecue**. Thus, the Casa Mexicana/Rancho del Zocalo space, which had been strictly a Mexican restaurant for almost two decades, started to offer Big Thunder's "Western barbecue specialties," which were served up here as Smoked St. Louis Ribs, Ranch Style Barbecued Chicken, and an El Grande Barbecue Platter.

The new Rancho is bigger and fancier than the old Casa Mexicana, with exotic tiles, fountains, a big mural on an exterior wall (see photo above), and more ironwork enhancing the Spanish architecture. In 2007, the menu changed again, this time reverting to mostly Mexican dishes supplemented by a few California specialties like "citrus fire-grilled chicken."

Thurl Ravenscroft

CHRONOLOGY: February 6, 1914–May 22, 2005

HISTORY: Like **Paul Frees**, Thurl Ravenscroft had one of those resonant voices everyone has heard in movies, TV commercials, and Disneyland attractions for decades. A Nebraskan born in 1914, Ravenscroft served in World War II and then established a Hollywood career as a singer. He was part of several different groups, including the Mello Men and the Johnny Mann Singers (one of his best-loved performances was "You're a Mean One, Mister Grinch" for the holiday classic *How the Grinch Stole Christmas*). As a successful voice actor, his single most famous line was Tony the Tiger's enthusiastic declaration "they're grrrrreat!" for Kellogg's cereal.

For Disney, Ravenscroft voiced characters or sang in numerous movies, among them *Lady and the Tramp*, *Mary Poppins*, *Cinderella*, *Alice in Wonderland*, and *The Jungle Book*. At Disneyland, he provided voices for the **Country Bear Jamboree** (he was the mounted buffalo head), the **Enchanted Tiki Room** (Fritz), the *Mark Twain* (narrator), and, most famously, the **Haunted Mansion** (not only did he sing lead on that attraction's theme song, "Grim Grinning Ghosts," but his face is still in the quartet of singing busts).

Southern California residents also knew Ravenscroft as the narrator of both *The Pageant of the Masters*, a living tableaux of artworks held every summer in Laguna Beach, and *The Glory of Christmas*, a holiday spectacular held every winter at Garden Grove's Crystal Cathedral. Thurl Ravenscroft was inducted as a Disney Legend in 1995; ten years later he died of cancer at age 91.

Redd Rockett's Pizza Port

MAP: Tomorrowland, T-16

CHRONOLOGY: March 21, 1998–ongoing

HISTORY: After the **Mission to Mars** attraction stopped flying in 1992, its large building in **Tomorrowland** sat empty for the next four years. In 1996, the **Toy Story Funhouse** set up here for a brief run, but two more years would pass before something permanent settled in.

Surprisingly, the new arrival wasn't an attraction, it was a restaurant serving big portions of fast food. Redd Rockett's Pizza Port and its new neighbor, **Honey, I Shrunk the Audience**, both debuted in 1998 in conjunction with a major Tomorrowland remodel. The restaurant's name alludes to both the big red-and-white rocket on the roof (the famed **Moonliner**) and the Space Port that was considered for Tomorrowland in the '60s (**Space Mountain** went up in the '70s instead).

Redd's has cafeteria-style counters and plenty of seating indoors and outdoors. Buitoni, a Tuscan pasta and sauce company that opened for business in 1827,

is the sponsor here, which means Italian food dominates Redd's menu. The menu items are anything but typical, as they all have humorous space-themed names like Celestial Caesar Salad, Starfield of Greens Salad, Mars-inara Pasta, Spacegetti, and Lunar Cheese Pizza. Proximity to the popular **Starcade** makes this a favorite spot for arcade-happy kids. The 10 classic **attraction posters** along the back walls make it a favorite for history-happy adults.

Red Wagon Inn, aka Plaza Inn

MAP: Plaza Hub, PH-3

CHRONOLOGY: July 17, 1955–ongoing

HISTORY: Supposedly **Walt Disney** preferred the posh Red Wagon Inn over any other Disneyland restaurant. In the '50s, it offered the park's priciest dining experience and was so elegant that it even had its own inviting **attraction poster**. Wide photos of the white-trimmed Edwardian exterior made it into all of the park's early **souvenir books**, their captions touting "tempting meals in the beautiful surroundings of Grandfather's day."

The Red Wagon name derived from the logo of the sponsor, Swift & Company, which debuted two other Disneyland restaurants, the **Market House** and the **Chicken Plantation**, along with this one on **Opening Day**. The full-service Red Wagon offered full-course breakfasts, lunches, and dinners in glitzy antiques-filled rooms lit by crystal chandeliers. It also had a terrace for alfresco dining, and, unbeknownst to most guests, there was a private room with a private entrance for Walt Disney and his VIP guests (this alcohol-serving area was a precursor to the exclusive **Club 33** he had built, but never got to use, in **New Orleans Square**). Disney's presence is all over the building's interior—in fact, some of the opulent curlicues and brackets on display came from a Victorian mansion he owned over near USC.

In July of 1965, with Swift ending its sponsorship, the restaurant got a new name, the Plaza Inn, and a new sponsor, the Columbian Coffee Growers. The Plaza Inn was more like a swank cafeteria that served roast chicken, turkey, pastas, Cobb salad, gourmet desserts, and other fancy favorites. A 1998 renovation kept the plush Victorian interior but introduced some new menu items, including a prix fixe breakfast with omelets, Mickey-shaped waffles, and the company of Disney characters. The Plaza Inn, incidentally, is the third Plaza-named restaurant in the immediate area—across the way are the **Plaza Pavilion** and the **Plaza Gardens**. Of this trio, the Plaza Inn is the only one on the **Tomorrowland** side of the **Plaza Hub**.

Reel-Ride

MAP: Frontierland, Fr-1

CHRONOLOGY: Never built

HISTORY: If an intriguing Disneyland legend is accurate, Willis O'Brien, the wizard behind the stop-motion special effects for *King Kong* and other early movie classics, once drew up some concept art for the park. Unfortunately, the Reel-Ride attraction he supposedly invented for **Frontierland** was never built.

As shown in the museum exhibition called Behind the Magic: 50 Years of Disneyland, O'Brien's color illustration depicted 10 kids on mechanical horses facing a movie screen. These young buckaroos would've ridden their horses while a rollicking movie of a cowboy star on his horse rolled in front of them. The ungrammatical caption described the synchronization of the horses with "a back-projection on a translucent screen, giving effect of actually traveling through the country. When chase is ended—horses stop."

Had it been constructed and implemented, the three-to-five-minute Reel-Ride might've been the world's first melding of motion-simulation and an amusement park attraction. O'Brien, who was about 68 years old when he purportedly made his 1954 drawing, died in 1962.

Refreshment Corner, aka Coke Corner, aka Coca-Cola Refreshment Corner

MAP: Main Street, MS-10

CHRONOLOGY: July 17, 1955–ongoing

HISTORY: The most durable fast-food location in the park has existed since **Opening Day** on the western corner where **Main Street** meets the **Plaza Hub**. The Refreshment Corner, also known as the Coke Corner and the Coca-Cola Refreshment Corner, bends around the intersection of Main and West Plaza Street towards the **Adventureland** entrance. Its neighbors have been the enduring **Candy Palace** just south on Main Street and, for a while, a small hat shop tucked over on the Adventureland side. The Refreshment Corner opens on the inside into the Candy Palace; the outside area with alfresco tables next to the **Plaza Pavilion** is called the Corner Café. The basic menu initially listed just sodas and was supplemented later by various hot dogs and snacks.

Three features have secured the lasting popularity of this otherwise simple eatery—its long hours (longer than most other food establishments in the park), its charming interior with ornate turn-of-the-century embellishments, and the presence of affable piano man Rod Miller. Miller, wearing old-fashioned clothes and a consistent smile, played exuberant ragtime piano favorites and chatted with guests on the patio for over 30 years dating back to around 1970 (he and his white upright piano were spotlighted with a large photo in the 2006 **souvenir book**). With Miller now retired, a handful of other pianists currently share the entertainment schedule.

As perky as the Refreshment Corner is in daylight, it's even brighter after sundown, when the lovely lights and lively music combine to make this perhaps Disneyland's cheeriest spot. Success here on Main Street led Coca-Cola to sponsor additional locations in the park over the decades, including 1967's **Tomorrowland Terrace** and 1998's **Spirit of Refreshment**.

Restrooms

CHRONOLOGY: July 17, 1955–ongoing

HISTORY: On **Opening Day**, **Walt Disney** almost had no working restrooms in Disneyland. A strike by local plumbers forced last-minute negotiations that got the restrooms, but not the water fountains, into operation (Disney made his agonizing choice with the realization that guests could do without the latter but not the former). A free map handed out to guests that day pinpointed only ten public restrooms (five men's, five women's) in the entire 60-acre park; the maps in the park's 1956 **souvenir book** accounted for just a dozen (six and six). That year, two pairs of restrooms were on **Main Street**, and then each land had only one pair of public restrooms each. Also that year the coin-operated stalls in some of the restrooms were converted to free stalls.

Today there are over 25 pairs of restrooms in Disneyland. Counting from the **entrance** up through Main Street and all the way to the **Plaza Hub** restaurants, there are six pairs of restrooms. The lands all have at least three pairs each, except for **Critter Country** and **Mickey's Toontown**, which have one pair each. The size of the restrooms varies from the spacious (like those at the **Golden Bear Lodge**, aka Hungry Bear in Critter Country) to the cramped (**Tom Sawyer Island** in **Frontierland**).

What never varies is the cleanliness. **Chuck Boyajian**, the original manager of custodial operations, and his staff raised the bar for cleanliness to a height that became the industry standard. Every bathroom is lightly cleaned every hour, even on the busiest days,

with thorough sanitizing cleanings every night. Not only are the facilities spotless, they're convenient for parents: most restrooms have baby-changing stations, and some even sell baby-changing kits (diapers, wipes, etc.). Disneyland accommodates special restroom needs at the **Baby Station** and **First Aid**, both along the Plaza Hub's East Plaza Street.

A delightful enhancement to each restroom's exterior is the sign that is usually themed to the area. For instance, Kings and Queens are depicted on a restroom by **Alice in Wonderland**, Roger and Jessica Rabbit adorn doors in Mickey's Toontown, aliens aim for the restrooms in **Tomorrowland**, and Gentlemen and Ladies use Main Street's restrooms. Prince, evidently, has his own restroom outside of the **Princess Fantasy Faire** in **Fantasyland**.

What's more, the theming occasionally even extends indoors—some restrooms in **Frontierland** have wood walls and antique hurricane lamps, and those in Tomorrowland have the same bronze-and-green color scheme that's used outside. The most opulent restrooms are inside **Club 33**, where the ladies' room features gilded seating arrangements that earn the nickname "thrones." The most conveniently placed might be the pair just outside the park by the ticket booths, giving guests who are headed for their cars a chance to go before they're gone.

Cicely Rigdon

CHRONOLOGY: Unknown—ongoing

HISTORY: Working her way up from 1957 ticket seller to 2005 Disney Legend inductee, Cicely Rigdon enjoyed a distinguished Disney career that included over three decades of Disneyland service.

In 1959, just two years after being hired at Disneyland, she was heading the new **Tour Guide** program. That success led her to **Guest Relations**, which she supervised in the '60s and '70s while also training and overseeing the ticket sellers out front. Among many other responsibilities during this time, Rigdon supervised the private **apartment** maintained for **Walt Disney** above the **Fire Department**, she was there at the 1964–1965 New York World's Fair to help with the debuts of the four new Disney attractions, and she worked closely with the park's "Honorary Mayor," **Jack Lindquist**.

In the '70s, Rigdon took on training responsibilities at Walt Disney World, and a decade later she was updating the **Miss Disneyland** program into the Disneyland Ambassador to the World program. After 37 years of working at Disneyland, Cicely Rigdon retired in 1994.

River Belle Terrace

MAP: Frontierland, Fr-7

CHRONOLOGY: 1971–ongoing

HISTORY: What had been **Aunt Jemima's** restaurant for over a decade, and the **Magnolia Tree Terrace** for over a year, became the stately, white-trimmed River Belle Terrace in 1971. The location on the corner where **Frontierland** rounds into **Adventureland** has dictated restaurant entrances in both lands—a cream-colored entrance on the Frontierland side, pale blue on the Adventureland side—and a roof with double theming.

After a late 2007 remodel, today the restaurant has two stories. On its Frontierland side the River Belle stretches all the way back towards the **Stage Door Café**, usurping spaces that used to be occupied by smaller eateries. The interior décor is still as pretty as always, and the umbrella-shaded terrace in the restaurant's name still affords guests attractive views of the **Rivers of America** only 75 feet away to the north. Oscar Meyer, Hormel, and Sunkist have all been sponsors over the years.

No matter which company has been participating, the cuisine has always had a down-home flavor to it, offering lots of basic American food themed to Mark Twain and his writings—the Mark Twain and Steamboat breakfasts, Aunt Polly's Chicken, sandwiches named after Huck and Tom, Becky Thatcher's Fresh Fruit Plate, etc. Lately tangy barbecue specialties have joined the lunch and dinner menus. The highlight, though, might be the Mickey-shaped pancakes (this mouse-eared specialty is said to have originated here). The park's own literature declares the River Belle Terrace to have been the preferred Sunday morning breakfast choice of **Walt Disney** himself.

Rivers of America

MAP: Frontierland, Fr-9

CHRONOLOGY: July 17, 1955–ongoing

HISTORY: The man-made Rivers of America area is a highly visible, much-traveled section of the park that debuted on **Opening Day**. While it's called the Rivers of America, the waterway might be more accurately called the Rivers of the Midwest, since the Missouri and Mississippi seem to be the main inspirations for the design and the landscaping.

Though the river area is technically in **Frontierland**, it is visible from, and bordered by, **New Orleans Square** (to the south and southwest) and **Critter Country** (to the west) as well. Some of Disneyland's most popular attractions, including **Pirates of the Caribbean**, **Haunted Mansion**, **Splash Mountain**, and **Big Thunder Mountain Railroad**, ring the perimeter of the Rivers of America. The river section most often viewed by pedestrians is the southern area where **Fantasmic!** is presented. A walk through this area, from **Fowler's Harbor** in the southwest corner of the river over to the launch site for the *Mark Twain*, covers about 650 feet of pavement.

The overall surface area of the Rivers of America (including the island in the middle) covers about 325,000 square feet. These eight acres represent roughly 13% of the total area of the original 60-acre park. Shaped vaguely like a kidney bean around **Tom Sawyer Island**, the waters stretch almost 1000 feet from the northernmost to the southernmost shore. Measuring across the water from the mainland to the inner island, the river varies from about 80 to 100 feet wide.

Five watercraft have sailed upon its waters (though not all simultaneously): the *Mark Twain*; the *Columbia*; the **Mike Fink Keel Boats**; the **Indian War Canoes**, aka Davy Crockett's Explorer Canoes; and the **Rafts to Tom Sawyer Island**. Boats that circumnavigate the island travel about a half-mile through approximately nine million gallons of water that's only about five feet deep. Despite being so shallow, the river has been the site of an accidental drowning, the tragic result of an inebriated guest entering the waters after dark. According to Disney legend, the rivers supposedly flow from the hill on Tom Sawyer Island where Tom & Huck's Treehouse is built.

A Disney hardcover **souvenir book** called *Disneyland: The First Quarter Century* described the main problem with the river's construction. The first time water was pumped into the bulldozed trenches, the water immediately seeped away into the soil. After different riverbeds were tried, eventually the river was given a hard clay bottom. These days the river is drained every few years for cleaning and maintenance. The water that's used to refill the river would look clear except for a chemical additive that makes it appear murky, thus concealing the submerged tracks that guide the *Mark Twain* and *Columbia* (and also concealing any cameras, clothes, or other items accidentally dropped overboard).

One of the misconceptions about the waterway is that it is kept stocked with fish. It's not. Occasionally tiny fish are seen in the river, but they haven't been placed there intentionally. The only time park officials introduced fish was in the early years, when a small sealed area at the southern end of Tom Sawyer Island was abundantly stocked; guests were then given fishing poles to try their luck, but the practice was soon abandoned when their odoriferous catches later sat in lockers or were abandoned in the park.

The Disneyland Data page in the park's 1956 souvenir book identified ad-

ditional fauna along the river: "Wildlife of North America have 'discovered' Disneyland. Flocks of wild geese, mallards, and other birds have found Frontierland's River a safe retreat in their pilgrimages south. The birds pause to rest here, and in some cases stay on for several months." Thus, the desultory ducks often seen drifting in the waterway aren't **Audio-Animatronic** mechanicals, as some guests might suppose, but are instead migratory waterfowl wintering at Disneyland.

Rock Candy Mountain, aka Candy Mountain

MAP: Fantasyland, Fa-15

CHRONOLOGY: Never built

HISTORY: One of the more sugary ideas that was considered for young Disneyland was something called Rock Candy Mountain, aka Candy Mountain. As sung by Burl Ives, the ballad "Big Rock Candy Mountain" had been a big hit in 1949, so the image of an abundantly sweet wonderland was probably still floating in the air when Disney designers began drawing concept illustrations for it in the early 1950s.

Their creation would've been incorporated into the **Canal Boats of the World**, which debuted on **Opening Day** without any kind of candy, mountain, or mountain of candy as part of the attraction. As it was envisioned, the low-slung sightseeing boats would've entered Rock Candy Mountain and found inside scenes from a *Wizard of Oz*-related movie that **Walt Disney** had in the works (the scenes would've been from his new movie based on one of L. Frank Baum's many *Oz* sequels, not the 1939 Judy Garland classic). Candy Mountain wouldn't have been the only site in the park's first decade to incorporate props and costumes from a Disney movie—the **20,000 Leagues Under the Sea Exhibit** was a long-running display of movie sets, and in '61 the **Babes in Toyland Exhibit** took over the **Opera House.**

Even more colorful than the interior was the mountain's exterior, which was to have been constructed with artificial candy as decorations. Oversized candy canes, gumballs, lollipops, and more would've coated the six-story mountain, and the **Casey Jr. Circus Train** would've wrapped around the base. Unfortunately, when the *Oz* movie plans died, so did the mountain. As the story was related in *Disneyland: The Nickel Tour*, the miniature model that had been made with real candy was taken outside, where birds put a quick end to any Candy Mountain dreams.

Rocket Man, Space Girl, and Space Man

MAP: Park, P-18

CHRONOLOGY: December 1965

HISTORY: For a couple of weeks in the winter of 1965, jet packs were all the rage. At the movies, James Bond was soaring out of harm's way in the opening sequence of *Thunderball*, that year's winter blockbuster. And at Disneyland, the park's Rocket Man was soaring above the **Flight Circle** in **Tomorrowland** for the holidays. Both Bond and the Rocket Man were using Bell-designed rocket-powered backpacks (also called rocket packs and rocket belts) intended for the Air Force. Both pilots wore white helmets, but the Disneyland Rocket Man wore a white flight suit as well (Bond wore his usual natty suit and tie). *Disneyland: The Nickel Tour* identified the Disneyland rocketeer as William Suitor, the same man who later flew a jet pack at the 1984 Summer Olympics in L.A.

The Disneyland Rocket Man is not to be confused with Space Girl and Space Man, who roamed Tomorrowland from the '50s to the '70s. In 2007, informed **cast members** in the **Opera House** identified this pair as K7 (Space Girl) and K8 (Space

Man), setting up a joke about a Space Dog named K9 that was never sprung. The fit, young space couple walked around, rode on attractions, shook hands with guests, and promoted a happy, energetic, technological future as the "symbols of Tomorrowland," which is how they were labeled in the park's '59 **souvenir book**.

As shown in that same book, Space Girl and Space Man wore big cartoony suits that were definitely futuristic but hardly realistic. These suits varied, at times including foil-looking material, sometimes all-white material, plus silver boots, huge glass helmets with antennae on top, thick padded rings on the forearms and shins, and little oxygen tanks on their backs. Space Girl sometimes wore either a white pant suit or a short white dress. Silliest of all was her cape, a super-fashion taken right out of superhero comic books. Randy Bright was one of those cast members who donned the Space Man's silver space suit; Bright later wrote a history of the park called *Disneyland: Inside Story* and eventually oversaw new attractions as VP of concept development.

Real spacemen arrived in Disneyland in 1969 when the **Tomorrowland Stage** broadcast a live TV feed of Apollo astronauts Neil Armstrong and Buzz Aldrin walking on the moon. Eight years later, Scott Carpenter, Gordon Cooper, Wally Schirra, and Alan Shepard were among the astronauts on hand for the debut of **Space Mountain**, as shown in the book *Disneyland: The First Thirty Years*.

Rocket Rods

MAP: Tomorrowland, T-8

CHRONOLOGY: May 22, 1998–April 27, 2001

HISTORY: "The Rocket Rods zoom above, through, and around Tomorrowland in the fastest and longest attraction in Disneyland Park. This thrilling experience puts guests behind the wheels of high-speed vehicles of the future as they tear along an elevated highway above Tomorrowland." So read the ambitious declaration in the park's 2000 **souvenir book**. "Ride the road to tomorrow" was the proud boast at the attraction entrance. Unfortunately, the Rocket Rods' disappointing reality never matched the printed hyperbole or ambitious potential. What should have been an exciting new 30-mph thrill ride for the 21st century barely sputtered through the last year of the 20th. Even more embarrassingly, the Rocket Rods were built to be a high-profile showpiece attraction at the front of **Tomorrowland**, making their failure all the more glaring.

In the spring of '98, what had been the **Circarama** theater opened as the Rocket Rods' spiraling queue area. Waiting guests learned about the history of transportation from numerous displays, among them movies, large blueprints, and vehicles from extinct Disneyland attractions. Guests also heard car-themed music, including a reworked version of "Detroit" from Disney's *The Happiest Millionaire*. The displays and music were fine, but not the long wait, which often stretched to well over an hour.

When they arrived at the old **PeopleMover** boarding area under the new **Observatron**, guests found sleek, five-passenger hot rods that looked suitably futuristic and sounded surprisingly loud. Originally they were called Rocket Rods XPR (Experimental Prototype Rocket), but the initials were dropped before guests could start inventing their own acronyms (Extremely Problematic Ride, for instance, or Exceptional Patience Required). Once they headed off along the PeopleMover's elevated tracks, the cars lurched from acceleration on the straightaways to sudden deceleration on the curves for a spastic four-minute trip that was as hard on the vehicles as it was on the passengers.

While some people liked the experience, nobody liked the frequent ride breakdowns.

After struggling through three trouble-plagued summers, park executives temporarily closed the whole attraction for repairs in the fall of 2000. At least, their intention was for the shutdown to be temporary. In April 2001, Imagineers finally gave up and moved the Rocket Rods from Disneyland's future to Disneyland's past. Four years later, the successful **Buzz Lightyear Astro Blasters** attraction moved into the Circarama theater building; outside, the elevated tracks still stand in mute testament to the fully realized PeopleMover dream of the '60s and the unfulfilled Rocket Rods dream of the '90s.

Rocket to the Moon, aka Flight to the Moon

MAP: Tomorrowland, T-16

CHRONOLOGY: July 22, 1955–January 5, 1975

HISTORY: Though it was displayed on **Opening Day**, the Rocket to the Moon attraction in **Tomorrowland** didn't truly open to the public for five more days. When it did debut, Rocket to the Moon was sponsored by TWA; in 1962, Douglas Aircraft took over sponsorship until September 5, 1966, at which time the attraction was closed for 10 months for refurbishing. For most of these previous years, Rocket to the Moon had cost a C ticket. When it reopened on August 12th of 1967 the old Rocket to the Moon was the new D-ticket Flight to the Moon sponsored by McDonnell Douglas, which is how things stayed until the whole attraction closed in early 1975 to make way for the **Mission to Mars** flight.

The location for the Rocket to the Moon attraction was behind the imposing *Moonliner* rocket. Rocket to the Moon boarded inside curving buildings that looked something like observatories. When Flight to the Moon debuted in mid-'67, the *Moonliner* was gone and the huge Carousel Theater with its **Carousel of Progress** show spun next door. Today **Redd Rockett's Pizza Port** is where Flight to the Moon used to launch.

When it was initially listed in the park's **souvenir book**, the attraction was dubbed "Rocket to the Moon, TWA—Round trip to the moon." The simulated "round trip" was indeed to the moon, but only to lunar orbit, not to the lunar surface itself. The attraction worked as a low-tech flight simulator. Guests sat in one of two steeply raked 102-seat theaters named *Diana* and *Luna*. Inside each cylindrical theater, large circular screens were mounted on the center of the floor and in the center of the ceiling. As described by an informative narrator, for 15 minutes the screens displayed views of the ship's previous location (the bottom screen began with footage of the launch pad and morphed into a receding Earth) and its approaching target (the top screen showed the oncoming moon).

Simple special effects, such as the raising and lowering of seats, along with views of a glowing comet and the backside of the moon, plus a noisy trip through a meteor shower, all made the space trip even more exciting. Disney Legends **Claude Coats**, **Peter Ellenshaw**, and **John Hench** had a hand in creating the space experience.

The Flight to the Moon update in '67 introduced a more authentic and technically advanced space journey. In addition to more and better special effects inside the ship (including a brief moment of weightlessness and views of astronauts on the moon), there was an elaborate new Mission Control area on display before the flight. Previously, the pre-flight show had been a room with a short film, but now it was a complex, computer-lined area populated with **Audio-Animatronic** scientists.

This busy team was headed by a sophisticated A-A character named Tom Morrow, the Director of Mission Control. Morrow described the about-to-launch Lunar Transport Flight 92 while directing guests to look at wall monitors, one of which was used to spring a joke about an incoming UFO that revealed itself to be a clumsy bird. As impressive as the Flight to the Moon update was, it fell short of the ambitious concept illustration sketched out by artist Bill Bosche, who showed the flight heading to Saturn and beyond.

That guests took a journey measured in thousands, not millions, of miles soon became a problem. Two years after it debuted, the Flight to the Moon was superseded by the real drama of *Apollo 11* in July of 1969. As the sight of men actually walking, riding, even swinging a golf club on the moon became more commonplace in the '70s, attendance for Disneyland's own lunar flight unfortunately began to dwindle, leading to the new-and-improved Mars mission of '75. While the Rocket and Flight to the Moon are long-gone, what remains is one of the most beautiful of all the park's **attraction posters**, one that shows the majestic *Moonliner*, swooping Tomorrowland buildings, a star-spangled sky, and tantalizing text that invites guests to "blast off aboard a rocket ship on a thrilling trip to the moon and return to Earth."

Roger Rabbit's Car Toon Spin

MAP: Mickey's Toontown, MT-11

CHRONOLOGY: January 26, 1994–ongoing

HISTORY: The first indoor dark ride to open in Disneyland since **Pinocchio's Daring Journey** debuted in **Fantasyland** in 1983, Roger Rabbit's Car Toon Spin was the biggest attraction in the park's new **Mickey's Toontown** area. The Car Toon Spin opened in 1994, a year after Toontown, and quickly became so popular that by the end of the decade it warranted **FastPass** ticket distribution.

At first the Car Toon Spin seems like other indoor dark rides that have little cars moving through decorated sets themed to an animated movie (think of the Pinocchio, **Snow White**, and **Mr. Toad** attractions). Yet Roger's ride offers something those others don't—guest-controlled cars that spin a full 360 degrees à la the teacups in the **Mad Hatter's Mad Tea Party**. After entering a garage and climbing into smiling cars styled like the cabs in *Who Framed Roger Rabbit*, guests begin a colorful excursion through that movie's Toontown. The trip gets spinny as soon as the cab slides through the slick that weasels have poured onto the road (movie fans will recognize this as the deadly Dip). From this point on, guests can whirl their cars in a circle, pointing them at anything they pass. Some five minutes and a dozen **Audio-Animatronic** characters later, Roger extricates guests from the dizzying spin by opening a portable hole that leads back to the garage.

From the entrance to the exit, frenetic energy, zany imagination, and madcap gags are bursting out of this attraction. The queue area rivals the **Indiana Jones Adventure** for wonderful touches: the wisecracking gorilla, Jessica on the phone, the pinup calendar, the recipe for Dip, the wall of Disney-themed license plates (2N TOWN, CAP 10 HK, 3 LIL PIGS, etc.), and many more, making the wait

Major Attractions and Exhibits Added in the 1990s

1991
Disney Afternoon Avenue

1992
Fantasmic!

1993
Aladdin's Oasis; Chip 'n Dale Tree House; Donald's Boat; Fantasia Gardens; Gadget's Go Coaster; Goofy's Bounce House; Jolly Trolley; Mickey's House; Minnie's House; *Partners*

1994
Roger Rabbit's Car Toon Spin

1995
Indiana Jones Adventure

1996
Toy Story Funhouse

1998
Astro-Orbitor; *Honey, I Shrunk the Audience*; Innoventions; Observatron; Rocket Rods

1999
Tarzan's Treehouse

an attraction in itself. The scenery along the cab ride is more detailed than it is in most attractions because of the freedom of movement enjoyed by spinning guests—Imagineers had to create fronts, sides, and backs to everything, since guests would be observing from all directions.

Guests may come for the twirl, but they'll come back for the barrage of jokes. Any attraction that culminates with a backwards journey through the Gag Warehouse has just got to be ridden more than once.

Wathel Rogers

CHRONOLOGY: 1919–2000

HISTORY: "Here rests Wathel R Bender, He Rode to Glory on a Fender, Peaceful Rest." That old tombstone at the **Haunted Mansion** was a nifty tribute to Wathel Rogers, a Disney Legend who worked for the company for 48 years.

Born in Colorado in 1919, Rogers studied at an L.A. art institute in the '30s and joined the Disney Studios in '39. There he started as a film animator on such classics as *Pinocchio* and *Bambi*. After a World War II stint with the Marines, Rogers returned to Disney to help animate *Cinderella*, *Peter Pan*, and *Sleeping Beauty*, among other great '50s films. Meanwhile, his expertise as a model-maker qualified him to help **Walt Disney** construct the miniature Carolwood Pacific train on Disney's Holmby Hills property in the early '50s.

Rogers then became one of the main model-makers at Disneyland, building small-scale 3-D versions of the architecture that would later fill the park. During the '50s, Rogers took on a special task at Walt Disney's request—create a mechanical man. His nine-inch dancing man, inspired by the lanky moves of Buddy Ebsen, was the prototypical **Audio-Animatronic** figure and set the stage for the remarkable achievements to come.

In the '60s, with technology becoming more sophisticated, Rogers made A-A birds for the **Enchanted Tiki Room**, animals for the **Jungle Cruise**, personable buccaneers for **Pirates of the Caribbean**, and the breakthrough Lincoln figure for **Great Moments with Mr. Lincoln**. In the mid-'60s, while developing new mechanicals for the attraction that would become Disneyland's **Carousel of Progress**, he was shown alongside Walt Disney on national TV to demonstrate how the elaborate programming harness strapped onto Rogers could manipulate the Audio-Animatronic character nearby.

There were still more achievements to come. In the '70s, Rogers build an A-A Ben Franklin figure for EPCOT, and in the '80s, he organized a team of core Imagineers to help solve technical problems at all the Disney parks. After retiring in '87, Wathel Rogers was inducted as a Disney Legend in 1995, five years before his death in Arizona at age 81.

Royal Street Bachelors

CHRONOLOGY: 1966–ongoing

HISTORY: Since the late '60s, the park's **souvenir books** have often flaunted photos, some at full-page size, of an authentic jazz combo on the streets of **New Orleans Square**. This trio is the Royal Street Bachelors, among the most enduring entertainers in Disneyland history.

As described in the souvenir books, the three Bachelors "recreate the sounds of old New Orleans." They play about five days a week, frequently at the intersection of Orleans and Royal Street in the back of New Orleans Square, but also near the **Royal Street Veranda**, at the **French Market**, and for special events elsewhere in the park. The men are invariably dressed in classy styles that can include matching red or green vests, plaid sports jackets, chalk-stripe suits, bow ties, and festive skimmers.

The three Bachelors who currently play at the park aren't the same three who started in '66. The original trio was comprised of Jack McVea (co-composer of the '47 hit "Open the Door Richard"), Harold Grant, and Herb Gordy (a relative of Motown founder Berry Gordy). McVea was the group's leader, clarinetist, and saxophonist; Grant played banjo and guitar; and Gordy plunked an upright bass. McVea stayed with the group for 27 years, finally retiring in 1992. A year before he left, a new CD called *The Official Album of Disneyland and Walt Disney World* included 86 seconds of the Bachelors' "Swanee River." This number typified their set, which relied on smooth, low-key arrangements of jazz and R&B standards.

Today saxophonist Kenny Treseder heads the Bachelors, supported by guitarist Terry Evens and bassist Jeffery Littleton. Other musical groups that have enjoyed long New Orleans Square careers include the Cajun-style River Rascals, the Bayou Brass Band, and the Side Street Strutters. Except for the Royal Street Bachelors, all these groups seem to have been dropped in the fall of 2006.

Royal Street Sweets

MAP: New Orleans Square, NOS-7

CHRONOLOGY: 1995–ongoing

HISTORY: Candy of all stripes, including many with Disney designs, is the specialty at this stall on Royal Street next to **Café Orleans**. In addition to the sweets, this spot gets in the **New Orleans Square** spirit with such Mardi Gras items as sparkly beads, necklaces, and masks. The actual cart sports different looks, sometimes coming across like a sweet **Main Street** flower cart, other times like a black coach making a ghoul delivery to the **Haunted Mansion**.

Royal Street Veranda

MAP: New Orleans Square, NOS-2

CHRONOLOGY: Ca. 1966–ongoing

HISTORY: The Royal Street Veranda is the first dining choice offered to guests as they walk into **New Orleans Square** from **Adventureland**. Located around the corner from the entrance to **Pirates of the Caribbean**, the little eatery is merely an open counter in the first-floor wall; the veranda referred to in the name belongs to what used to be the **Disney Gallery** upstairs and is not part of the dining spot below.

     The Royal Street Veranda is a fast source for non-fast food with a Cajun twang—hearty gumbos, clam chowder served in bread bowls, fritters, and fruit punch. Outdoor seating is abundant and scenic in this riverfront area.

Ruggles China and Glass Shop

MAP: Main Street, MS-13

CHRONOLOGY: July 17, 1955–March 1964

HISTORY: A gift retailer named Phil Papel debuted the Ruggles China and Glass Shop on Disneyland's **Opening Day.** Filling the small store with imported ceramics and gifts, Papel was successful enough to establish 19 other locations around Southern California. The derivation of the Ruggles name isn't clear, unless perhaps it refers to New Hampshire's Ruggles Mine, which was a major producer of feldspar, a key ingredient in fine ceramics.

     The park's early **souvenir books** listed its Ruggles store as the China Shop, Ceramics & China, the China & Glass Shop, and China & Glass, seemingly any combination of nouns that didn't include the actual Ruggles name. The shop's location was one door north of the **Intimate Apparel** shop and one door south of the hospitality center that was known from 1958 to 1975 as **Carefree Corner.** A year after opening, Ruggles expanded into the room that was made available when Intimate Apparel left. Nine years after opening, the Ruggles China and Glass Shop closed and was quickly replaced by the store that is still operating there today, the **China Closet.**

Herb Ryman

CHRONOLOGY: 1910–1989

HISTORY: "I look upon Walt as a conductor of one of the world's greatest symphonies," Herb Ryman said in the book *Remembering Walt*, "and I was part of the orchestra." Humble as Ryman was with that statement, the truth is that few artists who contributed to Disneyland were as important as he was. On September 26th and 27th of '53, Ryman drew out a detailed aerial view of the unbuilt park as it was being described to him by Disneyland's "conductor," **Walt Disney**. That remarkable sketch, which included a recognizable **Main Street**, a **Plaza Hub** with various lands radiating outwards, a castle, a perimeter **berm** and train, a river with a riverboat, and a **Jungle Cruise**-like attraction, was a key component of the successful presentations **Roy Disney** made to potential investors (Ryman's rendering was frequently displayed in the park's hardcover souvenir books, among them *Disneyland: The First Quarter Century*; it's also been displayed in the **Opera House,** see photo above).

Once Disneyland plans were underway, Ryman was one of the key designers of **Sleeping Beauty Castle**, the **Jungle Cruise**, Main Street buildings, and later **New Orleans Square**. On the *Disneyland: Secrets, Stories & Magic* DVD, Ryman claimed that he proposed one of the more notable design changes for Sleeping Beauty Castle—he's the one who spun the top of the castle around because he thought it looked better, and when Walt Disney agreed the castle was built with its original "back" facing the **Plaza Hub**.

Ryman's Disneyland creations were the crowning achievements of Ryman's long art career. He was born in Illinois in 1910, studied art, and then headed west to work in the movies. MGM got him first and hired him as an illustrator for some of its great '30s films, among them *A Tale of Two Cities* and *Mutiny on the Bounty*. In '38 Ryman joined the Disney Studios, where he worked as an art director on *Fantasia*, *Dumbo*, and *Victory Through Air Power*, among other animated films. During his Disneyland years, he was photographed for a feature story about the park in a 1963 issue of *National Geographic* (the photo showed him executing a concept illustration for New Orleans Square).

Ryman formally retired from the Disney Company in 1971, but he stayed on as a consultant for projects at Walt Disney World, Tokyo Disneyland, and Disneyland Paris, and he created art for the 1977 Disney film *Pete's Dragon*. A year after he died in 1989 in Los Angeles, Herb Ryman was inducted posthumously as a Disney Legend. At Disneyland, a tree near Sleeping Beauty Castle was planted in his honor, and up until 2007 his drawings and paintings were still sold in the **Disney Gallery**.

Safari Outpost

MAP: Adventureland, A-2

CHRONOLOGY: March 1, 1986–January 1995

HISTORY: Starting in 1956, one of the shops at the **Adventureland Bazaar** was a fabric-and-fashions shop called Guatemalan Weavers. On February 23, 1986, that shop closed; two weeks later, the more prominent Safari Outpost opened in its place. The location was the far left (west) end of the Bazaar next to the eatery known back then as **Sunkist, I Presume** (today it's the **Bengal Barbecue**).

Wacky for khaki, the Safari Outpost's main stock in trade was safari clothing, as you'd expect for a store across from the **Jungle Cruise**, but there were also plush animals and toys for young explorers. In 1995, the same year Indy's major attraction opened nearby, the store became the **Indiana Jones Adventure Outpost**.

Sailing Ship *Columbia*

MAP: Frontierland, Fr-17

CHRONOLOGY: June 14, 1958–ongoing

HISTORY: While most guests think of **Frontierland** as focusing on America's 19th-century Wild West decades, this area actually includes a prominent nod to America's 18th-century Revolutionary War years. The last major addition to Frontierland's roster of varied vessels, the majestic *Columbia* is, as described on the park's big **attraction poster**, a "full-rigged three-masted sailing ship" that has been taking "a voyage of discoveries on the **Rivers of America**" since 1958, the year it was dedicated in front of **Walt Disney** and naval officials. For most of the '50s, '60s, and '70s, the *Columbia* was a D-ticket attraction, occasionally upgraded to an E.

The ship's design was inspired by the original *Columbia*, a privately owned sloop that in 1790 became the first American windjammer to circumnavigate the globe. Some fans, however, have suggested that the actual design is closer to the *Bounty*, the infamous ship captained by William Bligh and commandeered by mutinous Fletcher Christian in 1789. Either way, Disneyland's *Columbia* is a wonderfully appointed replica accurately capturing the spirit, if not the propulsion, of the great age of sail (despite appearances, engine power, not wind power, drives the ship along the same half-mile-long submerged track used by the *Mark Twain*). The ship's main mast towers 84 feet, the decks hold 275–300 guests, and the 110-foot-long hull displays 10 cannons, one of which occasionally gets fired on the 12–14-minute tour around **Tom Sawyer Island**.

To accommodate the addition of such a large vessel on the Frontierland waterways, the park added a new dry dock and landing, **Fowler's Harbor**, to the southwest corner of the Rivers of America in front of what would later be the **Haunted Mansion**. To show off the ship's meticulously detailed interior, a walkthrough exhibit known as the Below-Decks Museum opened on February 22, 1964. Since then, guests who "mind thy head" (as signs warn) have been able to tour the cramped, low-ceilinged quarters endured by ancient mariners.

Today the *Columbia* sails in daylight hours on the park's busiest days, with narration and sailing music as accompaniment; at night it has figured prominently as the pirate ship in the **Fantasmic!** show presented off the southern tip of Tom Sawyer Island. Occasionally it has also been transformed into a ghost ship for Halloween-related special events. Despite a dockside tragedy in 2001 that precipitated new governmental safety regulations, the *Columbia* is still rightfully considered one of the proud flagships of Disneyland's diverse fleet.

Santa Fe & Disneyland Railroad, aka Disneyland Railroad

MAP: Town Square, TS-1

CHRONOLOGY: July 17, 1955–ongoing

HISTORY: Before there was a Santa Fe & Disneyland Railroad, there was the little Carolwood Pacific. This was the one-eighth-scale train that **Walt Disney**, with the help of Disney Legends **Roger Broggie** and **Wathel Rogers**, built in the backyard of his home in Holmby Hills, an upscale neighborhood near Beverly Hills (how upscale? Hugh Hefner's Playboy Mansion is also in Holmby Hills). That little train, named after the Carolwood street address, ran on a half-mile-long track that included a tunnel, a trestle, switches, and other realistic features that were sometimes crafted by Disney himself.

Walt Disney's love of railroads, which dated back to his teen years when he worked on trains in the Midwest, was one of the driving passions that inspired him to create a theme park. He wanted to ride/display/be around trains, and thus every concept illustration for the unbuilt Disneyland, whether the area was a small 16-acre rectangle in Burbank or a 60-acre triangle in Anaheim, included an old-fashioned train running around the perimeter.

Naturally, when it came time to design, construct, and operate the railroad line around Disneyland, Walt Disney was closely involved every step of the way. Most **souvenir books** of the '50s and '60s included a photo of Disney, wearing an engineer's hat and a red neckerchief, waving happily from the train. In fact, the Disneyland Data page of the park's 1956 souvenir book even claimed that Disney was so interested in the train that he "sometimes sits at the throttle of the *E.P. Ripley* on the Santa Fe & Disneyland RR to take the little train on its trip around the Park."

Like much of the rest of Disneyland, the railroad is built slightly smaller than full-size. Both the train and its track are about five-eighths scale, making Disneyland's railroad—its cars three feet narrower than standard train cars, its doorways closer to six than seven feet tall, its track about 36 instead of the standard 56.5 inches wide—friendlier and less

intimidating. The trains travel approximately 6,700 feet in a clockwise loop around the park. Making stops at three stations along the line, today each round trip from the **Main Street** station takes about 25 minutes, making a train tour the longest-lasting ride in the park.

12 Terrific Views

Disney Gallery (extinct, second-story balconies overlooked Adventure-land, Frontierland, and New Orleans Square, see photo below)
Fort Wilderness, Tom Sawyer Island
(second-story views of Critter Country and New Orleans Square)
Innoventions upstairs balcony (second-story views of Tomorrowland)
Main Street train depot
(a stationary second-story view of Town Square and Main Street)
Main Street omnibus
(a moving second-story tour of the entire Main Street area)

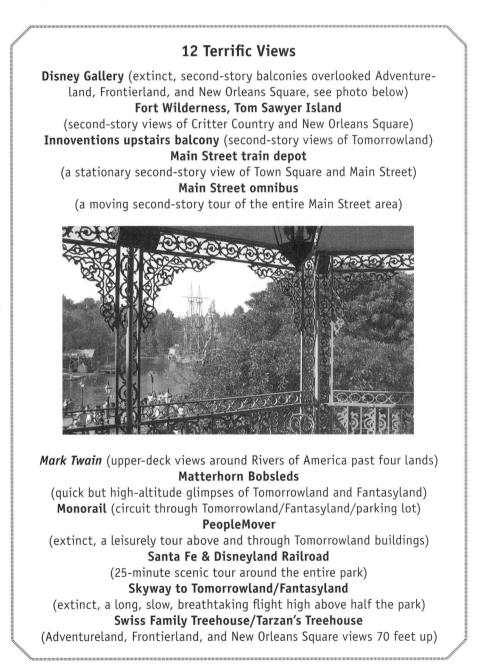

Mark Twain (upper-deck views around Rivers of America past four lands)
Matterhorn Bobsleds
(quick but high-altitude glimpses of Tomorrowland and Fantasyland)
Monorail (circuit through Tomorrowland/Fantasyland/parking lot)
PeopleMover
(extinct, a leisurely tour above and through Tomorrowland buildings)
Santa Fe & Disneyland Railroad
(25-minute scenic tour around the entire park)
Skyway to Tomorrowland/Fantasyland
(extinct, a long, slow, breathtaking flight high above half the park)
Swiss Family Treehouse/Tarzan's Treehouse
(Adventureland, Frontierland, and New Orleans Square views 70 feet up)

When it debuted on **Opening Day**, the train at Disneyland had a sponsor, the historic Santa Fe Railroad (more formally known as the Atchison, Topeka and Santa Fe Railroad). The Santa Fe & Disneyland Railroad also had only two stops—the high-profile Main Street station that greets guests approaching from the **parking lot**, and a rustic depot at the back of **Frontierland**. Like the tracks themselves, both the stations are perched on the tall **berm** that rings the park. Designed by **Bill Martin** and spreading 270 feet above the **entrance** into the park, the Main Street station can hold 300 guests; its interior displays include old photographs and the miniature engine and caboose from the Carolwood Pacific. The diminutive Frontierland station, renamed **New Orleans Square**/Frontierland station in 1996, is based on a design used for a station in the Disney film *So Dear to My Heart*. Attentive fans watch for the real, working water tower just outside this station, while at the building itself they listen for the quiet telegraph-coded version of Walt Disney's Opening Day speech. Curiously, the Main Street and Frontierland stations aren't at the same elevation; the sign at the Main Street station marks the park's elevation at 138 feet above sea level, while the New Orleans Square/Frontierland sign claims it's five feet higher (suggesting a gradual downward slope from the back of the park to the front).

A history of Disneyland's railroad is a history of change. A new medieval-looking station joined the line in **Fantasyland** in 1956, but this fanciful little building was removed when **It's a Small World** went up in 1965. Fantasyland got a new **Videopolis** station in 1985, its location a little further westward from where the old Fantasyland station had been (in '93, the Videopolis station became **Mickey's Toontown** depot). In 1958, an uncomplicated, futuristic platform (not a fully realized building) was added to **Tomorrowland**. Further additions to the line arrived in '58 and '66, the years when the tunnels containing the **Grand Canyon Diorama** and the **Primeval Canyon Diorama** opened in the section of track between Tomorrowland and Main Street (the trains noticeably slow down during this portion of the trip for sightseeing purposes). The name of the entire line was simplified to the Disneyland Railroad in the fall of 1974 when the Santa Fe Railroad, which had begun carrying only freight instead of passengers, ceased its sponsorship.

The trains are pulled by one of five brightly painted steam engines. Four of the five are named after former executives of the Santa Fe Railroad—the *C.K. Holliday* (named after the founder of the company), plus the *E.P. Ripley*, the *Fred Gurley*, and the *Ernest S. Marsh* (all former Santa Fe presidents). The fifth engine, the *Ward Kimball*, is named after a Disney Legend who was a train enthusiast and a close friend of Walt Disney's.

Machinists headed by Roger Broggie built the first two 35-foot-long engines, the *C.K. Holliday* and *E.P. Ripley*, at Burbank's Disney Studios in 1955 for about $100,000; these were the only locomotives operating on Opening Day. The

Fred Gurley was purchased, not built, by Walt Disney; it dated to 1894, was used in Louisiana, and had been sold for scrap before Disney purchased it for $1,200. He spent 30 times that for the major overhaul needed before it could go into Disneyland service in March of 1958. Built in 1925, the *Ernest S. Marsh* was still chuffing in New Jersey when Walt Disney bought it for $2,000 and had it refurbished; it started circling the park in 1959. The *Ward Kimball* is a refurbished engine that first began running in 1902; renamed and put into Disneyland service in 2005, it is the first engine added to the railroad in 46 years.

Re-dedicated simultaneously with the *Ward Kimball* was the *Lilly Belle*, a lavishly appointed observation car (see photo, previous page). Named after Walt Disney's wife, the *Lilly Belle* includes potted plants, stained glass, elegant woodwork, and velour-upholstered furniture. Though guests can't ride in it, they can still see the red car when it tags along at the end of some of the trains or when it's brought out for VIP events.

In 1955, guests sat in traditional forward-facing bench-seat passenger coaches with windows, or they stood up in wooden freight cars, glimpsing their views from openings or between the horizontal slats. By the time the Primeval World Diorama opened in '66, some cars had been converted to the open-walled side-facing design that afforded better starboard views (all these freight and passenger cars were built, not purchased, by Disney).

Today, different trains on the line have different passenger cars—some the forward-facing, others the side-facing. Upon request guests are sometimes allowed to sit up near the engineers or in the caboose. All guests can ride as long as they want without disembarking; many guests use the train, not as a full-circuit journey, but as a relaxing way to get part way around the park. As they ride, guests hear prerecorded deep-voiced narration. These announcements of upcoming stops and attractions are voiced by an actor named Pierre Renoudet, aka Pete Renaday (not **Thurl Ravenscroft**, as is sometimes rumored).

Guests boarding the trains in 1955 bought old-fashioned-looking tickets that had stubs for each leg of the 1.3-mile journey around the park. When A-E ticket books went into effect, a ride on the railroad usually cost a D ticket. By now the number of riders on the well-traveled Disneyland trains tops 300,000,000, and the 50+ years of train trips around Disneyland total over 5,000,000 miles (mileage equaling 10 round-trip flights to the moon). What began as Walt Disney's youthful passion and became his backyard hobby continues to thrive as one of the most venerated and visited attractions in Disneyland history.

Santa's Reindeer Round-Up

MAP: Frontierland, Fr-20

CHRONOLOGY: November 2005–January 2006; November 2006–January 2007

HISTORY: In recent years, the winter holidays have been celebrated in **Frontierland** with a six-week-long special event. Held from early November to early January, Santa's Reindeer Round-Up brings the Clauses (Mr. and Mrs.), their live reindeer, and Yuletide festivities to the **Big Thunder Ranch** area. Holiday arts and crafts, sing-alongs, an evening tree-lighting ceremony, and visits with Disney characters are among the daily events.

Richard and Robert Sherman

CHRONOLOGY: June 12, 1928–ongoing; December 19, 1925–ongoing

HISTORY: The two men behind such famous Disney songs as "The Bear Necessities," "Supercalifragilisticexpialidocious," and "It's a Small World" are the Manhattan-born Sherman brothers. Robert was born in 1925, Richard three years later, their father a Tin Pan Alley composer. After several cross-country trips, the family settled in Beverly Hills and began learning various musical instruments. Richard attended Bard College in New York, where he majored in music and began composing, while Robert joined the Army and was awarded a Purple Heart in the European campaign. After the war, Robert also studied at Bard, and when both brothers graduated they teamed up to begin writing songs together.

Their partnership would endure as one of the most prolific, successful pairings in music history. "Tall Paul" and "Pineapple Princess," sung by Annette Funicello in the late '50s, were their first hits. Quickly the Shermans were hired as the staff songwriters for the Disney Studios, and soon they were cranking out popular songs and soundtracks for such Disney screen projects as *Zorro*, *The Parent Trap*, and *The Monkey's Uncle* (during these early years they also had a notable non-Disney hit, "You're Sixteen," recorded by Johnny Burnette).

In the mid-'60s, the Shermans started getting Oscar recognition—their score for *Mary Poppins*, and that movie's "Chim Chim Cher-ee," both won Academy Awards. Also during the decade they wrote the classic songs for *The Jungle Book*, as well as Oscar-nominated music for a non-Disney movie, *Chitty Chitty Bang Bang*. Later Oscar-nominated film projects included *Bedknobs and Broomsticks*, *Tom Sawyer* (for which they also wrote the screenplay), and *The Magic of Lassie*.

Disneyland would benefit from several key compositions by the Sherman brothers. Hundreds of millions of guests can sing their familiar theme songs for the **Enchanted Tiki Room** and **It's a Small World**; other attractions showcasing their music have included **Adventure Thru Inner Space** ("Miracles from Molecules"), the **Carousel of Progress** ("There's a Great Big Beautiful Tomorrow"), and the **Many Adventures of Winnie the Pooh**. Interestingly, the Shermans composed the most famous of these attraction songs, the Small World theme, as a slow ballad, not as the peppy romp it later became.

By now Richard and Robert Sherman have been awarded several Grammy Awards, accumulated about two dozen gold albums, had blockbuster shows on Broadway, been named to the Songwriters Hall of Fame, and been inducted as Disney Legends (1990). Currently Richard lives in Beverly Hills, while Robert lives in London, where a popular exhibition of his paintings was held in 2002. Their autobiography, *Walt's Time: From Before to Beyond*, was published in 1998.

Silhouette Studio

MAP: Main Street, MS-13

CHRONOLOGY: January 19, 1956–ongoing

HISTORY: Just a few months after **Opening Day**, **Grandma's Baby Shop** suddenly departed from its tiny 100-square-foot spot on the right-hand side of **Main Street**. Fortunately, the business that replaced it was a little more durable—the Silhouette Studio has been operating in Grandma's old location since January of 1956.

The Silhouette Studio has always had a sparkly retailer one door northward. Originally that neighbor was **Ruggles China and Glass Shop**, and then in the mid-'60s Ruggles got renamed as the **China Closet**, the current occupant. And the Silhouette Studio has always done just one thing. The **cast members** here are experts at hand-cutting black paper silhouettes of guests' profiles. This art form was born in Europe in the mid-1800s, revived in America in the early 1900s, and transplanted to Disneyland in 1955 as an interesting souvenir appropriate to Main Street's turn-of-the-century atmosphere. It's an affordable souvenir, too, because the only added expense is the frame that can be purchased to enhance and preserve the delicate silhouette. What's more, the silhouette subject doesn't even have to be in the room, since the artists can work from only a photograph.

While this whole enterprise may seem like a minor novelty, it's actually gotten more exposure in the park's **souvenir books** than many other Main Street businesses. In the '80s, the souvenir books included a photo showing an artist at work with framed silhouettes in the background, and in the 2000s, the books displayed a photo of the silhouettes themselves alongside a caption about the "fanciful silhouettes made while you wait." That "while you wait" part is even easier than it sounds, because there's almost no wait-time at all. Amazingly, each customized cutout is created in only about a minute, with slightly more time needed for group portraits.

Silver Spur Supplies

MAP: Frontierland, Fr-3

CHRONOLOGY: Ca. 2001–ongoing

HISTORY: When **Bonanza Outfitters** replaced the **Pendleton Woolen Mills Dry Goods Store** in 1990, the single Bonanza Outfitters space actually had two additional areas inside it—the American Buffalo Hat Company and Silver Spur Supplies. Sometime in the early 21st century, American Buffalo left and Silver Spur expanded into its space, thus establishing itself as its own distinct two-room store, "the greatest round-up of wares in the West." Looking at the exterior from the **Frontierland** walkway, Bonanza Outfitters is to the left and the **Golden Horseshoe** is to the right.

The Silver Spur interior still connects to Bonanza, and the store's back wall is still dominated by the large wooden buffalo sculpture that was there when American Buffalo Hats were sold. A large upside-down canoe hangs from the ceiling, and historic photos of famous frontier figures adorn one wall. Today the Silver Spur is light on the silver and the spurs and heavy on the pins, fashionable Western clothes, mugs, and frames. To commemorate the store's ongoing success, in 2005 a new pin was issued that showed the Silver Spur sign and Mickey wearing his cowboy duds.

Martin Sklar

CHRONOLOGY: February 6, 1934–ongoing

HISTORY: Few people have been as closely involved with Disneyland for as long as Marty Sklar, whose Disney career precedes **Opening Day**. A New Jersey native who was studying at UCLA, Sklar was editor of the university's newspaper when he created an old-fashioned newspaper for the park called *The Disneyland News*. While this paper was being sold on **Main Street**, Sklar returned to school, graduated, and then joined the Disneyland publicity team in '56.

Working from offices on **Town Square**, he created a wide range of promotional materials, including *Vacationland* magazine, scripts for Disney TV shows, and text for Disneyland's souvenir books (he's listed as the sole author of the '64 and '69 hardcover anniversary editions). In the '60s, Sklar worked with **Walt Disney** on the new exhibits for the 1964–1965 New York World's Fair, and a decade later he became a vice president helping to steer the creations of EPCOT and Walt Disney World. Later he was promoted to resident and then vice chairman at Walt Disney Imagineering, roles that placed him in charge of the designers who create new attractions and concepts for Disney theme parks, hotels, and cruise ships around the world.

Still actively involved with the park, he is widely recognized as an authority on everything Disney and is frequently interviewed for TV documentaries. Martin Sklar's decades of leadership brought him recognition as a Disney Legend in 2001.

Skull Rock and Pirate's Cove, aka Skull Rock Cove

MAP: Fantasyland, Fa-14

CHRONOLOGY: December 1960–1982

HISTORY: Five years after the **Pirate Ship Restaurant** opened in **Fantasyland**, a fully realized lagoon was finally built around the ship. Named both Pirate's Cove and Skull Rock Cove in the **souvenir books**, the shallow turquoise pond was shaped like a lopsided rectangle and covered about a quarter-acre. The lagoon and the ship were well-placed in between some prominent attractions—the **Mad Hatter's Mad Tea Party** to the south, the **Casey Jr. Circus Train** and **Dumbo the Flying Elephant** to the west, and the **Storybook Land Canal Boats** cruise to the north and east. A **Skyway** tower on the western bank carried buckets full of passengers directly over the southwestern corner of the lagoon (but not over the ship). A narrow walkway led from the southern shore to the ship out in the middle of the lagoon, and dining terraces lined the northern shore.

Besides the beautiful pirate ship, the most famous feature of Pirate's Cove was Skull Rock. This artificial formation was a Disney invention for the 1953 *Peter Pan* movie; J. M. Barrie's original play didn't mention a Skull Rock (the only named rock in Barrie's *Peter Pan* was Marooners' Rock, a lagoon boulder that got swamped at high tide). Disney's Skull Rock probably owes its inspiration to *King Kong*, the 1933 classic that had a Skull Island topped by a prominent skull-shaped mountain. At Disneyland, Skull Rock was a 30-foot-tall rock-like sculpture rising on the north-eastern shore. As shown in an aerial photo in the park's 1968 souvenir book, Skull Rock shared the same rock formation that currently holds the head of Monstro, the gaping entrance into the **Storybook Land Canal Boats**.

The souvenir books frequently showed off Skull Rock in all its eeriness. It had an open mouth, craggy teeth, large open eye sockets that stared towards the ship, and a wide crack down its forehead. Waterfalls poured from the mouth and from either side of the skull. At night the eyes lit up with an unearthly green color. Abstract rock sculptures surrounded Skull Rock, and what looked like trails seemed to wind through the area; all of this landscaping would've made for great climbing if only guests had been allowed to explore it. Unfortunately, this wasn't **Tom Sawyer Island**, so Skull Rock and its rugged terrain were off limits to adventurers.

Skull Rock, Pirate's Cove, and the Pirate Ship Restaurant were all destroyed in 1982 for the massive remodeling of Fantasyland. Dumbo the Flying Elephant now spins on the site where the glorious pirate ship once sat in its exotic lagoon. Today visitors to Disneyland Paris will find a new ship and Skull Rock on Adventure Isle in that park's Adventureland.

Skyway to Fantasyland and Skyway to Tomorrowland

MAP: Tomorrowland, T-13; Fantasyland, Fa-12

CHRONOLOGY: June 23, 1956–November 9, 1994

HISTORY: Most modern guests wandering near the **Casey Jr. Circus Train** in **Fantasyland** are oblivious to the alpine chalet on a little hill half-hidden among lush trees. This chalet is the old Fantasyland station, and the sole remaining reminder,

of the extinct Skyway to Fantasyland/ Skyway to Tomorrowland attraction.

Guests who never got to experience the Skyway might find it hard to appreciate the wonder of this attraction. But wonderful it was, especially back in the '50s and '60s when cable-suspended gondolas were still a decade away from becoming ubiquitous transit systems at ski resorts (in fact, the park's **souvenir books** claimed that Disneyland's Skyway was "the first aerial tramway of its kind in the United States").

Like the **PeopleMover** and the **Monorail** that followed it, the Skyway was an ambitious attempt to introduce efficient public transportation into Disneyland. Unlike those or any other attractions, the Skyway afforded guests a lingering view of the park from high above. The hyperbolic **attraction poster** certainly emphasized the airborne vistas, making it look like guests were *hundreds* of feet aloft and rising on steeply pitched cables. While the ride was not quite that dramatic, the scenery could inspire guests to invent new adjectives, because as glorious as Disneyland looks from ground level, it was even more breathtaking when seen from an open-air Skyway bucket four stories above the ground.

The Skyway to Fantasyland and the Skyway to Tomorrowland were really the same attraction operating in opposite directions. Both Skyways ran on the same cable, both shared the same support towers, and both connected the same two stations in Fantasyland and **Tomorrowland**. The Fantasyland station (see photo, previous page) had a Swiss theme, though the inscription on the building came from *Alice in Wonderland*: "'Up above the World You fly Like a Tea-Tray in the Sky,' said the Dormouse." Meanwhile, the station a quarter-mile away and just to the right of the **Tomorrowland Autopia** entrance had a more spartan, futuristic design.

Guests paid their D tickets at either station and rode in small red, blue, yellow, and green buckets with no windows and a flat roof. Over the years, bucket design changed—originally they had individual chairs for only two people inside, and originally the buckets were cylindrical, but by the mid-'60s the chairs and cylinders had become four-person benches and rectangles. In the early years, the ride could be taken either one-way or as a seven-minute round trip, but in later decades all trips were one-way only. The altitude varied depending on where the 42 buckets dangled along their journey, but usually they averaged a height of between 40 and 60 feet (the central suspension tower, standing tall on the site where the **Matterhorn** would be built, topped out at 85 feet).

Along the way guests got incredible views of Tomorrowland and Fantasyland, views that were enhanced three years after the Skyway's 1956 debut when Matterhorn Mountain and the **Submarine Voyage** both opened. Because it straddled the Skyway's path, the Matterhorn was erected with holes in its west and east faces, thus enabling guests to make an exciting entry into the mountain's interior. Inside the Matterhorn, guests saw hurtling bobsleds that slashed down their angled tracks. Also on view directly below the Skyway were **Alice in Wonderland**, a corner of the pond that held the **Pirate Ship Restaurant**, the clear waters and submerged rails of the subs' lagoon, and the Casey Jr. Circus Train.

Fallacious rumors of severe accidents, and even deaths, have long swirled around the Skyway, but all of these rumors have been exaggerated, and none of them pertain to the reasons the attraction was finally closed in the fall of 1994. It's more likely that what did factor into the decision to ground the buckets for good was the irresistible temptation for some guests to spit, litter, or pour their beverage cups over the side. That messy temptation, added to the more serious possibility of an eventual calamity, plus the presence of the incongruous steel towers and cables in the charmingly remodeled Fantasyland, finally made the buckets expendable. After the Skyway's last celebratory run with Mickey and Minnie aboard, the Matterhorn's holes were sealed up, the Skyway's towers were removed, and the Tomorrowland station disappeared into memory.

Sleeping Beauty Castle

MAP: Fantasyland, Fa-2

CHRONOLOGY: July 17, 1955–ongoing

HISTORY: If Disneyland has a soul, it's probably within the walls of Sleeping Beauty Castle. Even without seeing the castle in person, many people around the world recognize it as the iconic symbol, not just for Disneyland, but for the entire Walt Disney Company itself. This was probably true even before Sleeping Beauty Castle was actually built—after all, back in 1954, a year before the park opened, viewers could glimpse an animated castle in the opening titles of the popular **Disneyland TV series** and thus could've easily equated the castle with Disneyland and Disney entertainment. Later, of course, a castle became the centerpiece of the corporate logo that prefaces Disney movies, as well as a prominent feature of countless commercials and print ads.

Pre-construction, the early concept illustrations usually placed some variation of a castle at Disneyland's center. **Herb Ryman's** landmark 1953 illustration showed a massive fortress, towering hundreds of feet high and ringed by tall battle-worthy ramparts, dominating the park. What was finally built was, of course, much smaller. Disneyland's 2000 **souvenir book** finally explained why the park's "regal sentinel" was scaled downward: "**Walt Disney** recalled that European castles of old were often built to intimidate the peasants. He believed a less-imposing castle would appear friendlier and more inviting to Disneyland guests, and thus Sleeping Beauty Castle is smaller than any of the other Disney theme park castles." Indeed, the castle stands only 77 feet high, making it half as tall as the **Matterhorn**, two-thirds as tall as **Space Mountain**, and only one basketball player taller than the **Swiss Family Treehouse**.

However, its position at the north end of the **Plaza Hub**, where it can be seen from **Town Square** and **Main Street**, makes Sleeping Beauty Castle the park's ultimate visual enticement (what Walt Disney called a "wienie"). Who hasn't walked through the **entrance** tunnels, gazed ahead to the castle, and been irresistibly drawn into the heart of the park? Guests looking through the castle's own entranceway can see the twirling, gilded **King Arthur Carrousel**, another alluring wienie, pulling them into the castle's courtyard.

During the actual design phase in 1954, architects intended the castle to evoke (and promote) the forthcoming movie *Sleeping Beauty*, but nobody knew what that movie castle looked like, since *Sleeping Beauty* was still early in production and wouldn't be released until 1959. Thus they used as their inspiration several European castles, especially the now-famous (but at the time relatively unknown) Neuschwanstein Castle in Bavaria. After squashing that fantastical sky-reaching structure down to a more intimate size, designers implemented the same forced perspective techniques they applied to the buildings on Main Street. For the castle, the optical trick of using bigger blocks at the bottom than at the top persuades viewers that the cement walls and fiberglass towers are stretching higher than they really are.

The front is broad yet intimate. At moat level, the majestic face presented to the Plaza Hub spans about 35 feet across the first pair of cylindrical turrets, with the next turrets angled about 15 feet back towards Fantasyland. A 35-foot-wide circular courtyard in front of the castle offers paths to the **Plaza Gardens** and the **Snow White Wishing Well and Grotto**, plus a famous song lyric, "When you wish upon a star, your dreams come true," embedded in its pavers. As shown in a wide photo in the 1955 souvenir book, the castle has always had a side entrance/exit that leads to a trail on the west (left) side of the moat.

The drawbridge entrance is the main path into and through the castle. Within this entry are two stores on either side, visible only upon crossing the moat—no distracting signage or supplemental doorways mar the exterior's integrity. Above the entrance is the top of the castle, which, according to a legendary story, was turned around, either by design or by accident, so that the true front of the castle is facing **Fantasyland**, not the Plaza Hub. Some experts claim Walt Disney asked for this change because it presented more spires towards Main Street, others suggest he wanted to differentiate his castle from Neuschwanstein, while still others suggest the reversal was a designer's or builder's mistake that Disney later approved.

Fascinating castle details are abundant, the Disney lore long. There's 22-karat gold leaf on the spires; for years one spire was colored differently from the rest; the heraldic crest of the Disney family adorns the entranceway; the courtyard side has spiraled columns and gothic arches; a time capsule was buried in the forecourt on Disneyland's 40th anniversary; a conspicuous bronze marker under the courtyard entrance denotes the park's original geographical center before **Mickey's Toontown** was added (some experts dispute the significance of this marker); downspouts are animal-shaped; swans occasionally glide across the moat; swan topiaries grow off to the side, and on and on. The drawbridge, incidentally, has officially been raised and lowered twice, once on **Opening Day**, and again for a re-dedication in late May 1983 (*Disneyland: The Nickel Tour* claimed that there were many raisings and lowerings during that May week, but only one was for the public ceremony).

Important modifications have been made to the castle since 1955. While guests expect to see the familiar blue and pink coloring, the castle originally had soft gray stones at the bottom. For some celebrations, the castle's taken on special decorations, as when it was trimmed in gold for the park's 50th anniversary. Of other modifications, the two biggest came in 1957, the year the charming **Sleeping Beauty Castle Walk-Through** debuted and the spectacular Fantasy in the Sky **fireworks** began to splash above the turrets on summer nights.

Ultimately, there's been no building more indispensable to Disneyland's history and image than Sleeping Beauty Castle. Upon its completion, Disneyland artists and editors immediately seized upon it as the building that best represented the park's truest self. As proof, the castle has been shown on far more souvenir book covers than all other cover subjects combined. Publicists have long recognized its significance, and thus the castle has often been the site of special events and holiday festivities. Guests also treat the castle differently—they don't usually linger at the entrance to any other land, but they do here. In short, ask someone to think of Disneyland, and there's a good chance that person will immediately, or by a quarter past immediately, think castle.

Along with the **Opera House**, Sleeping Beauty Castle was one of the first Disneyland buildings finished in 1955. The Opera House was required for its functionality as a lumber mill. The castle, it's said, was required as an inspiration to the park's construction crews. To prove that dreams really could come true. To show them what make-believe looked like. And to remind them, finally, where Disneyland's soul was.

Sleeping Beauty Castle Walk-Through

MAP: Fantasyland, Fa-2

CHRONOLOGY: April 29, 1957–October 2001

HISTORY: Almost three years after it opened, **Sleeping Beauty Castle** received a significant enhancement. Not that it was visible from outside the castle—in fact, the entrance to the Sleeping Beauty Castle Walk-Through is so unobtrusive in the southwestern corner of the castle's inner courtyard that many guests unknowingly walked right past it.

The Castle Walk-Through presented a narrow corridor and several stairways that led guests into the castle and past 10 beautiful dioramas. Designed primarily by **Ken Anderson**, these dioramas, similar to those that were later added in the **Emporium** windows on Main Street, peacefully retold the story of a movie, in this case Disney's *Sleeping Beauty*. Artist Eyvind Earle, who painted some of that movie's distinctive backgrounds, also helped create some of the Castle Walk-Through scenes. Large illustrated storybooks with ornate calligraphy, well-executed sets with dreamy colors and cinematic lighting effects, detailed figures with elaborate costumes and precise accessories, and delicate music from the Disney movie all combined to deliver both exposition and artistry. An update to the art in 1977 somewhat changed the look, but not the overall spirit, of the dioramas.

One of Hollywood's royals, Shirley Temple, and the **Disneyland Band** graced the opening ceremonies in 1957. Temple, it's said, donated some of the dolls used in the beautiful tableaux, so perhaps her presents preceded her presence. For the next 44 years, millions of guests investigated the passageway into the castle. Many of those guests, it's safe to say, weren't so much fans of dioramas as they were fans of the famous castle itself and were curious to see what it was like inside. The cooling, calming effects of the dark interior were additional draws on hot, busy days.

Though only an A-ticket attraction for most of its first two decades, the Castle Walk-Through was always a satisfying charmer. Unfortunately, a temporary closure in the fall of 2001 quietly became permanent, possibly because of accessibility issues or refurbishment costs. The loss of the Castle Walk-Through is a disappointing development for anyone looking to recapture some Disneyland history or trying to find some shaded serenity in **Fantasyland**.

Snow White Adventures, aka Snow White's Scary Adventures

MAP: Fantasyland, Fa-8

CHRONOLOGY: July 17, 1955–ongoing

HISTORY: Seemingly innocent but deceptively sinister, Snow White Adventures has been charming adults and terrifying toddlers since **Opening Day**. Throughout its long history, the attraction has survived several name changes: the first **souvenir books** called it the Snow White Adventures Ride, later books amended that to Snow White Adventures, and for a while the actual sign above the entrance read Snow White and Her Adventures.

The biggest name change, and an acknowledgement of the main issue some parents have always had with the attraction, came in May of 1983, when it was dubbed Snow White's Scary Adventures. Previously, the main warning of the ride's terrors appeared in the early souvenir books, which warned guests that they would "flee with Snow White from the Wicked Witch." Also, a small sign posted prominently at the attraction's entrance depicted the witch and announced that this was a scary ride, not the gentle, song-filled lark in eight cute little vehicles past smiling woodland animals that guests might be expecting.

Certainly some of those happy elements exist inside, since guests are basically being shown highlights of the classic

1937 Disney movie. Thus Dopey, Doc, and the other dwarfs do cavort to the joyous refrain of their "Silly Song," and the Prince does turn up at the end to inject some romance into the proceedings. But like the movie, the attraction's imaginative, detailed settings range from the cozy and assuaging (the dwarfs' cottage, the glittering mine) to the dark and menacing (the creepy forest, the castle dungeon). And between the dwarfs' cheery song and the arrival of the passionate Prince looms the evil Queen, who yanks the ride back to the Dark Side with a witch-transformation scene that has traumatized kids for decades.

Interestingly, like the **Peter Pan** and **Mr. Toad** attractions elsewhere in the **Sleeping Beauty Castle** courtyard, the attraction's namesake never appeared amid the scenery until the 1983 makeover of **Fantasyland**. Designers hoped guests would realize that *they* were playing Snow White during the ride, experiencing her adventures the same way they were supposed to be experiencing Peter's and Toad's. Since few guests saw it that way, and since many guests repeatedly asked where Snow White, Peter, and Toad were, all three were eventually added to their attractions. But even after she was introduced as a physical presence on the cottage staircase,

> **A Dozen Disney Movies Not Represented with Attractions or Exhibits at Disneyland**
>
> *Bambi*
> *Beauty and the Beast*
> *Cinderella*
> *Hercules*
> *The Jungle Book*
> *The Legend of Sleepy Hollow*
> *Lilo & Stitch*
> *The Lion King*
> *Mary Poppins*
> *Monsters, Inc.*
> *Pocahontas*
> *Treasure Island*

Snow White's appearances were far outnumbered by the witch's repeated manifestations (the handsome Prince is barely a presence at all). And when the souvenir books finally started showing photos of the attraction (something they never did until recent years) they devoted much less space to the young beauty than to Her Royal Ugliness. Scary adventures, indeed.

In addition to changing the name and showing off Snow White, that 1983 remodel resulted in some other notable improvements. The most obvious change was to the exterior, where the simple medieval-tournament façade built in the '50s was supplanted by a complex, detailed design that evoked the Queen's stone castle, complete with skull decorations and a half-timbered tower over the entrance (as shown in the photo, the Queen herself makes regular window appearances that in 2007 came every 24 seconds and lasted for eight).

Inside the queue area, guests are now prepared for the frights to come by eerie voices and a dungeon display. Within the attraction, the poisoned apple laced with "sleeping death," which had formerly been a much-stolen prop, has been replaced by a hologram of the apple. Disney Legend **Ken Anderson**, whose career had already arced from the 1937 animated movie to the 1955 attraction, also steered the 1983 enhancement.

To adults, Snow White is today more impressive than ever. To kids, it is still one of the most affecting two-minute experiences in the park.

Snow White Wishing Well and Grotto

MAP: Fantasyland, Fa-1

CHRONOLOGY: March 27, 1961–ongoing

HISTORY: Tucked into a tranquil corner to the right of the **Sleeping Beauty Castle** moat, the Snow White Wishing Well and Grotto site has been a bucolic hideaway since the spring of 1961. A heart-adorned wooden bridge leads from the north-eastern corner of the **Plaza Hub** to the old-fashioned blue-roofed wishing well. From the bridge and the well guests get clear views of the lovely garden enclave where a gentle waterfall trickles among the white marble statues of Snow White, all seven of the dwarfs, and assorted woodland creatures.

Disney Legend **John Hench** was responsible for this tranquil spot. He also solved the slight problem that arose when it came time to install the statues, which were created as a gift to **Walt Disney** from an unnamed Italian sculptor. Intended to represent the characters as they appeared in the classic Disney movie, all the figures are mistakenly about three feet high—Snow White, of course, should dwarf the dwarfs. To disguise the inaccuracy she is placed well at the back, the added distance and elevation giving the illusion of proper height disparity.

Romance is in the air here. Literally. The Snow White Wishing Well emits a soft, echoing rendition of the movie's "Some Day My Prince Will Come," as sung by the vocalist from the 1937 *Snow White* movie, Adriana Caselotti (1916–1997). Princes come by often, it seems, because a photo caption in the 2000 **souvenir book** identifies the well as the "site of numerous wedding proposals." More fairy tales come true when various Disney princesses make their regular stop to sign autographs and get their pictures taken. For all the romance, guests frequently respond to the well they way they do to other inviting receptacles and bodies of water—by tossing coins into it, all of which go to charity.

South Seas Traders

MAP: Adventureland, A-2

CHRONOLOGY: June 30, 1984–ongoing

HISTORY: Though the theming in **Adventureland** suggests exotic jungles and dangerous rivers, guests are actually in Southern California, one of the world's surfing capitals. Consequently, since 1984, Adventureland has offered South Seas Traders, a beachy-keen shop that's stocked with almost everything surfers and beach-going teens could need (*almost* everything—Disneyland is BYOB, Bring Your Own Board).

The bouquet of flowery shirts, the Roxy/Billabong/Quiksilver surf wear, the displays of sunblock and lotion, the flip flops and straw hats and sunglasses would all be appropriate wares inside an informal tropical shack in far-off Polynesia or nearby Huntington Beach. Best bets are the Disney-themed Hawaiian shirts, the safari gear, and Shrunken Ned, a "self-service witch doctor" whose decapitated head dispenses advice.

Open to the **Indiana Jones Adventure Outpost** next door, the store's interior is arrayed in "castaway casual," lots of nets and oars and bamboo, with **Hidden Mickeys** worked into the décor. Whether it's summer or not, South Seas Traders is a fun stop on the way from the **Jungle Cruise**, which is directly across the way, to the **Indiana Jones Adventure** a little farther down the trail.

Souvenir Books, aka Souvenir Guide Books, aka Pictorial Souvenir Books

CHRONOLOGY: 1955–ongoing

HISTORY: The souvenir books referenced throughout this encyclopedia were (and still are) official publications of The Walt Disney Company. As such, they are valuable resources for anyone researching the history of Disneyland. Sold throughout the park at many stores and souvenir stands, the books have come out nearly every year since 1955, usually with updated photos and text, and nearly always with a photo of **Sleeping Beauty Castle** on the front. In early years the books cost only a quarter, a price so low that the profit on each sale was just a single penny.

Sometime called souvenir guidebooks or pictorial souvenir books, most of the souvenir books are horizontal rectangles approximately 11.5 inches wide by eight inches tall. Typically they are softcover books, have 28–38 photo-filled pages, and are divided into chapters for each of the park's lands.

1955

For the Disney Company, the softcover souvenir books have served several purposes over the decades. First, they were created as beautiful pictorial keepsakes to help guests recall their visits to the park; perfectly positioned photos, imaginative artwork, and evocative text captured the spirit and atmosphere for guests who either had no cameras or had no luck using them (most of the books were issued when clunky, unreliable cameras generated as many dark/blurry/misaimed discards as they did treasured photos).

1956

In addition, for guests who hadn't yet been to the park, the books welcomed them with warm words from an avuncular **Walt Disney**, introduced Disneyland's novel hub-and-spoke layout, and described the kind of thrills to expect from each major attraction. Helpfully, in 1956 and 1957, each land was illustrated with a separate captioned map. But from 1958 until 1964, the entire park was depicted with a single two-page illustrated map in the center of each book. Though this single map was captioned by a thorough list of every attraction, store, and restaurant in Disneyland, unfortunately the single maps did not identify the location of every single item on the list, only a few landmarks. Subsequent souvenir books had no maps or lists at all, reducing their efficacy as research materials.

1962

1968

While the spirit of the books has been consistent over the decades, the format has changed substantially. The first souvenir book, called *The Story of Disneyland*, was finished before the park was, and so it was filled with artist renditions instead of actual photographs. A small eight-inch-wide by five-inch-tall photo-filled book came out later that year; revealingly, inside was a map of the freeways that led to the park, showing how foreign the whole Disneyland concept was in 1955. The '56 and '57 books, both tall verticals, were the first truly educational souvenir books and had on their back covers what amounts to a checklist of everything in the park. The '58–'64 books all had the same

1972

8x11 horizontal-rectangle shape, covers that blended photos with illustrations, and basically the same interior pages that got sporadically revised to accommodate important new attractions (the **Matterhorn Bobsleds** in '59 and the **Enchanted**

Tiki Room in '63, for instance—the '60 book even had a special wraparound cover devoted to the expensive new **Nature's Wonderland** area). These early books also incorporated preview pages that tantalized guests with concept illustrations for future developments such as the **Haunted Mansion** and **New Orleans Square**.

The '65 and '66 books were an odd, almost square-shaped 11 inches wide by 10.5 inches tall, and they added heavy design elements and borders to the pages at the expense of large photos. There were no '67 or '69 books; the '68 book returned to the format of the '58–'64 books but put on the cover, not the traditional castle portrait, but rather an informal photo of Walt Disney signing autographs on **Main Street** (that photo had originally run in *National Geographic* in 1963). In the '70s, the books all had the horizontal format and looked almost identical with their castle covers, save for the big photo on the back cover of whatever was the newest high-profile attraction—the **Country Bear Jamboree**, **Space Mountain**, etc.

Page counts dramatically increased in the '80s and '90s. While the covers varied to look high-tech or glossy or "magical," the interior layouts during these years didn't change much, and the center maps of the early decades were sorely missed. The 2000 book was a small squarish 8.5" x 9" edition dense with pages and photos. Later books returned to the horizontal format but were no longer just about Disneyland—by covering Disney's California Adventure as well, the books devoted less space to the original park and thus were more functional as generic souvenirs than as detailed planners or research tools. Happily, these recent souvenir books still only cost about $10, and older collectible editions (ranging in price from a few dollars for '90s books to over $100 for high-quality '50s books) are still abundantly available from dealers and online sellers as mementos of earlier, sometimes long-lost attractions.

Interestingly, Walt Disney himself has become less of a presence in the books over the decades. He's been on many, but far from all, of the covers. Books of the '50s and '60s included his portrait and welcoming letters, with four or five additional photos showing him laughing as a **Jungle Cruise** skipper, **Tomorrowland Autopia** driver, headdress-wearing Indian chief in **Frontierland**, kerchief-wearing train engineer, and waving passenger in a **Peter Pan Flight** galleon. Fewer photos of him appeared from the '70s to the '90s, and the 2000 book didn't include a single photo of the man the park is named after.

1986

Occasionally the softcover books have been supplemented with special hardcover editions that are oriented vertically, are about 9 inches wide by 11.5 inches tall, have over 100 pages, and commemorate special anniversaries (the 10th, 15th, 25th, 30th, etc.). These hardcover editions broadly retell the highlights from

2005

Disneyland's long history. While the historical perspective is always interesting, text and photos are often duplicated from book to book, limiting their usefulness. For the researcher the annual softcover books are more informative because, when compared side by side, they provide a more comprehensive picture of the year-to-year changes in the park.

Space Bar

MAP: Tomorrowland, T-14, T-8

CHRONOLOGY: Summer 1955–September 1966

HISTORY: In the park's first summer, a futuristic restaurant called the Space Bar opened on the eastern edge of **Tomorrowland**, a location just to the right of the spot where the **Skyway to Fantasyland** station would rise in 1956. The restaurant's name alluded to keyboards and outer space, two components of Space Age living, but it might also have been a description of the site itself, which did indeed take up a lot of space. So much space, in fact, that in 1961 a Space Bar Dance Area would be opened up out front, and in 1967 the huge Carousel Theater would rise above the ruins of the demolished Space Bar.

When it was being planned in early 1955, the Space Bar was going to be called the Stratosnak, an automatic vending service similar to New York's famed Automats. What finally did open was a small counter-service eatery offering fast food (burgers, chili dogs, sodas, etc.). A wall of vending machines offered some self-serve convenience, and an overall industrial design emphasized convenience over comfort.

A half-dozen years later, the whole enterprise was remade into a bigger, more inviting restaurant without vending machines. Rows of plastic chairs with little side tables provided functional seating on a covered patio with a Tomorrowland view.

In 1967, the Space Bar became the Displaced Bar when the **Carousel of Progress** started spinning inside the Carousel Theater, a major addition to that year's massive Tomorrowland redesign. A smaller Space Bar, reduced to a mere snack stand, reopened that year about 150 feet to the west underneath the loading area of the new **PeopleMover** attraction. A decade later, the **Lunching Pad** replaced this Space Bar sequel.

Space Mountain, aka Rockin' Space Mountain

MAP: Tomorrowland, T-18

CHRONOLOGY: May 4, 1977–ongoing

HISTORY: The second-tallest structure in Disneyland opened in **Tomorrowland** in 1977 at a cost of about $20,000,000. This dollar figure made Space Mountain the most expensive attraction in the park at the time and the first one to cost more than what the entire park had cost to build in 1955.

For its money, the Disney Company got a futuristic cone in gleaming

white that reached 118 feet high and covered approximately three-quarters of an acre. Built on the site of the old **Flying Saucers** attraction, Space Mountain's position triangulates evenly with the **Plaza Hub** and **Innoventions**; if a line were drawn from **Town Square** to Innoventions, Space Mountain would be halfway along the line. Viewed from what used to be the **parking lot** and is now Disney's California Adventure, Space Mountain and its crown of slender spires loom high above the southeastern border of the park.

The idea for a roller coaster attraction called the Space Port, which closely resembled Space Mountain but had tracks spiraling down the *outside* of the structure, was drawn up by Disney Legend **John Hench** around 1964. The Space Port

Estimated Costs of 20 Disneyland Projects
(and year opened)

Dollar figures represent approximate costs at the time and have not been adjusted for inflation.

$100–125 million: Indiana Jones Adventure (1995)
$85 million: Splash Mountain (1989)
$70 million: Finding Nemo Submarine Voyage (2007)
$30 million: Many Adventures of Winnie the Pooh (2003)
$30 million: Star Tours (1987)
$20 million: Space Mountain (1977)
$17 million: Disneyland (1955)
$17 million: Haunted Mansion (1969)
$17 million: *Captain EO* (1986)
$16 million: Big Thunder Mountain Railroad (1979)
$15 million: New Orleans Square (1966)
$8 million: Bear Country (1972)
$8 million: Carousel of Progress/Carousel Theater (1967)
$8 million: Pirates of the Caribbean (1967)
$2.5 million: Nature's Wonderland (1960)
$2.5 million: Submarine Voyage (1959)
$1.5 million: Matterhorn Bobsleds (1959)
$1 million: Monorail (1959)
$375,000: Grand Canyon Diorama (1958)
$250,000: Swiss Family Treehouse (1962)

would've been a dramatic new highlight for the mid-decade redesign of Tomor-rowland, but the high-priced attraction wasn't doable at the time, not with the nascent Walt Disney World project starting to eat up funds (in addition, computer technology still needed to catch up with the Imagineers' imaginations).

About three years after Walt Disney World opened, Space Mountain de-buted in Orlando in early 1975, where it immediately drew raves from guests and roller coaster aficionados. Construction on Disneyland's Space Mountain began that same year, though the Anaheim cone was about 60 feet shorter, and its 200-foot diameter was about 100 feet smaller, than its older sibling. Plus, the Disneyland mountain had only one interior track instead of the two in Florida. According to *Disneyland: The First Quarter Century*, over a million man-hours went into Space Mountain's design and construction in Anaheim. The finished product was shown off with a beautiful **attraction poster** of streaking rockets against a galactic back-ground, and the park's **souvenir books** of the late '70s presented glorious evening photos of the glowing building on their back covers.

Opening in May of 1977 to some of the longest lines in Disneyland's his-tory, Space Mountain propelled the park to an attendance milestone: 1977 was the first year annual attendance eclipsed the 10,000,000 mark. Guests were eager to see the second peak in the park's "mountain range"—the 147-foot-tall **Matterhorn** had been erected in 1959, 104-foot **Big Thunder Mountain** would follow in 1979, and 87-foot **Splash Mountain** would rise 10 years after that.

But Space Mountain wasn't really competing with the Matterhorn or any-thing else at Disneyland. Instead, it was competing with all the dynamic new roller coasters that were luring teens to other theme parks around Southern California in the 1970s with bigger/faster/louder rides. To zoom ahead of their rivals, Disney designers came up with a unique twist on the coaster concept that has now been validated with 30 years of success.

The Disney innovation—have guests ride in the dark—is simple in concep-tion but sophisticated in execution. After they walk through long, narrow pas-sageways, over 1,800 guests an hour can slip into sleek open-cockpit rockets and hurtle for three minutes on two-thirds of a mile of unlit indoor track. The darkness makes the velocity seem much faster than the 30 mph achieved by the rockets, and the banked curves and dips seem more thrilling because they're unseen and unan-ticipated. Air blasts from fans and the rushing sounds of the rockets themselves intensify the sense of speed. Enhancing the interstellar atmosphere are starry ef-fects (created by floor-mounted disco balls), spinning galaxies, asteroids that have at times looked suspiciously like cookies, and a huge loading-area prop that echoes the *Discovery* spaceship from *2001: A Space Odyssey*. Adding legitimacy to the whole enterprise were six of the original seven Mercury astronauts at the opening-day festivities (the seventh, Gus Grissom, had died in an *Apollo 1* fire in '67). And adding heft to the building were nearby space-themed structures that also debuted in '77, among them the **Space Place** and the **Space Stage**.

Two decades after it opened, Space Mountain started to undergo changes. Fast-paced on-board music was added in 1997. In 1998, the white exterior was painted in the bronzes and greens that adorned the **Astro-Orbitor** and other new attractions of the remodeled Tomorrowland. In preparation for the park's 50th anniversary, in 2003 the whole attraction closed for two years to replace the track, give the rockets a new look, update the queue area with a new silver ship, and restore the white exterior. The entrance ramp is gone, replaced with a walkway that goes behind and above the **Magic Eye Theater**. Souvenir photos are now snapped at the end of the trip à la the pre-splash photos at Splash Mountain, with Spaceport Document Control at the exit handling the transactions.

A new nighttime variation called Rockin' Space Mountain, which debuted as Rock-It Mountain in the summer of 2006, brings new energy, new psychedelic lighting effects, new narration from a rock DJ, and new high-powered music (the Red Hot Chili Peppers was one of the bands playing in 2007) to the spacey interior. If anything, today's Space Mountain is farther out of this world than it's ever been.

Space Place

MAP: Tomorrowland, T-16

CHRONOLOGY: Summer 1977–1996

HISTORY: When **Space Mountain** started drawing tens of thousands of people every day deep into the eastern corner of **Tomorrowland**, a new fast food restaurant opened up in the base of the Space Mountain complex to keep all those hungry space travelers well-fed. The Space Place was a large counter-service facility with seating for about 700. Pizza, hot dogs, fries, salads, and ice cream were the main menu items, plus special birthday celebrations and group parties were available.

Interestingly, the Space Place served Coke and Pepsi simultaneously—usually some kind of sponsorship arrangement at Disneyland's eateries has precluded one of the rival beverages. In fact, for years insiders informally divided the park in two, a western half where Pepsi was served, and an eastern half for Coke.

Unfortunately, the Space Place always seemed to have more space than space travelers, and as its popularity gradually dwindled, its operating hours gradually shrank. Early in 1996, the Space Place space was taken over by a temporary new attraction, the **Toy Story Funhouse**. Two years later this area was subsumed within the spacious **Redd Rockett's Pizza Port**.

Space Station X-1, aka Satellite View of America

MAP: Tomorrowland, T-5

CHRONOLOGY: July 17, 1955–February 17, 1960

HISTORY: In the spring of 1955, with more artists on hand than money, **Walt Disney** decided to install an elaborate painting instead of an elaborate attraction into the middle building on the left-hand side of **Tomorrowland**. In keeping with the land's Space Age theme, the exhibit room was called Space Station X-1, its position supposedly in orbit above the rotating earth.

The lovely but overly dramatic **attraction poster** showed guests thousands of miles up with all of North America below, but actually the "space platform" (as the **souvenir books** called it) was intended to be only 90 miles above the United States. For three minutes, the round room slowly revolved past a beautiful, detailed landscape painting that ringed the perimeter. Created by two artistic Disney Legends, **Claude Coats** and **Peter Ellenshaw**, the painting was necessary because photos from space had yet to be taken, since the first true satellite, *Sputnik 1*, wouldn't be launched until October of 1957.

From inside Space Station X-1, guests looked over a short wall at a view that began with the East Coast at sunrise, concluded with the West Coast at sunset, and showcased a daylight panorama of all the mountains and plains in between. Since the entire country was shown in three minutes, this implied that guests were orbiting at about 60,000 mph. Logically impressive, yes, but viscerally thrilling, no, and so admission into the languid, sparsely attended viewing chamber cost only an A ticket.

To keep current with all the exciting satellite developments of '58 (the year of America's own first satellite launch, *Explorer 1*), that year Space Station X-1 got renamed Satellite View of America. Unfortunately, audiences still weren't getting on board. Two years later, the lights went out on the space exhibit and went up on the **Art of Animation** exhibit just in time to promote the Disney Studios' latest animated movies.

Spirit of Refreshment

MAP: Tomorrowland, T-15

CHRONOLOGY: May 22, 1998–ongoing

HISTORY: The reintroduction of the red-and-white *Moonliner* rocket in 1998 brought a new little beverage stand with a matching red-and-white logo. That logo, of course, belongs to Coca-Cola, and their **Tomorrowland** counter next to **Redd Rockett's Pizza Port** is called the Spirit of Refreshment. Opened in 1998 with other new attractions and restaurants in the area, this is Coke's latest Disneyland establishment, the first being the venerable **Refreshment Corner** (aka Coke Corner) on **Main Street**, the second the **Tomorrowland Terrace**.

If presentation is everything, the Spirit of Refreshment has the most appropriate presentation of any snack stand in the park. Here at the base of a towering rocket, **cast members** will actually launch plastic Coke bottles into the air and catch them before serving. Somehow the sodas don't get all shaken up in the process, so they can be opened without the spray boldly going where it's never gone before.

Splash Mountain

MAP: Bear Country/Critter Country, B/C-9

CHRONOLOGY: July 17, 1989–ongoing

HISTORY: In the '80s, Disneyland designers were eager to put a high-profile thrill ride in **Bear Country**, which had become Bore Country for many guests. Something new and dramatic was needed to reinvigorate, even redefine, the northwestern corner of the park. That something was Splash Mountain.

The last and shortest of the four peaks in the Disneyland "mountain range" (**Matterhorn**, **Space**, and **Big Thunder** all preceded it), 87-foot-high Splash Mountain covers two acres of what was originally the **Indian Village** in **Frontierland**. Though it's in the same "thrill ride" category as the other Disneyland mountains, Splash Mountain is different from the rest in that its thrills aren't apparent until the very end of the ride. The other mountain attractions are what they are from the first minute of ride time and all the way to the end—fast-moving roller coasters with rapid twists, turns, and dips past quickly glimpsed scenery.

Conversely, Splash Mountain is, for the first 75% of the experience, a gentle musical cruise more akin to **Pirates of the Caribbean** or **It's a Small World**. Here guests drift in hollow logs for about a half-mile through amiable cavern settings reminiscent of the 1946 Disney movie *Song of the South*, with that movie's Oscar-winning hit, "Zip-a-Dee-Doo-Dah" a recurring theme (indeed, one of the names originally considered for the attraction was "Zip-A-Dee-Doo-Dah River Run"). Cute critters, ranging from possum families to croaking frogs, sing the happy "How Do You Do" song while a simple plot unfolds about Brer Rabbit eluding the bumbling villains Brer Fox and Brer Bear.

About seven minutes into the 10-minute cruise, however, the mood begins to darken. The faces on the singing creatures get worrisome, ominous vultures appear, and the river leaves its cozy interior and seems to point to the distant **Fantasyland** sky. Only in the last moments do guests fully understand what puts the splash in the name Splash Mountain. Diving down a 52-foot slope at a 47-degree angle, the logs hit about 40 mph as they zoom beneath an overhang of thorny briars and ram into a pool of water that sends waves splashing across the bow and gunwales. Guests are traveling so rapidly few remember the sign at the bottom that reads "Drop in Again Sometime."

The **souvenir books** of the late '80s and early '90s, which each proudly devoted two pages to the new attraction, touted Splash Mountain as a record-setter, "the world's steepest, highest, scariest, wildest adventure." "You may get wet," warn the signs along the queue, understating the soak factor achievable when a heavily front-loaded log noses even deeper into the splash pool. Attentive guests

13 Attractions, 13 Theme Songs

Adventure Thru Inner Space: "Miracles from Molecules"
Carousel of Progress: "There's a Great Big Beautiful Tomorrow"
Casey Jr. Circus Train: "Casey Junior"
Enchanted Tiki Room: "The Tiki, Tiki, Tiki Room"
Grand Canyon Diorama: "Grand Canyon Suite"
It's a Small World: "It's a Small World"
Haunted Mansion: "Grim Grinning Ghosts"
Mad Hatter's Mad Tea Party: "A Very Merry Un-Birthday (to You)"
Peter Pan Flight: "You Can Fly! You Can Fly! You Can Fly!"
Pirates of the Caribbean: "Yo Ho (A Pirate's Life for Me)"
Rainbow Caverns Mine Train: "The Mine Train Song"
Rocket Rods: "Magic Highways of Tomorrow"
Swiss Family Treehouse: "The Swisskapolka"

might notice that some of that splash isn't from logs plunging down, it's from water cannons shooting up. Inside the log, the thrill is perhaps the most intense in Disneyland; from the walkway out front, the screams, the five-story plummet, the explosion of water, and the sudden disappearance of guests and logs create as much concern as fascination. Fortunately, a happy ending built around an enormous set piece, the jubilant *Zip-A-Dee Lady* showboat, brings damp guests, and a laughing Brer Rabbit, home safely.

When it was dedicated on Disneyland's 34th birthday after five years of planning and construction, Splash Mountain brought with it **Critter Country**, a successful update of the Bear Country name and theme that had existed since 1972. Lines for the new attraction were immediately some of the longest in the park's history, but so were the strings of praising adjectives. Among the many satisfactual surprises along the way are the **Audio-Animatronic** characters themselves. Over 100 of them populate the caves, most of them recognized by veteran parkgoers as recycled entertainers from the **America Sings** attraction that spun inside the Carousel Theater in **Tomorrowland** from 1974 to '88. Chickapin Hill is the name of the mountain's peak, and the Brer Bear voice is provided by Nick Stewart, the same actor who vocalized that character in the 1946 movie. And just as guests begin their final drop, a camera snaps a photo that is viewable at **Professor Barnaby Owl's Photographic Art Studio** outside the exit. All this and more adds up to an immensely popular attraction that at full capacity pumps over

2,000 guests an hour through its caves, with **FastPass** tickets fortunately offering some line relief (for obvious water-related reasons, lines are longer in summer and in daylight than in winter and at night).

Some estimates say Splash Mountain cost an extraordinary $85 million to build, but few guests would say it wasn't money well spent. The **attraction poster** gets it right—it puts the three Brers (Fox, Bear, and Rabbit) into a hollow log splashing down the mountain, and only one of the three is laughin'. Terrifying to some, hilarious to others, entertaining to all, Splash Mountain is a zip-a-dee-doo-dazzler.

Spring Fling

CHRONOLOGY: April 14, 1962–ca. 1972 (seasonally)

HISTORY: Hoping to generate some off-season excitement, Disneyland executives created a special all-park event called the Spring Fling. It was first held on April 14, 1962, and was then repeated one weekend night each spring for about a decade.

Though the name conjures images of bright sunshine and gambols among blooming flowers, the Spring Fling was a nighttime event that began at 8:00 or 8:30 P.M. and continued past midnight to as late as 1:30 A.M. Guests needed to buy a separate ticket to attend (in 1972 that ticket cost $6 per person), but once they were in they didn't need to use any separate A-E tickets to ride on anything, because Spring Fling admission included "unlimited use of all adventures and attractions." "Unlimited use" was a new concept in the '60s and so made the Spring Flings popular events.

Adding to the fun were special musical acts, dancing, and "hundreds of free prizes, no purchase required" (as stated on the tickets). "Get into the Fling of Things," read the welcoming flyer, and guests did into the early '70s.

Stage Coach

MAP: Frontierland, Fr-21

CHRONOLOGY: July 17, 1955–February 10, 1960

HISTORY: Though it must've seemed like a good idea at the time, the Stage Coach proved to be one of the more problematical and dangerous attractions in the park. Also occasionally spelled as Stagecoach in the park's **souvenir books**, the three C-ticket coaches were beautiful wooden vehicles with large yellow wheels, gaudy yellow flourishes along the sides, the name Disneyland Stage Lines above the doors, and seating for about a dozen guests (half inside, half on the top, with even a "shotgun" space available next to the coachman).

As mentioned in a photo caption in the '57 souvenir book, these were Concord-style stages—that is, they copied the luxurious design created for the famous overland stagecoaches of the mid-1800s by the Abbot-Downing Company of Concord, New Hampshire. At the same time, the wilderness territory got remodeled and the neighboring **Mule Pack** got renamed the Rainbow Ridge Mule Pack, the stage got renamed in June of '56 to the Rainbow Mountain Stage Coaches.

Teams of four horses from the **Pony Farm** pulled the stages through the wilderness territory of **Frontierland**, the same area traversed by the mules and the **Conestoga Wagons** (all three attractions loaded their passengers in the vicinity of today's **Big Thunder Mountain Railroad** station). The operation was certainly photogenic—Disneyland's hardcover books showed Vice President Nixon smiling from a window, and **Walt Disney** wore a cowboy hat when he posed next to the stage. The hyperbolic **attraction poster** showed an illustration of galloping horses, even though they rarely broke out of a trot.

At least, that was the plan. Unfortunately, startling noises from trains, ship whistles, and other park attractions caused the horses to jump and run at times. When several of the top-heavy coaches capsized and spilled guests into the Frontierland dust, the whole operation was shut down permanently in 1960.

Stage Door Café

MAP: Frontierland, Fr-5

CHRONOLOGY: September 1, 1978–ongoing

HISTORY: The "stage" in the name Stage Door Café is next door to the left, the venerable **Golden Horseshoe** with its sit-down dining. To the right of the café is the **River Belle Terrace**, another fancy dining destination.

Sandwiched in between these two more formal restaurants, the Stage Door is an attractive option for a quick, easy meal to be eaten on outdoor tables with a view of **Tom Sawyer Island**. For years the fast-food fare didn't stray far from the basic burgers-dogs-fries theme; later some more varied items have appeared on the menu, including fish and chips, chicken strips, and fancy coffee drinks.

Starcade

MAP: Tomorrowland, T-19

CHRONOLOGY: May 27, 1977–ongoing

HISTORY: Guests waiting in line for **Space Mountain** may not realize that part of the upstairs queue takes them past Disneyland's main video arcade. Called Starcade, in keeping with the rocket themes of **Star Tours** and other space-named establishments in the neighborhood, the illuminated complex used to spread over two stories and at one time housed hundreds of arcade games. The upper story has been closed for years, however, which is why the Space Mountain line-waiters might not realize what used to be behind the now-dark glass. One reminder of the arcade's glory days is the 20-foot-long X-Wing fighter from *Star Wars* that still hangs above the escalator connecting the two floors.

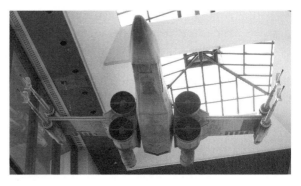

Even with only one floor of games, the Starcade is still a popular, noisy place. Among the current offerings are some old faves from decades past and all the newest technology that for over $4 a pop can send a guest on a simulated ride down a ski slope, on a racetrack, or into space. "Something for every player," touts Disneyland's Web site, a boast easy to believe considering the comprehensive range of games available here. This is the third, and still the largest, arcade in Disneyland history, the others being the durable **Penny Arcade** on **Main Street** and the extinct **Teddi Barra's Swingin' Arcade** in what was once **Bear Country**.

Star Tours

MAP: Tomorrowland, T-24

CHRONOLOGY: January 9, 1987–ongoing

HISTORY: In the 1970s, Disney's own live-action adventure movies, especially *The Black Hole* and *Island at the Top of the World*, failed to grab hold of huge audiences the way Universal's *Jaws* and 20th Century Fox's *Star Wars* did. This meant that in the early '80s, when Disney designers were considering a new attraction to replace the slowly decaying **Adventure Thru Inner Space** in the first right-hand building in **Tomorrowland**, they had to look outside the company's own film oeuvre for successful movie tie-ins.

The resulting pairing with George Lucas proved to be so fruitful, eventually three separate Lucas-assisted attractions would open in Disneyland—the *Captain EO* film of 1986, the following year's Star Tours, and 1995's **Indiana Jones Adventure**. Lucas himself must have loved the irony of helping to put Star Tours, a *Star Wars*-based attraction, in Disneyland, since he'd not only been a frequent park visitor in the '50s and '60s, he'd been rejected by the Disney Studios when he pitched his *Star Wars* script there in the mid-'70s.

Outside the Star Tours building, the curving exterior was thematically repainted to distance the new outer space attraction from the old Inner Space days. Currently the exterior mural shows StarSpeeders zooming past planets and moons, a hint of what's to come. Inside, Star Tours presents a high-energy amplification of what the old **Rocket to the Moon** attraction had started doing three decades before: sit guests in a flight simulator and show them a movie of a space voyage. Rocket to the Moon, Flight to the Moon, and **Mission to Mars** in the '70s all used primitive flexible-seat technology and small circular screens that paled in comparison to the intense, gut-wrenching effects possible for an estimated $30 million in the mid-'80s.

In Star Tours, 40 guests at a time are strapped into futuristic StarSpeeder 3000s with a wide movie screen in front of them. Ostensibly, guests are passengers on a quick, uneventful jaunt to the forest moon of Endor, but unfortunately the novice pilot (voiced by Paul "Pee-wee Herman" Reubens) quickly loses his way and crashes into the middle of a battle scene straight out of the *Star Wars* trilogies. Intimidating Imperial cruisers loom, enemy TIE fighters and friendly Rebel X-Wings dart nearby, and explosions echo as the StarSpeeder bursts through a glassy "iceteroid," frantically maneuvers through a lethal dogfight, negotiates the dreaded Death Star's claustrophobic trench, races up to light speed, and thunders back to its hangar for a final crashing career.

Supplementing the visuals are the realistic flight effects delivered by the seats, which shake and shudder with every thrust. So intense is the heart-pounding six-minute ordeal, **cast members** check seatbelts as assiduously as if Star Tours

A Dozen Cool Queues
(well-themed line and waiting areas)

Extinct Attractions
Adventure Thru Inner Space
(Mighty Microscope and many TV-sized display pods)
Circle-Vision 360 theater (phone exhibits and flag displays)

Current Attractions
Big Thunder Mountain Railroad
(antiques and Rainbow Ridge miniature town)
Haunted Mansion (cemetery with humorous tombstones)
Jungle Cruise (1994 remodel added two-story area with safari displays)
It's a Small World (fascinating façade and elaborate clock)
Indiana Jones Adventure
(underground archaeological dig site and hieroglyphs)
Mickey's House (displays and theater as preludes to the main photo op)
Roger Rabbit's Car Toon Spin (comical garage interior)
Space Mountain (spaceship display)
Splash Mountain (mountain interiors)
Star Tours (vacation ads and droid-assembly area)

were an inverted roller coaster, and the signs out front have some of the longest health warnings in the park.

Throughout the Star Tours experience, obvious and not-so-obvious references to the *Star Wars* movie universe, and Disneyland's own past, add fascinating fun to the thrills. The actual droids from the film, C-3PO and R2-D2, are on hand, Anthony Daniels reprises his C-3PO vocals, Admiral Ackbar from *Return of the Jedi* oversees the queue area, there's a page for a land speeder with the license plate THX1138 (Lucas's first feature film), and even George Lucas himself puts in an appearance—his name in reverse is pronounced over the intercom, and he's quickly glimpsed ducking as the StarSpeeder screeches to a final stop (some experts dispute this last Lucas sighting and say it's an anonymous actor). Sharp-eyed and sharp-eared Disneyland fans also pick out the Mighty Microscope from Adventure Thru Inner Space in the film's first hangar sequence, a page for Tom Morrow from Flight to the Moon, two armatures from **America Sings** birds in a droid-assembly room, and lots of interesting artifacts floating by on conveyor belts in the queue's Droidnostics Center.

When it debuted in early '87, Star Tours generated lines that extended all the way out to **Town Square**. In honor of its newest attraction, Disneyland even presented its inaugural guests with celebratory digital watches; exactly 10 years later, another special commemorative ceremony was held, this one with actress Carrie Fisher on hand. As expected, the park's **souvenir books** have always splashed big photos and Star Tours logos across their pages with enthusiastic text emphasizing the Lucas collaboration and the sci-fi thrills. The Mars candy company was the original sponsor, but Energizer has since taken over, its presence acknowledged with a series of "keeps on going" posters near the exit. That exit leads to an even more conspicuous commercial interest—still dizzy with Star Tours visions, departing passengers lurch straight towards a "duty free" shop, the **Star Trader** store, and its galaxy of *Star Wars* merchandise.

Star Trader

MAP: Tomorrowland, T-22

CHRONOLOGY: November 21, 1986–ongoing

HISTORY: What had been the **Character Shop** since 1967 became the Star Trader store in 1986. The new store's opening came six weeks before the neighboring **Star Tours** attraction started to take mil-

lions of guests into hyperspace. True to **Tomorrowland**, the colorful neon out front shows astronaut Mickey tumbling through space.

Just like the old Character Shop, the Star Trader boasts one of the park's biggest retail interiors, a space big enough to hold a 20-foot-long replica of a *Star Wars* X-Wing suspended from the ceiling (that model now hangs in the **Starcade**).

The Star Trader has spacey black light murals on the walls, glowing saucers above the floor, and shelves filled with futuristic T-shirts, stationery, jewelry, dolls, hats, and toys, much of it similar to what's found in the slightly bigger **Emporium** on **Main Street**.

The Star Trader, however, offers something no other Disneyland store does—the Force, in force. In a room in the back, hundreds of different Star Tours and *Star Wars*-related items are on display, everything from action figures and weapons to posters and collectible models. The most popular activity here might be the photo transformations that merge a guest's face with dramatic *Star Wars* imagery. When *Toy Story* and *Toy Story 2* became blockbusters in 1995 and '99, merchandise for those films joined the shelves throughout this fun store.

State Fair

MAP: Park, P-5, P-9, P-10, P-15

CHRONOLOGY: September 19, 1987–fall 1989 (seasonally)

HISTORY: In the 1980s, Disneyland officials tried out several long-running special events that were intended to boost off-season attendance. Following 1986's **Circus Fantasy** and preceding 1988–'89's **Blast to the Past** was a celebration called State Fair. Held in the fall of 1987 and '88, the park's fair was a spirited simulation of what is thrown annually in most states of the Union, including California, which has its own official state fair every summer in Sacramento.

Disneyland's State Fair filled **Main Street** and the **Plaza Hub** with traditional carnival attractions that ranged from ring-toss games to quilt displays. Guests were divided as to the suitability of such commonplace events in one-of-a-kind Disneyland. Some visitors were amused by the old-fashioned midway booths and the pig races over at **Big Thunder Ranch**. Purists, on the other hand, couldn't believe that such ordinary attractions were being prominently showcased in a park famous for its innovation. They also pointed out that **Walt Disney** himself had once declared Disneyland to be a Ferris wheel-free zone, but a Ferris wheel there was, right at the main **entrance** (in the second year, the 12-seat Ferris Wheel was moved to **Frontierland**).

Less popular in its second autumn than it was in the first, Disneyland's State Fair permanently closed with little fanfare, and the park quickly ramped up for its busy holiday season.

Storybook Land Canal Boats

MAP: Fantasyland, Fa-15

CHRONOLOGY: June 16, 1956–ongoing

HISTORY: About 11 months after **Opening Day**, **Walt Disney** finally got the charming boat ride he'd envisioned for his park. Limited on time and money early in 1955, he'd had to settle for the feeble **Canal Boats**

of the World attraction that sputtered noisily across one undeveloped acre at the back of **Fantasyland**.

However, even as that attraction was operating, plans were already underway for a huge remodel that began in the fall of '55 and lasted into the following spring. After some nine months of building and landscaping, official dedication ceremonies were held on June 18, 1956, with some of TV's Mouseketeers on hand to help celebrate.

When the seven-minute attraction started up again, it did so with verdant little knolls in place of the muddy slopes that had formerly rimmed the canals. Carefully manicured miniature trees and flowers grew everywhere, a patchwork quilt made of plants lined one hill, and dotting what were once barren banks were now adorable villages and palaces taken from classic Disney animation. Among the meticulously detailed displays on view were windmills and houses from *The Old Mill* and *Three Little Pigs* cartoons, gardens inspired by *Peter Pan*, Geppetto's village and toy shop from *Pinocchio*, the *Cinderella* castle and coach, and structures from *The Adventures of Ichabod and Mr. Toad* and *Alice in Wonderland*. All the architecture was built at 1/12 scale, meaning a six-foot doorway became a six-inch doorway. So well-crafted were the miniatures, the hinges on those tiny doors actually worked (a necessity for changing interior bulbs). To observe such intricate beauty cost only a C ticket in the '50s, then a D in the '60s and '70s.

Disney Legends **Ken Anderson** and **Fred Joerger** have received most of the accolades as the designers of the scenes and buildings on view since 1956. After their initial efforts, a 1994 update added scenes from more recent Disney movies, including *Aladdin* and *The Little Mermaid*, all built with the same careful attention as their predecessors to keep this an attraction that rewards close study. Among the subtle details guests like to watch for are the blinking eye on Monstro the Whale and the steam he periodically emits from his blowhole. Veteran parkgoers recognize the lighthouse out front as the old ticket booth used in the days when guests had to pay their way into each individual attraction.

As they did in the '50s, guests today observe the scenes while sitting in low-slung bateaux similar to the watercraft of Northern European canals and rivers (though Storybook Land's upgraded boats are battery-powered). Costumed **cast members**, usually sitting on the decorative motor housings, drive the

Names of the Storybook Land Canal Boats

Alice
Ariel
Aurora
Belle
Cinderella
Daisy
Faline
Fauna
Flora
Flower
Katrina
Merryweather
Snow White
Tinker Bell
Wendy

quiet boats along a track submerged in 465,000 gallons of water. These canal captains deliver live narration just like **Jungle Cruise** skippers do, though the Storybook script isn't fraught with the jungle's dangers and opportunities for punning humor.

Because guests are required to climb in and out of small free-floating boats, over the years this attraction has unfortunately generated a few bumps and bruises for both guests and cast members. Despite the occasional mishaps, the Storybook Land Canal Boats attraction has endeared itself to hundreds of millions of visitors, and it's long been said to have been one of Walt Disney's personal favorites.

Story Book Shop, aka Western Printing Book Shop

MAP: Main Street, MS-3

CHRONOLOGY: July 17, 1955–April 1, 1995

HISTORY: One of the original investors in Disneyland was Western Printing and Lithographing, a Wisconsin company also known simply as Western Publishing. Among Western's imprints were two popular Disney lines that dated back to the 1930s, Little Golden Books and Big Golden Books. With hundreds of children's titles in its back catalog, Western Publishing was there on Disneyland's **Opening Day** with a children's bookstore on **Main Street**. Located on the left-hand side of the first block, the Story Book Shop's small site was off the street and at the back of the **Crystal Arcade** building. To the left (south) was Main Street's **Glass Blower**, and to the right (north) was the **Candle Shop**.

Mattel bought up Western Publishing in the 1980s, and a decade later the Story Book Shop came to the end of its last chapter. After surviving almost 40 years of changes on Main Street, the shop disappeared during a 1995 remodel of the Crystal Arcade.

Strawhatters

CHRONOLOGY: Ca. 1955–ca. 1975

HISTORY: The Strawhatters was the name of a popular New Orleans-style jazz quintet that frequently played in Disneyland during the park's first two decades. Swingin' Dixieland tunes were their core repertoire. In its early years, the group generally played on a small gazebo stage in **Frontierland** several times a day; footage of the Strawhatters playing here while the *Mark Twain* glided behind them made it into the 1956 featurette *Disneyland, U.S.A.* (that gazebo disappeared in the early '60s when the area was remodeled). The Strawhatters also performed at special events such as **Grad Nite**.

Like the **Dapper Dans**, the Strawhatters replaced its members over the years, but there was always a pianist, drummer, trumpeter, trombonist, and clarinetist. The five men were shown in the park's 1965 **souvenir book** wearing gray plaid jackets, black pants, red bow ties, and the straw boaters that gave them their name. A Strawhatters record called *Dixieland at Disneyland* was released by Disneyland Records in 1956; the cover showed the group tootling away in front of the **Rivers of America**. They also made it onto the *Slue Foot Sue's Golden Horseshoe Revue* LP in 1957.

The group's name, by the way, isn't unique. For instance, a non-Disney TV variety show called *The Strawhatters* was a summer replacement in 1953 and '54. Additionally, other groups have used the Strawhatters name and worn the same hats, though they've featured different instruments (often banjos) and haven't performed at Disneyland.

Stroller Shop

MAP: Park, P-6

CHRONOLOGY: July 17, 1955–ongoing

HISTORY: Since **Opening Day**, toddler-laden guests entering Disneyland have been able to make a stop at the handy Stroller Shop their first order of business. The location outside of the park's east tunnel **entrance** is the first of two that rents strollers—the other one is at the **Star Traders** store in **Tomorrowland**.

Baby Jogger strollers with canopies rent for about $10 per day. If guests lose track of their strollers (but hopefully not the strollees), their claim tickets will get them free replacement strollers. Strollers must be returned to the front-entrance location upon exiting Disneyland, but park-hopping parents can get new strollers over at Disney's California Adventure at no extra charge. Also available at the Stroller Shop are wheelchairs (about $10) and ECVs (electric convenience vehicles, about $30).

Stromboli's Wagon

MAP: Fantasyland, Fa-10

CHRONOLOGY: Ca. 1983–ongoing

HISTORY: So the villainous puppet master in *Pinocchio* warrants his own souvenir stand, but wise Jiminy Cricket doesn't? How does that work? Guests can puzzle

over that conundrum while shopping at this big, elaborately decorated souvenir wagon that's parked at the back of **Fantasyland** near the Village Haus restaurant. Candy, T-shirts, sunglasses, postcards, film, and small souvenirs like pens and key chains are the staples here, making this a convenient stop before heading off down the Big Thunder Trail to **Frontierland**.

Submarine Voyage, aka Finding Nemo Submarine Voyage

MAP: Tomorrowland, T-10

CHRONOLOGY: June 14, 1959–September 8, 1998; June 11, 2007–ongoing

HISTORY: Technically speaking, they weren't submarines. Yes, they looked like real subs, were named after real Navy subs, were sponsored by a company, General Dynamics, that actually built subs, and were promoted as "the world's largest peacetime fleet" of subs. But if the true definition of a submarine boat is that it submerges beneath the surface, then what began circling Disneyland's one-acre, 9,000,000-gallon concrete lagoon in June of 1959 weren't true submarines.

In point of fact, the eight aluminum vessels were more like 52-foot-long sightseeing buses. They carried 38 passengers and ran horizontally, never at an angle, on wheels mounted on a rail. And the upper half of the vehicle was always, *always* above the waterline. None of this quibbling truly mattered, of course, because the original Submarine Voyage was a remarkable simulation of the undersea experience.

Built in San Pedro, outfitted at the "Navy Yards" in the park's northeast corner, and introduced simultaneously with the **Matterhorn Bobsleds** and the **Monorail**, the new submarines were part of the first big makeover of **Tomorrowland**. Since the ships were based, not on futuristic subs, but on existing U.S. Navy vessels, naval officials joined Walt Disney for the official June 14th dedication held a week after the subs had begun cruising. Eager crowds swarmed for decades, live **mermaids** occasionally splashed in the waters, and the park's **souvenir books** regularly showed off the photogenic qualities of the impressive attraction that had cost $2.5 million to build. Subs nosing out from a waterfall, or sliding gracefully through illuminated evening waters, made vivid postcard pictures, and a streaking sub viewed from the depths was transformed into one of the park's

Names of the Submarine Voyage's Subs

1959
Ethan Allen
George Washington
Nautilus
Patrick Henry
Seawolf
Skate
Skipjack
Triton

1985
Argonaut
Explorer
Nautilus
Neptune
Sea Star
Seawolf
Seeker
Triton

2007
Argonaut
Explorer
Mariner
Nautilus
Neptune
Scout
Seafarer
Voyager

most dramatic **attraction posters**.

The subs' loading area was underneath that of the Monorail, making this a particularly bustling corner of the park. After paying their E tickets, guests boarded a sub and descended through a hatch to sit in front of small portholes for a nine-minute voyage. Realistic shipboard sounds and bubbles streaming past the glass re-created a descent into "liquid space," and as each sub putted along at just under two miles an hour, such memorable sights as exotic mechanical fish, the ruins of Atlantis, tethered artificial mermaids, sunken treasure, the polar ice cap, and a googly-eyed sea monster were soon drifting past. Few guests recognized that some of what they saw wasn't in the open lagoon at all but was actually housed in a building underneath the roadway of the **Tomorrowland Autopia**. The subs entered and exited this building by going through a cascading waterfall.

Seemingly nuclear but really diesel-powered, the subs were decked in military gray until 1986, when they got repainted in the yellow livery of oceanographic research vessels. Then, deemed out of date in '98, the long-running attraction finally closed, and the queue area was replaced in 2001 by the **Autopia Winner's Circle** store. However, the subs' rail remained clearly visible from the Matterhorn Bobsleds into the 21st century, suggesting that the missing subs would eventually resurface. Though executives discussed paving over the lagoon, some Imagineers continued to work on plans that reinvented the attraction using themes from Disney films like *Atlantis: The Lost Empire* and *The Little Mermaid*.

Finally, after a nine-year closure and an upgrade that some rumors claim cost over $70 million, in the summer of 2007 the much-missed subs returned as the Finding Nemo Submarine Voyage. This time the fleet ran on electricity, not diesel fuel, the speed slowed to under 1.4 mph for a ride time of about 15 minutes, and the volume of water in the lagoon dropped by about three million gallons. The new story involved little Nemo, Dory, Crush, a beautiful new underwater coral reef made of 30 tons of recycled glass, 126 sea creatures, 10,000 artificial plants, a dazzling erupting volcano, and an Australian narrator who mentions the old attraction's mermaids and sea serpent. The crowd-pleasing result has generated some of the longest lines in park history, proving that yesterday can thrive today in Tomorrowland.

Sunkist Citrus House

MAP: Main Street, MS-6

CHRONOLOGY: July 31, 1960–January 3, 1989

HISTORY: For many years, a prime location in the heart of **Main Street**, just south of the **Penny Arcade**, existed as a bakery. In the '50s, that bakery was called **Puffin**, and in the '90s, it was called **Blue Ribbon**. In between the bakery years, the Sunkist Citrus House used this location to pour glasses filled with sunshine.

The Citrus House was the first of two Sunkist eateries in the park—**Sunkist, I Presume** over in **Adventureland** ran almost concurrently. When Sunkist took over for Puffin on Main Street in 1960, the dining room was enlarged to include adjacent space that had once been used for the **Sunny-View Farms Jams & Jellies** shop. Despite these interior changes that recast the two rooms as one business, from the outside the Citrus House still looked like two separate establishments with different paint jobs.

Uncomplicated Sunkist juices were the order of the day here, especially refreshing glasses of fresh-squeezed O.J. and from-concentrate lemonade. The juice bars were frozen favorites, and the short menu was rounded out by coffee and a few baked goods. Everything was served up by **cast members** in colorful striped costumes that featured bow ties and green pants for the men and aprons for the women.
The Citrus House cooled off hot guests for almost three decades. After Sunkist departed Main Street in 1989, the Blue Ribbon Bakery moved in the following spring.

Sunkist, I Presume

MAP: Adventureland, A-3

CHRONOLOGY: 1962–1992

HISTORY: Two years after the **Sunkist Citrus House** opened on **Main Street**, a nifty outdoor snack shack called Sunkist, I Presume debuted in **Adventureland**. Its name, of course, was appropriated from Henry Stanley's famous 1871 meeting with David Livingstone in deepest, darkest Africa. Stanley's first words to the reclusive missionary were "Dr. Livingstone, I presume."

In deepest, darkest Adventureland, I Presume's location was adjacent to what was then **Aunt Jemima's Pancake House** and across from the **Jungle Cruise**; previously the **Tropical Cantina** had stood on the spot. Appropriately enough for the jungle theming of this whole area, the little structure had a thatched roof, the male **cast members** wore Hawaiian shirts and Bermuda shorts, and the females wore long floral dresses.

Sunkist juices, especially the Jungle Julep medley, were the beverages of choice to go with the hot dogs served here. Behind the scenes, Sunkist, I Presume also whipped up and delivered the mint juleps that were served on the *Mark Twain*. Above the scenes, the upstairs balcony was used as a break area for cast members. The **Bengal Barbecue** replaced Sunkist, I Presume in 1992.

Sunny-View Farms Jams & Jellies

MAP: Main Street, MS-7

CHRONOLOGY: 1955–1957

HISTORY: This small **Main Street** business was listed in the 1956 and '57 **souvenir books**, but it finished out the '50s as a small unnamed candy shop. The location was on the left-hand side of Main Street in the middle of the second block, with the **Carnation Ice Cream Parlor** on the corner to the left (south) and the **Puffin Bakery** to the right (north).

The souvenir books identified the Sunny-View merchandise as "jams, jellies, fresh candied fruit." Meanwhile, a small brochure distributed in the shop described the goods as "delicious gifts," and a sign out front announced "preserves of distinction." Jams and candies gave way to juices and juice bars in 1960 when the **Sunkist Citrus House** expanded into this space.

Swiss Family Treehouse

MAP: Adventureland, A-5

CHRONOLOGY: November 18, 1962–March 9, 1999

HISTORY: What had been a landmark Johann Wyss novel in 1812 and a block-bustin' Disney adventure film in late 1960 became the world's most elaborate treehouse in November 1962. At the time, **Adventureland** sorely needed something to complement the **Jungle Cruise**, which had been operating as the only high-profile attraction in the area since 1955. The delightful Swiss Family Treehouse was a happy, clever addition to the northern border where Adventureland rounds towards **Frontierland**.

The treehouse took its design and décor from the *Swiss Family Robinson* movie's sets and props, which included items salvaged from the Robinsons' sinking ship and homemade creations fashioned from jungle materials. A B-ticket walk-through attraction, the treehouse offered a library, kitchen, private rooms, and viewing platforms, all of it furnished and functional, all of it toured via 137 steps on the wooden stairways. Most memorable was an ingenious water-delivery system that lifted hundreds of gallons of water per hour to the upper levels with pulleys, bamboo dippers, and bamboo chutes. Throughout the tour, a lively Buddy Baker composition from the movie, "The Swisskapolka," resonated as a buoyant theme song.

Almost as impressive as the treehouse was the tree it sprawled across. Whimsically named a *Disneyodendron semperflorens grandis* ("big ever-blooming Disney tree") by its designers, the massive steel-and-concrete structure rose "70 feet over the jungle" and spread "brilliant colored branches 80 feet in width," according to the park's 1964 **souvenir book**. These stats reveal a width greater than the height—unmentioned is the depth of the foundation "roots," which drove another 40 feet downward and, according to *Disneyland: The First Quarter Century*, helped give the whole structure a total weight of 150 tons. The 300,000 leaves were artificial, reddish at first until they lost their color to the harsh sun and were replaced by green plastic. True to the Robinson's heritage, a Swiss flag flew from the top.

The film's stars were on hand for the dedication, and a hand-painted sign in the Jungle Lookout welcomed guests with this inscription (the ellipses are included here just as they were presented on the sign): ". . . In this compound we often pause to contemplate our small world. . . . Here adventure beckons . . . with every view & every sound, the jungle & its river call out their mystery. . . . invite us to new discovery." That "jungle & its river" were indeed visible from the treetops, which afforded spectacular views of Adventureland and the **Rivers of America**.

Cherished as the treehouse was for almost four decades, it got a dramatic makeover in the spring of '99 and reopened that summer as **Tarzan's Treehouse**. Only a few souvenirs have been retained in the new domicile to remind of the departed Robinson family.

Sword in the Stone Ceremony

MAP: Fantasyland, Fa-5

CHRONOLOGY: Summer 1983–ongoing

HISTORY: Along with the much-ballyhooed 1983 architectural redesign of **Fantasyland** came a smaller, more intimate ritual held several times a day 10 feet south of the **King Arthur Carrousel**. The Sword in the Stone Ceremony derives from the 1963 Disney animated movie of the same name; that movie had already been referenced from 1955's **Opening Day** until early 1983 with **Merlin's Magic Shop**.

As in the movie and T.H. White's 1938 novel, the fabled sword Excalibur was buried in a stone (at Disneyland, a golden anvil) and could only be extracted by "the true-born king of England." These days, a **cast member** dressed as Merlin the Magician auditions crowd members for the regal role of Wart, the story's youthful sword-puller. During the ceremony another cast member nearby temporarily releases the sword from the anvil, and a boy or girl is heralded as royalty. Afterwards, the replaced sword is immovable until the next ceremony (the park's 1989 **souvenir book** showed kids standing on the anvil and tugging fruitlessly at the sword).

A free "Disneyland Today" brochure from 1986 listed three performances a day, a number that doubled in the 2006 holiday season. That brochure also named the Make Believe Brass as the musical accompaniment helping to "manufacture merriment."

Tahitian Terrace, aka Stouffer's in Disneyland Tahitian Terrace

MAP: Adventureland, A-12

CHRONOLOGY: June 1962–April 17, 1993

HISTORY: In the summer of 1962, visitors to **Adventureland** were greeted by a new South Seas restaurant. The Tahitian Terrace, also briefly known as Stouffer's in Disneyland Tahitian Terrace, was located just inside the Adventureland gates on the left-hand side.

The building had existed since 1955 and been filled throughout the '50s by the **Plaza Pavilion**. Though that big restaurant faced east towards the **Plaza Hub**, it had used the west-facing Adventureland side for a back patio that overlooked the **Jungle Cruise**. It's this back half that became the Tahitian Terrace. The unusual roofing revealed the building's dual function: half the roof had an old-fashioned **Main Street**-style design, while the other half was tropical thatch.

Until the **Blue Bayou** debuted in '67, the Tahitian Terrace was the fanciest restaurant in this half of the park. Guests sat at tables, were served by waiters and waitresses, and dined outside on exotic Polynesian cuisine under the spreading leaves of a three-story artificial tree. Created in the same kitchen used by the Plaza Pavilion, the Tahitian Terrace menu included island favorites like teriyaki steak, barbecue ribs with pineapple, marinated chicken skewers, shrimp tempura, and tropical fruit salad with pineapple ice cream. The famous beverage here was a nonalcoholic juice-filled Planter's Punch. And prices were so low back then that a full dinner could be had for under $4.

Not only was dinner included in that price, but so was live entertainment. From their tables guests could watch the *Polynesian Revue*, a long-running music-and-dance spectacular. Hip-swinging hula girls in grass skirts, male dancers dressed like island chiefs, a thrilling walk-on-fire display, and complimentary leis were all part of the show. Virtually every **souvenir book** from the mid-'60s to the early '90s showed a colorful photo promoting the restaurant and the show, identifying the entertainers as the "exotic Royal Tahitians dance troupe."

Since it was held outdoors, the *Polynesian Revue* didn't adhere to a steady year-round schedule, but it managed to stay popular for over three decades. The show and the restaurant finally closed in April of '93, to be replaced three months later by **Aladdin's Oasis**. From 1971 to 2003, Walt Disney World had its own *Polynesian Revue*, and today guests will find a Tahitian Terrace at Hong Kong Disneyland.

Tarzan's Treehouse

MAP: Adventureland, A-5

CHRONOLOGY: June 19, 1999–ongoing

HISTORY: Just as the **Swiss Family Treehouse** had been based on a Disney movie of a classic book, so too was its replacement, Tarzan's Treehouse, inspired by Disney's cinematic retelling of a popular story. In this case the movie was *Tarzan* and the book was Edgar Rice Burroughs's 1912 adventure novel *Tarzan of the Apes*.

The Swiss Family Treehouse and Tarzan's Treehouse debuted in very different circumstances. When the original treehouse opened in 1962, Disney's *Swiss Family Robinson* movie had already been a huge box-office sensation two years earlier; in contrast, when Tarzan's Treehouse opened on June 19th of 1999, Disney's animated *Tarzan* had been in theaters exactly one day, which meant that as the attraction was being planned and built in early '99 nobody really knew if the movie would be a success. Fortunately for the movie studio and moviegoers, for Disneyland and Disneyland guests, the new movie and the new treehouse were both instant hits.

Since the Tarzan and Robinson story locations are an ocean apart, and since each plot has its own distinct characters, Tarzan's Treehouse is a radical re-imagining of the 37-year-old Swiss Family lodgings. Serving as a fun new "foyer," a thin two-story tree now stands in the **Adventureland** walkway, with a rickety suspension bridge spanning above the crowds to lead guests to the main tree (see photo, previous page). That immense artificial structure, already 70 feet tall, 80 feet wide, and 150 tons heavy, has been modified to stand a little taller and broader. And to make it more African and less Caribbean it's been adorned with new leaves and hanging moss (it also flies a different flag, the Union Jack instead of Switzerland's). As always, views from the top can be spectacular for guests who make the 72-step climb.

The treehouse itself is completely new and mirrors the obvious maritime features, including the ship's bow and the hanging dory, of the 1999 movie. Also new is the presence of the movie's main characters. None of the Robinsons was shown in their treehouse, but Jane, Tarzan, and Sabor the leopard all appear here, with Jane's drawings imparting the tale. For younger explorers, the coolest enhancement is the hands-on interactivity of the new base-camp area, where musical pots and pans are offered up as a primitive but enlivening drum kit (movie fans will spot some recognizable *Beauty and the Beast* ceramics down here, too).

As with everything else at Disneyland, clever details delight veteran park-goers, especially those with emotional attachments to the Swiss Family Treehouse. The Johann Wyss novel sits on a table, some of the old hand-painted signs still hang on the walls, and several of the Robinson's furnishings have survived the remodel. Especially meaningful is the record playing softly on the ground-level gramophone—it's the familiar "Swisskapolka" song from the 1962 movie.

Betty Taylor

CHRONOLOGY: Unknown-ongoing

HISTORY: Before she was one of the most beloved entertainers in Disneyland history, Betty Taylor was a singin,' dancin' dynamo on nightclub stages. She was born in Seattle, had her own professional band while she was still a teen, landed a couple of bit parts in movies of the '40s, and played Vegas with Frank Sinatra in the early '50s.

Auditioning at Disneyland in 1956, Taylor quickly landed a lead role in the *Golden Horseshoe Revue* at the prominent **Golden Horseshoe** in **Frontierland**. She played the saloon's vivacious proprietor, Sluefoot Sue, alongside such other Disneyland stars as **Wally Boag** and **Fulton Burley**. Her showgirls, her knockout numbers, and her ever-spunky enthusiasm helped make the *Revue* a record-setting favorite, with Taylor herself putting in well over 40,000 performances. She performed for a national TV audience on a 1962 episode of *Walt Disney's Wonderful World of Color*, and in the '70s visitors heard her prerecorded vocals at **America Sings** in **Tomorrowland**

(Taylor belted out "Bill Bailey, Won't You Please Come Home").

After some 31 years of winning over Disneyland audiences, she formally re-tired in 1987, though she has continued to make special appearances. Betty Taylor, Wally Boag, and Fulton Burley were all inducted as Disney Legends in 1995.

Teddi Barra's Swingin' Arcade

MAP: Bear Country/Critter Country, B/C-6

CHRONOLOGY: March 24, 1972–April 2003

HISTORY: Teddi Barra, her name a play on the legendary silent-screen actress Theda Bara, was one of the **Audio-Animatronic** singing bears in the **Country Bear Jamboree**. Since she swayed on a big swing, the nearby arcade themed to her was named with an appropriate adjective.

Inside the small room the "games of chance" (as the sign out front an-nounced) had frontier themes as much as possible—in the '70s and '80s, that would've meant lots of old-fashioned pinball customized with Disneyland themes. Charming as they might have been, the selection was so limited that most serious gamers quickly made a beeline for the expansive **Starcade** as soon as it opened in **Tomorrowland** in '77.

Like the **Brer Bar** next door, the arcade got overrun by the Pooh invasion of the early 21st century. **Pooh Corner** now spills into what used to be Teddi's swingin' space, though Teddi's name is still on the building (see photo above).

Three Fairies Magic Crystals

MAP: Fantasyland, Fa-4

CHRONOLOGY: November 2006–ongoing

HISTORY: When the **Heraldry Shoppe** moved out of **Sleeping Beauty Castle** in 2006, the tiny Three Fairies Magic Crystals shop moved in. The first part of the name, of course, alludes to Flora,

Fauna, and Merryweather, the fairy trio from the 1959 *Sleeping Beauty* movie; the adjective "magic" refers to the images lasered into the interiors of small, clear-glass sculptures. These sculptures are in the shapes of cubes, spheres, even mouse ears, and make pretty gifts. The images inside them are either pre-inscribed and ready to go, or they're customized from guests' photographs for pick-up later that day.

Ticket Books

CHRONOLOGY: October 11, 1955–1982

HISTORY: During Disneyland's first summer, there were no ticket books. Adult admission to the park was $1, children were half of that, and additional admission prices between 10¢ and 35¢ had to be paid to enter each attraction. This meant that guests could pay for only park admission if they wanted to, with the added expense of attractions an option. However, it also meant that guests had to wait to buy an individual ticket any

time they wanted to ride something, they had to fish for change to pay for it, and **cast members** had to perform time-consuming ticket-selling and change-counting chores inside the tiny ticket booths stationed outside each attraction.

To make things easier for everyone, on October 11, 1955, the park introduced the first of its ticket books (sometimes called coupon books). These first books offered a total of eight A, B, and C tickets (or coupons) for $2.50. Nine months later, with **Tom Sawyer Island**, the **Indian War Canoes**, and other new attractions starting up in **Frontierland**, the ticket books were expanded to include D tickets; simultaneously, several existing attractions that had previously cost a C ticket, including the **Jungle Cruise** and **Rocket to the Moon**, were reclassified as D-ticket attractions.

The famous high-demand E ticket joined the ticket books in 1959 to coincide with the arrival of the park's biggest additions yet—the **Matterhorn Bobsleds**, the **Monorail**, and the **Submarine Voyage**. As before, several existing top-tier attractions, including the Jungle Cruise once again, were reclassified for the new higher ticket. For the next 23 years, no further tickets were added to the ticket books. However, new attractions were steadily added to the A-E lineup, and some existing attractions continued to shift around, sometimes going up in cost (the **Main Street Cinema**, from an A to a B), sometimes going down (the **Sleeping Beauty Castle Walk-Through**, C to B to A), sometimes doing both (**Snow White Adventures**, C-D-C). Only a few attractions, notably the A-ticket **King Arthur Carrousel** and **Main Street vehicles**, never changed their prices.

There's plenty of ticket trivia to bring smiles to nostalgic Disneyland fans. For instance, in 1957 the ticket books briefly included a small Special Bonus Ticket good for one free ride on any attraction. Then, in the '60s and '70s guests could choose between "Big 10" books with 10 tickets (one A, one B, two C, three D, three E) or, for a dollar more, "Deluxe 15" books with 15 (one A, two B, three C, four D, five E). If guests left the park with unused tickets, the tickets could always be used later but couldn't be refunded for cash. Over the years several attractions never needed tickets at all because either the park or a sponsor picked up the operating costs; these free attractions included **Adventure Thru Inner Space**, the **Golden Horseshoe** and its *Golden Horseshoe Revue*, the **Carousel of Progress**, and child admission to **Great Moments with Mr. Lincoln**. Conversely, some attractions still required the separate purchase of a special cash-only ticket, even while the lettered-ticket system was in place. Examples include the **Mickey Mouse Club Circus**, which cost an additional 50 cents during its brief run in late 1955; **Tom**

Ticketed Attractions, 1955–1982

Ticket prices often changed (Alice in Wonderland was everything from a B to a D, for instance), so this list gives the prices charged most frequently for attractions.

A Ticket

King Arthur Carrousel, Main Street vehicles, Satellite View of America, Sleeping Beauty Castle Walk-Through, Space Station X-1, 20,000 Leagues Under the Sea Exhibit

B Ticket

Alice in Wonderland, Art of Animation, Big Game Safari Shooting Gallery, Casey Jr. Circus Train, Conestoga Wagons, Main Street Cinema, Main Street Shooting Gallery, Mickey Mouse Club Theater, Midget Autopia, Motor Boat Cruise, Phantom Boats, Swiss Family Treehouse, Viewliner

C Ticket

Adventure Thru Inner Space, Astro-Jets, Dumbo the Flying Elephant, Fantasyland Autopia, Frontierland Shooting Gallery, Junior Autopia, Mad Hatter's Mad Tea Party, Mike Fink Keel Boats, Mr. Toad's Wild Ride, Peter Pan Flight, Snow White Adventures, Stage Coach, Tomorrowland Autopia

D Ticket

Flying Saucers, Indian War/Davy Crockett's Explorer Canoes, *Mark Twain* Riverboat, Mission to Mars, PeopleMover, Rafts to Tom Sawyer Island, Rainbow Caverns Mine Train, Rainbow Ridge Mule Pack, Rocket Jets, Rocket/Flight to the Moon, Sailing Ship *Columbia*, Santa Fe & Disneyland Railroad, Skyway to Fantasyland/Tomorrowland, Storybook Land Canal Boats

E Ticket

America Sings, Big Thunder Mountain Railroad, Country Bear Jamboree, Enchanted Tiki Room, Great Moments with Mr. Lincoln, Haunted Mansion, It's a Small World, Jungle Cruise, Matterhorn Bobsleds, Monorail, Pirates of the Caribbean, Pack Mules Through Nature's Wonderland, Space Mountain, Submarine Voyage

Sawyer Island, an additional 50 cents in 1956, a single D ticket thereafter; and the **Enchanted Tiki Room**, priced at an extra 75 cents in 1963 before graduating to a single E-ticket admission.

The ticket-book system ended in 1982 when all-encompassing **Passports** went into effect, offering unlimited use of all attractions. Today, leftover tickets can still be applied to the cost of park admission, but they can also be sold to collectors, who naturally place the highest premiums on complete, unused ticket books.

Tiki Juice Bar

MAP: Adventureland, A-11

CHRONOLOGY: Ca. 1976–ongoing

HISTORY: Talk about a match made in **Adventureland**—right outside the entrance to the **Enchanted Tiki Room** is the equally tropical Tiki Juice Bar. The TJB has been serving lots of J and other island-style refreshments from under its little thatched roof since 1976, the year Dole began sponsoring both this snack stand and the Tiki Room next door.

Unlike many of the other quick-stop eateries in the park, this one serves healthy treats like cool pineapple juice and pineapple spears, plus frosty Pineapple Whips that sound decadent but use no ice cream or dairy products. On a scorching summer day, a fortifying stop here is just the thing for overheated explorers heading westward towards the **Jungle Cruise** and beyond.

Tiki Tropical Traders, aka Tropical Imports

MAP: Adventureland, A-9

CHRONOLOGY: 1955–ongoing

HISTORY: Listed in the 1950s **souvenir books** as Tiki Tropical Traders, and renamed Tropical Imports around 1995, this little shop has been serving up **Adventureland** "curios for the curious" for five decades. Passengers about to disembark from their **Jungle Cruise** boats drift pass painted Tropical Imports advertisements that declare "all items guaranteed authentic" and "English spoken."

Always located in an exotic hut outside the Jungle Cruise queue area, for most of its history the shop sold merchandise less "Disney plush" and more "jungle unusual": rubber snakes, bamboo chimes, shrunken heads, exotic shells, etc. In the last decade, the imports have been from the food and beverage department, lots of juices, water, snacks, and fruit to go with the plush alligators, monkeys, parrots, and giant bugs. Sunglasses and sundries make this a convenient stop halfway between the Adventureland entrance and the **Indiana Jones Adventure**.

Tinker Bell

MAP: Park, P-16

CHRONOLOGY: Summer 1961–1977; 1983–ongoing

HISTORY: That a real live Tinker Bell was added to Disneyland in 1961 should come as no surprise— an animated version of the blonde fairy had already graced *Peter Pan* in 1953 (rereleased in 1958) and been the delightful (but mute) hostess on the *Disneyland* **TV series** as of 1954. Once **Matterhorn Mountain** was completed in 1959, **Walt Disney** knew it was time to bring Tink into the park.

The plan was to have someone in a costume take the elevator and stairway up inside the Matterhorn, strap on a harness, soar 784 feet from the mountain on a sloping wire, and land down on a mattress-padded platform near what is now the Village Haus restaurant in **Fantasyland**. Not coincidentally, the someone hired for the first flight had already flown in the correct costume. At the Hollywood Bowl in 1958, a 4′ 10″ circus aerialist named Tiny Kline had made a spectacular 1,000-foot glide from the hills to the stage while dressed as Tinker Bell for a special "Disney Night" concert. At the time, Kline, a Hungarian who was born Helen Deutsch, was 68 years old. Previously, her long career in show biz had included stints with the circus and stunts with airborne dirigibles and airplanes in which she dangled by her teeth above the ground.

Tiny Kline began at Disneyland in mid-'61. Every night of the summer she followed a flood of floating soap bubbles into the Fantasyland sky just before the nightly Fantasy in the Sky **fireworks** show. She performed until 1964, the year she died, with unconfirmed reports that the wand was taken up by her daughter.

Later Tinker Bells, who continued the nighttime performances until 1977 and then from 1983 onward, have worn the wings in shows similar to Kline's, with a few changes. In 2000's Believe . . . There's Magic in the Stars, for instance, Tinker Bell made her descent *during* the fireworks, not before. And Tink doesn't simply glide downwards anymore, she now moves back and forth across the sky. Finally, speculation persists that in recent years the person flying as Tinker Bell isn't a woman but is instead a man, a rumor that park officials haven't confirmed either way.

Tinker Bell & Friends

MAP: Fantasyland, Fa-3

CHRONOLOGY: November 2006–ongoing

HISTORY: The left-hand space within the **Sleeping Beauty Castle** entrance, where the **Princess Boutique** and the **50th Anniversary Shop** had both been, became a new Tinker Bell gift shop in late 2006. The pretty store is about 100 feet long and L-shaped, with exits to the castle entrance and the side path out to the **Plaza Gardens**.

Those friends named in the title aren't nearly as conspicuous as Tink, who dominates the shop (maybe that's the joke—perhaps she doesn't have many friends). There are Tink costumes, toys, jewelry, bags, blonde wigs, wands, and more, everything a girl needs to bring out her inner fairy.

Tinker Bell Toy Shoppe,
aka Once Upon a Time . . . the Disney Princess Shoppe

MAP: Fantasyland, Fa-7

CHRONOLOGY: 1957–ongoing

HISTORY: Since 1957, a charming toy and costume store has thrived along the northwest wing of **Sleeping Beauty Castle**. This location puts the store between the doorway to the **Sleeping Beauty Castle Walk-Through** and the **Snow White Adventures** attraction.

For the first 45 years, the store was called the Tinker Bell Toy Shoppe—an appropriate name for a cute castle store, considering Tink was sort of a cute castle mascot, thanks to the little blonde fairy's animated appearances at the opening of the **Disneyland TV series**. As the largest store in **Fantasyland**, this was for decades the area's main headquarters for enchanting gifts.

The two-part name change in 2002 to Once Upon a Time . . . the Disney Princess Shoppe again reinforced the castle connection. Once Upon a Time alludes to the beautiful love song "Once Upon a Dream" from the 1959 film *Sleeping Beauty*; meanwhile, the Disney Princess Shoppe suffix points directly at the store's target patrons. Little princesses, and parents of little princesses, could find much more merchandise in here than what was on view in the smaller **Princess Boutique** inside the castle entrance. Regal dresses, gilded crowns, magic wands, sparkly jewelry and tiaras, detailed dolls and statues, plush toys and furry purses, illustrated books, and Disney DVDs fill this store with the stuff wishful dreams are made of. What's more, in recent years the four classic Disney movie princesses—Snow White, Cinderella, Aurora from *Sleeping Beauty*, and Belle from *Beauty and the Beast*—stop by to meet guests, sign autographs, and even tell once-upon-a-time fairy tales. The picture window out front, with its displays of royal wardrobes and accessories, is a magnet few children can resist.

Tomorrowland

MAP: Park, P-18

CHRONOLOGY: July 17, 1955–ongoing

HISTORY: In Disneyland, no area was as problematical in the mid-'50s, and no area has undergone as many major revisions since then, as Tomorrowland. The land's main challenge for Disney designers is easy to grasp but difficult and expensive to resolve—create a futuristic, guest-friendly land that continually stays ahead of ever-advancing real-world technological achievements.

Unlike the rest of the park, which is set in the present (**Mickey's Toontown**) or the recent/distant/fabled past (**Adventureland**, **Critter Country**, **Fantasyland**, **Frontierland**, **Main Street**, **New Orleans Square**), Tomorrowland is set in the future. When Tomorrowland was first being designed and built, that future was pegged as 1986, the year of Halley's Comet's return. Later the target year was pushed into the 21st century. Consequently, with Tomorrowland mandated to stay fresh and innovative, many more new attractions have been introduced here than anywhere else in Disneyland. **Walt Disney** knew what he was talking about when he commented that "tomorrow is a heck of a thing to keep up with."

Once upon a yesterday, Tomorrowland almost didn't debut on **Opening Day** along with the rest of the park. Lacking adequate funds and time, Tomorrowland had empty buildings, the for-display-purposes-only *Moonliner* rocket, the **Circarama** theater, Monsanto's **Hall of Chemistry**, a barely functioning **Tomorrowland Autopia**, and not much else ready by July of 1955. For a typical amusement park or state fair, these attractions were acceptable, but for the stimulating Tomorrowland Walt Disney imagined, not so much, especially when compared to the ambitious descriptions that had been pitched to potential investors two years before. Those 1953 descriptions enthusiastically declared that "the World of Tomorrow" would have "a preview of some of the wonderful developments the future holds in store," including "a moving sidewalk, industrial exhibits, a diving bell, a monorail, a freeway children could drive, shops for scientific toys and a Rocket Space Ship to the Moon." Artist **Herb Ryman** had drawn a conceptual Land of Tomorrow entrance that included swooping architecture with wings and the suspended pods of some futuristic transportation system, and at one time some kind of "interplanetary circus" was discussed. Unfortunately, almost none of the things described or shown for the World and Land of Tomorrow was ready when the park opened.

Towards the end of 1954, with the park well under construction, Walt Disney resigned himself to opening Disneyland the following July with "coming soon" signs in front of a closed-off Tomorrowland. But early in '55, he decided to push

Major Attractions and Exhibits Added in the 2000s

2003
Many Adventures of Winnie the Pooh

2005
Buzz Lightyear Astro Blasters

2007
Finding Nemo Submarine Voyage; Pirate's Lair on Tom Sawyer Island

Tomorrowland to the Opening Day finish line. Alas, what was desired wasn't completely possible, and the public's first glimpses of Tomorrowland took in festive banners and balloons that camouflaged the embarrassing absence of high-profile, high-tech attractions.

Meanwhile, with guests streaming in throughout the summer, work continued apace to fill the land's approximately 13 acres with more to see and do. Within a month of Opening Day, **Rocket to the Moon** was flying, the **20,000 Leagues Under the Sea Exhibit** was displaying, and the **Phantom Boats** were sputtering. By that fall, **Hobbyland** and the **Flight Circle**, two pedestrian exhibits grounded in the present, were operating. Behind the scenes, Disney solicited more corporate sponsors and within six months had brought in Kaiser Aluminum for the **Hall of Aluminum Fame**, the American Dairy Association for their eponymous exhibit space, and the Crane Plumbing Company for the **Bathroom of Tomorrow.** Functional exhibits all, but hardly inspiring.

Inspiring attractions were on the horizon, however. The spring of '56 brought the **Astro-Jets** and the **Skyway to Fantasyland**, 1957 opened the doors on the **House of the Future**, and 1958 welcomed an attempt at mass transit, the gas-powered **Viewliner** train. A more audacious mass-transit system arrived in '59 with the first well-coordinated large-scale surge in Tomorrowland development. Debuting in June along with the **Matterhorn Bobsleds** (dubbed at the time a Tomorrowland attraction) and the **Submarine Voyage** was the **Monorail**. While the first two were visually stunning entertainments, the electric Monorail was the most significant addition, as it represented the most determined attempt yet to make Tomorrowland a testing ground for serious experiments in futuristic public transportation.

With this trio of attractions in place simultaneously, in one fell swoop Tomorrowland had three electrifying new E-ticket options to brag about. And brag the park's marketing department did, filling the **souvenir books** with lots of ebullient text and enticing photos. Additionally, this latest and greatest expansion was showcased in much-seen promotional films and TV specials. The Tomorrowland that Walt Disney wanted, one that would be a "living blueprint of our future," was finally here.

Eight years later, a dramatic facelift introduced the first "new Tomorrowland." This remarkable update, still one of the favorite moments in Disneyland history for many guests, re-themed the entire land as a shiny "World on the Move." Angular aluminum entrance gates 70 feet apart, the creative **Adventure Thru Inner Space** attraction, new **Rocket Jets**, a new **Tomorrowland Terrace** and **Tomorrowland Stage**, the immense Carousel Theater with its state-of-the-art **Audio-Animatronic Carousel of Progress**, and yet one more serious contribution to urban planning, the **PeopleMover**, all replaced familiar landmarks like the *Moonliner*, the Flying Saucers, the Flight Circle, and several long-running exhibits. New Tomorrowland's $20,000,000 price tag (according to the book *Walt Disney's Disneyland*) was about $3,000,000 more than what Disneyland itself had cost to build a decade before, but Imagineers got the impressive results they wanted, and dazzled guests felt like they'd suddenly time-warped into the 21st century. **Space Mountain** 10 years later made them feel like they'd time-warped into the mind-blowing StarGate sequence of *2001: A Space Odyssey*. And **Star Tours** 10 years after that had guests light-speeding into *Star Wars* territory. Who knew the future would be so fun?

The '90s brought an even newer "new Tomorrowland," but this one was as controversial as it was exciting. Rather than continually chase an ever-elusive future, Imagineers decided to reinvent a "retro-future"—that is, a future as it might've been imagined a century before. Long gone were the Skyway buckets, the Submarine Voyage, the PeopleMover, and the **Mission to Mars** flight (even the **Matterhorn** was missing, since the souvenir books were listing it as a Fantasyland, not a Tomorrowland, mountain). Jules Verne now seemed to be the main designer of neon-lit sci-fi attractions like the **Astro-Orbitor**, **Rocket Rods**, and **Observatron**, their warm colors the bronzes and coppers of the Industrial Revolution instead of the stark whites, blacks, and chromes of the Space Age. And with edible plants filling the flower beds and planters, the future at hand was as healthy and harmonious as it was scientific and gadgety.

For all the effort, somehow this future didn't work as well as it could have, and within a few years the disappointing Rocket Rods were Toy Storied out of existence by the fanciful **Buzz Lightyear Astro Blasters**, Space Mountain was being repainted white, and the submarines were getting new orders to find little Nemo. Rumors suggest that even the PeopleMover may eventually be resurrected. Tomorrowland's future, it seems, is firmly rooted in its past.

Tomorrowland Autopia, aka Autopia, Presented by Chevron

MAP: Tomorrowland, T-12

CHRONOLOGY: July 17, 1955–ongoing

HISTORY: Of the four Autopias that have existed in Disneyland, the Tomorrowland Autopia was the only one up and running on **Opening Day**. This original Autopia track curved and curled across approximately three acres of Disneyland's eastern edge, with most of the track design attributed to Disney Legend **Marvin Davis**.

With the nation's interstate-freeway system developing rapidly in the '50s, most of that decade's **souvenir books** labeled Disneyland's driving attraction the Autopia Cars and Freeway. The '59 book renamed it the Super Autopia Freeway, the super name differentiating the D-ticket **Tomorrowland** original from the C-Ticket **Junior Autopia** and B-ticket **Midget Autopia** that opened in **Fantasyland** in 1956 and '57, respectively. The large souvenir maps of the '60s and beyond used the site-specific designation Tomorrowland Autopia to avoid confusion with the **Fanta-**

syland **Autopia** that debuted in 1959.

During these early years, the Richfield Oil Corporation, "the official gasoline of Disneyland" and the company that in 1970 would become the "R" in ARCO, was the sponsor of the Tomorrowland Autopia, and the Richfield name was prominently displayed on the signage at the site. In 2000, the Chevron Corporation became the sponsor of the redesigned attraction that has been operating since then as the Autopia, Presented by Chevron.

The 1956 souvenir book called the Tomorrowland Autopia "Disneyland's cars of the future," though it's hard to see how these small, slow, noisy, gas-powered autos driven mostly by kids were futuristic. Fun, yes, but futuristic, no. For the first decade of operation the track did not have a guide rail running down the center, which meant drivers could veer their cars into each other, they could actually pass each other, and in some cases they even managed to go against traffic (a persistent legend has Sammy Davis Jr. being chased off the road into some bushes in 1955). Not until 1965 was a center rail installed down the middle of the Autopia freeway to keep cars aligned.

In contrast, the cars themselves, which were mostly designed by Disney Legend **Bob Gurr**, went through many modifications, starting almost immediately. The first, unused designs of the cars showed bulbous, heavy fenders and running boards, just like on classic American cars of the '40s and '50s, thus making the "cars of the future" really more like "cars of the recent past." The Mark I cars that hit the Tomorrowland road in 1955 were modeled on foreign sports cars, especially Porsches and Ferraris, to give them a sleek, low-slung look that anticipated styles of the next decade, if not quite the next century. Unfortunately, with bodies made out of fiberglass and bumpers made out of soft aluminum, the cars couldn't withstand anything more than slight impacts, even though they usually traveled at less than eight miles per hour. Consequently, when drivers showed a predilection for ramming other vehicles or bouncing off the side of the track rather than driving safely, the toll was both disastrous and immediate—according to the 2007 *Disneyland: Secrets, Stories, & Magic* DVD, 95% of the cars running at the start of Opening Day were disabled or broken down by day's end (that is, 38 out of 40 cars were not "usable").

Before the end of 1955, two more versions of the Autopia cars—the Mark II and Mark III—were created with sturdier engines and chassis. Yet another update, the Mark IV, appeared midway through '56, and an even heavier, slower (hence safer) version appeared in 1959. This iteration, the Mark V, was the longest-lasting design of its time and wasn't replaced until 1965, the same year that the center rail arrived on the track. Since drivers could no longer sideswipe each other, the side bumpers were taken off these cars. Then in 1967, in keeping with the dramatic remodel that was sweeping through all of Tomorrowland, new Mark VII Tomorrowland Autopia cars debuted that were, at over $5,000 apiece, the most expensive yet (by comparison, guests could've bought two brand-new full-size Ford Mustangs for that price). Looking like little Corvette Stingrays, these Autopia cars were also the most durable and rode the track until the end of the century.

After temporarily closing in 1999, the 2000 version of the attraction opened with a large video screen displaying animations, a grandstand viewing area, new cars that came in three different styles (Dusty, Suzy, and Sparky, to coincide with the TV ads of Chevron, the new sponsor), and a longer, more exciting, and more humorous driving experience. The new layout incorporated the extinct Fantasyland Autopia track, stretched the ride time out to over six minutes, and even included a bouncy "off-road" section.

No matter the era, guests of all ages have enjoyed the Autopia experience, and it remains today as one of the park's most consistently popular attractions (and the only one in Tomorrowland left from Opening Day). This popularity may seem ironic, since most guests have to fight their way through freeway traffic just to get to Disneyland, so it would seem unrealistic to ask them to then pay and wait for a chance to get behind the wheel of another car. However, many old photos show adults, prominent celebrities, and even **Walt Disney** himself happily taking cars for a spin (the 1957 souvenir book included a photo of Disney sitting alone in a car, waving merrily while wearing his standard gray suit and a rakish cap). Kids, naturally, have always jumped at the chance to take the wheel, especially if they were over 52" tall and could drive alone.

Decades of nifty enhancements have helped make the Autopia a utopia for trivia fans. Of the original Mark I cars, four were designed to look like patrol cars with black-and-white color schemes, sirens, and flashing lights. Also, in the '50s and '60s, kids could get a free Official Driver's License from Richfield Autopia certifying them as safe drivers (new Chevron Driver's Licenses were offered as of 2000, see photo above). And these days humorous signs punctuate the trip: there's one that warns of "Mouse Crossing" near a mouse hole, another that designates the road as Disneyland Route 55 (in honor of the inaugural year), another that posts a speed limit of 6.5 mph, and cartoony roadside billboards that advertise clever products. One of the dinky Midget Autopia cars is still displayed about a minute into the drive (see photo on page 284), followed shortly by an ancient car from **Mr. Toad's Wild Ride**. The Tomorrowland Autopia roadway may be only about a mile long, but for millions of drivers that's a mile of smiles.

Tomorrowlanding

MAP: Tomorrowland, T-8

CHRONOLOGY: 2006–ongoing

HISTORY: What had been the **Radio Disney** booth under the **Observatron** became a new **Tomorrowland** store called Tomorrowlanding in 2006. "Gifts from outer and liquid space" supposedly filled the small trapezoid that opened towards **Innoventions** according to the sign outside, but really outer space was far better represented than liquid space. *Star Wars* lightsabers and Disney-themed hats seemed to be the main stock in trade until the nearby **Submarine Voyage** started to generate some new merchandise in mid-2007.

Tomorrowland Stage, aka Space Stage

MAP: Tomorrowland, T-19

CHRONOLOGY: 1967–1986

HISTORY: The "new **Tomorrowland**" of 1967 introduced an intimate bandstand, the **Tomorrowland Terrace**, for smaller acts, and a showy new venue, the Tomorrowland Stage, for theatrical extravaganzas and nationally known rock bands. The Tomorrowland Stage filled the eastern corner of Tomorrowland where the **Flying Saucers** had hovered in the first half of the '60s. The stage itself was about 30 feet across and 12 feet high, and it was festooned with the same kind of arcs and abstractions that adorned the Tomorrowland Terrace.

The Tomorrowland Stage was a big setting for big shows. Among the large-scale musical spectaculars presented here on Sunday nights were *Show Me America* and *Country Music Jubilee*; the book *Disneyland: The First Quarter Century* described the former as a "fast-paced musical comedy" with "more than 120 sparkling costumes" and "favorite American melodies sprinkled with a touch of old-fashioned humor," eventually playing 124 performances "acclaimed by audiences and critics alike." Among the rock groups booked here were Herman's Hermits, Linda Ronstadt (backed by the newly formed Eagles), and the park's own **Kids of the Kingdom**. A high point may have been the live big-screen broadcast of the *Apollo 11* moonwalk on July 20, 1969. Not only was the event historic, for most people it was the first time they'd seen a large-scale TV broadcast. Despite these significant events, over the years the annual **souvenir books** gave the Tomorrowland Stage very little exposure, usually just an infrequent nighttime photo in the Disneyland After Dark pages and a nonspecific caption about "Tomorrowland's new stage" offering "top name talent in major shows."

With the completion of **Space Mountain** in 1977, the Tomorrowland Stage got rebuilt as part of that attraction's sleek new architectural complex. That December it also got a new name, the Space Stage, just one of the space-related names (**Space Place** and **Lunching Pad** were some others) that arrived with the mountain.

The kingdom-themed musical *Disneyland Is Your Land* began running here in 1985, but a year later the show and the outdoor stage were gone. Starting in 1986, outdoor shows were being held at the new **Videopolis** stage over in **Fantasyland**, and the Space Stage space was turned into the **Magic Eye Theater**, an indoor venue where *Captain EO* was soon to land.

Tomorrowland Terrace

MAP: Tomorrowland, T-9

CHRONOLOGY: July 2, 1967–2001; 2006–ongoing

HISTORY: When a "new **Tomorrowland**" opened up in the summer of '67, every addition was conspicuous—except one. Out in the middle of the plaza, a spot about 100 feet from the loading areas of the **Monorail** to the northwest and the new **PeopleMover** to the southwest, was now a futuristic design of some kind. Decorated with artistic pylons and flowing plants, guests could admire the serene 40-foot-long display without really understanding what it was or how it added to the Tomorrowland atmosphere.

Understanding came when, every few hours, the display began to ascend to reveal itself as the roof of a small oval stage where a spirited music group was already playing even as the stage rose up. Sometimes called the Coke Terrace or the Coca-Cola Tomorrowland Terrace in deference to its sponsor, the stage below was decorated with the same sleek arcs and op art abstractions that formed the sculptural planter on top. The performers, which included the pop-oriented Sunshine Balloon and beachy boys called Papa-Doo-Ron-Ron, got assembled, tuned, and started on the subterranean stage before they made their appearance at ground level.

Teens were the target audience, especially at night. During the days tables out in front of the raised stage offered seating for hundreds of guests; at night the tables got cleared away to open up the space as a dance area. The park's **souvenir books** of the late '60s and '70s showed off the Tomorrowland Terrace with photos in both the Tomorrowland and the Disneyland After Dark sections to showcase its youth appeal.

Nearby a counter-service eatery offered fast food staples like burgers, sandwiches, fries, and Cokes (natch). About a decade after the Tomorrowland Terrace opened, this menu got supplemented with a Tomorrowland-themed Moonburger, and two decades after that (the late '90s) the lunch and dinner menus got updated with healthier wraps, fruit, and salads.

Coca-Cola shifted its sponsorship from the Tomorrowland Terrace to the nearby **Spirit of Refreshment** when another "new Tomorrowland" remodel arrived in 1998. The Tomorrowland Terrace music and fast food continued to operate, though a new sculpture crowned the roof and the colors were updated to the same golds and bronzes of other area attractions like the **Astro-Orbitor**. In 2001, **Club Buzz** reinvigorated the stage and dining with a new name and new musical presentations with *Toy Story* themes.

The name Tomorrowland Terrace returned in 2006 when a new hit show arrived. Sponsored by Hasbro and performed a half-dozen times a day, *Jedi Training Academy* brings *Star Wars* themes and characters to life by training earnest young guests to "master the ways of the Force." Kids learn the art of lightsaber fencing and square off against Stormtroopers and two evil Darths, Maul and Vader. The confrontations are more hilarious than terrifying thanks to the intense kids and the fast-paced narration. At night, dance music is often provided by either a deejay or a live band. And these days the menu of sandwiches and burgers is called "Flight Command Cuisine."

Tom Sawyer Island, aka Pirate's Lair on Tom Sawyer Island

MAP: Frontierland, Fr-16

CHRONOLOGY: June 16, 1956–ongoing

HISTORY: Walt Disney never produced a movie based on *The Adventures of Tom Sawyer*, but he certainly had an affinity for that adventure novel, and he shared a Midwest background with its author, Mark Twain. Disney was born in Chicago, about 350 miles from Twain's Florida, Missouri birthplace; both men grew up in small Missouri towns (Marceline, Hannibal); both were alive concurrently (Disney was eight when Twain died in 1910). And both created an island in the middle of a river.

Twain's *Tom Sawyer* did not include a place called Tom Sawyer's Island. But it did have a fictional Jackson's Island "about three miles long and a quarter of a mile wide" out in the middle of the Mississippi River. There Tom, Huck, and their friend Joe Harper cavorted as pirates and escaped the constraints of "civilization." Once they reached the island via log raft (chapter 13), the three boys eagerly roamed the woods (chapter 14) with "plenty of things to be delighted with."

In early 1956, with Disneyland up and running, Walt Disney turned his attention to completing the visible-but-unvisitable island he'd left unfinished out in the middle of the **Rivers of America**. Early ideas would've fashioned either a Mickey Mouse Island or a Treasure Island based on Disney's 1950 movie. Once the Sawyer concept was set, Disney did what he typically did for new attractions: he turned over the actual creation to an individual designer, who used his boss's general suggestions to map out the details. Tom Sawyer Island, however, got some extra attention.

According to Bob Thomas's *Walt Disney: An American Original*, the island was the only early Disneyland attraction personally designed by Walt Disney himself. Disney did let artist **Marvin Davis** have first crack at it, but the results weren't pleasing. Thomas quotes Disney as telling Davis to "give me that thing," before taking away Davis's drawings. That same night Walt labored "for hours in his red-barn workshop. The next morning, he laid tracing paper on Davis's desk and said, 'Now that's the way it should be.' The island was built according to his design." Added Disney's daughter, Diane Disney Miller, in her book *The Story of Walt Disney*, "He [Disney] kept on adding things until he felt that there weren't any missing parts."

The result is something close to Twain's rough-hewn Jackson's Island. Just as Twain's island was 12 times longer than it was wide, so too is Disney's island long and narrow. Disney's island stretches 800 feet from top to bottom and varies in width from a sleek 50 feet in the middle to about 250 across the northern end, a total land mass of almost three acres. The surrounding shore, most of it belonging to **Frontierland**, is 80–100 feet away, with **Rafts to Tom Sawyer Island** conveying guests back and forth.

Walt Disney added his own flourishes to Twain's undeveloped island, of course. A play structure called Tom & Huck's Treehouse stands on a hill at the southern tip (in the early decades the island maps handed out to guests declared this to be the "highest point in Disneyland," meaning that the treehouse was for many years the highest point guests could access). Some 250 feet to the north of the treehouse was Fort Wilderness, a two-story log fort straight out of a Western movie. In its first years the fort was replete with stairways, a passageway down to the trails, a display of Davy Crockett and Andrew Jackson mannequins that had once been in **Davy Crockett Frontier Museum**, a refreshment stand, and lookout towers with rifles that used to deliver a bulletless bang (in the 21st century age finally caught up with the fort, and it's gone from being closed to being demolished). Additional island features, all of them shown on the free island maps drawn by **Sam McKim** (see photo above), included smooth sculpted rocks for climbing, shaky pontoon and swaying rope bridges, Merry-Go-Round Rock, Pirate's Den, Castle Rock, Smuggler's Cove, Teeter-Totter Rock, and a fake cemetery behind the fort with antique headstones. And then there was Injun Joe's Cave.

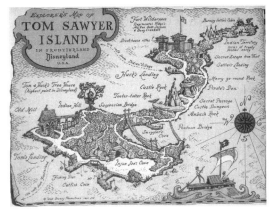

McDougal's Cave was the scene of the thrilling climax to Twain's *Tom Sawyer*. While writing the book in the 1870s, Twain could recall his childhood days when he'd played in a cave outside of Hannibal. This cave, which exists today as a national landmark, was his model for the cave where Tom, Becky Thatcher, and other revelers made a giddy procession into marvelous subterranean rooms with exotic names like The Cathedral and Aladdin's Palace. Twain's vivid descriptions created a "romantic and mysterious" world. The "main avenue" was "eight or ten feet wide," "crevices branched from it on either hand," there was "a vast labyrinth of crooked

Tombstones in the Tom Sawyer Island Cemetery

Most of the following names seem to be fictitious. Feignoux and Clemmings, however, were real employees of the Disney Studios; Sacajawea, also sometimes spelled Sacagewea, was the Shoshone woman famous for helping the 1805 Lewis and Clark expedition. The cemetery disappeared in the island's 2007 remodel.

Thaddeus Walker, 1812

Rufus Finley

Amos Wilson, 1797–1862

Wing Lee, 1811

W. Pierre Feignoux, *j'y suis j'y reste*, 1809

Lieut. Laurence Clemmings fell here defending the right

Jno. C. Sawyer, 1813

Eliza Hodgkins died June 7, 1812, 27 years

Unknown Remains found 1808

Sacajawea Indian Scout

Ebinizer Browne, 1812

Unknown Guest

aisles," a "tangle of rifts and chasms," a "multitude of shining stalactites," "glittering crystals," and "fantastic pillars."

The Disney cave, while not quite as elaborate and only about 100 feet long, captures the natural wonder and adventurous potential of Twain's creation. Guests duck through dimly lit passageways, creep along a dirt floor, negotiate slender side paths, and stand at a rail before a Bottomless Pit. The island maps included this description of the cave experience (ellipses are the map's): "Explore the labyrinth of passages . . . look for the fossils in the walls . . . crawl through secret tunnels . . . discover the hiding place of Injun Joe's treasure 'under the cross' . . . Glistening stalactites and stalagmites form weird shapes in the Chamber of the Bottomless Pit . . . some have said that from the depths they have heard the mournful sound of Injun Joe, crying out in the darkness . . . but others claim it is just the wind moaning in some lost subterranean passage."

When the island finally opened in July of '56, it did so with two winners of Hannibal's "most typical Tom and Becky of the year" contest. The two kids received a trip to Disneyland, courtesy of one of the park's sponsors, Western Printing. Once in the Magic Kingdom, the pair, dressed as Tom and Becky Thatcher, met Walt Disney and helped dedicate the new attraction.

That first year guests couldn't use any of their A, B, or C tickets to enter the island—they had to buy special 50-cent tickets for admission. Once on the island guests could pursue one additional adventure: fishing. Using the park's poles, hooks, and bait, guests could fish off the Catfish Cove docks at the island's southern tip. Because they dropped their lines into a penned area of water that had been stocked with live catfish, guests were pretty assured of success. That, unfortunately, was the problem, since neither guests nor **cast members** knew what to do with the fish once they were caught. After enough odoriferous carcasses were found abandoned in lockers, trash cans, and bushes, the rods were reeled in.

For many guests, Tom Sawyer Island has remained one of the most unique, and most entertaining, locations in Disneyland for at least 10 reasons: lines to get on and off the island are usually short; on hot days, the island's a good place to sit and relax near cool water and under real trees; there are no big stores or restaurants on the island to distract guests away from the fun or presidents away from wallets; as a confluence of four different lands (Frontierland, **Adventureland**, **Critter Country**, **New Orleans Square**), the island offers grand views of such landmarks as the **Haunted Mansion**, **Splash Mountain**, **Big Thunder Mountain Railroad**, the *Mark Twain*, and the *Columbia*; unlike most other attractions, Tom Sawyer Island is not a three-minute experience—the only time limit is "dusk"; other attractions take guests indoors, away from the California sunshine, but this one encourages them to stay outside; unlike high-profile, high-tech attractions that have been known to break down, the island is so low-tech it's almost *no*-tech and is nearly always open; since there's no set path or pattern to the adventure, untrammeled guests get to invent the island experience themselves (many a game of hide-and-seek has been played here); the island doesn't automatically reveal itself the way many other attractions do—with all the hidden areas, secret passageways, multiple paths with short cuts and long cuts, every visit can be different; finally, because they're not relegated to a boat or a car, guests have no "safety bar" to stifle imaginative impulses.

Not all of those imaginative impulses have been well-received. For one thing, several guests have unsuccessfully tried to hide on the island overnight. More bizarrely, chanting protesters invaded Fort Wilderness in 1970 and briefly raised a Viet Cong flag, forcing the park to temporarily suspend raft trips to the island.

The inaccessible cabin north of the fort (see photo below) has generated headlines of its own. In September 2001, the *L.A. Times* called the cabin "perhaps the most altered attraction" in the park. "For nearly 20 years, the victim of an Indian arrow lay sprawled in front of a burning settler's cabin," explained the paper. "In the 1970s, in the middle of the gas crisis, Disneyland turned off the flames for roughly a decade. . . . In 1984, the park began using a simulated flame and the settler was replaced with a moonshiner passed out on the porch.

Then . . . the theme became how an animal habitat was endangered by a fire caused by a careless settler." Today's cabin is still off-limits, but its flames no longer flicker. The most durable blaze in history was finally extinguished in 2007, and the cabin was restored to look like an unseen settler actually lives there.

At the other end of the island, changes came in 1992 when the southern tip was remodeled to accommodate **Fantasmic!** More dramatically, in February of 2007, the entire island closed for an extensive renovation that brought out the Bobcats (the earth-moving machines, that is). Reopened on May 25, 2007, as Pirate's Lair on Tom Sawyer Island, the island now sports wider paths, a sunken pirate ship, hidden treasure, ghostly apparitions, and other changes themed to the *Pirates of the Caribbean* movies.

Purists may deride any tamperings with Walt Disney's original vision of his Twain-inspired island, but as long as the island still exists at all, it will always be one of the best old-school attractions in the park. Missouri's legislature agrees—it has officially annexed Disneyland's island as part of the state.

Toontown Five & Dime

MAP: Mickey's Toontown, MT-9

CHRONOLOGY: January 24, 1993–ongoing

HISTORY: Sharing a bright yellow two-story building with the **Gag Factory** is the Toontown Five & Dime, a cheery retail operation within laughing distance of **Roger Rabbit's Car Toon Spin** in **Mickey's Toontown**. Outside the Five & Dime are some of Toontown's signature jokes and surprises, including talking mailboxes, wacky phones, Dr. Drillum's dentist office, and a broken clock on the clock-repair shop.

Unfortunately, there's no item in the Five & Dime that costs only one or two nickels, but there are lots of inexpensive pens, key chains, and other small souvenirs. In the hundreds-of-nickels/hundreds-of-dimes category are mugs, picture frames, and charm bracelets, with Toon-themed clothes, bags, and plush toys requiring big bags full of coins.

Toon Up Treats

MAP: Mickey's Toontown, MT-7

CHRONOLOGY: December 13, 1997–ongoing

HISTORY: About four years after **Goofy's Gas Station** opened in the heart of **Mickey's Toontown**, a small open-air "snack stop" opened up at Goofy's place. Toon Up Treats is always there but not always open (only the busy seasons seem to require regular hours). Basic sandwiches, pre-made salads, chips, some desserts, candy, and sodas provide fast fuel for guests on the go, with outdoor seating available nearby.

Topiary Garden

MAP: Fantasyland, Fa-21

CHRONOLOGY: May 28, 1966–ongoing

HISTORY: A topiary is a bush or tree trimmed into some recognizable shape, usually a geometric figure or an animal. An arrangement of many small plants into a single pattern is not considered a topiary, and thus the quilt planted on the shore of the **Storybook Land Canal Boats** and the large flower-formed face of Mickey Mouse at Disneyland's **entrance** don't qualify as topiaries. Disneyland does boast several true topiaries, including the joyful pachyderms by **Dumbo the Flying Elephant** and the giant swans outside of **Sleeping Beauty Castle.** But by far the most famous topiaries are those gathered in front of **It's a Small World** in **Fantasyland.**

So unusual was this array when it opened along with the instant-classic attraction in the spring of 1966, the area came to be known as the park's Topiary Garden. Certainly that's what **Jack Wagner** called it in his narration for guests riding the **Santa Fe & Disneyland Railroad** through Fantasyland: "From our train, you can see the boats sailing past the Topiary Garden, where trees and shrubs grow in the shapes of animals." The best views, though, weren't from the train, they were from the Small World boats, which still loop around the garden to show off the topiaries from different angles.

Three key factors make the Disneyland Topiary Garden so memorable. First and foremost, the whimsical subjects perfectly suit the imaginatively designed building and "the happiest cruise that ever sailed 'round the world." The animals have included a soaring giraffe, an elephant balancing on its front legs, a laughing hippo, a fuzzy-headed lion, a prancing reindeer, a striped zebra, a horned bison, a rhino with a bird on its back, a dancing bear, a seal balancing a ball, leaping dolphins, and a three-part sea serpent. There are also densely verdant trees cut into cones and corkscrews, domes and lampshades, plus decorative hedges trimmed into cubes and spheres. The fanciful greenery makes the garden look like a child's play area filled with wonderful toys and blocks.

The second factor is the scale of the sculptures. So much work goes into topiary creation, other parks often keep their topiaries small and simple. At Disneyland the sculptures in the Topiary Garden are almost all life-size, and they're all finely detailed.

Finally, painstaking effort is carefully applied to keep the plants in immaculate condition every day of the year no matter the weather conditions. Most of the plants are tight-growing, small-leafed shrubs that are grown for several years and then pruned constantly once they're in the park. Disneyland's own landscapers and gardeners maintain the topiaries, but a San Diego company called Coburn Topiary & Garden Art claims responsibility for first growing and shaping some of the plants.

Tour Guides

MAP: Town Square, TS-4, TS-2
CHRONOLOGY: 1958–ongoing
HISTORY: To help novice guests, or guests short on time, navigate the overwhelming park, a small team of tour guides was added as a Disneyland guest service in 1958. Early on, the tours began at **City Hall** and were informal presentations by a few **cast members** wearing their own casual clothes. But the increasing popularity of the tours resulted in a large team of trained guides, official uniforms, and formalized spiels.

By 1960, the Tour Guide program, led by **Cicely Rigdon**, was operating from what was called the Guided Tour Garden, a small landscaped area to the left of the **Police Station** on **Town Square**. Conveniently, this would've been the first location guests would've walked past had they entered Disneyland via the west tunnel. A 1964 park flyer described how the "enchanting" guided tours enabled guests to "enjoy several exciting Disneyland rides" while getting "interesting information about Disneyland from your attractive Disneyland Tour Guide." The "Happiness Trip" lasted two hours and cost $3.25 in '58, $5 in '64; these prices included park admission and a free ticket good for "another ride."

Tour guides were first presented in a **souvenir book** in 1962. That book showed a prim, 20-ish woman standing and smiling alongside a family of six on **Main Street.** She wore a red-and-black plaid skirt, a red double-breasted vest, a white short-sleeve blouse, red knee-high socks, and black flats (not shown was a cape, a cold-weather option). In the photo, the guide's black riding hat and the riding crop in her upraised hand added an equestrian influence to the amalgamation of styles. The laconic caption identified her duties: "Pretty Disneyland Tour Guide points out highlights of Main Street as part of entertaining, informative journey through the Magic Kingdom." Eventually the Tour Guides became popular and recognizable enough for Disneyland to sell a Tour Guide doll, "a true reproduction of the popular Tour Guide Girls" in the traditional plaid skirt/red vest outfit.

Just as the park has become more complex over the decades, so too have the tours, which now have themes. While they don't automatically move their groups to the front of attraction lines, tours usually include some priority seating for a parade or a show, plus extras like pins and free lunches. In the early years of the 21st century, the tour options bookable at City Hall included a "Premiere Tour" (four-hour minimum at an hourly rate, guests created the route); a "Welcome to Disneyland Tour" (two and a half hours, a general layout of the park); a "Holiday Time

Tour" (two and a half hours, highlighting winter holiday traditions); a "Discover the Magic Tour" (three hours, an interactive treasure hunt with a story line about finding Mickey); a "Disney's Myths, Mysteries and Legends Tour" (two and a half hours, held at night); and "A Walk in Walt's Footsteps" tour (three and a half hours, a fact-filled walk-and-talk that added dimension to the visuals, offered a look inside **Club 33**, gave a special train ride around the park, and provided a private lunch at the **Disney Gallery**). Prices, of course, have escalated from what was charged in the '60s; for instance, "A Walk in Walt's Footsteps" cost $59 per person in 2006, a price that did not include park admission.

Town Square

MAP: Park, P-8

CHRONOLOGY: July 17, 1955–ongoing

HISTORY: The early concept sketches of Disneyland were very consistent in their representations of Town Square, and usually what those drawings showed closely resembled the Town Square that was finally built in time for 1955's **Opening Day.** The famous **Herb Ryman** illustration executed in '53, showing a square-shaped one-acre plaza, a triangular third-of-an-acre green in the center with a soaring flagpole, and a few landmark buildings around the perimeter, was virtually a blueprint for Town Square.

As historians have noted for years, **Walt Disney** carefully crafted Disney-land as if he were a movie director laying out movie shots. Moviemaking techniques are still on view at Town Square. For one thing, guests can't see Town Square until Disney reveals it to them—they enter the park through one of two dark, confining tunnels that are lined with tantalizing **attraction posters** and then emerge upon a wide, dramatic vista. The move from tight close-up to breathtaking panorama is a cinematic strategy that intensifies the surprise and fixes the sight in memories.

That the first view of Disneyland is of an open, relatively calm area is no accident. Back in the '50s, remember, nobody in the general public knew what Dis-neyland was or how it worked, so Walt Disney gave disoriented guests a chance to acclimate gradually to his dramatically different park. Town Square was something they would've already been used to—a small town's civic center (at one time plan-ners were even thinking of calling Town Square the Civic Center). Mind-stretching options like **Tomorrowland** and **Fantasyland** could wait; here at the beginning of the Disneyland experience, it was enough to get one's bearings while being sur-rounded by such stable institutions as the **Police Station**, **City Hall**, and **Fire Sta-tion** on the west side of the square, Old Glory and inviting benches in the middle, and the **Opera House** and **Bank of America** to the east. Ahead of Town Square stretched what looked like an old-fashioned street in any American small town, and on the horizon, about three full football fields north of the **entrance** tunnels, was the first fabulous, yet safely distant sight: **Sleeping Beauty Castle.** Karal Ann Marling called this kind of environment "the architecture of reassurance" in her book *Designing Disney's Theme Parks*. Novice guests entered Town Square quizzical and left it comforted.

There's one other Town Square strategy worth mentioning. Besides orienting his guests, Walt Disney had to manage the crowds. By spreading guests out across a broad square, he nimbly averted the instant bottleneck that would've occurred every day had guests walked straight from the tunnels into narrow **Main Street**.

In addition to the "civic" buildings, Town Square is also home to formal entertainment and ceremonies. The Opening Day dedication, the flag-lowering tribute every afternoon, the lighting of the annual **Christmas** tree, even visits with Santa were and still are held in Town Square. Because of the wide range of events and its prominent placement at the head of the park, Town Square buildings and ceremonies have been shown in every one of the park's **souvenir books** and virtually every photo book about Disneyland. Old photos reveal little change in the exterior architecture (though some of the interior functions have changed over the decades). Town Square, thankfully, is timeless.

Town Square Café

MAP: Town Square, TS-7

CHRONOLOGY: December 1976–spring 1978; October 1, 1983–August 23, 1992

HISTORY: Making an **American Egg House** sandwich were the two iterations of the Town Square Café, which existed before and after the Egg House in the same spot overlooking **Town Square**. The Town Square Café first set up in 1976 as a replacement for the **Hills Bros. Coffee House and Coffee Garden**. This choice site had **Disneyland Presents a Preview of Coming Attractions** on the corner to the left and the **Mad Hatter** and **Opera House** to the right. As a full-service sit-down restaurant for breakfast and lunch, the sponsorless Town Square Café was the only eating establishment on Town Square.

After two years, the American Egg House took over the location. Five years later, the eggs were out and the previous café was back in, this time for almost a full decade. The Town Square Café redux closed in 1992, and the site eventually became the **Dalmatian Celebration** store and a character-greeting area. Gone but not forgotten, the Town Square Café has been honored with its own beautiful Disney pin.

Town Square Realty

MAP: Town Square, TS-10

CHRONOLOGY: 1955–1960

HISTORY: Listed in all of the park's **souvenir books** through 1959 was, of all things, a business called Town Square Realty (aka simply Real Estate in some of the books). Located to the right of the entrance into the **Opera House**, this was an actual office for an actual realtor who was selling land in Apple Valley, a largely undeveloped area some 80 miles northeast of Anaheim.

According to *Disneyland: The Nickel Tour*, the office dispensed information, handed out free maps of Disneyland, and gave away little pouches of authentic California dirt. With the novelty worn off by 1960, that year's souvenir book didn't include a mention of Town Square Realty, and in '61 the space was absorbed into the **Babes in Toyland Exhibit**.

Toy Story Funhouse

MAP: Tomorrowland, T-16

CHRONOLOGY: January 27, 1996–May 27, 1996

HISTORY: With *Toy Story* a hit in theaters as of late 1995, a play area based on the movie went up in **Tomorrowland** in early 1996. The site was next to **Space Mountain** in the old **Mission to Mars** building, which had been closed since 1992. The Toy Story Funhouse was never meant to have a long run at Disneyland, and it didn't, ending about five months later.

Disneyland's version of the Funhouse was based on an interactive exhibit that had been set up for the holidays at the Disney-owned El Capitan Theatre in Hollywood, the glitzy movie palace where *Toy Story* was being shown. After seeing the movie, patrons there could explore the exhibit next door for more *Toy Story* fun. At Disneyland, the Funhouse was spread over several rooms where guests could play video games, negotiate clever obstacle courses, interact with different displays, and get photos with the movie's characters. An ever-present gift shop, this one themed to the movie, was also part of the fun. Outside the Funhouse stood a temporary stage where a musical show called *Hamm's All-Doll Revue* was presented regularly to standing-room-only audiences (the standing-room wasn't because the show was so popular, it was because there weren't any seats).

With spring about to become summer and *Toy Story* gone from theaters, the whole Toy Story Funhouse complex was removed in favor of . . . nothing. Two years later, **Redd Rockett's Pizza Port** would start serving up fun pizzas from the old Funhouse location.

Tropical Cantina, aka Adventureland Cantina

MAP: Adventureland, A-3

CHRONOLOGY: 1955–1962

HISTORY: Listed in the park's **souvenir books** of the '50s was a spot in **Adventureland** called at times the Tropical Cantina, Adventureland Cantina or simply the Cantina (the latter name was painted on the building). Whatever the name, it was situated near **Aunt Jemima's Pancake House** and across from the **Jungle Cruise**.

The signage out front said this establishment served "ice cold tropical drinks" (the souvenir books proclaimed "light refreshments"). The thatched roof and outdoor tables were retained when the **Sunkist Citrus House** set up here in 1962.

20th Century Music Company

MAP: Main Street, MS-19

CHRONOLOGY: June 20, 1999–ongoing

HISTORY: That cigar-store Indian standing on the right-hand side of **Main Street** may seem out of place today, but it's there to remind guests of the **Fine Tobacco** shop that had existed next to the **Main Street Cinema** for the park's first 35 years. Then, after spending the '90s as different collectibles shops, at the end of that decade the space became a fun and fascinating music shop.

Offering "new sounds for a new century," according to the sign out front, the 20th Century Music Company is all about tunes (not to be confused with toons). Antique instruments are displayed on upper shelves, a century-old symphonion music box stands against a wall, and drawings of classical composers hang on the walls.

For Disney aficionados, the store is nirvana (though that band isn't represented here). The jam-packed room showcases new and vintage Disney-related music, including all the soundtracks from Disney films and Disneyland attractions a fan could want. The nicest surprise might be the albums recorded by Disneyland entertainers like the **Dapper Dans**, Billy Hill & the Hillbillies, and ragtime pianist Rod Miller from the **Refreshment Corner**. Movies and books are also available to help round out collections. For a while special kiosks enabled guests to burn their own customized CDs of Disney sounds, speeches, and announcements; today's version of the kiosks puts long-extinct Disney vinyl albums onto discs that are adorned with the original LP artwork.

20,000 Leagues Under the Sea Exhibit

MAP: Tomorrowland, T-23

CHRONOLOGY: August 3, 1955–August 28, 1966

HISTORY: Possibly the very last attraction **Walt Disney** worked on before **Opening Day** was the 20,000 Leagues Under the Sea Exhibit. According to Neal Gabler's *Walt Disney: The Triumph of the American Imagination*, Disney hastily conceived of the exhibit the night before the park's televised opening and worked on it late into the night with Disney Legend **Ken Anderson**, both of them donning masks for a flurry of 11th-hour spray-painting. They were desperately trying to get something, anything, into the circular building on the right-hand side of **Tomorrowland** that in the late '60s would house **Adventure Thru Inner Space** and in the late '80s **Star Tours**. Unfortunately, this building was, in mid-July of '55, mostly empty, and would remain so for the next two weeks.

When it was finally installed, the exhibit didn't really have much to do with the future, which supposedly was Tomorrowland's domain. Instead, the exhibit offered a walk-through tour of the 19th-century-styled sets and props used in the *20,000 Leagues Under the Sea* movie. While a movie-set exhibit might seem like a run-of-the-mill concept today, it was unique for its time, and guests were elated to be closer to moviemaking magic than they'd ever been before. Adding to the excitement was the propitious timing. The immensely popular *20,000 Leagues* movie had come out in December of '54, and on March 30, 1955, it had won an Oscar for Best Art Direction-Set Decoration. Thus Jules Verne's tale was still a very hot property in the summer of '55.

The sets guests saw included some of the actual iron-and-antiques interiors from the *Nautilus*, and among the props was Captain Nemo's famous pipe organ in his lavishly appointed parlor. A large, detailed model of the sub and Vulcania paintings by **Peter Ellenshaw** contributed cinematic special effects, and a view of the tentacle-flailing giant squid through the sub's circular viewing window contributed some genuine thrills. **Harper Goff** designed the sub and some of the sets, and golden-throated **Thurl Ravenscroft** provided the narration.

What was intended to be a temporary Tomorrowland placeholder, and never more than an A-ticket attraction, was ultimately so durable it lasted until 1966 and generated a dynamic **attraction poster** of guests facing off with the squid. Finally, after 11 years the sets were struck to make way for the huge remodel that was on Tomorrowland's near horizon. In Disneyland, the lone surviving reminder of the exhibit now resides in the **Haunted Mansion**, where a ghostly musician in the ballroom still plays Nemo's organ.

Upjohn Pharmacy

MAP: Main Street, MS-4

CHRONOLOGY: July 17, 1955–September 1970

HISTORY: On **Opening Day**, **Main Street** had a bank, a department store, a candy shop, a general store, and other businesses that would've legitimately appeared in an early-1900s downtown area. To add even more authenticity, it even had an apothecary. The Upjohn Pharmacy wasn't a joke or a fake—the Upjohn Company was a huge pharmaceutical manufacturer founded in 1886 (they're now part of Pfizer), and the Disneyland pharmacy they sponsored was a detailed re-creation of what a pharmacy would've been like at the turn of the last century.

The shop's location was halfway down Main Street on the left-hand side; more specifically, it was on the corner of West Center and Main, with the **Crystal Arcade** one door to the left (south), the **Carnation Ice Cream Parlor** across Center, and the **Market House** across Main to the east. Old-fashioned medicines lined the shelves and antique pharmaceutical equipment decorated the counters and walls, but it was the jar teeming with leeches that riveted guests' attention. While nothing was actually for sale, pills—actually free samples of all-purpose vitamins—were freely dispensed in small jars inside a red-and-yellow box.

The Upjohn Pharmacy got a mention and an illustration in the Special Shows and Exhibits section of the park's 1958 **souvenir book**, which noted something about "a unique look into the micro world." This "unique look" was probably a reference to an up-to-date side-room display of 1955 pharmaceutical technology. When Upjohn ceased its Disneyland participation in 1970, the whole corner site was soon split up and transformed—the side room became the **Hurricane Lamp Shop** and the main pharmacy became **New Century Watches & Clocks.**

Ursus H. Bear's Wilderness Outpost

MAP: Bear Country/Critter Country, B/C-6

CHRONOLOGY: March 24, 1972–November 23, 1988

HISTORY: Disneyland has had three Outposts in its history. Preceding the **Safari Outpost** and the **Indiana Jones Adventure Outpost** was Ursus H. Bear's Wilderness Outpost, a new store for the new **Bear Country** that opened in 1972. The formal name honors a character who supposedly founded the nearby **Country Bear Jamboree**. More realistically, *ursus* is the Latin word for "bear," and "outpost" is the Disney name for "retail store."

The Wilderness Outpost shared the long wooden building in the back of Bear Country with the **Brer Bar** and **Teddi Barra's Swingin' Arcade** (Ursus's spot was in the southwestern corner). The wilderness merchandise available here included country-style gift items, plus the T-shirts and souvenirs found in other park shops. In 1988, when Bear Country went Critter, the mammalian Outpost transformed into the reptilian **Crocodile Mercantile** on its way to becoming the Winnified **Pooh Corner** in 2003.

Videopolis, aka Fantasyland Theater

MAP: Fantasyland, Fa-18

CHRONOLOGY: June 22, 1985–October 2006

HISTORY: When the indoor **Magic Eye Theater** replaced the outdoor Space Stage in 1986, Disneyland was left without a venue for large open-air concerts. Voilà Videopolis, a new state-of-the-art concert area that opened in **Fantasyland** even before the Magic Eye was completed. Videopolis, the au courant name capitalizing on the

10 Live Stage Shows at the Fantasyland Theater, 1989–2006

1989–1990: *One Man's Dream* (based on the life of Walt Disney)
1990: *Dick Tracy Starring in Diamond Double-Cross* (based on the '90 movie)
1991: *Plane Crazy* (starring Baloo)
Winter 1991 and winter 1992: *Mickey's Nutcracker* (for the holidays only)
1992–1995: *Beauty and the Beast* (based on the '91 movie)
1995–1997: *The Spirit of Pocahontas* (based on the '95 movie,)
1998–2001: *Animazement—The Musical* (a tribute to Disney animation)
2001–2002: *Mickey's Detective School* (Disney characters search for Pluto)
Winter 2001 and winter 2002: *Minnie's Christmas Party*
(for the holidays only)
2004–2006: *Snow White—An Enchanting Musical* (based on the '37 movie)

new videocassette technology that was emerging in the '80s, opened to the north of the **Storybook Land Canal Boats** and to the west of nearby **It's a Small World.** A new train depot, the Videopolis Station, along the **berm** made the site accessible to train-traveling guests.

Catering to teenagers for the first 10 years, the park offered boisterous nighttime concerts, with bands performing up on the brilliantly lit stage in front of large dance areas totaling 5,000 square feet, a space about the size of a basketball court. Perimeter bleacher seats, light shows, special effects, big video screens, and dozens of monitors ringing the dance area with music videos and visuals of the crowd all combined to make concerts here just as dazzling as those in any rock arena. And just as loud, too, but fortunately the location at Disneyland's northern boundary kept the noise far from guests in the rest of the park.

By the '90s, however, with teens losing interest, the theater got 1,200 new first-come, first-served floor seats and a new purpose. Rather than provide live concerts for dancin' teens, Disneyland started trying out live stage shows for sitting families. The results were so successful that in '95 Videopolis received a video-less, more traditional new name. Actually, the new name wasn't all that new—Fantasyland Theater had been given to the **Mickey Mouse Club Theater** from 1964 to 1981 (the arrival of **Pinocchio's Daring Journey** into that building in '83 made the theatrical appellation available). Later changes to the theater included the addition of a tent high over the seating area in 1998.

The Spirit of Pocahontas was the debut stage show for the revived Fantasyland Theater. Shows usually lasted one or two years and became increasingly spectacular: *Snow White—An Enchanting Musical* boasted Patrick Stewart as the Magic Mirror, elaborate sets, and a producing team straight from Broadway. Late in 2006, the theater finally closed and was reinvented as a new themed area called the **Princess Fantasy Faire.**

Viewliner

MAP: Tomorrowland, T-10

CHRONOLOGY: June 26, 1957–September 15, 1958

HISTORY: Not satisfied with the old-fashioned **Santa Fe & Disneyland Railroad** orbiting Disneyland, the miniature **Rainbow Caverns Mine Train** chuffing through **Frontierland**, and the charming **Casey Jr. Circus Train** winding through **Fantasyland**, **Walt Disney** decided to add a more modern train to the park in 1957. What was modern in 1957 hardly looks modern now, of course, and so the inelegant Viewliner is usually remembered as one of the oddest contraptions ever to run on Disneyland tracks.

The new **Bob Gurr**-designed train had lots of similarities to other vehicles. The figure-8 track, for instance, was only 30 inches wide, the same as Casey's and the Mine Train's tracks. The sponsor was the Atchison, Topeka and Santa Fe Railroad, as it was for the park's main railroad. The cab on the front car was a cutdown version of a '54 Oldsmobile 88, which meant a height of under six feet, two swinging car doors, a car-like windshield, and the semblance of a car's blunt nose and headlight assembly. Inside the cab, the engineer shifted gears with an automobile clutch and drove with a steering wheel. The gas-powered V-8 engine from a Chevy Corvette could get the train up to about 30 mph and was strong enough to pull five cars behind the locomotive.

When the Viewliner debuted as a B-ticket attraction in Disneyland's third summer, it had two complete trains, one blue and one red, running on the same track. There were stations in Fantasyland and **Tomorrowland**, with each train operating from just one (blue in Fantasyland, red in Tomorrowland). Not only were the trains painted differently, their 32-passenger cars had themed names—*Alice*, *Bambi*, *Cinderella*, *Pinocchio*, and *Tinkerbell* for the Fantasyland cars, and *Mars*, *Mercury*, *Jupiter*, *Saturn*, and *Venus* for the Tomorrowland cars (no *Pluto*, since that name applied both to Disney characters and planets). The trains looped through the two lands and around the sites of what would become important attractions in 1959—**Matterhorn Mountain** and the **Submarine Voyage** lagoon. The park's 1958 **souvenir book** featured two photos of the Viewliner and described it as "low" and "speedy."

Almost 1.5 million guests rode the trains, but just a year after the first run the Viewliner's days were already numbered once Walt Disney began investigating an experimental new monorail line in Germany. Only 15 months after opening, the Viewliner was closing, and nine months after that Disneyland's **Monorail** was up and running, its loading area right where the Viewliner's Tomorrowland station had been (the actual Viewliner station moved to the back of the **Tomorrowland Autopia** to become the Tomorrowland station for the Santa Fe & Disneyland Railroad; the Viewliner's Fantasyland station disappeared altogether). Attempts to recycle the Viewliner trains into other civic projects around Los Angeles fell through, and two decades later they were demolished.

Uillage Inn, aka Uillage Haus

MAP: Fantasyland, Fa-10

CHRONOLOGY: May 25, 1983–ongoing

HISTORY: Back when the **Mickey Mouse Club Theater**, aka the Fantasyland Theater, was drawing guests to the northwest end of the **Sleeping Beauty Castle** courtyard, the closest thing to an eatery in the immediate area were the little **Welch's Grape Juice Stand** and the quick-serve **Character Foods** hut. Everything changed in the spring of '83 with the landmark remodel of **Fantasyland**. The theater became **Pinocchio's Daring Journey**, Welch's and Character Foods disappeared, and **Dumbo the Flying Elephant** moved eastward where **Skull Rock and Pirate Cove** had been. The area's main restaurant became the alpine-styled, gable-roofed Village Inn, attached to the back of the Pinocchio building and sprawling out to Dumbo's former space. Later the Inn became the Haus, which is how it's named today.

Two food companies, Sun Giant for the first decade and Minute Maid thereafter, have sponsored what is Fantasyland's main dining destination. Inside, wood carvings punctuate the décor and wall murals depict the plot of Disney's 1940 *Pinocchio* movie. The menu has gotten increasingly well-rounded over the years, shifting from basic burgers and fries to pizzas, pastas, sandwiches, and salads, with even egg breakfasts occasionally available. Seating is available inside and out, with the outdoor tables offering views of the nearby **Casey Jr. Circus Train**. Guests dine aware that below them is a subterranean maze of storerooms, offices, food-prep areas, and more.

Uillains Lair

MAP: Fantasyland, Fa-30

CHRONOLOGY: October 3, 1998–July 1, 2004

HISTORY: For such a choice location—first store on the right as guests walk north from **Sleeping Beauty Castle** into the **Fantasyland** courtyard—this building sure has gone through lots of tenants. **Merlin's Magic Shop**, the **Briar Rose Cottage**, **Quasimodo's Attic**, and the **Knight Shop** have all operated here with varying success and varying longevity. Notable among the prior occupants was the **Disney Villains** shop, purveyor of villain-themed merchandise from '91 to '96.

In '98, the bad guys rebounded with a new shop in the old location. This one, the Villains Lair, reprised the dark themes from earlier in the decade. After four years of selling lots of scary costume accessories, apparel with images of wicked queens, and creepy glow-in-the-dark gifts, the Villains Lair started to operate on an infrequent schedule and was closed completely by the end of 2004. Though the

Heraldry Shoppe is now in this building, rumors persist that evil still lurks here on the south side of the **Peter Pan Flight** attraction and that some kind of villainous store may eventually reopen.

Jack Wagner

CHRONOLOGY: October 17, 1925–June 16, 1995

HISTORY: "The Voice of Disneyland" was born in California in 1925. Surrounded by a musical family, Jack Wagner was in show business at a young age and was working for MGM in his teens. As an adult Wagner got many supporting parts on popular TV shows of the '50s, among them *The Adventures of Ozzie and Harriet*, *Dragnet*, and *Sea Hunt*. Fluent in several languages and possessor of a warm, resonant voice, Wagner was also a popular radio personality in Southern California, which brought him invitations to do some announcing for Disneyland's parades and special events in the '50s and '60s.

He began working at Disneyland full-time in 1970 as its official announcer, replacing actor Rex Allen in that role. For the next two decades, it was Wagner's friendly, welcoming voice that was heard narrating the train trip around the park, politely requesting riders on the **Matterhorn Bobsleds** to "remain seated please," giving cheerful safety spiels at numerous other attractions, delivering official announcements over the park's loudspeakers, and introducing the **Main Street Electrical Parade**. Most of these performances were recorded at Wagner's home studio a few miles from the park.

In addition to his Disneyland work, Wagner produced Disney-themed records, made announcements for Disney special events, and did voice-overs on TV commercials. He also performed the announcements for other Disney theme parks and for other public entities (his voice can still be heard on Walt Disney World's Monorail and at the Orlando International Airport). Jack Wagner retired in 1991 after undergoing vocal cord surgery and died from a heart attack four years later. He was named a Disney Legend in 2005.

Tommy and Vesey Walker

CHRONOLOGY: 1923–1986; 1893–1977

HISTORY: Together and apart, the son-and-father team of Tommy and Vesey Walker was closely tied to Disneyland for almost two decades. Of the two Walkers, Tommy was hired first, his title Director of Entertainment. Starting in 1955, he helped invent the famous **fireworks**, **parades**, Candlelight Procession, and other special events that quickly became crowd favorites and long-lasting Disneyland traditions. Prior to his Disneyland career, he'd been a decorated World War II vet, a drum major at USC, and the kicker on the school's football team. He's credited as the composer of the familiar six-note "da-da-da-DUT-da-DUH . . . CHARGE!" fanfare that's still heard in virtually every stadium in America.

In '65, Tommy Walker was credited at the end of a *Walt Disney's Wonderful*

World of Color episode as the "Disneyland Co-Ordinator." Two years later, after a dozen years at the park, he left to form his own entertainment company. Walker eventually orchestrated such events as the opening and closing ceremonies of three Olympic Games, Super Bowl halftime shows, the fireworks at the Statue of Liberty celebration in '86, the annual Independence Day fireworks shows at the Rose Bowl, and special performances at Radio City Music Hall. Tommy Walker died at age 63 in 1986 while undergoing heart surgery.

In July of '55, when he was looking for someone to organize and lead a marching band for the **Opening Day** festivities, Tommy Walker didn't have to look outside his own family. Vesey Walker, an Englishman born in 1893, had already led dozens of marching bands in the U.S., including the one for Marquette University. Vesey Walker's original Disneyland gig was supposed to end after two weeks, but it wound up lasting until 1970.

According to Bob Thomas's biography *Walt Disney: An American Original*, **Walt Disney** gave these instructions to Vesey Walker about the band's repertoire: "I just want you to remember one thing: if the people can't go away whistling it, don't play it." Whistling they were, and Vesey Walker's **Disneyland Band** in its crisp uniforms is a fond memory for millions of Disneyland guests. He was also a familiar presence in the park's **souvenir books**—from '55 to '68, he was in every single one, sometimes with two photos, and usually he was the only individual besides Walt Disney to be identified by name in the entire book. Working in pain in the late '60s, Walker overcame a rare paralyzing disease to make some final park appearances before retiring in 1970. Vesey Walker died seven years later and was inducted as a Disney Legend in 2005.

Walt Disney Story, aka Walt Disney Story, Featuring Great Moments with Mr. Lincoln

MAP: Town Square, TS-9

CHRONOLOGY: April 8, 1973–spring 2005

HISTORY: The **Legacy of Walt Disney**, a tribute to **Walt Disney** and his many accomplishments, ran on **Main Street** from 1970 to '73. When that corner space became **Disneyland Presents a Preview of Coming Attractions**, the awards and biographical material that had been there moved into the ground floor of the **Opera House** and received a new name. The Walt Disney Story was an expanded version of the previous Legacy display and for Disney fans constituted one of the most absorbing exhibits in the park. It replaced the Opera House's previous show devoted to another legendary American, **Great Moments with Mr. Lincoln**, though the Great Emancipator wouldn't be gone for long.

As the sign out front announced, the Walt Disney Story included everything "from Mickey Mouse to the Magic Kingdoms" and was "presented free by Gulf Oil." The Opera House's lobby area was filled with Disney artifacts and awards that celebrated his diverse roles as an artist, international ambassador of good will, naturalist (by way of the *True-Life Adventure* documentaries), TV pioneer, and moviemaker. Original art from Disney's animated films, props from his TV shows, family photos, early Mickey Mouse merchandise, and even the horseless carriage Walt Disney rode in for parades were all on view.

Disneyland itself was part of the show, as a fascinating high-speed film showed the park under construction. The most unusual display was also the most elaborate—a detailed re-creation of Walt Disney's actual office at the Disney Studios, with authentic furniture and decorations all accurately in place (some biographers state that though this office did exist at the studio, Disney usually preferred to work in a spare side room with a simple desk).

The second part of the exhibit was presented in the 500-seat Opera House theater. There a 28-minute film retold Walt Disney's life story. Rare film clips and Disney's own narration took guests from his Midwestern upbringing through his movie career and all the way up to the beginnings of Walt Disney World in Florida. As entertaining as the film was, guests expressed nostalgia for the **Audio-Animatronic** Mr. Lincoln. So, after closing on February 17, 1975, for a four-month remodel, on June 12, 1975 the exhibit reopened with Lincoln supplementing the film, making this a long presentation with a long compound title: The Walt Disney Story, Featuring Great Moments with Mr. Lincoln. In the '70s, the park's **souvenir books** proudly showed off the entire exhibit with several photos per book and detailed descriptive text.

Modifications came to the exhibit over the next decades—a huge, meticulous model of the U.S. Capitol was added to the lobby area, Mr. Lincoln was updated with new technology and a new Gettysburg presentation, and eventually the Disney film stopped showing. For 2005's "Happiest Homecoming on Earth" celebration of Disneyland's 50th anniversary, Lincoln was retired once again and the theater was turned over to a well-received film called *Disneyland: The First 50 Magical Years*.

In 2007, guests would find a big change in the lobby, where an intricate 180-square-foot model of **Opening Day** Disneyland had replaced the U.S. Capitol model, but no change in the theater, where the anniversary film still ran in place of Lincoln. Happily, history buffs can study lots of classic Disneyland art, early **cast member** uniforms, and fascinating park memorabilia inside the lobby's display cases.

Watches & Clocks, aka Timex Shop

MAP: Main Street, MS-13

CHRONOLOGY: July 17, 1955–1971

HISTORY: In 1954, exactly 100 years after its founding, Connecticut's Waterbury Clock Company renamed itself U.S. Time. That was the company's name when its new Watches & Clocks store debuted on Disneyland's **Main Street** on **Opening Day**. The shop's location was a small room one doorway south of the **Silhouette Studio** on Main Street's second right-hand block.

Timex watches, which U.S. Time had put on the market at the beginning of the decade, were the store's timeliest attractions; already ads were touting their hardiness as the affordable timepiece that "takes a licking and keeps on ticking." In fact, the shop was even informally referred to as the Timex Shop, even though the park's **souvenir books** of the '50s and '60s invariably labeled it Watches & Clocks.

Whatever it was called, many of the timepieces on display had Mickey Mouse faces and are now considered valuable collectibles. However, after 15 years time finally ran out on Watches & Clocks. **Crystal Arts** moved into this space around 1971, and soon Elgin's **New Century Watches & Clocks** across the way would become Main Street's primary watch store.

Welch's Grape Juice Stand

MAP: Fantasyland, Fa-9

CHRONOLOGY: 1956–1981

HISTORY: In the park's first three decades, **Fantasyland** had few eateries and even fewer eateries with a name sponsor. One of the latter was the Welch's Grape Juice Stand (as the park's **souvenir books** usually labeled it). Welch Foods, the juice company founded in the 1800s, also sponsored the Mickey Mouse Club, and thus the stand's location was especially appropriate—it shared the same building that housed the **Mickey Mouse Club Theater**. More precisely, Welch's was between **Snow White Adventures** and the theater and had an entrance that faced the original location of the **Mad Hatter's Mad Tea Party** (if Welch's was still there today, it would be facing the **King Arthur Carrousel**).

Exclusively promoting the company's main product, the Welch's concession was painted with grape-themed murals. The counter sold cold cups of purple, red, and white grape juice, with frozen grape bars an even icier option.

In 1982, the massive remodel that upended Fantasyland finally brought the Juice Stand's 26-year run to a halt. In May of '83, the beautifully styled **Pinocchio's Daring Journey** and **Geppetto's Arts & Crafts** opened where the theater and Welch's had been.

Westward Ho Conestoga Wagon Fries

MAP: Frontierland, Fr-18

CHRONOLOGY: November 16, 1998–ongoing

HISTORY: Even though it's a relatively modest little eatery in what seems like an out-of-the-way spot alongside the **Rivers of America**, Westward Ho Conestoga Wagon Fries (the cumbersome name used on the signage) has several connections to Disneyland's past. In the '50s, back when the nearby **Big Thunder Mountain** area was called the **Painted Desert**, the **Conestoga Wagons** attraction operated near this part of **Frontierland**; those wagons had the words "Westward Ho!" painted on them.

Another connection is to something that still exists, the similarly named **Westward Ho Trading Co.**, which has been operating about 300 feet away at the Frontierland entrance since 1987. Both Westward Ho spots echo *Westward Ho, the Wagons!*, a 1956 Disney movie about pioneers on the move. The Conestoga Wagon Fries stand actually resembles one of those wooden plains-crossing vehicles from the 1800s.

There's yet one more connection between the Conestoga Wagon Fries stand and something else in the park. The stand's sponsor, McDonald's, has another eatery, the **Harbour Galley**, on the other side of the river in front of **Splash Mountain**. Both places sell virtually the exact same thing—McDonald's fries and sodas.

Westward Ho Trading Co.

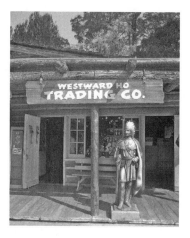

MAP: Frontierland, Fr-27

CHRONOLOGY: September 2, 1987–ongoing

HISTORY: What had been the three-decades-old **Frontier Trading Post** was transformed into the Westward Ho Trading Company around Labor Day in 1987. The rustic sign out front announced the shop as the rhyming Westward Ho Trading Co. The first part of the name alludes to a 1956 Disney movie starring Fess Parker called *Westward Ho, the Wagons!*

A small exterior sign describes the merchandise, which used to be souvenirs but then switched to sweets. The wide candy selection has included gourmet chocolates, jelly beans, cookies, and more. In recent years the store has also pushed pins and frontier-style hats, including classic coonskin caps and Mouse ears. At times the store has also been filled with the holiday ornaments and decorations that were formerly in **La Boutique de Noël** over in **New Orleans Square**. That five-foot-tall cigar-store Indian on the front sidewalk, incidentally, is a twin of the one in front of the **20th Century Music Company** on **Main Street**.

Wheelhouse and Delta Banjo

MAP: Frontierland, Fr-6

CHRONOLOGY: 1974–ca. 1990

HISTORY: In the mid-'70s, these two fast-food eateries replaced the tiny **Malt Shop and Cone Shop** next door to the **River Belle Terrace**. The Wheelhouse, its name an allusion to the nearby *Mark Twain*, was mainly a weekend spot for burgers, sodas, and ice cream; the Delta Banjo, its name an allusion to a restaurant that had been in this location in the late '50s, **Don DeFore's Silver Banjo Barbecue**, was a sandwich-and-snacks seller of limited menu and hours. By 1990 both had been lost to remodels.

Wonderland Music, aka Main Street Music

MAP: Main Street, MS-13; Town Square, TS-8

CHRONOLOGY: 1960–1972

HISTORY: After briefly trying out a spot in the second right-hand block of **Main Street** near the **Kodak Camera Center**, in 1960 the Wonderland Music store settled into a space on **Town Square.** This new location was just north of the entrance into the **Opera House**, a room that from '56 to '59 was **Jimmy Starr's Show Business Souvenirs.**

With Wonderland there in place of Jimmy Starr, the business on show was all Disney's, since Wonderland sold the company's own movie soundtracks on vinyl records, more vinyl by Disneyland entertainers, and sheet music of Disney songs. From '63 on, the park's **souvenir books** labeled this shop with the generic name Main Street Music, perhaps to help guests better locate it.

Wonderland wandered off in '72, leaving the space vacant for three years until it was used as a hospitality center into the '80s and as an infrequent guest-relations office in the '90s. Today those Disney musical classics can still be found nearby in the **20th Century Music Company** next to the **Main Street Cinema.**

C.U. Wood

CHRONOLOGY: 1922–March 14, 1992

HISTORY: One of the almost-forgotten members of the core Disneyland-planning team was Cornelius Vanderbilt Wood, a Texan born in 1922 (some profiles call him an Oklahoman). Though only in his early 30s, Wood was hired to be Disneyland's first general manager as the park was being constructed.

Wood's background was in industrial engineering. Prior to his Disneyland years, he was a manager at the Stanford Research Institute, the same firm where **Harrison Price** worked (**Walt Disney** hired Price in 1953 to scout out locations for Disneyland, and Wood then helped persuade Anaheim landowners to sell their plots to Disney). Joining up with Disney full-time, Wood quickly brought **Joe Fowler** and **Van Arsdale France** onto the nascent Disneyland project—Fowler would rise from a position as consultant to become supervisor of the park's construction, and France would eventually be in charge of training all Disneyland employees.

Harrison Price called Wood one of the "boldest, smartest, most shameless and colorful characters ever to career through this business" in his book *Walt's Revolution!* Working with Wood, concluded Price, was "never dull." In his memoir *Window on Main Street*, Van France described Wood as a "masterful salesman" who "could easily compete with the legendary P.T. Barnum." France also claimed that it was Wood's idea to bring in corporate lessees like Swift and TWA to help loosen the park's tight financial situation.

It was Wood who oversaw the daily logistics: pre-opening, these included such details as having the official **Opening Day** invitations printed up, and post-opening it meant that Wood and his team were going to run Disneyland, setting everything from park policies to park hours. However, soon after Opening Day (within a week, according to Harrison Price), Walt Disney relieved Wood of his duties so that Disney himself could oversee daily operations. Some stories suggest they had a serious falling out, possibly because Wood had taken credit for designing Disneyland; Price claimed that a separation was inevitable because of Wood's and Disney's immiscible personalities (the scabrous Wood easily offended the conservative Disney with off-color jokes).

Wood responded by starting his own amusement parks in Colorado, Massachusetts, and New York. Of these, the one in the Bronx was the most famous. Called Freedomland U.S.A., and promoted as "The World's Largest Entertainment Center" because it sat on 205 acres (as compared to Disneyland's 160), the park operated from 1960 to 1964. Wood, dubbing himself "The Master Builder of Disneyland," was aided by former Disneyland employees. His park even echoed Disneyland's themed layout, though Freedomland's themes all derived from American history. Unfortunately, a fire that destroyed some of the buildings three months before the park opened, a serious ride accident in the first month, and a robbery in the first summer all contributed to the park's immediate financial problems. When the 1964–1965 New York World's Fair opened in Queens, Freedomland U.S.A. was declared bankrupt, and some of its rides were scattered to other amusement parks.

Later Wood cofounded the International Chili Society, he helped bring London Bridge to Lake Havasu in Arizona, he co-designed Lake Havasu City, and he even landed a small part in a B movie. After a lifetime of heavy smoking, C.V. Wood died of cancer in 1992. Despite his early contributions to Disneyland, there's no mention of him on the **Main Street windows**, and official references to Wood seem to have been purged from Disney's public literature.

World Beneath Us Exhibit

MAP: Tomorrowland, T-6

CHRONOLOGY: Summer 1955–December 1959

HISTORY: In 1955, the Richfield Oil Corporation sponsored two different locations in Disneyland. One—the **Tomorrowland Autopia**—used gas, while the other—the World Beneath Us Exhibit—promoted it. The World Beneath Us was located in a rectangular building on the left-hand side of **Tomorrowland**. To the left (back towards the **Plaza Hub**) was the circular display of **Space Station X-1**, and to the right (towards the lagoon) was the **Art Corner**.

The park's 1956 **souvenir book** described the exhibit as a "Cinemascope Technicolor Cartoon & Diorama" telling "the story of oil." That cartoon, titled *The World Beneath Us*, had prehistoric cavemen teaching modern audiences how oil is formed, with dinosaurs alongside to help illustrate the process (the '58 souvenir book emphasized the connection between decaying dinos and plentiful petroleum by placing a drawing of a dinosaur in front of an oil rig). The exhibit ended with a diorama and a map of the L.A. basin that highlighted the oil fields along the coast.

The Richfield exhibit ran out of gas at the end of '59. Two months later, the next-door neighbor, Space Station X-1 (renamed the Satellite View of America) came back to Earth, and three months after that, in May of 1960, the **Art of Animation** exhibit filled the building with a display promoting Disney's animated movies.

Wurlitzer Music Hall

MAP: Main Street, MS-20

CHRONOLOGY: July 17, 1955–September 1968

HISTORY: In the park's first decade, guests streaming northward from **Town Square** onto **Main Street** encountered the Wurlitzer Music Hall on the first right-hand corner. Eastward, to the right, of the Wurlitzer shop on Town Square was the **Maxwell House Coffee Shop**, while to the north along Main Street was the **Main Street Magic Shop**.

The Wurlitzer space was big, for a big product—as the signage out front declared, this shop housed pianos and organs. The shop was listed in the park's 1958 **souvenir book** in the Special Shows and Exhibits category in back, the announcement there describing "daily organ concerts and display of pianos and organs" and the illustration depicting a pianist at an upright piano. Pianos were indeed played in the shop by pianists, mechanical player pianos rolled out traditional tunes, and guests were invited to sing along, though how many bought pianos while shopping at Disneyland is debatable.

The Rudolf Wurlitzer Company pulled out its sponsorship and its instruments in 1968. About a year later, the prominent corner was refashioned as an awards-filled celebration called the **Legacy of Walt Disney**.

Yacht Club, aka Yacht Bar

MAP: Tomorrowland, T-10, T-7

CHRONOLOGY: Summer 1955–September 6, 1966

HISTORY: At one time Disneyland had its own Yacht Club, though it wasn't as posh or exclusive as it sounds. Basically a place for fast food, the Yacht Club was a freestanding eatery alongside the **Tomorrowland** lagoon and the short-lived **Phantom Boats** (hence the "yacht" reference). The aquatic theme was effected with an exterior display of nautical pennants; the rest of the building looked more like an old McDonald's franchise with its counter service and an angled roof extending out over the customers.

In '57, the Yacht Club got a new location—not just a different place that the name transferred to, but literally a new site for the entire structure. With the **Viewliner** and its station about to be built, the Yacht Club was lifted and moved about 75 feet away from the lagoon (two years later, the **Monorail** station would stand where the Yacht Club had been). The Yacht Club restarted as the Yacht Bar, though the burgers-and-fries menu stayed about the same.

The 1959 **souvenir book** listed a Yacht Bar Dance Area adjacent to the Yacht Bar, a foreshadowing of future developments. In '66, a major remodel of Tomorrowland sank the Yacht Bar for good, and near its place the **Tomorrowland Terrace** arose with a zesty dance area of its own.

Yale & Towne Lock Shop

MAP: Main Street, MS-19

CHRONOLOGY: July 17, 1955–1964

HISTORY: Looking for sponsors to help launch his park, **Walt Disney** enticed the Yale & Towne Lock Company to set up business on **Main Street**. Inventor Linus Yale had patented pin-tumbler locks in the mid-1800s and then partnered with Henry Towne in 1868 to build a Connecticut factory. Soon Yale & Towne was America's premier lock manufacturer, successful enough to diversify later into forklifts and industrial vehicles.

At Disneyland, the Yale & Towne Lock Shop was located just to the south of the prominent **Market House** on the right-hand side of Main. Y&T was listed in the Special Shows and Exhibits section in the back of the park's 1958 **souvenir book**; there an illustration showed a lock and a key, and the text described "a complete display of the locksmith's art, from the oldest to the newest." One wall in the store told "The Story of Locks," another displayed hundreds of keys. As unexciting as all this might sound, the Lock Shop lasted for almost 10 years. A short-lived gift retailer called Fantasia moved in around 1966 but soon got absorbed into the **Jewelry Shop** next door. In 1986, **Disneyana** settled in for its ongoing stay.

Year of a Million Dreams

CHRONOLOGY: October 1, 2006–2008

HISTORY: In 1971, Disneyland became the site of a special event called the Year of a Hundred Million Smiles. Some special giveaways helped count down the wait for guest number 100,000,000 to walk through the park's turnstiles, a moment that finally occurred on June 17th of that year. Thirty-five years later, as soon as the 18-month celebration of Disneyland's 50th anniversary concluded, the park introduced its Year of a Million Dreams, all of them undoubtedly leading to a million smiles.

Among the million gifts and opportunities offered to guests were special pins and Mickey Mouse ears, free meals in the park, invitations to march along in Disneyland **parades**, and instant **FastPass** badges for quick access to attractions. The biggest giveaways were overnight stays in the Mickey Mouse Penthouse at the adjacent Disneyland

Hotel and world-tour trips to other Disney parks. No purchase was required, and no special qualifications or competitions helped guests anticipate the sudden, surprising appearance of wish-granting Dream Squad members who toted black bags with special Year of a Million Dreams logos.

Originally, the Year of a Million Dreams was scheduled to last 15, not 12, months, going from October 1, 2006, to December 31, 2007. But halfway through 2007 the promotion's ongoing popularity prompted Disney execs to extend the Disney Dreams Giveaway to the end of 2008 and to dangle a new dream in front of guests—a chance to stay overnight in the **New Orleans Square** rooms formerly occupied by the **Disney Gallery.**

Yumz, aka Louie's, aka Meeko's, aka Fantasyland Theater Snacks, aka Troubadour Treats

MAP: Fantasyland, Fa-17

CHRONOLOGY: June 19, 1985–ongoing

HISTORY: The tradition of serving fast food next to the big outdoor theater at the north end of **Fantasyland** began in mid-1985. That's when Yumz, a small snack stand, opened at about the same time as **Videopolis**, a new dance and concert area. The food at Yumz, just like the music next door, was teen-friendly. Basic nachos, pizza, popcorn, and sodas were the quick-serve items available at the compact counters.

Another tradition, that of updating the name of this eatery to match whatever was happening on the adjacent stage, began in '91. When Videopolis began presenting a live show called *Plane Crazy*, Yumz briefly changed its name to Louie's in keeping with the stage show's TV connection (Louie, of Huey, Dewey, and Louie fame, was also on the *Disney Afternoon* program that had spun off *Plane Crazy*). Yumz was soon restored, and then in '95 everything in this area got revised: Videopolis became the Fantasyland Theater, *The Spirit of Pocahontas* moved onto the stage for a long run, and the snack stand, while retaining its simple menu, was renamed Meeko's after the talking raccoon. Meeko's offered the same basic snack food as its predecessor, all the quick carbs and drinks a busy theatergoer could want.

Some two and a half years after opening, when the theater began showing *Animazement—The Musical*, Meeko's got remodeled first into Fantasyland Theater Snacks and then later into Troubadour Treats. As usual, the hours of operation generally coincided with those of the neighboring show. In 2004, when *Snow White—An Enchanting Musical* moved into the theater, Troubadour Treats got a new name, some new décor, and a new transformation into **Enchanted Cottage Sweets & Treats.**

Appendix
Land by Land in Disneyland
(this book's entries listed by category)

Adventureland

Attractions
Aladdin's Oasis
Big Game Safari Shooting Gallery
Enchanted Tiki Room
Indiana Jones Adventure
Jungle Cruise
Magnolia Park
Swiss Family Treehouse
Tarzan's Treehouse

Restaurants
Bengal Barbecue
Indy Fruit Cart
Sunkist, I Presume
Tahitian Terrace, aka Stouffer's in Disneyland Tahitian Terrace
Tiki Juice Bar
Tropical Cantina, aka Adventureland Cantina

Stores
Adventureland Bazaar
Indiana Jones Adventure Outpost
Safari Outpost
South Seas Traders
Tiki Tropical Traders, aka Tropical Imports

Bear Country/Critter Country

Attractions
Country Bear Jamboree, aka Country Bear Playhouse
Many Adventures of Winnie the Pooh
Splash Mountain
Teddi Barra's Swingin' Arcade

Restaurants
Brer Bar

Critter Country Fruit Cart
Golden Bear Lodge, aka Hungry Bear Restaurant
Harbour Galley
Mile Long Bar

Stores
Briar Patch
Critter Country Plush
Crocodile Mercantile
Pooh Corner
Professor Barnaby Owl's Photographic Art Studio
Ursus H. Bear's Wilderness Outpost

Fantasyland

Attractions
Alice in Wonderland
Baloo's Dressing Room
Canal Boats of the World
Casey Jr. Circus Train
Disney Afternoon Avenue
Dumbo the Flying Elephant
Fantasia Gardens
Fantasyland Autopia
It's a Small World
Junior Autopia
Keller's Jungle Killers
King Arthur Carrousel
Mad Hatter's Mad Tea Party
Matterhorn Bobsleds
Matterhorn Mountain
Mickey Mouse Club Circus
Mickey Mouse Club Theater, aka Fantasyland Theater
Midget Autopia
Motor Boat Cruise, aka Motor Boat Cruise to Gummi Glen
Mr. Toad's Wild Ride
Peter Pan Flight, aka Peter Pan's Flight
Pinocchio's Daring Journey
Princess Fantasy Faire
Skull Rock and Pirate's Cove, aka Skull Rock Cove
Skyway to Fantasyland and Skyway to Tomorrowland
Sleeping Beauty Castle
Sleeping Beauty Castle Walk-Through

Snow White Adventures, aka Snow White's Scary Adventures
Snow White Wishing Well and Grotto
Storybook Land Canal Boats
Sword in the Stone Ceremony
Topiary Garden
Videopolis, aka Fantasyland Theater

Restaurants
Carrousel Candies
Castle Candy Kitchen, aka Castle Candy Shoppe
Character Foods, aka Character Food Facilities
Enchanted Cottage Sweets & Treats
Pirate Ship Restaurant, aka Chicken of the Sea Pirate Ship and Restaurant,
      aka Captain Hook's Galley
Village Inn, aka Village Haus
Welch's Grape Juice Stand
Yumz, aka Louie's, aka Meeko's, aka Fantasyland Theater Snacks,
      aka Troubadour Treats

Stores
Arts and Crafts Shop
Briar Rose Cottage
Castle Arts
Castle Christmas Shop
Clock Shop
Disney Villains
Fairytale Arts
Fantasy Faire Gifts, aka Fantasy Shop, aka Fantasy Emporium,
      aka Fantasy Gift Faire
50th Anniversary Shop
Geppetto's Arts & Crafts, aka Geppetto's Toys & Gifts,
      aka Geppetto's Holiday Workshop
Heraldry Shoppe, aka Castle Heraldry
It's a Small World Toy Shop
Knight Shop
Le Petit Chalet
Mad Hatter of Fantasyland
Merlin's Magic Shop
Mickey's Christmas Chalet
Names Unraveled
Princess Boutique
Quasimodo's Attic, aka Sanctuary of Quasimodo
Stromboli's Wagon
Three Fairies Magic Crystals

Tinker Bell & Friends
Tinker Bell Toy Shoppe, aka Once Upon a Time . . . the Disney Princess Shoppe
Villain's Lair

Frontierland

Attractions
American Rifle Exhibit and Frontier Gun Shop
Big Thunder Mountain Railroad
Big Thunder Ranch, aka Festival of Fools, aka Little Patch of Heaven
Conestoga Wagons
Davy Crockett Arcade, aka Davy Crockett Frontier Arcade
Davy Crockett Frontier Museum
Fantasmic!
Fowler's Harbor, aka Fowler's Landing
Frontierland Miniature Museum
Frontierland Shooting Gallery, aka Frontierland Shootin' Arcade,
    aka Frontierland Shootin' Exposition, aka Frontierland Shooting Exposition
Golden Horseshoe
Indian Village
Indian War Canoes, aka Davy Crockett's Explorer Canoes
Mark Twain Riverboat
Marshal's Office
Mexican Village
Mike Fink Keel Boats
Mineral Hall
Miniature Horse Corral
Mule Pack, aka Rainbow Ridge Mule Pack,
    aka Pack Mules Through Nature's Wonderland
Nature's Wonderland
Painted Desert, aka Rainbow Desert
Petrified Tree
Rafts to Tom Sawyer Island
Rainbow Caverns Mine Train, aka Western Mine Train Through Nature's Wonderland
Rivers of America
Sailing Ship *Columbia*
Santa's Reindeer Round-Up
Stage Coach
Tom Sawyer Island, aka Pirate's Lair on Tom Sawyer Island

Restaurants
Aunt Jemima's Pancake House, aka Aunt Jemima's Kitchen
Big Thunder Barbecue, aka Festival of Foods
Casa de Fritos, aka Casa Mexicana

Chicken Plantation, aka Plantation House, aka Chicken Shack
Don DeFore's Silver Banjo Barbecue
Magnolia Tree Terrace
Malt Shop and Cone Shop
New Orleans Barbecue
Oaks Tavern
Rancho del Zocalo Restaurante
River Belle Terrace
Stage Door Café
Westward Ho Conestoga Wagon Fries
Wheelhouse and Delta Banjo

Stores
Bonanza Outfitters
Bone Carving Shop
Calico Kate's Pantry Shop
Davy Crockett's Pioneer Mercantile, aka Pioneer Mercantile
El Zocalo, aka El Zocalo Park
Frontier Trading Post
Indian Trading Post
Leather Shop
Pendleton Woolen Mills Dry Goods Store
Silver Spur Supplies
Westward Ho Trading Co.

Main Street

Attractions
Carefree Corner
Disneyland Presents a Preview of Coming Attractions
Legacy of Walt Disney
Main Street Cinema
Main Street Electrical Parade
Main Street Shooting Gallery
Main Street vehicles
Main Street windows
Penny Arcade

Restaurants
Blue Ribbon Bakery
Candy Palace, aka Candy Palace and Candy Kitchen
Carnation Café
Carnation Ice Cream Parlor
Gibson Girl Ice Cream Parlor

Main Street Cone Shop
Main Street Fruit Cart
Puffin Bakery, aka Puffin Bake Shop
Refreshment Corner, aka Coke Corner, aka Coca-Cola Refreshment Corner
Sunkist Citrus House

Stores
Candle Shop
Card Corner
Carriage Place Clothing Co.
China Closet
Coin Shop, aka Stamp and Coin Shop
Cole of California Swimsuits
Crystal Arcade
Crystal Arts
Disneyana
Disney Clothiers, Ltd.
Disney Showcase
Ellen's Gift Shop
Emporium, aka Disneyland Emporium
Fine Tobacco
Flower Mart, aka Flower Market
Gallen-Kamp Stores Co.
Gibson Greeting Cards
Glass Blower
Grandma's Baby Shop
Hallmark Card Shop
Hurricane Lamp Shop
Intimate Apparel, aka Corset Shop
Jemrock Shop
Jewelry Shop, aka Rings 'n' Things
Kodak Camera Center, aka GAF Photo Salon, aka Polaroid Camera Center
Locker Area, aka Main Street Lockers & Storage
Mad Hatter of Main Street
Main Street Magic Shop
Main Street Photo Supply
Market House
New Century Watches & Clocks, aka New Century Timepieces and
    New Century Jewelry
Patented Pastimes, aka Great American Pastimes
Pen Shop
Ruggles China and Glass Shop
Silhouette Studio
Story Book Shop, aka Western Printing Book Shop
Sunny-View Farms Jams & Jellies

20th Century Music Company
Upjohn Pharmacy
Watches & Clocks, aka Timex Shop
Wonderland Music, aka Main Street Music
Wurlitzer Music Hall
Yale & Towne Lock Shop

Mickey's Toontown

Attractions
Chip 'n Dale Tree House
Donald's Boat, aka *Miss Daisy*
Gadget's Go Coaster
Goofy's Bounce House, aka Goofy's Playhouse
Goofy's Gas Station
Jolly Trolley
Mickey's House
Minnie's House
Roger Rabbit's Car Toon Spin

Restaurants
Clarabelle's Frozen Yogurt
Daisy's Diner
Pluto's Dog House
Toon Up Treats

Stores
Gag Factory
Toontown Five & Dime

New Orleans Square

Attractions
Disney Gallery
Haunted Mansion
Pirate's Arcade Museum
Pirates of the Caribbean
Portrait Artists

Restaurants
Blue Bayou
Candy Cart
Chocolate Collection, aka Chocolat Rue Royale
Club 33

Creole Café, aka Café Orleans
French Market
Le Petite Patisserie
Mint Julep Bar
Royal Street Sweets
Royal Street Veranda

Stores
Bookstand
Cristal d'Orleans
Jewel of Orléans
La Boutique de Noël
La Boutique d'Or
Laffite's Silver Shop
La Mascarade d'Orléans
Le Bat en Rouge
Le Chapeau
Le Forgeron
Le Gourmet, aka Le Gourmet Shop
L'Ornement Magique
Marché aux Fleurs, Sacs et Mode
Mlle. Antoinette's Parfumerie
One-of-a-Kind Shop
Parasol Cart
Pieces of Eight
Port d'Orleans
Port Royal

Plaza Hub

Attractions
Baby Station, aka Baby Center, aka Baby Care Center
Bandstand
First Aid and Lost Children
Partners

Restaurants
Little Red Wagon
Plaza Gardens, aka Carnation Plaza Gardens
Plaza Pavilion Restaurant, aka Stouffer's in Disneyland Plaza Pavillion
Red Wagon Inn, aka Plaza Inn

Tomorrowland

Attractions
Adventures in Science
Adventure Thru Inner Space
Alpine Gardens
American Dairy Association Exhibit, aka Dairy Bar
American Space Experience
America Sings
Art of Animation
Astro-Jets, aka Tomorrowland Jets, aka Rocket Jets
Astro-Orbitor
Avenue of the Flags
Bathroom of Tomorrow
Bell Telephone Systems Phone Exhibits
Buzz Lightyear Astro Blasters
Captain EO
Carousel of Progress
Circarama, aka Circle-Vision, aka Circle-Vision 360,
     aka World Premiere Circle-Vision
Clock of the World, aka World Clock
Club Buzz
Corridor of Murals
Cosmic Waves
Court of Honor
Fashions and Fabrics Through the Ages
Flight Circle, aka Thimble Drome Flight Circle
Flying Saucers
Grand Canyon Diorama
Hall of Aluminum Fame
Hall of Chemistry
Honey, I Shrunk the Audience
House of the Future
Innoventions
King Triton Gardens, aka Triton Gardens
Magic Eye Theater
Mermaids
Mission to Mars
Monorail, aka Disneyland-Alweg Monorail , aka Disneyland Monorail
Moonliner
New York World's Fair Exhibit
Observatron
Our Future in Colors, aka Color Gallery
PeopleMover
Phantom Boats

Primeval World Diorama
Radio Disney Broadcast Booth
Rocket Man, Space Girl, and Space Man
Rocket Rods
Rocket to the Moon, aka Flight to the Moon
Skyway to Fantasyland and Skyway to Tomorrowland
Space Mountain, aka Rockin' Space Mountain
Space Station X-1, aka Satellite View of America
Starcade
Star Tours
Submarine Voyage, aka Finding Nemo Submarine Voyage
Tomorrowland Autopia, aka Autopia, Presented by Chevron
Tomorrowland Stage, aka Space Stage
Tomorrowland Terrace
Toy Story Funhouse
20,000 Leagues Under the Sea Exhibit
Viewliner
World Beneath Us Exhibit

Restaurants
Lunching Pad
Redd Rockett's Pizza Port
Space Bar
Space Place
Spirit of Refreshment
Yacht Club, aka Yacht Bar

Stores
Art Corner
Autopia Winner's Circle
Character Shop
Fun Fotos
Hobbyland
Little Green Men Store Command
Mad Hatter of Tomorrowland, aka Mod Hatter, aka Hatmosphere
Premiere Shop
Star Trader
Tomorrowlanding

Town Square

Attractions
Apartments
Babes in Toyland Exhibit

Bank of America, aka Bank of Main Street, aka Annual Pass Center
City Hall
Dalmatian Celebration
Fire Department, aka Fire Station
Flagpole
Great Moments with Mr. Lincoln
Guest Relations
Lost and Found
Opera House
Police Station
Santa Fe & Disneyland Railroad, aka Disneyland Railroad
Tour Guides
Walt Disney Story, aka Walt Disney Story, Featuring Great Moments
    with Mr. Lincoln

Restaurants
American Egg House
Hills Bros. Coffee House and Coffee Garden
Maxwell House Coffee Shop
Town Square Café

Stores
Jimmy Starr's Show Business Souvenirs
Mad Hatter of Main Street
Mickey Mouse Club Headquarters, aka Mickey Mouse Club Shop
Town Square Realty
Wonderland Music, aka Main Street Music

Other Park Locations

Berm
Entrance
First Aid and Lost Children
Holidayland
Ken-L Land Pet Motel, aka Kennel Club, aka Pet Care Kennel
Marquee
Newsstand
Parking Lot
Photo Collages
Pin Trading Stations
Pony Farm, aka Circle D Corral
Restrooms
Stroller Shop

Park Areas and Attractions Never Built

Chinatown
Discovery Bay
Duck Bumps
Edison Square
International Street
Liberty Street
Lilliputian Land
Peter Pan Crocodile Aquarium
Reel-Ride
Rock Candy Mountain, aka Candy Mountain

Profiles of Disneyland Pioneers

Milt Albright
Ken Anderson
Hideo Aramaki
X Atencio
Buddy Baker
Mary Blair
Chuck Boyajian
Roger Broggie
George Bruns
Harriet Burns
Claude Coats
Bill Cottrell
Rolly Crump
Marc and Alice Davis
Marvin Davis
Roy O. Disney
Walt Disney
Don Edgren
Peter Ellenshaw
Morgan "Bill" Evans
Joe Fowler
Van Arsdale France
Blaine Gibson
Harper Goff
Yale Gracey
Bob Gurr
John Hench

Richard Irvine
Ub Iwerks
Robert Jani
Fred Joerger
Mary Jones
Bill Justice
Jack Lindquist
Bill Martin
George McGinnis
Sam McKim
Edward Meck
Dick Nunis
Jack Olsen
Harrison Price
Cicely Rigdon
Wathel Rogers
Herb Ryman
Richard and Robert Sherman
Martin Sklar
C.V. Wood

Profiles of Disneyland Performers

All American College Band
Wally Boag
Fulton Burley
Charles Dickens Carolers
Dapper Dans
Disneyland Band
Dixieland at Disneyland
Firehouse Five Plus Two
Paul Frees
Kids of the Kingdom
Thurl Ravenscroft
Royal Street Bachelors
Strawhatters
Betty Taylor
Tinker Bell
Jack Wagner
Tommy and Vesey Walker

Events and Celebrations

Blast to the Past Celebration
Christmas
Circus Fantasy
Date Nite
Dream Machine
Fireworks
Gift-Giver Extraordinaire Machine
Grad Nite
Halloween Time
Love Bug Day
New Year's Eve Party
Opening Day
Parades
State Fair
Year of a Million Dreams

Films and Television

A Day at Disneyland
Disneyland: The First 50 Magical Years
Disneyland TV series
Disneyland, U.S.A.
Gala Day at Disneyland
The Magic of Disneyland

Miscellaneous

Attraction Posters
Audio-Animatronics
Cast Members
Disney Dollars
FastPass
Hidden Mickeys
Miss Disneyland, aka Disneyland Ambassador to the World
Omnimover
Passports
Souvenir Books, aka Souvenir Guide Books, aka Pictorial Souvenir Books
Ticket Books

Bibliography

Anonymous. *Disneyland: The First Quarter Century*. Burbank, CA: Walt Disney Productions, 1979.

Anonymous. *Disneyland: The First Thirty Years*. Burbank, CA: Walt Disney Productions, 1985.

Bailey, Adrian. *Walt Disney's World of Fantasy*. New York: Everest House, 1982.

Bright, Randy. *Disneyland Inside Story*. New York: Harry N. Abrams, Inc., 1987.

Broggie, Michael. *Walt Disney's Railroad Story*. Pasadena, CA: Pentrex Media Group, 1997.

Childs, Valerie. *The Magic of Disneyland and Walt Disney World*. New York: Mayflower Books, Inc., 1979.

De Roos, Robert. "The Magic Worlds of Walt Disney." *National Geographic*, August 1963.

Dunlop, Beth. *Building a Dream: The Art of Disney Architecture*. New York: Harry N. Abrams, Inc., 1996.

Finch, Christopher. *The Art of Walt Disney*. New York: Harry N. Abrams, Inc., 1975.

France, Van Arsdale. *Window on Main Street*. Nashua, NH: Laughter Publications Inc., 1991.

Gabler, Neal. *Walt Disney: The Triumph of the American Imagination*. New York: Alfred A. Knopf, 2006.

Gordon, Bruce and David Mumford. *Disneyland: The Nickel Tour*. Santa Clarita, CA: Camphor Tree Publishers, 2000.

Gordon, Bruce and Tim O'Day. *Disneyland: Then, Now, and Forever*. Santa Clarita, CA: Camphor Tree/Disney Editions, 2005.

Green, Amy Boothe and Howard E. Green. *Remembering Walt: Favorite Memories of Walt Disney*. New York: Hyperion, 1999.

Greene, Richard and Katherine. *The Man Behind the Magic*. New York: Viking, 1998.

Hench, John with Peggy Van Pelt. *Designing Disney: Imagineering and the Art of the Show*. New York: Disney Editions, 2003.

Imagineers, The (text by Kevin Rafferty with Bruce Gordon). *Walt Disney Imagineering: A Behind the Dreams Look at Making the Magic Real*. New York: Hyperion, 1996.

Koenig, David. *More Mouse Tales: A Closer Peek Backstage at Disneyland*. Irvine, CA: Bonaventure Press, 2002.

Koenig, David. *Mouse Tales: A Behind-the-Ears Look at Disneyland*. Irvine, CA: Bonaventure Press, 1995.

Kurtti, Jeff and Bruce Gordon. *The Art of Disneyland*. New York: Disney Editions, 2006.

Lefkon, Wendy, ed. *Disney Insider Yearbook 2005*. New York: Disney Editions, 2006.

Maltin, Leonard. *The Disney Films*. New York: Popular Library, 1978.

Marling, Karal Ann, ed. *Designing Disney's Theme Parks: The Architecture of Reassurance*. New York: Flammarion, 1998.

Marling, Karal Ann with Donna R. Braden. *Behind the Magic: 50 Years of Disneyland*. Oakland, CA: The Henry Ford, 2005.

Martin, Steve. *Born Standing Up*. New York: Scribner, 2007.

Miller, Diane Disney. *The Story of Walt Disney*. New York: Henry Holt and Company, 1957.

Moore, Charles, Peter Becker, and Regula Campbell. *The City Observed: Los Angeles*. Santa Monica, CA: Hennessey + Ingalls, 1998.

Mosley, Leonard. *Disney's World: A Biography*. New York: Stein and Day Publishers, 1985.

Price, Harrison. *Walt's Revolution!: By the Numbers*. Orlando, FL: Ripley Entertainment Inc., 2003.

Ridgway, Charles. *Spinning Disney's World*. Branford, CT: The Intrepid Traveler, 2007.

Schroeder, Russell, ed. *Walt Disney: His Life in Pictures*. New York: Disney Press, 1996.

Sehlinger, Bob. *The Unofficial Guide to Disneyland 2000*. New York: Macmillan Travel, 1999.

Sklar, Martin A. *Walt Disney's Disneyland*. Anaheim, CA: Walt Disney Productions, 1964.

Sklar, Martin A. *Walt Disney's Disneyland*. Anaheim, CA: Walt Disney Productions, 1969.

Smith, Dave. *Disney A to Z: The Official Encyclopedia*. New York: Disney Editions, 1998.

Smith, Dave, ed. *The Quotable Walt Disney*. New York: Disney Editions, 2001.

Thie, Carlene. *Disneyland . . . the Beginning*. Riverside, CA: Ape Pen Publishing, 2003.

Thomas, Bob. *Walt Disney: An American Original*. New York: Simon and Schuster, 1976.

Trahan, Kendra. *Disneyland Detective*. Mission Viejo, CA: PermaGrin Publishing, 2005.

Watts, Steven. *The Magic Kingdom: Walt Disney and the American Way of Life*. Boston: Houghton Mifflin Company, 1997.

Yee, Kevin and Jason Schultz. *Magic Quizdom*. Anaheim, CA: Zauberreich Press, 2004.

Yee, Kevin and Jason Schultz. *101 Things You Never Knew About Disneyland*. Anaheim, CA: Zauberreich Press, 2005.

Zibart, Eve. *This Day in History: Disney*. Cincinnati: Emmis Books, 2006.

Two Recommended DVDs

Walt Disney Treasures: Disneyland: Secrets, Stories & Magic. DVD-ROM. Walt Disney Video, 2007.

Walt Disney Treasures: Disneyland USA. DVD-ROM. Walt Disney Video, 2001.

Ten Recommended Web Sites

The Disneyland Encyclopedia (the site associated with this book) = encycoolpedia.com
Disneyland Resort (official Disney site) = disneyland.com
Disney Legends (official Disney site) = legends.disney.go.com/legends/index
DLDHistory (unofficial fan site) = dldhistory.com
JustDisney.com (unofficial fan site) = justdisney.com
LaughingPlace.com (unofficial fan site) = laughingplace.com
MiceAge (unofficial fan site) = miceage.com
Santa Monica Press (this book's publisher) = santamonicapress.com
Walt's Magic Kingdom (unofficial fan site) = waltsmagickingdom.com
Yesterland (unofficial fan site) = yesterland.com

About the Author

The Disneyland Encyclopedia is Chris Strodder's seventh book, the sixth published since the year 2000. Several of his books before this one have some connection to Disneyland: *Lockerboy*, an adventure novel published in 2002 by Red Hen Press, uses an invented Disneyland-like park as a major setting; *The Encyclopedia of Sixties Cool*, a nonfiction compendium published in 2006 by Santa Monica Press, includes text about Disneyland in the 1960s. Among Chris's other works are the children's book *A Sky for Henry*, the comic novel *The Wish Book*, the short story collection *Stories Light and Dark*, and the popular nonfiction book *Swingin' Chicks of the '60s*, which garnered international attention, coverage in dozens of magazines ranging from the *National Enquirer* to *Playboy*, and exposure on national TV and radio shows. Chris lives in the green hills of Marin County, California.

About the Illustrator

Coming from a family of artists and scientists, Tristan Tang enjoyed a wonderfully creative childhood where she was encouraged to have a strong sense of curiosity and to fully develop her artistic self. She was able to combine her interests in mixed media art forms with cultural anthropology while completing her fine art degree. After enjoying rewarding work experiences in photography and scientific illustration, she found a love for visual effects and has worked as an artist on many films, commercials, and games. Some of her past Disney projects include the film *Pirates of the Caribbean: The Curse of the Black Pearl* and commercials for Disney's Animal Kingdom and Cruise Line. Tristan dedicates the illustrations in *The Disneyland Encyclopedia* to her children, Trey and Anya. She thanks her husband, Alex, for his artistic contributions and inspiration on this project and her extended family for their infinite support.

Index

Books Available from Santa Monica Press

The Bad Driver's Handbook
*Hundreds of Simple Maneuvers
to Frustrate, Annoy, and
Endanger Those Around You*
by Zack Arnstein and
Larry Arnstein
192 pages $12.95

Calculated Risk
*The Extraordinary Life
of Jimmy Doolittle*
by Jonna Doolittle Hoppes
360 pages $24.95

Captured!
*Inside the World of
Celebrity Trials*
by Mona Shafer Edwards
176 pages $24.95

Dinner with a Cannibal
*The Complete History of
Mankind's Oldest Taboo*
by Carole A. Travis-Henikoff
360 pages $24.95

**The Disneyland®
Encyclopedia**
*The Unofficial, Unauthorized,
and Unprecedented History
of Every Land, Attraction,
Restaurant, Shop, and Event in
the Original Magic Kingdom®*
by Chris Strodder
480 pages $19.95

**The Encyclopedia
of Sixties Cool**
*A Celebration of the
Grooviest People, Events, and
Artifacts of the 1960s*
by Chris Strodder
336 pages $24.95

**Exotic Travel Destinations
for Families**
by Jennifer M. Nichols
and Bill Nichols
360 pages $16.95

Footsteps in the Fog
Alfred Hitchcock's San Francisco
by Jeff Kraft and
Aaron Leventhal
240 pages $24.95

**Free Stuff & Good Deals
for Folks over 50, 3rd Edition**
by Linda Bowman
240 pages $12.95

Haunted Hikes
*Spine-Tingling Tales and Trails
from North America's
National Parks*
by Andrea Lankford
376 pages $16.95

**How to Win Lotteries,
Sweepstakes, and Contests
in the 21st Century**
by Steve Ledoux
240 pages $14.95

James Dean Died Here
*The Locations of America's
Pop Culture Landmarks*
by Chris Epting
312 pages $16.95

L.A. Noir
The City as Character
by Alain Silver and James Ursini
176 pages $19.95

Led Zeppelin Crashed Here
*The Rock and Roll Landmarks
of North America*
by Chris Epting
336 pages $16.95

Letter Writing Made Easy!
*Featuring Sample Letters for
Hundreds of Common Occasions*
by Margaret McCarthy
208 pages $12.95

Mark Spitz
*The Extraordinary Life of an
Olympic Champion*
by Richard J. Foster
360 pages $24.95

The 99th Monkey
*A Spiritual Journalist's
Misadventures with Gurus,
Messiahs, Sex, Psychedelics, and
Other Consciousness-Raising
Experiments*
by Eliezer Sobel
312 pages $16.95

Redneck Haiku
Double-Wide Edition
by Mary K. Witte
240 pages $11.95

**Route 66 Adventure
Handbook**
by Drew Knowles
312 pages $16.95

**Route 66 Quick Reference
Encyclopedia**
by Drew Knowles
224 pages $12.95

**The Ruby Slippers,
Madonna's Bra, and
Einstein's Brain**
*The Locations of America's
Pop Culture Artifacts*
by Chris Epting
312 pages $16.95

**Rudolph, Frosty, and
Captain Kangaroo**
*The Musical Life of
Hecky Krasnow—Producer
of the World's Most
Beloved Children's Songs*
by Judy Gail Krasnow
424 pages $24.95

Self-Loathing for Beginners
by Lynn Phillips
192 pages $12.95

Silent Traces
*Discovering Early Hollywood
Through the Films of
Charlie Chaplin*
by John Bengtson
304 pages $24.95

The Sixties
Photographs by Robert Altman
192 pages $39.95

Tiki Road Trip, 2nd Edition
*A Guide to Tiki Culture
in North America*
by James Teitelbaum
336 pages $16.95

Tower Stories
An Oral History of 9/11
by Damon DiMarco
528 pages $27.95

**The Ultimate Counterterrorist
Home Companion**
by Zack Arnstein and
Larry Arnstein
168 pages $12.95

Vanity PL8 Puzzles
*A Puzzle Book Where
You Solve the Vanity Plates*
by Michelle Mazzulo
96 pages $8.95

**"We're Going to See
the Beatles!"**
*An Oral History of Beatlemania
as Told by the Fans Who Were
There*
by Garry Berman
288 pages $16.95